ProActive Archery

Advance Praise for ProActive Archery

"*Pro Active Archery* by Tom Dorigatti is a book whose time has come. Tom has finally gone and done what should have been done a long time ago. An incredibaly in-depth and very well written 'How-To,' Tom`s book will take away every excuse devised by archers for failing to reach their goals. ***Pro Active Archery*** is written by a pro, for pros and amateurs alike who are looking for ways to improve their game and gives a sometimes humorous insight as to why certain things should be done to avoid problems before they start. With attention to detail not seen in previous works, ***Pro Active Archery*** demystifies the path to archery excellence that confounds so many new archers just getting into the sport or returning after a long absence. Tom's book is well worth the read and has something for everyone of all skill levels. Tom is a teacher and, if you will let him, he will show us how to get to a higher level of archery skill than we have ever been to. I highly recommend this book for 'newbies' and 'experts' alike!"

Steve Boylan—First archer in NFAA history to win all WAF events in a professional division in one season (Vegas Shoot, Indoor Nationals, and Stanislawski Open), won the Vegas Shoot three times.

"Tom Dorigatti's new book, ***ProActive Archery*** is great! It reminded me that I don't always remember all the important stuff. This book is a must for newbies and veteran archers alike."

Dave Barnsdale—Won Vegas Championship (Unlimited Men) in 1984 and 2005. Won the MFS Pro division at the 1983 NFAA Indoor Nationals; Owner of Barnsdale Archery Manufacturing, maker of custom bows and limbs

"I am sure after reading Tom's book, ***ProActive Archery***, you will be able to cope with multitude of situations that you as an archer can get into and find cures for a number of the problems we as archers incur throughout our shooting careers."

Tim Gillingham—Three time winner of the NFAA Unmarked 3-D (Pro Division), 2010 NFAA 3-Star Car Shoot-Off Winner, and member of the 2010 United States Archery Team.

"If you seriously intend to make progress with your archery game then you'll read this book. If you intend to actually become 'ProActive' about your archery game then you'll read this book with a notebook and pencil in your hand and take notes. You'll be "doing" what Tom lays out in each chapter and section of his book because these are the very things I had to learn to do in order to reach my highest level of archery performance. And now when I teach them to my students, I can just refer them to this book.

Tom's book isn't a lot of made-up hype, it's real! You have to pay attention to these kinds of details if you plan on elevating your performance. Just paying attention to getting yourself into proper full-draw-position with your drawing forearm in line with the arrow is a really good place to start. Tom lays it out for you by teaching you all the methods of measuring your draw length and then correctly points out that those measurements don't help if you aren't lined up correctly. Take action now to get pictures of yourself at full draw and then make the correction needed—and then measure it and record it in your notebook.

Your plan for success must begin with "action" or it's no plan at all. Read this book and commit yourself to act on what you learn.

Become ProActive! It will make the difference!"

Larry Wise—1986 World Field Champion with five books (180,000 copies) in print, ten major video productions, hundreds of magazine articles, and has coached in the U.S. and seven other countries.

"The sport of archery involves many intricacies that Tom Dorigatti explains in a clear and insightful manner. This book covers methods that will guarantee improvement in an archer's scores and consistency. I have applied Tom's techniques in this book not only to students I have coached, but to my own practice regime as well. ***ProActive Archery*** is a book every target archer should own."

Jon Eide—Holder of three NFAA indoor national records, winner of over 35 state championship titles while also setting multiple state records

"There are so many instances in this book I could have applied to my long archery career, but ***ProActive Archery*** is about 30 years late! I sure could have used it during my competitive years. It contains a wealth of information and tips that could have saved me many disappointments due to simple small things that exploded into big things. Vick Leach once said: "The will to win is only exceeded by the will to prepare to win." I have never forgotten this. Every imaginable aspect of preparation is covered in the book. This book is the ultimate guide for preparing to excel!

As I read through different chapters I kept thinking 'Why didn't I think to do that?' Many situations in my career would have been less painful had I only kept records of my bow setups. When you are in the middle of a round and you have the slightest change in your setup, you are in for some bad scoring. Unless you have all your setup recorded and with you for quick reference. The average and even a lot of the top archers never did that. The book will train you to follow these simple steps to eliminate the breakdowns that rob you of victory."

Gene Lueck—was the second person to shoot a perfect 300 Vegas round at Vegas (1974), 37 time state champion, winner of many NFAA Sectional Championships, as well as the 2002 NFAA national Marked 3-D Championship, President of the Professional Archers Association (1985-86).

"Usually, when you read a 'how-to' archery books, you end up with two or three pages tagged with 'Post-It Notes' or 'dog-eared' to mark points of interest to revisit later. Sadly, you can't do this with ***ProActive Archery***. If you did, you'd end up with a veritable 'Post-It Note Jungle,' as each page contains multiple hints and tips. With ***ProActive Archery***, Tom has condensed years of practical experience down to the fine points that will help you 'Eat the Elephant' and make you a better archer. A definite must read for anyone wanting to 'up their game.'"

Larry Clague—Author and programmer of "OnTarget! Software for Archers," 1975 US Collegiate Archery All-American

"In my 65 years of archery, I have read innumerable 'how to' bowhunting and archery books. ***ProActive Archery*** is hands down the most detailed, comprehensive book yet published. Tom Dorigatti has covered it all and in great detail as well. Even the most experienced archers will find new and useful information inside the cover, and any serious archer, from neophyte to pro, will benefit by reading Tom's book. In short order, ***ProActive Archery*** should receive acclaim as one of the best archery books ever published."

Roger Wheaton—Author, National Champion, Vegas Shoot Champion, winner of six international championships, and holder four World Records

ProActive Archery

by Tom Dorigatti

WATCHING ARROWS FLY, LLC

ProActive Archery

Library of Congress Cataloging-in Publication Data

ProActive Archery / Tom Dorigatti.
p. cm
ISBN 978-0-9848860-2-9 (softcover)
1. Archery. 2. Training I Tom Dorigatti, 1947-

ISBN 978-0-9848860-2-9

The web addresses cited in this text were current as of August 2012, unless otherwise noted.

Cover Photo This 5X-25 end, shot on the NFAA Five Spot Indoor Target, is one of hundreds, if not thousands, of such shot by professional archer Steve Boylan of Chillicothe, IL.

Writer: Tom Dorigatti; **Copy Editor**; Steve Ruis; **Proofreader**: Claudia Stevenson; **Graphic Artist**: Steve Ruis; **Cover Designer**: Steve Ruis; **Book Designer**: Steve Ruis; **Photographers** (cover and interior): Tom Dorigatti and Steve Ruis unless otherwise noted; **Illustrator** Steve Ruis

Printed in the United States of America 10 9 8 7 6 5 4 3 2 1

Watching Arrows Fly
3712 North Broadway, #285
Chicago, IL 60613
800. 671.1140

Dedication

This book is dedicated to my wife of 45 years, Sherry, and my two daughters, Kari and Teri. They gave up much over the years to allow me to be involved in competitive archery and bowhunting which literally became "The Only Sports Allowed on Sundays" during my younger years.

Tom Dorigatti
August 2012

Contents

con't

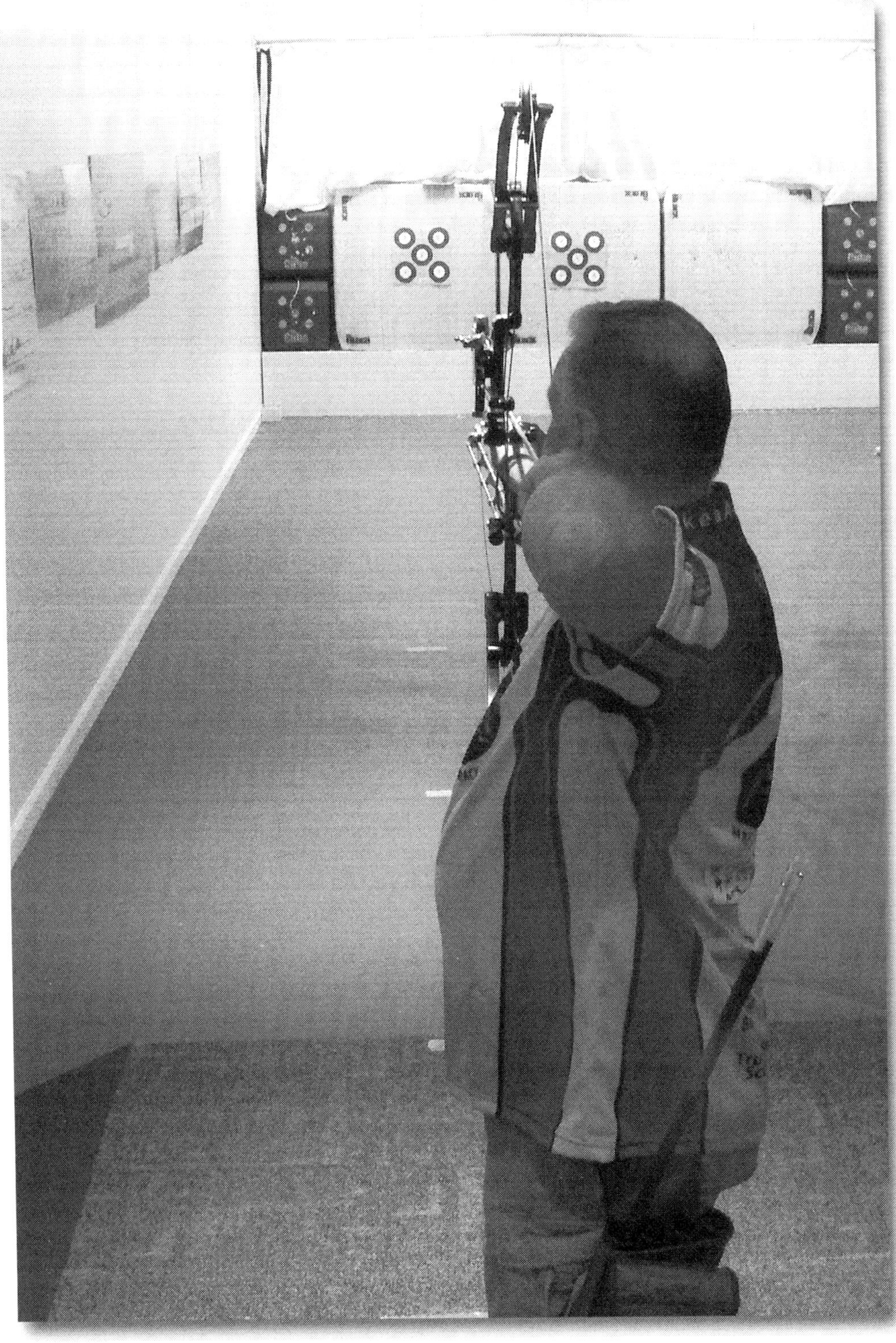

Preface

This book is the culmination of many of my writings over the years, mostly for *Archery Focus* magazine, but other archery magazines as well. In addition, it also includes many of my own experiences accumulated since I started shooting a bow and arrow in 1958, when I was only 10 years old. It didn't take long for me to realize that if I wanted to hit what it was I was shooting at and to bring home cotton-tailed rabbits, something had to become consistent. There wasn't anyone around to help me figure things out so most of what I learned from these raw beginnings was completely by trial and error.

I'm not a former Olympic, world, or national champion. I don't have a list of National, Sectional, and State titles to offer up. I have, over the years, won my share of tournaments. What I offer you are many years of experience in the sport of archery from many perspectives and experiences in many shooting styles and venues.

A Short Personal Story Sometime in 1958, I purchased a 50 pound Ben Pearson solid fiberglass semi-recurve bow and some wooden Port Orford cedar arrows from a local gun shop. I had been eyeing that bow for months and finally had the money for the bow and some arrows to go with it. I shot it nearly every day and quickly realized it was smarter to shoot into some sort of dirt backstop rather than out on the prairie; I spent less time chasing arrows or losing them that way.

The first really memorable experience the first time I came home with several cottontail rabbits on my belt. My father was not very happy and asked me how come I took the "gun" out without his permission. I told him I didn't take the gun out and that it was still in the gun cabinet. He asked me, "Then how did you kill those bunnies then, with rocks?" I told him, "No, I shot them with the bow and arrow I bought from Bill's Gun Shop." He was absolutely shocked that I was accomplished enough to do this, but he was also glad to have fresh rabbit for dinner the next few nights, too. If only he knew how many shots I had but missed and then had to chase down my arrows! I had to do something to get more consistent so I could shoot more accurately. It didn't take long for me to figure out that if I placed the arrow on the string at the same spot every time, then I could figure out how to aim better. My first "nocking point locator" was born by me tying fishing line onto the bow string above and below the arrow nock. I didn't know anything about tuning a bow, so I simply eyeballed the arrow until it looked sort of level and tied it in from there. My consistency, but not necessarily my accuracy, improved immediately. Those were the raw beginnings of me "figuring things out on my own" and making most of my archery gear. My first quiver was fashioned from some linoleum remnants and some yellow string used to sew the edges together and to use as a sling to place over my back. That quiver served me well for quite some time, too. I couldn't afford broadheads yet, so I got some field points and then learned that expended shell casings placed over the ends of the arrows made great blunts and zapped rabbits and prairie dogs pretty well. After a time, I was able to purchase some cheap steel broadheads and learned that dull ones worked more than adequately on rabbits and put them down in a hurry when you hit them with one. I had learned to stalk up close, so most shots were 15 to 20 feet or less; very few were more than 15 yards. I also fashioned a sight pin by taping a 6d finishing nail to the back of the bow and moving it until I was hitting consistently at about 20-30 feet. This made a huge difference in my success rate, too. Of course, some days I was "on" and others, I was "off," but I was having fun.

You are probably wondering, "So what does this past history of your experimentation have to do with this book?" Those and many more experiments and self-made solutions were, for me, the beginning of my life-long philosophy of being "ProActive" and not "reactive" when it comes to most things. Oh, yes, I can be reactive, too, but when it comes to something I can plan for or work to prevent from coming apart, I'm very ProActive. I have a temper, just like most people, and sometimes that temper can surface even when I've tried to be as ProActive as possible. Let's move on,

It is my hope you will want to read the entire book, cover to cover, however, I also know full well that you will probably skip around, so I set the book up so that you could pick and choose what you want to read and still be able to understand each topic. Consequently, you will find a bit of repetition, some of it verbatim, but most of it re-worded in several ways. It is essential, at least in my opinion, that I tell you what I'm going to tell you, tell it to you, and then tell you what I told you. This all comes from 40 plus years of teaching and/or managing people, and repeating things is about the only way to make sure things get across sooner rather than later. I also realize that some things, no matter how often they are repeated will never get across, but I won't fault myself for trying.

This book's intent is not to give you the answers to the "What to Do" aspects of archery; there are countless books written about that. It also isn't going to necessarily give you all the answers on "How to Do" whatever, but I surely intend upon giving you alternatives you may not have tried in order to resolve archery-related problems. You may find quite a few things you are already doing with regard to your archery equipment, your setup, your shot sequence, and even your practice regimen and mental attitude. This is good, since we all deal with problems of one sort or another on a daily basis. But others may not know of thise things, so please be patient.

You are not going to find information on "Paper Tuning." You are not going to find "how to French Tune." You are not going to find out "how to hold your release aid," or "how to align your bow arm and elbow." I won't be delving into weight and balance, and all those other hosts of things volumes of recommendations have been already written.

What I am offering you in the pages that follow is a means of helping to ensure that you can avoid so many of the road-blocks, trials, and tribulations I've gone through over the years. You are lucky, because back when I started, there were very few shooters in my area, and those who were around tended to be very secretive about the "how" and the "what" they did to hit their target more frequently. None of us knew what a perfect score was, because frankly, nobody had ever shot a perfect score to show us it was possible! We were happy to hit the target, let alone the bull's-eye!

People like to be told stories; that is one of the best ways we learn. Thus you will find that I often relate personal experiences, and tying them into the current topic. I may even pose a question or problem to pique your interest and then explain how a solution to a problem was figured out. As I have always told my students and subordinates, "I'll never give you something to do that there isn't a reason behind it," and I sure won't give you "busy work" just to keep you occupied.

This book is divided into seven sections:

A New Relationship with Your Equipment
ProActive Bow Ownership and Maintenance
ProActive Form & Execution
ProActive Practice & Tournament Preparation
Getting More Accurate Sight Settings
ProActive Attitude & Mental Game
Making Archery Fun (Again)
Making Your Own "Stuff"
Benchmarks, Goals, & Performance

I have re-worked and updated any older material, keeping the essence of the original material as the foundation.

The premise of this book will always be to become "ProActive," because in this individual sport, it is not "if" something is going to break, go totally out of kilter, fall off your bow, etc. it is "when" that is going to happen to you, always unexpectedly.

Those of you who ProActively prepare for the inevitable "things that go wrong" are going to be well ahead of your competition when it comes to identifying problems and correcting them with as little loss of time and, more importantly, fewer points lost because you are prepared and ready to handle them almost without missing a beat.

When you have ProActively prepared for "things that go wrong," your mental game cannot be totally disrupted because of some malfunction, the wind, the rain, a hang-nail, or whatever. So many shooters out there never prepare for the inevitable, figuring that "if" it happens, they'll deal with it at that time and place. Then, "when" it happens, they are obviously ill-prepared and clueless as to what to do or where to go; other than back to the clubhouse or car and try to recover within the few minutes allowed.

I keep using the word "ProActive" don't I? I will explain when you begin.

So, if you want to learn some easy things you can do to make your archery more fun (as in better scores are fun) and find out how to help yourself to be better prepared to handle the things that will go wrong while you are practicing or shooting, then this is the book for you!

My Thanks

I have procrastinated for nearly three years after having been asked over and over again by Steve Ruis, Editor of *Archery Focus* magazine, and Claudia Stevenson, of Watching Arrows Fly, LLC to sit down and put this book together. Obviously they have put in a tremendous amount of work assisting me in pulling this book together. Steve and Claudia also reviewed and edited the manuscrip and offered very valuable suggestions as to how to improve upon what I had initially put together. I also must thank my wife, Sherry, and my daughters Kari, and Teri for putting up with me being out on the archery ranges, sometimes more than I was at home. They gave up most weekends while I was attending archery tournaments, making it truly, "The Only Sport Allowed on Sundays" for me and the family for many years! I would be remiss if I didn't thank my fellow archers, far and wide, for all the experiences they've shared with me. To list them would take pages upon pages, and I would still be unable to list them all due to simply forgetting their names; there are so many. Rather than to attempt to name any of them, I'll simply give a heart-felt "thank you" to anyone reading these pages who knows me, since you likely helped bring this to fruition in one way or another.

Tom Dorigatti
Pekin, IL
August 2012
Email dorigat@comcast.net

Section 1

A New Relationship with Your Equipment

One would surmise that the way to start any book about archery would be to start at the beginning with the receipt of the new bow and work on through the set-up process, arrow selection, and tuning steps (be those paper testing, French tuning, or a host of other tuning methods). Then would follow specifics for fine tuning processes, developing or furthering different skills for different shooting environments, working on specific form items, miscellaneous do-it-yourself items, and finally, working on the mental game. That outline makes sense, almost.

My approach to this book will be different and hopefully those differences will pique your interest and allow you to better grasp not only the intricacies of this game of exacting finesse but also how one thing depends on another and the effects of one seemingly small thing can have on a host of other important items.

I am calling my approach to archery "ProActive Archery." So, what do I mean by "ProActive"? Here is a common definition:

Proactive

"Action and result oriented behavior, instead of the one that waits for things to happen and then tries to adjust (react) to them. Proactive behavior aims at identification and exploitation of opportunities and in taking preemptory action against potential problems and threats, whereas reactive behavior focuses on fighting a fire or solving a problem after it occurs."

(*Source* www.businessdictionary.com/definition/proactive.html)

So, before I get into all those nice things that can help a person improve their bow mechanics skills and their archery prowess, I will address some of the common things archers do that have a negative impact on their development and their ability to solve their problems quickly and efficiently. In every part of the book I am focused on removing problems before they become problems (in your equipment, technique, everything). And since problems cannot be completely eliminated I also focus on how you can quickly and inexpensively get back on track when something untoward does occur. This is what I mean by ProActive Archery. If you aren't a ProActive archer, you will be stuck, puzzled every time something goes wrong, having to invent a solution by trial and error.

Also, you progress through this book, you are going to see many points repeated. This is intentional because so many things are interrelated – if you change one thing, a host of other things will also be affected. So, because of this complexity I repeat points rather than make you slog back through other chapters looking for the information you need.

Tom Dorigatti

1

Common Things Archers Change "On the Fly" (and Shouldn't)

All of us are guilty of trying to change more than one thing at a time, mostly because we are always in a hurry to hit the spot. What ends up happening, though, is that you do too many things at once and never know which of them is good and which of them is the culprit when things don't work out. The items below are not listed in any particular order nor are they prioritized. I think you will find that you are guilty of at least some of the following; most of which are not ProActive, but rather reactive.

Are You Guilty of *Any* of These?

1. *Changing Your Stance* without regard to how it affects your body alignment and draw length. Most archers don't realize how closely their stance is related to their upper body shape and flexibility. I always tell my students that "the stance is tuned to the draw length, and the draw length is tuned to the stance." For example, your body shape and flexibility can restrict you from shooting a very open stance, while other people must shoot an open stance and cannot effectively shoot a closed stance.

   Here is something to think about: your body has what is called bilateral symmetry. In effect, this means that the left side of your body is pretty much the same as the right, a mirror image, so to speak. This leads me to ask the following question: Do you know which of your arms is longer than the other? This over-looked item has an effect on your stance positioning, your anchor, the positioning of your bow arm elbow and shoulder, and, believe it or not, even your required draw length. This can throw off the different measuring techniques used to establish a starting point for your draw length, especially the "wing-span method." In my particular case, my right arm is over 1″ longer than my left and has a lot to do with why I require a 1½″ longer draw length when shooting left-handed than I do when shooting right-handed. The wing-span method worked fine for me when I was shooting right-handed, but with the change to shooting left-handed, the wing span method starting point and my required draw length were far apart. This is especially interesting if your longer arm happens to be your bow arm! I will discuss this later on.

2. *Indiscriminately Changing Your Bow's Draw Weight* without considering the other effects this has on your equipment and your ability to shoot that bow. Doing this will affect the bow-to-arrow spine match. With some cam systems, cam synchronization can also be affected. With all systems, your nocking point, brace height, and axle-to-axle length (ATA) can change as well. How significantly these are affected depends on how much you change the poundage. In addition, these are also affected by how "unevenly" you move the limbs bolts. Many people make these adjustments in quarter turn increments and don't pay attention to the exact position of a limb bolt before they start cranking on it. It isn't long before the limbs are way out of balance with one another. I always align both limb bolts by using the long end of the Allen wrench parallel with the long axis of the limb. When I change draw weight, it is always one sixth turn at a time on each limb, always maintaining that Allen wrench's longitudinal alignment with the limb. (Just insert the wrench so its shank is 60° off from the limb and turn the wrench so that it lines up with the limb.) I also always use the same Allen wrench and no other when I'm adjusting my limb bolts. (There are differences between one Allen wrench and another.) Worn ends of Allen wrenches should be either cut off or a new Allen wrench should be obtained. Never use someone else's Allen wrench to make draw weight changes on your bow (for more on this see Chapter 3)!

   Did you ever wonder why your bow feels so different after you've changed your draw weight? It isn't all about the increase or decrease in peak and holding weights! The other critical thing about this indiscriminate changing of peak weight is that the bow's draw length will be changed. The rule of thumb is that for every full turn of the poundage bolts, the draw length can change between ⅛″ and ¼″ depending upon the cam system and limb angle. If you increase the poundage, you decrease the draw length; if you decrease the poundage, you increase the draw length!

3. *Twisting Up Strings or Cables* without considering what this does to the tune of the bow. I've seen people just up and start twisting their bowstring and/or cables without paying attention to how many twists they are putting in or taking out! In addition, instead of taking twists evenly at both ends (especially with a single cam bow), they just twist one end and then wonder why their peep alignment goes "south" on them and they have to fiddle with that. Of course, at this point, they have also changed the cam timing/synchronization, the draw weight, the ATA, the brace height (slightly), and the bow's draw length, as well as the nocking point location! Is this practice ProActive? I think you know the answer to that question already.

4. *Moving the D-Loop Up or Down the Bowstring* without regard to the effect this will have on the bow's aiming characteristics and shootability. Once you have your D-loop set so that it doesn't deform when used (indicating it is free of off-axis stresses on it), you don't want to be changing the pulling point on the bowstring (see Chapter 7). Nocking point adjustments should, after the D-loop is set, be made

by moving the arrow rest up or down ever so slightly. It doesn't take much to make a large change down range! Of course, you should have marked and written down where you started, just in case you have to put it back where it was. If you don't document and mark the starting point, then good luck in finding "it" again.

5. *Moving the Arrow Rest Back* (away from the riser) without regard to its effects on other things A current trend is moving the arrow rest back toward the archer. This isn't something earth shattering and new. Those of us who were shooting archery back in the 1970's did this; we did it again in the 1980's (during the overdraw craze), and again in the 1990's. I'm not saying it doesn't work or that it can't help; however, you had better have a good reason as to why you are doing it and then give it time to prove itself. Many shooters will move their rest back, and then turn around and cut off their arrows. If you do it this way, you have just massively changed the spine of your arrows. Your previous "tune" is pretty much shot (pun intended). Whoops, yet another reactive change that creates several more reactive effects.
6. *Making Large Draw Length Adjustments* without regard to your alignment, head alignment, anchoring position and stance requirements. I see people make ½″ or greater draw length adjustments, shoot a couple of shots, and say, "Well that isn't working." How do you know for sure? After all, you've only shot a few shots this way. Your muscles are used to the longer (or shorter) draw length and alignment. If you don't give this more than a few arrows, if you don't give this more than one round or one practice session, you cannot be sure of anything other than "the old way felt better." (The old way always feels better!) What you need to do is give this adjustment at least two to three weeks of time for you and your muscles to adapt to it. Sure, go ahead and score your rounds, take pictures of your target, and write down what your sight picture looks like during each practice session (seriously, write things down). Keep your scoring target faces and date them or, even better, take pictures of each scoring end. This will give you documented proof of whether "this is working" or not. Graphing your results is even better, and so easy to accomplish (see Chapter 48). It will also give you a clue as to whether or not you went the wrong way, or simply too far. You can then try something in between that ½″ you made and where you started, but only if you know and have documented and marked where you started from. Being ProActive means practicing with a "plan," an hypothesis, and then testing for the results, one variable at a time. This scientific method is invalidated if you test more than one "variable" at a time.
7. *Severe Bending of Your Bow Elbow* because you see some other shooters doing this After all, more is better, isn't it? It is next to impossible to maintain good, solid shooting form at distance with a severely bent bow arm! The ideal situation, as expressed by the majority of the top echelon shooters, is that the elbow, while not locked is indeed slightly bent. At this point, the anchor, stance, and draw length are set for this and it keeps your shoulder positioning down and in the "bone and bone" alignment. Severely bending your bow arm places pressure on your hand

and forearm and also the tops of the shoulder. It causes you to invoke muscles for control and static maintenance of pressure instead of letting your skeleton resist the load. The skeleton is designed to resist the load, while the muscles are designed to move the load. Think about this: in order to be consistent with regard to arrow impact points, you must be able to replicate the same procedure shot after shot. How can you replicate the bend in your elbow when instead of bone on bone alignment and skeletal support, you are using muscle support? No two shots in a row are going to be the same when shooting with a severely bent elbow; regardless of what you might think. Hard stops, you say? Well, we'll discuss the myth of "hard stops" phenomenon at length later in this book (see Chapter 14).

8. *Attempting to Raise or Lower Your Drawing Elbow* simply because you see some other shooter doing well that way You see an archer with either a higher or lower than "normal" drawing elbow or you hear someone talking about raising the draw elbow to achieve "scapular alignment" and you think "I've got to try that!" If you have a shorter upper arm, then you are automatically going to shoot with a higher elbow than most people. If you shoot a higher anchor point, you will normally shoot with a higher elbow. In addition, if you are trying to raise your elbow for "scapular alignment," whatever that is, the tendency is to pull upwards by using your forearm and shoulder muscles, which forces your bow hand downwards, and your sight will start dropping out the bottom of the bullseye.

   If your draw length is too long, then your elbow will have to be below the line of the arrow. Your bow shoulder may come up toward your chin as well, along with several other "body adaptations" you have to make to support a draw length too long (such as bending your drawing wrist). You will see more of the "drawing hand wrist bending" with shooters using wrist-strap releases than those shooting with hand held releases, however. I mention this from the perspective of "too long" because well over 90% of the compound archers in the game today are shooting too long on draw length along with too much peak weight for them to handle. This is due to improper training, and a "speed craze" that is dominating shooters' minds of late.

9. *Adding or Taking Off Large Amounts of Mass/Weight* or side weighting/V-bars all at once You see some top shooters who shoot a lot of mass weight or wide angled, heavy V-bars or counter weighting and you think that would help you. What you don't see are the pros increasing such weights in small increments (I suggest one ounce increments), checking each setup out, one at a time, before settling on what they are shooting now. Adding a large amount of mass to your bow all at one

time is a recipe for disaster. Sure, you can "check out" a new weight distribution for on the spot "holding appearances," but as the adage goes, "everything works great . . . at first." When it comes to mass weight, if you add too much too fast, you are going to end up with some very sore shoulders. You are going to end up with inconsistencies the first several times you try this new combo. What you need to do is take your time, shoot several rounds for score using a given weight combination, take target pictures, (document, document, and document some more what you are doing). Have "proof" before you make any conclusions as to whether or not a weight combination is working. The proof is in the tightness of the hold and the consistency of your groups or X-counts. ProActive? You bet!

10. *Increasing "Tip Weight" on Your Main Stabilizer in Large Increments* Because you see some other shooters who have theirs this way, you. . . . etc., etc. See item 9 above.
11. *Indiscriminately Changing the Tension (Speed) on Your Release* I see shooters going to a super light "hair trigger" because a top shooter does it that way; or the reverse, going to a super heavy trigger tension without regard to how your alignment, anchor, and draw length are set up in the first place. This also applies to changing the positioning of the "moon" or cam on triggerless releases. Most shooters, when they are having problems getting their release to fire, will speed up the release. By doing this, you are creating a monster because subconsciously, you will now be thinking that the release is going to be touchy, so you will, as you settle in, start to let up or stop pulling on the release and subsequently will have more problems getting it to fire. Then you will fire it by cheating it. The more correct thing to do, in most cases, is to slow down the speed of the release aid. This will force you to continue to pull more without stopping the process and to maintain back tension, because subconsciously, you know you won't get it to fire unless you do so. If the release was firing just fine the last time you shot, and this time it isn't, what is to blame? Obviously, the release itself hasn't changed, now has it? Obviously you have changed something with how you are executing your shot sequence. So, instead of being ProActive and working on that solution, you become reactive and change something with the setup instead of checking out what you are doing differently. You now have taken a step backwards and created several other problems, solving nothing. Doesn't make sense now, does it?
12. *Changing from a First Finger Wrist Release to a Hand-Held Release* and trying to maintain the same anchor point that you had with the wrist release You can go from a wrist release to a hand-held release without changing the draw length of your bow. However, you most likely won't use as high of an anchor point with a hand-held release aid. Therefore, you will have to move your peep sight (upwards).

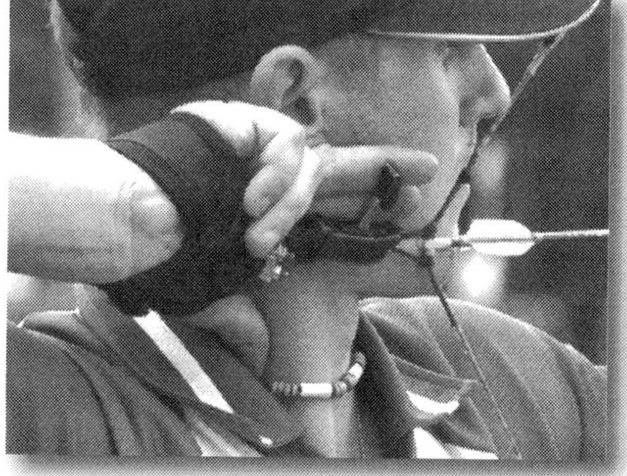

You most likely will be moving your anchor downward below the line of your jaw bone when you go to the hand-held release aid. This anchor is much more solid and much more repeatable, once you get used to it. So, make the commitment, put the wrist release into a drawer at home and then shoot many scoring rounds and document things before you say "It isn't working." You can get close, if not exactly the same, positioning with the hand-held that you had with the wrist strap, but only if you measure and match the distance from the string to the trigger between those two release aids. Most always it will be "close," but rarely exacting enough. You can be ProActive with this change if you stop to think about what you are trying to accomplish.

13. *"Skying" the Bow* or coming in to the target from a very high bow position; turning your head away from the target and swinging your shoulders and hips; drawing the bow with a low elbow down nearly to your waist, etc. These are dangerous practices and in some places you will be warned once and if you repeat these, you will be asked to either turn down the bow's poundage or to get off the shooting line. (*Note* If you are a FITA/WA/ NAA shooter, FITA rule 7.7.7 strictly prohibits this practice and if, in the opinions of the judges, you are pointing the bow beyond the "safety zone," you can and will be asked to leave the shooting line. And, no, your entry fees will not be refunded.)

A bow is a weapon, and as such, you must keep control of the "muzzle" (arrow direction) at all times! If you can't draw your bow easily while the arrow is level and pointed at a target, then you need to be turning the poundage of the bow down until you can. The excuse used by those doing this is normally that they used that positioning to "set their bow hand and get their shoulders into position." Well, how did this get started when the majority of shooters don't perform this contortionist's maneuver and do as well or even better than those few who do? Be ProActive here, because the reactive part of it can get embarrassing, expensive, and result in you being disqualified, even banned from a range. Imagine the results indoors when you hit a sprinkler head and set one of those off? The owner's reaction is going to be instantaneous.

14. *Switching to an Extremely Light Launcher Blade with Heavy Arrows* because some of the top professionals are doing this successfully This practice creates severe problems for shooters who don't have the form or know-how that professional level archers have. You will have a lot of chattering and bouncing of the arrow along the launcher blade as you draw the bow back. Often the arrow will fall off the rest as you start to draw back the bow, later during the draw cycle, or even when you hit your anchor point. None of these are a good thing and all are sure-fire ways of losing your confidence and concentration during a scoring round or tournament.

In addition, this is yet another unsafe act practiced by many shooters today.

15. *Trying to Shoot a Larger Diameter Shaft on a Very Narrow Launcher Blade* because many of the best shooters are doing this If you do this, you will probably experience arrows falling off the rest as you start to draw back the bow and at other times during the draw cycle, even as you hit your anchor point. In addition, launching a large arrow off an extremely narrow blade can cause what I refer to as "skidders." A "skidder" is a less than perfectly executed shot whereby there isn't enough "guidance" given to the arrow by the arrow rest. Subsequently, the arrow will skid off the launcher or the rest to one side or the other, resulting in a wild "flyer." This can range from the shot being slightly out to a complete miss depending upon the distance being shot and, of course, the severity of the shooting flaw. ProActive? No.
16. *Trying to Shoot a Bow Set Up for High Arrow Speed* because some of the best shooters are successful with it You really need to know your limitations with regard to the amount of draw weight you can safely and consistently handle. You also need to know your capabilities with regard to "handling" speed out of a bow. All too often, when you try to get more speed out of your bow, you do it by going to a lighter arrow that isn't correctly spine matched to your set up. Then you will go to the lightest point weight possible in an effort to "stiffen up" the spine of that arrow, completely disregarding how that affects the arrow's front of center (FOC) balance and how the bow will handle this type of arrow. These changes are often done "on the fly" without regard to safety or the tune of the bow to the arrow. Are you being ProActive, or are you responding to a self-image you want to create for yourself?
17. *Changing from a Low Magnification Scope to a High Magnification Scope* because you think you will be able to see better and hit more X's that way What you fail to realize is, that while you do "see less of the target," you will also see more movement of your dot, circle, or fiber optic pin. You will also have a blurrier view of the target as well. Changing magnification can sometimes help you, but it isn't an overnight thing. In addition, you may well have to make other changes, among these being peep hole diameter, sight extension distance, and sometimes, you might even have to get new sight settings. If you haven't indexed your lenses so that you get them back into the same place when you change them, then you could have changes in your impact points, even when you put the original lens back into the housing! If you try this, give it time, and lots of it. You might well go down in score during the period of adjustment. Be ProActive about it. Anticipate the obstacles and be prepared to take that step backwards. Be prepared to give up "what you are now" for "what you could be."
18. *Indiscriminately Changing to a Super Long Sight Extension* to emulate some of the Pros who do this Should you copy these archers, you will also see more "perceived" sight motion and movement. Additionally, you will have to get new sight settings. With a longer sight extension, your scope or pins move down on the sight (vertical) bar creating, in some instances, a lack of clearance for the longer

targets. In addition, with some brands of sights, you may have to re-set your 2nd and 3rd axes more often due to the increased vibration and movement of the extension bar. You might even have to change the aperture in your peep sight to a smaller aperture to help you center the housing in the peep sight; for some, the reverse may be true.

19. *Doing any or all of the above (#1-#18) and then trying some or all of them for only a few shots, a few ends, or a few rounds, and not giving your muscles and psyche enough time to adapt to the radical changes you have made* When something "doesn't work" you abandon some or all of them because there isn't instant gratification and instant improvement in your scores and X-counts. Worse, when you think they "do work" you don't notice the effect was temporary and no real benefit occurred.
20. *Doing any or all of the above without any plan, well thought out reasoning, or documentation of where you started, where you are, and what you expect to achieve* Archers often abandon changes in their equipment, form, or execution without having any real proof of their success or failure. Most archers will not try a "change" for more than a round or two, and often even less than that. Taking the time to shoot several full scoring rounds and take pictures of the target(s) and documenting how the archer, the bow, the groups, and the consistency have really changed is what the pros do. I'm not saying that there aren't effects that will immediately show up. More often than not, though, most archers rarely give the changes they make any sort of a chance to prove themselves, especially with regard to "form changes," release aid speed changes, mass weight changes, and draw length changes. If there isn't instant gratification, then "it isn't working," so you try to go back to where you were, but you haven't written down or marked "where it was" so now you are lost! You will be offered more information on this in later Chapters, and a quick and fun method for you to monitor this and other aspects of "changing things" (see Chapter 48). The ProActive part of this is obvious, isn't it?

Summary

If any of the items described above sound like you, then perhaps you could use some help, especially with regard to determining "where you are" and "where you want to go." If you are making more than one change at a time, you are asking for problems trying to figure out which of the several changes is working, and which are not.

If you want to watch a pro, have an organized approach of what to look for and document while you are scouting what you think you might want to emulate or copy (see Chapter 37 for suggestions as to how to do just this). Those top shooters didn't get to where they are by not experimenting. They didn't get there by having a "shoot from the hip" approach. They didn't get there by changing everything all at once. They might have started there, but eventually they got to where they are by changing what needed to be changed, but in a systematic and well organized fashion, one thing at a time. Then, they verified that each change was for the better or worse by sticking with it and shooting many, many arrows or scores, comparing those to where they were before. If they have proof that a change didn't pan out, they make the decision to return to the previous situation and move to the next potential improvement.

In this game, if you are making change after change and you haven't got any documentation of where you started, you are guaranteeing you will end up lost. You will be without a "map" of how to get back to the beginning.

Is this you?

If so, it can be different.

Tom Dorigatti

2

How Do You Eat an Elephant?

Most archers who hit a shooting slump attack it with gusto, or put the bow up for a few weeks or months and then come back to it, or flail away at trying to correct everything all at once because they just have to get ready for the next tournament or league score and can't afford the time. Many of these archers, unfortunately, can't solve their problem quickly just fade away and take up something less stressful. (Bernie Pellerite says that most archers are fishermen in training.)

Other archers simply feel that they can't get any better and become stagnant and satisfied with how they are shooting. They tend to sit back and enjoy the ride and have fun regardless of score or how they place in a tournament. They claim they are in it just for the fun of it, but you still hear them mutter the same comments those of a more competitive nature utter; they just aren't quite as vocal about it is all.

If you are one of those, like me, who have a competitive spirit and cannot just sit back and take whatever comes, then perhaps you may be enlightened by this chapter. You aren't going to be exposed to pictures of a "what to do" or "how it should look" nature. You won't be exposed to a pep talk about getting your head into the game, or urged to read a couple of books on "mental attitude," or watch several videos about how to "get it done." I'm not going to tell you the magic cure for what ails you, or to start over if it doesn't feel right. You've read and heard all those things countless times before.

In my classroom (Did I tell you I was a teacher?), when my students were having difficulty solving a problem or were trying to figure out a new concept, I always asked them a simple question: "How do you eat an elephant?" The first time I ask this question, I get lots of funny looks and at least one student will ask, "What does eating an elephant have to do with what we are trying to learn?" I will then go into the "Problem Solving" techniques that we have discussed time and time again. You know, breaking a problem down into smaller pieces and working on them, one at a time. It quickly becomes clear to the students that I'm telling them not to tackle the "elephant" and try to eat it all at once, but rather to take the elephant (the problem) one "bite" or step at a time and no more or less than that. I tell them that it will take time to solve the problem or learn the material, but doing it one bite at a time is by far the better way of getting the results you want and achieving your goals.

Problem solving techniques are nothing new or at least they shouldn't be. Some problems are simple to solve and don't require thorough analyses or loads of data to figure them out. Still others, well, are complex and many have multiple steps and each step will have an effect on the previous and subsequent steps. Does this sound like I'm heading somewhere in particular?

Getting Up Front and Personal, Embarrassingly So

Let's take a case that is up front and personal and very, very close to someone special, since I'm most familiar with it; that case being my own. I've been "eating the elephant" in the wrong fashion for quite some time; in fact, in some instances, I'm still doing it to this very day! You see I, too, wanted to jump right up from being down and vault back to the top as quickly as possible. I attacked my problems with gusto only to fall right back down and fail to get anywhere. I changed things around, often several of them at once in an effort to hurry up the process so that I could quit being so embarrassed with my low scores.

After all, I had shot perfect 300 scores with 60X's. I had shot 555+ field scores; although not in several years. I had shot 890+ scores on the 900 round. The problem was that I had done all this before I had a major heart problem and the subsequent heart surgery left me with an intentional tremor. I was competitive at the top of my division before all this happened, so why shouldn't I be "king" again? I was convinced that I knew enough about myself and shooting to solve this problem in a heartbeat! Well, folks, that was 10 long years ago and up until I took my own advice (the same I gave to my students) and put myself into proper perspective, I hadn't gotten past square one! I even spent time getting a coach, or should I say coaches, to try to help me figure this mess out. What happened? I wanted it right now! No, actually, I wanted it yesterday. And I wanted it all corrected all at once and was mentally trying to force a physical thing into submission. As I write this, I realize that forcing the mental to try to fix a physical thing isn't something that is going to happen. This is especially difficult when you can't see yourself perform and you are reluctant to bother your friends, or worse yet, your friends are reluctant to bother you because they figure you know more about this than they do, and they don't want to give you "bad advice." The difficulties of becoming ProActive, even when you know about the consequences, can and will be frustrating, to say the least.

Doing Everything at Once

After flailing about for nearly eleven years, I came to the conclusion that I most likely won't see those 60X 300's or 550 field scores anymore. I also started to realize that I was trying to eat the entire elephant at once and was trying to fix everything at the same time and, thus failing to fix anything at all. I let the intentional tremor rule my mental game. I let the "comments" of other shooters who were saying things such as "Do you know your bow arm and bow hand are shaking?" or "Good grief, look at that guy shake, they should get him off the line before he hurts somebody," rule my shooting. I became so self conscious about the shake that the "shake" ruled my shooting and what I looked like was more important to me than trying to just hit the middle. I know for a fact that most other archers would have quit long ago and not stayed with it. However, after nearly 50 years of shooting a bow and 42 years of competitive shooting, some "physical thing" or some "competitors who don't really understand" are not taking me out of this game without a fight, and fighting is exactly what I'm now doing. But you know what? I'm winning this fight! How am I winning it?

One Bite at a Time

The last time I shot at Vegas, my scores were atrocious. The comment about me being taken off the shooting line because I was "dangerous" is real; that was said. I haven't competed in a major event since then but that is going to change . . . hopefully, soon.

So, what does this all have to do with "eating an elephant?"

Remember earlier that I said that I told my students that you eat an elephant one bite at a time? Well, about a year and a half ago, I decided to eat my elephant; better known to me now as my "little problem" one step and only one step at a time. I finally decided, with the help of some close friends, that the "shake" was there and I could do nothing about that. So, the first plan of living with the tremor and dealing with it failed. I never learned to accept it and made a decision to go back to shooting left handed. That was the first "bite" of the elephant: accepting that the shake was not to be overcome; I had to do something different as opposed to trying to force regaining my previous form. You see, the shake was visible to spectators, but guess what? It was not visible as any real consequence to my aiming; that is, unless I let it get to me and I tried to control it. Then it became highly visible and my hold was only as good as the 8-ring on a Vegas target face, but I could still hit mostly 9's and 10's if I "let it happen" and didn't fight it.

Now that I've made the change back to left-handed shooting (yes, I had changed from left to right before), the shake isn't in my bow arm but rather in my release hand, but the tremor is a pressure type problem and isn't a "pulling" type of problem. The bigger elephant has been put out to pasture, and I'm tackling another smaller elephant and trying to tackle it one bite at a time. I still catch myself trying for too much, too soon and have to constantly rein myself in and take stock of "giving up what I am for what I potentially could be." It is a school of hard knocks; do not let anyone kid you!

Writing the Problems and Prioritizing the Steps

All too often, especially in archery, we don't really formulate any sort of real plan for our problem solving. We just flail about, trying this or that for a quick and short experiment to see if it helps or not. Most of the time, we don't even give the changes a real chance. We choose to shoot an end or two with a release setting or a form change and if the results aren't instantaneously better, then we cast it off as not working at all. Sound familiar? You know it does; we've all been doing this for years, so fess right on up with me. I finally decided that my entire form was a wreck. I started by keeping track of where my misses were occurring and what I was thinking about when I had the bad misses. Then, I wrote down those things that I figured were causing the lousy shots and the wild misses I was suffering through. I left out the intentional tremor, since that is accepted and cannot be eliminated.

I organized and attended a Larry Wise Core Archery Seminar and got the shock of my archery life! More on that subject later. I then organized and helped teach a second Core Archery Academy with Larry Wise and came away with even more insights into this and how to incorporate ProActive Archery into what I've re-learned.

I revised my shot sequence to include those elements. Many of the steps in my shot sequence were correct and automated. When I added the problem elements to it, I ended up with a shot sequence that read more like a book! More than one bite of the elephant here, for sure. This wasn't going to work. I needed something better.

I wrote out the list and then tried to prioritize them into some order of preference as to which were bigger problems and which may be things that could eliminate other problems below them. This, as it turned out, was easy to organize, and it quickly started making sense to me. Organization and "black and white" works for me! Being ProActive works even better.

The First Bite: Blind Shooting and Getting My Body Alignment Right

I can "blank bale it" with the best of them. On a targetless bale, I can execute shots with proper back tension all day long. However, for me, put up a target face and it is an entirely different ball-game. So, I needed something better. I call it the "Blind Bale" technique. (We'll discuss this at length in Chapter 18.) Blind bale shooting clearly demonstrates that a person can and will shoot perfect ends of 25/25 (NFAA 5-Spot Target) with their eyes closed. It is that simple. You might not shoot a perfect 300 round with your eyes closed, but it sure will teach you a lot about your body alignment, draw length, shot flow, and follow through. You will quickly learn to feel your entire shot, but you are shooting at a target instead of just flinging arrows at the bale and feeling the release. You are learning to memorize the smallest aspects of a perfect shot and not just one phase of it. In addition, you have a goal and some fun in the process. I don't spend a lot of time doing this. Just enough to get my body alignment correct and develop some feel for what was happening to me during the shot process with the target there, but not having the visual reference of seeing my sight move; but rather feeling it. I instruct my archery students to shoot a few games every month or so by using this valuable training tool. It is a very quick way to re-evaluate your form and feel for the shot and shot sequence. This might be shot visualization at its best.

Reading Old Journal Entries

Then, I got out my old shooting journals from when I was shooting at the top of my game and started reading. If I had been there before, then perhaps what I needed would be written in the old journals. I soon found out that some pretty cool stuff was contained therein. One key element to my current "problem" involved some high/left and low/right misses that were bothersome to me back in the early 1990's. The problem solution? Simple, thanks to the journal entry that was also short and simple: "Keep your left eye shut and don't even squint it." I've been having wild high left and low right misses for a long time and couldn't figure it out. That was also on my current "elephant list" as one thing to solve and solve quickly. So, the one bite became "Keep the left eye shut," and I went to work on that and only that element. I tended to keep my left eye open slightly and when I do, it will take over and the sight will jump high left. Of course, if the shot breaks then, that is where the arrow goes. If I catch it in time, I'm moving the sight low right quickly to try to correct it. If the shot breaks then, I'm moving low right and the arrow goes there. Simple problem; but a one-minute correction to this was by no means simple.

Fast forward to the past year and a half of learning to shoot left-handed again. That particular eye problem raised its ugly head again recently. I have been shooting left-handed again for over a year; not out of wanting to but out of necessity. The right side used to be the follower and the left side the leader. The right eye is used to doing the work and had done so for 25 odd years. So now we have the situation of the left eye having to do something that it wasn't used to doing; trying to focus and do the aiming! What I ended up with, because I couldn't keep the right eye closed, is seeing two scopes, two circles (or dots, doesn't matter), and also two targets that the upper one is diverging from the lower one at about a 45 degree angle to the 2 o'clock position! They are not side by side, so the Vision Blocker won't work. I tried taping the right lens in my glasses and got vertigo. This problem was getting more and more out of hand. I tried an eye-patch and got squeamish and vertigo. I was getting wild low left misses and then out of nowhere, high right misses. Just a short time ago, a friend told me to just try shooting without my glasses. I am far sighted, so my distance vision is still 20-20. So, I took off my glasses, drew back the bow, anchored, kept both eyes open for the first time in years, and voila; I saw one target, one scope, one ring (or dot), and things settled quite a bit. Only after this was I to realize that my glasses were creating the double vision problem and that the right eye was simply taking over. I couldn't keep it closed and even a squint would allow that eye to take over. The "moving" target was my right eye (the one moving to the 2 o'clock position), the stationary one was my left eye's view, and they were fighting each other for attention. New bite for the elephant: if you cannot see, you cannot focus. This reminded me of a comment made by Larry Wise at his Core Archery Seminar: "Man who chases two rabbits catches neither. Man who chases one rabbit, normally catches it." If you see two things, which one is real, and which one is fake? Out of necessity, I had to change my plan. The vision problem went to the top of the list.

Following the Plan

This is the hardest part. For me, it has become more of a mission than anything. I realized that I do not have to compete to have fun at archery. I do not have to "get ready" for anything. Time might be against me, but yet it is on my side. I don't have to do anything I don't want to do with my archery; it is my hobby, not someone else's. "The Plan" has me competing again on the list, but at some point in the future, as yet undefined. I have more important bites of that elephant to complete before the competitive mode kicks in. Competing again is obviously way down on that list and will not move above any of the other items on that list until those little bites of the elephant are completed. I have, over the course of the past six months completed many of the items on The Plan. There are still several more steps to complete before I'm to the item where I will compete in an event again. However, I'm getting closer and closer, and each time I shoot, I follow The Plan for that day.

Some Interesting Facts

In the past two years, I have found out some very interesting things about myself and my shooting. One of the early things I discovered was that I can shoot great with just about any bow I put into my hands. I have had only one bow recently that I couldn't get to shoot for me. For whatever reason, after eight months, I simply couldn't get things even close to working with it. I got rid of it and picked up something else and things went back to plan quickly.

Stick with the plan, and don't let a rush job short-circuit it. I veered away from the plan a couple of times, and got set back: not a day or two but by several weeks. I've become a firm believer in the adage that breaking or forming a new habit takes a total commitment of at least 21 days. Believe it, and live by it, it works!

Maintain your cool and don't let snide comments or "you have to go to this shoot and compete" short circuit what you are trying to accomplish. You are going to have bad days, and you are going to have good days. You'll have times when you don't think you've accomplished a thing. There are some days I go to the range and shoot 20 shots and spend the rest of the time chatting. However, in those 20 shots, I've accomplished what I set out to do, so that session was over. Yes, I do have practice sessions where nothing is going right and I have to drop back to the previous step in the plan; sometimes even more. Sometimes when working on one thing, it changes another and you have to move backwards in order to move forwards. This is normally perceived by those observing you as a "helter-skelter" approach, but it is your hobby and your plan, so just document what you changed and why, and move on with the new plan.

You don't have to satisfy anyone but yourself. You have nothing to prove to anyone but yourself. I already know I probably won't beat my lifetime personal best scores; so I'm not pining away trying. My plan calls for me merely becoming somewhat competitive. My plan calls for me finding the elements that minimize the effects of "my" intentional tremor (I accept it now.) on my shooting psyche and maximize the scoring potential in dealing with that tremor. Being realistic has gone a long ways in my formulating The Plan. This isn't too bad for a person who was so knotted up after the "Vegas Incident" that I was afraid to even step onto a shooting line again with anyone around for fear someone would again say, "Do you know your bow arm and hand are shaking."

So, realize that we all have an elephant to eat when it comes to our shooting and life in general. The best option is to eat that elephant one bite (and only one bite) at a time. Approach your problem(s) with a plan. Maybe it doesn't have to be written, but for most people writing it down and breaking the problem down into little bites is the only way to really see it for what it is. It is fine to have a goal, but without a plan of how to achieve your goal you won't have much to document or even measure your progress . . . those "bites" are that important.

Tom Dorigatti

3

Archery Instrumentation—Tools for Tens

All of us have instruments/tools that we use to assist us in setting up our bows, be they recurve or compound. How we use those instruments can make the difference between keeping a set-up in proper tune or thinking that the setup has changed, when in reality it hasn't changed at all. The source of such illusory changes is in our selection of the instruments we use and measurements we get from them.

In this chapter, I address just the common instruments we all use as part of our tuning and checking processes. It may seem silly for me to even mention this, but if you don't know how to utilize your instruments or understand basic measuring techniques and practices, then becoming ProActive about this becomes problematic. Some of these instruments are:

- bow scales
- limb bolt wrenches
- bow squares
- calipers.

Bow Scales

First let's address the bow scales you use for setting the draw weight of your bow. Instead of offering basic instruction on their use, I am going to focus on common problems and misjudgments made by archers. This will be followed by some recommendations to help minimize error.

Using a Shop's Bow Scale One of the biggest problems I see is that most archers will pretty much use any bow scale that happens to be handy. Lots of archers have a scale at home, which is fine. However, they come into an archery shop thinking something has changed. They go to the shop's bow scale, weigh the bow, and say, "Yep, just as I thought, my peak weight has changed. This darned bow isn't staying the same." They don't stop to think that since they are using a different instrument, that perhaps it is the instrument that is giving a different reading and not the bow. (Spring based bow scales, like the ones in most shops, are notoriously inconsistent.)

Here are some additional poor practices:

- Taking only one reading to ascertain the peak/draw weight setting. Most shop staff who I have observed, and also most shooters, will take only one reading and that is what they think the actual draw weight is.
- Not pulling straight away from the scale, failing to realize that the angle that they pull the bow down changes the reading.
- Pulling the bow/scale too fast, failing to realize that how fast they draw the bow down on the scale changes the reading.
- Failing to check the "zero setting" of the scale. This is difficult, since most shop scales are set pretty high above the archer's field of view, so you can't tell if the scale is pre-set at zero or not.
- Trying to pull past the peak weight and all the way down to holding weight all at once. If you are checking peak weight, then get it to peak weight and then let the bow down. If reading for holding weight, go straight to the minimum value in the valley; do not bounce back and forth to let the scale settle. You've introduced hysteresis into the equation, and the reading is invalid.
- Failing to read the scale's pointer at eye level when they take their reading.
- Failing to take before and after readings on the scale they are using to make the adjustments. It can be okay to use a different scale to check your bow; however, it doesn't make much sense if you don't write what that scale tells you before as well as after you make a change, also recording how many turns, or sixths of turns, you have moved the bolts. Writing down those numbers allows you to put the bow on your scale when you get home and determine if you were really off in the first place and, if not, to be able to put it back.

Recommendations for Using Bow Scales

- Always check the zero setting of the bow scale before you start.
- Always take three scale readings when using a bow scale. Toss out spurious readings. This is especially important if you are using a wall hung scale, such as Hanson or Viking bow scales. These are accurate but only within 1-2 pounds or so.
- Always write down *what you started with* as indicated on the instrument you are now using.
- Always write down *what you finish with* as indicated on the instrument you are now using.
- Always read the scale's pointer at eye level. If you don't, you can be off as much as two pounds by reading it at an angle. (You can see from the Hanson bow scale photo that even being slightly off will give you a slightly inaccurate reading. The camera angle was not perfectly at eye level (This was done on purpose.).)
- Always pull the bow down at the same angle every time and at the same speed. Be smooth with it and don't just simply try to get to peak weight quickly.
- If possible, use a digital scale. At least they give you a readout without a pointer needing an eyeball reading. It is important here, however, to make at least three readings (maybe even five). Digital scales are very susceptible to pulling angle variances.

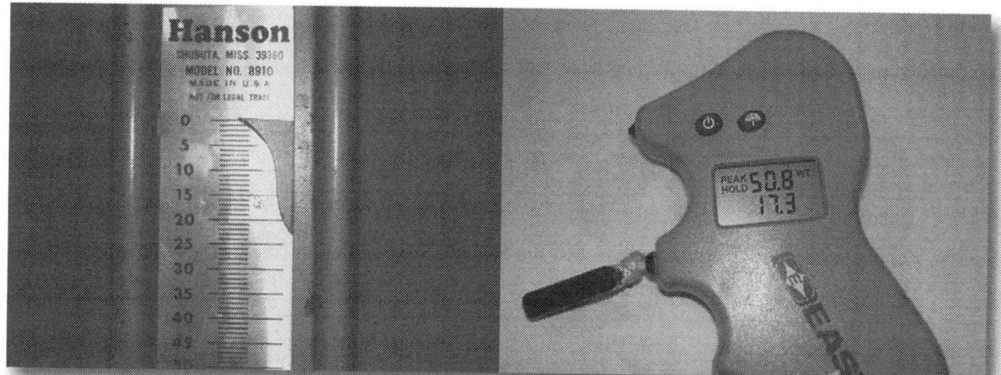

- Better yet, get an Easton Digital hand-held bow scale. Besides giving you peak and holding weights, it holds the last one in memory, and is much less susceptible to variances due to pulling angle. It is light, portable, and accurate to within 0.1 pound. I've converted over to this scale after my experiments described in an *Archery Focus* article (Volume 12, No. 6) concerning the Carter *Evolution+* release aid.

Limb Bolt Wrenches

How often have you borrowed another archer's Allen wrench set to re-set the poundage of your bow? Do you mark your limb bolts? Do you move those limb bolts in ½ and ¼ turn increments like most people? If so, you are introducing error into what you are doing and literally changing the tiller and cam timing (among other things) by doing it in this manner!

Just like with the bow scale, it is imperative for a well-rounded ProActive bow tuner to use the same Allen wrench for setting limb bolts every single time. It is imperative to mark those limb bolts. I've also found that it is more accurate and consistent between limbs to align the end of the Allen wrench parallel with the center of the length of the limb. If you look at the photos of the four different Allen wrench sets inserted into the same limb bolt, you will see a huge variation in their relationship to the longitudinal axis of the limb! The first in the series is the Allen wrench I always use to set my limbs and I never use any other one to do this. When you look at those pictures closely, it will become obvious as to why I've done this for many years. While they may look to be at the same angle, when you "reset" the limb bolts to have their long ends parallel to the longitudinal axis, each of them differs quite significantly from the others! Four wrenches and four different positions of the limb bolts. Recommendations for ProActive use of limb bolt wrenches follow.

Recommendations for Using Limb Bolt Wrenches

- Buy good quality, long-handled Allen wrenches similar to the one I favor. This longer handle gives you better leverage, prevents the wrench slipping out of the key while you are turning the limb bolts, and prevents you from expanding the Allen socket on the limb bolt and/or stripping it out. With today's bows, the limb bolts are tougher and tougher to move, so you need leverage to provide the necessary torque to move these bolts.
- Keep this Allen wrench "new." If it starts to get sloppy or shows wear, replace it. Obviously, check the starting point with the new wrench before you use it to make any adjustments.
- Align the long end of the Allen wrench along the center of the longitudinal axis of the limb.
- Make your adjustments in "lands." Lands are the flat surfaces on the Allen wrench. Since there are six of them, you will see six lands in one full turn, hence one "land" is ⅙ of a turn, or 60 degrees of rotation. First, this is more accurate; second, it allows you to align the long end of the Allen wrench in line with the longitudinal axis of your limb. Third, and most important, it allows you to work in smaller increments than quarter, half or full turns, thereby reducing the risk of getting very far out of balance or having the wrench slip out of the key in the Allen bolt head.
- Mark your limb bolts. This is done for many reasons but, in this instance, the primary one is to help you keep track of how far you've moved it since the last time and, also, if your Allen wrench slips, you know where you are with it. This also gives you a quick visual reference if you think something has moved. By having the bolts marked, a quick glance will confirm that either they have moved, or they are okay.
- Never use someone else's Allen wrench to adjust your limb bolts. This is especially important if you don't have your limb bolts marked so that you can know where you started.
- Always write down everything that you have done and how far you moved each limb bolt.
- When you get the bow tuned and the limb bolts are where they are going to stay, re-mark them with a line that is parallel with the longitudinal axis of the limb. I mark mine on the opposite side of the bolt from the long side of the limb.

The Famous (Infamous) Bow Square

Here is yet another common mistake made by many an archer. I know of many archers who have asked another archer, "Can I borrow your bow square? I forgot mine." This can be a huge mistake. This is especially true if you believe the reading you get off the other archer's bow square is going to be the same as yours! When I first started in archery many years ago, I did this all the time because I was too lazy to carry a bow square with me. However, as I improved my skill level, it wasn't long before I selected one square and used it as the only instrument I used to check things on my bow; from tiller to brace height, to peep height, to nocking point. (I recently adopted a completely different, and in my opinion much more accurate method, for checking my nocking point (*see Chapter* 6).)

Different bow squares can and will give different readings! Different brands and different styles, and even bow squares of the same brand will differ; sometimes very significantly. Take a look at the two bow-square readings in the picture. The blue square is my "master," the green one is my "spare" that sits in a drawer. I think you will see why the green one was put away. The blue one is nearly 35 years old; it obviously shows the wear, doesn't it? Actually, it is even kind of ugly, but the wear is not in places that affect it's accuracy.

You can even get different readings with the same bow square, depending on how you set it onto the arrow rest to position it for the reading! I use a piece of arrow with a slot cut in it that matches the current arrow diameter I'm using. This allows me to put the long arm of my bow square on the arrow rest not relying on remembering whether my arrows just touch the points of the prong, or if it sets down in the groove, etc. (*Note* As long as you have the setting written down or marked, it really doesn't matter that the piece of arrow matches your current arrow size or not – it represents a constant point of reference, which is the key to all of this).

The "Blue" Bow Square
The "Green" Bow Square

Recommendations for Using Bow Squares

- Consistency in setting and checking a nocking point is the primary reason I changed to the more accurate method. I still have that bow square in my bow case, and it is marked with the setting used with the "arrow" on the string. It also has my peep height and brace height marked on it, along with the tiller markings. I carry it with me at all times when I'm shooting outdoors.
- When you make a reading, do it at eye level; that is with your eye square to the scale and not at an angle to it. Bridging the "gap" between the bow square and

the nocking point is tough enough. Doing it when out of line decreases your accuracy. *Note* Do you remember in science class reading the bottom of the meniscus of a liquid in a graduated cylinder? Same idea for accuracy applies: eye level only.

- Take at least three readings every time you do a check. If you have a "ringer" toss that reading, or take two more to confirm. Never rely on just one reading.
- Pick one way, and only one way, of setting that bow square on the arrow rest, and practice it so that you know you are consistent with it.
- Write everything down. If you think you need to make a change, take three measurements, and write them down first. Then make the change, take three new readings, and mark those down too. This way, you know exactly where to move things back to if you've made an error or something doesn't work out.
- If you have to use a different instrument, write down what you are getting as a reading with that instrument before you do anything else. Make the change and write that down too. If you have to make a change that doesn't work, you can go back to where you started without any question in your mind.
- If you've used a different bow square and written the measurements down, it is easy when you get home to take out your bow square and make comparisons and note the difference between the two instruments' measurements.

Calipers

I don't see many archers using calipers for tuning or measuring items on their setups. People probably think I'm nuts because I do use calipers a lot. However, when I tear down and re-build a bow, they cease to think I'm crazy when the first shot fired out of the re-built bow normally goes into the bullseye and quite frequently into the X-ring. I will discuss the changing of strings and cables later in this book (*see Chapters 11 & 12*). It should go without saying that you should use one instrument as your master instrument; always zeroing the instrument before you make a measurement. If you have to use someone else's instrument, simply write down the setting(s) that you start with based upon the reading of that instrument.

I use calipers for several important items, such as:

Changing D-Loops I use a caliper to make sure that the finished D-loop length is exactly the same as the old one. There are new pliers available that make this super easy since I can tighten the loop to exacting tolerances. Here's how:

Procedure for Changing D-Loops

- Make sure to zero the instrument first (*see photo*).
- Measure the D-loop length and mark the reading down (*see photo*).
- Lock the caliper when you remove it, since you can then save time; or should you forget to write it down, you still have the "numbers" right there, still on the instrument.
- Install the new D-loop, one knot at a time, and when the nocking point is properly set, tighten the new D-loop to the same specification indicated by the caliper. This can be done in less than two minutes.

Pressure Point Setting Measuring the positioning of the inner arrow rest "prong" I follow much the same scenario here. Of course, I have the original setting written down and marked. Even with the Short Arrow Technique (*see Chapter* 6), it is a good practice to mark those prongs or center "V" onto your bow square. This will save your bacon out in the field should something happen to your arrow rest! ProActive archery can and often does involve a backup plan. I will discuss this in a later chapter, so watch for it.

Procedure for Setting Arrow Rest Position

- Make sure to zero the calipers first.
- Re-check the measurement to make sure it has really moved.
- Don't move the caliper when you remove it, since you can then save time.
- Reset the arrow rest to specification and lock it down.
- Arrow rest height setting: I also have the original setting marked on my bow square and the setting is also written down.
- Make sure to zero the instrument first
- Measure the rest height setting to see if it really has changed or not. Don't move the caliper when you remove it, since you can then save time. Reset the arrow rest to specification and lock it down.

Recommendations for Using Calipers

- Don't go out and spend a ton of money on a set of calipers. Those depicted in the pictures didn't cost an arm and a leg, but they do a great job for what I use them for. (I have a very expensive set of calipers that are certified, however, they stay at home and are used for loftier purposes.)
- Always zero the instrument before you use it.
- Always take three measurements and toss out any "ringers."
- Always write down the setting you started with in case you have to go back to the original setting.
- When using a different instrument it is vital to write down the readings from that instrument, both before and after. This allows you to go home, get out your instrument and make the comparisons, corrections. Then you are good to go again with your instrument.

Summary

We have addressed four of the most commonly used instruments for checking and setting our bows: bow scales, limb bolt wrenches, bow squares, and calipers. When using any of these instruments:

- Select and use one and only one instrument as your standard instrument.
- Keep them in good shape. If they get worn, replace them. This is especially true of the Allen wrench used for limb bolt adjustments.
- Always zero an instrument before using it. I cannot stress this enough.
- Always check any "reading" to make sure adjustment is really needed before proceeding.
- If you need to make a change, mark down the starting reading, make the change, and write down the ending reading.
- Always take at least three measurements, more if the readings aren't consistent.
- Always read analog instruments (ones with pointers) at "eye level" meaning eyes square to the scale. Reading them at any other angle can create a huge inaccuracy.
- Pick one method to use for moving limb bolts, setting up the bow square, setting and measuring the D-loop length and so on, and always use that method.
- Be consistent and focus while making your measurements. This will save you on the day when something has failed and you are under the pressure and stress to get it repaired and back into specifications again.

Tom Dorigatti

Section 2

Proactive Bow Ownership and Maintenance

In this section of the book, we will be discussing many of the intricacies involved with bow ownership and maintenance. ProActive archery isn't just about fending off the inevitable out on the range; it is also about utilizing a step-by-step planned process to check new bows out and fulfill the warranty requirements. Then you need processes to follow for mounting the accessories properly and also to measure, mark, and document each of your bow's settings before you fine tune the bow. Last, you must then carefully measure, mark, and document those settings once you have completed the fine tuning process. You are not going to be given a lesson in walk-back tuning, French tuning, or paper testing. Instead you are going to be given simple processes that, if followed, will give you the means of replicating your bow's settings with confidence that even if you change the strings and cables and install a new D-loop, the first arrow out of the bow is most likely going to go into the bull's-eye and even likely into the X-ring. You may not even have to get new sight settings—if you follow these simple, ProActive documentation and measuring processes.

50.516

Tom Dorigatti

4

Proactive Bow Ownership—Your New Compound Bow Has Arrived!

In the previous three chapters, I addressed common things people do on the fly 9and shouldn't), and then talked about breaking things down into doable steps (Eating an Elephant) and the importance of maintaining a plan and sticking to it. Finally I discussed archery instrumentation and how important your tools and their proper use is to truly becoming a ProActive archer. Now, it is time to get into bow setup, maintenance, and adjustments, from the time you receive your new bow in the shop or via mail on through to becoming proactive about your bows' maintenance, adjustments, and preparing for the inevitable changes that will occur sooner or later; some sooner, and some later. The better prepared you are by becoming ProActive, the easier it will be to recover when something either changes or fails, or wears to the point of having to be changed.

You have ordered a new bow and you've waited four, six, eight weeks or more to receive it and it has finally arrived! At last it is here and you cannot wait to shoot it. How "ProActive" are you in your bow ownership? Do you want to be able to fend off those inevitable involuntary "changes" that are going to happen as part of bow ownership?

In this chapter, I'll outline some things to do with a new bow before you so much as draw it back. Many of these things are overlooked by new owners in their rush to get that first arrow loosed down range. Doing these things can save you many difficulties later and give you peace of mind about your new bow's condition upon its arrival. They will also help you to protect that new bow's warranty. This chapter introduces "Proactive Bow Ownership" from its natural starting point, the coming of a new bow. I'll be covering what to do upon arrival and the bow registration process, along with many tips concerning those. The following chapters in this section will deal with ProActive bow setup and maintenance. In subsequent chapters, I'll provide tips for mounting accessories, initial bow setup, measuring and documenting all of the important settings for the bow, accessories, and even your arrows, along with those all-important first few hundred shots out of a new bow. Enjoy this chapter and that brand new bow you just received!

Upon Arrival

Here are the first things I recommend a person do when they get their new bow and before installing anything on it. If you are going to the pro shop to get your bow, take your camera with you! You should also tell the archery shop that you prefer that they do not open the box to look at your bow before you get there. If they have, you can deal with that, but still always take your camera with you. Important Note Never just grab the box at the store and take the bow home with you without opening it to inspect the contents. This could be a very costly mistake in the event something is wrong with the bow or attachments that may be missing, etc. After all, you now have several hundreds of dollars tied up in this new piece of equipment; you need to protect that investment.

1. *Before opening the box, inspect the condition of the box.* This can be a tip-off to shipping damage and where to look for it if there is any. If you see a damaged box, take a picture of it before you open it. Be sure to have a time and date stamp on that photograph as proof of when that photograph was taken. Most digital cameras have this feature as do many cell phones with photo capability. Simply turn that feature "on" for these pictures.
2. *When opening the box don't rush it and do not cut into the box with a knife.* Cut the packing tape (only) at the end of the box and open the end flap. Then, carefully remove the bow from the box by lifting it out. Don't try to get the bow out of the box in a hurry. There is no rush here. If you see anything wrong at this point, stop, take a time stamped photograph and even include the shop person in the photo as proof that this is witnessed.
3. *Remove the bow from its protective plastic bag.* Many bow manufacturers wrap the riser with bubble wrap and then place the bow into a full length plastic bag. Don't cut into this bag prior to getting it and the bow out of the box.
4. *Check for the location of any miscellaneous parts, the owner's manual, and other items.* Normally they are in the bag with the bow. Sometimes, however they are lying in the bottom of the box in a separate package or bag. Things to look for with bows are: the cable guard glide and cable guard (if not on the bow already), attachment brackets and bolts for the cable guard and, of course, the registration form and the owner's manual.
5. *Check the entire bow over several times, from top to bottom and back again for mars, marks, dents, and dings.* If you find any problems, take date and time stamped pictures of them. Do this in VGA mode (lowest resolution) so that you can send them via e-mail if need be. It is best to do this right there at the shop so that the shop owner or vendor can see that you didn't mess with the bow before reporting the problem. Here are some key things to look for (actually there are many things, but over the years, these are the most common problems I have found):

   a. *Check for dings or rough spots on the cams.* These are serious and can cut up a bowstring or serving in no time. Don't tolerate even a minor ding or dent in any cam surface that is near or in close contact with the bow string or the cables. These are unacceptable and the bow should be returned or the cams replaced, if new cams are in the shop. Do not let them talk you out of this; it is not okay that things are like this.

b. *Check for limb scratches, dings, or cracks.* Again, these are unacceptable depending upon, of course, how severe they are and their location. You paid for a "mint condition" new bow, not one that is marred up or blemished. If they don't want to accept a bow return, then demand a discount for a "blemished" bow.

c. *Check for missing "e-clips."* This is a very common problem and must be addressed immediately. It is not a big enough concern to return the bow, but the bow shop should install any "e-clips" missing from the axles immediately upon discovery (*see photo*).

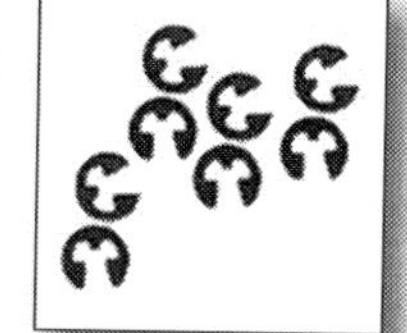

d. *Check for missing nuts and bolts.* It might not seem like a big deal, but missing nuts and/or bolts are more common than you might think. They are also easily overlooked when you first get the bow. It is better to find out now, in the shop, and get them replaced right away than it is to discover a day later that something is missing.

e. *Check the peak weight.* Most bows come in today set at maximum draw weight. Measure the bow on the shop's draw weight scale before touching anything and record what the bow peaks at. If it is above what you ordered by more than 4 or 5 pounds, be concerned. Many come in peaked out at 2 – 4 pounds over what the limb states as maximum. Personally, I hope for that, but won't accept 5 or more pounds over what I ordered.

f. *Check the cam modules for positioning and that the cables are, if on a twin or hybrid cam bow, on the same "slot" on the module(s).* Check that both modules (twin or hybrid cam bow) are the same size. It has happened before that one module is one size, and the other module doesn't match! Check to make sure both cams are the same size, too. Also check those modules to be sure they are tightened, but not over-tightened. Those screws can be stripped of their threads quite easily, or the Allen key can be rounded off. If you over-tighten them, then the two dissimilar metals can bind together and you might not be able to get them loose.

g. *Check the let-off.* If you ordered 65%, make sure the bow is set for that. If you ordered 80%, then check for that. Many bows have the option of both on the same module. Check that you got the let-off you ordered or that you can set the bow to the ordered let-off. Some bows ship with a 75% let-off cam as standard, and if you wanted 65% and didn't specify it on your order, you may be surprised and have to order a set of 65% let-off cams or modules separately.

h. *Check the draw length by* measuring *it.* Don't trust the limb tag! The intent of this caution is to make you aware of this situation, if you didn't already know it. The bow you received may or may not be set to the draw length you ordered. That isn't necessarily a big deal on a modular system. However, on a draw length specific cam this is serious stuff. You need to make sure that with minimal adjustment you can get the "ordered" draw length. Many, many bows come in on a longer setting than they should for any given cam type/size. Some bows run ½″ long while others run ¾″ or more longer that what the order says it is or what the limb tag says it is. Never, ever trust the limb tag as being gospel; more often than not, it is not correct. If you have "room" to get the draw length you want on the delivered cams and/or modules, then everything is fine. On bows with adjustable modules, you may end up away from the "middle of the range," but normally, unless they shipped the wrong cam size totally, you are probably going to be just fine. However, if you cannot get your draw length without radically twisting up the strings and/or cables, or putting the cam out of "optimal position," then return the bow immediately and tell them to send one with the correct draw length or to exchange the cam for the correct one. Exchanging cams can be problematical if the limb deflection is such that the next smaller cam will put your specified (ordered) peak weight out of the range you ordered.

Note that I'm recommending that you check the draw length as the bow sits right now and that you have room to go either way. There is a method to this apparent madness. Since the bow probably came in maxed out in poundage and you are likely to be reducing that draw weight some, you must be aware that when you lessen the draw weight to what you want to shoot, the draw length setting is going to increase by about ⅛″ per half turn of those limb bolts. This being said, can you imagine the impact on this if you ordered 28″ AMO, but maxed out the bow is already 28½″ AMO and you plan on letting it down 6 or 8 pounds or more (that is two full turns or more on the limb bolts) for shooting it? That means that when you "set the poundage" your draw length will now be somewhere between 29″ and 29½″ of draw, which on a draw length specific cam is way out of specification and you won't achieve your "ordered draw length" very easily with that cam without changing the bow string and/or putting the cam out of its optimal range. This is only of major concern if you are really going to be dropping that poundage a lot from maxed out to your planned shooting weight. On a draw length specific cam, this can really be a major problem since new cams will need to be ordered, and as a result, likely at least a different length bowstring, and in many cases even the cables. Then comes the problem of the limb deflection (a measure of limb stiffness) not matching the cams.

j. *Check the axle-to-axle measurement and the brace height while the bow is maxed out.* This can give you clues as to whether the string and cables are "in spec" or not. Most people change to new strings and cables almost immediately nowadays, but as you will see, I differ regarding this item. Write down these measurements. There is a reason for this as part of your ProActive approach to bow ownership and set-up.

k. *Read the Owner's Manual* before doing *anything* with the bow. Even if you think you know all about the bow, it won't hurt to check things out in the manual. There are good things in there such as how to properly install the cable guard, how the cam system adjustments work, marks for cam synchronization, recommended starting point for nocking point and centershot. Then, of course, many manuals have a documentation section for the bow's measurements to be recorded.

l. *Check the limb mounting bolts and cam module bolts for tightness.* Do not over tighten these bolts; just make sure they are snug before doing anything. Occasionally, the bolts that attach the limb pockets to the riser are loose. It is a good idea to check these out and make sure they aren't stripped out or exceedingly loose. When it comes to checking your bow over, leave no stone unturned and no bolts or screws not checked. It can save you a lot of grief and hassle.

Registering your Bow with the Manufacturer

If everything above checks out and you are happy with your purchase, now is the time to register your bow. Always take care of this as soon as possible. Most failures occur within the first few thousand shots. If the bow is registered right away, and you've shown the dealer any "flaws," etc., it makes it much quicker and easier to make a warranty claim. Of course, you did take those time-stamped pictures, right?

1. *Remove the bow's "Information Tag" from the end of the box it was shipped in.* Most bow companies have a computerized shipping and inventory system. When the bow is shipped, it has a removable label on the end of the shipping container that has the bow's serial number and other information on it, along with bar-coded information. They have made this tag easily removable for safe-keeping. I have discovered however, that few bow shops and even fewer new owners pay any attention to this all important shipment and inventory tag. I always remove this tag and stick or tape it onto the manual's registration form or the front of the owner's manual (*see photo of a box shipping label*). Compare the serial number and bow specifications on this tag to the actual serial number that is on the bow. Do not throw away that bow box. Take it home with you. You never know if you'll have to ship the bow back for a warranty claim. You might also need that box to ship out the bow when/if you sell it to another person. It is a good idea to keep the plastic packing bag and bubble wrap, if any.

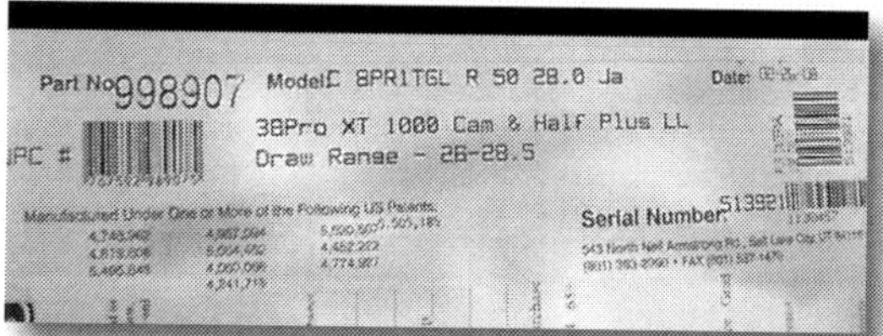

2. *Fill out the registration form and then attach your store receipt for the payment of the bow to the owner's manual.* This is often overlooked by bow-owners. However, down the road, should a problem arise, this can be very important. Many bow companies are going to want to see that store receipt (to make sure you are the original owner and you didn't pick the bow up second-hand)! Fill out the Bow Owner's Data form in the instruction manual (*see photo next page*). Keep your time-stamped photographs as part of the owner's manual materials. You never know when you might need them.

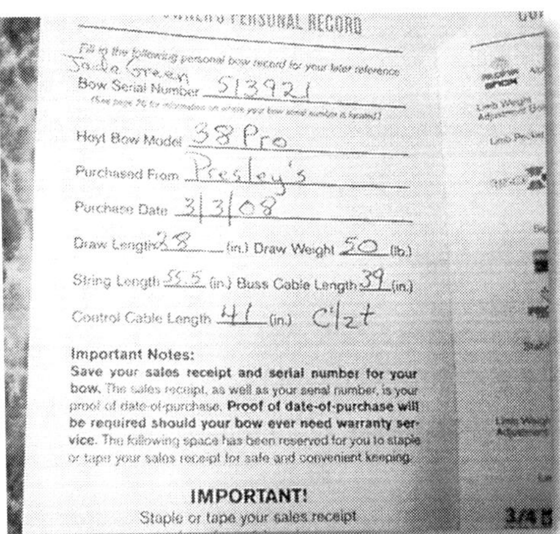

3. *Mail in the registration form or register the bow online.* I prefer to register my bows on-line and save the postage stamp. In addition, I don't have to make a copy of the registration form, so I have that form, the sales receipt, and the bar-coded manufacturer's label in one place for safekeeping, along with the owner's manual and those all important time-stamped pictures.

With all of the above items accomplished, you are now ready to begin installing accessories. In the chapters that follow, I'll discuss some tips and ProActive steps to take in order to make this initial set-up a bit more hassle free and reliable.

Summary

In this chapter, the following were recommended:

- Inspection of the bow's shipping box prior to opening the box. Taking date/time stamped photographs if there are damages to the exterior of the box.
- Checking for all the items that are supposed to come with the bow.
- Checking for missing nuts and bolts or other parts and accessories.
- A list that cannot be totally all-inclusive was given for the inspection of the new bow for scratches, dents, dings, and blemishes at the shop before you so much as draw the bow back safely for the first time. Don't forget those date/time stamped pictures of any dents, dings, mars, abrasions, or blemishes that may show up during the inspection. These are your visual proof of said damages.
- Checking the peak draw weight to insure that it isn't way over or under what you ordered.
- Checking the cams for dings and rough edges and that the cam sizing is correct for the draw length that you ordered.
- Checking that the let-off percentage is what you ordered and/or that you can set the bow to the let-off that you want.
- Checking the bow's draw length while at full, bottomed-out peak weight to insure it won't be way too long should you desire to lower the peak weight. (Lowering the peak weight lengthens draw length about 1/8″ (3 mm) per half turn of the limb bolts). This is probably the most important item of the lot, other than dings, dents, and blemishes or flaws. On a fixed draw length cam, this can be a crucial item necessitating a return of the bow or a cam switch if it is too far off from what you ordered. Remember, many times, the bow will come in longer on draw length than ordered. It depends upon the manufacturer and the style of cam system involved.
- Checking the axle-to-axle length and the brace height. This gives clues as to

whether the string and cables are reasonably close to specifications or not.

- Reading the owner's manual first. There are several do's and don'ts contained in the owner's manual. In addition, there easily could be some important instructions concerning cable guards, draw stop pegs, and the like. You need to be well aware of these things before drawing the bow for the first time.
- Registering your bow with the manufacturer and saving all the shipping information, receipts, and recording bow specs in the manual

If you do the above, you will find that this simple ProActive approach to bow ownership will give you a lot of peace of mind as you proceed to setting up that new bow.

Owner's Guides—either as a booklet or now often as a download off of the Internet—read them, keep them.

Tom Dorigatti

5

Proactive Bow Ownership—Mounting Accessories

In Chapter 4, I addressed how ProActive bow owners check out a new compound bow newly arrived at home or archery shop. If you haven't read Chapter 4, here is a summary (or if you just read the danged thing you can skip over the summary).

Summary of What You Should Be Doing Upon Receipt of a New Bow

Inspection of the bow's shipping box for damage prior to opening the box is very important. Taking date/time stamped photographs if there is any damage to the exterior of the box is well worth your time.

- Check that all the items that are supposed to come with the bow are included.
- Check for missing nuts and bolts, "e" or "c" clips, or other parts and accessories.
- In addition, a list that cannot be totally all-inclusive was given for the inspection of the new bow for scratches, dents, dings, and blemishes before you so much as draw the bow the first time. Don't forget to take date/time stamped photos of any dents, dings, mars, abrasions, or blemishes that show up during the inspection. These are your visual proof of said damages. If in a shop, be sure to include photos and the name of the shop person witnessing the photographs and bow's condition.
- Check the peak draw weight to ensure that it is what you ordered.
- Check the cams for dings and rough edges and that the cam sizing is correct for the draw length that you ordered.
- Check that the let-off percentage is what you ordered and/or that you can set the bow to the let-off that you want.
- Check the bow's draw length while at full, bottomed-out peak weight to insure it won't be way too long should you desire to lower the peak weight. (Lowering the peak weight lengthens draw length about ⅛″ per half turn of the limb bolts). This is probably the most important item on the list, other than identifying dings, dents, blemishes and flaws. On a fixed draw length cam, this can be a crucial item necessitating a return of the bow or a cam switch if it is too far off from what you

ordered. Realize that, typically, bows come in longer on draw length, but not always (it depends upon the manufacturer and the style of cam system involved).
- Check the axle-to-axle length and the brace height. These give clues as to whether the string and cables are reasonably close to specifications.
- *Read the owner's manual.* There are, often times, important do's and don'ts contained in the owner's manual. In addition, there easily could be some cautions and warnings concerning cable guards, draw stop pegs, and the like. You need to be well aware of these things before drawing the bow for the first time.
- Register your bow with the manufacturer and save all the shipping information, receipts, and record all bow specs in the manual.

If you adhere to the above, at a minimum you will find that this simple ProActive approach to bow ownership will give you peace of mind as you proceed to set up that new bow.

Now let's get to the meat of this chapter. If you are sloppy about mounting your accessories, you are opening yourself up to all sorts of what you think are malfunctions but, in reality, are oversights you made in your rush to shoot that new bow. Consider the following story.

A True Story I had started scoring on target #1 of a 14 target unit on a field round at a Sunday tournament. I got to target #14 without hitting anything out of the 5-ring; I was, as we called it, "clean" so far. That last target was a 40 yard, "flat as a pancake" target with good level footing in the trees and out of the wind. My X-count was out the roof that day, already in the mid 40's, and things had been pretty easy. I set my sight, drew back, and caught the left edge of the x-ring. I thought it should have been center, but hey, an "X" is an "X", right? Wrong. The next arrow went solidly into the 4-ring, again dead left. I was absolutely shocked. To miss a "5" at 40 yards on the last target? What the heck is going on? I had not collapsed on that shot and my execution hadn't felt any different. I had checked all four arrows on the previous target and the arrows and nocks were just fine. The next shot went into the 3-ring, dead left, but good elevation. Three points down in two shots after not missing up to this point. What the heck was going on here? I checked the scope to be sure it was tight, checked the cable rake, all checked out okay. What the heck was going on? I found out "what was going on" while drawing the next shot back in that the arrow fell off the arrow rest. I let down, collected myself, and drew back again, with the same result. Now obviously, I knew something was amiss. I was shooting a Golden Key *Golden Premier* arrow rest with the "fishing pole wire loop." On the second let-down, it became obvious to me that the arrow rest itself was the culprit! Sure enough the "fishing pole wire loop's" holding set screw had worked loose and now the loop was tilted sideways, not allowing the arrow to stay upon it any longer. Dang it. Why hadn't I seen that sooner? I got out my Allen wrench and re-tightened the set screw, which automatically went into the detent made in the opposite end of the arm from the loop. The next, and last shot went dead into the X, just like the others "should have" since they were all good, solid shots. This little oversight had cost me not only three points on that half, but also a perfect 14 half as well! All from one little set screw coming loose and me not picking up on it immediately. Everything else on the bow and arrow rest had been marked for a quick glance check. I had been ProActive, but not quite ProActive enough.

I marked that one down in my memory banks and you can bet that the particular set-screw at fault was marked and checked frequently after that fiasco. Well, yes and no. In fact, I got away from that type of launcher arm the very next day and never went back to it. If you over tightened the set screw, you bent the arm; obviously the set screw worked loose quite a bit to allow the loop to twist out of position. Yes, I could have used blue Loctite®. Lesson lived, lesson learned. I had been so, so, diligent about mounting my accessories onto my bow. I had been almost diligent enough in marking everything that "mattered" and some things one would think didn't matter on the bow, on the arrows, on the release aid; but one measly little ole set-screw had cost me dearly. I think I ended up with a 555 that day, dropping two more points on the second half, but I don't remember that nearly as well as the single set screw that cost me a perfect 14 target score of 280 out of 280. I'll remember those two shots the rest of my life.

Another True Story We were shooting a Sectional Tournament some years ago. One of the members of my group started shooting high for no apparent reason. It wasn't particularly hot outside that day, nor was there any obvious external cause for his problem. As we progressed, it was like his arrows were simply walking their way up the targets. He'd move his sight to correct for this and his next arrow would still be high. What do you supposed he checked and in what order to resolve the problem? Do you think he moved his indicator pin and all was well? You might jot down the items you would check, in order, to try to figure out what is going on. I will tell you the resolution of this problem later on in this chapter.

Mounting the Accessories onto Your Bow ProActively

Now that you have thoroughly inspected your shiny new bow, you are ready to begin the task of mounting your accessories. Note The photos I provide use masking tape to mark the positions of various accessories. The use of masking tape is not recommended for marking your positions on the bow or accessories. I only used the tape to give the contrast necessary for clarity in the photos. What I actually use is a fine-tipped permanent magic marker that is in a contrasting color and easy to see. This ink will come off simply by using an alcohol swab.

Caution *For safety reasons, resist the temptation to draw the bow back at all until you have at least the arrow rest and nocking points or D-loop installed!* If you attempt to draw it with a release aid, you have nothing to stop the release from sliding on the bowstring, and this can cause a potential serious injury. Drawing back the bow with your fingers is also risky, since you don't have an arrow rest on the bow. You should also resist drawing the bow with your fingers on the string and no arrow; both practices are accidents waiting to happen. Since you are not familiar with the draw cycle, nor, if you are a release shooter, are you familiar with how to properly let down a compound bow with your fingers on the string, it is best to just wait. Today, it is commonplace for people to dry-fire their bow, or worse yet, to torque the string so badly that they actually derail the strings/cables from the cams. This can cause irreparable damage to a bow, its cams, and even its limbs. If you do this damage, then you have just "bought" the now damaged bow and will have to pay for the repairs due to your negligence.

Mounting the accessories doesn't have to be in any special order, but you should be ProActive and take care in how you do your work and document what you do.

Things to Check Here are some things to check before you begin the process. If any of these are over-looked they can cause you problems, either immediately or (worse) later on.

1. *Check the condition of the mounting bolts and screws.*
   - Are the threads on the bolts clean and unobstructed? It would pay to clean them up. Remove old "Loctite®" or grime from the threads now. It can save you the potential problem of cross threading and stripping out the holes in the riser!
   - Are the bolts too long or too short? This is often overlooked. If the screws are too short, the potential of stripping out the mounting holes in the riser are compounded. Simply checking for this will save you some headaches. To be long enough, the screw threads have to penetrate a distance equal to the diameter of the screw itself. If they are too long (the holes are not drilled all the way through), then you won't be able to get the bolts tight or, worse, you will distort the metal at the bottom of the hole. If you have to cut bolts off, be careful that you don't score the threads or create burrs or edges that won't mesh with the internal threads!
   - Are the Allen-heads on these screws in good-shape, or have they been rounded off from previous use? If they are not in good-shape, then replace them now. Be ProActive and fend off this problem before it has a chance to get you.
   - Color mismatches? It should go without saying that black screws with silver hardware or silver screws with black hardware can look "tacky." However, if you aren't concerned about this, then obviously it isn't such a big deal. It is better to change them now rather than later.
2. *Check the condition of all threaded holes in your riser.*
   - Sometimes during the dipping, painting, or anodizing process "gunk" finds its way into the mounting holes and will cause problems when you try to put the bolts into them. It is a good idea to either take the correct sized tap, or the correct bolt size and simply turn it into each and every mounting hole on the riser that the particular tap, screw or bolt fits into in order to help clean out the threads. Taking care to do this now is a lot easier than having problems later.
3. *What, if anything, will I use on the threads to help keep the bolts tight?*
   - ***Danger*** The use of *red Loctite®* is "verboten" when it comes to the mounting accessories on your bow (sight, rest, anything that is mounted on that bow or equipment).
   - You should never consider using hot melt glues for this purpose.
   - You should never consider using "fast-set" gel glues for this purpose either. They

aren't designed to handle this type of application.

- Blue *Loctite*® or its equivalent has gained in popularity over the years. It normally allows for the removal of the screws or bolts with "some resistance." However a word of caution is in order: for any bolt size 10-24 or smaller, I don't recommend the use of blue *Loctite*®! This is your choice, but with the smaller screws/bolts of that nature, you are at a high risk of having the Loctite® hold too well and as a result, you won't be able to get those screws and/or bolts loose without stripping out the bolt heads! More is not better, so, if you use this stuff, use it sparingly!
- *Caution* Be especially cognizant of over-tightening screws and bolts; especially those on cams, cam modules, or bow sight parts! Often the two metals are dissimilar and this alone can cause the screws and bolts to "seize up." What you normally have is a steel screw or bolt (a harder substance) being tightened into a softer substance (typically aluminum). As a result, the harder substance can score up the softer substance and the bolt's threads get particles pulled into them. As vibration occurs and eventually moisture sets in, the bolts can, if over-tightened, seize up or at least make their removal exceedingly difficult. *Loctite*® or the excessive use of it could magnify this problem. Ruined cams and modules are bad enough, but imagine the damage done when a bow's riser sight mounting holes are stripped out, or you have stripped out the bolt/screw heads themselves, or worse yet, broken one off inside the hole?

  Yet another caution, especially for smaller bolts: *never use an old Allen wrench that appears to be even slightly rounded off* when trying to loosen or remove these smaller bolts on accessories, such as on sight mounts and especially cam modules! If those bolts are over-tightened or have "seized up" from rust or too much Loctite® then by using a worn Allen wrench, you could round out the Allen heads and create a difficult problem. A new Allen wrench is far less expensive than a new module or cam or trying to find a tool to get the bolt loosened up!
- I'm not saying that using blue (not red) Loctite® isn't a good idea; it is just that I prefer not to use it on my equipment. If you are comfortable with this product, or similar ones, then fine. Just be aware that with this product "More is not always better" and can cause potential problems. Use it sparingly.
- I've found that simple bowstring wax placed upon the threads of the bolts/screws works quite well in allowing you to mount the accessories. It provides some lubrication to help the screws go in easier, can help provide a moisture barrier, and also seems to help prevent the screws from working loose.
- Clear finger-nail polish also works well on bolt threads. In my opinion, while it may not be better than blue *Loctite*®, it is safer.
- Yet another thing I've used is *Fletch-Tite*® fletching glue, but when I did use it, I used it sparingly. More is not always better.
- Finally, there is the old standby, which I've really come to prefer: this is applying nothing at all on those threads! My preferred method is simply not over-tightening the screws and snugging them up after 100–500 shots or so out of the

new bow. It has been my experience that after about 100-500 shots, if bolts are going to come loose, that is when they will do it, so I snug them up. I have found that after snugging up accessory screws/bolts, I've not had any issues with them coming loose. Once again, as you'll discover when you go through the mounting of these accessories, becoming ProActive reaps many benefits down the road when (and not if) you need such benefits.

- Yes, I know I covered this before, but I cannot stress this enough, so I'm saying it again. When mounting any accessory, use an Allen wrench that is in good repair. Do not use Allen wrenches that have rounded edges on them. You are asking for problems. Become ProActive and use only good equipment.
- You can purchase replacement set screws with nylon tips on them, but finding them in smaller sizes can be difficult. Spott-Hogg, with their *Premier* and *Infinity* series arrow rests, provides a nylon-tipped set screw that is ideal for placement through the threaded portion of those rest extensions and into the second hole on the riser (if there is one—see photo of cushions below). However, the threads are not 5⁄16-24, so this needs only to be snugged up to stop the arrow rest from movement on the vertical plane. It is still a good idea to use the suggestions below.
- There is another way to assist in mounting accessories that have dead end holes in the riser, or the bolts/set screws come in contact with the riser or carbon/steel components. This method will not only help to keep those bolts or screws snug, but it will also help prevent marring the riser (if mounting arrow rests), or will help keep you from fracturing the carbon (such as a cable guard rod) with solid metal screws. You can deal with this situation by making your own "mounting cushions" especially for cable guards made of carbon fiber or you want to use the set screws that are in the mount for your arrow rest, but do not want to mar the riser. Here's how: If you have a leather punch, then this is an easy task to cut out a piece of rubber or leather slightly smaller than the bolt hole. Simply cut it out and place it into the screw hole before putting in your mounting or set screws. If you don't have a leather punch, you can use a drill bit that you have ground the chuck end of the bit to a flat and sharp surface. Find the size bit you need, place the leather, rubber, or whatever soft material, onto a piece of waste wood, tap the drill bit solidly with a mallet and cut out the "cushions" of the proper size to fit the bolt/screw hole. Some people even use wadded up tape or cut outs from plastic milk cartons for this purpose. You'll be amazed at how well this works! This isn't anything that I invented. These have been used for multi-rod carbon stabilizers with sliding weights for years. It stops the set screws from damaging the carbon rods and holds the sliding weights in place much better. I simply picked up on it when mounting other types of accessories (*see photos above right*).

Mounting Cable Guard Rods

Many bows today come with cable roller guards. However, many others still use

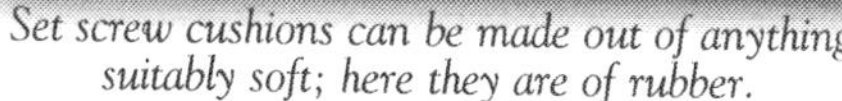
Set screw cushions can be made out of anything suitably soft; here they are of rubber.

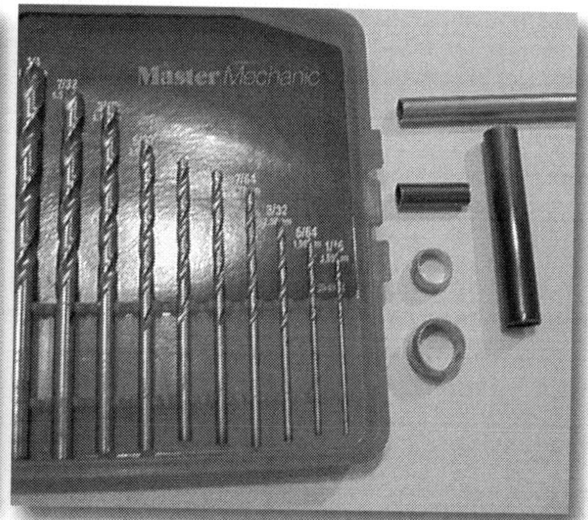

All kinds of things can be used to "punch" out disks if you don't have a leather punch (see text).

straight cable guard rods and still others have "angled" or "bent" cable guard rods that allow you to adjust the rake. Question: "What are you going to do when the bent or angled cable guard works loose and you lose your rake adjustment? While proper mounting of the cable guard can help delay this, having a "plan" on how to make sure that when it comes loose, you won't lose your tune and draw length, and have vane/feather contact on the cable guard. You should be capable of putting it back in place; and I mean the exact place where it was before it came loose, shouldn't you? Think it through. If you are sloppy about mounting this accessory, then you are asking for problems.

Yet Another True Story This time, the story isn't about my shooting. This happened only a few short weeks ago during a league. One of our top shooters, who has shot numerous 60X indoor rounds was shooting along just fine, when all of a sudden an arrow went off out into the 4-ring on him. He said, "What the heck?" He went to draw back the next shot and noticed his feathers were rubbing deeply on his cables. He mentioned to me that his feathers were hitting his cables and he just shot a "wide four." I glanced over and immediately told him to check his adjustable-rake cable guard, that I'd bet it had come loose on him. Sure enough, that was exactly the case. Problem is, he didn't know where it was set before it came loose. He hadn't ever marked it or even thought about marking it before. Well, he eye-balled it to get clearance back, shot two solid 5's, adjusted the rake a bit wider, and got into the X ring again. He ended up with . . . a 56X-299! Had he not lost the rake on that cable guard, he'd have likely had yet another 60X-300. Simple problem, high cost for a bungled fix. Obviously, he now has that cable-guard rake marked for when it comes loose again.

1. If your bow comes with a bent or angled cable guard rod or straight rod with an adjustable "rake," I feel it is imperative to perform a few simple steps while mounting this item to the bow.
   - Read the owner's manual concerning the attachment of the cable guard! This

will likely give you the configuration for the cable routings, especially if you have a "roller guard." Sooner or later you will have to change cables, so you need to know how to properly do this anyway.

- Put the bow into a good quality bow press and press the bow so that the cables and string are loose.
- After having checked that the mounting hole's threads are clean and clear, simply attach the cable guard bracket and cinch it up and then, after using some cushions into those set screw holes (see above), lightly tighten the set screws holding the guard rod is held into the riser or mounting bracket.
- You will be establishing the correct "rake" later, once you have mounted the arrow rest.
- Install the cable glide onto the cables, being certain to follow the correct crossing pattern for the cables. For most cable-guarded bows, this is extremely important and should not be reversed. Yes, I know I just repeated myself, it is for good reason.

Question You are shooting for score and suddenly your "bent-angle" cable guard rod comes loose and you have zero cable clearance. What have you done ProActively to insure you can get your cable guard rake back to where it was before the cable guard came loose? See the photo below—it is so simple, yet few people bother to mark the location of their cable guard and wonder why they can't get their grouping quite right for quite some time due to rotation of the guard, or worse they set it "close enough" and go on. Be ProActive and don't make this mistake!

The tape is a stand-in for a permanent score or pen mark (tape will wear off).

2. If your bow comes with a straight-rod cable guard, I still recommend that you put the bow into a bow press to relax the cables. It can be quite difficult to put the cables into the glide, orient the cables, and then try to hold the bow and pull the glide and cables over the end of the guard rod. I've seen many a set of brand new cables chafed or strands even cut while trying to do this the "hard way."

Pressing your bow makes it easier to get the rod onto the riser and precludes pre-loading the set screws so that you can cinch those bolts down tightly without any bias on them. You can permanently damage a carbon cable rod by over-tightening those set screws. I recommend the use of the cushions I suggested above.

Now you can install the cables into the glide in their correct orientation, and then place the cable glide onto the cable rod. Some cables route through the cable glide, while others snap into slots on the cable glide. Either way, it is much easier to install the cables into the glide if the bow has been pressed so the cabling system is loose. *Caution* Before backing down or releasing the bow press, make sure the cables and bow string are correctly mounted into the cams. Failure to do so could seriously damage the cables and string and/or damage the bow or cause injury to you when you attempt to draw the bow back after taking it out of the bow press.

Mounting the Bow Sight Mounting Bracket

Do you recall the scenario at the beginning of this chapter concerning an archer suddenly shooting high? Well, this particular problem source ends up being one of the last things shooters check when you start shooting high, then higher, and higher. Most fail to check this item until finally they've run out of things to check! Think about what happens when your sight mounting bracket comes lose. The weight of the aperture causes it to drop causing the archer to raise his bow higher which results in . . . high shots. A tiny slip at the bow gets amplified greatly down at the end of the extension bar. Read on for some hints to help alleviate the problem during your accessory mounting routine. But first:

- Have you checked the riser mounting holes to make sure they are clear and that the bolts you will be using work easily in those threads?
- Have you checked the lengths of the bolts?
- Have you checked the Allen heads to make sure they aren't rounded off or worn?'
- Are you using an Allen wrench that is in good shape and not rounded off or worn?
- Have you checked that you have the correct mounting bracket for your sight? (And, yes, I've seen people use the wrong mounting bracket.)

Now you are ready to mount the sight bracket to the riser. This is no big deal; or is it? Many of you will simply place the mounting bracket directly onto the riser without anything between the riser and the bracket. This gives you a metal on metal mounting; not necessarily all bad, but a "cushion" of some sort will not only provide you with something to prevent the bracket from coming loose, but when it does come loose, something that protects the bracket from marring the riser. There are several things you can use to make such a cushion. Some of those are, and in no order of preference:

- A thin piece of rubber that has holes in it matching those on the sight mounting bracket is very, very effective; in fact some sights (very few, unfortunately) still come with these. You can make one easily, just trim it to size after you've made the holes in it.
- Use a piece of plastic from a milk jug to make a cushion. This is very easy to do. The soft plastic provides a nice, soft cushion for that mounting bracket and, if done right, is nearly invisible, too (see photo below).
- You can also use clear plastic from any of a variety of packaging components, even from "blister packs." The plastic packaging from your arrow rest or release aid can be used to make this cushion.
- In the past, lots of shooters used clear silicone cement or caulking as their cushion and then once they had the sight mounting bracket tightened down, they

would caulk around it with the clear cement. By far, this is my least favorite method for providing a cushion to keep the sight mounting bracket from moving. I don't see this much anymore, but the problems with this method are: getting the caulk into the mounting holes, having an uneven spreading of the caulk on the back of the bracket, causing a "bias" in the mounting of the bracket to the riser (this will play havoc with proper leveling of the vertical bar to the riser and also your 2nd and 3rd axis alignments), and temperature variations, should the bolts become loosened, will cause varying degrees of movement and have you really guessing, thus, you won't be checking for this when the scenario above happens.

Making a Sight Mounting Bracket Cushion So, I've talked about the advantages of a "sight mount bracket cushion" and now I'll tell you how to make one for your sight mounting bracket. Since I favor using milk carton material, I'll go through making your cushion out of milk carton plastic. You will need the following: A milk carton; a sharp hobby knife or a sharp box cutter blade; a drill bit of the right size, a mallet; a piece of wood to use as a cutting board (so you don't tear up your table or desk top); a metal ruler or straight edge; your sight mounting bracket; the sight mounting bolts, and your Allen wrench that is in good condition.

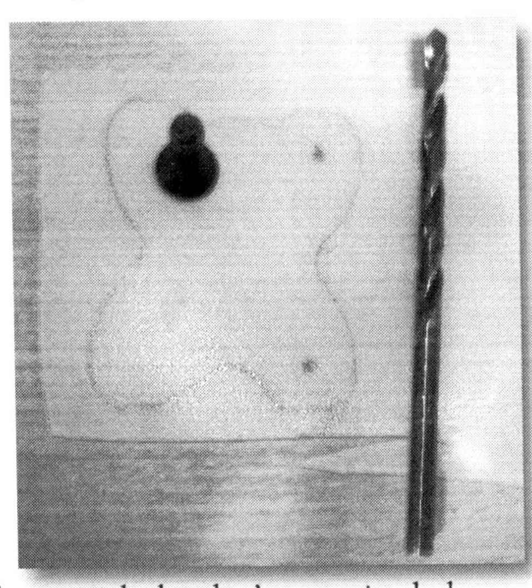

Steps

1. Cut out an over-sized piece of the plastic from the flat side of the milk carton.
2. Place this plastic onto the piece of wood you are going to use as a cutting board.
3. Place your sight mounting bracket on top of the plastic. If you want, you can clamp the bracket down on the plastic for the next step, but you don't have to.
4. You can either use a fine-tip magic marker to mark the spot where the holes go, or if you have your butt-end of the drill bit flattened down, you can use your mallet and bit now to "Punch" the two holes through the plastic that match your sight bracket's mounting holes.
5. Outline the outside edges of your sight mounting bracket onto the plastic.
6. Cut out your cushion using the straight edge to get things cut cleanly. I don't recommend you trying to cut around the bracket itself. I cut myself pretty badly one time trying to hold the bracket and do the cutting at the same time. That was not fun and hurt like the blazes. In addition, the danged bracket, even when clamped down seemed to want to move just at the wrong time forcing me to start over.
7. If you haven't made the holes from step # 4 yet, now is the time to make the holes by using the drill bit, or even a hand held paper punch, or, if you have one, a leather punch. I do not recommend using the drill bit in a high speed drill right through your sight mounting bracket. One slip of the drill, and you could oval out

that mounting hole, which isn't a good idea at all!

8. Once you have holes in the cushion, use the sharp blade to smooth out both sides of the plastic so it is totally flat.
9. Put both mounting bolts through the bracket; put the bracket cushion onto the mounting bolts. Then, put two of the punched leather or plastic cushions into the mounting bolt holes in the riser. (Unless your riser is drilled completely through, in which case you don't need "cushions.")
10. Attach the sight mounting bracket to the riser and tighten the two bolts. Caution Do not over-tighten these bolts. I do not recommend the use of any Loctite® on these two bolts! In my opinion the heads on these two bolts are too small and too easy to "round out" if you even slightly over-tighten them and then later try to remove them (for whatever reason). Remember what I said about dissimilar metals and steel against aluminum? There is a lot of stress placed on this mounting bracket from lateral movement of the sight extension bar and also in the vertical plane just from the weight of the scope and vertical bar. The longer the sight extension, the more stress is placed upon the mounting block! It seems that the vibrations from the riser, once the bolts are set, seem to tighten them even further! If you want to use bow string wax or fingernail polish on the bolts before placing them into the riser; both those will work (see comments made earlier on this). My experience has been that if I snug up these two bolts without really "reefing" on them, they might come loose slightly after the first 100 shots or so, but once they are snugged back down they normally don't come loose, even without the use of Loctite® or a similar product.

Yes, I know you are thinking, "didn't he say *when* they come loose?" Yes, I certainly did. So now comes the question: "So what can you do to be ProActive and have a visual check that these two bolts are staying in position?" Think about it. I had the situation a few times in the past, but not anymore. Usually on a new mounting, the screws, if they come loose at all, will come loose after 100 shots or so. I snug them (not reef on them) to get them tight again, and I've not had them come loose again. This is not to say it can't or won't happen, but it hasn't; at least not yet. However, I'm "set up" so that I will know instantly at a glance if these bolts are a culprit for me suddenly shooting high or not. Figure it out yet? *Solution* mark the bolt head with a matching line on the bracket (*see photo*). So simple. You now have that visual reference.

So, there you have it, a simple solution to prevent marring of the riser by the sight mounting bracket, a cushion to help keep those bolts tight, and a means of having a ProActive quick visual check to see if those bolts have moved or not. And, you also should know the first thing to check if, out of the blue, you start shooting high! I have seen this cause this problem and yet not be isolated until the shooter has lost a lot of points on their score; sometimes they've even finished their lousy score and don't

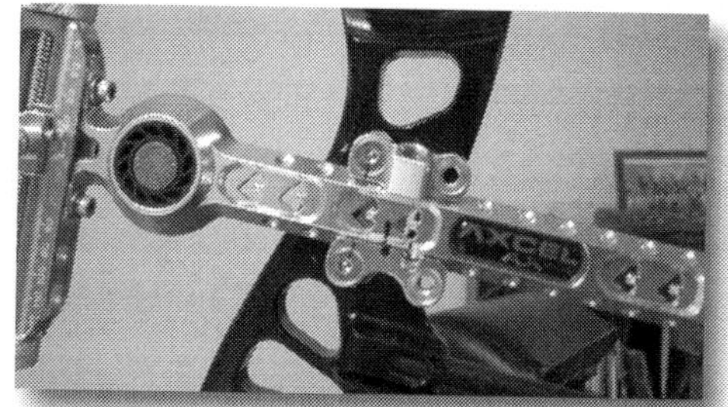

discover the cause until much later. Some have even made the error and moved their indicator pin and now, they are really "lost." They've taken a perfectly good set of marks and thrown all of them off and now have to find the indicator pin placement on the fly.

One last thing, you should also consider is to mark the position of the sight extension bar in a contrasting color, so that you aren't trying to remember which extension hole you are using (see photo previous page and look for mark on extension bar)! I've seen more than one shoot-off lost because when a shooter pulled out his bow to re-assemble for the shoot-off, in the excitement of the moment he forgot to put the sight extension where it belonged. I even seem to remember a Vegas shoot-off being lost in one of the divisions and also an Iowa Pro-Am shoot off being lost in the BHFS Division because of this very problem. The shooter simply didn't put the sight back on with the correct extension and only discovered it after the fatal miss. It may have gone better for them, had a simple visual cue been used.

Mounting the Arrow Rest to the Riser

The proper mounting or any arrow rest is extremely important. To get it right, preferably right the first time, is not as difficult as you would think. However, too many archers simply go through the motions when they mount their arrow rest and don't really think about this process ProActively.

Most bows have only one mounting hole, also called the "Berger Hole," for the mounting of the arrow rest to the riser. Some bows, such as those from Merlin, Barnsdale, and some models from BowTech and Elite have two mounting holes for the arrow rest. Some arrow rests accommodate the use of two bolts, while most don't. If your bow has two mounting holes, it is up to you to decide how you want to mount the arrow rest, either with one bolt or with two bolts. There are even some arrow rests that have individual mounting holes for the placement of that rest forward or back onto the riser (Spot-Hogg *Premiers* and *Infiniti's* are examples). Others, such as the Hamskea *Versa-Rest*, the Brite Site *Pro Tuner Jesse Mount*; the AAE *Freakshow*, most models of the Trophy Taker arrow rest line, and others have a mounting slot cut into them so you can position those rests at any point between the two ends of the slot. Still other bows have arrow rests available that mount solidly because the rest is designed to be attached to a particular brand of bow (Hoyt and Mathews come to mind). If the arrow rest can be solidly mounted and pretty much lock into place, then you only need to take care concerning not marring the riser, over-tightening those 5⁄16–24 bolts, and/or stripping out the Allen heads.

So, let's discuss some particular arrow rests and how to attach them to your riser with a minimal risk of them coming loose or moving. Along the way we'll address the second screw issue.

Arrow Rests of the Spott-Hogg Premier or Infiniti, 3-D Rover Type These have two or more threaded mounting holes on the rest arm itself. They also include a nylon tipped set screw that you can use as a second bolt lock-down in the event your riser only has one hole. All you have to do is to select which mounting hole, based upon the riser shape and/or how far back you want the arrow rest to sit behind the riser. Then, depending upon how many holes you have in the riser, consider the hints below:

1. *One Mounting Hole on the Riser* If you don't have to set the arrow rest all the way back, then I would recommend you use the mounting hole on the arrow rest that places the rest closest to the riser. This leaves the other hole available for use of the threaded set screw. That screw is nylon tipped, but I still recommend that you use either a thin rubber insert, or a thin leather insert, or even multi-layered pieces of masking tape inserted into the hole before tightening down the set screw. This helps prevent marring the riser and actually can help in keeping both the set screw and the main mounting bolt tight as well.

   If you use a single bolt alone, then the use of a larger washer (I recommend stainless steel or blued steel) along with an "internal Star Washer" to help keep the mounting bolt tight. I've never had an arrow rest mounting bolt come loose when using a "Shake-proof Internal Star Washer" (*see photo*).

   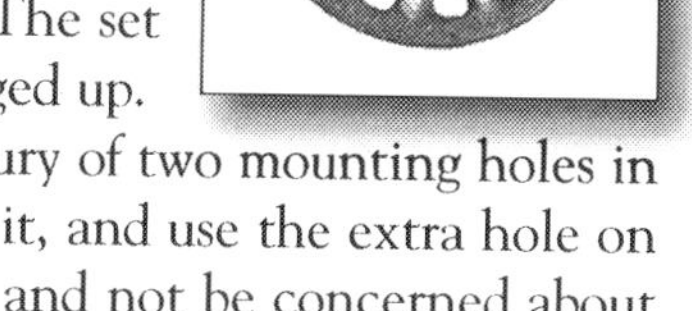

   If your arrow rest has only a solid mounting bar and one mounting hole, it likely has threaded set screw holes in the mounting bar. This is okay, but again it is a good idea to make small rubber or leather inserts and place those into the set screw holes before tightening up the set screws. The set screws don't need to be super tight, just simply snugged up.

2. *Two Mounting Holes on the Riser* If you have the luxury of two mounting holes in the riser, you can set your arrow rest how you want it, and use the extra hole on the arrow rest mounting bar to insert a second bolt and not be concerned about a set screw marring your riser. Options here include:

   - If the rest is of the Spott-Hogg variety, you can use the nylon-tipped set screw through the hole in the arrow rest and simply tighten it snugly enough to hold the arrow rest's level mounting angle. Caution The threads on this bolt are not 5⁄16 -24, so don't expect to tighten it far. It only needs to be snug in order to hold the arrow rest in place!

     If the arrow rest doesn't have extra holes for a large bolt to go through but the end of the mounting bar extends beyond that second hole, then you can simply use a normal 5⁄16-24 set screw through the sight window side of the riser and snug it up to the arrow rest mounting bar! This works well, and also doesn't stick out into the sight window.

   - If the arrow rest's arm has a slot in it which allows for you to move the arrow rest forward or back in any increment, then I've found that you can use a "Button head" bolt in one of the holes (with a smaller washer) and then a cap screw as the other mounting bolt. This will give you an absolutely solid mounting of your arrow rest that will not come loose or, if it does, the arrow rest will not slip out of position.

Some Other Hints On Arrow Rest Mounting Some people, in order to help prevent "slipping" of the arrow rest should it come loose, will use a thin layer of double

stick tape cut to the shape of the arrow rest mounting bar. Others use masking tape to accomplish this but beware: masking tape breaks down quickly and should never be used on the riser itself. You will not be able to get the glue from the masking tape off the riser later on! Double stick tape also breaks down after a time, and I don't think this is advisable either.

Of course, you do have the option of a thin rubber liner or one made out of milk carton or plastic packaging material. This does provide the cushion between the riser and the arrow rest, doesn't break down, and doesn't require an adhesive. All you would have to do is to make the hole in the cushion larger to accommodate the bolt(s).

Question How can you create a quick visual check to see if your "single bolt mounted arrow rest" has slipped from its initial alignment? (This can happen; it happened to me.) *Answer* Outline the contours of the arrow rest with a fine-tipped marker of a contrasting, visible color. A simple procedure and it will save you a ton of problems in isolating what has happened, as well as points on your scorecard, because you can easily identify this problem now and fix it in seconds. Without the marks, you will likely not know for sure whether your rest has moved nor will you know where to put it back. I'm sure you realize the impact on the nocking point and tune of the bow should that arrow rest come loose and start moving around.

Again tape was used here (instead of permanent pen marks) for clarity in the photo.

A Quick Note Regarding Limb-Driver Style Arrow Rests In my opinion, it is a good idea to measure and mark the positioning of the limb clamp(s) on any type of split-limb mount for the *Limb-Driver* style or Hamskea *Versa-Rest* that you are using. When that mount works loose and slips, it will wreak havoc with the "tune" of that arrow rest.

In addition, once you have established the position of the lanyard on a cable-driven fall-away arrow rest (be it a *Trophy Taker*, a *Ripcord*, or whatever), it is a good idea to not only tie it in solidly, but also to tie it in with something that won't slip. When the lanyard moves, it normally gets moved up the cable, and this will really cause problems if not caught immediately. I have also measured that distance down from cable guard to the lanyard and then marked this on my bow square and in my notebook of settings. When that lanyard moves, it will change the "timing" of that arrow rest and really mess things up!

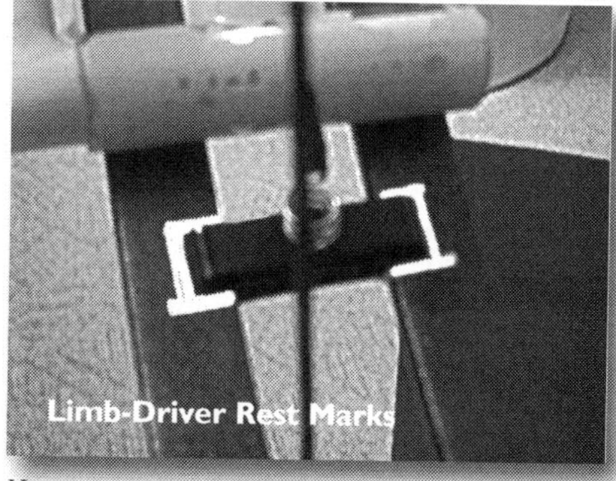

Yet again tape was used here (instead of permanent pen marks) for clarity in the photo.

Pressure Point "Starting Point" One last thing to mark is the "starting point" of the in/out positioning of the launcher blade from the inside of the sight window. It is necessary to know where you started so that you know how much you have moved it. Once the bow is finally tuned, however, you then remove the "starting point" marks and mark the "tuned ones." Simple, no? Well, I'm here to tell you that I've seen countless mid to high level shooters who haven't a clue where their center shot or nocking point are when the bow is shooting well. Then, when their rest moves or they move it, are totally lost as to where it was when they started! This is a major oversight committed even by some top shooters quite often! The photo below shows what I'm talking about. This particular photo is for my Hamskea *Versa-Rest* launcher and represents my final tune point. I also have this marked with my "short arrow technique" (see next chapter) and also a sight window template that I built. However, this provides me with a quick visual check on the rest itself and a second from a rear view behind the launcher. You are likely thinking, "Why two visuals?" The arrow rest may not have moved, but, especially in the case of some single bolt models and some "sloppiness" in two bolt blade mounts, that blade can get "bumped" and knocked out of position quite easily, or the single bolt comes loose and you don't know it. Remember the story of me losing three points in two shots at the beginning? Having this second visual is a worthwhile backup plan and once again "ProActive Archery" at work.

Launcher blade marks (indicated with tape) seen from front and rear.

Mounting Bow Slings, Quick Disconnects, and V-Bar Mounting Brackets

I can read your mind! You are thinking, "Marking the position of my bow sling, quick disconnect and V-bars? Is this guy nuts?" Well, the positions of those V-bars and yes, even your bow sling can affect your shot! You work hours and weeks getting the angle of the V-bars just right and making sure that the mount is square to the riser, correct? Do you really want to trust your memory as to the "numbers" those things are set upon? I would hope not! Mark them with a visual reference that is easy to check quickly. When they move (and in the case of V-bars, it is definitely a "when") you can put them right back in a jiffy with a visual reference. Without these markings you are trusting memory, which in times of pressure becomes faulty. My setup is much easier, since my particular V-bar set has the back stabilizers in one plane alone. Thus, I only need to know that the mount is still correctly positioned.

There are large varieties of bow-slings, stabilizer quick disconnects, and stabilizer V-bars and back bar mounting brackets and it seems like something different is released on a daily basis. Things to concern yourself with, in order to be Pro-Active, are:

Bow Slings I recommend your bow mounted bow sling (that you put your hand through) be mounted permanently and either use a quick disconnect, or a V-bar/side bar mounting bracket to keep the bow sling in place. I see people who remove their stabilizer and wrist sling after every shooting session and then re-install them the next time they shoot. One would not think that something as superficial as a measly bow sling could cause a problem, but I know from experience that even a small misalignment of the bow sling can cause you problems with your repeatability which will cost you points. This game is all about repetition and anytime you have something that can move or is moved from one session to another will cost you points. So, I recommend that if you use this type of bow-sling, mount it permanently. I've seen a lot of shooters going to simply a length of D-loop material, parachute cord, or ⅛″ nylon rope and tying it through a hole in the riser. Nothing wrong with this other than you being aware that sooner or later it will wear off the paint, dipping, or even anodizing from the area around that hole in the riser.

Quick Disconnects I recommend that if you are using a quick disconnect with a slot in it (that you insert a short metal dowel rod into) that this opening be on top, and not on the bottom or on the side of the bow. The reasoning is simple: When you forget to snug it up tightly enough, if you have the slot pointed downwards, your stabilizer will hit the floor and not only disrupt you, but it will disrupt the shooting line, too. If it is mounted so the slot is to the side, then you have the potential when you forget to snug it up tight enough, to have the stabilizer "waggle" left and right, and/or the stabilizer will work itself off center and cause slight misses until it falls out. I also mark my quick disconnects, when I use them to line up with a line on the riser that is visible. Might be obsessive, but ProActive archery leaves as few stones unturned as possible.

V-Bar and Counter Balance Brackets It is impossible to discuss these, since there are so many variants out there. The best piece of advice I can give on these is to mark their locations clearly so that when one of them gets bumped or comes loose, you can get the unit back into the same position it was in before it moved. Stabilization can be very sensitive and even a small change in the angle up, down, left or right can cause significant "drift" in how the bow steadies down and it really can affect your impact points. Be ProActive and mark their positions. It will save you in the long run.

Note in the photos (*below*) that the main stabilizer mount and the two V-bar mounts all have a 'blue dot" on them? Do you know why? I always put those units on in the same orientation! Blue dot is up, always up. Notice I use a 3-rod MAC (Merlin Archery Centre) stabilizer. I make sure that this unit is in the same orientation every time. The positioning of those three rods does indeed affect the shot, especially in the wind. Being ProActive leaves as little as possible to "chance" or "forgetfulness." For round stabilizers, this might not be so critical . . . or is it? I've seen some stabilizers out there that the positioning up and down and left to right vary depending upon the orientation of the quick disconnect of the style I'm using now. Thus, once tuned, you don't want to vary the position, so you mark it and put the thing on the same way every single time. I have seen people's stabilizers stick out at an odd angle, and the people are blaming the bow's stabilizer bushing, when in reality, it is the stabilizer itself and the end of the stabilizer has not been cut square! I have also seen a few (very few) bows in which the stabilizer bushing was installed crooked. Simple ProActive Archery.

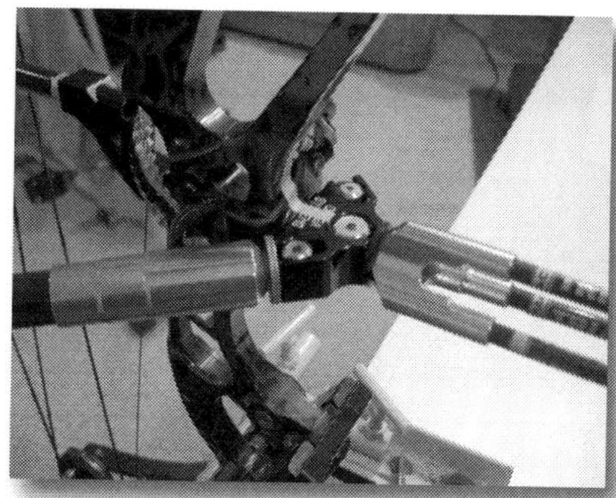

A wide piece of tape was used here (instead of permanent pen marks) for clarity in the photo.

Again a wide piece of tape was used here (instead of permanent pen marks) for clarity in the photo.

String Stoppers/Suppressors Many bows have "string stoppers" on them now. Most instructions call for you to adjust the string stop so that it either lightly touches the bow string (at brace) or that you have a "credit-card thickness" space between the string at rest and the string stopper. Many shooters don't give much consideration to the fact that this is yet one other item that can/will move (and wear) with continued impacts from the bowstring. It is a good idea to mark the position of the string stopper just like you do anything else. If (when) that string stopper moves it can affect shots and the tune of the bow. So, once set, mark it. This item takes a beating, and sooner or later it is going to be moved or get jarred loose. I know many shooters who take off their suppressors without any ill effects. However, if you are using yours, then mark its position so when it moves, you can put it back.

Summary

So, there you have it, ProActive mounting of the accessories onto your shiny new bow. We discussed:

1. How important it is to be careful with the mounting holes in your bow's riser. Inspect and insert the bolts and screws into the mounting holes before trying to mount your accessories into them.
2. How important it is to inspect the mounting bolts and screws that came with the

accessories before using them, especially if you are using old bolts or screws to make sure they are in good repair.

3. It is important to check the lengths of the bolts and screws to make sure they are neither too short nor too long. Different accessories may well require different lengths of bolts from what you had before. Screws and bolts that are too short are much more prone to stripping out threads in the mounting holes, so beware.
4. How important it is never to use red *Loctite*® on any parts that relate to your archery equipment, but especially your accessories cams, limb bolt locks, limb bolts, etc. I recommended that you avoid the use of even blue Loctite® for anything smaller than 5⁄16-24 threads, since even this product could seize up and cause you to strip out an Allen bolt head. We also discussed that the use of any instant glues is also not recommended for these applications.
5. The use of finger-nail polish, bow string wax, or *Fletch-Tite* glue were discussed as means of helping to hold bolts and screws snug.
6. The mounting of the cable guard rod and bracket to the bow's riser including to place the bow into a bow press to take the tension off the string and cables to make this process easier.
7. Using a thin piece of rubber or leather as an insert into the set screw holes for the cable guard rod to alleviate loosening and protect the carbon or soft aluminum cable guard rod.
8. Proper installation of sight mounting brackets by using a cushion either cut out of thin rubber or from a plastic milk carton or soft plastic bubble pack material, cut to the shape of the mounting bracket. Then the bolts and the mounting bracket are marked so you can tell at a glance if they have worked loose. It has been my experience that normally after 100-200 shots they'll work loose, but once they have been snugged up a second time those bolts normally won't come loose again. By being ProActive and marking them, a quick glance will eliminate that possibility when you suddenly start shooting high.
9. Proper mounting of the arrow rest to the riser with several examples given. Among these were: the use of two bolts in there are two mounting holes in the riser; the use of a nylon tipped set screw into the second hole in the riser if you can do so; also, if your arrow rest has a mounting bar that only has one hole in it and your riser two holes, simply place a 5⁄16-24 set screw through the sight window side of the riser and snug it up against the arrow rest mounting bracket. If you only have one mounting hole and only one hole in the arrow rest, then it was strongly suggested that you use a larger stainless steel or blued steel washer and on top of that a shake-proof, internal star washer to tighten down the arrow rest. Also we recommended that you outline the arrow rest mounting bracket with a fine tipped permanent marker of an opposing and/or visible color.
10. Mounting of the wrist sling, quick disconnects, and V-bar or counter weight stabilizers. The ProActive part of this being: mounting the wrist sling permanently and then for the quick disconnects and V-bar/counter balance brackets, clearly marking their angles up/down, left right so that when they move or get moved you

can put them back into place.

11. How critical knowing the positions of all accessories, especially the "cable guard rake" can be, and how to ProActively mark them so you have one or more visual references/quick checks when something goes haywire.

If you have ProActively mounted your bow's accessories, you will have avoided stripping out the bolts and screws associated with them, and when they do come loose, move, or get bumped out of position, you will, with a quick visual check, be able to put them back exactly where they were without losing many points, if any. It goes without saying that anything can happen; bows fall off of bow racks, bows fall over even when leaned up against a tree. A lot of vibration is absorbed by your accessories and things eventually work loose and move. If you know where they were in the beginning, it is a snap to check them and put them back into their original positions. I intentionally did not discuss securing D-loops onto the string, items on the sight itself, such as 2nd and 3rd axis adjustments, vertical bar mounting to the sight extension bar and other related items. That is beyond the scope of this chapter, and I will discuss those in a subsequent chapter. Now, go out and enjoy your shiny new bow with the assurance that, in being ProActive concerning how you mounted the accessories, you can have many rounds of enjoyment on the range and will spend more time shooting arrows than fixing your equipment.

6

The Short Arrow Technique

Now that you have your accessories mounted on your bow, you can get down to the real nitty-gritty and begin the finer aspects of bow setup. The first among these is that pesky D-loop or nocking point installation. However, before you begin this process in your normal fashion, I have suggestions to reducing the amount of time and effort you take in getting a tune for your setup. This will reduce the hit-or-miss procedures folks use that sometime take hours or even days to work through. The methods I'll outline in the next few chapters will insure you can duplicate your setup when changing arrow rests, D-loops, and/or bowstrings and cables on your compound bow without having to re-tune your bow! They work almost perfectly for your initial bow set up and even better once your bow has been set up, and you need to replace a component (D-loop, peep site, or even the bow string and cables). I will also outline some other ProActive techniques that will get your arrow aligned perfectly. I provide you with a series of "instruments" you can make to insure you have an exacting method of setting up and replicating your nocking point and arrow centershot position, along with your arrow rest alignment.

You will no longer have to "eye ball" whether you are "centered" over the pressure button hole or "eyeball" the centershot of any size arrow. If you want "super accuracy," you can use both this method in combination with others. I call the first method the "Short Arrow" Technique for arrow centershot and nocking point placement (horizontal).

The Short Arrow Technique

How many times over the years have you wanted to figure out a way to get things more exacting with regard to your nocking point location and centershot when you first set up your bow? Sure, we all own a bow square, and most of us have used them exclusively for years for their intended purpose. However, setting the bow square onto the bowstring and then figuring out where and how to place it on the arrow rest the same every time is a real headache (see that discussion in Chapter 3). Then, there is that gap to read across. You are never really sure if you have duplicated it or not, are you? Those pesky clips eventually get sprung and your bow square no longer sits on the string properly. Sometimes even the D-loop interferes with proper placement of your bow square onto the bow string, knocking it out of square or allowing the bow square to slide where it will as you try to get it settled in. If you would like a fool proof method of setting that arrow where you want it and being able to duplicate it every time, so you will be able to check it in seconds, and know for sure you did it right, read on.

Setting up and Making a "Short Arrow"

I actually got this idea when I was digging through some drawers and cleaning out old archery items. I ran across one of those home-made "pen arrows" that are commonly used to write down scores during leagues or tournaments. (You've all seen them. It involves the use of a piece of fletched arrow into which a ball-point pen cartridge has been inserted.) I'm always looking for ways to get things more exacting on any bow setup. I realized that a person could easily fashion one of these short arrows to set their centershot and their center arrow height exactly! Since most people cannot afford two or three bows to shoot for indoor, 3-D, and outdoor target rounds, most of us have gone to shooting one bow with different arrow sizes and then moving the arrow rest to accommodate the different arrow diameters. (We will discuss this in subsequent chapters.) You should by now be anticipating the solution, no?

My description below is assuming that you have your bow finally tuned and are wanting to simply get everything "marked" and documented for easy and immediate duplication or cross-checking. However, this works well for an initial set up as well; the same principles of measuring and marking apply to both. They key being that you mark and document your starting point, and then, once the bow is finely tuned, you simply mark and document your exact measurements again so that when something goes awry, you have the means to instantly check those critical settings. Once again, ProActive Archery at work.

Setting Up For a Bow That is Already Tuned What you are intending to do here is to get your bow riser marked and to make exact measurements based upon the current "tune" positions of nocking point height and centershot with your current arrow size. Obviously, the more exacting you become, the easier it is to return things to their previous settings when something comes loose, moves, gets bumped or wears out.

1. The first thing you do is to transfer your brace height to the inside face of the riser on your bow (*see photos top of next page for how to do this*). If you don't want to use a permanent marker on your riser, then simply use some writable invisible cellophane tape. In many of my examples, I use thin strips of masking tape only so that you can see the lines. Do *not* leave masking tape on your bow riser; in time you won't be able to get it off without sandblasting! Once you have transferred your brace height to the face of the sight window, you now have a means of measuring your true draw and also for setting the minimum length to make your Short Arrow.
2. Now that you have the vertical line, you can measure out how long you want to make your Short Arrow. In the photo (*right bottom*), you can see that I've made the length of my Short Arrow to be just past the "true draw" vertical mark, but

Measuring the grip-to-string distance. You must choose whether to measure to the inside, outside, or center of the string. Here the measurement is to the inside of the string. Mark this distance on your bow square.

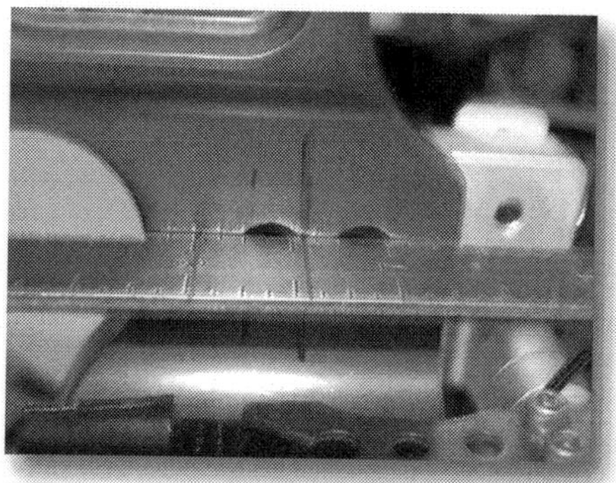

Then turn the bow square around and transfer that distance to the inside face of the riser and make a mark. If you do not want use a permanent marker on your riser, then simply use some writable "invisible" cellophane tape.

still within the sight window of the bow. This simply makes it a tad bit more accurate, but isn't necessary. Just do not go beyond the end of the riser away from the bow string when determining the length of the Short Arrow.

3. Make up an arrow of the size you are shooting so that, with a nock and a point installed, when placed on the string and rest its point extends to somewhere within the width of your riser/sight window. It really isn't necessary to have the size you are shooting, but I personally prefer to have a short arrow for each size I use in the bow; especially for the 25, 26, or 27 diameter arrows. Most of us bang up or ruin a shaft or two, or we "cull out" an arrow that won't hit with the others. Many of us don't shoot a 32″ long arrow, so it is easy to get a short 4-7″ piece of shafting, add a nock and a point, and there you have it; your "short arrow." How long it needs to be, of course, is dependent upon your bow's brace height, and the width of that riser.
4. Next, you will set your "horizontal line" at the tip of your short arrow as it now sits on the bow string. This is in reality your "tuned" nocking point height. Put the short arrow onto the string and rest and then simply mark the riser at the very tip of the arrow, or, if you want then measure up exactly from the shelf to the tip of the arrow and transfer this measurement to the riser and extend the line horizontally as far as you want. On a new setup, I always mark the riser at each end of the arrow rest mounting holes and make a horizontal line connecting the two dots. I always start my setups with the arrow center down the middle of the arrow rest mounting holes in a horizontal plane.

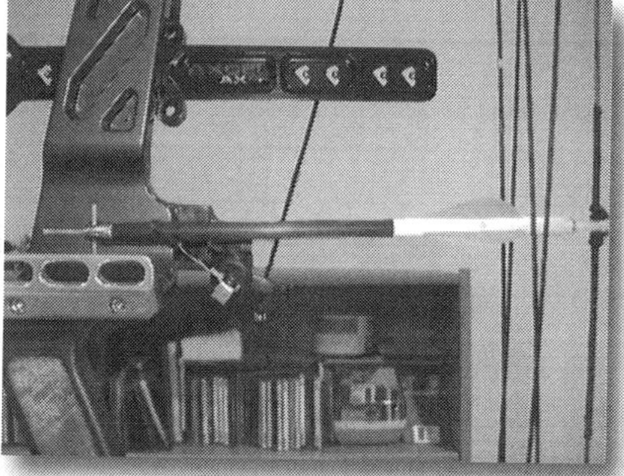

5. Then, you can level the bow vertically, and taking a short level, extend that "dot"

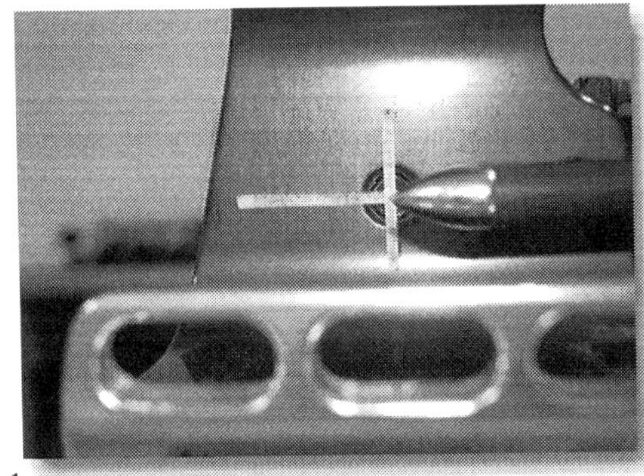

horizontally and level towards and away from the bowstring for as far on the riser as you want. An alternative is to simply measure up from the arrow shelf to the tip of your short arrow and make marks at each end of the site window and connect the marks. Some Pros prefer having the arrow at the bottom or top of the Berger hole. If you want your arrow centered on the bottom of the hole or on the top, then simply make your line there.

How to Finish Your Set Up and Mark Your Settings

Once you have made your Short Arrow and completed your initial settings, you are ready to fine tune things. At this point, you probably won't have much to do other than very minor refinements. Once you have your bow "paper tuned" (if you choose to do things that way), or "group tuned," or "French tuned," you are now ready to mark your measuring instrument for those all important final settings of that particular bow/arrow combination. If you are just starting out, you now can measure and mark your starting point and have a base reference of comparison to where you start and where you end up after the tuning process is completed. How simple ProActive Archery can become, huh? Templates are a handy thing when it comes to replicating or complementing all sorts of things.

6. Using your Short Arrow on the bow string you have just set up on your bow, you can now simply use the tip of your bow square, or a machinist's ruler to measure "up" exactly from the arrow shelf to the exact center of the tip of the short arrow (see photo below). This gives you an exact vertical measurement for arrow tip center. If you have had something move on you, it is a simple check and adjustments of the arrow rest or nocking point to get it back where they belongs.
7. Using your Short Arrow again, you can also mark the "out" from the face of the riser to the exact center of the tip of the "short arrow." You now also have an exact measurement of your centershot setting you just completed tuning to. (You may note in the pictures that I used metric measurements instead of inches. I just happen to prefer metric measurements.) However once you have your instrument marked, you adjust things so the point goes back to the line, so it really doesn't matter what system you use (*see photo right top*). Your Short Arrow obviously allows you to put everything back exactly as it was before you moved it.

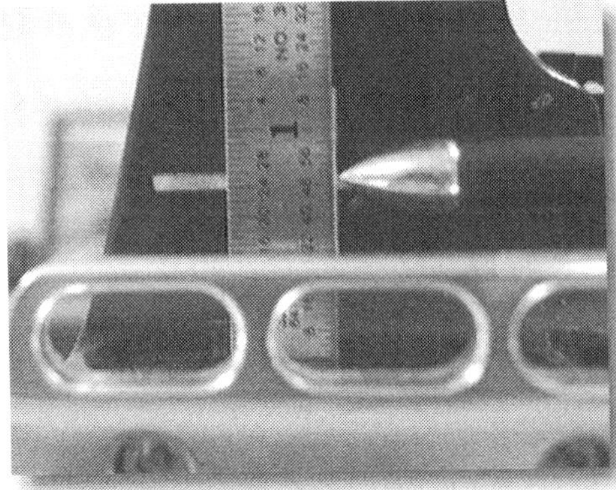

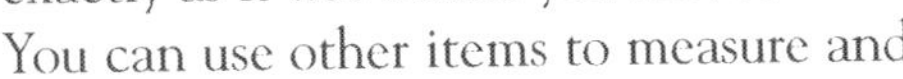

You can use other items to measure and

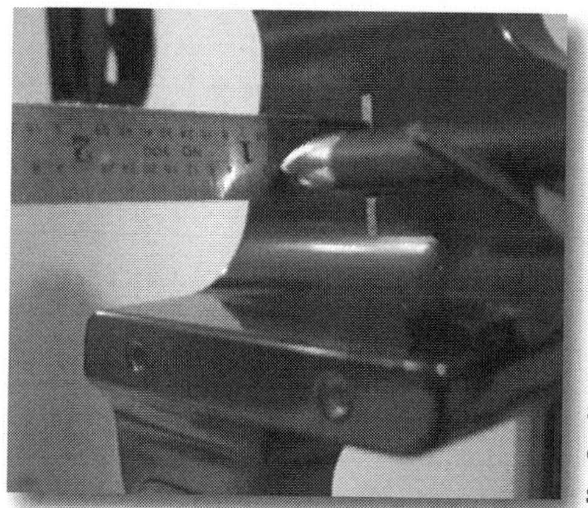

mark your short arrow's point center measurements, but since most of us carry a machinist's rule or bow square, I simply suggested those as a means of insuring you have something with you that you can use in a jiffy to check if a rest has moved or something has changed.

Obviously, you will make another Short Arrow and measurements for the next arrow shaft diameter change when you make a changeover for the outdoor or indoor season. These adjustments, you will soon find, are not really as complicated as you would anticipate! Often, you simply place the new size Short Arrow onto the arrow rest and then move the arrow rest so that the new arrow matches the setting of the old arrow and then fine tune from there. If you have already done this, then you should already have a mark on the template or bow square for that size of arrow too! Changing over from one shaft size to another with the same bow can be this simple, if you are ProActive about it and don't trust your memory. Using this technique will allow you to change over from fat shaft to small shaft and back again in a matter of minutes and should require zero "re-tuning" as long as you are exacting in your initial measuring and documentation.

Summary

In this chapter I have outlined and discussed the following:

1. How the short arrow technique is a modification of the stabilizer technique for nocking point placement. The stabilizer technique is more accurate and can be done in addition to the "Short Arrow Technique." However, the stabilizer technique doesn't give you the option of having your exact centershot measured and marked to the very center of your arrow. Only the Short Arrow technique allows you to accomplish this more quickly and with greater accuracy and without the use of electronics or a laser. This is precisely why I recommend using both of the techniques in unison with each other. The horizontal/lateral positioning (centershot) of the arrow won't normally move unless you physically move that arrow rest in or out. However, the vertical component can easily shift due to D-loop slippage, serving separation or failure, or a host of other things. So, if you've moved the arrow rest in or out and it isn't working, how to you get it back to the original setting? It is quick and easy if you have been ProActive and have measured and marked it before you started piddling. If you haven't, then as they say, "Lots of Luck!"
2. How to measure up and mark the bow riser for exact horizontal center of the Berger hole. We will discuss this further in subsequent chapters.
3. In addition, I have again reiterated the use of a vertical line that is a transfer of the brace height of the bow to the riser. This is critically important to help you

ascertain if you have had a cable or string stretch that has affected your draw length, and ultimately, even the poundage of your bow. This is a double purpose line of great importance to the ProActive archer. Of course, there is a backup/quick check system to this that will be discussed later in the book; a ProActive archer never proceeds without a backup plan.

4. How to make yourself a Short Arrow that will allow you to have a means of replicating your set up for each arrow size you opt to shoot out of a given bow. If you are ProActive, you measure everything and mark it. You also back those markings up by writing them down in your journal, or by taking pictures of those measurements.

The "Short Arrow Technique" offers you a very inexpensive means of setting up your bow without the use of electronics or lasers. Creating one involves a minimal expense and gives you exacting measurements for every size shaft you tune to a given bow, from the fattest "27 diameter" arrow to the smallest ACE or X-10 arrow!

Realize also that you don't have to use the exact arrow size in a Short Arrow. One size of Short Arrow will work for all applications as long as you measure and mark each accordingly. That is to say, you can use an X-10 short arrow for all of this if you want. I just find it quicker and easier to have a "Short Arrow" for each diameter of arrow I use out of a given bow.

Another option is to place a tag on your short arrow documenting those measurements. Avery labels work very well for this and you can place the label on your Short Arrow and then cover that label with cellophane tape to keep it from getting obscured (*see diagram at right*). Otherwise, be sure to "color code" your marks on your measuring instrument for the "up" and the "out" for each arrow size and note which color mark represents which arrow.

Shaft Size	Center Shot
Point Weight	Dist. Up

One last thing to remember is that you started with the tip of your arrow centered on the Berger hole (or at the top or the bottom of the Berger hole). Most likely, you won't end up with the tune being exactly there when you finish up. What matters is that you have the ability to measure it within the confines of the arrow shelf (height) and face of the riser (centershot) and replicate this every single time without having to re-tune the bow. Once your tune is finalized, all you have to do is measure it and write it down or mark it, or both. Better yet, make a template; oh, that is the backup instrument I will discuss later on.

In addition, don't you just relish the idea of changing your complete harness and D-loop on your bow and putting your first arrow right into the bullseye or X-ring? Don't you just relish after the outdoor season, changing over to your "fat shafts" for indoor shooting and not having to completely re-tune your shooting rig? Don't you just relish the fact that you can even change arrow rests and go right back to perfectly duplicating your centershot and nocking point settings even with a new arrow rest mounted on your bow? Don't you relish the fact, that if you are exacting in these measurements and documentations that you could, in reality, switch from fat shafts to tiny shafts in the middle of a scoring round and not lose anything? Of course, most tournaments these days won't allow you to change shaft diameters in mid-competition and definitely won't allow you to change shaft sizes for the "shoot offs." That isn't to say however, that you shouldn't become proficient at change-overs in the effort to be able to go from an indoor "fat shaft" setup to your outdoor setup in minutes rather than hours, correct?

ProActive archers are religious in their bow and arrow setup and documentation. Being ProActive can and will save you countless hours of trying to find a sweet spot again when something moves or you change it and it doesn't work out for whatever reason.

Tom Dorigatti

7

Proper D-Loop Placement

Please realize that if you adopt this approach you are not going to be moving the D-loop during your bow set up regimen. You will be moving the arrow rest when you change arrow sizes and/or during your tuning process instead. This is what I feel is the beauty of this system. You move the arrow rest up and down to allow for different shaft sizes. Obviously before we can begin D-loop installation, the arrow rest has to have been mounted onto your bow and the blade angle (assuming a launcher rest is used) set the way you would like it (I recommend a 30-35° angle). If it is a fall away rest, sometimes that angle isn't adjustable, not to worry. If you align your arrow with the top or bottom of the Berger hole, then you will set your D-loop up or down on the bow string that same distance. We are going to discuss setting the D-loop up in such a position that yields no deformation of that D-loop when you have drawn and let down the bow or have shot arrows out of the bow. What follows will have the arrow centered on the Berger hole.

This technique may also serve as a cross-check of your equipment setup, especially if after trying mass redistribution, draw length adjustments, creep tuning, and the like, and you are still having problems holding steady or getting consistent grouping. If you are shooting your bow already, you can skip step #1. However, if you are setting it up for the first time or if you are changing your string and cables or center serving, it may well pay you to try this technique.

Step #1 Initial Positioning of the D-Loop

Before you can safely draw back your bow you need to have a nocking point locator installed. To draw a bow without a solid nocking point is a high risk operation with the probability of serious injury as a result. Also you must always have an arrow on the bow to avoid the risk of a dry-fire.

The initial positioning of the D-loop can be done by eye but this is not recommended, as it can be done much more precisely. Most shooters simply place the arrow on the arrow rest, attach it to the string with the nock, and "eye ball" it so that the arrow is running through the center of the rest attachment hole and is "dead level." Then they tie in some serving thread above or below the arrow nock, tie in the D-loop knot above and below that, and go paper test. I used to do it in this same way. However thanks to some conversations with a knowledgeable guy, Mike Cooper, I soon found out that for single cam and hybrid cam bows and especially binary cam bows, this common technique might be good enough for a hunting rig, but for pin-point accuracy, this was far less than the best technique. Since that time, I have put together what I feel is an accurate procedure for setting your D-loop in very close to a perfect position the first time and thus I don't have to deal with nock travel problems cropping up later in the tuning process due to improper D-loop placement.

Here's the step-by-step procedure I came up with for the initial placement of a D-loop on the bow string.

1. If you have a bow with a loop on it, it is simple to measure the installed length of the D-loop. Do so, and write this down. If not, then you can start with a length of D-loop material that is 4″ to 5″ long, melt down each end to form a "ball" and start from there. You can measure up the final stretched length of your loop later on. If you know the starting length of your D-loop, then start with that length.
2. Mount your bow square on the bow string.
3. Line the bottom of the bow square even with the horizontal line you made on the riser during the sequence in Chapter 5, or use the center of the rest mounting hole (or bottom of the hole if you choose to shoot your arrows down that low).
4. Take a piece of masking tape, about ⅜″ to ½″ wide and place the approximate center of the masking tape in line with the bottom edge of the bow square as it relates to the string (*see photo right*).

5. Wrap the masking tape around the bow string. You will have to remove the bow square to accomplish this. The reason for this is that the extra thickness of the tape will help hold the nock in place on the string. However, if your nock doesn't slide on the string, you can mark the serving itself with a contrasting color of ink.
6. Replace the bow square on the string and re-align the bottom edge with the center of the arrow rest mounting hole (*see photo below*).
7. Mark the masking tape with a red or blue line that you can see that aligns with the bottom edge of the bow square.
8. Place an arrow nock on the bowstring, using the mold line on the nock to align it with the ink mark on the masking tape or center serving. It is going to fit tightly and that is what you want!
9. Using a sharp knife. Carefully trim the masking tape even with the top and bottom of the arrow nock. You only need to "score" the masking tape around the string to get an even edge.

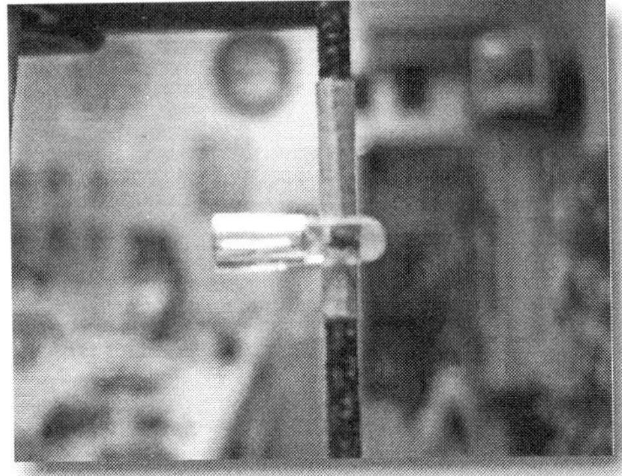

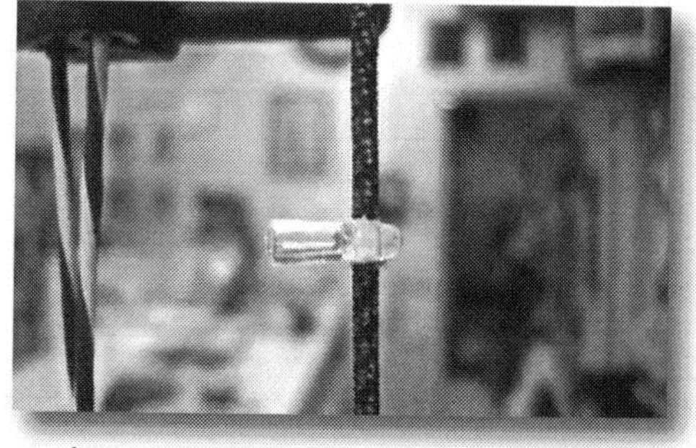

You do not have to cut very hard, and then you can remove the excess with your fingernail (*see photo right*).

10. If you serve in a nock locator above the nock with serving thread do it now, without moving the nock. If not, then place and tie in the top D-loop knot there. I like to start with the top knot since then gravity assists you in tying in the bottom serving spacer or bottom D-loop knot correctly (*see photos below*).
11. If you serve in below the nock, then do it now, without moving the nock. If not, then tie in the bottom knot of the D-loop. It is a good idea to leave about ¹⁄₆₄″ (the approximate width of one strand of serving thread) gap between the bottom serving thread or D-loop knot to help prevent nock pinch at full draw. If the gap is much more than this, then your vertical accuracy down range suffers a lot (*see photos again*).

12. Remove the arrow nock and tighten up the D-loop to get it to the exact length you normally shoot. You have written down that piece of information, haven't you? I mentioned before that I make my initial D-loop length to accommodate the use of D-loop pliers to tighten (extend) the D-loop length to my previously known setting. I have found, over time, that doing it in this prevents any stretching of the D-loop as I shoot the bow and it also prevents slippage of the bottom knot once I have it set. (Note: my particular finished D-loop opening is 0.550″, and I start with an initial length of 4″ of release rope). *Caution* Many of the D-loop pliers out there today are made for the fitting of normal nocks such as Easton G-nocks, *3-D* nocks, etc. If you are shooting with "Pin nocks" which are narrower, then this gap will be too wide; so be careful in how you tighten up that D-loop! I have taken a motor tool and ground down that width of the "spreader portion" so that my set of pliers will tighten my D-loops to the correct width for the nocks I'm using.

What you have accomplished here is to place your D-loop so that the center of the arrow is really centered on the arrow rest mounting hole. This may or may not be the positioning you will end up with after tuning, but it is the starting position recommended by most bow manufacturers. You can quickly check this by placing your short arrow onto the string and arrow rest and then move the arrow rest up or down until the tip of the short arrow is centered (*see photos in previous chapter*). You are not quite ready yet to go out and paper tune this rig, however—so don't rush off!

Step #2 Checking your Cam Synchronization/Timing

Now that you have installed your D-loop, you can safely draw back your bow, as long as you have followed the instructions in your owner's manual for the installation of the cable guard, cam stops, etc if the bow is new. It is likely that during the stretch in process one of the "units" in the harness has changed in length slightly. Before proceeding with "D-loop tuning" you need to make sure your cams are in synchronization and/or properly timed. You can either have a friend watch as you draw the bow back to the stops. He/she must carefully observe whether or not the cams hit the "stops" at the same time or if one is ahead of the other one. Another way to check this is through the use of the drawing or crank board. This allows you to have the crank board hold the bow string back while you check the cam synchronization/timing. For obvious reasons, the crank board is the better choice. I don't recommend that you have a friend draw your bow back so you can check the cam timing. He/she might well hold the bow quite differently than do you, and thus the "timing" may be different for him/her than it is for you.

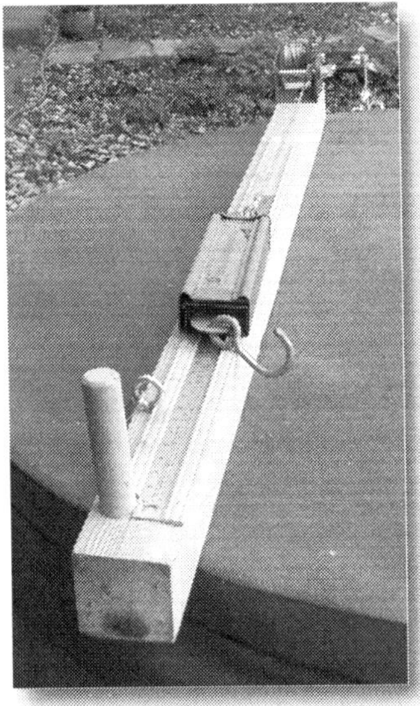

A crank board can be made with a board, a nail, and a pulley or be more complicated. They are very handy for checking and setting eccentric timings.

For a single cam bow, getting the cam in "time" isn't as difficult, since the manufacturers give you "timing holes" to line up and there is a little fudge room. The one cam controls pretty much everything, including draw length. Thus, if the cam is the correct size for your draw length, you can set it exactly by twisting the power cable and/or the bowstring to get it where you want it without radically affecting the "timing."

With the hybrid cam system, however, since the two cams are working simultaneously, cam synchronization is imperative. If the cams are out of synch, you will feel mushiness at full draw, and the bow will be difficult to tune as well. Additionally, you won't be able to hold as steady on the target. When the cams are in synch, the wall is solid, and the holding qualities at full draw are quite noticeably better.

If the Top Cam is Late What I've found is that if the top cam is late, it is easier if you let out twists of the control cable, one half twist at a time, to get the cams in synch. This doesn't change the bow's draw length as radically as adjusting the power cable to retard the bottom cam. Many shooters want the top cam to be very slightly ahead of the bottom cam as they come into full draw position, but this type of fine tuning is accomplished during a "creep test," which is an advanced technique and isn't part of this chapter. Many top shooters prefer to have the top cam "lead" the bottom cam very, very slightly so that it hits the stop first and then the bottom cam comes in. This is not much, but can have a large effect on the hold and shootability, along with accuracy at long distances. When creep tuning a hybrid cam bow, one half twist on a power or control cable can make a huge difference in the grouping of the bow at long distance, so you make adjustments in small increments.

If the Top Cam is Early Follow the manufacturer's recommendations.

Step #3 Measure the Bow's True Draw Length

Having your bow's draw length matched to your full draw body position is probably the most overlooked and yet critical aspect of shooting a bow accurately. My personal preference is to use the true draw setting of my bow as opposed to the AMO draw length (AMO draw length is equal to the True Draw Length + 1¾″). In my opinion, not enough emphasis is placed upon draw length and how critical this is for you to get proper alignment and proper full draw position in order to shoot your shots with proper back tension. At this juncture, you won't be tuning the draw length, you will just be measuring the length the bow is actually set at.

Measuring a Bow's True Draw Length If you placed a mark on your riser as I recommended in Chapter 6, that now comes into play and will be used to accurately measure and record your bow's true draw length. This setting can now be easily replicated, time and again, unless you change grips (or add a grip, or remove the grip). Note in the accompanying photo that I marked both brace height measurements. I feel that it is more accurate and useful than marking at the tip of the arrow rest or launcher blade, mostly because this can be used regardless of the arrow rest you mount on the bow and won't have to be redone unless you change brace height. This will help measure the True Draw Length (not the AMO Draw Length) of the bow. Again, from my experience, while measuring to the center of the bolt hole will give you a consistent measurement, it is not necessarily the correct True Draw measurement that you really need to enter data into arrow selection software and/or data entry for the generation of sight tapes. You need to know where your starting point was and document it for future reference. ProActive archers always try to think ahead of the game. Making this measurement is simple:

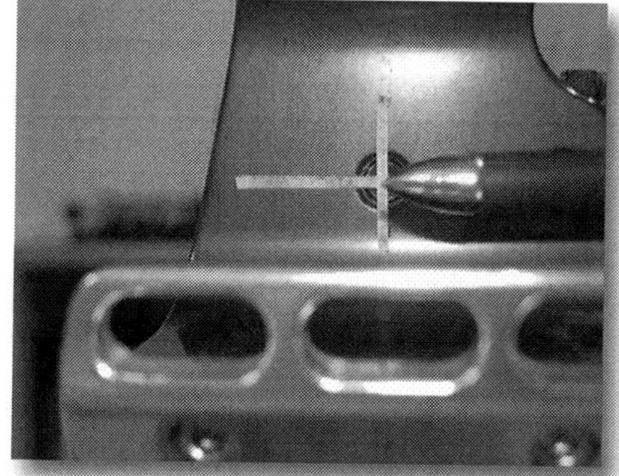

a. Load an arrow on the string and then using your release aid, draw the bow back to the stops either with your release aid (*Caution* Never draw back your bow without an arrow on the bow string. Dry fires can totally destroy a bow and void the warranty. In addition, personal injury can result.), or use a crank board and mark the arrow at the vertical line (or if you are using a draw length measuring arrow, read the scale). You should repeat this at least three times to insure it is the same each time. If the mark on the arrow "moves" relative to the line then you are not pulling consistently and must "average" the positions of the marks (go for the middle) or start again. We will be talking about the role played by "hard stops" and your "to anchor draw length" later in this book.

b. If you are not using a measuring arrow, then measure from the bottom of the nock's slot to the line on the arrow and write this distance down as exactly as your measuring instrument allows. *Note* Remember that you are after the cur-

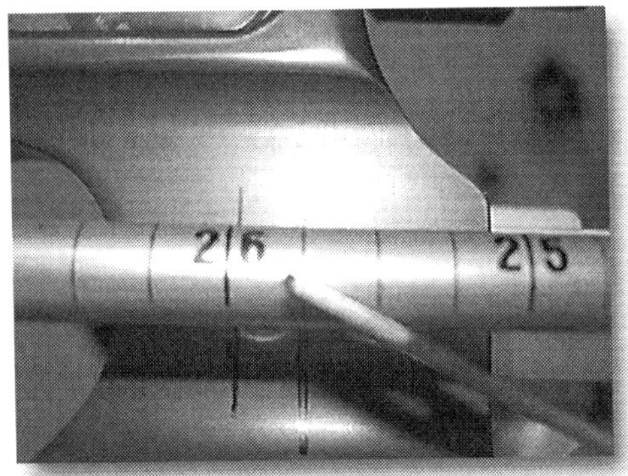

rent setting—as the bow is set now—and that it is rare that the strings and cables are exactly perfect! As a matter of clarification, don't expect to have the vertical line on your riser come out exactly in the center of the arrow rest's mounting hole. I've found that most times, it doesn't happen this way. If there are two arrow rest mounting holes, don't expect this line to be exactly in between the two holes either. It could be closer to the mounting hole closest to the shooter. In addition, remember that ⅛″ of draw length is indeed critical to your accuracy, so getting this "true draw" length measurement as exact as possible is imperative (*see photos above*).

c. You now have the True Draw Length that your bow is set for at the current time. If you want the AMO Draw Length, simply add 1¾ inches to this measurement. (Remember, if you change your brace height, then your mark on the riser needs to be re-done).

d. Unless you have a measuring arrow you can mark on, it is a good idea to set aside that arrow that you marked as a permanent reference, available in case you suspect the string or buss cable has stretched, thus changing the bow's draw length. If you suspect a change, all you have to do is draw back this arrow and see if the lines on the bow and the arrow still match or not. Note: this works even if you have changed or moved your arrow rest, since the line is based upon the bow and not related to the positioning of the arrow rest itself. You have a constant reference this isn't going to move or be moved.

e. Remember, changing the length of the D-loop does not change the draw length of the bow; it simply moves your anchor point and makes it feel like the bow has changed. Changing the length of the D-loop is a good means of fine tuning your "to anchor" positioning to get proper body alignment for the execution of proper back tension.

Step #4 Testing for Proper D-loop Placement

You are probably thinking, "I placed my D-loop so that the arrow passes through the center of the arrow rest hole, so it must be on right." Maybe, maybe not, but there is a way to check.

D-Loop Position Tests Keep a sight on the bow, but remove all stabilizers and

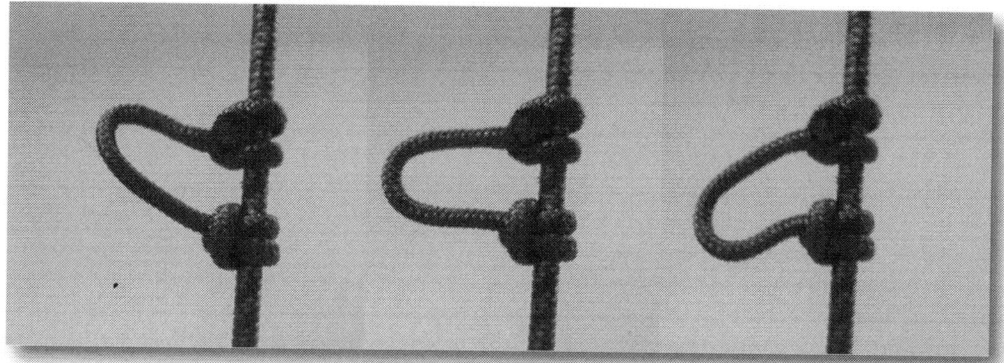

The D-Loop on the left is deformed "up," the one on the right is deformed "down," and the one in the middle is "just right."

counterweights from the bow. Then, draw the bow back, hold, aim, and shoot an end of arrows. Don't pay any attention to impact points at this time. After each shot, look at the D-loop carefully, without touching it. Is that D-loop deformed? By this I mean, is the end of the loop higher or lower than the center of the space between the knots (see the montage of photos above)?

If it is deformed, then your D-loop is not in the "center of the pulling area" and thus, your nock travel is being thrown off; along with the stability of the arrow and your holding ability! If the D-loop is angled up from center (*left photo*), move the loop down slightly (not much) on the string. Shoot several more arrows and this time, also pay attention to the holding qualities of your sight picture and what the loop looks like after each shot (don't touch the loop to "re-shape" it). Repeat the process until that D-loop is not deformed after a shot or even a let down. Now, once the D-loop is not being deformed by the shot process, shoot an end paying careful attention to your aiming. *Note* You are still doing this without stabilization. Once you get this done and put your stabilizers, etc. back on the bow, you aren't going to believe the difference in your sight picture!

More than likely, you will not have moved that D-loop enough to affect your cam synchronization or timing but, if you want, go ahead and re-check it. What you have done here is to get your nock travel as close to level as you can based upon how you hold the bow.

One other thing I've learned is that if you are having problems getting your release to fire, or if you struggle with a shot or shots, a quick look at your D-loop will tell you a lot about what you are doing during your immediate past shots. This information helps immensely to analyze whether or not you are plucking, pulling your elbow up, chin down, elbow down, etc. In my particular case, if I'm struggling with my shot process, and I either shoot a bad shot, or I let the shot down, in nearly all cases, my D-loop is deformed upwards. However, on the shots that go cleanly or without much of a struggle, I have no D-loop deformation at all. Yet another example of ProActive Archery and paying attention!

During tuning, never move the D-loop once you have it finalized. Now that you have your D-loop placed in the proper location on your bowstring, it is imperative that if you need to adjust the angle of your arrow in relation to the bowstring to get arrow flight and grouping (paper testing, or whatever) that you move the arrow rest and not the loop. I repeat—the key here is that "nocking point adjustments" (now a misnomer) are to be made by moving the arrow rest and not the D-loop on the bowstring.

Summary

We have reviewed a step-by-step technique for placing a D-loop on your bowstring. The technique in step #1 (above) can also be applied to those wishing to shoot a release rope around the bowstring and below the arrow nock. However, most of the time, the arrow rest will have to be dropped significantly to accommodate the different pulling point imparted on the bowstring by this method of release attachment and anchoring. With the release rope around the string, you will be pulling below center and will have to accommodate that with a different tuning process than that used with a D-loop. You will also "lose yardage" on your vertical site bar and change your required peep height because you will actually be raising your anchor point, by raising the back end of the arrow in relation to your touch point at full draw.

We also reviewed techniques for checking cam synchronization/timing and the importance of having your bow set at your correct draw length. You are probably wondering why the cam timing and draw length aren't checked before placing the D-loop onto the string. The answer is simple; first, drawing the bow with an arrow in it without a nocking point of some type on the string is unsafe. The release and arrow will slide upwards on the string and you can/will get injured, possibly severely. You can make those adjustments upon initial placement of the loop. It simply makes sense to try to minimize how many times you loosen and tighten the D-loop to get it into final position. If you place the D-loop and it is very far off, you will have to do the cam synchronization/timing and draw length over again anyway. Anytime you adjust the cam synchronization/timing, you also can affect draw length slightly, depending upon how much you have changed the synchronization/cam timing thru the use of the cabling system.

Finally, we gave a technique for determining if that D-loop is really placed correctly for how your hand is in the bow and you are drawing it back, actually becomes a part of the "shooting machine." It is very sensible to realize that if that bow shoots and holds steady in your hand without any stabilization and the D-loop isn't deformed, then when you put on the stabilization, things can only get better! Again, let me make it clear that checking this is best done with you drawing your own bow and using a trusted friend who knows what to look for, or, through the use of a draw/crank board. I do not recommend taking your bow into the pro shop, dropping it off, and having them "tune" the bow to a bullet hole for you. Since it is not you shooting the bow, then how can you expect their tune to work for you? Furthermore, a "bullet hole" does not necessarily mean that the bow will group for you either up close or at distance.

We finished by driving home the point that the D-loop is the one thing that does not get moved during the subsequent fine-tuning process. The arrow rest is what is moved up and down, not the D-loop.

Tom Dorigatti

8

More Accurate Nocking Point & Peep Height Settings

Since your shooting accuracy is based upon your consistency setup documentation is essential to ensure you can quickly check any part of your setup. If something changes while you are shooting, you need to be able to rapidly detect what changed and restore your correct settings with confidence. This chapter deals primarily with how to get very accurate nocking point height and distance of your peep height above the nocking point measurements. Using these techniques I have been nearly "dead-on" when I had to make a string and/or cable change, change a D-loop, or had to re-serve the center serving on the bow string (thus requiring me to re-establish my correct nocking point and the peep height exactly like the pre-existing setup). Realize that it is not a matter of "if" something changes or needs to be rebuilt, it is a matter of "when" you are going to have to perform these very tasks.

The procedures below are based upon the assumption that you have set your correct draw length, peep sight height, nocking point, and arrow rest positioning and that the bow is ready to shoot. Once you have documented and marked everything, you should be able to duplicate these settings with ease; especially during a bow string and/or cable change or a change of your D-loop. In addition, by having these settings measured and written down, it is obvious that if need be, you can go back to home base should some change(s) made during the tuning process do not work out. This becomes a double-edged sword: if you eat more than one bite of the elephant at a time and don't keep track of every bite, you soon become overfull and lost. It will be next to impossible to go back to exactly the same previous setting. This can result in a lot of lost time and effort.

Items Required

1. your new bow that hasn't been fine tuned or your bow set up with correct draw length and reasonable grouping already established (or final tune completed). The new bow regimen will only differ because you will be documenting where you started. You will repeat this process once you have established a "better tune." Keeping a history like this will reap benefits down the road and keep you from losing track of things as you go through the maze of finding a sweet tune of the bow

to you and the arrow to the bow.

2. a bow square
3. a millimeter gauge or ruler marked in 1/64 inch increments and calipers (optional, but preferred for accuracy)
4. a tape measure
5. a fine-tipped permanent marker and masking tape
6. one of the arrows that you are currently using in your bow.

Measuring and Documenting Nocking Point Height

This is a critical part of your documentation. Most people try to match up a mark on their bow square with placing the tips of the launcher blade just nicking the bottom of the bow square then reading across a small gap to the lines on the "T" of the bow square. Others use a split arrow shaft of the same size they are shooting and place it onto the bottom of the bow square and then place that onto the launcher or other arrow rest to get their nocking point as a close check (actually, this is my "backup" method, but this method is my primary method). In Chapter 6, I outlined the Short Arrow Technique as a means for establishing a fine reference for centershot and nocking point height. This is especially useful in a new setup, or when you've changed your arrow rest specifications (the thickness of the blade, the angle of the launcher or even when you have changed styles of arrow rests). This will get you back very close to the original setup provided, of course, you were ProActive and document those settings.

I have recently found a way of duplicating your nocking point setting nearly perfectly with a single positive measurement, as long as the arrow diameter and arrow length are not changed! Here's what to do:

a. Attach your stabilizer to the bow and tighten it to its normal tightness. A fully round stabilizer works best, but you can use a multi-rod stabilizer provided that you always place the same (previously) marked rod into the same tightened position every time. This can easily be accomplished by marking the stabilizer and either the bow's bushing or the quick-disconnect so that the lines match up. *Note* I briefly mentioned this in Chapter 5, "Mounting Accessories," but by design, I did not mention marking the stabilizer and bushing positions. (I have to save some things for the appropriate time and place.)
b. Place your bow into a bow vise or get it set into a steady vertical position.
c. Place an arrow that your bow is tuned to on the bowstring and also onto the arrow rest.
d. If a fall-away rest, raise the rest to the full up position and hold it solidly there. No need to draw the bow back to full draw. In fact drawing the bow isn't necessary, is risky and besides this, it is also less accurate because you can't hold still and the person assisting you cannot chase the measurements down quickly enough.
e. Using a square or a level to establish a 90° angle between the tip of your arrow and the long stabilizer, place one edge on the stabilizer and the other vertically to the tip of the arrow. It is important that you have the instrument perpendicular to the stabilizer to insure accuracy and allow you to mark the stabilizer properly.

f. Mark the stabilizer with a magic marker where the square now contacts the stabilizer. For clarity, I put masking tape on the stabilizer to denote this point (*right and below*).

g. Using a good ruler (marked in 32nd inch increments, or better, 64th's) or your bow square, place the "T" of the bow square on the top of your stabilizer directly under the tip (point) of the arrow and on the stabilizer mark you made in step f.

h. Make sure you use the same length arrow and measure perpendicular to the stabilizer without pushing down on the stabilizer or moving the arrow when you mark the bow square or instrument you are using.

i. Be sure you are perpendicular to the stabilizer and not pushing down on the stabilizer, deforming it. Yes, I repeated myself, but it is important.

j. Then make a mark on the measure or bow square at the exact sharp tip of the arrow. Then, write down the measurement.

k. Last, extend the mark on your measuring instrument (*see photo below*).

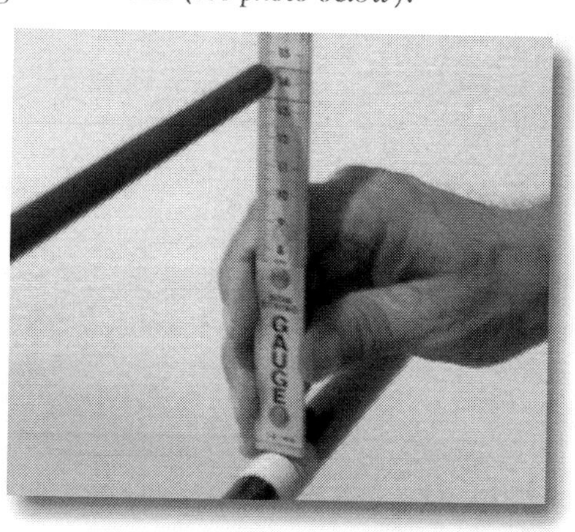

You will be able to use this anytime that you change servings, strings, cables, or D-loops and/or make any changes to the arrow rest. It should, if you measure it correctly, return your nocking point to its original position. I've used it to re-set several bows after a string/cable change or a center serving change, and it has worked perfectly every time. In every case, the first shot has impacted, at worst in the bullseye, but most often, in the X-ring. Normally, if I make a mistake, that first arrow is high, but in the bull's-eye. (I haven't yet figured out why yet.)

Measuring and Documenting Peep Height from Top of Nock

You really need to know your exact peep height setting when the bow is at brace. If the peep moves or gets moved, you must know exactly where to put it back to.

One More True Story This may be interpreted as bad sportsmanship, but it has happened to me twice over the years. I'll talk about only one of them, since the end result on both was only one lost shot, and a couple of points on my scorecard, but could have been worse if I had not been ProActive.

I had left my bow in the bow rack and went in for lunch. I normally don't leave my bow out of my sight, but in this case I had done just that. I finished my lunch and went to my group and we went down to our assigned target to start our animal round. I was in the lead by several points coming off the hunter round. The first target was a raccoon at some 30 odd yards. Back then, you simply aimed at the nose of the raccoon since it was in the center of the vital. I set my site, aimed at the nose, and released the shot. To my shock, the arrow managed a "16" just inside the body line high. I noted that one of the shooters in the group sort of smirked after the obviously shocked look on my face as a result of the severely high miss. I knew it was a good shot and that the arrow was just fine. We finished shooting and after the arrows were scored, I lagged back and took my time. The first thing I checked was my peep height, since I had a gut feeling that something was awry. Sure as shooting, when I pulled out my marked bow square and checked the pre-marked peep height, the peep site had "slipped" upwards quite a bit. Yeah, right, "slipped up" my foot. So, I re-set the peep height and went on to the next target. I had just lost four points off my lead and couldn't afford any more than that. I said nothing about this to anyone; nobody really had a need to know, especially the culprit. On the next target, I slammed the first arrow dead into the vital right where I was aiming, and noted a rather surprised look on that person's face. Obviously, I knew, and he now knew that a shenanigan had been pulled, but the joke was on him and not upon me. I didn't say anything to him at all, nor to anyone else. Why ruin everyone else's afternoon by being a cry baby; just let your bow and shooting do the talking. I finished the animal round with that "16" being my only miss (276 out of 280) and managed to scrape out the victory. However, as I said above, "If the peep moves or gets moved, you must know exactly where to put it back to." Had I not been ProActive and had that peep height marked exactly, I could have been chasing demons for several targets and lost that tournament as a result of this. Marking the location on the string is not enough, in my opinion; you need an exact measurement and need to be able to check it quickly, positively and accurately.

Measuring the Peep Height You should use the top of the nock as it rests against the top knot of the D-loop as the zero point for this measurement. This is a very repeatable and positive reference point. For the measuring point on the peep site itself, it is next to impossible to accurately measure to the "center of the peep hole" and get it accurate enough! On a peep site such as the Fletcher *Tru-Peep*, you should use the lowest portion of the peep site where it will first contact your measuring instrument; this is an absolute positive reference and no "eye-balling" or "guess-work" is involved. On a hooded peep site, I suggest you measure from the top of the nock to where the "hood" contacts the measuring tool; again another positive, consistent, and exact measurement (*see photo*). I recommend that you mark this in millimeters, but some archers mark it using a steel measure

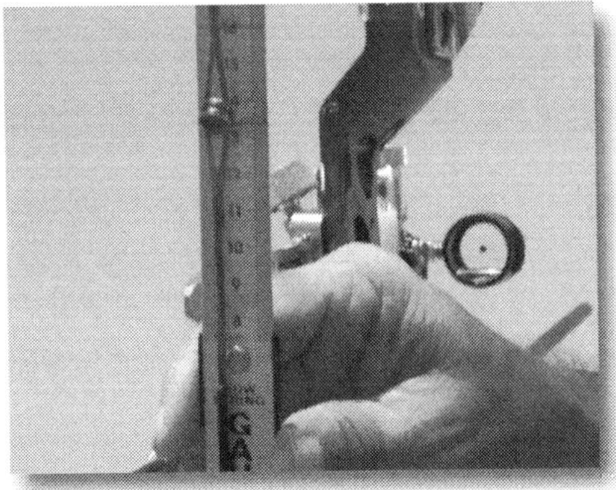

in 64ths of an inch, which is just fine.

Note I might make mention here that your peep height for your indoor setup and your peep height for shooting longer distances will not be the same! The average distance on an NFAA field or hunter round is around 44 to 45 yards. Thus, to avoid having a severely floating anchor point, you need to move your peep down slightly for outdoor shooting. I normally will set my peep height outdoors for a comfortable and solid anchor with the site set at around 48 yards or so. This gives me a repeatable anchor on the longer yardages and a tighter anchor for those shots at 20 yards and under. If setting up for FITA, then the peep height is set differently. For my setup, I know to lower my peep height for outdoor shooting by 2 mm from what I normally shoot indoors at 20 yards. You will be amazed at how much better you control your lefts and rights (along with elevation) by lowering the peep when you go outdoors! I have always taught that a bow tuned for 20 yards is just that; a 20 yard bow. It will likely not shoot nor group well at distance.

Summary

I have address several techniques of marking measuring tools and/or your bow to insure accurate duplication of the critical tune settings for arrow rest positioning, nocking point positioning and peep site height, thus saving you time and aggravation when something moves or needs to be replaced. In summary, the most important aspects of this documentation are:

- Document items only when a new bow has been "shot in" and the new strings and cables have had some time to "seat" themselves.
- Once the bow is group tuned and your draw length is set, then you will measure and document everything in a "Master Bow Configuration Table" (coming in Chapter 10).
- It is important to not only write the measurements down, but also to mark as many of the measurements onto the bow or a measuring instrument such as your bow square. This gives you a quick reference any time you want or need it to verify that everything has remained the same.

  For example, it is time for a little test: if you suddenly start shooting low on most all your shots and you know you are aiming well, what items would you check? Well, you might first check your sight setting. Then you would check the peep height. Then you should be checking the limb bolts for movement. Then check the nocking point height with the Stabilizer Method or Short Arrow Method. Next, you should check the mounting bolts on the sight block itself, these commonly come loose (you'd know about this one, if you've read Chapter 5). What state of mind are you going to be in if you didn't know any of the answers mentioned above for sure? From those last few points, are you starting to see a pattern of where we are going with this "ProActive Archery" stuff?

You now have the knowledge and methodology so that:

- Your draw length can be quickly checked by using a mark on the riser and a marked arrow or a measuring arrow.

- The nocking point can be checked and/or re-set by using your stabilizer and measuring up to the tip of the arrow and matching the number you jotted down, or, better yet, the distance marked right onto your measuring instrument. You won't even have to leave the shooting line or waste your only "equipment failure" for the round (at least not yet).
- Remember, as a standard of accuracy and repeatability, measurements should always be made with the same instrument and always made to a positive and consistent point of reference that can be duplicated and that minimizes error. Always use your instrument and never someone else's; it is your instrument that counts.

Next I will address critical measurements on the arrow rest, cams, and cable guard. Some, out of necessity, will be repeated, while others will be brought forth as we build the Master Bow Configuration Table, one bite at a time, piece by piece.

Tom Dorigatti

9

Measuring and Documenting Other Critical Positions

Sometimes, a quick visual check of important settings is needed without having to leave the course or the shooting line. For this purpose I tend to use templates and placards as backups to the "numbers" recorded in my archery journals and in a "Master Bow Configuration Table." ProActive archers also give their bow a complete inspection whenever they take their bows out of their cases and after they have mounted their sight, scope and stabilizers. Here are some techniques making that easy.

Arrow rest positioning, cam rotation, and the position of a moveable cable guard are yet another set of critical elements of a well-tuned bow. How many times have you had an arrow rest come loose, or had a cable or string stretch, or had the cable guard move? If you have been ProActive and have these things marked and documented, putting these items back in place is not a problem and shouldn't cost you very many points, if any. However, I'm sure you have seen many shooters who have had this happen and been totally clueless as to how to put things back where they were to start with. They will unnecessarily claim their one and only official equipment failure, find themselves completely flustered and any chances of recovery are cast into the wind.

In the chapters up until now, you have been given detailed recommendations on how to document and mark many of the important items that 'run' your equipment set-ups. Again, there are also several ways to accomplish the same tasks I have proposed prior to this and will propose in the following chapters. The techniques below have worked for me for many, many years, having refined them from rather rough beginnings. I'm also sure you may well have other techniques that may be easier. I have learned, however, that when it comes to compound bows, if something can move, sooner or later it will move; if something can come loose, sooner or later it will come loose. In many instances, if something can break, sooner or later it will break. You had better be prepared to put things back together. Otherwise, you will either have to quit for the day or end up with a terrible score and a lot of frustration. To make matters worse, without documentation, you are going to be really lost and, basically, you will have to start all over and re-tune. Why not be ProActive and avoid the grief?

This should be sounding familiar by now, but it bears repeated yet again: the procedures below are based upon the assumption that you have your bow tuned and set up properly and that the bow is grouping well for you. Once you have documented and marked everything, you should be able to duplicate these settings with ease, especially during a bow string and/or cable change, a rest change, or if something just comes loose. If you are doing a new setup, the same applies since you will need a documented starting point to which you can return if something isn't right.

Measurements Being Addressed

1. Center Shot From Window to Edge of Launcher or Rest
2. Launcher Height from Arrow Shelf to Tips of Launcher
3. Marking the Cam Positioning
4. Marking the Angle of the Cable Guard (Cable Guard Rake)

Items Required

1. A tuned bow with correct draw length and proper grouping already established (final tune completed). Or if a new setup, you still need a starting reference point, so continue to read on.
2. A bow square
3. A millimeter gauge or ruler marked in 64ths inch increments, calipers (optional).
4. A fine-tipped permanent marker and masking tape.

Measuring the Center Shot From Window to Edge of Launcher or Rest

Place the edge of your bow square or a business card against the inside surface of the sight window and angle it so the launcher blade contacts the bow square or the card. Mark either your bow square or a business card by outlining the nearest edge of the launcher blade and the "V" of the launcher. Notice, in the photo below, how I have completely outlined the shape of the "V" launcher on my bow square. It is a much more positive reference that "eyeballing" the center of the arrow. You now have a positive and quick verifiable constant reference of your current setup's launcher/rest positioning (in-out from the riser).

Measuring the Launcher Height from Arrow Shelf to Tips of the Blade

This is yet another critical measurement that is easy to acquire and document visually as well as numerically. The angle of your launcher blade has an impact on the stiffness and tenability of the rest. If this angle is off, not only is your nocking point affected, but the entire arrow tune can be radically affected. You might get "contact" with fletches as they slide by where there was no contact before, or the rest could now start "spring-boarding" the arrow causing wild fliers.

a. Take your bow square or a business card (trim it if necessary, always keeping a squared edge) and place it against the side of the sight window and slide it down onto the arrow shelf. The important part is the distance up from the arrow shelf.
b. Mark at both the tips of the prongs of the launcher or the tip of the vertical support for your arrow onto the card or the bow square, whichever you choose to use (or both).
c. Measure this distance up from the bottom of the bow square or the business card to your mark.
d. Record the distance on the "Master Bow Configuration Table" (*see figure in Chapter 10*), and then retain the card for future reference.
e. You now have this important setting on both your bow square and on a card for a double check. I have included a photo of how I use the business card method for centershot and for "tip up" marking for checking launcher angle (*see photos below*).

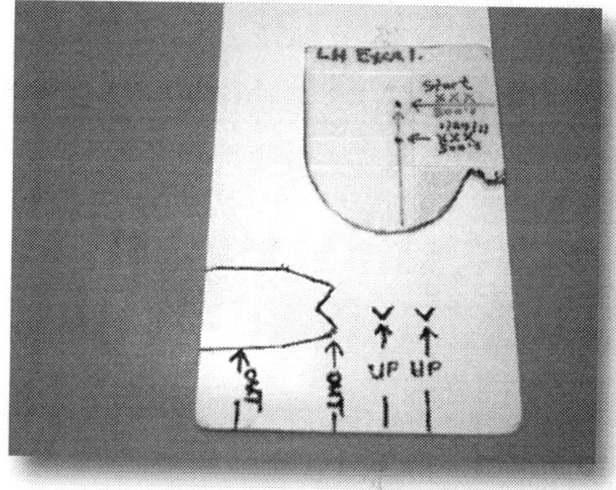

Marking the Cam Positions

There are a few other items a person should mark with reference lines once the bow is finally tuned and set up. These are marks made directly on the edges on both of the cams.

It is a good idea to mark both cams with a piece of tape or preferably a fine point magic marker line at the exact point where the cam is visually lined up with both the leading and the trailing edges of the limb. Many cams have "timing marks" that use the leading edges of the limbs as their points of reference. It is too hard to remember which line and which edge, and if your bow is set between the lines, you need a more accurate indicator. Marking both the leading and trailing edges of the limbs as they align with the cams gives you a more positive and accurate visual reference for checking this alignment and posi-

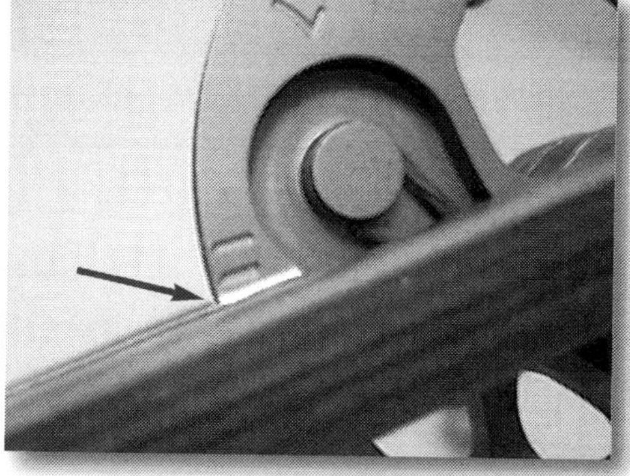

tioning and readily tells you at a glance which way the cam has "slipped" (*see photo*).

On hybrid cam bows, it is also preferable to mark two lines, one on each side of the buss (Power or Y-split) cable across from where it attaches to the bottom cam. This gives yet another positive visual reference that you can quickly check if you suspect something has moved (*see photos*). Do you remember what I said about one half

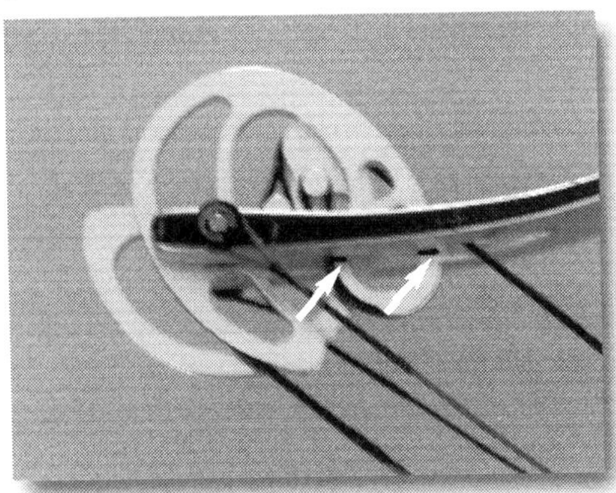

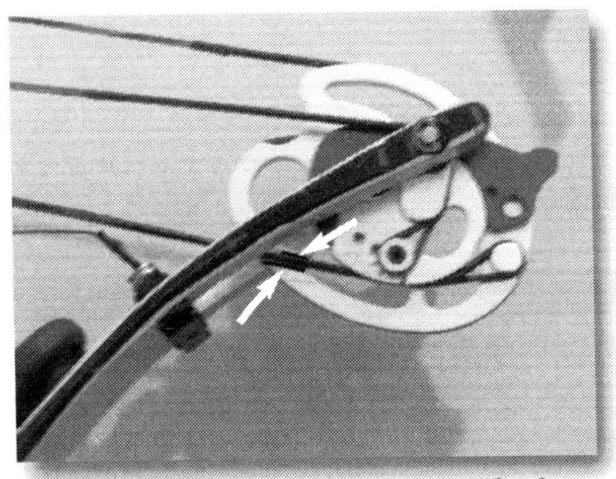

twist radically affecting the impact point at longer distances on a creep tune? The buss cable controls your draw length and in effect, your nocking point and poundage. If the buss cable stretches or breaks down (gets longer), then your poundage will drop, your draw length decreases, and your nocking point will move up; all of which can cause you to aim unsteadily and give the bow the tendency to shoot low.

Marking the String Off Point on Both Cams It is also a good idea to mark both cams with a piece of tape or a fine point magic marker with a dot or an arrow at the exact point where the bowstring "leaves" each cam. This way, if the bowstring stretches, you will have another reference from which you can see the change without having to use your measuring arrow to determine the change in draw length. Sometimes it is quicker and easier to have this backup set of markings as a means to double check the cam positioning marks on the cams themselves that align with the limbs.

Marking the Limb Bolt Positions

Limb bolts can and do move. (This problem has not been "solved" in modern bows or even addressed by many manufacturers as far as I can tell.) Generally, if they move, they wind outwards, thus reducing poundage and increasing draw length of the bow slightly. (There is tremendous outward pressure on limb bolt heads and vibrations causing movement of these bolts will cause that pressure to go down, which means the bolts will work loose.) If the bolts back out unevenly, it can really upset the tuning and shootability of your bow. In addition, this drop in draw weight will seriously affect your sight marks! Without marking the limb bolts, you will have no idea if they have moved and certainly no idea how much they have moved. Always mark the limb bolts with either a magic marker or even liquid paper correction fluid. Some bows now have "limb bolt locks," some have limb pocket locks, some even have both, however, many bows have no limb bolt locks of any type. I recommend that you mark limb bolt position lines in line with the center of the limbs, towards the center of the bow. Another thing I always recommend is that you have the Allen wrench handle parallel to the longitudinal axis of the limbs as well. In other words, I make my limb bolt adjustments in ⅙th turn increments (and never quarter turns, for example). This is more accurate, and if you have the bolts marked you know exactly how much they have been moved should the wrench slip out of the key in the Allen bolt head.

Marking the Angle of the Cable Guard

If your cable guard is movable, it is a good idea to place a mark on the riser and a matching line on the cable guard. This way, if the cable guard does move, you will pick up on it quickly; or if it has come loose, you can put it back exactly where it was. Eyeballing it back into position isn't close enough. I've witnessed many a shooter who has fought this during a scoring round because their cable guard wasn't marked or documented. The amount of cable rake can and will affect cam synchronization and thus, could really foul up the tune of the bow and also your sight marks and left/right impact points. In addition, if the cable rake moves very close to the bow, you could have vane or even arrow contact with the cables, which could be a dangerous situation.

I recommend again that you use a fine tipped permanent marker to mark this position (*see photo*). Masking tape was used in the photo for clarity. *Caution* Never use masking tape on your bow. The adhesive will harden and make the tape adhesive next to impossible to get off the part of the bow the tape has been placed upon. The use of magic marker allows you to remove the old mark(s) using an alcohol pad or a rag dampened with alcohol, and then put on your new marks.

Summary

We have discussed several techniques of marking measuring tools and/or your bow to insure accurate duplication of critical tune settings, thus saving you time and aggravation should something move or needs to be replaced. The most important aspects of this documentation are:

- Before shooting your bow always cross check the settings you have marked down to make sure something hasn't come loose or changed since the last time you shot the bow. This alone can save you a lot of grief and give you assurance that things are indeed still "on the money."

- Once your new bow has been shot in and the new strings and cables have had some time to "seat" themselves, it is time to document all the measurements and settings, mark the cams and limb bolts, and re-tighten the bolts and screws.
- Once the bow is group tuned and your draw length is set, then measure and document everything in the Master Bow Configuration Table isn't cast in stone, and there may well be other items you wish to include in the table (see Chapter 10).
- If you have two bolt holes in your riser for securing an arrow rest, it is likely possible to use a button head bolt in one hole to secure the rest, and a "cap screw" in the other hole to make sure it doesn't move. If not, then the use of an "inside" star washer between the rest and the bolt head will help secure the rest. In order to preserve the re-sale value of your bow, I personally don't recommend you use the "set screws" that some arrow rests have as part of their mounting process. This doesn't work all that well, and will always mar the riser's finish, thus affecting the aesthetics and the re-sale value. Even though my bows have a two-bolt system, I still outline the arrow rest's mounting bracket with a fine-tipped magic marker in a contrasting color to that of the riser.
- Measurements should always be made with the same instrument and always made to a positive and consistent point of reference that can be duplicated and that minimizes error. Always use your instrument and never someone else's; it is your instrument that counts.
- Always carry a spare launcher blade, or spare prongs, depending upon which type of rest you are using.

Tom Dorigatti

10

Proactive Bow Setup Documentation

A target archer's accuracy is based upon their consistency and upon making quick and correct analyses as to whether it is he/she who erred, or if something in his equipment has changed. Setup documentation involves making sure you have the means at your disposal to quickly check any part of your setup and then, if something has changed, to accurately duplicate the correct setting with confidence. Keep the above in mind as you read through many variables and facts about equipment setup documentation that I have used myself and/or learned from others over the past 50 years. This chapter deals primarily with what to document and how to mark the items down for quick use and future reference. There are a couple of "special items" I have used for quite some time that are somewhat different, and these have proven themselves time and time again to be nearly "dead-on" when I make a string and/or cable change, or have to re-serve the center serving on the bow string.

For Example

(*I told this story back in Chapter 8, so if you have already read that chapter, you can just skim this to refresh your memory.* TD) I came off an NFAA field course with a very solid score and was in first place after completion of the field and hunter rounds. We only had the animal round to go, which shouldn't pose a problem. Normally, I don't let my bow and equipment out of my sight, but this time, we were at my home course and the bow racks were just outside the door, so I put my bow in the rack and went in to get something to eat. I thought it strange that my bow wasn't in the same spot in the rack when I came back, but didn't give it much of a thought at the time. We walked down the path to the first animal target, which was a medium distance raccoon. At that time, you simply aimed at the tip of the nose on the 'coon and that was getting you that "20." I set my sight for the distance and shot the arrow. It landed barely inside the upper body for a "16!" I knew full well that I had shot a good, solid arrow, but to make sure I indeed would score, I shot my second arrow and it, too, was high but a tad lower, in contact with my first arrow. Now, I knew something suspicious was going on. We went up to score and sure enough, the first arrow had scored me a 16. My closest competition had just picked up four points on me in one shot. I decided to lag back and do some immediate checking, because I knew something had changed, and it wasn't me. I knew it couldn't be a loose indicator pin, since it would have fallen downwards and I would have shot way, way low. I checked the arrow rest and it was fine. Checked the nocking point, and again, it too, was perfect. Checked the marks on the cams, and they, too, were dead on. That left only one thing it could be and that was the peep height. Fortunately for me, I had the peep height marked on my bow square and also had a card in my quiver that had the measurement written down. There was the culprit! The peep height had gotten raised by quite a bit, thus causing the high shots. I re-set the peep height and finished off with the 276 animal score, much to the chagrin of one of the shooters in my group. He didn't understand how I could "recover" so quickly from shooting so high on that first target. Obviously, by being ProActive and having those "numbers" marked and written down, I saved myself from losing a lot more points and most likely losing that tournament, too. To this day, when at a field our outdoor event, my bow does not get out of my sight and before starting a new half after a break, those items are checked first, not afterwards. Are you "ProActive" and do you have your setup positions marked and written down? Can you replicate those settings when needed?

As I have already demonstrated, I am going to be repeating some things in this chapter, but at the same time, provide you with a form you can use to document the important items in your setup that will allow you to detect when they change and get them corrected immediately and correctly. The form is obviously not cast in stone, and you may well add to it or depart from it as you so wish. After all, it is your equipment set-up to do with as you so choose. I see so many shooters who don't have anything marked down or measured and when something goes haywire, they don't have a clue as to where to start, let alone knowing what has changed or how to fix it. You will have a major advantage over those archers if you are ProActive.

The System in Detail

Whenever an archer gets a new bow, regardless of brand, first and foremost, in my opinion, the bow needs to be set to the proper draw length and then properly tuned. It is often a good idea to get a "basic setup" without too much attention to groups or impact points for at least the first 200 shots or so. This allows the strings and cables to get set into the grooves on the cams, and also for any "stretch" of string and cables to take place. It also allows you to get used to the feel of the new bow and cam system so that you know what to expect as you work through your fine tuning process. Sometimes there is some stretch in the system, even with today's "pre-stretched" or "pre-stressed" strings and cables, so adjustments will need to be made in that case. Once the bow is properly set up and you are satisfied with the grouping, forgiveness, and shootability, then it is time to write the settings down, and get the bow marked so you have quick visual references to see whether something has changed or not. (You have already gone through and marked your starting positions at this point if you have been working through the early chapters). You should never change anything without having first marked and documented your starting point(s) on a "Master Bow Configuration Table."

We have already discussed the items to measure out and write down and those which you really need to have marked on the bow and equipment to give you that quick visual reference for checking out your equipment before, during, and after your shooting session or tournament. What you are doing here, with a new bow or "Old Reliable," is simply establishing accurate starting points and documenting those. Many of the items won't change; this is good. Many of the items will change and this, too, is good. You need a road map to avoid getting lost when things do change, so let's build one.

Things To Write Down

Many shooters have a notebook or journal to write down everything concerning their bow. This includes, of course, all the settings and measurements obtained before (initial setup) and after the bow is properly set up and shooting well for them. The following Master Bow Configuration Table (*see next page*) lists the most common items to measure and provides a handy system to keep track of these measurements.

You already know the measurements to make and how to make them from the previous chapters and your general knowledge. You now also know the marks you need to make on the cams, bow square, and other measuring instruments. Now you are ready to go over your equipment and measurements with a "fine toothed comb" and get the documentation down on paper. It is easy to duplicate the table below and either put it on a printable adhesive label for filling out and attaching to a bow case or journal, or simply print out a copy and use tape to place it. Any time you make a change to anything with regard to your bow, arrows, accessories, or your release, and I do mean anything, this change must be, at the very least, documented in your journal. At the best, changed in your Master Bow Configuration Table. This is one way you have of assuring yourself that you can duplicate your current set up and/or go back to what it was before "something happened."

Yes, I know I am repeating myself somewhat from previous chapters, however, I thought you would prefer I repeat things here rather than sending you back repeatedly to Chapter X and page YZ. Read on, the information here, by design, is not necessarily verbatim from the previous chapters.

1. *Axle-to-Axle Length* Many of today's compound bow instructions state that the axle-to-axle length (ATA) is more important than the brace height. Axle-to-axle length (ATA) should be measured from the center of the top axle to the center of the bottom axle to the nearest 1⁄16″. Most bows allow a range of ATAs, but once your bow is tuned, you need to know for sure the best shooting ATA of the bow. It might be off manufacturer's specification by ¼″ or more. So what? If the bow shoots better there, you need to know it and to be able to replicate it. By the way, you don't have to measure from the center of the axle to the center of the other axle. I prefer to measure from farthest from center edge of one axle to the farthest from center edge of the other axle. This is simply more consistent. Just make sure you set your own "standard" method of measuring your ATA. If you go center of axle to center of axle, fine, but just like you try to do with your shot sequence, do

Master Bow Configuration Table

Bow ____________________ Date __________

Item	Measurement	Item	Measurement
Axle-to-Axle Length		Power Cable Length	
Top Tiller		Arrow & Length	
Bottom Tiller		Centershot	
D-loop Starting Length		Launcher Height from Shelf	
D-loop–String to Inside		Launcher Blade Thickness	
Brace Height		Peep from Top of Nock	
True Draw Length		Size of Peep Aperture	
String Length & #strands		Cam Size & Module	
Control Cable length		Nocking Point Height	
Peak Weight		Holding Weight	

Feel free to duplicate this table and use as you will.

it that way every time. It won't hurt to measure both sides of the bow. If one limb is ever so slightly twisted you can get a different value from one side to the other. You don't want to measure the left side and later measure the right and think your ATA has changed when really the two sides just differ by a small amount.

2. *Top Tiller & Bottom Tiller* I normally measure the top and bottom tiller from the limb at the top of the limb pocket to the inside or outside of the string (at right angles to the string, of course). An example: 9⅛″ **I** ("I" = Inside of string; "O" would indicate outside edge of string). With some bows, tiller measurements are not really exact since the cams are different sizes, but can be duplicated, so as long as you are consistent in how you measure and document it, it works just fine. I won't get into "exacting and for real" tiller measuring, because so few bows today deal with tiller in this fashion anymore. It is still important to have these measurements, however.
3. *D-loop Starting Length* You should measure the starting length of the untied D-loop to the nearest 1/16″, and write it down. It is also a good idea to set up a couple of spare D-loops to that length. It will save you time and trouble when your D-loop finally fails or needs to be changed. This is not a case of "if," it is a case of "when;" be ProActive and be prepared.
4. *D-Loop–String to Inside of Extended Loop* As discussed previously, my personal preference is to use a set of calipers to measure the "length" of the tied D-loop from the outside of the bow string to the inside of the stretched out loop. This is a very important measurement, because it does affect your anchor point, which directly affects how your draw length feels as well. When changing a D-loop, if you have pre-made your spare D-loop the same length as #3 above, then this should fall into place when your D-loop is secured. A word to the "wise" on changing D-loops bears repeating: it is a better practice, when changing D-loops, to remove only one end at a time. First place a nock on the string, and then remove one end of the D-loop. Tie on that end against the nock or tied on nocking point, and then tie on the other end of the D-loop. However, if you tie in serving above and below the arrow nock, and then place the D-loop on the outside, then this is not necessary.
5. *Brace Height* Many bow manufacturers specify a given brace height range for optimum performance of each particular model of bow. However, if the brace height changes, then it also changes your true draw length, thus affecting your performance as a shooter. As described before, I've come up with a sure way of establishing a consistent measuring point for obtaining True Draw Length, based upon the brace height of the bow. By doing it that way, you always have a positive reference point that is the correct True Draw of the bow. I use this method in lieu of simply measuring to the tip of the launcher blade or arrow rest because this method works even when the arrow rest has been changed! I discussed transferring the brace height to the inside of the riser before, so I won't list a step-by-step procedure for it here.

Things to remember here are: that the center of the arrow rest mounting hole is not always the spot directly above the deepest part of the grip (the so-called "pivot point") and that if you have two mounting holes, this point is not necessarily directly half-way in between those two holes. That point could be somewhere in the nearest hole, somewhere in between the two holes, or even somewhere on the hole farthest away from you! Thus, if you just pick a spot, you could be off by ¼″, or even ½″. Using a consistent point of reference, marked on the riser, should be acceptable, but if it is off ¼″ or more, then when you order up a new bow, you could end up way off with your draw length specification! Do not use the prongs of the arrow rest to establish this! What happens if you move your arrow rest or change to a longer or shorter launcher blade? You also will not know the True Draw Length of the bow accurately, and obviously your calculated AMO Draw Length will also be wrong.

6. *String, Control Cable, & Buss Cable Lengths and Numbers of Strands* Many shooters today do not shoot the strings and cables that come on their new bows, opting rather to order a custom made set of strings and cables. Thus, most shooters opt to make sure that their strings and cables are indeed the length specified in the specifications for the bow. I've found from experience that the strings and cables on new bows and what is marked on their limb tags are not necessarily the same! Measuring these is not difficult. However, once you have twisted up the cables and strings to get the bow tuned and set to proper draw length to get these "numbers" as they really are without pulling them off the bow to measure them. This is the subject of a future chapter, so for right now for your initial Master Bow Configuration Table (called "Table" from this point forward), use the factory string and cable specifications from the limb tag or the Tune Chart for your particular bow model and cam size. This is important, and will come into play later in this book.
7. *Peak Weight* The standard means of measuring a bow's peak weight is to use a hanging bow scale, and, placing the string or loop on the hook, pull down on the bow until you reach full poundage and it starts to let down. Do not let up and then pull back down on the same pull, this introduces error into the reading (called hysteresis). Some people also use their "crank boards" to measure their peak weight. The important part here is to use your own scale to measure the poundage or, if not your own, then always measure your poundage on the same scale all the time. If you have to make a change and you aren't using your scale, then before making the change, always check the poundage before you start, write it down, and then make the change and weigh it again and mark it down. Be sure to write both readings on the Table or in your journal and the date of change. Then, when you get home, immediately make the measurements on your scale and write them down. You might consider some type of digital bow scale, such as the Easton *Hand-held Digital Bow Scale*. This unit not only gives you peak weight, but also displays the holding weight. In addition, unless you zero the scale, it will hold the last readings in memory. Remember my rule of thumb: Always take three (3) measurements, toss out ringers and average the other two. Five (5) measure-

ments are even better.

8. *Arrow & Length* Which arrow your bow is tuned to is self-explanatory. You could expand this to include fletching, tip weight, nock, etc. Too much information, in my opinion is better than too little information.
9. *Centershot From Window to Center of Arrow* Place an arrow on the rest, and measure directly above the rest from the center of the arrow (or from center of the "V" if a launcher) to the inside of the sight window. We discussed several means of marking and documenting this in previous chapters, so now all you have to do is record this measurement into the Table.
10. *Launcher Height from Arrow Shelf to Tips of Launcher* This is a critical measurement that is easy to attain.
11. *Launcher Blade Thickness* Many shooters today are using custom thicknesses of launcher blades. Some use 0.008″, 0.010″, or 0.012″ thickness blades. It is imperative that you write down the blade you are using and its thickness. If you change blades, then change your table entry. You might even write down which brand of launcher blade it is and where you purchased it from! Don't forget to mark down whether or not you are using a support blade and its length as well.
12. *Peep Height from Top of Nock* This is a very important measurement. You will recall how I recovered from a peep height movement? I use the top of the nock because it is a very repeatable and positive reference point. I also shoot an angled peep site, so I measure from the top of the nock to where the leading edge contacts my measuring tool; again another positive and consistent, exact measurement. It is impossible to accurately measure to the "center of the peep hole." If using a hooded peep, then the edge of the hood on the peep is about as consistent of a reference point as you can come by!
13. *Size of Peep Aperture* This is self explanatory. If a clarifier or verifier, don't forget to write down which "color" or size you are using! This saves you trying to remember it, because in all likelihood, you won't remember what you changed from!
14. *Cam Size and Module* Write down which cam size and module (if required) you have on the bow. Don't forget to write down the let off percentage of this module too! It isn't a bad idea to write down your actual percentage of letoff, since most of the time, your setup is not giving you the letoff the cams say you should get.
15. *Nocking Point Height* This is one of the most critical parts of your documentation. Most people try to match up a mark on their bow square with placing the tips of the launcher blade just nicking the bottom of the bow square then reading across a small gap to the lines on the "T" of the bow square. Others use a split arrow shaft of the same size they are shooting and place it onto the bottom of the bow square and then place that onto the launcher to get their nocking point. Tip If you have read the previous chapters you will know that I prefer to use the "Short Arrow Technique" coupled with the "Stabilizer Method" to assure I have the most accurate measurement I can achieve. Document both in your Table. These measurements will save your bacon way more often than you would ever imagine.
16. *Holding Weight* This is sometimes difficult to ascertain. Again, be sure to use the

same scale you measured peak weight with. Also be certain to never "bounce" the scale back and forth. This introduces "hysteresis" into your measurement and it will not be accurate. If you weigh your bow on a crank board, then you also will check the holding weight on a crank board. Again, the Easton Scale will take care of this for you; all you have to do is to take the measurements, average them, and write them down in the Table.

Items to Mark on the Bow Itself Anything that could come loose and move should be marked! Here are some other items a person should mark with reference lines once the bow is finally tuned and set up:

- cams and limb bolts,
- V-bar or counter weight brackets,
- sight block mounting bolts on the riser,
- cable guard "rake" and alignment,
- which cam module "holes" you are set for,
- limb positioning for your limb pocket locks,
- the setting for how far out your scope is mounted on your windage turret,
- your sight extension hole, and
- the angle out and/or up and down on your v-bar counter stabilizers.

By having these things clearly marked, when something comes loose or gets moved, you can put it back exactly where it was without skipping a beat or losing many points because you can't figure things out. Eyeballing these settings simply isn't close enough. You shouldn't ever set yourself up for being frustrated when something like this happens. Unless something breaks (literally), you never have to use your "equipment failure time out" to get things back in order. In fact, you'll expect to continue right on shooting should those happen!

Summary

We have discussed how to measure the most important bow tune criteria, from axle-to-axle length on through to holding weight. In addition, several techniques of marking your measuring tools or the bow have been discussed. In conclusion, the most important aspects of this documentation are:

- Always document these items, even with a new setup. (You always need a starting point.) Don't document items as being "in stone" until a new bow has been shot in and the new strings and cables have had some time to "seat" themselves.
- Once your bow is group tuned and your draw length is set, then measure and document everything in the Master Bow Configuration Table.
- The Master Bow Configuration Table isn't set in stone, either, and there may well be other items you wish to include in the table. Make a table of your own; you have the basis and reasoning for the items contained therein, so improve upon it.
- It is important to not only write these measurements down, but it is also important to mark as many of the measurements onto your bow or onto a measuring instrument, such as your bow square.
- Draw length can be quickly checked by using a mark on the riser and a marked

arrow or a measuring arrow.

- Nocking point location can be nearly exactly re-set by using your stabilizer and measuring up to the tip of the arrow and matching the number in the Table, or the mark on your measuring instrument.
- Further document the cam settings by marking the cams with dots and reference lines with regards to limb and cam alignment, power cable positioning, and the cable guard rake.
- Measurements should always be made with the same instrument and always made to a positive and consistent point of reference that can be duplicated and minimizes error.
- Anytime you make any change to anything on your bow or equipment, write it down in the journal and also make the change in your Master Bow Configuration Table.
- Always mark the date and time on your journal entries and especially on the Master Bow Configuration Table.
- Remember, changing one thing can and often does change several others!! Thus, always make a new dated copy of the Master Configuration Table any time you make more than one or two changes to your setup.

Tom Dorigatti

11

How to Measure for Custom Strings and Cables

Today's bows, while they are great shooters, are very sensitive to having their brace heights and axle-to-axle lengths within very narrow ranges of values in order for them to shoot their best. This chapter is a guide to help you to measure up your current bowstring and cables (without removing them from the bow!) for ordering a custom set or for building a set yourself that will almost perfectly match what is on the bow now.

Preliminaries

I assume that you have the bow properly setup and tuned and also have taken the time to mark down all the settings mentioned in the previous chapter (things such as brace height, axle-to-axle length, peep height, nocking point height, etc.). Items #1 and 2 on the list below can be factory specifications, however #3 thru #7 are seldom known by archers. If you really want to match up the new set with the old, these need to be measured out carefully. This helps to insure that the new string and cable combination are as close as possible to what is on the bow now. Your tune can be saved, and also your bow's draw length and speed can be preserved closely, since the weights of the string/cables will be close as well.

The following will be addressed in this article:

1. Measuring string and cable lengths (if not known for certain).
2. Counting the numbers of strands (if not known for certain).
3. Sizes of the end loops (very few people even consider this, but it is important).
4. Whether or not to serve end loops for cam or axle pegs
5. Serving lengths, end loops, "Y" splits, or special circumstances.
6. Determining center serving location, length and thickness of the serving material.
7. The power cable ("Y" split).

Measuring Up the String and Cables

The first step in the process is to either look up the specifications for the particular bow model and cam size you are currently using. If you have changed the specifications for any reason, then you should use the new measurements for the new setup.

1. *String & Cable Lengths* Normally most people will opt to stay with the specifications indicated by the manufacturer. However if you don't have that information or have tuned your bow differently, it is a simple process to determine your string length without removing your current string from the bow. Simply:
   a. Take a piece of string that doesn't stretch, making it long enough to do the job. Center serving material works really well. Another thing that works well is a seamstress's cloth tape measure.
   b. Tie a loop on one end and loop it over the string peg on the cam, then wrap it around the cam and down to the other cam, wrapping it around that cam, too. Then, at the end of the cam peg for the string, either mark the string, or pinch it off between your thumb and forefinger (*see photos*).

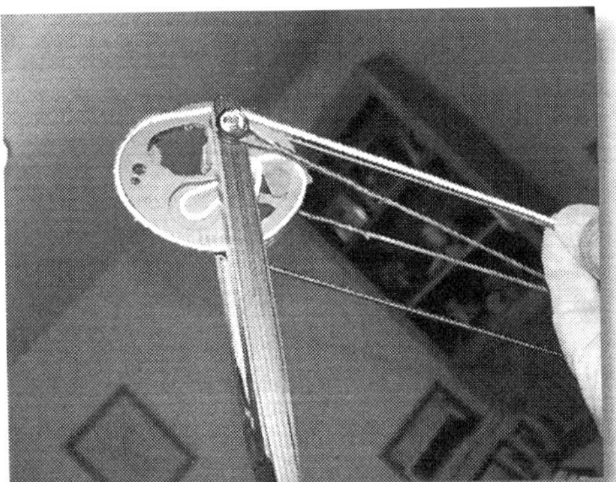

   c. Measure the length of the piece of string and record that length. Compare this to the manufacturer's specifications if you have them or to the limb tag on the bow. This measurement will allow you to get the length of string you need based upon the tune of the current bow and allows for the "stretch" you get when the string is under pressure (*see photo below left*).

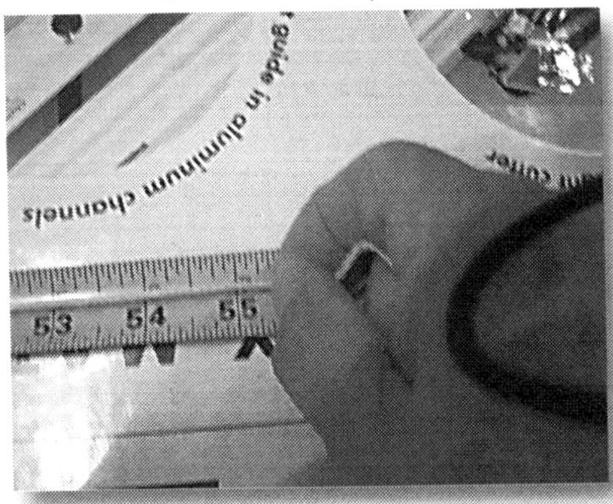

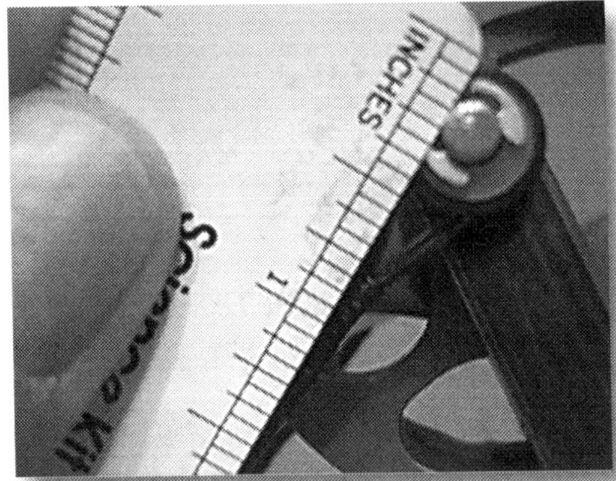

2. *Counting the Number of Strands in the String and Cables* You should have counted these as part of your initial bow documentation and recorded this information on your Master Bow Configuration Table. However, if you haven't, you can still count the strands. It is easiest to place the bow into a safe bow press and loosen the string enough so that you can spread out the strands and count them. Do not

remove the string or cables from the cam pegs or the bow.

3. *Sizing the End Loops* This is more important than you might think. The size of the opening of the end loops can have a huge impact on how easy they fit onto or come off of the pegs. Too small, and you could tear the loops up getting them on and off. Too large and the "over serving" could interfere with the string/cable fitting into the grooves on the cams. To measure the opening of the end loop, simply place a thin ruler marked off in 1⁄16″ or 1⁄8″ increments at the end of the cam peg and measure to where the long serving starts down the end serving of the string or cable. Most loops that I've seen are about 3⁄4″ long, but some are a bit longer than this. Smaller than 3⁄4″ is rare and is usually too tight to fit on today's cam pegs (*see photo above right*).
4. *To Serve or Not to Serve the End Loops* Many strings and cables that come with bows today do not have the ends of the loops served. However, many of the custom string manufacturers automatically serve these so that the end loop will fit cleanly over the cam peg and you don't have to worry about a "stray strand." You need to make this decision on your own. Personally, I prefer to have those loops served.
5. *Measuring Serving Lengths* This is an easy thing to measure so that your new string and cables have the same amount of serving on them and that the center serving is in the same location on the string as the original set. You can do this also without removing the string or cable(s) from the bow.
   a. Using the same piece of serving with the loop that you made to measure string length, again place that onto the cam peg and wrap it around the cam.
   b. Pull it tight and pinch it off with your thumb/forefinger where it comes to the finish off of the end serving.
   c. Write this measurement down to nearest 1⁄8″.

   Repeat a-c, above, for all the end serving lengths for the both the string and the cables (*see photos below*).
6. *Center Serving Measurements* The center serving's location can be a very important matter, especially on today's high performance bows and the very "slippery" nature of today's string materials. The length of the center serving is one of personal preference, with 3-D shooters normally putting as little center serving on the string as possible and FITA style shooters putting as much as 12 inches of center serving onto the bow. However, it is a wise idea, in my opinion and experience, to position that center serving so that no less than 1½″ of serving is above the nocking point location. Release shooters tend to put a lot of upward pressure on a nocking point or D-loop. Therefore, any serving separation or movement will be upwards. If there isn't enough serving above the nocking point to "resist" this movement or to lock the serving down, then the entire serving can move and ruin a good tune in no time. Here is one way of duplicating the location of the center serving by measuring it while it is still on the bow (*see photo on right next page*).
   a. Choose one cam or the other. On a single cam bow, you have no choice; it is the bottom cam for both ends of the string.

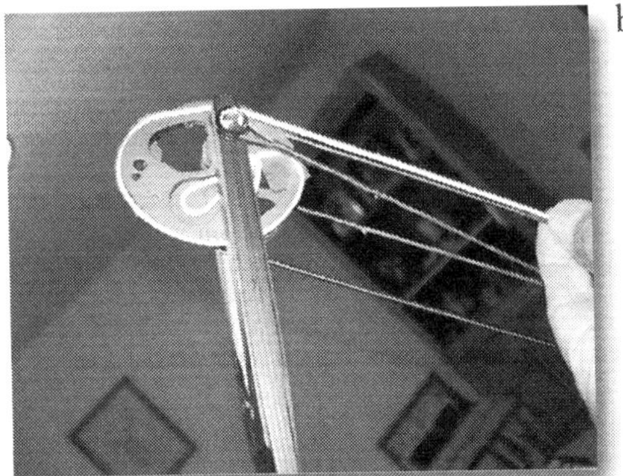

b.

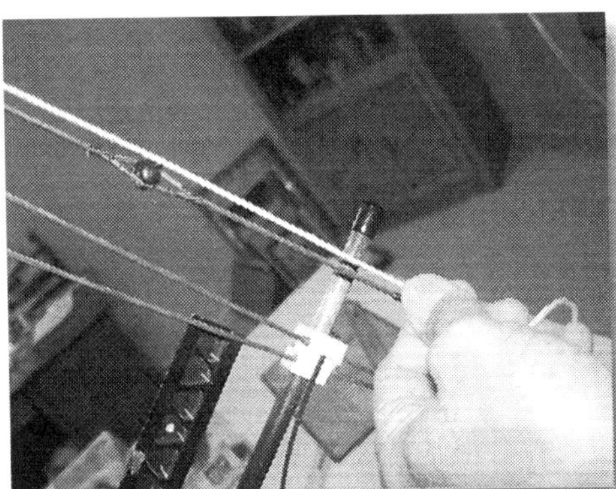

Place the loop of the measuring string you've been using on the cam peg.

c. Wrap that string around the cam and follow the string to the start of the serving. (I always use the top cam on a cam and a half bow or twin cam bow).

d. Pinch off the measuring string where it contacts the start of the serving.

e. Measure and record this distance.

f. Measure the length of the serving down towards the bottom cam and then write this down.

g. When ordering your string, specify how far from the end of the top loop to go before starting the top of the center serving and how long to make the center serving. It is also a good idea to tell the string maker the size and type of nock you are using and ask them to serve the serving so that type of nock has proper fit onto the center serving. You are paying them good money for your string and cables, so this should be easily accommodated. It is way more important than you think it is! *Tip* One other thing you might ask your custom string manufacturer to do as I do when I reinstall a new center serving myself. I always ensure that the "tag end" of the serving runs the entire length of the center serving. I start the serving from the top and wind down to the bottom, serving right over the tag. I've found that this really helps to lock down the center serving and nearly eliminates any chance of the center serving moving up the bowstring. You must ask for this; otherwise your string maker will make a short tag of only an inch or so in length when they start the center serving.

7. *The Power Cable ("Y" split)* The power cable has one other specification that can be very important. Some "Y" split cables are not served at all from where the split of the cable occurs to the axle on the top limb. Other manufacturers have their splits served. I personally like to have mine served at the split. Measuring the "Y" split is a simple process:

a. Using a ruler, write down the length of each leg of the "Y from the end of the axle loop to where the "split" occurs (*see photo below left*). Write down this length. Another technique is to also mark one of the two sides so that you know which is the left or right side of the split (or which is the longer of the two). This helps with consistency once you have adjusted your cam lean.

b. Measure how long the serving is from the split down the string. Most are from

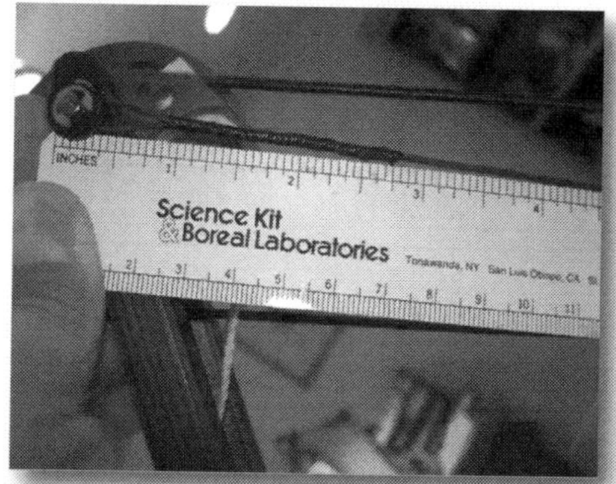

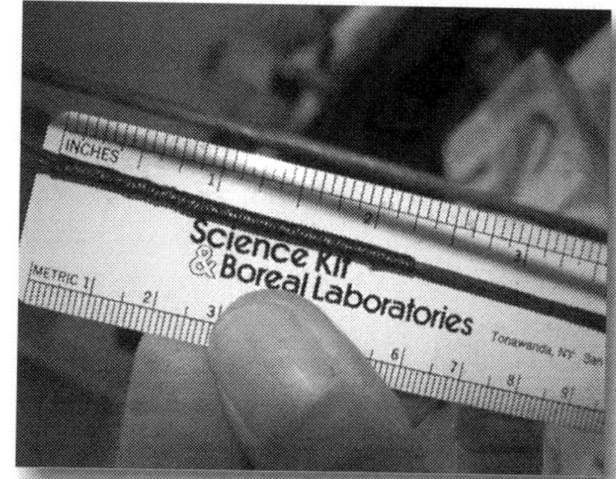

1½″ to 3″ in length. Remember, the closer to the axle end you go with the "Y" split serving, the less limb clearance you are going to have with your "pigtails" (see photos below).

The pigtails can be twisted to align the top cam lean or the idler wheel lean. In addition, the "pigtails" can be used for fine tuning draw length as well. Always remember that changing the length of the power cable by twisting it will change the nocking point height and, therefore, its travel.

Summary

In this chapter, I outlined seven basic steps needed to order or make a new bowstring with the same loop sizes, loop serving lengths, Y-split lengths, and with the center servings as close as possible to being the same as on your original string. You can do all this without removing your bowstring from the bow.

As in all measurement systems, consistency is the key. If you are uncertain, take the measurement again, always being sure to write the numbers down. I also recommend that you always start from the top of the bow and work towards the bottom of the bow; do the bow string first, then the power cable (Y-split), and then, if an assymetric cam bow, the control cable.

If you know, for certain, that you have changed the string and cables away from factory specifications for whatever reason, or that the bow is shooting so well with how you have it set now, that you want to duplicate what is on there, then order them up as measured. If you are wanting to start completely over, then I'd recommend that you go with factory specifications. However, in doing this, you must realize that if going with the factory specs constitutes a change of those dimensions, you are basically going to be starting completely over with that bow's set up. If you are in doubt, you can look up the specifications for the strings and cables on the bow manufacturers' website.

Through the use of nothing more than a piece of serving thread or a seamstress's tape and a tape measure, you now have the means to do this without disrupting your bow's current setup and tune! (That is unless you change the dimensions.) You can now measure up for the new strings and cables and continue to shoot while you await your new set to arrive. Once completed, if you have written all of this down on your documentation record, ordering or building a new set of strings and cables is an easy and repeatable process.

Tom Dorigatti

12

Changing Your String and Cables

Many shooters agonize over having to change the cables and bow string on their bow. Even worse is the fact that they often put off doing it until there is a failure of a cable or string thus forcing the issue for this change. Thus, instead of being ProActive about the inevitable, these shooters tend to think about it only when disaster happens, pushing their equipment to the limit and beyond, often times to the point of complete failure. Then when the time to change string and cables finally comes, they want to hurry up and get the bow "re-tuned," thinking all along that changing the strings and cables means that they have to start all over. Nothing could be farther from the truth, my friends! This really isn't something to get all exasperated and flustered about! There is a light at the end of the tunnel, so read on.

The steps below are based on the assumption that you have read the previous chapters or you have established your correct draw length, peep sight height, nocking point, and arrow rest positioning and that the bow is grouping well. Once you have documented and marked everything, you should be able to duplicate these settings with ease. Once again, the focus is upon "eating the elephant one bite at a time," and being ProActive about the process.

Introduction

All too often, when a person goes to change bowstring and cables on their bow, they put their bow into a bow press, pull off all the strings and cables and then replace them all at once. Once this is done, they put on their D-loop; put the peep in, "eyeball" the nocking point and go attempt to either paper or group tune or both. This is basically starting from scratch, is it not? It doesn't have to be that way. If you have taken the time to document your settings, you only need to make a final check of where they are right now, update them, and then proceed in a step-by-step fashion and you will be shooting into the X-ring right from the get-go with your new string, D-loop, and cables. Even if you have had a failure of a component, if you have been ProActive, you have the "before the failure" settings documented, so it should be a snap to put on the new component and move forward, should it not?

Here is the method I've come up with and used for quite some time. Each time, after following this procedure, the bow's owner has been able to shoot their first arrow into the bull's-eye or X-ring and then only have to verify their "fine tune." Hours of work are saved by following this basic and simple sequence of steps. The order in which you replace the string or cable is of little consequence, however, I tend to do the bowstring last, opting to replace the cables one at a time first. If it is a single cam bow, I replace the power cable first. If a hybrid bow, I replace the power cable first, then the "control" cable, and finally the bowstring.

Before you start, re-check and re-verify everything to make sure it matches what you have marked and written down in your Table. If anything has changed, go with what the setting is now; that is unless you have a broken or stretched string or cable. Don't move anything; just write down things the way they are right now.

Items Required

1. Your tuned bow with correct draw length and proper grouping already established (final tune completed)
2. A bow square
3. A millimeter gauge or ruler marked in 1/64″ inch increments, calipers (optional)
4. A tape measure
5. A fine-tipped permanent marker and masking tape
6. A long arrow or measuring arrow
7. Some lengths of serving thread to tie in the peep sight and if you so choose to tie in the nocking points for your arrow
8. The set of new cables and bow string of the correct lengths as per your documentation form (your "Table") or the bow manufacturer's specifications if you are indeed choosing to start over and change back to manufacturer's recommended harness sets.

Steps for Changing the Cables and Strings of a Twin-Cam Bow

a. Check the bow's poundage on your bow scale and mark this down. Do not make any poundage adjustments at this time; remember, you are trying to duplicate the way the bow is set up now. You have been shooting it well, so why change it?

b. Check the other measurements in your "Master Bow Configuration Table" to make sure they are still the same. Just a quick check should suffice, but if you are very particular or made changes since the form was filled in, make out a new one documenting the most current settings. Remember to always place the date on the Table.

c. Check the nocking point using the "stabilizer method" that I previously introduced. See the photos top right as a review.

d. Check your peep sight height. See picture below on how this is more accurately accomplished rather than just trying to eyeball to the center of the peep hole. Hint: You can also measure from the base of the top cam to the peep sight and write this "rough measurement" down for use in step k (below).

e. Check your D-loop length. I measure from the outside of the bowstring to the inside of the D-loop using a set of calipers. This measurement is more important than one might think, so be careful with it.

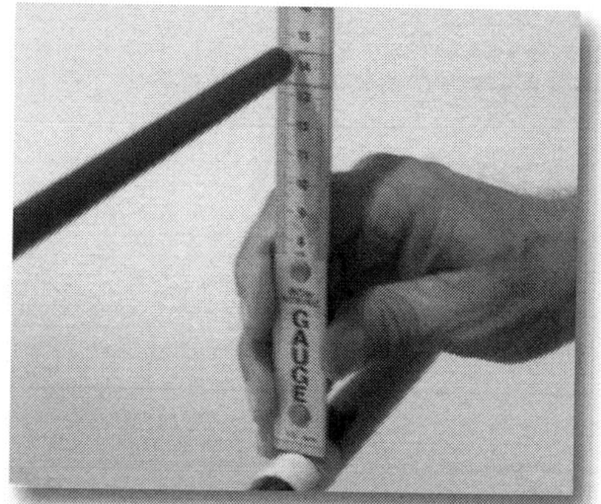

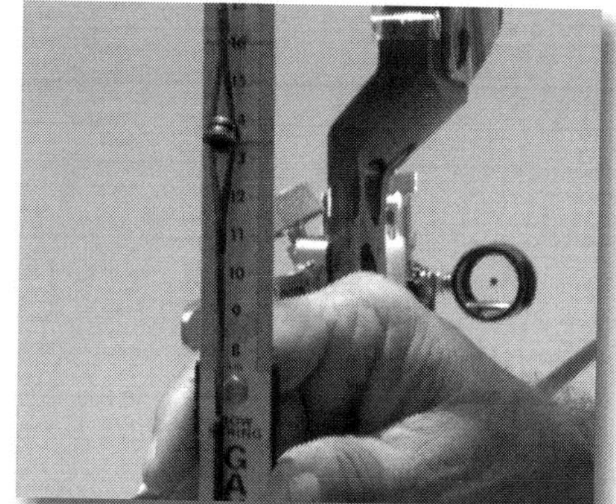

f. Remove the cable that controls the top cam first. Then put the new cable on the cams. Twist up the new cable until the bottom cam is back on your marks you previously documented and made.

g. Remove the cable that controls the bottom cam. Put the new cable on the cam. Twist up or untwist the new cable until the top cam is back on the marks you previously documented and made.
h. Check the ATA to insure that it is where it was before you began the replacement process. It should be identical if you have documented things correctly. If not, get it there before proceeding by twisting or untwisting the both cables equally. If you have to do this, watch the marks you placed on the cams before starting this process. If you ordered the correct length cables, and the maker fulfilled his obligation, it should be a simple matter of twisting them (shorter) or untwisting them (longer) to bring your cams back to where they belong.
i. Remove the bowstring.
j. Put the new bowstring onto the cams. Most often, the new bowstring is going to set in on the long side, and will "settle in" a bit as the end servings get into the cam grooves. This is usually not a problem with BCY 452X or 8125 material. Make sure that you are twisting that bowstring at each end in the right direction to tighten the end serving! If you rotate it in the wrong direction, then the end servings will come loose. Sometimes, the string makers do overlook this and "pre-twist" the string in the wrong direction. Not many people pay attention to this minor detail, and this can cause the end loop servings to come loose and separate prematurely as a result of this over-sight!
k. Twist up the bowstring to bring your cams back onto the marks you made before you started.
l. Check the ATA to make sure it is back into specifications from your documentation record.

m. Insert your peep sight into the bowstring. At this point, don't worry about the exact peep height; just use the "rough measurement" from step b (*above*). You will get the final peep setting later.
n. Let down the bow press making sure that the cables and string are all in the appropriate orientation and in the cam grooves.
o. Remove the bow from the press. Then carefully draw the bow back and let it down several times without dry firing the bow. This can easily be done, either by drawing the bow with your fingers and letting it down, or by using a release aid that will not "fire" so that you can accomplish this task.
p. Put the bow into your bow vise. Attach the stabilizer, and get the bow into the vertical position.
q. Attach the top knot of the D-loop (or the top tied in nocking point) loosely, so you can move it.
r. Establish your proper nocking point using the stabilizer method previously described. Place an arrow of the size and length you shoot onto the bowstring. Slide the D-loop (or top knot of the tied in nocking point) so it contacts the nock of the arrow. Simply move the knot until the tip of the arrow matches your previous nock-height setting you recorded.
s. Tie in the nocking point or top knot of the D-loop securely. Re-check using the stabilizer method, and move the D-loop or tied in knot accordingly.
t. Tie in the bottom nocking point or bottom knot of the D-loop. Re-check the nocking point height using the Stabilizer Method. Be sure to leave a slight gap between the bottom of the nock and the bottom D-loop knot or the bottom tied-in serving. This will help prevent nock pinch.
u. Set the peep height. Use the method in step b (*above*) or whatever you normally use to establish your peep height. You may well end up with the peep sight out of rotation. If so, put the bow back into the press, and by twisting each end of the bowstring a twist or two evenly at both ends, you will get the peep rotation correctly accomplished. Once you have this done, tie in your peep sight.
v. Re-check the cam positioning, peep height, nocking point height, and draw length. Remember that the brace height can be transferred to the riser thus making your true draw very easy to measure quite exactly without the use of a crank board to draw the bow. You previously established your True Draw length by transferring the brace height measurement to the inside of the sight window, remember? Now you can use this once again to make sure you have this all important setting accomplished. If you have done your homework in the steps above, your draw length will be dead on, or at least extremely close to what it was before you started.
w. Re-check your draw weight to make sure it is still where it belongs.
x. Re-check the ATA on both sides of the bow.

At this point, you should have the bow with the new string and cables on it set as close to the way things were before the change as is humanly possible. Some things might change as a result of the string and cables settling into the grooves, but these should be minor and correctable with simply a few twists of the bowstring or cables. You might also get some peep rotation change overnight, but normally with today's custom strings and cables this isn't a problem. Your first shot, if you have been careful, should go at least into the bull's-eye, and most likely into the X-ring. Only minor adjustments should be needed, if any.

Steps for Changing String and Cable on a Single Cam Bow

a. Follow steps a through e as was done for a two cam bow to insure that you have everything correctly recorded on your documentation form.

b. Check how far down the "Y-split" is from the ends of the axle on the top limb. See the photos below, and you will get the idea. I measure from the top of the retainer on the axle. It matters not, as long as the same basic reference points are used on each side of the bow. Note, however, that the lengths of the "Y-split" legs do matter. You need to get these as close as possible to the "old" cable's settings.

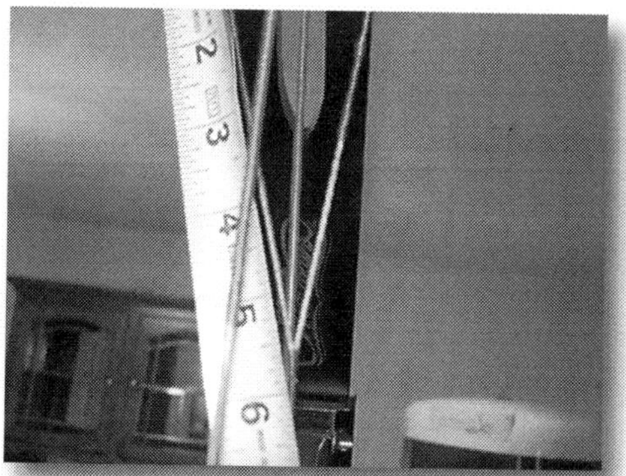

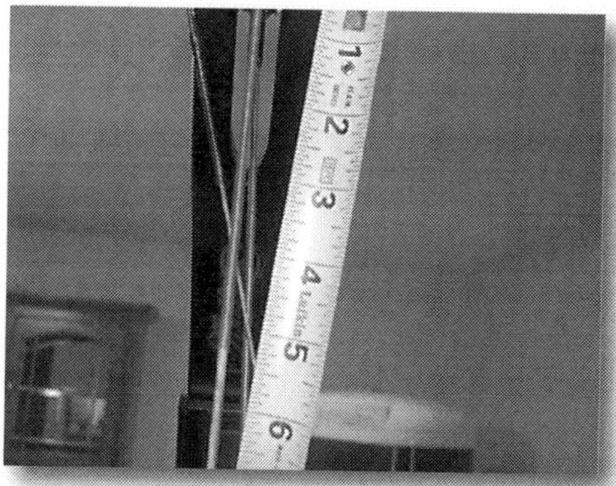

c. Note the position that the string rolls off the cam, and mark it with a piece of tape or contrasting paint pen. Also mark the cam in line with the limb, or note where the timing marks are located (*see photo below*).

d. Place the bow into the bow press and take the pressure off the string and cable.

e. For a single cam bow, I like to replace the power cable, (the "Y-Split" cable) first.

1. Remove the old cable and then place the new cable onto the lower cam.
2. Put the "Y-split" onto the axles. At this point, it gets a little tricky to get the "Y-split" length just right while at the same time getting the cam back into position. However by doing this with the old string still on the bow, it makes string replacement a cinch.
3. Work with the twists in the power cable and removal of one leg of the "Y" until you get the split length and cam timing back into position.
4. Be sure to match up the ATA (axle-to-axle) on both sides of the bow to

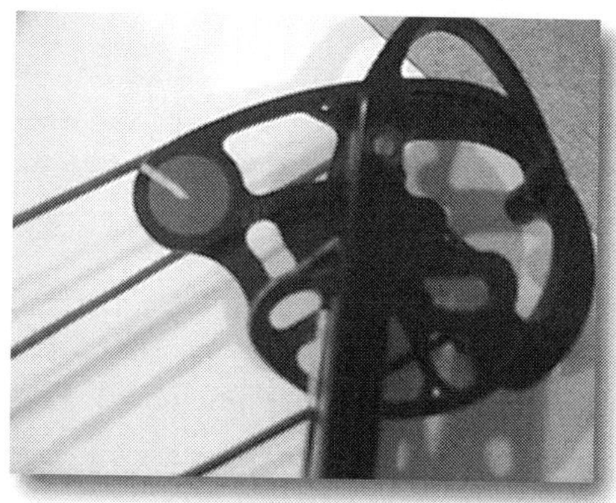

what they was before you replaced the power cable.

f. Follow steps j. through x. as was done for a two cam bow (above) to complete this process.

g. To keep the single cam peep rotation correct, always remember to put the same number of twists into the string at both ends of the string. You can get a partial correction with using only one end, but it takes a while for those twists to "take over" due to the length of the string (sometimes as many as 50 shots or more!) but your peep will move because of it.

h. When completed, check the ATA, brace height, and draw length. Remember that the brace height can be transferred to the riser thus making your true draw very easy to measure quite exactly without the use of a crank board to draw the bow.

i. Recheck the draw weight and then double check that the nocking point is where it belongs using the Stabilizer Method.

Steps for Changing the String and Cables on a Hybrid Cam Bow

Hybrid cam bows have a string and two cables; one cable is the "Y-split" or "power" cable, while the other is the "control" cable and links the two cams together. I prefer to change the power cable first, and then get the bow set back to original with the new power cable. Then, I change the control cable and get the cams back to their marks with that new cable is in place. Then I change the bowstring last and get the ATA and brace height correct again.

a. Follow Steps a. through e. in the twin cam sequence. Be sure to check your ATA on both sides of the bow.

b. Measure up your "Y-split" length and mark the lower cam along the limb line with contrasting tape or magic marker (*see photos above*).

c. Mark your cam positioning for the top limb and string roll-off point in the same manner as you mark them for a single cam as described and shown above.

d. Remove & replace the power cable. Twist or untwist the power cable to bring the lower cam into its proper position and marks. Be sure to check the "Y-split" length. You may have to jockey this by removing one end of the "Y" from the axle and wrapping it around the other leg of the "Y" to twist it up or down.

   1. Remove the old cable and then place the new cable onto the lower cam.
   2. Place the "Y-split" onto the axles. At this point, it gets a little tricky to get the "Y-split" length just right while at the same time getting the cam back into position. However by doing this with the old string still on the bow, it makes string replacement a cinch. You might as well adjust the cam lean (if any) now as opposed to later.
   3. Work with the twists in the power cable and removal of one leg of the "Y" until you get the split length and cam timing back into position.
   4. Be sure to match up the ATA on both sides of the bow to what it was before you replaced the power cable.

e. Check the ATA on both sides. If you adjust this by twisting or untwisting the legs of the "Y" as needed, you can get this back to where it belongs, unless it is a gross adjustment. If you are way off, then you will have to twist or untwist the power cable from the cam end in one half twist increments. A little goes a long ways, so be careful.

f. Remove & replace the control cable. The "control cable" is the one that ties the two cams together. Twist/untwist the cable to get the cams back to their "timing marks" that you put on the cams.
g. Remove & replace the bowstring. Follow steps "j" thru "x" in the twin cam sequence above.
h. Double check your draw weight, ATA, and brace height.
i. Double check that your draw length is what it is supposed to be. Remember that your brace height measurement can be transferred to the riser thus making your True Draw Length very easy to measure (quite exactly) without the use of a crank board to draw the bow.

Steps for Changing the String and Cables on a "Binary Cam" Bow:

This procedure is nearly identical to that followed for a twin cam bow, since once again, both cables are the same length. Simply follow the steps for twin cam bows above, steps a through w.

Summary

Introduced in this chapter were step-by-step procedures for replacing cables and string without having to re-tune from scratch. We started by re-checking all of the important measurements, writing them down in the documentation form (the Table), and then marking everything before removal of any of the cables or strings. The keys to this are first, replication and duplication of those settings, working one step at a time, and second, replacement of the cables and string, one element at a time. As a review, here are the steps to document before tearing the bow apart, one cable at a time, with the bow string being the last item replaced and replicated.

- Document items only when the new bow has been "shot in" and the new strings and cables have had some time to "seat" themselves.
- Once the bow is group tuned and your draw length is set, then measure and document everything in a Master Bow Configuration Table. Remember, the Table isn't fixed; there may well be other items you wish to include in that table.
- It is important to not only write the measurements down, but also to mark as many of the measurements onto the bow or onto measuring instruments, such as your bow square. This gives you a quick reference any time you want or need to verify that everything has properly positioned.
- Your draw length can be quickly checked by using the previously discussed mark on the riser and a marked arrow or a measuring arrow. You should always have the measuring arrow or marked long arrow with this setting as a constant reference point. When something goes amuck, you then have that critical measurement to quickly check and compare.

- The nocking point can be nearly exactly re-set by using your stabilizer and measuring up to the tip of the arrow and matching the number in the Table, or the mark the distance right onto your measuring instrument.
- Measurements should always be made with the same instrument and always made to a positive and consistent point of reference that can be duplicated and minimizes error. Always use your instrument and never someone else's; it is your instrument that counts.

Cable and string replacement does not have to be a gut-wrenching experience! If you think the process through and replace only one element at a time, then get the bow back "to specs" with that element, and then go to the next element, you should have little difficulty getting the bow back up and running in a matter of minutes. It should not require a "re-tune" and it should also not require a completely new set of sight marks . . . if you are careful and follow a sequence.

This documentation process is an on-going thing. You should shoot your new strings and cables for about 100 shots, and then re-check your settings, making sure they are get back to where they were (as closely as possible to the set you just took off). Other helpful hints:

- Don't throw away the original Master Bow Configuration Table. Simply mark the original date, along with the date you made the change(s).
- Fill out a new Table. Most of it will be copied from the old one, but there may well be some new measurements that must be documented so they are available for next time.
- Always put a date on each Table for each bow you own. It is also a good idea to have a completely different Table for each bow that you own, since no two bows will likely end up being identical with regard to "tune setting", no matter how hard you try.
- Whenever you make a change, make sure you mark the new setting on the documentation form and date that change.

I have been very successful with my own equipment and that of many other archers with the use of this step-by-step system. In most cases, the first arrow will go into the bull's-eye, and many times the first shot is into the X-ring. I have had the pleasure of watching the bow owners' eyes light up when they shoot those first arrows right into the bull's-eye. You can see a look of relief in their eyes, as well as a welcome surprise! There is no guarantee of this, of course, because so much depends upon how well you have things measured and marked. The more careful you are and the less of a hurry you are in, the better the results and the quicker you are back to shooting normally.

Tom Dorigatti

13

The Most Overlooked Piece of Equipment—Nocks

Most middle-to-upper echelon tournament archers and bowhunters spend an enormous amount of time setting up their equipment. The best are diligent about getting their draw length set as perfectly as possible. They are careful about arrow rest placement and peep sight setting (and rotation). They make certain that all axes of their sight are precisely aligned. Many also are scrupulous about their arrow weights and lengths, point weights, spine, and vane placements. What is amazing is the number of archers who all but ignore the nocks on their arrows—except, of course, when one gets broken or finally fails to properly fit the bow string. Only then do they become alarmed enough to take action. Some will go along for several rounds with an arrow that isn't hitting where it should and not even think to check the nock in that arrow! If you are interested in learning some of the finer details about your arrow nocks, read on. What do you have to lose besides the few points in your score you might be losing because of overlooking . . . the nocks of your arrows?

I am not writing this to give information or statistics about any particular brands of nocks, although I do have such information. I won't even be mentioning brand names in this chapter, since that is not the point. However, over the years, I've used many different types and brands of arrow nocks. Some of them have been very inexpensive types, while others have been very expensive indeed. What I have found is that it pays to be ProActive; even when it comes down to the little piece of plastic affixed to the back of the arrow that is the connection point to the bowstring. Something that takes the load of accelerating a projectile from zero to around 200 miles per hour in a distance of only 20 inches is bound to give out sooner or later and, often, this is much sooner than you might think, especially if the arrow is not spined correctly or the bow is poorly tuned! I won't go into the "g-forces" this little piece of plastic undergoes, but it suffices to say that if that happened to you, a mere human being, you likely wouldn't survive the massive dose of acceleration! Yet you rely on them for several thousand shots and never consider it just might be . . . the nocks that are undermining your otherwise finely tuned system.

As always, we take things step by step.

Step #1 Checking the Fit of Your Nocks on Your Bowstring

My recent research into various types of nocks (of the same brand and also of different brands) has revealed to me that there are sometimes very significant variances in the size of the throat of the nocks out of the same package! I've found that in the same package, it is highly likely to find a few, and sometimes several, that are of a completely different throat size than the majority of those in the same bag. If you don't check them, you won't know there is a problem it until it is too late and an arrow that you just changed a nock on doesn't fit the string correctly. You do change your nocks now and again, don't you? Whoops, I'm getting ahead of myself here! Here are a couple of techniques I've been using for years. I cannot remember who put me onto these tricks, but the use of them has saved my score countless times.

1. I always check an entire package of 100 nocks for appropriate nock fit when I first open the package. All nocks that are too loose are immediately culled out. Sometimes, I've had to cull out a dozen or more for loose fit.
2. All nocks that are too tight are grouped and set aside by themselves. I don't use a tension meter for this, but you can get pretty close by feel alone; close enough for as well as I can hold, anyways. If you have a good collection of drill bits you can use a bit with the same diameter as the hole in the nock as a "bowstring substitute."
3. When I change a nock on an arrow, before I shoot that arrow out of the bow, I will place the arrow on the bowstring and pull it off the string, repeating the process 15 times. Then, I consider that arrow okay to shoot. This allows for at least some breaking in of the arrow nock to the bowstring; not perfect, but better than a first timer when all the other arrows have been shot numerous times. It doesn't take much to affect the impact point of an arrow. This also gives me yet another cross-check concerning nock fit of the "new" nock. I guess you could also just do the 15 clicks when you open the package too and save the trouble of doing it later, but I've always done it upon changing a nock.

Step #2 Weigh Your Nocks

You are probably thinking, "All nocks of the same brand and type weigh the same." Well, have you checked that belief? I've done some extensive work weighing bags of 100 nocks of the same color and type among several different brands, types, and colors. I'm surprised at how inconsistent some of them are; some nocks in the same bag have differed by as much as three grains in weight! So, when I purchase a new package of nocks (I always purchase bags of 100 count), I sit down and weigh each nock in the bag and group them according to matching weight. Out of a bag of 100, there are going to be some that are way out of

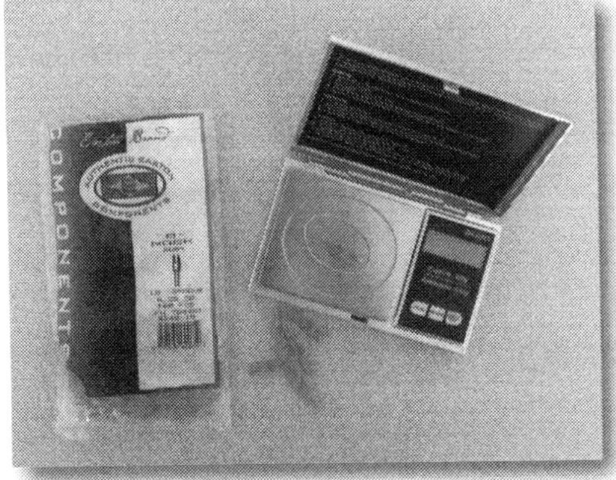

line, and those get tossed. You might think that two or three grains won't matter much; but, if your nocks are off 1 to 3 grains, and then your points differ another 2 or 3 grains, and the arrow shafts themselves differ, and then the vanes differ, it doesn't take long for a set of arrows to come up mismatched quite a bit in weight, and not from the fault of just the shaft itself!

1. As you weigh up the nocks, separate them into groups by weight, and then put a piece of paper with each pile stating what the weight of those nocks are. It is easy to do. Then simply put like-weight nocks into packages of their own (tiny Baggies work well). A tenth of a grain isn't going to rob you for much of anything, but I have found variances of much more than this in the same package of nocks, so it becomes significant. I always keep a package of nocks that are weight matched in my bow case and also some in my quiver. I always know that they are the same, and that they fit pretty much the same on the bow string. (Why? Because I bothered to check them. This is a key ProActive principle.)
2. It is also interesting to note that different colors of the same type and brand of nock will weigh differently; just like different colors of vanes can weigh differently. Thus, unless you know for sure that different colors of nocks weigh and fit the same, don't mix them. I won't borrow nocks from a fellow archer for this very reason; plus, some shooters keep old used nocks around, just in case! I've even seen some people pick up nocks from the floor indoors and from in front of the bales outdoors and check them. If they think the nocks are good, then they put them into their bag or quiver and use them! Oh, my!

Step #3 Setting an Arrow's Nock Alignment

Most archers, and especially those shooting fall-away arrow rests, are lackadaisical about arrow nock alignment, thinking that a little bit won't matter much, even off of a launcher arrow rest. You probably know about the powder test for checking arrow clearance, yes? Well, there is more to it that just checking clearance on the arrow rest; you are also supposed to be checking to see if the arrow nock is aligned correctly so that the vanes are clearing the rest or, if they are contacting the arrow rest, that all arrows are contacting the rest the same amount. Some archers will "paper tune" with only one or two of the arrows out of their quiver, and never ever bother to check the entire quiver full of arrows for "paper tune." Very few will even check anything about the nock of the arrow if one or more of those they used to paper tune have the same nock orientation or not. I learned this lesson many years back while shooting with the famous "springie rest". With that arrow rest, identical nock orientation from arrow to arrow was essential; if you didn't have this accomplished, you weren't going to get consistent grouping of that set of arrows. This is better related to checking each and every arrow so you know that they all have the same vane orientation, or, realistically, the same nock alignment. There are many ways to accomplish this:

1. *You can "eye-ball" your nock rotation from arrow to arrow and get it close*. This works after a fashion for fall-away type arrow rests. However, for launcher rests or arrow rests with prongs, eye-balling nock rotation is not close enough; that is if you like

to shoot higher scores and tighter groups!

2. *You can use one of various nock alignment tools available for purchase.* Bjorn used to make a quality nock alignment tool that worked really well (*see photo in montage*). Now and again one will show up on eBay.
3. *Other manufacturers also make nock alignment tools that are readily available for a modest cost.* Apple Manufacturing has a nice nock alignment tool, as does Archery Technologies (*see photos in montage*). I happen to know that another manufacturer is working on prototypes of an updated nock alignment tool that they used to manufacture some years ago, but I cannot get information from them as to when it will become available.

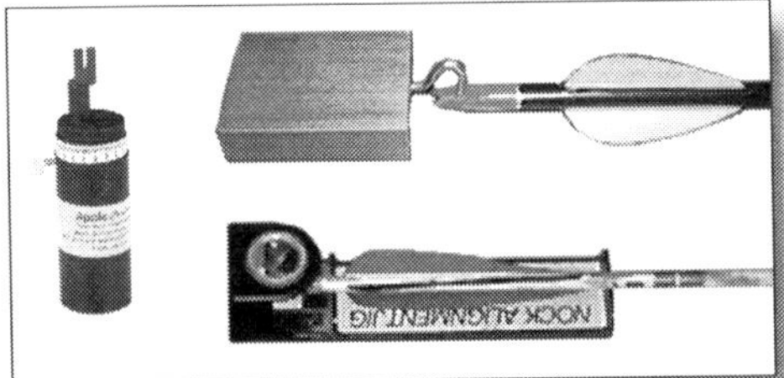

4. *You can make a nock alignment tool of your own.* All it takes is a means of supporting the arrow and the nock, and then having a consistent "indicator" to align with one of the vanes of the arrow in order that you can orient all of the arrows in the same nock orientation. A friend recently made me a nock aligner out of a ½″ PVC plastic elbow. He simply placed a stove bolt that had been spun down to the same size as the throat of my arrow nocks through the PVC elbow with the depth of the bolt matching up so that my cock feather could be aligned with a mark placed on the end of the opening. This works perfectly for my GoldTip XXX shafts. We are in process of making me a set for my GoldTip Ultra-lite Pro 500's and my Gold Tip 22 Series shafts as well. It isn't difficult to make something like this to get consistency, and I honestly think this consistency of nock rotation is critical; especially if you are using a launcher blade arrow rest! Contrary to popular belief, in my opinion, you do not absolutely have to have zero vane contact. Consistent contact is the key, and if the nocks aren't aligned the same, then this consistency is next to impossible to achieve. In other words, if you have contact, it must be consistent (and of course minimized) vane contact for all the arrows in your shooting set.
5. *Simply lay that first arrow you powder tested and that shows the best or consistent vane clearance down on a flat surface with the cock vane up* (it is your "standard"). *Lay the other arrows out of your set down with the same vane orientation, and simply look at the orientation of the string groove of the nock*; or the flat part of the nock. All of them should be the same. Keeping your "master" safe, simply work with each arrow, one by one until all of them have the same groove orientation as the master. With practice, you can get them nearly identical. I've had much success with this; to the point that when I borrowed a friend's nock alignment tool and set it with my master arrow, all of the others were very, very close; not all were perfect, but extremely close. If you look closely at photo (*next page top right*), you can see that the nock alignment on the second and third arrows from the left are slightly off. This was done purposefully for demonstration purposes.) The use of cam-

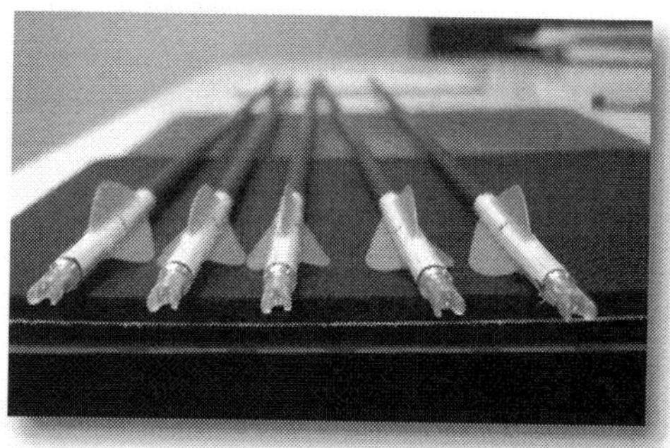

era with a macro function can really be a big help on this item! Take a similar picture and let your eye find the ones that don't match. (Which of these is not like the others?)

Step #4 How to Mark Your Nocks

So, now you have nocks on all of your arrows. Those nocks all weigh the same. They also fit onto your bowstring with as close to the same amount of resistance as you can get without using sophisticated instruments. You have the nock orientation on each and every arrow the same. So, how do you go about making sure that, should you have to replace a nock on an arrow out in the field, you get the new nock oriented exactly the same as the rest of the arrows in your quiver? Sure, you could just put that arrow into the "penalty box," but what happens if you suddenly need that arrow? Then what do you do? ProActive archery doesn't allow for "punting." Remember, ProActive archery has a system! This "system" is very simple and easy to accomplish. It is a simple case of marking the nock orientations on the shafts, or if you have inserts in the back of your shaft (such as for Easton G nocks, *Super* nocks, or pin-nock inserts), you mark the insert; either with permanent ink ultra-thin point marker, or, with a very fine pointed scratching instrument such as a sharp hobby knife. Where to put this mark or scratch, you ask? This is very simple as all nocks have a mold line on them. I simply make my mark on my arrow and/or insert to match up with the mold lines on both sides of the nock, and voila; a nock orientation indicator for that arrow that won't change (unless you mess up the bushing, that is). However, if you mark the shaft and the bushing, then even a bushing movement won't affect your indicator. (In the photo, I used a much thicker marking line than normal for clarity purposes).

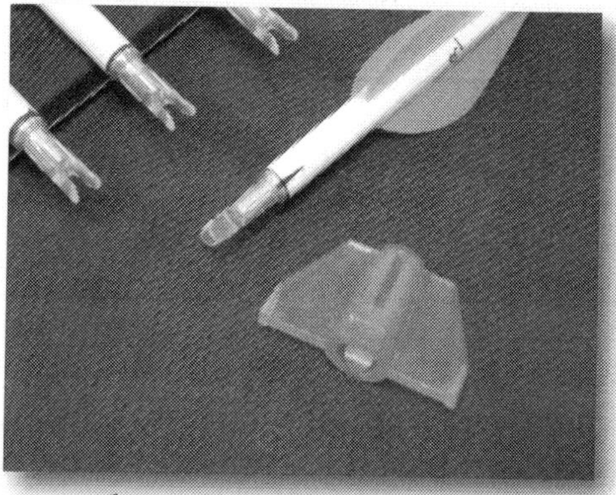

Step #5 When to Change Your Nocks

As I mentioned earlier, most archers seldom change their nocks, even when shooting today's super-heavy, aluminum "fat-shafts" such as 2512, 2613, or the new 2712s or equivalents in the carbon arrow world. Some of these arrows weigh upwards of 700 grains! Release shooters place a very strong downward pressure on the arrow rest with such weights, which then cause an up pressure at the back, or nock-end, of the arrow. The only thing absorbing that pressure is; you guessed it, the soft, plastic nock. Just like anything else under pressure loads, sooner or later, it fatigues and starts to give out. In the case of pin-nocks, problems are pretty easy to detect, because they simply will not fit the string and normally will fall right off the string when they are cracked or about to fail; not always, but most of the time, the cracks are apparent and clearly visible. However, in the case of a nock that is inserted into an arrow shaft directly or through an insert, the invisible part of the nock can soon become bent, or brittle, and/or even start to bend out of line, or crack. Ypu might not realize it until when the arrow goes "out," and then blame yourself instead of the nock and continue shooting. I've encountered people who will shoot the same nocks in their arrows one, two, or even three indoor seasons without changing them! Most archers fail to even consider all the strain and stress placed on those tiny pieces of plastic. They don't stop to realize that not only does the serving wear, but so do the "ears" of the nocks themselves. They don't stop to think how many times that slight miss or even a flier wasn't them at all, but easily could be a worn, bent, brittle, or cracked nock!

Miscellaneous Nock Tips

Here are some tips I've picked up through the years with regard to arrow nocks:

1. *Always number your arrows and always shoot them in order.* I do this for many reasons. First off, it is part of my shot routine. Secondly, it slows me down and makes me pay attention. For indoors, it helps me to know exactly which spot (for a 5-spot or a 3-spot target) I should be shooting at that time. Additionally, it is that ProActive backup of which arrow it is that is going out of the group. This is especially important for outdoor shooting when you are shooting all of your arrows at one or two spots. Without those numbers, you have no way of telling if it is your #2 arrow or your #4 arrow that is acting up. ProActive archery also should require you to become involved with your equipment and keeping track of said equipment.
2. *Unless you are certain you made a bad shot, always check any arrow that is out of the main group.* I also use the "penalty box" method, especially outdoors. If an arrow is away from my group and I even have a thought that the reason might involve that particular arrow, it goes into the penalty box Some people use the penalty box system whereby they put the "questionable" arrow upside down in one of the quiver tubes. I will do that only if I know that the arrow has a bent pin or a loose vane or point. However, most of the time, since I have a numbering system, an arrow that is in the penalty box may well end up out of the penalty box later in the round. I use the penalty box as a means of putting a "bad?" arrow out of my mind so that I don't think about, "Oh, my, here is #1-3 arrow, it might not be a good one. It shot high left on the last target." That is a negative thought, and if you think this through, then you don't want to ever put a bias into your mind about any arrow before you shoot it. If you think the #1-3 arrow shot high left last time, then in all likelihood, it will be there on this shot, too. I like to call this "out of sight, out of mind." This prevents me from doubting that arrow. Sooner or later in a round, it might come out of the penalty box, but typically it doesn't get another chance that day. I can't take the time right then and there to break concentration and start doubting things, so I rid myself of that thought; at

least for the short term.

3. *Always make sure that this arrow check includes checking the nock completely for alignment, for string-fit, for cracks, and for straightness.* A bent, cracked or misaligned nock is a miss or even a "dry fire" waiting to happen. Safety Tip Never forget the "safety check" for today's carbon arrows, you know, "flex & check," especially if you are shooting with a group of archers on a field or target course. You just never know when you might end up with an exploding arrow that will shatter and impale your bow hand! You've seen those gruesome pictures; don't take this risk.
4. *Always start a new indoor season with new nocks, correctly aligned.* I also make it a point to change inserted arrow nocks about every 3,000 shots or so. I will change pin nocks about every 4,000 shots or when I even slightly suspect a problem with one. Some archers change them more often than that. You are thinking, "Wow, that's going to get expensive." Do you realize that indoors, for a Vegas Round, 3,000 shots get you 75 rounds including practice shots? If you shoot 4 times a week, then that is about every four and a half months you should be replacing those nocks. If you are shooting field or hunter rounds, then obviously, you should be checking and replacing nocks monthly! That is a lot of abuse and a lot of shooting. This gives ample time for those plastic units to fatigue.

Summary

Years ago, most of us would routinely "spin" our aluminum arrows all the time to check for straightness. Those at or near the top of the leader board were also checking for loose vanes and bent or broken nocks (even though they weren't saying anything about that)! Today, you see very few shooters spinning arrows or checking them over much at all. However, if you really pay close attention to the ones who consistently win tournaments, both indoors and outdoors, you will see them closely inspecting their arrows after they have been pulled from the targets, including "flex and check" and, wiping them down from end to end if they've been shot into foam type bales or targets! Again, however, you might see some bending and flexing of the shafts as recommended by carbon arrow manufacturers, but you don't see much checking of the arrows by spinning or blowing on them to spin the vanes and watching for nock misalignment. It seems like a lost art for the most part especially for beginners and mid-level shooters.

The better archers have learned from experience and from the school of hard knocks (pun intended) what to look for and how to tell if it is "them" or if there is something amiss with their equipment when problems occur. Many of them will check their arrow nock details off first when something appears to be amiss. Why? Because, especially outdoors, nocks can become damaged very easily, and sometimes you might not notice it. This is just checking for sources of problems in the order of their likelihood. This is why I never allow anyone to pull my arrows when I'm shooting, especially when I'm shooting outdoors. Proactively, I'm paying attention to details, and the condition of my arrows is not a minor detail; arrows are the business end of my shot. When Uni-bushings first came into being several years ago, I was wary about people pulling my arrows, and would universally ask them not to pull my arrows. I had noticed many times that people were pulling arrows with one hand against the bale and the other wrapped around the vanes and too close to the nock for my comfort. It would be easy for them to give a bit of a twist to the end of the shaft and . . . turn the arrow nock on the arrow out of alignment. Nope, I'm not giving them that chance; besides I like to pull my arrows in a certain fashion and in a certain order for psychological reasons. I'll talk about this technique later on in this book.

I discussed weighing and batching nocks of the same weights. I outlined how to group your nocks with regard to proper string fit and to get rid of those that are too loose. I recommended "pre-loading" a new nock 15 times on the bowstring before shooting it for the first time. I mentioned how critical nock alignment is and gave you examples of the different tools and techniques available to insure identical nock alignment. We discussed how to proactively mark the nock's position by using the mold lines and matching these with a mark on your shaft and/or insert. Last, I gave you some suggestions about when to change nocks, because . . . nocks are the most neglected, yet among the most important, pieces of your archery equipment.

Intentionally, I did not discuss the placement of the nock insert bushing into the back of the shaft. However, much the same system applies there as it does to the nocks. With aluminum arrows, one is pretty safe to use hot-melt glue to hold them in. However, for aluminum/carbon or all-carbon arrows, some prefer to use instant glues, while others, especially when they are using pin nocks use Saran Wrap or plumber's tape to make sure the inserts fit tightly and won't move within the shaft; but yet are easily removable should a pin become damaged or bent. I have recently switched over to very low temperature 'hot-melt' glue in order to place my pin nock bushings into the arrow shaft. This has been working out very, very well, and holds much better than plastic food wrap or plumber's Teflon tape. ProActively think your way through the nock insert issue, based upon the discussions in this article. You will gain some insight simply by thinking this through. Your arrow nocks get knocked around much more than you think!

It would be a pity to be knocked out of a competition because of a piece of plastic — knocked out by a nock? Think about just how many times you have lost points from your score because they got knocked off by a nock.

Tom Dorigatti

Section 3

Form & Execution

As indicated by the title of this section, over the next several chapters, we will be discussing form and execution. You are about to embark upon what I hope is an enlightening and very valuable learning experience. However, you will not be getting a course in anatomy with sketches of what proper alignment looks like. You won't get an explanation of all the "what's" and "what if's" concerning pushing, pulling, squeezing or pinching the shoulder blades together and other related items. It is my intent to give you a no-nonsense ProActive approach that will provide you with methods that will help you to be able to replicate shots more precisely so that your consistency from shot to shop improves. After all, this sport is all about replication: shot to shot, end to end, and round to round; is it not? Some of the information may seem old hat or common knowledge. It might be for you but not necessarily for all. Other items I'll discuss may well surprise you and have you thinking; "Why haven't I heard of this before?"

You will learn that "hard stops are not really hard stops." I'll discuss how to correctly measure your draw length; or at least how to get it closer to perfect. Then I'll discuss how to go about adjusting your stance to your draw length bow setting and how to have a backup system in place to check it. There is also a discussion on an expanded practice technique that significantly differs from "blank baling." I call this "blind baling." With this technique you can learn to shoot a perfect "25" or "30" indoor ends with your eyes closed, and it is easier than you ever imagined! Finally I will cover the often times feared "Changing Over Bow Hands". You will find that even this is something that is achievable should you choose to go this route. Of course these chapters are written by someone who has experienced this changeover; not once, but twice over the course of the past 25 years.

Tom Dorigatti

14

Do You Think "Hard Stops" are Really "Hard Stops"?

Many of the cams on today's bows have gone from the soft, smooth, "long-valleyed" systems of the past in favor of higher letoffs and thus higher speeds. Few manufacturers offer letoff percentages below 65% anymore, and those that do have it only as a special order option. The term "hard cam" is more common in dewcriptions, as are "hard wall," "solid stops," or "short valley." Along with this trend, archers of today are thinking that since our bows have the "solid stops" and a "hard wall," then we don't have to concern ourselves much with watching or working for tighter consistency in draw length. We figure that since we have the hard wall, then that means if we pull the bow back to the stops, we are being consistent in draw length and don't have to worry about it. This chapter is not going to address the fact that most shooters today have their draw lengths set from one half inch to two or more inches too long. It assumes that you already have your draw length very close to where it is supposed to be and that the bow is already tuned It will deal with, however, the fact that hard cams are not as easy to be consistent with as we think. It will also offer an explanation of how to set up a visual reference to make yourself more consistent with your draw length. I call it the "Triple Tape System for Improving Draw Length Consistency."

There are six important questions I pose at this point:

1. Do you know how close you are each time to being at exactly the same point in the draw cycle of your bow when you hit your anchor point and your full draw position?
2. Do you know how much "room" you have in your cam system to "wander" from the short side to the long side of your bow's valley and to how far that cam can be drawn back to?
3. Do you know if you are at your "sweet spot" or if you are really coming in too short or perhaps too hard into those stops?
4. Do you know that this can be set up to be more controllable for little or no cost and with little or no adjustment to the bow (unless one is really needed).
5. Do you have any idea at how variances in your full draw position and/or "to anchor draw length" affect your impact point on the target?
6. Do you realize that ¼″ or even as little as ⅛″ variance in this position is a "big deal"

and is not "close enough?"

7. Do you know that if you pull harder into the "stops" on today's modern cams that for every 1/20th of an inch into the limbs (1/20th of an inch, by the way, is less than 1 millimeter!), your holding weight goes up one pound?

Most newer archers and even a lot of mid-level shooters will answer "no" to most or all of these questions. Higher echelon shooters are aware of many, but not all of the answers.

A Case in Point I will bet that you have noticed that during an end indoors you have some "just high" impacts at the beginning of the end and then by the 4th or 5th arrow, you are impacting lower. You also notice that during the round, this changes and you are steadily impacting lower and/or to the right as the round progresses. Of course, you realize that some of this is fatigue, which is natural . . . or is it? What you are about to read and learn is that a lot of it relates directly to the seven questions posed above and how well you are controlling your draw length. As you progress thru the next five chapters, you are going to learn techniques to help you alleviate or possibly even eliminate many variances in your full draw positioning that you previously were unaware of. Obviously, we start with the "stops."

Reexamining Your Full Draw Position

Since most of today's bows are no longer of the "soft cam" variety, we think most bows and cam systems have very little room for variation in how far back we pull back the string to get to our anchor. We think we have our draw lengths set correctly and that everything is peachy keen. We tend to put that part of the shot out of our minds. However, upon careful investigation, I've discovered that even with a hard cam and a "hard stop," a shooter can and will vary their draw length by as much as 3/4″ and some even more than that. What I mean by this is simple: we all can come into the stops, or we can *come into the stops*, or we can come *HARD INTO THE STOPS*, or we can pull until we cannot draw the bow any farther. In addition, we can do anything in between at any time or on any shot and not realize we are doing it. What I discovered in researching this is that "average" or "beginning" compound archers vary the most, and the better shooters vary the least. This isn't surprising, no?. According to the video **Secrets of the Pros** (*www.carterenterprises.com*), one can paraphrase that "draw length is probably the most critical aspect for accuracy control." The not so obvious is how much this variance really is among bow brands, cam types, and among different levels of shooters; even when time is taken to try to get it right!

I won't drag you through all of the data, since that really isn't the focus of this book, however, there are some key elements that I need to stress with regards to the cam type, the cam size, and how aggressive the cam is. What I discovered isn't rocket science, and it makes complete sense.

1. *How Much Variance is in Cam Itself?* What I have found from extensive checking on my own equipment arsenal, and from several cooperative other shooters clearly shows that even the hardest cams can be pulled from softly into the stops all the way back through to where you cannot pull any further. This can and does

change one's draw length more than one would think. You can easily ascertain this on your own bow in a matter of minutes by use of a measuring arrow and an assistant to mark that arrow at any common point of reference. I would recommend the True Draw reference point transfer I described in Chapter 6. I highly recommend that you do so. What you are going to find will shock you!

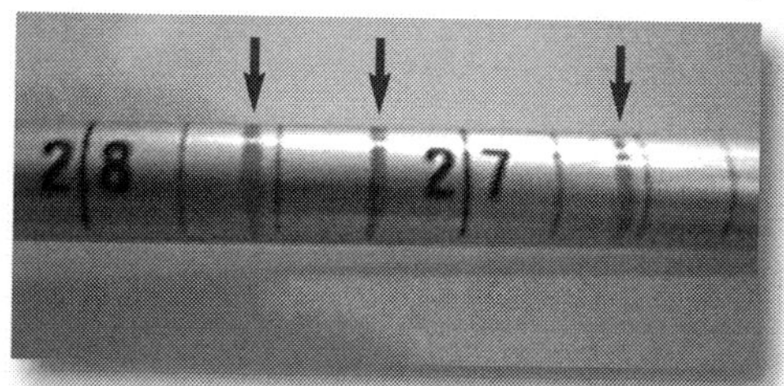

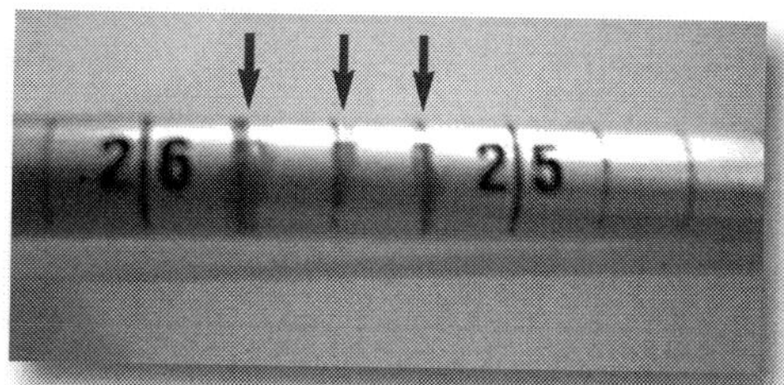

Conclusions on Cam Variance

- The larger the cam (the longer the draw length) and the less aggressive the cam, the more a shooter can vary the distance pulled "into the stops." This was anticipated (it makes sense), but I didn't expect the numbers I found. The differences in draw length ranged from just over 1¼″ on the larger, less aggressive cams to just under ¾″ on a 27″ draw cam (which is the shortest draw length that I measured). The bow with the ¾″ variation has "pretty close to very aggressive" cams with a very short valley.
- I also found that the norm for the shooters I checked, including myself (on four different bows and three different cam types), the initial draw length variance was from ¼″ to ¾″!

2. *How Much Does Your Draw Length Vary?* Most of the archers I have approached with this question haven't a clue. Some didn't seem to care. Most that cared told me that since their bows were hard stop cams and that they set their draw lengths up to the stops, they figured they probably weren't varying very much at all. When asked how far into the stops they drew, most couldn't tell me, they just said "where it feels good." Those who I measured were appalled at how far their draw lengths could vary, and even more by how much they differed either from shot to shot or from the beginning of an end or round to the conclusion of the end or round! It was a real eye opener for them to see that they were running anywhere from ¼″ to ¾″ or more variation when all the time they thought that they were coming to the same point in the draw cycle every time by "hitting their anchor point and going by feel alone." If you are not shocked by this, look at any arrow spine chart you have around. A difference in draw length of 1″ almost always puts you into a new spine group for your arrows!

Conclusions Concerning Shooters' Thoughts on Their Variances

- First off, most thought they had draw length under control with little to no variation. They had been misleading themselves!
- Most good shooters' draw lengths varied within a reasonably consistent range no matter which bow or cam style was involved. But on average it is nearly ¼″

between long and short draws for good shooters and ½″ or slightly over for average shooters.

- This difference doesn't vary on every single shot, but it does vary depending upon the following (and probably other variables as well):
  1. How early into the round you are. Early in the round, people tend to overdraw (they aren't tired yet).
  2. How early into the end you are shooting. The first arrow is normally drawn farther than the last arrow of an end.
  3. Indoors, whether they are shooting the higher target or the lower target and how high those targets are from the floor! (I'll be supplying a method of dealing with this problem later on).
  4. The time of day they were shooting. Oh, yes, if you've worked or done a lot of physical activity that day, you tend to came in "short." If you are fresh, such as in the morning, then you tend to come in long for a longer period of time during a round.
  5. The shooters never had a "sense" that their draw lengths varying, since most are going by feel alone of their anchor touch point and a few other potentially variable parameters. The bow feels the same but if you take the time to actually check this, a different story will emerge all together.

So, now that raised questions as to just how good you are at achieving a consistent draw length, I provide a ProActive system to help you control your draw length, minimizing your variation using a simple visual check. In addition, this system will help you learn the muscle memory associated with your draw and give you a visual cue to use on those tough uphill, downhill, side hill, or shots with poor footing or body positioning in the field.

The Tape System for Improving Draw Length Consistency

This system is not new, nor did I invent it. It has been around since the mid-1970's, in the days of the wheelie bows (round wheeled "soft cams"). There are many variants of this system. It was pretty much abandoned by most shooters with the advent of harder cammed bows, solo-cam bows, and the development of hybrid cams. Again, as mentioned before, people don't see the need for watching their anchoring draw length, since things feel like they are in the stops so it is "good enough." Most set themselves up to where they figure they are right on, and practice from there, never thinking about a potential source of variance which can be a potential point or X robber. You often hear pros talk about being able to "feel" a difference of one half twist in the bowstring or a cable and, if that is true, you should realize how they are able to shoot such consistently high X-counts both indoors and outdoors. It isn't all in those "fat arrows" or their stabilization systems, releases, scopes, and accessories; it is more basic than all that stuff.

Most archers who use a "tape system" use two tapes, one on each cable, and either they set them to draw even with each other (less precise) or they set them to draw the top of one tape to the bottom of the other tape (more precise). There was even a set of "cable stops" back in the early 1980's that one could place on the cables as a "draw stop" to help control the anchor point draw length (see photo right). You simply set the stops to come together when you were either in the center of the valley or at just the back of the valley. However, most of the time, we found ourselves coming off those stops, or that they would come loose or slide down the cables with use. (Does "coming off the stops" sound familiar to you? You've had this problem with your setup from time to time, haven't you?) Those gimmicks didn't last long. Once people started setting themselves up to the wall or back of the valley, then creep tuning came in and it became apparent that absolute draw length control, especially indoors wasn't as critical . . . if (and it's a big "if") the bow was properly creep or tiller tuned. Outdoors, however is an entirely different story, but nonetheless, people still shoot mostly by "feel" and pulling to "somewhere in the stops." Either way, that draw length control is extremely important.

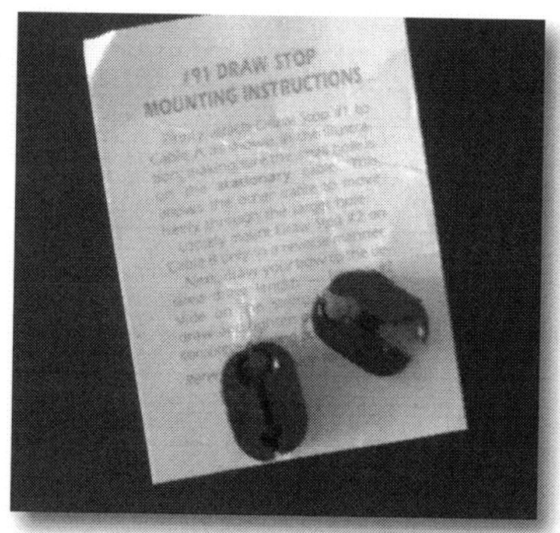

The Triple Tape System for Improving Draw Length Consistency What I have made is an improvement on the two tape system and one that is much more accurate to apply and use. It costs only a few pieces of ⅛″ wide masking tape about 3″ long, a little time, and some super glue or *Fletch-Tite*®. Instead of only two pieces of tape to align, I recommend the use of three tapes, two on one cable, and one on the opposing cable. The idea is to space the two pieces of tape apart just a little wider than the single piece of tape on the opposing cable. Then, when you are at the "sweet spot" on your draw and anchor, the single tape is aligned between the two pieces of tape on the other cable. In order to learn the muscle memory, one simply draws back the bow to anchor, visually checks to make sure those tapes are aligned correctly, sets their shot sequence (with back tension), and finishes the shot. A telltale signal that you are "losing it" is a tightening of the release hand or forearm. A quick glance at those tapes at this time will show, more than likely, that the single tape is now aligned with the top tape, which is an indi-

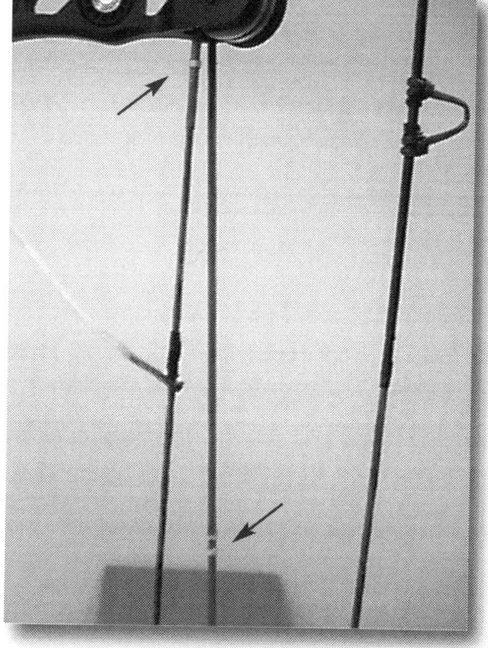

cation you have "crept" at least ¼″. Some people set up to draw to align the single and bottom tape half-way and come into the "in between position." This is fine, but remember that any loss of draw tension must be regained.

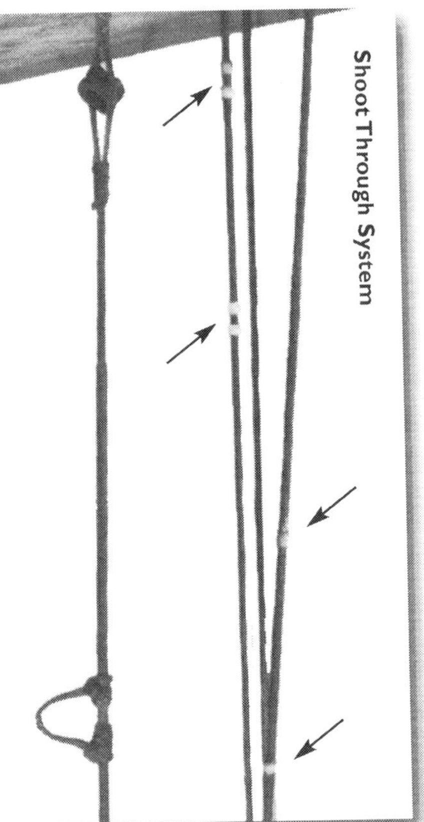

How to Set up the Tapes Cut two pieces of masking tape (it works the best in most cases) ⅛″ wide and about 4 inches long. The wider you make these tapes, the less precise you will be. You will be cutting all three tapes from the same 4″ long piece of masking tape so that the widths are identical.

1. If your cable guard is above the bow grip, then it is best to mount the single tape on the down cable about ½″ to ¾″ below the cable guard. This insures that this tape isn't disturbed or moved by the cable glide or roller guides. It also insures you get the aligned tapes as close to the rest level as possible. To mount the tape, simply wrap it tightly about five or six layers thick around the cable, pressing it firmly with your fingers. Do not glue it into place just yet.

   For "shoot through systems" or bows with their cable guard below the grip, strive to have it set so that the down cable tape aligns as close as possible to the height of the peep at full draw. This will give you a view of the tape alignment in your peripheral vision as you come into your scope, which is a big help.
2. Draw back the bow to what you feel is the correct point and have someone mark the other cable (the up moving cable) or in the case of a single cam, the back side of the bowstring, right where the single cable aligns. Since you have all three pieces you will use the same width, mark the opposing cable for the full width of the single piece of tape.
3. Place the two tapes on the "up cable" or back side of the bow string where you have it marked. Again, do not glue them down just yet. Five or six layers is plenty, just be sure to roll them tightly onto the cable.
4. Draw back the bow to your "normal" anchor draw length and check for proper tape alignment. It is your choice as to which of the tapes to move to get the single tape into the center of the gap.
5. Repeat drawing the bow several times to verify alignment and that it is indeed "comfortable."
6. If the tapes are properly aligned and you are happy, then use either *Super Glue* or *Fletch-Tite*® glue to coat the tapes and the nearby cable and let it dry a few min-

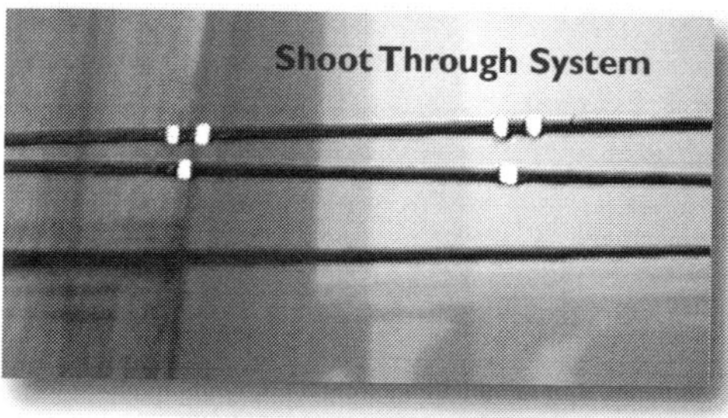

utes. This will hold the tapes in place.

You want the tapes on a single cam or a bow with its cable guard above the arrow rest to align as close to the rest as possible.

You want the tapes to align on a shoot through system as close to peep height level at full draw as possible.

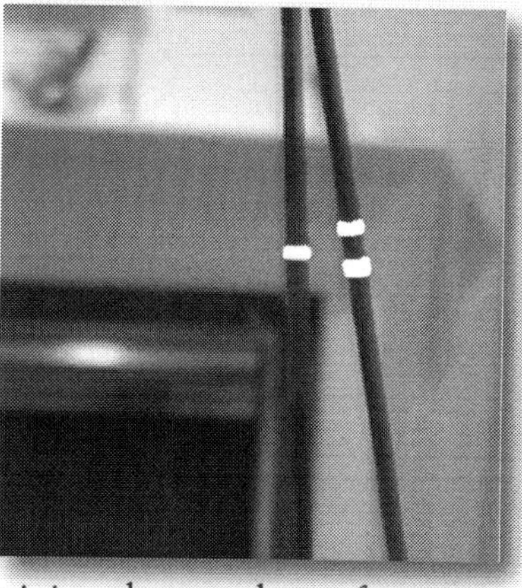

If you so choose, you can use two sets of tapes. This gives you a backup just in case one set moves or you move a set only to find you don't like the new alignment. You can then return the moved set more quickly by simply measuring the other set's distance apart.

7. Shoot this setup for several days, paying strict attention to drawing those tapes into alignment every single time, time and again, accepting nothing less. Normally, in a few hundred shots you will be getting used to it. Over the course of a week or two, you will find yourself pulling to those tapes pretty much automatically and only giving them a glance for assurance you are "there." After a few weeks, you are going to find your X-counts going upwards, along with your "inside out" hits and "inside out" X's to boot!

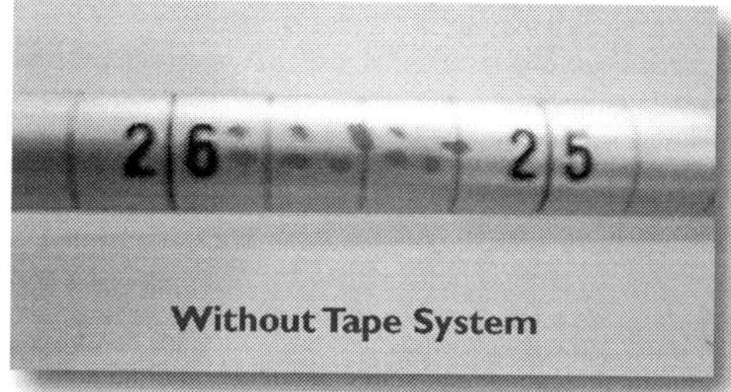

8. When outdoors, religiously draw to those tapes! You will find that your consistency and control outdoors on those uphill, downhill, side hill, and poor footing shots will improve dramatically. You will have significantly improved draw length and anchor control no matter what the situation.

Summary

What I have described is not something that is a quick and easy way for you to improve upon your draw length consistency and gain better control of your cam system. This method will also help get you to find that real sweet spot in your draw stroke (your personal draw length sweet spot) much quicker and easier than just shooting groups and shooting by feel alone. You will achieve a better level of muscle memory and will have the additional benefit of a visual reference that can be used for a check of your "feel" for your shot.

This might not necessarily turn a 555 field round shooter into a 560 shooter and a professional archer who is already shooting at that level may not benefit either. However, take a close look at the last two photos again. Which would you prefer to have happening during your draw and shot sequence?

What do you have to lose by trying out this "triple tape system?" Only a few near misses that are keeping you out of the winner's circle.

Tom Dorigatti

15

What is My "Correct" Draw Length? Pt I

This is the first of a two chapters concerning how to arrive at a near optimal starting value for your AMO draw length. This discussion is intended for compound/release aid archers. Many things about the positioning of the draw hand for fingers shooters differ dramatically from those of compound/release aid shooters, so I will focus only on my area of greater expertise.

The subject of draw length and which method is the best to use in estimating one's draw length has become a major source of contention among top echelon archers, mid-range archers, beginners, and even among archery shops and coaches. So, I decided that it was time to discuss, all in one place, many of the main methods commonly in use for measuring draw length, using pictures and data to demonstrate the results of these methods. I'll address several of the pitfalls of each method and how to avoid them. I will also offer up some suggestions to help you establish something that will likely get you even closer to an optimal answer to the question, "How do I determine my AMO draw length?"

I will not be presenting drawings of archers' triangles, muscle anatomy, or any of that. I'll merely present some very interesting data that I acquired measuring six different archers using common methods for determining draw length, comparing those measurements to their already established draw lengths.

I'm not going to tell you which method is the best; that choice will be yours. Of course, I also won't tell you which of the shooters is the best shooter either. I will, as I said, offer up a solution that uses combinations of the methods (this will be in the next chapter) to assist you in narrowing down that starting point for your AMO draw length.

A precaution that all readers should heed if you are in the process (or even just thinking of) purchasing a new bow: Do not get caught up in the hype of having to have a high peak weight bow with a long draw length so that you can get more speed out of the bow. If you are of short stature and the shop tries to sell you a 70 pound bow with a 30″ AMO draw length, beware! In addition, be especially cautious when it comes to the limb tag that is on each bow. Those limb tags typically give: peak weight range, string and cable lengths, and the "AMO draw length" at which the particular bow is supposedly set. This last item is not necessarily accurate! Most of the bows I have checked run ½″ to 1″ longer than what the limb tag says! You should have your shop physically measure the draw length of the bow to make sure it is indeed what the limb tag says it is. This becomes even more important if the type of cam on the bow is "draw length specific," meaning that the bow has a very narrow range of adjustment for draw length. If the shop won't physically measure the bow's actual AMO draw length for you, then perhaps you should be more insistent or seek out another shop. Selecting a bow that is out of the range of your AMO draw length starting point could cost you a thousand dollars or more. You must realize what all of the top professionals tell us over and over, "Having a correct draw length is the most critical aspect for shooting consistently high scores and tight groups."

It will become apparent why I do not accept the practice of sizing up an archer by asking how tall they are, what they think their draw length is, and then picking a bow off the rack that is "close" to what they think (or I might think) would be a fit for them for them to "try." What I've discovered is that as long as the bow isn't way too heavy in peak weight for me, I'm going to draw back that bow to the stops (or back all the way) without regard to form or proper positioning even though my particular draw length is just over 28½″ AMO! I can comfortably draw a 31″ AMO draw length bow back and it "feels good" when I get it all the way back, too. I wouldn't be able to shoot it accurately, but hey, it feels good! And I think you are much the same.

This chapter will address the three most common methods in use today.

1. The "Wing Span Method"
2. The "Wing Span Calculation Method" This relates directly to your measured wing span, but as you will see, the result differs significantly from the "Wing Span Method"
3. The use of a "Light Weight 'Draw Length' Recurve Bow"

In Chapter (16) we will deal with three other methods which are not as common, but still used today; namely:

4. The 45 degree Upward-angled Measuring Arrow Method
5. The Horizontal Measuring Arrow Method
6. The Fist Against the Wall Method.

Test Archer Acknowledgments

Before getting started, I acknowledge the shooters who volunteered their time for data gathering, picture taking, and putting up with me during this process. They are students of the game, and I do coach them. They are also close friends. Their names, not in any order, are: Mark Cooper, Mike Vaccaro, Cody Engle, Dan Terrill, and Earl Raymond. Without their assistance, this study wouldn't exist. Like me, they have a special interest in this in that they, too, would like to find a means of getting closer to that magical "correct draw length" starting point.

The Wing Span Method

The vast majority of compound shooters in archery today are selecting and shooting a bow with a draw length that is 1 to 3 inches too long. This is robbing them of their potential to perform at a higher level.

If your bow is improperly fit to your draw length you will never shoot as good as you could with a proper fit. In addition, with today's higher peak weights and higher let-off cams, the risk of serious injuries to shoulders and other joints is increasing. Improper fit on draw weight and draw length can, and normally does, result in serious and sometimes career ending injuries!

The data below was shown to me in the early 1970's by Denise Libby, who was then a top Professional Archers Association (PAA) Professional archer and coach. It was finally put into a chart format and improved upon by Bernie Pellerite sometime in the 1990's. Listed below are the starting points for AMO draw length based upon your wingspan (arm spread). You do not add or subtract from this based upon the length of a D-loop so commonly used today. The length of the D-loop changes how soon or late you come into the anchor point and not your needed AMO draw length on the bow (This of course assumes a somewhat standard D-loop opening length of ½″). When you shorten or lengthen the D-loop, you have done nothing to the bow's draw length setting. Shortening or lengthening the D-loop is one means of fine tuning your anchor point without having to put the bow into the press and adjust the cables, poundage, and cam timing. This also does not force you to reset your nocking point and/or move the arrow rest up or down. However, it could result in the movement of the peep height up or down and the resulting adjustment of your sight settings.

How to Measure your Wing Span Your wing span is measured by standing with your shoulder blades against a long wall. It is best to select an area where you can consistently keep the finger tips of one hand against an object, such as the edge of a door casing (molding). This allows you to have a standard location for one side of your body, which gives a consistent starting point for measurements. (You all are well familiar by now that I always require some known standard or starting point for everything.) Keep your shoulders relaxed and down; do not hunch up, do not over-extend. Raise your arms to a "T" formation making sure both arms are extended, but not over

extended, and level to shoulder height (*see the photos above*). In the first picture, Mark Cooper (a mid-to-upper level shooter), has his shoulders hunched up, his head tilted upwards and his arms well over-extended. In the second picture, he has his shoulders down and relaxed, his head is level, and his arms are normally extended without being overextended or tight. Doing this wrong can make an error of inches in the final result. The next step is to have someone mark the wall at the tip of your other middle finger.

Do this five times, measuring this distance to the nearest ⅛ inch, recording each measurement, even if most are the same. Then, average the result of those measurements. If you have a wild measurement, it is okay to toss it out and average the four others. Then consider the table below, in which wing span is matched to a beginning draw length. You can easily interpolate within the table to establish your starting point to the nearest ⅛″ if you so choose. (For example, if your wing span is 73½″, halfway between 73″ and 74″, your draw length will be halfway between 29″ and 29½″ which is 29¼″, etc.) Remember, being ½″ off on your draw length is not close enough, but it can be refined as you work through the process. The intent of this is to get you at least within ½″ of your correct AMO draw length and then fine tune it from there.

Wing Span / Draw Length

WS	DL	WS	DL
67″	26″	76″	30½″
68″	26½″	77″	31″
69″	27″	78″	31½″
70″	27½″	79″	32″
71″	28″	80″	32½″
72″	28½″	81″	33″
73″	26″	82″	33½″
74″	29½″	83″	34″
75″	30″	84″	34½″

It is important to note (again) that this is a starting point and assumes you are normally proportioned (your height and wing span are close to each other). You will soon see, however, that height and wing span can be quite different from one another, among other things that I will discuss in the next chapter.

The chart above also assumes that with bow in hand, the shooter is utilizing proper form: both shoulders are down and relaxed, head is erect, chin is level, bow arm is relaxed and unlocked, with no leaning back at the waist, no tucking of the head back to reach the string, tip of the drawing elbow even with or very slightly above the plane of the arrow, and the drawing elbow in line with the arrow when at full draw (when viewed from behind or directly in front). It should be noted, however, that the "elbow in line with the arrow may have to be partially disregarded if the shooter is older, has a shorter upper arm than lower arm, is "barrel chested," or lacks the flexibility to get that elbow around. If you don't have proper form, the chart can't work to give you any sort of reliable results. Are you beginning to see why this method can be difficult to use accurately and consistently by an archery shop? Shop employees will have different opinions as to what the "correct positioning" of all the items mentioned above is.

If you are normally proportioned and have proper form, then this chart will often get you to a starting draw length easily within ½″ (within certain limitations). As with almost everything in archery, this will work for most people, but it will not work perfectly or for everyone.

If you've got your mind made up you can shoot a 30″ draw bow when your wing span is 71 inches, then you need to reevaluate your own situation. Just remember, if your draw length is out of whack, so is your alignment and therefore your groups, scores, and accuracy will suffer drastically and in proportion to how far "off" your bow's draw length is set!

This method has been in use for over 40 years; it is not new and can be reasonably accurate if used correctly. Just don't get caught up into using this as the most accurate way to go.

I'll repeat this one last time: the wing span method gives you a starting point for your AMO draw length. You will then need to set the bow to this AMO draw length and then the fine tuning of your bow's draw length can begin. Don't trust the limb tag, but rather measure and set the bow's draw length to this starting point for your AMO draw length.

The Positive Aspects of the Use of this Method

- It is quick and easy to get the measurements and average them.
- The table is straightforward.
- In many cases it gets you within ½″ from where you ultimately end up on your bow's draw length, but not always.
- It can be used to make sure you order a bow that, if it has a cam module for adjusting its draw length, you are within the longest and shortest limits of the cam. Experience tells me that this works to make sure you don't get a bow that is too short. More on that later.

The Negative Aspects of this Method

- It is easy for the person being fitted to defeat the system by over stretching themselves or otherwise skewing the measurements. Remember, today people think "speed" above all else, and they are well aware that a shorter draw length means less speed, so they will do just about anything to get as long of a draw length as possible.
- It is difficult to interpolate the table correctly, since each inch of wing span

changes the AMO draw length starting point by ½″.

- If you use just a single measurement, you could easily end up way off, costing you much time and money.
- Figuring out how much to add or subtract for the many variables in your proportions can be time consuming and difficult, if not impossible! This is precisely why it is claimed to only get you within ½″ of your AMO draw length starting point. I will discuss this further in the next chapter, so keep it in mind.
- Since most bows run "long" on their draw length tags, it makes it very difficult to decide whether to order the bow "short" or to order it "long" and pray for the best. On a "draw length specific" cam bow, this can result in a lot of expense with having to get different cams. In some cases, it could mean having to also get a stiffer or weaker deflection on the limbs, which is an expensive proposition.

The Wing Span Divided by 2.5 Method

I don't know the source of this method or even how the magic number of 2.5 got into it. I do know, however, that just like the other five methods I'll be discussing, there are people who swear by this method. Is it accurate? How far "off" is it when compared to the other methods? Should you favor this method over the tabular wing span method I just described? Doing it isn't so hard as you know how to get your wing span, so that part doesn't need repeating. Obviously, once you get your averaged wing span measurement, then divide that by 2.5. It is definitely simple, quick, and perhaps efficient. However, we can't call this good or bad here. The biggest disadvantage to this method is that it doesn't address any of the variables of body symmetry contained in the normal wing span method, but then again, neither does the regular Wing-Span Method. In addition, I haven't found out where that 2.5 came from (someone probably knows, but it wasn't my intent to research the subject that far).

Remember that I said that I had data and comparisons? Be patient. I have one more method to go through before said data are presented and those comparisons are presented.

The Light Draw Recurve Bow Method

This method has been in use for a number of years. It is an easy one to use, and can be used effectively for finger shooters, since finger shooters don't use D-loops. You place your fingers around the bowstring, draw the bow back using proper form, anchor, and head and shoulder positioning, hold for a second or two, and let it down once the observer has written down the measurement. The person taking the measurements then adds 1¾″ to the "true draw" measurement taken from drawing the bow and arrives at the archer's AMO draw length estimate. The prospect can easily draw this bow without the risk of dry-firing an expensive compound bow. This light weight bow "fits" everyone, so a shop only needs one of them. What can be easier than that, right?

I think you probably understand that cheating the system with this light bow is fairly easy to do, especially if the person taking the measurement only uses one or two observations to get it "close" and then proceeds to the bow rack to find a bow with a range of draw lengths that matches (only rarely will that "off the rack" bow be physically measured to see if it is correctly marked or not). If the person taking the measurement isn't knowledgeable with regard to proper form, proper alignment, proper head and shoulder positioning and alignment, proper stance, and a host of other items, it will be very easy for the person to end up with a measurement that is way, way too long and, obviously, very inaccurate. Also, the grip of this recurve bow is quite different from the grip on most compound bows, so hand positioning is tricky.

Is this method feasible? or even useful? Absolutely, but only in the hands of a shop person or coach who knows what to look for while the prospective buyer/student is doing their part. It is quite easy to be way off in the measurement, and being way off can cost that person/student/potential customer, even to the point of a total bow replacement. So, when using this method, you must be very, very careful and make many, many measurements. You are going to find that even the most experienced shooters are going to shimmy and shake once they hit their "anchor point" and they won't hold this bow for long. Why? Simple, in nearly all cases they are going to be holding more peak holding weight with this bow than they are currently holding with their compound bows. This is exactly why, if things are properly done and the observer takes his/her time, this method can be better than the two previous methods or, if done improperly, is going to come in way off. It is critical that the full draw position be checked closely. The drawing elbow needs to be in line with the arrow when the prospective customer is at full draw position, and the bow shoulder needs to be down and also the standard "T-formation" needs to be properly set up; otherwise this system is also destined to give erroneous readings.

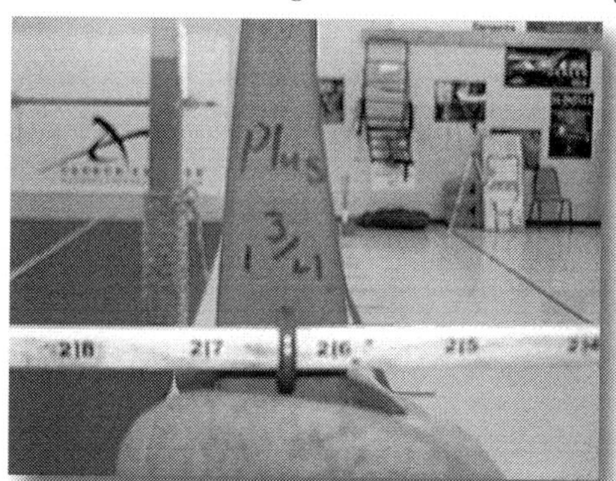

Mike Vaccaro draws back light weight bow.

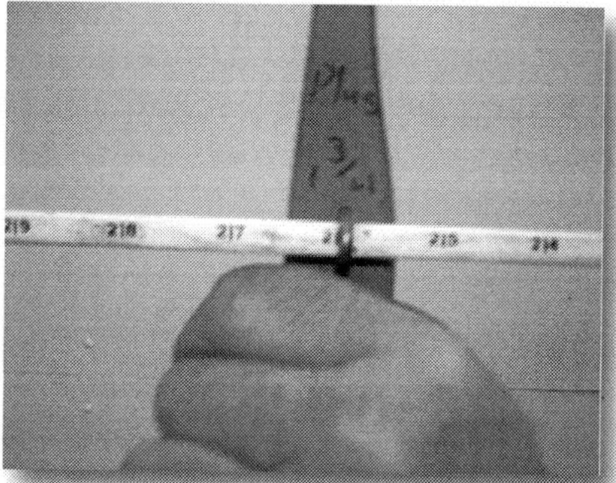

Cody Engle draws back light weight bow.

The Data

For the purposes of this investigation, each measurement was done five times and an average taken. The reasons I use the current draw lengths of these shooters are many, but foremost among them is that all six have shot numerous perfect 300 scores indoors on the NFAA five spot target. In addition, all six have consistently shot those scores with their X-counts in the range of 52-58 X's. One of the shooters has shot numerous 60X scores on the NFAA face and many perfect 300 scores on the Vegas face as well.

As a result, their bows' draw length settings, while still works in progress, are very close to their optimal draw lengths (or so their scores and X-counts so indicate).

Comparisons of These Three Methods

I have compiled the data above from only three of the six methods (*see the next chapter for the other three*). It is clear that there is a lot of variation among the three methods. All three of Dan's were somewhat close, but Mark's are all over the place. Remember that all measurements were taken five times for each method and then averaged. None of them was taken from a single measurement (so commonly done by most people and bow shops). Since we need a "known standard" of comparison, that is the "Bow's Current Measured AMO Draw Length" of these very accurate archers.

Let's look more closely at the table and see what consistencies and/or inconsistencies there are when comparing the methods to the shooters' bows' current draw length settings.

Data Table of Wing Span, Wing Span Divided/2.5, Light Bow Draw Length, and Shooter Dimensions (all Measurements are in inches)

Name	*Height*	*Ave Wing Span*	*Ave Wing Span AMO*	*Ave Wing Span / 2.5*	*Ave Light Bow AMO*	*Ave of the Three Estimates*	*Bow's Current AMO Setting*
Mark	71	70.62	27.625	28.250	30.35	28.74	29.00
Cody	70	69.15	27.125	27.660	28.8	27.86	28.00
Mike	66.5	67.56	26.325	28.025	27.5	26.97	27.375
Dan	69	71.51	28.250	28.625	28.2	28.35	28.00
Tom	67.5	67.61	27.310	27.045	27.75	27.37	27.875
Earl	70	69.325	27.125	27.730	29.33	28.06	28.50

Average Wing Span Compared To Bow's Current Draw Length You will note that in all but one case (Dan) the Average Wing Span AMO comes up short when compared to the current draw length setting of the archers' bows. If you take a closer look at these differences, the Wing Span Method comes up short by an average difference of 0.998 inches (ouch!). The range of variance for this data set using the wing span method is a total of 1.625″. However, it must be noted that both Earl and Mark are shooting release aids with the new "shorter throat" design, which requires a change in draw length to accommodate the release aid, thus skewing the results somewhat. Tom, on the other hand elected to lengthen his D-loop slightly beyond the "standard" ½″ opening length rather than go with a draw length increase on his bow. If we take those into consideration, then the numbers are much closer than 0.998 inches and back within the ½″ criterion we ask of any of these methods. We will discuss "Tom's situation" (that's me) more closely in the next chapter.

Wing Span Divided By 2.5 Compared To Bow's Current Draw Length You will note that in all but two of the cases (Cody & Tom), the wing span divided by 2.5 appears to be really scattered, with this method being short four times and long two times. However, when you work the average of the differences, the 2.5 method averages out at only 0.487″ (or nearly ½ inch) short. But this is misleading, being an inch short one time and an inch long another doesn't "average out" because those are two different archers being measured. Each got a draw length estimate that was wrong by one inch. If you take only the four readings that average out short, this changes to 0.831″ short on average, and 0.445″ long for those two for whom the 2.5 method came out longer than the bow's current setting. The range for these data is 1.58″, only slightly better than the wing span indication.

The Light Bow AMO/ATA Measurements Compared to the Current Draw Length This comparison gives some very interesting results. Four out of the six measurements come out long by an average of 0.951″, while two came up short by an average of 0.312″. What is more interesting, however, is that the actual five measurements taken by drawing the light bow correctly, paying special attention to proper form and body positioning, etc., did not vary among the measurements more than 1/4″ for any of the shooters. Three of the six shooters actually drew the light bow to the same point for all five measurements!

The jury is still out as to exactly why they ended up longer with the light bow; especially since they complained that the "holding weight" of the light bow was really making them feel which muscles they really needed to use due to the "burning sensation" between their shoulder blades as opposed to their use of arm and forearm/hand muscle to get to the same point, with no "burn" between and towards the lower side of their shoulder blades. They admitted that there is such a tendency for them to not utilize those larger muscle sets in their backs because they can hold the bow back much "easier" with their arms, even though they know this is poor technique. (Basically this is just favoring what you are used to over doing something different.) Perhaps there may well be something about those recurve bows that make you cognizant of which muscles you need to use and forcing you to do so in order to come to anchor correctly.

Comparing the Average of All Three Methods to the Current Bows' Draw Lengths This comparison also gives some very interesting results. In four out of the six cases, the average of all three methods comes up short. However the gap is only by 0.55″ with a range of 0.32″ for the entire group. For the two shooters for whom the average of all three methods turned out to be longer than their bow's current setting, the difference was only 0.355″. So far the average of the three methods appears to be a better estimate than any single one of the methods used as a stand-alone. Will it be superior to any one of the other three, also? I think it is too early to draw that conclusion; we'll await the results of the other three methods (*see next chapter*).

Summary and Conclusions

Let's pretend that each of the six persons who were measured for this study were purchasing a new bow, and they didn't know which draw length to order. That is to say that they don't already have a bow that they are shooting to a high level.

Based upon the data above, and ignoring the "Bow's Current Draw Length" in the table above (since that bow doesn't exist for this scenario) I would either find a bow on the rack that could be measured and set up to the specifications below or I would order their bows with the following draw length range:

Mark AMO range 28″ – 29½″
for a draw length specific bow: 28½″ AMO

Cody AMO range 27″ – 28½″
for a draw length specific bow: 28″ AMO

Mike AMO range 26½″ – 28″
for a draw length specific bow: 27″ AMO

Dan AMO range 28″ – 29½″
for a draw length specific bow: 28″ AMO

Tom AMO range 27″ – 28½″
for a draw length specific bow: 27½″ AMO

Earl AMO range 27½″ – 29″
for a draw length specific bow: 28″ AMO

Based upon the data for just the three methods discussed, the draw length specific cam's AMO draw length recommendation would give each shooter some room for adjustments either shorter or longer from the "Average of the three methods" used. Of course, this also assumes that the manufacturer is going to ship the bow "as ordered" and not send one that actually comes in longer than specified (which occurs quite frequently).

At this point I think you can see why using just one measurement or only one method can really cause a lot of problems, hassle, and expense to shooters as well as to archery shops and manufacturers. Can you see why so many shooters end up with a bow they will never be able to shoot really well? Remember, the bow needs to be fit to the shooter, not the shooter fit to the bow.

However, before ordering a bow for them, I would check the shop's stock for a bow that can be measured and then adjusted to fit the shooter's draw length requirement, and if I were lucky enough to have one, set it up exactly at the requirement indicated by the average of the three methods and go from there.

Better yet, of course, is to use another method or methods that may better determine this thing and narrow it down further.

So, are we to conclude from this data that none of the three methods is reliable? Absolutely not. Are we to conclude that the Wing Span Divided by 2.5 Method is completely unreliable, especially for a person with a longer wing span?" Not necessarily. You will already note that averaging the three methods, and then comparing that average to what the bow is set for brings things into a better light and appears to perhaps support that using only one of the methods or only one measurement of each is likely not to be the best route to follow. The more data you have and the more cross-checks, the more accurately you can find that somewhat elusive "starting point for your AMO Draw Length" for shooting a compound bow.

You are likely to form your own conclusions based upon the data above, and there is nothing wrong with that. If you want to have some fun, while at the same time

Mike Vaccaro draws back the light weight bow showing the D-Loop.

learning something about your own setup and how close you might be, then make yourself a blank table similar to that one above, gather your personal data (don't forget to take at least five measurements of each item in the table, including when you measure the "true draw" of your bow and convert it to AMO Draw length). Realize that a single measurement or use of a single method almost always will not be as accurate as many measurements and a combination of methods. You have already seen in the review of the three most common methods that the results differ greatly; even when used by an experienced archer/coach! Imagine what will result if the person taking the measurements is not experienced or as well-versed and the person wanting a bow doesn't know the first thing about what to do or what to expect.

In the next chapter I'll discuss three more methods and provide similar data for those as well. Then, we can combine all the data for each shooter, average all six of the methods' data, and then compare them to each shooter's actual draw length and see what comes out. As is said, "the more the merrier."

Tom Dorigatti

16

What is My "Correct" Draw Length? Pt II

In Chapter 15, I offered up three of the six methods commonly used to determine a "starting point" for a person's AMO/ATA draw length requirement. Here I will, as promised, offer up a solution that uses all six of the methods in combination.

Some precautions that all should heed if you are in the process (or even just thinking of) purchasing a new bow are worth repeating once again; they are that important:

- Do not get caught up in the hype of having to have a high peak weight bow with a long draw length so that you can get more speed out of the bow. If you are of short stature and the shop tries to sell you a 70 pound bow with a 30″ AMO draw length; beware!
- Be especially cautious when it comes to the limb tag that is on each bow. Those limb tags typically give: peak weight range, string and cable lengths, and the "AMO draw length" at which the particular bow is supposedly set. This last item is not necessarily at all accurate! Most of the bows I have checked run ½″ to 1″ longer than what the limb tag says!
- You should have your shop physically measure the draw length of the bow to make sure it is indeed what the limb tag says it is. This becomes even more important if the type of cam on the bow is "draw length specific," meaning that the bow has a very narrow range of adjustment for draw length.
- If the shop won't physically measure the bow's actual AMO draw length for you, then perhaps you should be more insistent or seek out another shop. Selecting a bow that is out of the range of your AMO draw length starting point could cost you a thousand dollars or more. You must realize what all of the top professionals tell us over and over, "Having a correct draw length is the most critical aspect for shooting consistently high scores and tight groups."

Test Archer Acknowledgments

Before continuing, in case you haven't yet read the previous chapter, I acknowledge the shooters who volunteered their time for data gathering, picture taking, and putting up with me during this process. They are students of the game, and I do coach them. They are also close friends. Their names, not in any order of priority or level of expertise, are: Mark Cooper, Mike Vaccaro, Cody Engle, Dan Terrill, and Earl Raymond, and, of course, myself. Without their assistance, this study couldn't have been created. Like me, they have a special interest in this: they, too, would like to find a means of getting closer to that magical "correct draw length" and be able to help someone they know get things closer from the very beginning.

This article deals with three more, but less commonly used, methods:

1. The Measuring Arrow 45° Method
2. The Measuring Arrow Horizontal Method, and
3. The Fist Against the Wall Method

Descriptions of the Three Other Methods of Estimating Draw Length

The Measuring Arrow 45° Method This method has been in use as long as I can remember. It is a very simple method to use. Once again, the person taking the measurements has to be very observant. In addition, if only one measurement is taken, then things will not be as accurate which could result in you costing a customer (or yourself) a lot of trouble and money.

Procedure Once again, the key is in taking at least five (5) measurements. (*Note* I will discuss one other probable oversight at the end of this Chapter.) Using a pre-marked measuring arrow that most archery shops have on hand (if one isn't available, then you can use a long or uncut arrow and simply place marks with a fine point magic marker of a contrasting color):

1. Have the archer place the nock end of the arrow in the notch at the juncture of the collar-bone and throat. Placing it in the notch will help simulate the bow-string's positioning. Placing it on the chest bone (sternum) gives a measurement shorter by ¼″.
2. Have the archer place both palms against the arrow shaft and elevate to about a 45 degree upwards angle. Tell them to pick an object on the wall to which they can "mark" their hand positioning.
3. Making sure that the person is not overstretching or hunching up their shoulders, mark the measuring arrow at the tip of the middle finger that gives the longest measurement. The archer is going to likely try to match up the tips of his two middle fingers, so as I've since learned, you must really watch them closely! Oh, yes, it is normal for one arm to be longer than the other; sometimes as much as ½″ or even more! (See the end of the chapter for a personal discussion of issues that can come into play!)
4. Make a dot on the measuring arrow, and tell the person to let down and relax a few seconds.
5. Repeat steps #1-4 at least four more times, marking the arrow each time at the middle finger-tip that is the longest.
6. Write down the measurements and average them, being sure to toss out any "ringers" that are way off. If you so choose, you can take more measurements. The average of these measurements is supposed to closely estimate the person's AMO draw length requirement.

Once again, if the person stretches out too far goes up too high, locks their elbows, hunches their shoulders upwards or any combination of those (*see Cody in the photo below*), the measurement is going to be way off. It should be obvious why it is important that the second part of step 2 be consistent. The archer should be more in the position of Dan, rather than that of Cody.

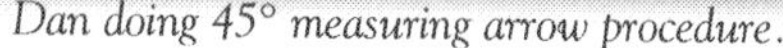

Dan doing 45° measuring arrow procedure.

Cody doing 45° measuring arrow procedure.

The Measuring Arrow Horizontal Method This method is nearly identical to the Measuring Arrow 45 Degree Measuring Method, but yields quite a different measurement. You follow the same procedure as the 45 degree up method, except that the shooter holds his/her arms level, just as if they are shooting holding their bow. Again, it is critical that the person not be overly stretched out, that their shoulders are down and relaxed, and that their elbows are not locked. Once again, you mark the measuring arrow at the tip of the middle finger that ends up being the longest. Make sure that you take at least five measurements and that the shooter brings those arms up to the same point every time. Write down the measurements, and then average them.

Cody doing level measuring arrow procedure.

The "Fist Against the Wall" Method This method is a bit more time consuming, but is also perhaps a more accurate means of obtaining a person's AMO draw length estimate. Once again, this is a two-person operation, and the person taking the measurement needs to know exactly what they are doing and how to get the person properly positioned, with regard to stance, shoulder alignment, full draw positioning, hand position against the wall, head position, chin position and bow-arm extension. If any of these are incorrect, then the subsequent measurements will be way off. Once again, take at least five measurements, allowing the person to reposition themselves between measurements. After all, while shooting their bow, they do indeed reposition themselves as they set up from shot to shot to shot.

Procedure

1. Find a post or open wall space.
2. Have the person, with a properly positioned and extended bow arm, move forward so that their fist is against the post or wall.
3. Have the person stand in their normal stance as if addressing the target, with their bow arm extended just as if they are holding their bow, and with their fist against the pole/wall. Make sure they don't open or close their stance from their normal positioning, it will make a difference.

4. Make sure that their bow shoulder is down and that the bow arm is relaxed and not over extended, nor "bent." Make certain that the shooter is not leaning back and that their head is positioned just as if they are at anchor. (Their aiming eyeball should be above their navel or gig line.) It is a good idea to have the person simulate that they are indeed at anchor, by actually placing their release hand at anchor. This is more likely to get them to adopt proper positioning of their head, chin, bow arm, both elbows, and both shoulders (see photos below).
5. Make sure the shooter also has their chin level and not tucked downwards or upwards.

   Note If the shooter assumes a vertical hand position on the post, the head, chin, and shoulder position will change dramatically! In the photos below, Mike demonstrates the positioning he has if he uses a "vertical grip" on the wall/post. You can see this hand position on the post, and then Mike's head, chin, and shoulder position. This is not the ideal position and, as a result, yields a quite different measurement, but not what you would expect (*see Data Table #1 below*).

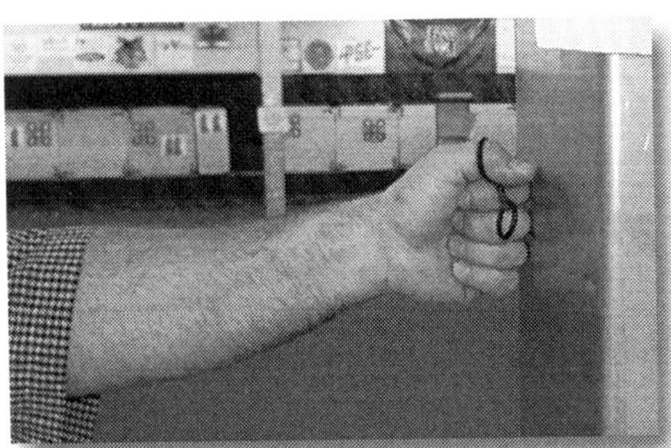

In the next pair of photos, Mike assumes his best hand positioning with his knuckles at about 45 degrees to the floor, the same hand position he uses on his bow. Note the distinct difference in the head, chin, and shoulder positioning from when the bow hand was vertical. This is a more ideal position for solid shooting form, and one you should strive for before taking any measurements.

6. Once the shooter is in a correct, relaxed position, simply measure from the post

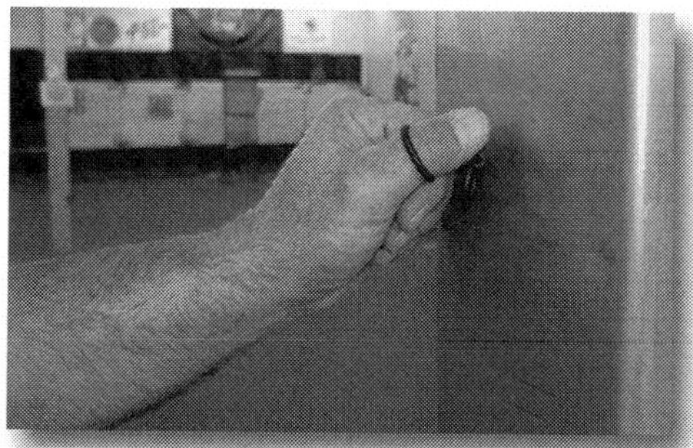

or wall to the corner of the shooter's mouth. This is the "standard" position of the bowstring for most shooters shooting compound bows.

Place the end of the tape measure against the post, and then extend the tape measure to the corner of the shooter's mouth (*see photos below*). Record the measurement from the wall/post to the corner of the mouth to the nearest 1/16″.

7. Without having the shooter move their feet in relation to the post, have them lower their bow arm relax a few seconds, and raise the bow-arm and release hand into anchor position for the next measurement. This simulates them doing the next shot. Check that elbow alignment every time. He/she needs to be in correct full-draw-position.
8. Repeat steps 1-7 at least four more times, making sure that each time proper positioning is attained before you make the measurement.

Record each measurement and then average them. Calculate your measurements in decimals since that makes averaging them easier (1/16″ = 0.0625″, 1/8″ = 0.125″, etc). See Table #1 top of next page for my results.

Comparisons of These Second Three (now Four) Methods

Looking at the actual data above is most interesting, but hard to decipher. Comparisons become much clearer, though, if we compare the average of each measuring method against the measured AMO setting of the shooters' bows (see table below). The results below include the differences + or – between the measured estimates and the shooters' bows' actual measured draw length, the given standard.

Comparison of Differences Between Each Method and the Bows' Current Draw Length It is interesting that if one averages the differences of all three of the

Table #1 Data Table for Measuring Arrow 45° Method, Measuring Arrow Horizontal Method, & Fist Against the Wall/Post Methods (inches)

Name	*Bow's Current AMO Setting*	*Avg. Diff. of the 3 Estimates*	*Measur. Arrow @ 45°*	*Measr. Arrow Hort.*	*Vert. Fist Against Wall/Post*	*Angled Fist Against Wall/Post*
Mark	29.00	27.97	27.40	27.55	28.15	28.80
Cody	28.00	26.59	26.45	26.35	26.51	27.05
Mike	27.375	27.09	27.25	26.05	27.25	27.83
Dan	28.00	27.87	27.30	27.30	28.19	28.69
Tom	27.875	28.21	28.50	28.00	27.875	28.50
Earl	28.50	28.63	29.00	28.50	28.24	28.80

Table #2 Comparison of Differences Between Each Method and the Bow's Current AMO Setting (all measurements are in inches)

Name	*Bow's Current AMO Setting*	*Avg. Diff. of All Estimates vs. Bow's AMO Setting*	*Avg. Diff. Arrow @ 45° vs. Bow's AMO Setting*	*Avg. Diff. Arrow Hort. vs. Bow's AMO Setting*	*Avg. Diff. Vert. Fist vs. Bow's AMO Setting*	*Avg. Diff. Angled Fist vs. Bow's AMO Setting*
Mark	29.00	-1.03	-1.60	-1.45	-0.85	-0.20
Cody	28.00	-1.41	-1.55	-1.65	-1.49	-0.95
Mike	27.38	-0.29	-0.13	-1.33	-0.13	0.45
Dan	28.00	-0.13	-0.70	-0.70	0.19	0.69
Tom	27.88	0.34	0.63	0.13	0.00	0.63
Earl	28.50	0.13	0.50	0.00	-0.26	0.30

methods and then compares this average to the bow's current draw length, in four out of six cases, this average comes up with a shorter draw length estimate than that being currently used by the shooters. This was unexpected. This holds true through all of the data until one compares the Difference of the Angled Fist Against the Wall vs. the measured draw length of each shooter's bow. In that case, the differences come in longer than the current bow setting in four of the six cases. In addition, the result is also much closer to what the shooters are currently using. This is not to say that the shooter's bows are set at their optimal draw lengths, nor is it to say that those shooters need to increase their bows' draw lengths. However it could be that those shooters, should they need a change might increase, rather than decrease their draw length in small increments to see if they get closer to the sweet spot. This data clearly shows that even without knowledge of which method was used to determine where to set the bow's draw length, the angled fist against the wall method ends up being the closest of the three depicted in the table.

Table #3 Data Table for Wing-Span, Wing-Span Divided by 2.5, Light Bow Draw Length, Versus Current Bow Setting (all measurements are in inches)

Name	*Bow's Current AMO Setting*	*Avg. Diff. of the 3 Estimates Combined*	*Diff. Wing Span Est. vs. Bow's Setting*	*Diff. Wing Span / 2.5 vs. Bow's Setting*	*Diff. Light Bow Est. vs. Bow's Setting*
Mark	29.000	-0.260	-1.375	-0.750	1.350
Cody	28.000	-0.140	-0.875	-0.340	0.800
Mike	27.375	-0.405	-1.050	0.650	0.125
Dan	28.000	0.350	0.250	0.625	0.200
Tom	27.875	-0.505	-0.565	-0.830	-0.125
Earl	28.500	-0.440	-1.375	-0.770	0.830

Again, note that the Vertical Fist Against the Wall Method consistently yielded a substantially shorter draw length requirement than the Angled Fist Against the Wall method. I had thought that with the head angle being off, the shoulder up, and other alignment problems, that the vertical fist would have come in longer, not shorter. However, we noticed that when we placed the bow hand against the wall vertically, then entire feel in the bow arm and shoulder was tensed up and the only way to get even a bit more comfortable was to move the bow shoulder in and up, the head back slightly, and the chin downwards, thus shortening the measurement result significantly (*see photos above*).

The next table depicts the differences between the three methods discussed in the previous chapter and the shooters' bows' current draw lengths. It is important to bring these data up again so that they can be compared with the other methods discussed above.

Comparisons of the First Three Methods

As seen in this table, using the average of the first three methods shows that in five out of six cases, the methods come up short, but in all cases but one, less than ½″. In all but one case, too, those measurements regarding Wing-Span also came up well short when compared to the shooters' actual draw length. The Wing Span Divided by 2.5 Method doesn't fare much better, but is more consistent. Note that the use of the Light Bow Method versus the bow setting comes in long in 5 out of 6 instances, and is pretty well scattered. While this apparently shows that each method comes in short, using all three does net a closer "figure" than any one of these as a stand-alone.

I have had some further investigations concerning the Wing Span Method, mostly as a result of my having depended upon this method quite heavily over the years. According to the data, the Wing Span Method comes up short by an average difference of 0.998 inches. (Ouch!)

It has since also been discovered since the previous chapter that for me (Tom in the tables), the wing-span method does indeed come in nearly an inch short as well. Further investigation thus far is also beginning to show that perhaps the Wing Span Method wasn't really designed for AMO draw length, but rather true draw length. If this is true, this could well explain the "adjustments" that some claim need to be made for the many variables such as finger length, body shape, hand-size, etc.; you know, those adjustments of "some" taken off or added for variances in normal body symmetry.

Wing Span Divided by 2.5 Estimates Compared to Current Draw Lengths The wing span divided by 2.5 estimates appear to be really scattered, with this method being short by over ¼″ four times and long two times by ⅞″. The average of these is misleading, being almost an inch short one time and an inch long another doesn't "average out" because those are two different archers being measured. I would gather that this method can be pretty unreliable. That does not refute this method, however, since it does seem to work for some people.

The Light Bow Estimates Compared to Current Draw Lengths This method yielded some very interesting results. Five out of the six measurements come out long by an average of 0.951″, while for one of the shooters the light bow measurement came up short by 0.312″. What is more interesting, however, is that the actual five measurements taken by drawing the light bow correctly, paying special attention to proper form and body positioning, etc., did not vary among the measurements more than ¼″ for any of the shooters. Three of the six shooters actually drew the light bow to the same point for all five measurements!

As stated earlier in this chapter, the person observing Tom the second go around noted that Tom's drawing elbow was well short of proper alignment positioning, which turned out to be the root of Tom's shooting stability problem! From this example, it is apparent that simply drawing the bow back several times to get a "number" isn't necessarily accurate. The person performing this measurement must be very careful to get the shooter into proper alignment from all sides and from the ground up. In Tom's case, muscle memory for poundage prevailed, regardless of the "drawing position." This muscle memory threw the measurement way off and Tom has paid a price for it.

Comparing the Average of All Three Methods to the Current Bows' Draw Lengths This comparison also yields some very interesting results. In four out of the six cases, the average of all three methods comes up shorter than actual draw lengths. But, so far, the average of the three methods appears to be a better estimate than any single one of the methods used as a stand-alone. However, you must note that one method came in well short, one method was very "scattered," and the light bow method came out long when compared to the shooters' draw lengths. Thus, further investigation may well be needed.

The Culmination: All Seven Methods Compared

Here is a table comparing all of the methods draw length estimations with the actual measured draw lengths. There is also a column whereby the average difference of all seven methods is compared to the current draw length. Remember, I stated that sometimes more than one method should be utilized, along with at least five separate measurements for each method employed. The more data you have, the closer you may well be to that starting point for your draw length. Read on, since these results are quite interesting.

First, the premise here is that the archer's current AMO draw length setting is indeed correct (or very close to being so), to make them our standards of comparison. Of course, in reality we realize that this may or may not be the case. However, we must also note that if we weren't searching for a method of getting this determination closer, then we wouldn't have all these various methods of trying to ascertain this magical number!

Summary and Conclusions

According to the data:

- If one were to use all seven methods, in most cases you would come up only slightly short. However, we all realize that very few people and even fewer bow shops are going to go to all this hassle to try to fit oneself or a customer to a new bow. This was included only to show that the use of varying methods can "average out" and perhaps get you closer to an optimal starting point.
- *The Wing Span* and *Wing Span Divided by 2.5 Methods* apparently come in well short and by more than the ½″ that is claimed for their accuracy.
- *The Light Bow Method* tends to come in long by a large amount (when compared to the person's current draw length). Could this possibly be a source of so many persons being long on draw length after they've been "measured" for a new bow? It is obvious that even a trained eye for detail can miss with this method.
- *The Measuring Arrow* comes in short, which may lead me to believe that using the measuring arrow may give you

Table #4 Comparison of All Methods Studied vs. the Current AMO Draw Length Setting of the Bow (all measurements are in inches)

Name	*Bow's Current AMO Setting*	*Avg. Diff. of All Methods*	*Avg. Diff. Wing Span Method*	*Avg. Diff. Wing Span / 2.5 Method*	*Avg. Diff. Meas. Arrow 45° Method*	*Avg. Diff Meas. Arrow 45° Method*	*Avg. Diff. Meas. Arrow Hort. Method*	*Avg. Diff. Vert. Fist Wall/Post Method*	*Avg. Diff. Angled Fist Wall/Post Method*
Mark	29.000	-0.696	-1.375	-0.750	1.350	-1.6	-1.45	-0.850	-0.200
Cody	28.000	-0.608	-0.875	-0.340	0.800	-1.6	-1.65	-0.490	-0.150
Mike	27.375	-0.199	-1.050	0.650	0.125	-0.1	-1.33	-0.125	0.455
Dan	28.000	0.079	0.250	0.625	0.200	-0.7	-0.70	0.190	0.690
Tom	27.875	-0.021	-0.565	-0.830	-0.125	0.6	0.13	0.000	0.625
Earl	28.500	-0.111	-1.375	-0.770	0.830	0.5	0.00	-0.260	0.300

a "true draw" length as opposed to a AMO draw length estimate. The same goes with the horizontal measuring arrow method.

- *The Vertical Fist Against the Wall* also comes in short, but not as bad as the other methods tested.
- *The Angled Fist Against the Wall Method* on the other hand apparently came in slightly long, or did it? The reason I bring this up is because more and more coaches and shops are starting to utilize this method because of its close similarity to getting the person to correct body positioning while not under a load of any sort. Remember what I said before concerning a person drawing a bow to the stops and saying it feels good even if the draw length is set 2″ or even 3″ too long for them? If the person doing the measurements makes sure the customer is properly aligned and in the proper body positioning, and has them simulate anchoring, it appears that this relaxed method can work quite well.

Thus, in order to accommodate your curiosity, I'm going to use the raw data and not my personal preference or opinion, to prioritize the methods based upon "how close" each method came to the shooters' actual AMO draw lengths, based upon the average difference, variance, and to some extent, the standard deviation of the set when compared to the standards.

A Prioritized Listing The winners are, in order of "most reliable" to "least reliable:"

1. *Wing Span Divided by 2.5 Method* The average comes in short by only –0.236″, the variance is 0.125″, and the standard deviation is only 0.518″. However, there is a caution in that the range of the sample set was significant.
2. *Vertical Fist Against the Wall Method* The average comes in short at –0.256″. The variance is 0.660″, and the standard deviation is 0.712″. However, as discussed, this method does cause problems due to stress placed upon the arms, shoulders, head, and neck and could end up being way off, if the measurer were not careful, since proper positioning is the key to accurate and comfortable shooting form.
3. *Angled Fist Against the Wall Method* The average comes in long at 0.287″. The variance is only 0.490″, while the standard deviation is 0.821″. This method bears out further testing, since it uses a no load situation on the body and assumes correct angling of the bow hand and how a person should be gripping the bow.
4. *Measuring Arrow 45° Method* The average comes in short by 0.475″. The variance is rather large at 2.300″, and the standard deviation is 0.818″. This too bears watching when measuring a person because of a person's tendency either not stretch enough or to stretch out way too far. (The person could be thinking "I want a longer draw length" from a pre-conceived notion they want more speed because their buddy told them so).
5. *Light Bow Method* The average comes in long at 0.530″. The variance is bothersome in that it is 1.550″ and the standard deviation is 0.904″. This method is very difficult to use with new shooters because of all the elements of proper body positioning involved to get reasonable results. Remember the data was gathered by utilizing mid to top echelon shooters with lots of shooting experience.

6. *Measuring Arrow Horizontal Method* The average comes in short by 0.833″. The variance is at 2.150″, while the standard deviation is 0.955″. Once again be aware of the constraints of this method.
7. *Wing Span Method* This method, while the one I personally condoned for many years, doesn't fare well in this investigation. The method came in short by nearly ⅞″ (0.832″), while the variance was 1.125″ and the standard deviation was 1.523″. Indications are that this method should be investigated much further (*see the Post Script below*).

Post Script

To my knowledge, nobody has undertaken the task of really determining a reliable methodology for determining an accurate starting point for an archer's AMO draw length. The research involved in data gathering does tend to show that of these seven methods tested, all seven vary quite a bit and are dependent upon a lot of variables. It is difficult, if not impossible to control all those variables and to only test one at a time, per the scientific method. However, I do feel strongly that further testing is in order for the Fist Against the Wall Method to gather data from top echelon shooters and compare those measurements to their bows' measured AMO draw lengths. Most all top echelon shooters have come by their draw length settings via trial and error and have it down to a fine art. They are able to tell the difference in a twist of a cable or bowstring and whether or not their draw length or cam synchronization is off by as much as one half of a twist!

This research, started as a result of me having such a tough time with the changeover back to shooting left-handed. My "old" data from the right-handed side turned out not to apply to me shooting from the other side of the bow; perhaps because I wasn't as diligent in documenting things as I thought I was, and also due to my age and health deterioration.

This has opened a real can of worms, hasn't it? I had occasion to work with Larry Wise in between the publication of the first chapter of this section and writing this second chapter. The data gathering for both chapters was complete and quite frankly, in most cases, that data stands as it is and is reasonably accurate as presented in spite of the fact that all but one person represented in the data went through the Larry Wise courses. The others, besides myself, actually had minimal changes, if any to their draw length setting, but nearly all had "bow hand" issues.

What we discovered was, like I thought, I was way short of my optimal draw length. I thought that I was only "slightly" short; how wrong I was! For many years I had been relying on the Wing-Span Method, thinking it was a good estimate of AMO draw length. In my particular case, this method wasn't cutting it. Based upon Larry's assessment, I was over 1″ (actually closer to 1½″) short of the draw length I should be shooting in order to have the best possible shoulder and elbow positioning! For me, it obviously didn't work as claimed (getting me within ½″ of my final ending point). In fact, it cost me a larger set of cams for my bow and, of course, a new bowstring, plus a lot of lost time fighting with too short of a draw length and wondering why I was being so inconsistent. I'm finding out that yes, indeed, you can teach an old dog new tricks; all the old dog has to do is listen! In order to teach myself how to get the drawing elbow around and into position, I had to go to an even longer draw length for a period of time, nearly 29½″ AMO, in fact. After a few months of learning this correct positioning, I've now been able to get the draw length shortened and also still achieve correct full-draw-position with my left elbow alignment and to be able to relax the bow arm. It took a huge effort to turn things around, but it has been worth it. My scores were out the window, but, as the focus of this book prescribes, "one bite of the elephant" at a time and practicing with a plan.

I've discovered that the data indicates the Wing Span Method does indeed come in "short" more often than not (the data indicates 1″ or more short). This leads me to believe that perhaps the Wing Span Method really was intended for your True Draw (AMO minus 1¾″) starting point and not the AMO draw length starting point and somehow got changed around over the years. I honestly cannot remember what I was taught way back in the 1970's when I was introduced to the Wing Span Method.

A Personal Note I found some discrepancies not mentioned before! Remember when using the Measuring Arrow Techniques I recommended marking the arrow at the tip of the middle finger that gave the longer measurement? I mentioned also that this could have a huge impact upon your estimated draw length, so let's open yet another can of worms regarding finding that "starting point" for your optimal AMO draw length.

I very recently discovered yet another important pitfall associated with the Wing-Span Method and the Wing-Span Divided by 2.5 Method. Neither method covers the fact than a person's arms are not necessarily the same length. I only happened upon this potential huge discrepancy while trying to figure out how and why, in order to get into the "real and proper" Full Draw Position that allows me to have my drawing elbow directly behind the arrow, I was having to increase my bow's draw length setting from the 27½″ mentioned above to nearly 29½″ AMO! The above information worked to near perfection for me shooting right handed, but using this draw length setting shooting left handed simply wasn't working out at all, and I was struggling in every phase of my shot sequence. In addition, I also found out that of five archers I know who have had open heart surgery, all five of us have had an increase in our draw length by 1″ or more! Interesting stuff, and the tables don't compensate for this at all. But there is more to this.

Let's get back to the a person's bilateral symmetry, meaning that the left side of our body seems to be an exact duplicate of our right side, just reversed as in a mirror. It is a fact that one leg is normally slightly longer than the other, one ear is bigger than the other, etc. I never gave this much or even any thought during the long process of my change to left-handed shooting. When I shot left-handed in the past, I used the same draw length I started back with and the same as I was shooting so well right-handed. I only happened across this totally by accident while trying to figure out exactly why my AMO draw length that we came up with in the Larry Wise Course was what I considered to be "way out of whack." In order to help me figure this out, I was using a the measuring arrow technique, not out of necessity, but out of ease of use so that my wife could work with me on figuring just what was going wrong all these months. I put the measuring arrow in the correct location and then put both my arms out in front of me comfortably and asked her to please mark the measuring arrow at the tips of my middle finger. She asked me, "Which middle finger, the left one or the right one?" I asked her why and how much difference it makes? She told me that the tip of the middle finger on my right hand was nearly 1″ farther down the measuring arrow than the tip of the middle finger on my left hand. I was well aware that it could be ½″, but when she told me it was well over 1″, it immediately sent up a red flag, so I relaxed, repositioned and tried again, and got the same result. My right arm, for this system, seems to be just over an inch longer than my left arm. Think about this for a second. I'm shooting left-handed and my right arm is over an inch longer than my left? The right arm is . . . my bow arm and it is extended out 1″ farther without any "stretching" than the left would be if it was my bow arm. This puts that bow out away from me an inch farther, and now makes perfect sense of why I'm having to have that 1″ or more of draw length shooting left handed now as opposed to what I had shot for years shooting right handed (with the shorter arm as my bow arm). That coupled with the five of us I know that have had open heart surgery now makes perfect sense on this enormous draw length change.

The "charts" don't cover this, and even while performing the test with the digital scale and coming to the same holding weight didn't register either, because people were not watching my full-draw-position. Interestingly enough, however, now that I have finally learned to get the elbow around the 28½″ AMO draw length is working well indeed. So many months of working with this one bite of elephant at a time, occasionally taking two bites and having to spit one of them out and go back.

They key to all this is simple: No matter what system you use, it would be a good idea to find out which of your arms is the longer and how much longer it is than the other one. If it is your bow arm (or intended bow arm) that is longer, and if you are using the Wing-Span or Wing-Span Divided by 2.5 Method, you need to add that difference in; if the bow arm is shorter, then the "Method's" numbers are probably pretty close, but don't trust them fully! The use of several methods, and then averaged will get you closer, but the final proof is still obviously in the consistency and the grouping and the shooter's scores, and not some number or measurement out of a chart or off the wall (pun intended). As stated before, all of this only gives you a starting point; it is just that some methods are far better than others, as demonstrated by the data presented in this small sampling set.

You are probably thinking: "So is there a "reliable method?" for getting a starting point for my optimum draw length?" The answer? Yes, there is. For now, based upon what I have learned, if I'm setting up a person for a bow or checking them, I'll use Wing Span divided by 2.5, and then the Fist Against the Wall technique along with personal observation of their body positioning from all angles to make an assessment of where they should adjust (if any) concerning their draw length setting. As you well know, I don't depend upon a single measurement, nor a single method, but opt for more data to help me make a more informed decision. I will, however ascertain which arm is the longer and if it is the bow arm, then I know to add in that difference and go from there with that person's set up parameters.

If nothing else, you are certainly more knowledgeable concerning those methods being used to getting anyone a proper starting draw length; which is the exactly the point of the past two chapters. You now have a basis for what is likely the best method to get you the closest, and then once that is accomplished; you shoot your way in to finding that sweet spot, just like the upper echelon shooters will do to get "there."

Remember in this shooting thing, one or two samples are not going to cut it; you need lots of data. Make a small adjustment, and then shoot it there for several days without touching a thing. Take notes, take pictures of your targets and groups and then compare those to the previous pictures and notes. Make an "educated guess" and not a "wild guess" based upon how you feel that day. If you succumb to a simple feeling that you are shooting better, you are going to lose to the guys who demand proof they are getting better, because from time to time you will be wrong and they won't.

You have to, as I keep saying, "eat the elephant, one bite at a time."

Tom Dorigatti

17

Tuning Your Shooting Stance to Your Draw Length

There has been a lot of discussion about several top shooters having "opened" their shooting stances. However, little is said about what goes on behind this decision or how one should go about doing this. The "what to do" is discussed openly; but the "how to do it" and the consequences of changing your stance are left unsaid.

Your stance is the basic foundation for shooting consistently. In my opinion, taking your stance and your ability to repeat that step every time you shoot an arrow, especially indoors, is one of the most overlooked aspects of basic form, second only to getting the correct draw length. Yet, believe it or not, the two go hand in hand with each other. One of the very first things I was taught when I took up field archery was, "once set, never move your feet while shooting on any field target until you have shot your last arrow from that stake." When a top pro archer says he "opened his stance," he hasn't given the rest of the story, that story being that their draw length is tuned to their stance and vice-versa!

This chapter is intended to help beginning to intermediate or even advanced archers decide whether or not a more open (or even just a different) stance is good for you. It will help you find out where you are, help you to make a change in your stance, and if it doesn't work, help you to get back to your original stance without a lot of hassle or spending a lot of time.

A Little History Lesson

At this point, I think it wise to go through a little history lesson concerning how I've come up with my procedure to "fine tune" a stance, then to fine tune the draw length and the stance, thus ultimately getting the two working together for you.

I was shooting a FITA tournament in Ohio back in 1975. At that time, FITA had not yet accepted compound bows as legal in competition. In fact in 1975, Ohio had finally "legalized" the shooting of release aids and compound bows in their State Target Rounds, American Rounds, and FITA rounds (separate division, obviously)! Prior to that, if you were shooting on the multi-color FITA target face in Ohio, you had to shoot a recurve bow with your fingers on the string! FITA, however, for official events, really didn't want compound archers and recurve archers on the same shooting line or even in the same area at the same time. Thus, a dispensation was made to allow this, but only if there was a "dividing line" between the "legal" FITA shooters and the, heaven forbid, "compounders." In this case it was a rope line with flags on it that bisected the shooting field. Compound shooters were relegated to their side, and the real FITA shooters were relegated to the other side. Yes, this was true in 1975 in Ohio!

I was over watching the FITA Olympic-style archers during warm ups because I had never really been around the cream of the crop of the FITA (Olympic-style) archers. As luck would have it, Olympic Gold Medal winner Darrell Pace was on the shooting line warming up, along with many others. I always keep my eyes and ears open when top echelon shooters are within range. While Darrell and the others were warming up, I noticed that they were placing golf tees in the ground at the tips of their toes. I knew that they were allowed to do this, but didn't understand the exact reasoning behind it. I soon found out that it wasn't only for how far apart their feet were spread (which is what I initially thought). What they were doing was, in essence, adjusting their "windage" by leaving the back foot alone and moving their front foot back and forth parallel to the shooting line. Once they were "centered up," then the tee (of their color) was placed in the ground at their spot on the shooting line. Then, for the next end, they simply stepped up to their spot on the shooting line, set their toes on those tees, and they had their exact foot positioning and could repeat it every time. These guys were not going to adjust their windage on their sights; they did it with body alignment via their shooting stance on the line! The guys were shooting 90 meters and were centering up consistently with their windage and simply moved the front foot to make this "adjustment." I also later found out that if they were shooting "strong," then they closed their stance, so that the extended push or pull they were giving would center them back up; if they were shooting "weak" that day, and then they opened it slightly, to move their body alignment accordingly. We are not talking inches here, fellow shooters; we are talking one quarter inch increments! At 90 meters it doesn't take a large stance adjustment to make a big difference down range.

By the end of that practice session, I realized several things, the most important item was that, finally, I fully understood why one of the very first things I learned about shooting field rounds was to "never move your feet" once you were comfortable. If you were having left/right troubles, the first thing to check was your stance. The same was driven into my head indoors, as well. Get that stance comfortable and never move those feet until you leave the shooting line. How many of you move your feet when you reach for your binoculars to gaze at your arrows after a shot? Uh, huh, I thought so. How many of you shoot very well one day, and then come in the next and you have to make a windage adjustment one way or the other? Yes, this is exactly what I expected and it isn't always the lighting difference from lane to lane indoors, this is an opportunity to put ProActive archery to work.

Keep this little history lesson in mind as we go through this procedure. You are about to embark on what I hope will be enlightening and also something to add to your "checklist" of things to consider when something has gone wrong and you are scrambling to figure out what it might be. Once again, you will have the knowledge and also a "tool" to use to make sure your form hasn't slipped and if it has, how to get it back without starting over.

Ascertaining Your Rough Shooting Stance or "Addressing the Target"

I am not going to take the time or space to address head positioning, posture, bow arm positioning, and the like; at least not directly. I'm going to operate on the premise that you have gotten your draw length down and already have the shoulder position, head alignment and those other aspects of the "T-form" pretty well mastered.

A very common simple method still used by many coaches today is: they have the shooter address the shooting line with their "normal" positioning and posture. The shooter points his/her bow down range level with the target and in line with it. Then, the shooter is instructed to draw back their bow, but as they are doing so, to turn their head back directly away from the target. They then come to full draw to the point they feel they would anchor. Then, they are instructed to turn their head back to the target and anchor, then to look down range and see if they are left or right of the target face they are supposed to be shooting. If they are pointed to the left of their target (right-handed shooter), they are asked to move their front foot forward keeping it parallel to the shooting line (close the stance) and repeat the process. (Some coaches have shooters move their entire bodies, if the alignment error is severe). They keep moving that front foot forward until they are no longer left of the target face or are roughly "centered up" on the same. If the shooter is pointing to the right, then they are instructed to open their stance by moving the front foot (or turn the body the other direction) backward keeping it parallel to the shooting line until they are roughly centered up on their own target.

This is a great starting point to at least establish a reasonable foot position for one's current draw length and bow balance and gets the body alignment pretty close to optimal to start with. However, if the shooter's draw length is too long (normally the case), most are going to end up with a "closed stance" and their feet nearly perpendicular with the shooting line. Some will even end up with an extreme closed stance to help the body align with the target due to over extending the bow arm to reach anchor! Of course, they will quickly learn when they have gone too far; they will slap their bow arm with the bowstring. Very few archers are initially set up with too short of a draw length. (I'm personally one of the few exceptions to this.) The most common occurrence is having the draw length set too long by ½″ to upwards of an inch! If this is the case, the coach should shorten the draw length of the bow before proceeding.

Subsequent to this "coarse" method of arriving at a shooting stance, the next step I've seen commonly used to tune the stance even closer is for the shooter to then make up a target that consists of five or more spots, either NFAA blue face, or Vegas spots set on a single sheet, but placed horizontally across the bale with little space horizontally between the spots. Remember that most shooting lanes indoors are 24″ to 30″ across, so you don't want the spread of those five spots any wider than that (3″ x

5 spots = 15″ across). The shooter then shoots multiple ends, each end using the same stance and shooting from left to right, right to left, and then mixing the shots up on which spot they are aiming at during that end. After five or six ends, the shooter then gets a pattern on each of those five spots, and further adjusts their stance to accommodate shooting at the extreme left or extreme right without having to move their feet. Small adjustments are made to the foot positioning until the pattern is centered up from one foot positioning all the way across those five spots. Yes, this is time consuming, and yes, I know you will say you see "pros" move their feet during an end. However, if you watch them closely, you will find that this movement, if any, is consistent and they are doing it the same every time and for reasons specific to their shot sequence.

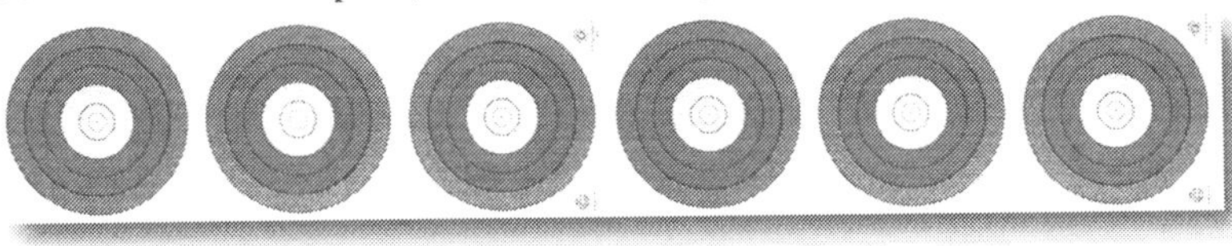

It is easy enough to take two FITA three-spot indoor targets and pin them up side by side, like this.

A Short Digression: "The Blind Bale" Technique

Have you ever found yourself in the position of shooting well during a practice session and the very next time you shoot, you are shooting left or right, sometimes by a lot? (You know that you have.) What many shooters normally do is to gripe that something has changed, which is entirely obvious. Much of the time, the shooter won't move his sight's aperture and continues to struggle with shooting to one side or the other, losing points and X-count and saying, "Well I gotta figure this out; it was good yesterday, so I'm not moving my sight." What they fail to realize is that this attitude is costing them points and X-count and by moving that sight, or making another adjustment (soon to be discussed), they can save the points and X's quickly and easily by using the whole "X-ring" rather than just one part of it!

I'm going to jump ahead for a brief moment, and then come back to the crux of this chapter: in the next chapter I will show you my "Blind Bale Technique" for learning your shot sequence and mastering your stance to an even finer degree. The Blind Bale Technique differs from ordinary "blank bale technique" in several ways, the major one being that you are shooting at a target for score. In addition, once you acquire the target and settle your sight, you then completely close both eyes and concentrate on finishing your shot process from target acquisition until you hear the impact of the arrow in the target. I don't want to get ahead of the game any further but, obviously, if you are shooting for score with your eyes closed, you must keep your alignment the same every single time. You must also have a means to "memorize" this positioning so it becomes automatic. I will also address later how you go about checking to make sure your stance and alignment haven't slipped back from the new to the old. Does this sound like ProActive archery at work once again? Absolutely! You should always be prepared for the inevitable.

The challenge to the above is to find out if you can indeed shoot a perfect "25" on an NFAA Five-spot target (or a perfect "30" on a Vegas Face) with your eyes closed. I'm not able to do it every time but, even with my intentional tremor, I can, and I have recorded many 25's by shooting the Blind Bale Technique while taking the visual cues out of the shot. It is so simple, even you can do it! The best I've ever done for a complete game, however, is 98 out of 100 with 15 X's. I have friends that have shot perfect 100 games, but none that I know of have ever shot 20X's for the game. Pretty impressive development of muscle memory and consistency, isn't it?

This technique does not allow you to think only of the feel of the release. Feeling the release is for the blank bale technique; but in my opinion, shooting by feeling the release when shooting for score means you are "thinking" release and you are not concentrating on the shot. Remember, you can only think of one thing at a time; if you are thinking release, you are not thinking about the shot and hitting the middle of the middle, correct (or more correctly, executing this shot with proper back tension)? The Blind Bale Technique allows you to concentrate on the entire shot sequence and memorize that full shot experience once you have acquired the target and settle the sight. After a short time doing this, you will begin to feel those nuances that creep into the shot as you run your sequence. You will also find that the direction of your misses "Blind Bale" are in the same direction that you tend to miss when you shoot with your eyes open, the big difference being that they are magnified, because all visual cues are taken out of the matrix. Your shot becomes an open book for you to read! But first, we need to get a base stance set and memorized before progressing to the Blind Bale Method. Digression ends here.

Fine Tuning Your Stance: Making a Template

So, how does one "fine tune" your shooting stance? This is easily done (assuming your draw length is reasonably close to what you should be shooting and your basics are pretty much automated and consistent). Part of this is also tuning the draw length to your stance; however, we have to start somewhere. We don't know if you need a draw length adjustment, foot position adjustments, or both.

1. You need a two foot square piece of butcher paper or poster paper. Color doesn't matter. I used white for my photos in order to get the contrast needed to show the markings.
2. Place the paper on the floor in the shooting lane you are going to use for the practice session and then tape it down (*see photo*). You will want to mark the position of the shooting line on this paper.
3. Next, take your "normal stance" on the paper, or at least what you think your 'normal stance' might be. Mark an outline around your shoes far enough around to make sure you establish your foot angles. Simply draw an outline from instep around the toe of your shoe to the other side at the instep (*see photos below*).

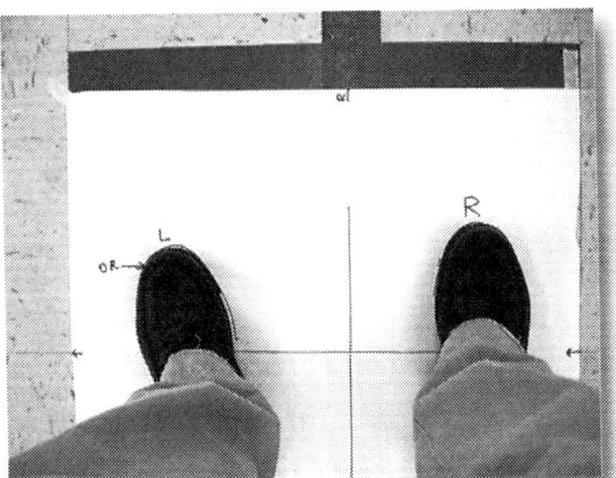

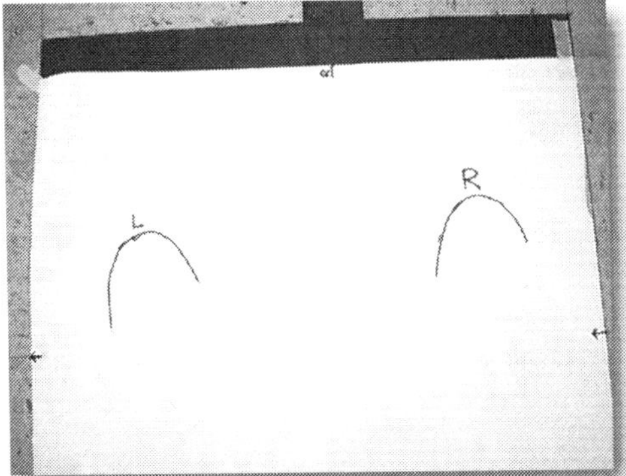

You now have a template to insure that your Stance remains constant for the upcoming steps. Without this, you cannot accomplish the goal of this series of exercises.

4. A little action and fun are in store for you now. Using this stance, you are now ready to "Blind Bale" it. The important things here are to keep your feet still and never adjust your sight's windage or elevation (that is a huge no-no). Only one variable at a time can be changed and the sight is not a variable to be tossed into this process at all.
   a. Put up a single spot target face.
   b. Take your stance (that you just marked on your paper). Do not change anything yet! Patience, grasshopper, patience!
   c. Draw an arrow back, anchor, acquire the target and settle the sight.
   d. Close both eyes completely and finish the shot sequence. Do not under any circumstances "punch off" or get rid of the shot as soon as your eyes are closed. If you do this, you are wasting your time and won't learn a thing. No cheating here. Shoot the entire shot sequence. I warn you that your first end's score is not going to be pretty, that is unless you are already a top echelon shooter and there are no guarantees for them either! I've seen 60X shooters who struggle with this for several ends, shooting 19's, 20's, or 21's! Talk about humility. In fact, one "60X shooter" upon trying this only scored 13 on his first end! It didn't take him long, however, to get that score up, and eventually shoot his first "25" with his eyes closed.
   e. Shoot several 5-arrow ends and score them. Also take pictures of each end you shoot. You need a photo record so that you can see what you are doing and review it. The following photo (*next page top left*) demonstrates an end of five arrows and subsequent impact points. It is followed by the marking of a new foot position on the placard and then shooting another end (this was made by an expert shooter, Jon Eide, from North Dakota).
5. You are now in a position that you should see a trend concerning your lefts and rights. Notice in the photos just below, that Jon is shooting high and right while shooting blind. (If you are down the middle nearly all the time, then you won't be changing your foot position.) You will continue on Blind Bale to get the total

shot sequence down so you can indeed shoot 25's quite often (not all the time, don't expect it). If you are not yet "centered up" with your lefts/rights then go to step 6. Most of you will be doing step 6 and onwards.

6. If most of your arrows (toss out the wild flyers if you have any) are going to the *left* and your toes are way past even (closed stance already), then either you are punching the release, or you are pushing way too hard with your bow arm, and/or the draw length is too long. Nearly all shooters do not go beyond or dead on perpendicular when they address the target. Do not move the back foot as part of this process. That back foot is your stance's "anchor" so to speak. Some coaches have you moving that back foot, but I've found that by moving both feet at once, it takes twice as long and the shooter also tends to widen his stance when doing that. It isn't necessary just yet, if at all. This can also result in creating other stance related problems. Thus, one step at a time.
7. Let's assume that you are not perpendicular to the shooting line with your feet when you address the target. Your stance is slightly open already. At this point, if you are shooting to the right (*see photos above*), you would "open your stance" slightly by moving only the front foot to the left about ¼″. Mark this new foot positioning in a color different from your original outline (*see below left*). You now

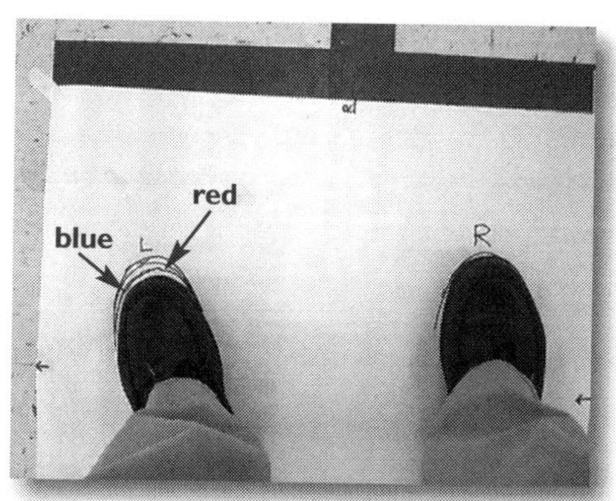

repeat the process of shooting several ends of "Blind Bale" scoring and taking photos once again. If still to the right, then you will move the front foot ¼" more and mark it again. Then repeat the process. We are fast forwarding to save space, but Jon's success, as indicated in the below right photo, was after his third foot movement. You can see that, indeed, Jon was now able to shoot a 25 with his eyes closed. And all he changed was his front foot position! The sight was not moved, and no adjustment to the bow was necessary. He has now "tuned his stance" to his draw length.

8. Once you are pretty much centered up with your lefts and rights, mark that final foot position again and label it so you know which foot position you are now using. As you are probably tired at this point, it would be a good idea to take up your placard with your foot positioning marked on it and call it a day. If you want to, however, you can further open your stance, marking each front foot position until you reach a point of negative return. At this point, your stance will become too open for your draw length. You will start shooting left and have wild shots. In addition, you will start to experience some left knee pain and a pain in your lower back as you try to struggle for the shot. You will know quickly you have exceeded your range of motion for that draw length and stance position. Mark that so that you know the limit (see photo at right).

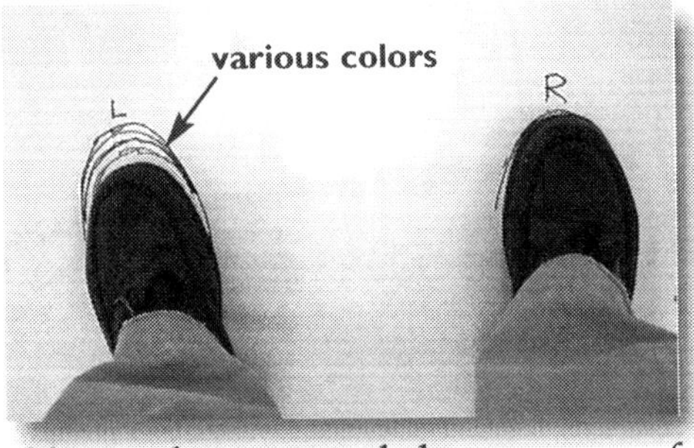

9. Each time you come to shoot for the next two to three weeks, you should put down the placard on the floor and then use the "new" foot position you established. Continue to do this until you have it "memorized" and you can pretty much duplicate this "new" foot positioning every time.
10. Start off the next several practice sessions by shooting a game of 20 arrows "Blind Bale," always using your placard. Then put up a regular target and go ahead and shoot for score. After all, this isn't all about shooting all your shots with your eyes closed. You need some real "eyes on" shooting practice too. You will find that the blind bale feeling will already be having a positive effect on your shot execution.
11. If you find yourself shooting highs and lows while Blind Baling, then Stance Width could be the culprit, but in my experience, it more likely is related to slight weight/balance issues with your stabilization system than stance width. However, if you are shooting slightly low, you can try widening your stance slightly; if you are shooting slightly high, then narrow up the stance width slightly, always maintaining the "open or closed" foot positioning and of course marking the template.

By Design

You may have noticed that I intentionally set my photos up to have the stance "opened" by moving the front foot to the left. This is by design. Remember at the beginning I said there has been a lot of talk about many top shooters opening up their stances? Remember I also mentioned that there was more to this than just opening up the stance for the sheer sake of emulating the pros?

As in everything else in archery, more isn't always better. If your draw length is already too long and you up and open your stance, you are going to make things worse. You can easily strain a muscle because you are already overextended and now you are trying to be over-overextended, then forcing your bow arm to the right to get it back over on target. You are going to shoot way left when you Blind Bale it! Doesn't take a rocket scientist to figure that one out now, does it?

What I am saying is this: if you want to open your stance, that is fine. However, in many, if not for most beginning to mid-level shooters, the draw length of their bow is going to have to be shortened some. In most cases, it won't be over ¼″, but in today's competitions in which you cannot afford to miss an X-ring, 1⁄16″ of draw length can mean the difference between an X and a normal run of the mill 5 or 10! In addition to this, if you are moving your feet around on the shooting line between shots, or you are unknowingly changing your foot positioning between practice session or ends, then you are costing yourself X's. You are not shooting one shot 60 times, but rather shooting a different shot after each foot movement.

ProActive Archery recommends you take things one step at a time. ProActive Archery says to always have a backup plan and a backup for each instance of when something goes wrong. By following the foot placard routine outlined above, you have a documented record of your original foot position. In addition you have your "new" foot position down on paper and can use it during your practice sessions.

Take note that in the example pictures, Jon Eide is a 60X shooter. My point with Jon was to let him see for himself what was happening to his shot and why his misses were nearly always high and right. By shooting Blind Bale, Jon's misses were magnified, and he was able to see just that. When I questioned Jon about his stance change and his ability to now shoot "25's" with his eyes closed after such a dismal start, Jon was quick to add that once he got rid of shooting to the right while blind; he simply had to place emphasis on shooting the shot and not using more muscle than necessary; in other words to relax, "let it float," and shoot the shot. He said he could feel those tendencies while shooting blind, and when it wasn't right, he stopped the shot sequence, let down, and started over. Does that sound familiar to you? If you can let-down shots that aren't "right" while shooting "Blind," then why won't you do it when the visual cues and the shot sequence are breaking down? Mind over matter, my friends. ProActive archery at work once again.

What about People Who Shoot with Glasses?

Few people who shoot with glasses realize the differences in the shapes of what you see when looking through the corner of the lens versus what things look like when you look through the center of the lens. Many shooters who wear glasses actually lose some vision because the edge of the lens and frame just so happen to be where they want to see the target/peep/scope alignment! Yes, special shooting glasses are available. You can also order a set of lenses and have them grind a "sweet spot" that is the same prescription that is in the center, but also ground in on the edges. I have two sets of those glasses and the larger sweet spot in the corner does the job, but not enough. The problem lies with the blamed edge of the lens and the resulting loss of target acquisition and distortion that causes misses because I'm not seeing where it really is, but rather the distortion makes me think it is there when it really is more to the right! Thus, my lefts and rights suffer. I was told by the person who did my custom lenses that without the enlarged sweet spot, if I was off in my head placement high, low, left, or right on that lens by even as much as 1⁄16″, that my impact point will change due to the distortion of my prisms on what I see and where it really is. He offered to build yet another larger sweet spot on my right lens which will give me room for error. He did suggest, however that I change my head position to avoid the edge of the lens because nothing can be done about the distortion and misrepresentation of the image next to the frame/lens juncture.

As we age, our eyes get weaker and, believe it or not, our body is shrinking as well. We aren't as flexible, so we can't draw the bow back as easily and we also can't get that younger person's shoulder and arm alignment at the same draw length we shot just a few years ago. Do you see where I'm going with this one? In come those glasses and now you need to change your head position to get away from the corners of that lens/frame and keep away from the distortion and parallax caused by this. How do you accommodate all this?

I'll bet that you've guessed it. You work on opening your stance and getting that draw length shortened to accommodate it, if necessary while shooting pain free and engaging fewer muscles than before! This is a case of needing to open the stance and also to shorten the draw length to accommodate body changes due to age, injury, or illness. Not only are you now accommodating a change in head position, but also the change you just made in your shoulder, arm, and body alignment. You cannot just open up your stance a bunch and keep that same old draw length. Be advised that you can carry this too far and end up with your drawing elbow out of line. This will create much too much muscle tension in your entire system, from your bow arm right across and on through your drawing arm and shoulder, so be very cautious about this adjustment! Once again, opening your stance very much will require you to retune your draw length to the opened stance in order to minimize the tension on your arms and shoulders. It is a balancing act, but once again, we aren't talking inches; we are talking very small increments. Sometimes, you can simply lengthen the D-loop by 1/8″ or so and this relieves the tension and keeps your "Blind Bale" centered up. (I've done this often rather than changing my bow.) Often, however, if you are already shooting a longer loop, it pays more rewards to shorten the draw length of the bow and leave your anchor point alone! You have to make that judgment and decision, but one or the other will have to be done in order for this rapid change to an open stance work to your benefit.

Summary

- We covered a little history about how FITA shooters used golf tees to mark their foot positions so that they could return to the exact same spot and that they "adjusted their windage by front foot positioning." We also discussed that once set on the line, a person should never move their feet unless they see they made a positioning error and know something is out of line.
- I discussed the rough addressing of the target used by some coaches and how this is a great starting point to get a person's body aligned so that they don't waver off their target and have to use more muscles to maintain target alignment. While very effective and a great starting point, this technique, in today's competitions isn't close or exacting enough, more refinement is needed.
- I then outlined how to document your "normal stance" in order to get it down on paper before making any decisions to change your stance. Then, we discussed details of the "Blind Bale Technique," the 10 steps to follow to find your correct blind shooting foot positions and how to document this on your foot placement placard. After this is established, you then practice for several weeks using this new foot positioning after having started each practice session with one game of Blind Bale shooting.
- I emphasized the fact that the draw length and your stance need to be matched to one another and that suddenly opening your stance without taking draw length into consideration can cause more problems than it can help.
- I discussed that, often, people who shoot with glasses have to open their stances to accommodate the glasses. This allows you to get your line of sight away from the edges of the lenses and frames, where there is severe distortion.

You are again reminded that "more is not always better" in archery. Also remember that what is right and working superbly for some shooters may not be the course of action that will work for you.

Thus, you can move to a bit more open stance and, if it is within the range of your given draw length, you might get by without strain developing in your lower back or your upper shoulders, arms, and forearms tightening, and some pain developing on the inside of that front knee. A "little" more open stance can work wonders, but only if your stance and draw length/anchor are in tune with that open stance. If they are out of tune with each other, you will neither be more accurate nor more consistent. In addition, you will never be able to shoot a "25" with your eyes closed; because you won't have the proper form for it.

You can't advance to the finer points of the Blind Bale technique until you have your stance tuned to your draw length and your draw length tuned to your stance. Your body and your results when shooting blind are going to tell you when you've done too much of a good/bad thing!

Making it to the winner's circle requires that the finer points of form and shot execution be mastered and automated. I have outlined yet another item of interest where the "What to Do" is discussed freely in the target archery community, but the "How to Do It" is completed ignored.

Tom Dorigatti

18

"Blind Bale" Practice for More Accurate Shooting

Can you shoot a "25" on the NFAA blue face at 15 or 20 yards . . . with your eyes closed?

It might not be as hard as you think or as easy as you think either. Have you often wondered why your misses tend to be in one particular area of the target face, either indoors or outdoors? Sure, we all have tendencies, but sometimes those small misses nag away at us until we get to thinking more about the small misses and end up messing things up to the point of frustration. We've all been there and had it happen over and over again. So, this chapter deals with a means of magnifying what is going on so you can solve and this nagging problem. I'm not telling you to intentionally miss big on purpose, quite the contrary. We begin by working through a real life story about a shooter who was having problems with small, slight misses in the 1 o'clock to 2 o'clock position on the target face. These misses were driving him nuts just trying to figure out what was going on. Cue the "Blind Bale Technique" to help resolve the problem.

While this may appear to be the same topic as Chapter 17, it really is an expansion of that discussion. You are going to see some of the photos from Chapter 17 again, only this time with a bit more explanation of what was going on as Jon Eide worked through the regimen . . . this time with a plan. (Having the photos right in front of you is easier on you than flipping back and forth among pages.)

This technique incorporates stance alignment (covered in the last chapter), the use of a target face (no blank bale here, folks), and complete integration of your entire shot sequence and not just one part of it. The notable exception is: you close your eyes completely after you have "centered up" on the bull's-eye. You then finish your shot by concentrating on the shot process and not the release aid or the feel of that item alone. This also incorporates, once you have established your baseline pattern, a means to more precisely align your stance, not to just the target, but to the bulls-eye or even the X-ring on that target. So cast your doubts aside, you may well be on your way to being able to say: "I can shoot a 25 on the NFAA face with my eyes closed," and then proceed to prove it. Heaven only knows, but you may acquire the expertise and muscle memory to be able to tell your friends that the NFAA blue face is so easy that "I can shoot a 25 with my eyes closed," and then take on bets and go out and prove you can indeed not only talk the talk, but also walk the walk. This can be fun as well as a great learning (earning?) experience.

Background

Blank bale technique has been around for a number of years. This technique has worked for many archers to resolve things ranging from target panic to shot sequence automation. There are many variants to blank bale technique and it can be adjusted to fit the needs of any given archer. Of course, the key element of blank bale techniques is the lack of a target face. I, for one, can "blank bale it" with the best of them. I can shoot hundreds of shots this way and execute nearly all of them smoothly and without a hitch. However, if I put a target face back up there and open my eyes, this becomes a different story and old problems soon raise their ugly heads again. Does this sound familiar?

A Story Involving a Bet About 25 years ago at an outdoor field tournament some of us were conversing over sodas when a top professional archer said how easy indoor 300 rounds were for him. He then made the statement: "It is so easy, that I can shoot a 25 with my eyes closed." I told him that I didn't think he could do this at 20 yards. He asked me if I was willing to bet him $20 or not. I took the bait and bet him the money, because I did not think it could be done. The rules were simple: He was to draw back the bow, anchor, settle his sight, close his eyes completely, and finish the shot; not by punching off the shot, but by completing his shot sequence. The rules were fair, since a person must be given the opportunity to line up first and then close their eyes. To make a long story short, this person not only shot a perfect "25" score on his very first end; he shot a 4X-25 with the other arrow just barely out of the X-ring.! He promptly collected my $20. I've never forgotten that or how well this person had his shot sequence and feel of his shot incorporated as "automated" items.

I definitely think that blank baling is fine and, within limits, very useful. Proper alignment of your stance is also essential, if not a vital key to consistency. Coaches have students shoot with their eyes closed all the time. But nobody I know of has integrated all of these together into a practice regimen with the added benefit of not just concentrating on the release, but concentrating on one's form and the completion of the shot process and using fine motor skills to accomplish it. My expectation is that if you are just blank baling, then you are probably concentrating on your release. If you are moving your body alignment, you are concentrating on your stance. If you are closing your eyes to shoot, you are back to concentrating on the release again and not paying attention to finishing the shot with your complete release sequence, bow arm maintenance, and followthrough. You might be thinking, "I have no reason to worry about impact point, so why concentrate on the finer motor skills and shot process?" I'm thinking, "Let's be ProActive and use a system that allows you to practice and learn muscle memory for the entire shot process from target acquisition right up through the followthrough," or as well-known professional archer Dean Pridgen says, "Followthrough, the last thing to happen, but the first thing to go."

Tom Dorigatti

Items Required

1. Single spot NFAA face or Single Spot Multi-color target face
2. Masking or electrical tape
3. Magic marker
4. Patience & willingness to accept some humility

The Blind Shooting Technique in Detail

Selection of the distance to begin this process is entirely up to you. I've worked with several people doing this and some were very comfortable with it at 10 yards, some wanted to do it at 15 yards, and others went to the full 20 yards. It is important that you use a single spot face, since we want to get your shot sequence, body alignment, and thought process all onto only one location and one bulls-eye, and also establish a definite pattern and have a "picture" of your accomplishment (the target face with 20 holes in it).

After you've selected your distance and put up your single spot face at about shoulder level on the target butt:

1. We are not concerned too much with body alignment at this stage of the procedure. You will be shooting arrows at a target from the very beginning. This is blind shooting, but at a target face.
2. You will be shooting a full end of five arrows each time, and shooting a full game of arrows (20 shots).
3. Keep score. There is nothing wrong with this. In fact, you will find this fun to see if you can break 90 or better for a full game (20 arrows).
4. Do not move your feet or your sight during this first 20 shot sequence. You are trying to establish a tendency pattern, much akin to group tuning your compound bow.
5. Address the target in your normal stance. Then, using masking tape, have a friend mark the positions of your feet in relation to the shooting line (or you can mark the tip of each foot). This is important so that you use the same foot positioning each time and repeat it for the four ends you are about to shoot.
6. Address the target like you always do. Draw back the bow and anchor as normal, then settle in to the bulls-eye and X-ring. Once settled in, quickly close your eyes completely and then continue your shot process, keeping your eyes completely closed. Do not punch off the shot. To do so won't accomplish your objectives. It is vital that you complete the shot just like you do with your eyes open. Don't worry where the shot ends up.
7. Shoot the full end of three or five arrows and go to the target and write down your score. Mentally note (or it is even better that you take photos) where the shots went. Again, do not move your sight or change your body alignment during these ends of arrows.
8. Finish the 20 shot game, writing down your score after each end and, preferably, take photos after each end. (They are worth their weight in gold.)
9. After completion of the 20 shots, you should now have a pretty good pattern of

what you are doing with regard to shot pattern and alignment. Now it is decision time before you repeat the process.

a. If you are shooting to the left, then when you address the target move your left foot (right handed shooter) to the right slightly. Mark this new toe position with another piece of tape. Leave the original tape where it was. How much depends upon how far left you are shooting. One half of an inch moves me from the middle of the 4-ring over to the bull's-eye at 20 yards.

b. If you are shooting to the right, then move your front foot to the left slightly and mark your new foot position with another piece of tape. Leave the original tape where it was.

10. Follow steps 6 & 7 above again, but for only one end. Score your arrows (and take a photo), and then come back to the shooting line. This time, however, if you aren't "centered" or went too far, realign your front foot to counter the trend (steps 9a & 9b above). Then shoot another end with the new foot alignment. Be sure you mark any changes with new tapes at the tips of your toes.

Once you are centered up for a couple of ends, you should be finding your scores going up for each end and your groups tightening up. You will soon discover that by concentrating on the shot process and not just the release, you can indeed shoot 25's with your eyes closed. It is that easy . . . but your technique has really got to be "spot on" (pun intended) in order for you to accomplish this with any kind of consistency. You will find after doing this exercise that your shot technique is improved and you most likely will have fun doing it. Then you can challenge your friends to a bit of a wager as well.

Pictorial Results

The photos below are from the first "game" of 20 shots that a "student" of mine, Jon Eide, from North Dakota agreed to try using the "Blind Shooting Technique." He chose a distance of 15 yards for his first game of blind shooting. He did not adjust his foot positioning for the first game of 20 arrows. Jon is a very solid shooter and has won national titles and set state records for many years. He won second place at the NFAA Indoor Nationals in the AMFS class. Jon also placed ninth at the Iowa Pro-Am, sixth at Vegas, and in 2006, he was ninth at the NFAA Outdoor Championships (AMFS). In addition to all this, in his home state of North Dakota, Jon set new state records at the State Indoor, the State 900 round and the State Field tournament in 2007. Jon is also a student of the "Shot Timing Technique" that I previously published in *Archery Focus* magazine and will cover later on in this book.

Notice during this first end that Jon was a bit unsettled. His shots were mostly to the

right during this end of shooting. He got a dose of humility by shooting a "19" (*see photo previous page*).

For the second end (*see above left photo*), Jon improved some, but he had one arrow impact away from the right side group: score 21, 1X.

The third end (*above right*) shows some dramatic improvement. Jon shot a 25 with three Xs with his eyes closed! He's obviously getting somewhere.

The fourth and final end for Jon was another 25 with two Xs; but look at the tendencies (*see photo below left*).

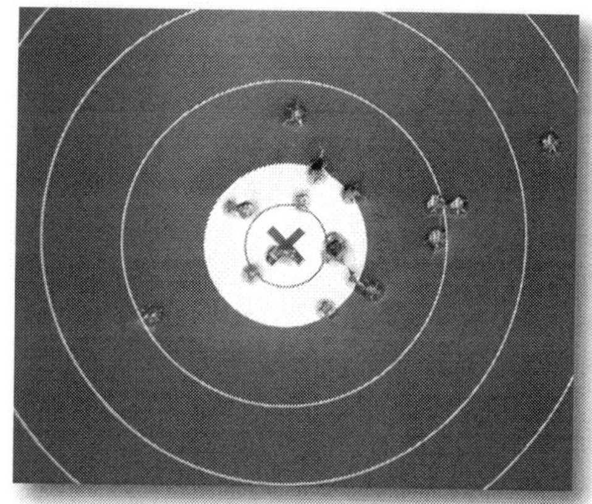

Jon's pattern definitely shows a tendency to shoot to the right when he is shooting "Blind" (*see photo above right*). What is more interesting, is that in speaking with Jon prior to introducing him to this practice regimen, he has had problems with his misses of the X-ring indoors or the bull's-eye outdoors being to the right most of the time.

An Added Recommendation

Once you have established that your alignment is correct and you are shooting pretty much down the middle with your eyes closed, it is a good idea to make yourself a placard or cardboard template of your foot positions for use during your practice sessions. Blind Bale practice can be habit forming; I've found that most of the people I introduce this to end up enjoying this challenge and will use it quite often. Just like the FITA shooters using. golf tees to mark their foot positioning on the shooting line I described in Chapter 17, you can use the template of your foot positions so that you eventually memorize your correct footing. This is yet another muscle memory training task and getting it right will take some repetition and conscious effort on your part. Once learned, you can keep your template on hand to check yourself once in awhile repeating the "Blind Shooting Technique."

Another Success Story

Another friend of mine, Nate Ulrey, also tried the Blind Bale Technique. Nate, just like Jon, started out with a dose of humility and he was also victimized by a mid-level shooter when both of them were working on this for their very first time. This is a funny story, and I hope Nate doesn't mind me telling it to you. Earl Raymond had been working on his game for quite some time. I wanted Earl to give the old college try to the Blind Bale Technique so he could see and feel exactly what I was speaking about. Nate was listening in and he also wanted to try it. So, we put up single spot faces and got onto the shooting line at 20 yards. Well, what happened next really shocked me. The first end, Earl scored a 21, while Nate scored a 19. The very next end, to my amazement and to Nate's shock, Earl scored a 25, while Nate only gets a 21. This was the first time I'd ever seen anyone new to this score a 25 on their second end of trying it! That gave Earl an added boost in confidence that he was indeed doing things really well, and provided Nate with the motivation that if "Earl can do it, then I know I can do it." Several weeks later, Nate contacted me giving me the bad news and the good news. The bad news was that Nate had to quit doing this on a single spot face because he was ruining arrows due to groups being too tight. The good news was that he was now shooting more 60X rounds than ever, with more "inside outs" and that he was able to shoot 25's with his eyes closed even on 5-spot faces! Obviously, he was following the rules of setting up the shot visually and then properly finishing his shot execution. Fortunately for me, this time around, I did not bet either of these guys $20 that they couldn't shoot a 25 on an NFAA 5-spot with their eyes closed!

Summary

I have used this technique with much success with several shooters, including myself. My particular tendency is to shoot high and to the left. I corrected the left problem by moving my front foot to the right. I can and do shoot 25's at twenty yards while shooting with my eyes closed. I've even had some shooters shoot a 25 their first time trying this; but they are the exception; most shoot in the high "teens" on their first end of blind shooting. In nearly all cases, however, only a minor adjustment to their stance was needed and they discovered that the "tendencies" of a particular miss pattern were reduced after the adjustment. High and low adjustments can be made by narrowing or widening how far apart your feet are, but most shooters are not having that problem unless they are punching off the shot. None of the shooters I've used this technique with required a draw length adjustment due to their stance becoming way too "open" or too "closed" so as to be impractical or uncomfortable.

One final note of importance here is a quote from Jon after having shot his first "blind shooting" game at 15 yards: "I found when I first started shooting with this technique I was thinking way too much about the shot and hold with my eyes closed. As I continued on I found that I needed to acquire the target and shoot the sucker . . . not really rush it, but get the arrow out of the bow."

How many times have you read or heard that from coaches, top shooters, or even said to yourself: "Shoot the shot" or "take the shot"? I know for a fact that I hear this all the time and say it under my breath when I hold too long and don't let down. This is not punching a shot, it is "taking" the shot; and the longer you hold, the worse it becomes. The shot sequence breaks down, your concentration goes from one thing to another. Then your muscles fatigue and tighten up, and about the time you hit a limit, the shot goes off and you tell yourself, "Dang, I should have let that shot down."

This practice regimen, when applied correctly and with vigor, will teach you how to focus; but not just on your release (for which blank bale technique is useful), or on the stance (for which the body alignment technique works), but rather on the entire shot sequence from target acquisition all the way until the arrow is in the target. This technique gives you a "magnifying glass" into what is really going on during your shot sequence. Without your vision to correct the slight errors you are making, you don't really know for sure what small thing(s) you are doing that are resulting in those slight misses. Using this technique, it won't be long at all until you will be able to "feel" what your shot is like. We can have an uncanny sense of muscle memory and feel as a result of numerous repetitions of the same motions or set of circumstances; our shot becomes second nature to us and, in archery that is exactly what we are striving for. Using this technique you will be able to "feel" and know even a slight difference in your shot. You will know in advance whether the shot went high, low, left, or right by feel. Yet you will be doing this with your eyes closed! You will be well on your way to mastering your shot sequence like you never imagined you could. Yes, you can shoot a 25 (or 30 on the multi-color face) with your eyes closed, and do it consistently. Shooting a perfect 100 game is achievable, but is a perfect 300 round shot with your eyes closed possible? That might be stretching things a bit too far; but try it, you never know.

Tom Dorigatti

19

So You *Think* You Are Right-Handed?

Have you hit a plateau in your scores and don't seem to be getting any better no matter what you try or do to improve? Do you have problems seeing double and even using an eye patch or double vision blocker doesn't work out well for you? Do you have tremors in your bow arm or bow hand that disrupt your aiming and slow down your shot sequence, thus resulting in frustration and comments from your fellow shooters about the "shake?" Have you contemplated undertaking the change over from right-handed to left-handed shooting or vice-versa? If you answered "yes" to any of these questions, then these next few chapters are for you. Even if you aren't contemplating the "big change," there will be things in these chapters that may well help you break though the "peaked out" syndrome, helping you to improve your scores without shooting from the other side of the bow.

For the next few chapters, I am going to switch gears and address something many shooters contemplate but few are brave enough to try. You will likely suspect from the title of this chapter what this change in the flow of this book is all about, since when it comes to which side of the bow you should shoot on, the advice is "always go with your master eye dominance." While it is generally accepted that this is the way to go, many archers, including some of the top professionals, have been extremely successful in doing just the opposite, opting rather to go with another principle: "the strong arm should be used as the bow arm." This particular subject is something I've personally gone through, not once, but three times. I'm left-eye dominant and very dominantly left-handed, so I can strongly relate to this switching gears thing. Before we begin to dissect this changeover, I need to relate my first personal experience in dealing with the change from one side of the bow to the other after having shot left-handed for nearly 25 years.

What Led to the Change

In the mid 1980's, I had reached a plateau in my shooting and could not improve my scores above the mid 520's on field or hunter rounds. I was shooting in the 54-56X range on the NFAA 300 round, with my best ever being 58X. Basically I was in a rut and had been for several years. I was not competitive enough to win any major events beyond the local or state levels. I had placed second in a couple of NFAA Sectional shoots, but always seemed to come up short. I had certainly won my share of tournaments, but while I was consistent, I was far from being competitive at the next level. I had joined the Pro Division in Iowa in hopes of that helping me to break through to the next level, and while it did move me up a notch or two; it wasn't the breakaway I was looking for.

Then, in 1984, I was at the NFAA Midwest Sectionals in Waverly, Iowa that would end up changing my archery career forever. I was also the tournament chairperson for this event, so not only did I have my hands full from shooting, I also had them full with administrative tasks involved with managing the tournament. I was afforded (or should I say rewarded by request?) the honor and privilege of shooting with one of the finest and most knowledgeable field shooters of that era (and even today, he still holds his own on any field course or indoor venue), Dean Pridgen. Dean was in my shooting group for both days of the event and watched me shoot arrow after arrow just barely out to the left. I wasn't missing very far, but hey, a 4 is still a 4 be it ⅛″ out or an inch out. I was having a tough time of it shooting 4's and not knowing why. About two-thirds of the way through the Sunday hunter round, I remember Dean making the comment, "Tom, if you could see yourself doing what you are doing, you would stop it in an instant." Nobody had ever offered up anything in the sort of any kind of help with regard to my constant left misses, so this caught me by surprise, since the last person I would ever suspect to do this would be a top professional archer. I asked him what it was, and he told me that it was best to keep shooting, finish the day, and that we would discuss it later. He told me to just focus on trying to hit the middle, "let it float, and shoot the shot" and that was all he said.

At the end of the day, we were sitting around talking and I asked Dean what he had meant with his comment. He asked me what it was I thought I was doing that may not be right. I told him that I thought I was losing back tension. He then told me that if he had as good of back tension I had on every shot, he himself would be working a lot less and probably would never miss a shot. I thought this strange, since he had shot over 555 on both days! He then proceeded to tell me to quit "sagging the bow arm" or, as we say today, bending the bow arm by amounts varying from shot to shot). He also said that if by working on this I couldn't get it going after 45-60 days, then to consider changing over from left-handed to right-handed shooting and just go for it. I told Dean exactly what most of you are thinking as you read this, "But I'm dominant left-eyed and way dominant left-handed. Everything I do is done left-handed." Dean then told me that, in his opinion, lots of shooters should be shooting the opposite side of the bow because as he then put it, "The strong arm, in my opinion, should be the bow arm and most people have overdevelopment of their dominant side, so should use that to their advantage." He went on to tell me that he isn't really left-handed, but his strong arm is his bow arm and he went with the flow of that instead of worrying about the dominant eye side. I had noted that Dean's bow-arm was rock solid and that nothing moved. He could drive an arrow up into the upper leg of the X, or to the lower right leg of the X, or could plant it in the center of the X, and all by how he managed his back tension and bow arm control! I worked on that sagging bow arm diligently for nearly five months, and wasn't really achieving much success at all with moving my scores up; the misses on the left side got smaller, but they were still sporadic and inconsistent, and lots of times I didn't know what to expect on even some darned good shots.

In thinking about this over the years, and especially shortly after I made the decision to switch over a few months later, I realize that Dean was absolutely correct in his assessment. I am, or at least was, way stronger from the left side than from the right. I was, at the time also playing tournament racquetball left-handed, which added to the strength of my left side; not only of my arms, but my legs and left shoulder as well. So, finally, after hunting season was completed for the year, I made the leap on March 15, 1985.

How I Accomplished the Change

So, for those of you who have considered changing over, let me outline what I did in order to insure that the changeover would be effective. Before going any farther, a word of caution is in order: this is what worked for me at that time and also for several other shooters I've helped through "the change." This approach may not work for everyone, but there are certain essentials that I strongly feel you must accomplish in order to make the switch permanent and effective and to maximize your success; namely:

- Remove any possible bailout of "if this doesn't work, I'll simply go back to left (or right) handed" by selling off or trading in everything related to left-handed (or right-handed) shooting, including even your quiver. In my case at the time, it involved selling off all five of my left-handed compound bows and purchasing two new right-handed bows.
- If you are indecisive concerning your release aid, then pick a completely new release aid and get rid of the ones you used to shoot (other than those of sentimental value), and start completely new. I think a totally unfamiliar, fresh start is the way to go.
- Make a complete separation in your body and mind of what you used to do. This is a completely new ball game, and things are going to have to change; so, out with the old and in with the new.
- Make a total commitment to the new regimen. That is why the other equipment had to be disposed of—you want to leave yourself no means of going back to the old ways. Now, I might add that with nearly all of today's bows, you can shoot a right-handed bow left-handed or a left handed bow right-handed! There is an exception here, however, and that is the "Tec-Risered" Hoyt bows. Those are next to impossible to shoot "wrong-handed" because the bridge gets in the way of your wrist. Most any other bow, however will work out just fine, and often times, you won't even have to move your sight or tune much, if any at all. Obviously, if you want to make that commitment, you really need to get rid of the old and go in with the new, but you can start the change process while you are waiting for the new bow(s) to arrive.

- Be prepared for surprises, and take them as they come. In my case back then, the surprises were few, but very obvious, eye-opening, and memorable.
- Get ready to work from square one and be prepared for a bit of humility, but this humility isn't going to last long—if you have and maintain the proper positive attitude. The words "I can't" should be removed from your vocabulary. Actually, I try to coach my students that negative connotations such as "I can't" aren't really acceptable and to change it to, "I'll give it a try."
- Don't get frustrated if this doesn't work in a day, or a week; it will come around and likely faster than you would have thought it would. Anyone can learn to do this if they simply get their head into the game and stick with it.

After selling all my left-handed bows and getting rid of all my releases (excepting my two original Stanislawski releases and home-made rope-spike releases out of sentimentality), I selected a pair of Dean Pridgen Fail-Safe II release aids, with pinky trigger, and while I don't shoot these release aids today, I still have both of them. I then ordered two Astro Regency compound bows, both right-handed. However, I wasn't prepared for what happened next. The hardest part of the transition for me was the simple task of transferring the arrow from the quiver and loading it onto the bowstring! The first night out, for every arrow I successfully transferred from the quiver to the bow string, I probably dropped between five and ten onto the floor. It got to be so funny that even I started laughing about it. Hey, this was already more fun than I had had in months. I was swimming all over the bullseye with my aperture but, hey, even that was better than I had anticipated it would be. The first night, I was hitting the bull's-eye more often than not, so things were good. Why was I hitting so many bull's-eyes right out of the gate? I was relaxed and not bent on forcing the issue (letting it float and shooting the shot). So, I shot about 90 arrows every night, and every night I was getting more settled. I learned to transfer arrows from quiver to string and that, too, got better every night.

One week later, I decided to try my first scoring round on the NFAA Blue Face right-handed. I simply shot my game, without high expectations (sound like a plan?) and didn't push it. Seven days after making this complete transition, my first score was a 297. I had been struggling with doing that left-handed for years! Sure I had shot many perfect 300's, but each of those was way more difficult than this 297 on my first try right-handed! The very next night, I had a 299, missing early in the round, and was in the low 50's on X-count. We had our first outdoor tournament, an International Round, coming up that weekend, so I had to get sighted in at least through 65 yards. I got my sight settings and checked them over many times, but weather prevented me from getting a scoring round in, so I didn't know how I'd fare in Sunday's event. I sure wasn't going in with high expectations. (Does this sound like something maybe you should incorporate in your day to day shooting?)

Come that following Sunday, only 13 days after the changeover, I went to that outdoor shoot and shot a lifetime personal best of 291 on the International Round. Nobody was told I had switched over and nobody even noticed. They were all just commenting on what an improvement they were seeing in my groups and consistency. Needless to say, I was on cloud nine, this thing had been so easy that it was ridiculous. Finally, much to my chagrin, a friend of mine opened up and spilled the beans and said, "Yep, and Tom did all this right-handed, too." People were shocked that anyone could basically start from scratch and do this well in less than two weeks time. After that Sunday, I never looked back for nearly 17 years. I shot all of my lifetime personal best scores while shooting the bow right-handed – 557 Hunter, 556 field, numerous 60X-300s on the NFAA Blue Face, numerous perfect Vegas 450 rounds (all with small arrows), 891 on the American 900 round, and of course numerous perfect Vegas 300 and 600 rounds. These were all things I had never and probably would never have accomplished while shooting left-handed.

I'll discuss my current state of affairs in a subsequent chapter, but first, I feel that it is extremely important to relate several behind the scenes things that I came up with to get the most of what I had.

Eye Dominance I am very left-eye dominant, so I had to learn to close my left eye so that I could acquire the correct target face. Shooting right-handed, I still must close my left eye to this very day. In addition, in all the years of shooting right-handed, I never once lost points because of shooting the wrong target face. Yet, while shooting left-handed, I had done this several times over the years. For 3-D I obviously use both eyes to acquire the distance, but after that, I don't find the loss of depth perception to be a detriment. One thing is for sure: on a 3-D course it is next to impossible to shoot the wrong target anyways, since most all the time, there is only one sitting out there for you to shoot at! Some people will be able to train themselves to overcome their eye dominance and learn to shoot with both eyes open, even after they changeover. I have been unable to do this, so I just close my left eye while aiming. I tried eye patches, eye shields, and tape over the lens of my glasses; you name it, I tried it; but closing my left eye was the only thing that worked and allowed me to not feel claustrophobic or impeded while shooting.

A Possibly Contradictory but Informative Anecdote I did have one problem that occurred twice while hunting that very first year, however. On opening day, a very nice buck came in and I decided to go ahead and take him. He offered me up a quartering away shot at about 15 yards. I pulled back the bow, anchored, and . . . no peep sight. I could see nothing thru the peep. So, rather than take the risk of a wound, maim, or miss, I let down and the deer went by the wayside. What the heck? I pulled back the bow, and the peep alignment was just fine. About an hour later and even larger buck came down the same trail and once again, I was offered up another quartering away shot at about the same distance. I drew back, anchored, and . . . no peep sight again. I let down again and this deer too went by the way side. I let him get clear, looked around to make sure nothing was around and drew back the bow, and things were peachy keen. It then hit me what had happened. You got it! The "buck fever" and excitement had put me back into my comfort and habit zone, and I had gone back to my left eye being open and the right eye (the peep sight eye) being shut! No wonder I couldn't see thru the peep; my right eye was closed and I was doing the aiming with my left eye. At least I didn't take the shot and wound or maim the deer. At that distance it would not have been a killing shot, and I likely would have made a terrible hit on the animal. I still laugh about it to this day, but that mistake never happened again, because it was such a well-learned lesson about eyes and eye dominance and, in addition to that, how under pressure we fall back to the old way of doing things, most times without even consciously thinking about it. This is a clear demonstration of the power of the sub-conscious mind. Keep this in mind when or if you decide to make the switch, or if you even make any changes in your shot sequence: Under pressure you will, if not well-versed and practiced, fall back into the same old habit you thought you had just broken. If you are aware of this, and are ProActive, then you will likely pick up on it quickly and not have it spoil your entire round.

Solid Bow Arm Since my stronger arm was now my bow arm, it was easy to concentrate on a solid, but relaxed bow arm and to keep things as static as possible until the arrow was into the target. I had previously had a "sagging bow arm" which was a habit I couldn't break. This time, I had learned the bow arm thing completely anew, so new that I wasn't about to get into that rut again. I didn't have a bad habit to break so I started out by doing it correctly from the very beginning. In my opinion, Dean is 100% correct in saying that the bow arm is the key to a lot of what is ailing you. It is simply amazing what you can get away with if you have a solid bow arm and followthrough. I remember Dean's saying, "Followthrough—the last thing to happen, but the first thing to go." I know I have quoted him once already say this, but you'll see repeated again because I feel it is that important.

Personal Confidence I think that confidence is the key to more of this than most would like to admit. I have learned (but often times don't practice), that you don't necessarily have to be the most talented shooter on the course to win or to make a podium finish. You don't have to shoot a fast bow, or the fattest arrows you can find, or the heaviest poundage in order to shoot top level scores. However, personal confidence is worth its weight in gold. One other thing Dean had told me, during those two days way back when, "If you step up to the stake (line) with any doubt, if you are at full draw and think the word "miss" or have a doubt, if you sway in concentration, you must learn to let that shot down and start completely over. If you don't have full confidence that you can put that shot in the middle, then let it down and start over." This is positive and great advice from a great shooter. One big problem with all of us and what separates us from those on the podium is our confidence and, of course, getting it right nearly 100% of the time and if it isn't right, then letting it down and starting over. How many times have you known that a shot wasn't right and went ahead with that poor sequence and had a bad result? Uh huh, I thought so. Sure, once in a while, we get away with a bad shot and end up with a good result; that happens. However, if you keep going along with those knowingly bad shots and keep expecting good results, you are only fooling yourself. The quickest way to destroy your confidence is to take bad shots expecting good results or practicing bad habits. Either way you look at it, once your confidence is gone, you are in deep trouble. Sometimes keeping things positive is extremely difficult for one to do, but you should strive to find something positive to come out of every tournament or every practice session. It could be something as simple as an inside out 25 (without touching the blue) on an end during a scoring session where your total score was terrible. It could be that 19 or 20 you shot on a 40 yarder during a bad field round. Always find something positive to put down in your journal and to come away from a practice or scoring round with. If you constantly dwell on negatives, then you will become a negative shooter and slide downhill in a hurry. I know. I've been there and I would imagine many of you have been there as well!

Training Regimen and Database While working on my game right-handed, I did develop a training regimen and even a database for determining what my personal shot timing was, but that will be covered later in this book. Everyone has a personal rhythm and what one shooter's rhythm is will probably not work for the next shooter. You should never try to use somebody else's rhythm based upon how well you perceive they are shooting; just because they shoot quickly or they take 11-12 seconds doesn't mean that it will work for you; so don't get yourself caught up in that trap; it can destroy your archery. You will have to shoot your game and not somebody else's and that includes not allowing a "fast line" or fast group of shooters to influence how you conduct your game. Making a change in your rhythm at a tournament is as bad as changing a form element during a scoring round or moving something on your bow; in fact, it may even be worse. What I found for me and for most all of the students I work with is that there is a window of opportunity where, if the shot breaks within the window, you will not likely miss the X-ring. When I was at the top of my game, I had taught myself to shoot 96% or better of the shots within that envelope of opportunity, the result being the winning scores I was shooting and the brimming confidence in my ability that made all the difference in the world. This was acquired and learned from my own sequence and not somebody else's – you are your own key to your own success. This will be discussed further in a later chapter.

Summary

So, you think you are right- (or left-) handed do you? If you are in a rut, if you have reached a certain level and cannot get better, if you have lost your confidence in the way you now shoot, then consider a changeover from one side of the bow to the other. I and many other shooters have been successful with a switch over from one side of the bow to the other and never looked back. All it takes is a positive attitude, a full separation from the old way and commitment to the new, and a little time and effort. I did it in only 10 days. I know a few others who have done it in even less time. You do not have to shoot on your dominant eye side to excel in this sport, but you do have to shoot with confidence and a strong, steady bow arm to get the most out of what talent you have. You also need to do everything you can to maintain a positive self-image and attitude. Nothing can be worse than a lack of confidence or negativity with regard to how you view yourself. This one has let me down many times, and is costing me dearly (I'll discuss this later, when we fast forward). I've personally been at both extremes. One thing I know for certain is that this sport is very easy when you do have confidence and just let things happen; but if you don't and you are shooting poorly and are trying to force things, then you end up working ten times harder to shoot a poor score than you ever will during the shooting of a 550+ field score or even a 55+X 300 round. Relax and let the force be with you on the side of the bow you choose—you aren't as "handed" as you might think.

Tom Dorigatti

20

Switching Bow Hands—Preparing for the Change

When it comes to which side of the bow we should shoot on we often hear, "Always go with your master eye dominance to determine which side of the bow you should be on." While it is generally accepted that this is "the way to go," many archers including some of the top professionals have been extremely successful in doing much the opposite, opting rather to go with another principle, "your strong arm should be used as your bow arm."

In this chapter, I will discuss in more detail the mental preparation necessary to begin the transition to the other side of the bow. I hear so many say, "Tom, I could never make the switch to the other side of the bow; it would be impossible for me to even try."

And, while I don't assume you have read the previous chapter, this will be much easier if you read Chapter 19 first.

Some More recent History (Around 2004)

So, in the previous chapter I detailed my experience changing from left-handed shooting to right-handed way back in 1984. It is time to "fast forward" from 1984 up to about 2004 and on from there.

All of Chapter 19 was true at the time as of my writing it in a magazine article in 2004 and, actually, most of it still holds true today. However, things in life are in a constant state of change or flux, so . . . nearly everything from this point forward I have written mostly in the first person because it relates my direct personal experience as someone who has done this changeover both ways; from left to right first and from right back to left. I've experienced all of the hardships and stumbling blocks described firsthand. My methods may not be 100% correct for everyone, but they are working for me and they are, at present, still a Work in Progress.

I had open heart surgery in 2000. My "neurological reaction" to the heart-lung machine was the development of what is called an "intentional tremor" that affects my left (dominant) hand. Any slight amount of pressure on my left hand, or if I get stressed or excited at all, that hand is nearly uncontrollable from shaking. There are times that I cannot even write my own name with that hand because it is so shaky.

Stapling papers is a chore and those staples could end up anywhere on the paper! If you translate this into trying to shoot a bow right-handed, where my left hand is my bow hand, you can well imagine what happened to my sight picture while I was trying to shoot! I fought this for almost 10 years, before it became a matter of either switching back to left-handed shooting or quitting the sport forever.

After all, I was the guy on the line at Vegas a few years back (my last competitive event, by the way) about whom a couple of people said, "Good grief, look at that guy shake! He's shaking so bad they'd better get him off the shooting line before he hurts somebody."

So, finally in December of 2009 I took the plunge and made the commitment to switch back to shooting left-handed. My assumption was that since going from left to right back in the 1980's had only taken a couple of weeks, then going back to left-handed should be like falling off a log. I mean, good heavens, I'm left-eye dominant and my right hand would now be the bow-hand, so the shaking should stop and I'll be back up to shooting 300 indoor rounds in no time. Best of both worlds, correct? Do you see the huge mistake I was making? If you don't re-read above and it stands out like a sore thumb: High Expectations! I violated my own rule, didn't I?

What better person to tell you the facts about making the switch to the other side of the bow than someone who has made this switch both from left to right and then again from right to left? What better person to advise you on how to prepare yourself philosophically and mentally to set up for this change? What better person to tell you about how to make the change in a step by step fashion in order to help you avoid pitfalls that will trip you up and make you want to give up on the whole idea, if not archery entirely?

It Starts in Your Mind, Not Your Hands

I've come up with an acronym to help you deal with setting up your new shooting philosophy and mental attitude. Making such a major switch provides you an opportunity to really start fresh. With the right philosophy and mental attitude, you are about to embark on something startling and very satisfying, albeit frustrating from time to time. I have dubbed this the "E-PETCARE" acronym.

E-PETCARE stands for:

Establish a new frame of mind leading to a new . . .
Philosophy about your archery by . . .
Establishing new and realistic goals that are reinforced by . . .
Telling yourself there is no going back to the old ways of doing things, and that you can do this by making a . . .
Commitment to yourself and to this hobby to . . .
Aggressively practice, by working on one thing at a time, in a planned and organized fashion and . . .
Refining your technique, one step at a time while at the same time . . .
Evaluating your performance versus your goals each step of the way.

Sounds complicated, but it is simple enough that, to quote a popular series of television commercials, "Even a caveman can do it." You are going to have fun on the way to accepting this new challenge and opportunity to continue your archery career! Archers are a breed that seems to be able to accept humility (at least most of us anyways or we would have quit long ago) and definitely are willing to accept new challenges. Why else would so many of us stand on a shooting line and shoot arrow after arrow knowing full well that sooner or later we are going to miss? All of us "miss" sooner rather than later, so accept it!

Setting up E-PETCARE

Establish a new frame of mind. Creating a new frame of mind is simple: you aren't going to be shooting 300's right out of the box, so accept it. Your sight's aperture is not going to sit dead on the middle at the beginning, so accept it. You aren't going to necessarily have an easy time even loading arrows onto your bowstring for awhile, so accept it. So what if you drop arrows on the floor? It is something to chuckle about; it will improve if you don't let it get to you.

And Now I Backtrack I said earlier, in the previous Chapter, "Get rid of anything and everything associated with the side you've been shooting on. In my case, that was to rid myself of all five of my left-handed compound bows." Uh, not so fast on this one my friends. This is something you will be very pleased to know! Back in the 1980's the arrow rest selections weren't wide open like they are today, thus it was difficult to try to shoot a left-handed bow right handed because of difficulties getting the arrow to stay on the rest, and also the difference in cutouts on the bow risers.

Fast forward to 2010. We now have drop-away arrow rests and launcher blade arrow rests. The bows are cut-out deeper past center, and the grips aren't as radical as in the 1980's. When I made the switch in December 2009 I had several right handed-bows, one of which was a "shoot-through" model. So, because of my past thinking processes and while waiting on my left-handed model to arrive, I opted to abandon my preferred model, a Merlin Excalibur, and selected the shoot through model to set up and shoot "off-handed." The bow shot superbly, and I found that I could also switch over back to right-handed (all of the time shaking like crazy, that is), and still hit the bull's-eye! (Yes, I really do keep hoping to be able to go back, but it isn't happening!) Finally about two weeks into this, a friend asked me why I wasn't shooting my right-handed Merlin Excalibur left-handed. I told him that I didn't think I could because the cable guard was in the way and the grip was wrong. He asked if I'd even tried it. I said that I hadn't. He told me he knew a couple of people who were shooting right handed bows left-handed and shooting 300's indoors, and into the 540's outdoors without incident. I had nothing to lose, so I took out the Excalibur and started shooting it left-handed. The bow was still "sighted in" for right-handed shooting, by the way. I used the same arrows the bow was set up and sighted in for, and to my surprise, my first shots went right into the bull's-eye, with literally no change in impact point!

A Personal Note Of course you will remember what I said earlier on concerning the huge difference in draw length between shooting right- and left-handed? I didn't know this in 2009, so for a long, long time, I was struggling by trying to shoot the same draw length left-handed that I was shooting right-handed (and which is way too short).

This was sweet, my friends. I had wasted two weeks of good time shooting a different bow brand and didn't have to. I can shoot the Merlin Excalibur either right- or left-handed and don't even have to touch the sight! I've since allowed right-handed people to shoot my left-handed bow right-handed, and they, too, have no change in left/right impact point. If they use my peep sight and arrows, they will hit the bull's-eye. I've since tried other brands of bows shooting them wrong-handed and they too shoot just fine. A Cautionary Note This does not work well at all with the Tec Riser bows, made by Hoyt. The bridge on the riser gets in the way, and it hits and puts pressure on your wrist. I do not recommend you try to shoot a Tec Riser bow wrong handed.

So, put away that excuse! You can start to learn to shoot left-handed with your right-handed bow (unless it has a Hoyt Tec riser) or your right-handed bow left-handed and do so while you are waiting on a bow of the correct hand to arrive! How about those apples? There is now no reason not to at least try it while you are waiting. You could even get pretty good at it well before your new "correct-handed" bow arrives.

In 2004, I also wrote, "If you are indecisive on a release aid, get rid of the ones you've shot for years and start anew. A totally unfamiliar, fresh start is a good way to go. Make a complete separation in your body and mind of what you used to do. This is a new ball game, and things are going to have to change."

Fast forward to 2010—in my honest opinion, this still holds true. In other words, pick just one release and stick with it. Toss the other ones in a drawer, since there is no need to try anything else. Keep away from the temptations of having something else to try. You haven't even begun to learn with the one you've selected, so you have no need for more equipment at this juncture. I also would recommend that you leave the setting on that release totally alone. It is new to your "other" hand, so learn how to deal with it.

You are basically flip-flopping everything over to the other side. There is no need to change draw length unless your new "bow arm" is significantly longer or shorter than your old bow arm. This, my friends, I've discovered the hard way, is something that can significantly affect things. There is also no need to change your shooting stance from anything but being the mirror image of your old stance at the start. There is no need to change your anchor, peep height (unless you have to radically change your draw length), poundage, and arrows. There isn't even a real need to change your quiver. So what if that quiver pouch rests against your leg and looks funny? You will have time for that later. You want to shoot, correct? So, shoot!

A Further Aside Setting up your stance and other form items will be covered in the next chapter. This part is for the Philosophical and Mental Aspects of preparing for this changeover.

. . . leading to a new . . .

Philosophy about your archery This starts by coming to the realization that you are not likely to shoot perfect 300's right out of the gate. In fact, you probably wouldn't be considering this changeover if you were shooting 300's consistently anyways. You should establish, however, that it is not about winning; it also isn't about impressing people or your friends; it isn't about trying for that elusive 60X-300 round. This change is more about exactly that—change. Something you've likely needed for quite some time. Something that is going to keep you in the sport by offering up an entirely new series of opportunities. You will have to decide upon your new philosophy about your archery on your own, but the above offers up some starting guidelines for you to work with.

Establish new and realistic goals. I can start by telling you that your first goal has already been established, namely, "to make the changeover from left to right or right to left." Remember, these goals must not only be realistic, but also achievable and measurable. However, making the changeover from left to right is really too broad and not really measurable. Thus, from experience, the first goal I suspect you'll have is to be able to correctly load every arrow onto the string without dropping one on the floor. The next goal might be to work on being able to hold steady on the bull's eye (don't worry about that X-ring, you will not be holding that steady for a few weeks). You can measure those goals simply by marking down those which were held pretty well on the spot, and not marking those where you were all over the place. Remember, you can also add or upgrade goals as the previous ones are achieved. In 1985, it took me seven days to shoot a 297 and 12 days to shoot a perfect 300 after my change from left to right. That didn't happen on this changeover in 2010, however. So, don't set your goals so lofty they aren't achievable. I would also not set an outcome goal like "I'm going to get at least third place in my first tournament after the changeover." While that could happen, I wouldn't hold my breath; especially if that first tournament is only a month or two away. So, maybe set your goal to shoot 290 within the first month, 295 within six weeks, and 300 within two months. Then work on goals for "X-count," etc. I might make mention of the fact that the night I shot my first ever 60X 300 round in league, my planned goal was to simply shoot all 60 arrows without a single arrow touching the "blue." I was only after an inside-out 300 and ended up shooting 60X's that night; a clear demonstration about how powerful "letting it float and shooting the shot" can be. I had to let down the 59th arrow twice and the 60th arrow once. But that final shot for the 60th X turned out to be the easiest of the night! Everything came together all at once and the shot broke perfectly. There was no doubt in my mind when I hit anchor on that sequence that the arrow was going in the X-ring.

Telling yourself there is no going back to the old ways of doing things. This one will trip you up big time. If you have a bad start or you have a bad night, or a bad week sometime during the change, it is not to be used as an excuse to abandon the effort. Remember the basics of any change: "It takes at least 21 days to form a new habit, and even then, you will tend to go back to what is comfortable when under pressure."(Remember my story about my deer hunting experience? S'truth!) Don't succumb to this temptation to go back to what you "used to do" or what "used" to work.

You made the change for many reasons, primarily because your shooting had gone to heck in a straw basket in the first place. Why would you want to go back there? You have an opportunity to start anew and to form habits that are correct and properly executed. Thus you are going to tell yourself daily that there is no going back to the old way, period. Good times, or bad times, no going back. If you have to get tough about it, then sell off the old-handed stuff once your "replacement equipment" arrives. That way, you will have nothing left to go back to. That is how I've done this both times, but this time, with the new types of bows, I really "could" go back if I wanted to with little expense and just shoot wrong-handed!

You have made the . . .

C*ommitment to yourself and to this hobby* to make this change, so stick with it. This is your "hobby" and not your life. You have probably already gone through the phase where your score was determining your spirit more than the fun and love of the game. Your commitment was probably that you had to get ready for the next big tournament or league, so the pressure was always on. You now have a golden opportunity to move your score back up there, possibly more than you ever imagined, but you must make the commitment to stick with this thing and commit to yourself to give it your best. You don't have expectations at this point, because you've no baseline from which to measure it.

A*ggressively practice, by working on one thing at a time, in a planned and organized fashion.* I cannot stress this enough. I fell into the trap of trying to work on too many things at once and still do from time to time. After all, I shot left-handed for 25 years (starting over 25 years ago, when I was a young man, that is), so this is so simple I should be able to conquer it in a week . . . I thought. How wrong I was/am on this very point. I was/am practicing too aggressively and while organized, I was putting the cart before the horse and trying to do too many things at once. I hate to admit it, but this very item has set me back months on my initial goals. Of course, my goals have been adjusted accordingly and I quickly learned (once again) to practice what I preach, and work on one thing, and only one thing during a practice session. When I lose focus, I sit down. If I lose focus due to students asking for help, or I just don't feel like it, I sit down. You must recall that I always preach "eating an elephant one bite at a time." There is no rush in this, even though you might think there is. After all, even your friends have provided you with the classic and the best excuse of all time, "Gee, you know you've just switched over, so what do you expect?" So, let them handle the excuses and you just sit back and take it one step at a time. Don't try more than you can bite off and chew. Enjoy the process and this new challenge you've taken on. It may well be the best thing that happens in your archery career.

R*efining your technique, one step at a time.* This ties in directly with all the steps above. As you progress through E-PETCARE, each step builds upon the previous step. Refining your technique will pretty much be automatic as your other side learns the new things it has to do to correctly and consistently to perform your shot sequence. Your sequence isn't likely to change from what it was on the other side of the bow, but your mind and body will have to reprogram themselves to accomplish these new and strange feeling things. The next chapter will focus quite a bit on this item of E-PETCARE.

E*valuating your performance versus your goals each step of the way*. As you progress through E-PETCARE and onward, always keep in mind that you need to evaluate and reevaluate your actual performance versus the goals you have set for yourself. This is your hobby, however, if you set those goals too high, then it is much too easy to get untracked and frustrated because you aren't making progress toward meeting those goals. So, if you go along for awhile with a goal that is too high, re-evaluate that goal and set it a bit lower. You don't want goals set so low that you don't have to try hard to achieve them, but you also don't want them so high that it will be next to impossible to achieve them. You don't want to create more expectations than you can realistically achieve in a short amount of time. Thus, while your long term goal might be to shoot a 55X 300, a shorter term goal might be, depending upon where you are, to shoot a 45X 300, with a time frame of a couple of months. Don't expect, if you've never shot above 55X 300 on your "main side" of the bow, to set a goal of 60X 300 only a few months after this change you've undertaken. Unless you are an anomaly, you would be in for a big disappointment. I personally had great success with the first changeover in the 1980's. However, age, health, and yes, having expectations too high has got me to the realization that had I properly used E-PETCARE at the very beginning instead of trying a "rush job," I'd be farther ahead than I am at this point in time.

Another Word of Caution You are going to have some days where it is like someone flipped a light switch. You are going to shoot fantastic and figure, "I got this thing whipped now." Don't get too caught up in that, however, as they say "results may vary." For example, only a month or so ago, I came in for a practice round. My goal for the day was to shoot for score and see how I would do on a Vegas round. The focus was on shooting with the working point of "keeping the drawing elbow engaged." So, I started scoring "cold turkey," meaning that the first end was for score, no practice arrows. After 15 arrows on the top of the bale, I had shot an absolutely perfect 15 Baby X, 150. I was on "cloud nine." I had kept my drawing elbow engaged for all 15 shots and had a perfect/perfect first half Vegas Round. I hadn't done that in years, even when I shot right-handed with the shakes! So, as normal, I moved the target face to the bottom of the bale, and I took a short break to get a drink of a soda. After that five minute break, I got back up, and promptly proceeded to shoot three arrows out in the 8-ring at 12 o'clock! I was disappointed. However, I hadn't focused on the task at hand and my drawing elbow had come forward slightly, causing other problems, one of which for my particular form is a straight high arrow. I finished the round with 33, 32, 33, and 32. However, dropping 9 points in 3 shots sure took the wind out of those sails! A 294 "real" Vegas score at this juncture for me isn't shabby, but the way it was done was shoddy. Shooting a 319/330 Vegas isn't too shabby either, but the way it was shot was shoddy. I fell victim to excessively lofty expectations, a bit of arrogance, and complacency, and paid the price. To make matters even more ironic, I might add that I also haven't come even close to shooting that kind of score since. I still have a lot of work to do.

Summary

The above is written mostly in the first person by design and directed at you, the reader, because it relates my direct personal experience from someone who has done this changeover both ways; from left to right and from right to left. I've experienced these hardships and stumbling blocks first hand. My methods may not be entirely correct, but they are working for me and are a Work in Progress, too. Don't let me discourage you; that isn't my intent at all. I'm simply trying to focus you on some pitfalls to avoid and to follow E-PETCARE and enjoy the experience, because I can still say that in spite of the work and some frustrations, changing back to left-handed beats the alternative of giving up on something that I have spent over 50 years of my life doing. That, my friends would be a travesty and I would be very unfair to myself by giving up now.

I fully described the rationale behind an acronym that I designed in order to help you deal with setting up your new shooting philosophy and mental attitude. You have an opportunity to really start fresh and with the right philosophy and mental attitude, you are about to embark on something startling and very satisfying; albeit frustrating from time to time. I have dubbed this the "E-PETCARE" system.

There are so many key elements above that are so important that I simply ask that you re-read the chapter, keeping in mind the words: "commitment," "aggressive," "one thing at a time," "refining your technique," and finally "evaluating your performance" versus your goals. You do not have to shoot any tournament; you do not have to push yourself beyond your means and, by heavens, I certainly hope you don't try to force the process and end up taking one step forward and two steps back. That leads to quitting to go fishing.

It is important not to overload any one practice session. It is important to know ahead of time that there are going to be bad practice sessions, and that there will be good practice sessions. I related a story about how complacency can get to you quickly when you prematurely think you've finally got the change in hand.

Remember to be ProActive. Remember to "eat the elephant one bite at a time." But mostly, remember to have fun with this change over, because it is going to be what you make of it.

In the next chapter, I will address the mechanical and technical issues of switching bow hands.

Tom Dorigatti

21

Switching Bow Hands—The First Two Transitional Steps

In Chapter 20 I thoroughly discussed the acronym that I came up with to help you establish a working philosophy for this new undertaking of switching from one side of the bow to the other. I have dubbed this "E-PETCARE." This is a foundation for what is to come, so if you haven't yet read Chapter 20, please do so before taking on this chapter.

I must also restate that two of the main keys to success in this or any other change concerning your archery are "personal confidence and "repetitive consistency." One thing Dean Pridgen told me and had repeated more than once was: "If you step up to the stake with any doubt, if you are at full draw and think the word "miss," if you sway in concentration, let the shot down and start over. If you don't have full confidence that you can put that shot in the middle, then let it down and start again." (Confidence and the ability to be consistent are inseparable.) You will soon find that, with the change-over underway, there are going to be frequent occasions when you should let down and start over. Doing so is a part of the learning curve and is to be expected. However, being religious about letting down when you should and to commit to not taking what you know to be bad shots is critical. If you do this you are just saying to yourself "bad shots are okay" and making it harder to let down in the future. Once again, I speak from experience on this. Do not let worry about the shot clock disrupt your rhythm or make you rush through things; take your 4 minutes to shoot your five shots. They are yours for the taking. Certainly, during practice scoring sessions, you must work on making sure you are well within that time limit constraint, but during routine practice sessions, the emphasis must shift to doing it right or letting down and starting over. If it isn't right at the beginning, you are not going to recover it, and in fact it will only get worse instead of better. Your confidence that you only shoot good shots and your consistency in doing so are built upon this principle.

I hope I have also convinced you that you do not have to shoot on your dominant eye side to excel, but you do have to shoot with confidence and a strong, steady bow arm to get the most out of the talent you have. I've been at both extremes, and one thing I know for certain, this sport is easy when you do have confidence; but if you don't and you are shooting poorly, then you end up working ten times harder to shoot a poor score than you ever will during the shooting of a 550 field round. Relax and let the Force be with you on the side of the bow you choose, even if it isn't what the experts and "gurus" or your friends say is supposedly correct for you.

So, I am going to assume you have decided to take the plunge. I'm also very particular and regimented in the way I approach or teach things (as if you hadn't noticed this by now!). Measuring, writing things down, and having physical references for nearly everything is an integral part of what and who I am. Sometimes this can hinder progress. However, one thing for sure, being careful and documenting all of the small changes allows you to not be caught in losing what you had before you made that last change or adjustment! If you record and mark those previous settings, putting something back when (notice I say "when" and not "if") the new change doesn't work is a snap and you can return "home" in a few seconds. Without this discipline, it is easy for you to become totally lost and frustrated. In my younger years, I had been known to "gravel tune" more than one bow, release, or arrows, so I know all about frustration skipping this vital practice can cause.

I will now approach two important foundational and key items:

1. *Your Visual Adjustments* If you are switching away from your dominant eye, these visual adjustments can be very difficult for some of you. There are several things you can do to help alleviate, and even potentially eliminate, visual problems. Some of these will work even for folks who are shooting with their dominant eye and having problems focusing on the intended point of impact, seeing double, or their vision blurring or graying out.
2. *Your Stance/Shooting Foundation* Houses are built from the ground up, and your new form is just like building a new house. This discussion will include some potentially alarming things I've discovered only recently. In spite of my many years of experience, I simply didn't take the time to get video or photographic evidence so I could see what is going on and wasted about 10 months of practice because of it!

Your Visual Adjustments

You will recall that I told you all that I am left eye dominant and also very dominantly left-handed. The only things I do right handed are playing golf, batting baseballs (as a switch hitter), and using ratchet wrenches, crescent wrenches, scissors, and screwdrivers. Yes, I can shoot a rifle left- or right-handed, but cannot use a left-handed bolt action rifle. With a rifle scope I can shoot with both eyes open, but give me open sites or a peep-sited rifle, and one eye is going to have to be closed regardless of the side of the stock I am on, with our without my glasses.

When I mention switching over to almost any fellow archer, one of the first things mentioned besides the normal "Oh, I could never do a switch over like that; it would be next to impossible," is a big concern about the master eye and how shooting on the other side of the bow is going to affect their eye dominance. They have had it pounded into their brains that you must shoot with your dominant hand, and often, the reality of it is that just because you are right-handed doesn't mean that you are always right-eye dominant. Of course, you probably already know this. Many people are just cross-dominant (right-handed and left "eyed," etc.) and never realize it or even think about it much until they get involved in a shooting sport of one sort or another. So much for this "shooting with your dominant eye" rule being absolute.

When I first made the switch to right-handed shooting 27 odd years ago at the time I am writing this, that switch was done knowing that I had to learn to keep my left eye shut. For 25 years prior to that, I had always shut my right eye to aim with open sighted rifles, pistols, and yes, bows. Thus, I already knew that closing my left eye would have to be done if I was to stand any chance of doing well right-handed. So, that is how I accomplished it. I learned from day one to close my left eye just as I acquired the target in my scope. It wasn't a difficult practice for target shooting. Fast forward to 2009 when I was forced to make the change back to left handed. This time around, I was actually going back to my master eye side of the bow. I figured I would have it knocked and it would be like falling off a log. How wrong I was on that account. Yes, for the year and a half or so, I closed my right eye, but after 25 years of having it open, I find myself sometimes opening that eye during the target acquisition phase of my shot sequence. I have come to catch it and get the eye closed quickly. However, it does seem to tend to "squint or flutter" open during the aiming process and I'm dealing with trying to just let it ride, since the sight didn't move off the bull's-eye when my right eye comes open . . . my vision improved! The drawback here is that I see two targets, one below the one I'm aiming at, even if one of them isn't there along with scope and dot or circle that are within the scope body. It got worse. The "target/scope set" that is the upper one appears to move toward two o'clock as it diverges. Talk about a major distraction! As time went on, I discovered that this had a lot to do with why my shot was taking so long to trip, and also that when I grabbed at the "moving target" I would sail a very high flyer at 2 o'clock. If I was caught transitioning to the one image that wasn't moving, and the shot tripped, the impact area could be anywhere from the X-ring to low left at 7 o'clock or anywhere in between. In addition to all this eye movement, the other problem was I was seeing "floaters" (specks of dust on my eyeball) across my open eye if I have to aim too long, because my eye was drying out, and even sometimes my vision was blurring to the point the target becomes almost obscured. Of course, the thing to do is to let down and start over, correct? Well, that is the right thing to do but, as I said before, few of us really follow that "rule" anywhere near as much as we should, now do we?

We'll get back to what I've ended up doing that has really worked out much for the better, thanks to a suggestion from a friend who was literally watching my bow move in from the lower left to upper right and back to the lower left while I was into my shot sequence.

For those of you that are worrying about seeing double or your dominant eye taking over, there are several measures you can take to alleviate or eliminate this potential problem. I'll list them, but only discuss them briefly, since each has its advantages and disadvantages, and I don't want to sway you one way or the other; at least not too much. These are not listed in any order.

1. *Use an eye patch.* I see more and more shooters these days utilizing an eye patch. I've tried one, but I get some claustrophobia and I also get some vertigo if the light to that eye is completely blocked off. In a short time, I also get a headache. Once again, many people are able to use the eye patch quite effectively, it is just not for me.
2. *Close the other eye.* This has been my preferred method for 50 years. That is not to say it is correct or incorrect. One must realize, however, that like the eye patch, blocking off the vision in one eye really messes up your depth perception and does increase eye strain on the remaining eye. You must learn how to deal with it, and when to close that eye and keep it closed. The tendency of most of us that close one eye is to allow the closed eye to flutter or squint. You will be constantly fighting with this because your dominant eye is going to want its way. Initially it is a forced thing, and when you aren't thinking about it, that off eye takes over and fouls you up. Suddenly, you find yourself not seeing your peep sight and wondering why. That is because the peep isn't in front of your off eye; it is in front of the eye you are not used to using. Live and learn, remedy it, and have a laugh or two. If you've shot with the "other" eye for years, then that opposing eye is going to tend to take over, so you have to be vigilant about it; it isn't impossible, just difficult. I did this for many, many years quite successful until recently. Things change as we age, and one simply has to learn to deal with new sets of circumstances.
3. *Use a "flip blocker" on either your glasses or the brim of your cap.* I've tried these, too. A flip blocker close to my eye doesn't work for me. The shooting eye blind that clips to a baseball style hat is pretty effective, and doesn't totally block the vision to your non-shooting eye. Below are pictures of two types of eye blind clips offered by Gun Star Sighting Solutions. The web-site URL and Gunstar's explanation of how this works are below. The unit is well made and if positioned correctly works great. (Of course, I quickly learned how to work around the thing.) They offer two versions, one is non-reflective, and the other is translucent and allows light to get to the off eye, thus relieving eye strain, vertigo, or claustrophobia. I've not tried the translucent one.

   This eye blind is for those who prefer to block out a smaller area of their vision, features a translucent blind material allowing full natural lighting to access the eye pupil. Features a non- reflective surface toward the eye. Clips to the bill of a baseball style cap the same as the standard model. For left or right handed shooter.

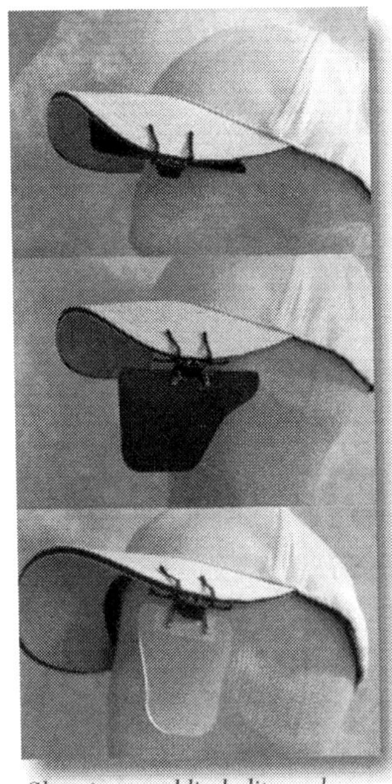

Shooting eye blind clips to baseball style hat allowing for the shooter to keep both eyes open while preventing double vision.

4. *The use of a piece of tape on the lens of the non-shooting*

for eye glasses wearers. There are many people today who are using this technique as well. It doesn't block the light out of your non-shooting eye, and it sure will stop it from seeing clearly, or taking over your aiming process. But my the vertigo problem persisted and I caught myself moving my head around to try to see around the piece of tape.

It is important to mention here that wearing glasses presents all sorts of problems with regard to having both eyes open or just one eye open while aiming. Many shooters who shoot with glasses don't even realize some of the more serious implications, some of which are:

a. First and foremost is ensuring your glasses are in the same position on your nose from shot to shot. If this means pushing them up between shots, then do it. If it means wearing some sort of restrainer to stop your glasses from sliding down your nose . . . do it.

b. Learning a new head position to get your line of sight to the target away from the edge of your glasses where the frame meets the lens. Most people who shoot in glasses have them adjusted so that the side of the frame is as close to the nose as they can get them. Still others get shooting glasses that are designed for this purpose. Most, however just learn a new head position. A person can spend hundreds of dollars on a set of shooting glasses and end up with little to no gain in score or the tightness of their groups. For some, it makes all the difference in the world. I will say, however, that ordinary glasses don't do as good a job off axis as do shooting glasses. Shooting glasses make sure your prescription goes right to the edge of each lens. Thus, you get a decent image, and you might only have to make a slight head position adjustment in order to get them to work.

3. *Getting the position of the peep sight in the same location on the lens, every time.* My particular prescription has a lot of prism in it. Thus, if your head is rotated off vertical, which I think many of you may well be, then you have the worst case scenario for archers; or so I am told. I have something similar a to lazy eye, so without the prescription, I see two images that are diverging from each other at a 45 degree angle. Believe me when I tell you there is not an easy way to shoot with my prescription glasses! I was told that if the position of the peep in my lens was off by as little as ⅛″ that my impact point on the target is going to shift ½″ or more at 20 yards and it gets progressively worse as the distance increases, or my head position differs. Thus, I have to be very conscious of not only making sure my glasses are tucked up, but I also have to really watch my head position as well. I strive to keep that peep hole in as close to the same position on my left lens as possible.

4. *Getting Custom Shooting Glasses or Lenses* There are opticians out there who can take your prescription and then take the prescription for the "sweet spot" on the lens to your shooting eye, and build a big "sweet spot" off in the corner of the lens for your shooting eye. They use an old set of frames and you just have them make the lens for the shooting eye side. I had a pair of them when I was shooting right-handed and they worked great! I didn't have to worry any where near as much

about peep sight position with regard to the corner of my lens in the shooting eye. The disadvantage was that the tri-focal was taken out of that lens, so I was reading and writing with only one eye, because the other was blurred for close vision work. Since I made the switch to shooting left-handed, that set of glasses cannot be used. I've chosen not to spend the money for another set.

5. *Acquire a lens positioning aid.* I tinkered with making my own positioning reference in the left lens corner of a spare pair of glasses. I used a small piece of markable cellophane tape, stuck it in the corner of my lens with a hole the size of a paper punch in it about where the peep sight should be. Then, I had my wife mark on that tape with a marker when I'm centered in the peep and comfortable. After that, I moved the tape around so that the center of a slightly smaller punched hole coincided with the mark on the lens of my glasses. That hole was the size of a standard paper punch and while it does have some merit, I quickly found out that this wasn't the best of things for me personally. I still had problems moving my head to that instead of being able to bring that into position the same every time.
6. *Not wearing glasses while shooting.* I mentioned earlier that a friend was watching me shoot one evening and he observed I had very significant motion while aiming. This movement was from lower left to upper right and back down again. He noticed it started at about the two second point, stopped for a moment, and then started shifting again. He asked me if I could see this in my aiming and obviously I could. I explained all the "stuff" that was going on with regard to the two images and my right eye squinting open and closed and open and the sight gyrating around this. He already knew that I'd tried the other things in an attempt to remove the non-dominant eye from the matrix. He also knew that my right eye had been so used to being "the eye" for aiming that it was natural for it to take over, since that is what I let it do by closing my left eye while shooting right-handed. He asked me if I was near or far sighted and how good my distance vision is. I told him my distance vision was 20/20, but up close at reading distance I don't see squat clearly. He asked me to simply try shooting without my glasses and to use them or "cheaters" when scoring arrows or writing down scores. I figured I had nothing to lose by trying this, so gave it a whirl. I'm here to tell you that the result was instantaneous. I was seeing the target more clearly than with my glasses on, and in addition to this, and this will 'blow your mind', I can shoot with both eyes open now, and don't see double anything! I found out later that this works because the peep sight restricts the light coming into the eye to a small region in the middle of the eye's lens, so small that there are no distortions in the lens needing correction. For me, the problem of shooting with glasses and having those problems was resolved in moments, after years of struggle trying to shoot with prescription glasses hanging on my face. There is some bad news here, however—I must put on my glasses(or use cheaters) to set my sight or write down scores. The other remaining problem is seeing the numbers on my arrows clearly enough so I load the correct arrow in sequence. This is a small price to pay for eliminating a

huge distraction and vision problems from my shot. That bite of the elephant was eaten quickly; it is too bad it took so long to resolve the problem.

7. *Use the Double Vision Blocker* (*www.topbowarchery.com*) It is said that a picture is worth a thousand words and the photos (right) tell you all you need to know about this device.

The NFAA Board of Directors upheld a ruling of the Rules Interpretation Committee that use of the *Double Vision Blocker* is legal in Bowhunter Freestyle and Bowhunter Freestyle Limited as long as the archer does not have more than five fixed reference points visible in the sight window.

I've seen several shooters using the *Double Vision Blocker* and most are having much better success with it compared to the other alternatives. Since it is far removed from your hat or your eye or face, it is much less intrusive. It also does a good job of blocking the double vision. This is a far less expensive alternative to purchasing special glasses or resorting to the other alternatives that interfere with your normal view of the world, and messing up your depth perception.

Try any or all of these alternatives if you are having difficulties with keeping your dominant eye or your "off shooting eye" from interfering with your aiming process. The easiest way to deal with the problem is to relieve or eliminate it from the very beginning. Those alternatives are out there, so don't let worrying about your "dominant eye taking over" stop you from making the switch. After all, if you weren't having shooting problems, vision problems, or health problems, you wouldn't be considering the switch as the alternative to quitting archery, would you?

The Stance and Your Shooting Platform

As I mentioned previously, in December of 2009 I took the plunge and made the commitment to switch back to shooting left-handed. My assumption was that since going from left to right back in the 1980's had only taken about two weeks, then going back to left-handed should be like falling off a log. I mean, good heavens, I'm left-eye dominant and my right hand would now be the bow-hand, so the shaking I experience from my open heart surgery should stop and I'd be back up shooting 300 indoor rounds in no time, right? Unfortunately, no.

There are pitfalls with regard to your stance and foundational alignment that I've come to understand and will pass on to you so that you don't fall into the same traps that I fell into. After making the switch, I went from shooting pretty well to having difficulties keeping the bow up in the bull's-eye and also started having increased difficulty getting the release to break. Yes, a lot of it had to do with my vision problems mentioned above. I always felt like I was straining and at the end of the "pinch" in my shoulder blades. There was tension in my bow arm and tension also in my pulling forearm and upper shoulder. I was told that my drawing elbow wasn't coming around. The natural thing to do in that case is to make sure your feet are square or slightly open, correct? Then, if the elbow isn't in line, you increase draw length, correct? Then, if still not in line, you consciously pull the elbow around farther, correct? Answers to all of these questions: not quite correct on any of them.

Let's go back to December, 2009 when I set my stance foundation. I simply took my stance template that I used to keep my stance correct when I was right handed. It was a simple matter of flipping said template over, taping it to the floor and then planting my feet and learning that stance as a lefty; so I thought and so I did religiously. The stance I took was the mirror image of the stance I always used when I shot really well right-handed; thus, so was the draw length of the bow. My stance was tuned to the draw length, and my draw length was tuned to the stance. Unfortunately things were not so cut and dried. My elbow would not come around to be in line with the arrow even if I closed my stance severely. In fact, the only way I got my elbow to come around was by standing in front of the mirror in the basement with my "Firing Line" and increasing the draw length on it until it was in line . . . at 31½″ of draw! I am 57″ tall, and my wing span and measuring arrow and tape measure check of approximate AMO draw length all indicate 26½″ to 27″. At this point, a red flag went up, since I knew it was impossible for me to hold or shoot a 31½″ draw length. I started looking elsewhere, but did increase the draw length on my Merlin Excalibur to 27½″, then 28½″, then 29″. My draw elbow was not any more in line and the shooting strain kept getting worse, with my sight dropping out the bottom causing low arrows, and lots of right arrows unexpectedly.

What is worse is that the "Blind Bale" test (shooting at a target, but with my eyes closed) indicated my stance was correct, in spite of my elbow being out of line. I was shooting right down the middle. However, there was a lot of vertical variance while shooting Blind Bale. Have you figured out what was wrong yet? I didn't think so. Read on, because you are about to learn the real reason it is so critical that you build that foundation and platform correctly from the get go and not have 14 months go by before you find the fault! I will tell you that the timing of the cams, or "tiller tuning" of the bow, or "pulling point" of the D-loop are not issues here. Those were checked and re-checked over and over and over again.

Another friend was watching me shoot (no, it really wasn't shooting, it was struggling) one afternoon. He mentioned my elbow wasn't in line just like we knew was happening. I told him I was struggling to even hold the bow back at this draw length and the story about the 31½″ draw length being the point my elbow would come around. He didn't say anything and continued to watch. After about 15 arrows or so, he said, "Tom, I'm not a knowledgeable coach or anything, but I think I might see what your problem is." He then went on to tell me that while my feet were squared up, my hips and shoulders were not squared up and were pointing 2-3 bales over to the right of the target bale I was shooting at. Yes, a stance square, but hips and shoulders twisted right severely.

What we have here is something that I had had problems with 25 years ago while shooting left-handed, but had forgotten about. It also showed its teeth early on when I made the switch to right-handed shooting, but I had forgotten about that, too. I'll bet you are now interested in avoid this problem when/if you make the switch, aren't you? (Or maybe your interest is piqued because you are struggling with your release and tight forearms, and your drawing elbow isn't coming around?) Remember also, that 95% of the shooters today are over-bowed and over-drawn.

What happened was at the beginning I started by simply flipping over the stance template, set my feet the same as always, and started at the same draw length I had shot for years. What I didn't do, however was to think through this entire process and what my body had been used to for 25 years as "automation" or nearly such. What I didn't realize was that this change over was not as simple as making a mirror image or as easy as falling off a log because I'd done it before. Here is my analysis and why/how this happened. As Foghorn Leghorn would say, "Pay attention, son, you might learn something:"

1. This was brought up earlier in the chapters on draw length, but applies here again and needs to be mentioned. You need to know if your bow arm is the longer of your two arms and by how much. If you are changing from your shorter to your longer arm, your draw length can go up considerably. This will allow you to not get so deep into the changeover that you have to step back and go back through the draw length adjustment process.
2. My knees and hips were used to the muscle memory from the opposite side of my body. What was more work on my right side is now more work on my left side, and vice versa. My knees were used to the loads being just the opposite of what the loads now being placed on them. They responded by going to where they were comfortable.
3. Shoulders normally follow hips, but if you've ever shot a recurve bow, you know that in order to draw the bow, you have got to have your draw shoulder behind the bow and use skeletal support. With today's high let-off compound bows, you don't necessarily have to have your bow shoulder behind the bow; in fact if you watch new shooters, most all of them are indeed supporting the bow with their arms. Some of them are even bending the bow elbow severely, which makes it obvious that it is arm support and not skeletal support that is bearing the load. Their inconsistent shooting and constant left/right group distribution is the proof of the pudding; especially once they get out past 25 yards or so.

   This forces the bow shoulder out to the right (left-handed shooter) and the shoulders won't necessarily follow the hips. So, you can get your hips aligned, but unless you make sure you are behind the bow with your drawing shoulder, you are putting a twist in your upper torso that is counter to your knees and foot positions. I recall that when I was shooting my best both left- and right-handed, I had maybe an inch of clearance on my chest and would sometimes slightly brush my bow arm with the bow string. This time around, there was 3″ to 4″ of clearance between my chest and the bow string, and about the same clearance from my bow arm! A huge red flag should have gone up . . . and didn't.

4. When I shot my best right-handed, I had slightly more weight on my back foot than on the front foot. Thus, my body and legs were/are used to having that weight distribution on them. So, guess what? I have more weight on the right leg, all right but, the right leg now is my front leg, so I'm leaning forward slightly, and as I tire, more weight goes that direction because it is natural after 25 years for my body to respond that way. It is also normal for my body to respond to the stress of the draw by the right leg gathering slightly more to accommodate the resistance. We often see shooters leaning back when they are tired or leaning back to draw the bow, especially if it is too heavy or too long for them. That is the normal state of affairs. If you turn around 180 degrees, however, you now have the reverse problem and that doesn't allow you to correctly draw your bow. You cannot correctly position your shoulders and hips, let alone your head and chin position. You cannot get your bow shoulder behind the bow. Well, maybe it isn't "can not," but rather a "will not." Remember when I said that my sight was dropping out the bottom all the time? I'd bet you can see why, also why it had nothing to do with the weight distribution and balance of the bow.

When I widened my stance on the shooting line, I quickly discovered that I had more weight on my right (front) foot/leg and was leaning forward toward the target. It became immediately apparent that I was actually tilting forward and twisting my hips and shoulders to the right because that is what they were used to doing when I was positioning 180 degrees the other way. My alignment right-handed was feet and shoulders square, draw shoulder behind the bow, and the draw elbow in line, all at 27½″ of draw, not 28½″, and certainly not 31½″!

My Remedy?

Now that it is a habit, the remedy is for me to literally force my hips to line up with my feet, then drawing the bow, and at the same time trying to put my bow shoulder behind the bow and support the bow with my skeleton, which is what is supposed to happen. My elbow automatically comes around and into line at my correct draw length. But, habits are tough to break so if I don't think about keeping my hips and shoulders square and my bow shoulder down and in to the left, then I will "leak" with the right hip, the shoulders follow, and so does my draw elbow. I'll lean forward, and the bow will drop out the bottom. I'm torquing the bow to the right, so the arrow will drop low and right when the struggled shot breaks.

So, how is this all to help you? This answer is simple, but involved.

- Make sure you use a stance template. Use it until your new foot positions are memorized. Then from time to time use it to ensure you are still using the correct stance. Don't move your feet between shots.
- Make sure that your hips and shoulders, and "gig line" are perpendicular to the shooting line or only very slightly to the right (if left-handed) or to the left slight-

ly (if right-handed). (You know, the old "T-form" exercise.) You can easily fall off this wagon as time goes on and you start to get into other details or move too quickly and change more than one thing at a time.

- Make sure you are behind the bow with your bow arm and bow shoulder. Don't let high let-off and low holding weight suck you in to holding the bow with your arm and allowing the bow shoulder to go out away from the mid-line of your body. If it does, your elbow is not going to line up, even if your hips and shoulders are square. You won't hold the bow steady either.
- Find your balance point. Since you've changed over, you must remember that your legs are very used to your old balance point, so if you had more weight on the right foot while shooting right-handed, you will now tend to do the same thing, only now you are leaning forward and the bow is going to drop out the bottom. I now know that if the sight drops out the bottom, I need to get my body weight distribution right again, and if I don't move the bow, the weight distribution correction puts the sight right back up to the middle without any arm movement.
- Make foot position, stance width, hips and shoulder rotation, bow arm and bow shoulder placement behind the bow, and weight distribution top priorities from the beginning of the transition. Get that "T-form" right, exercise it religiously, and don't take it for granted, because your body is going to tend to revert to what it is used to doing.
- Your draw length likely isn't going to change much if at all so, if you are having trouble getting the release to trigger, check the above. I think you will find the root of the cause right there. It only took me ten months and the help of several observers to find it, in spite of me having shot for nearly 50 years. I wouldn't wish that kind of problem on anyone.

Summary

After the mental preparation (E-PETCARE) to shoot from the other side, the change over doesn't have to be difficult, and it will be what you make it. The first two major obstacles, in my experience, are not learning the new release aid and how to draw the bow. It is more basic than that. First, you have to decide at the beginning how you are going to deal with the change in your visual perspective. Do it right the first time and you'll end up saving months of time and effort. You can't hit what you can't see, especially if you are trying to figure out which of the two objects you see is the one you want to hit. Just because it happened to me, doesn't mean it will happen to you, but now, if it does, you have several means with which to tackle such a vision problem. ProActive archery in action once again.

Secondly, when/if you make this switch, do not take for granted that you will know how to draw the bow and get it and your body parts aligned correctly. I made that mistake and I paid a dear price for it. I thought I knew what I was doing, but didn't think the process through. My body was telling me bad things all along, but I was blaming it on this and that, and not paying heed to my body. Now that you know this,

I'll bet you will not make that particular mistake.

By heavens, when my alignment is correct, does that sight ever lock onto the bull's-eye (no, not dead still for several seconds like some people brag about), and does that release ever go off so crisp and clean when the foundation and alignment of feet, knees, hips, shoulders, bow arm/shoulder, and elbow are all in synchronization with one another. When that all happens, it doesn't get any better.

It is important not to overload any one practice session. It is important to know ahead of time that there are going to be bad practice sessions, and there will be good practice sessions. I related a story about how complacency can get to you quickly when you prematurely think you've finally got the change in hand.

Remember to be ProActive. Remember to "eat the elephant one bite at a time." But mostly, remember to have fun with this change over, because it really is so simple even "a caveman can do it." It is going to be what you make of it.

Tom Dorigatti

22

Switching Bow Hands—Pitfalls to Avoid

This is my concluding chapter on the topic of changing over from one side of the bow to the other. While what I have been writing about may seem to you like it might be more trouble than it is worth, it can really be an easy process if approached with the correct mental and physical attitudes. Even if you aren't "changing over" to the dark side of the bow, there well may be some of the same pitfalls that you have already fallen into with your shooting, so it may be worth your while to continue reading this and even to go back to re-read the previous chapters. While I've had more than my fair share of problems going back to the original side of the bow from 27 years ago, it hasn't all been a bad experience. The amount of knowledge that I have gained about shooting archery, about equipment, and mostly about me as an individual is well worth any and all of the hassles, even if I tend to complain about how my scores were "in the toilet." I'm not a quitter, nor should you be. You shouldn't give up something you've spent your entire life doing, nor should you let some inanimate thing force you into submission. After all, how can an inanimate object, like a bow, control a living, breathing, thinking human being? Only if we allow it to, that's how!

Normally the main parts of the changeover from one side of the bow to the other aren't all that difficult to accomplish. However, the finer points require additional attention to detail and, if not planned out and considered properly, can become a major hassle. As they say, "Rome wasn't built in a day," and with a changeover being a complete re-building of nearly everything to have to do with your bow, you cannot expect to go through this without any hitches. As previously mentioned, my first change went extremely easily. I was a young man. I was healthy and hadn't had major heart surgery or other ailments. My vision was very good, and I also had a much deeper motivation to become the best I could be.

In this chapter, I'm going to discuss the remaining pitfalls, those that occur from the shoulders up, including those involving your bow arm and, of all things, your nose! Many people accuse me of "over-thinking" everything and "over-analyzing" it as well. They are probably right. However, those criticizing are also very young. They still have their vision, they still have their flexibility. Not a one of them has ever changed over from one side of the bow to the other, let alone doing that both ways, separated by 25 years! Only a couple of them have ever shot the elusive 60X 300 indoor round or 550+ on a Field Round, thus it is easy for them to think that things are simple as pie. They are right about the "simple as pie" in some regards, but not so with regard to when it comes to learning something 180 degrees out of phase of what you are very used to doing. I hear comments of "just do it the same way you've always done it, only in reverse." Wow, is that comment ever something loaded with contradictions with regard to learning to shoot a bow from the other side! To these I say, "Well, then since you bowl right-handed, just go onto the lane and bowl left-handed by doing everything in reverse, then tell me your bowling average hasn't changed one iota." You can well see what a debacle that would be.

I do tend to "over-think" everything and "over-analyze" it as well, but it is a dirty job and somebody has to do it. You may be very glad I have.

Your Shoulders

Ah, your shoulders. I've already discussed hips and shoulders alignment and how they tie into elbow rotation in Chapter 21. However, there is more to the shoulders than meets the eye. Remember I mentioned something about one side of the body was used to being the "lead" and the other side to "follow" and how that could affect your balance and alignment? Well, this applies to your shoulders too. Think about this. You switched from right to left. While shooting right-handed, your left shoulder was used to being down and in, while your right shoulder was used to being slightly higher than the left, correct? Well, guess what? They are still going to tend to adopt those positions now that you are shooting left-handed. As you fatigue, your body will just naturally revert to doing what it has always done, and you will now find both shoulders fighting each other over their "correct" (but now backwards) positions, that being the left shoulder is going to want to move down, and the right shoulder is . . . yes, going to want to move up . . . thus, screwing up your sight picture and body alignment. There is a simple fix, stop the shot sequence, let down, and start over. Simple, but arduous. Remember, you are new to this, and it is going to take time and work before it becomes ingrained enough so as not to keep going back to the old status quo.

Your Bow Arm

There is a lot of discussion (and arguing) concerning "proper" bow arm positioning; everything from a totally locked bow elbow on through to a significantly bent bow elbow is recommended. I will tell you this, however: It is next to impossible to replicate shots with a significantly bent elbow with enough consistency to shoot 60X's indoors or to shoot 540+ on a field course, or to consistently hit 10's at any distance on a FITA round. Most prefer the "not bent, and not locked" bow elbow position. However, this is not my point with regard to switching bow hands. My point here is, once again, what your body is used to doing versus what loads you are now placing on it. While you were shooting right-handed, your left arm was straight and extended; now that you are shooting left-handed, it is bent in half (or nearly so) and not extended. It was pushing, and now it is pulling. The right arm was the one bent in half (or nearly so), and pulling, while the left one was the straight one (or nearly so), and now you are asking it to push or at least to resist bending or "caving in." If you don't remember, earlier I mentioned my bow arm, while shooting lefty before was caving in and was inconsistent and causing left arrows all the time? Be cognizant that there are going to be breakdowns of your arms with the old habits cropping up and leading to creeping and collapsing shots. It is common nature. This is going to happen on occasion, especially under pressure; until you have it all finally incorporated and automated into the finely tuned shot sequence which is your ultimate goal not, as many think, "I'm going to shoot an "X" with this arrow." Hitting the X with that arrow is in the future, but you can only control the present! So, as Larry Wise says, to control the present with appropriate goals and thoughts, such as: "I'm going to execute this shot with proper back tension," then let the rest fall into place. If you do that one thing often enough, it will become a habit and a good habit indeed. And, you must indeed focus on the positives and saying "I'm not doing this", or "I'm not doing that," isn't going to cut it. Wouldn't "I'm going to do. . . ," be a more positive approach? If you tell yourself you are going to do a particular thing in a certain manner often enough, it becomes a habit, won't it?

A few more thoughts on this issue as it relates to your hands and fingers.

- All the while you were shooting right-handed, you had worked on relaxing your left hand and fingers so you didn't "grip" the bow, correct? Well, now, you are asking the left hand to "grip" the release. This hand is probably rebelling every now and again, and you are "losing the grip" on the release as you over-relax your left hand. You are also now asking your left hand to change its rotation from downwards at 45 degrees to upwards at 15-30 degrees or more; this requires rotation of the forearm well beyond what it is used to! Be aware of this if you are suddenly finding yourself having problems getting the release to trip. When this happens, it is likely you have over-relaxed the left hand and are chasing the release, along with a resulting increase in tension of the left forearm, which means the release is not going to trip or, if it does, you will shoot low and right as the sight sinks in that direction.
- All the while you were shooting right-handed, your right hand was used to gripping the release, and now you are trying to tell it to relax completely and not do gripping. It was also used to being rotated upwards 15-30 degrees and now you are telling it to rotate 45 degrees downward and to relax? No wonder it is confused! Well, from time to time, it too is going to rebel and tighten up. When it tightens up, so does your right forearm, then your shoulder, and the shoulder does what it is used to doing (coming up), Argh! If you sense your bow hand tightening up, it isn't the end of the world, but it should be the end of that try for a shot. Acknowledge the error, let down, and start over. Simple solution. But I have more about this release hand positioning! I have a student who was complaining about his shoulder and forearm actually hurting while he was at full draw and that he was having problems with back tension. I had seen this and was hoping he would ask, but if he didn't, he was about to be asked to try something differently. His

"pain" was a direct result of him over-rotating his release aid, pinky up against his face/cheekbone. This was raising his elbow and forcing him into a position that was outside of the normal comfortable and relaxed range of motion of his particular structure.

What did I do, you ask? I gave him a demonstration of a very simple exercise concerning release hand positioning at anchor. It is so simple and yet I've seen so few coaches every use this most simple exercise to drive home the point. With my student, it only took a couple of tries, and his release hand position was corrected almost immediately, because he knew what to look for and how it felt if it was out of kilter. Give this a try, and I think you may well realize what the pros are talking about when they say that their drawing hand, forearm, upper arm and shoulder are "mush" and relaxed while at full draw and the correct muscles are what are "taking up the slack" and contracting to make the release aid rotate—not the hand, lower arm, upper arm and shoulder.

The Exercise

1. Assume "T-form" with your arms out, relaxed and at shoulder level.
2. Make sure both your shoulders are down and relaxed.
3. Put your bow hand out like a stop sign and then rotate your knuckles to about 45 degrees.
4. Making sure your head is centered and your chin is level, turn your head to your position you normally assume and draw the string for anchoring. By the way, you do draw the string to your head and do not move your head to the string, correct? As such, this is likely your "real" correct anchor position for you based upon the length of your upper arm and lower are skeletal structure.
5. Now, for the fun part. Simply take your release arm and bend it to your anchor position without moving your head or moving your drawing shoulder. Just bend the release arm until your hand, imitating you are holding your release touches lightly under your jaw bone (if you go tight, then the drawing shoulder is going to come up). Think about how that feels, and how relaxed the forearm, upper arm, and upper shoulder have become.
6. Relax, shake that off and follow steps 1-5 above again. This time, however when you come to the nice comfortable anchor, rotate your pinky finger towards the cheekbone or top of your head. Feel the tightening up of that pinky side of your forearm and the top of the shoulder? Do you think this is helping your rhomboids to work properly for the execution of back tension? Do this a couple of more times, rotating the pinky even further upwards and note how the tightening up increases.
7. Repeat this again, only this time come to the comfortable anchor and rotate your pinky finger to the horizontal or slightly beyond horizontal. Feel the tightening up of the thumb side of the forearm and once again the tightness of the upper part of your shoulder? Do you think this tension is helping your rhomboids to work properly for the execution of back tension? Do this several times at varying

degrees of pinky "down" towards the floor and take note of how that tightness also increases.

8. Repeat this several times until you find your most comfortable positioning of your release hand at your anchor point. Note how relaxed you are there as compared to going too far pinky toward the top or your head or pinky overly horizontal toward the floor. Each of us is going to vary slightly in this position, but most of us will be at or around the 30 degree pinky up towards the cheek bone.
9. Now, memorize this release hand to bowstring orientation, but learn to do this at release hook-up and not as you draw the bow, and definitely not once you come to anchor. Why do I say this? This is simple mechanics and also a huge time and movement saver. The less gyrating around you do with things once you hit anchor, the more time you have left in the window of opportunity for your shot sequence completion! Why waste time bouncing your head around, jostling around with release hand angle, bumping your jaw bone with your release hand knuckles, re-setting the hand angle and all that?

Does it make sense now? Just like the bow hand being set with some pressure on the bow before you draw, the release hand should be set to its proper angle when you hook up the release to the sting and as you begin the draw cycle. Oh, but you are thinking, "I can't draw the bow that way." First off this is a negative thought, you know, saying "I can't" when you need to think 'I'll try it" or "I'll do it." Secondly, you may have some difficulty doing it right away, but believe me, if you think this through and think about that hand positioning at anchor, you will feel the difference, and you will come to not like having your release hand rotated too far either direction, because you will discover that if this happens, the release is going to become much more difficult to trip, and that you will generate a particular "miss pattern" based upon that seemingly minor little detail. (That and the position your hand is in is biomechanically stronger than your old position (tension = weakness).)

Trust me, if you do this 9-step exercise several times, both without your bow and then with your bow (without shooting an arrow), you will quickly come to realize exactly the angle your release hand needs to be set in order to minimize those tight muscles.

On another note, if you relax both the thumb and pinky, along with having the release hand at the correct angle for your build, the forearm and upper arm will relax more. If you tighten up the thumb, you will feel it on one side of the forearm; if you tighten up the pinky, you'll feel it on the opposing side of the forearm; if you tighten them both up the rest of your hand tightens up, and so does the entire drawing arm. Try it, you'll feel it quickly.

Your Nose

Where do I get off nosing into your business? Those of you who don't wear glasses don't have to worry much about the position of the string relative to your nose; or do you? At full draw most people center the string on their nose, but there are those who are off to the aiming eye's side of the nose, either slightly, or even along side of the nose, if they're seeking out maximum draw length or a special anchor point. What I'm driving at here is that, especially for those of us who wear glasses, is that we tend to place the string slightly off center on our nose to help get the peep over and away from the edge of the lens in our glasses and to also help get away from the frame. Thus, on this change-over, if your nose is used to having the string on the right side of center, then it is going to feel natural for the string to be over there in spite of the fact you are now needing it on the left side of the nose due to the change from right- to left-handed (especially if you wear glasses). But doing this positions your head angle improperly and forces you to be off-set in the wrong direction. This can cause sudden and seemingly uncalled for lateral misses. In addition, this makes centering the peep and your scope housing much more difficult. That tiny fraction of an inch in head placement can cause those lateral misses, some of which are large and which you would tend to blame on bow hand torque. This can even induce some muscle pain in your neck! So, if you are having sudden and inexplicable lateral misses or you are sometimes having difficulties getting the peep centered, check out your nose position on the bowstring. You may well have gotten yourself back into your old position without even thinking about it. The error might be quickly corrected simply by correcting the string placement on your nose. Poke your nose into your own business; you just might find the culprit right in front of you. It also can cause a bad habit, instead of drawing the string to you and your anchor, you end up moving your head around at full draw trying to find "that nose on the string position." This leads to the inevitable bouncing around of the head and release hand and with that those errant shots and in fact, instead of shooting one shot 60 times in an indoor round, you are really shooting 60 different shots and no two are really the same. The less movement, the better, in my opinion.

Summary

The proper building of your shooting platform was addressed in Chapter 20. Visual adjustments you can make to accommodate the change-over away from your master eye or even to your master eye if you have been shooting opposite your master eye were addressed in Chapter 21 as well as troubles you may encounter in your stance and shooting foundation and how your body will signal you when things aren't right.

In this chapter, I discussed the pitfalls that can happen from the shoulders up and the common sense reasons why your arms, shoulders, and hands are wanting to do just the opposite of what they are newly being asked to do. Those units were so used to doing one thing, and now you are telling them to do just the opposite. If you aren't careful, things will end up backwards and you will feel lost and frustrated when your shooting starts going downhill in a hay basket. To remedy this, you just need to think it back through one step at a time. You will quickly isolate the error(s) if you are systematic about it and understand the implications.

From the archer's "T-formation" I taught you an exercise to help you find your correct release hand position, without really getting into physics or an anatomy or schematic diagram lesson, as promised.

Last, I even got your nose into the act. Sooner or later your nose may well be integrally involved; especially if you have been used to shooting with your nose on the string. Once again, a body part that is essential for "centering up" is being asked to reprogram itself to the opposite side. Sometimes, without you even realizing it, your nose will seek out what has been most comfortable in the past, but is now not the place it needs to be for the new situation at hand.

From the top: you eat an elephant one bite at a time, use E-PETCARE, formulate and write down a practice plan for each and every practice session. Write down items in your journal. When needed, re-write your shot sequence checklist and put a placard on your bow in a spot you can read it in between shots. This constant review is essential to reprogramming not only your mind, but also your body parts . . . from the ground right on up through the tip of your nose. Once again, this changeover may sound complicated, but actually, it is going to be what you make of it. It can be as hard or as easy as you make it. It is indeed so simple that a caveman can do it; if you go into it with a positive attitude and take it one step at a time.

Section 4

Practice & Tournament Preparation

In this section of the book, I will be get into a lot of details concerning planning your shooting sessions, setting goals, and practicing properly to prepare for the things that inevitably happen during competitions. But, you are not going to get a course in distance tuning. You aren't going to be told how to "French Tune." You aren't going to be shown how to set up your 2nd and 3rd axes on your bow sight, either. Volumes of books, articles, and Internet posts have been written concerning those types of activities and while I use those things, I certainly don't think it necessary to delve into those one more time.

You are also not going to be seeing and interpreting anatomical drawings or schematics of how things work or are supposed to work. What you are going to read about is a common sense approach to becoming ProActive with regard to practice and tournament preparation so that you are ready for the inevitable and can avoid pitfalls before they strike. Most of you, I am sure, have a collection of bad experiences run into while shooting in competition. How well you prepare yourself to accommodate different ranges, shooting conditions, and types of competition will make a large impact on how you deal with those things and ultimately in how well you perform. There are only a few points separating winners and losers. You can't afford a problem you can prevent, nor can you afford losing points because you got rattle from something that almost went wrong.

What I will do is ask you questions about yourself and how you go about your "game." I will address stretching and exercising before you shoot. We'll talk about your personal shot sequence (if you have one at this stage), how to develop your personal shot sequence and how to go about practicing what you preach with regard to your shot sequence. I will discuss a means of determining your personal shot timing and rhythm based upon actual data and not anyone's "opinion" of how you think your are doing ("think" is not a part of the scientific method). I'll then delve into the meat of ProActively preparing yourself and your equipment for indoor and outdoor competitions, along with ProActive preparation for improving your outdoor performance.

What I have to contribute on these topics is not the only means of going about your business, but it is indeed what has worked for me and my students over the course of time. It represents years of learning through the school of hard knocks and by observing, listening, and paying attention to detail, all of which are an integral part of becoming ProActive in archery.

Tom Dorigatti

23

Do You Practice with a Plan?

Becoming ProActive about your shooting is just as important as becoming ProActive when it comes to your equipment, equipment setup, and changes to your form or shot sequence.

Archery is fun but practicing for score every time you shoot can be unnerving and become laborious and end up actually taking you out of your own game before it even begins. It gets even worse when you find out how ill-prepared you are for so many of the things that will happen out on the course. Let's begin by addressing the subtle, but important things, you can do to actually practice accommodating the inevitable unfavorable conditions you will encounter. So, hitch up your wagon, and let's delve into ProActively "Practicing with a Plan" and how to begin planning for more meaningful and less boring practice sessions.

How Do You Practice?

Having been in the sport of archery for the better part of my life, I have to admit that there were times when going out to shoot and going out to "practice" were two entirely different things. Just like many of you, in the beginning I would to out and "practice," but in reality I was simply shooting a lot of arrows without any real purpose other than to try to shoot a better score this time out. I didn't approach any practice session for any other real reason. Sometimes I shot a better score, but most times I didn't, and in fact ended up shooting worse by practicing mistakes.

As I moved up the ladder competitively, however, I came to realize that simply shooting arrows for the sake of shooting wasn't a very wise idea. I began to understand that shooting a great many targets a day or a set number of arrows for a practice session didn't do much good as far as score goes; those only increased my stamina but not my effectiveness. Does this sound familiar? I am a professional educator and even when I wasn't teaching, I was always involved in working from a "plan," be it written or mental. I always have a plan for what I am doing and what I am going to do in the future. You may say it has been a way of life for me for well over 40 of my 43+ years in the sport. I become quite non-functional if I have no idea as to why and how I am going to go about what I "plan" to do! Of course, you must also realize that having a plan and sticking to that plan from the standpoint of practicing archery are things very hard to keep in perspective and also keep on track. If you aren't careful, one thing leads to another, and before you know it, you plan is gone and you are back to trying to do more than one thing at a time. This results in frustrations and wastes of time and effort. This takes a lot of discipline, which I'm sure you all realize is one of the biggest separators between the professionals and top echelon archers and the mid-level and beginners. At this level, archery is no longer a sport, but rather a discipline to be mastered.

Are you one of those archers who goes out to practice and shoots a round for score every time you do so? Are you one of those persons who shoot "Y" shots and goes home? Are you one of those shooters who, if during a practice scoring round you shoot a bad end or arrow you quit "before it becomes a habit?" Are you one of those persons who writes down your score and X-count for each end on either a score card or on the target face? Are you one of those who also religiously counts your "inside-out X's" and doesn't really have any idea as to why you are doing it that way? Are you an archer who keeps a mental journal, and who doesn't really have a clue as to what you were feeling, thinking about, or what you attained at your last practice session? Are you an archer who really doesn't have a handle on where your misses are occurring? Do you know how many "quality" shots you are shooting per round? Do you know how many of those X's you just shot were mistakes instead of perfect shots? How many arrows did you see obliterate the X as they went into it? How many shots did you "punch off" or get rid of? How many times you let down and started completely over versus how many times you should have let down and started over? Are you a shooter who doesn't keep a journal of your daily practice and scoring rounds, how you felt that day, what you did right? Do you focus on negatives of what you are doing wrong as opposed to what you are doing right? If you answered "yes," "I don't know," or "I'm not sure" to any of the above, then I am here to help with some suggestions to help you develop a plan for each and every shooting session you undertake from this time forward. If you couldn't answer many of the above questions in the positive, perhaps you need to break your current pattern and try something different.

Developing a Plan Before Each Shooting Session

Starting & Keeping a Journal I cannot emphasize enough how keeping a written journal or log book of your practice sessions can help you keep yourself on top of your game. This journal should include more than just your scores, your X-counts, and your inside-out X-counts. Certainly these are important, but they are really just the tip of the iceberg as far as getting to the top and staying there. (I won't reiterate the importance of keeping any changes in equipment setup documented as I have covered this in the past.) Here are some more items to jot down in that written journal:

- Plan for this Session (more on this later).
- End for end scoring, arrow by arrow. You need to know this information. Most shooters have tendencies of when they start to tire or tend to miss during an end, game, or round. Remember, you don't keep score every time you practice. Focusing on score as opposed to working on just one form or execution element can actually bring your scores down and ruin your confidence quickly.

- How you felt physically & mentally. Did you have a long day at the office? Were you tired before you even started shooting? Did you have an argument or upsetting situation prior to arrival at the range? You need to learn how you are dealing with these issues that can upset your rhythm and mental focus. They arise again and again and also during tournaments and league outings. You have to learn how to deal with them, and then work on getting around them.
- Did anything that happened on that shooting line irritate you or disrupt your concentration? You need to be aware of the "little things" that disrupt your concentration so that you can learn to deal with them and get them out of your mind.
- What caused your "misses" (for any out of the bull's-eye)? All too often, a person will miss a shot and just talk to themselves and move on to the next arrow or end and never give it a second thought. The only way to avoid missing two in a row is to know what caused the mistake and correct it. You will rarely see a top echelon shooter miss two shots in a row. Sure it happens, but very rarely. There are a reasons for this and this is one of the things that separate the winners from the "also rans."

Setting up a Session Plan Here's how you then use that information: you review your shooting journal from your last practice session before you arrive at the range. Then, you should:

1. Write down the weak items documented from that last practice or scoring session. (Don't use negative descriptions!)
2. Prioritize them in order of importance to your shot sequence and consistency.
3. Pick one item and only one item and make that item the focus of today's practice session. You can only concentrate on one thing at a time. Thus, opting to try to correct three or four things during any one practice session will only frustrate you. In addition, you won't know which one of them is the "key" and which others may be leading you astray into yet another bad habit.
4. Make a short-term goal for that one item and make it measurable. It doesn't have to be for the entire practice session; sometimes more isn't always better. Always make your goals positive in nature, and set them reasonably. A poor goal would be one which is unachievable based upon what your last performance was. Example: "I intend to shoot 58X or better today" when your last score was a 46X. This could be a long term goal, but you won't achieve this in only one practice session. Long term goals need to be planned out as to how you are going to accomplish them.
5. Keep track of that one item. Document what you accomplished, find something positive and jot it down. Sure, you probably made some mistakes, but you had to have done something right, too. Nobody says you have to shoot a full round for a practice session; in fact, it is often times better if you don't do this. This is a common mistake made by so many shooters; they think that the only way to practice is in "full round sets." This is quite the contrary, my friends.

If you sense you are tending to sway away from correctly performing your shot, be religious about stopping, letting down, and starting over. After all, you are not there to shoot a certain quantity of arrows; you are there to improve the quality of arrows you are shooting! Remember what I said earlier that at this stage archery becomes more a discipline as opposed to being just a sport?

An Example of Setting Up a Practice Plan Let's assume that during your last practice session, you shot an NFAA 300 round with a perfect score of 300 and with 50X's. You felt pretty good, but you noticed that your "misses" were just out of the X-ring in no specific pattern; they were just out. You noticed that you were "seeing" many of the arrows that were in the X dive right in there (perfect shots), which was the best feeling you had for that round. You never touched the blue nor had any fliers.

1. List items you might work on (Hint: keep this list short so as not to discourage yourself). For example:
   - Extending your followthrough
   - Focusing more on the X (seeing more arrows appear in the X) and perfect shots.
   - Increasing X count to 52 or better (short-term goal?)
2. Prioritize the above items (This example shows how I would approach this; you may differ.)
   a. Focusing more on the X (seeing more arrows appear in the X); "Let it float and shoot the shot" is a great cue for this one!
   b. Extending the follow thru (never a bad idea)
   c. Increasing X count to 52 or better (short-term goal?)
3. Pick one item and make it measurable. This is where a technique I use can really put some fun into a practice session and give you something directly measurable to strive for! Here it is:
   a. Focusing more on the X and seeing more arrows appear in the X and counting them. Yes, you are reading this correctly . . . actually counting them . . . or counting arrows that were perfect, whether scored an X or not. Haven't you had some arrows shoot high that you wish you could have them go off like that every time and simply adjust the sight for them? Be honest with yourself, we know you have had this happen. Let's digress here and talk about something that I recently picked up from Coach Larry Wise during one of his seminars. He asks, "Were you aware that only four results can happen as a result of any one shot?" Of course, we got a puzzled look on our faces. I can't give you his exact words, so I'll paraphrase what he summarized to us in my own words:
      1. *Good Shot, Good Result* You executed that shot properly and were rewarded for it. Good for you, but don't get complacent or break your arm patting yourself on the back. Do everything you can to repeat it 59 more times in a row.
      2. *Good Shot, Bad Result* You executed what felt like a good shot, but it didn't score maximum value. "Stuff happens"—don't dwell on it; regroup and execute the next shot once again with correct back tension.
      3. *Bad Shot, Good Result* You got away with one. Don't think you will do it again or that you can learn to get away with it every time. You got lucky this time. Take a deep breath, gather your wits about you and execute the next shot with proper back tension and don't think about that bad shot that caught the

bull's-eye or X-ring. Maybe you have a "forgiving setup" and maybe you don't; try not to bank on this thing called "forgiveness."

4. *Bad Shot, Bad Result* What did you expect? You messed up somewhere during your shot sequence. Forget it, re-group, run your shot sequence through your mind, then follow your shot sequence on the next one and execute that shot with proper back tension.

b. Make it measurable. Set up "rules" for and keep a count of the above. I purchased a Hand Tally Counter many, many years ago, and have put it to great use in many ways. In this case, you set up a game to play during this practice session as follows:

1. You are only allowed to click the counter if you (a) see the arrow appear in the target "through your line of vision," or (b) have a shot explosion that you would wish for 60 in a row of. Yes, those good shots with bad results can count as a "clicker," so make sure you don't fall into the trap of clicks only occurring on X-ring hits. This practice session will establish a base-line for this measurement. Subsequent practice sessions working on this one item give you an opportunity for measuring your improvement. Ah, the beauty of this type of goal; you can measure improvement in an easy and positive fashion and document it! Remember, you don't click a shot if it is just an "X," you only click it when it is a perfect X or perfect shot (even if it doesn't hit the X). No cheating yourself, only perfect counts. You also do not have to be scoring to use this trick.
2. Complete the practice session/round. Then write down the number of times you were able to click the counter. You may end up lower than what you expected, or you could surprise yourself with how well you shot. Again, this is your baseline for the next several practice sessions. You can now measure your improvement in "Focusing more on the X" when you practice doing that.
3. Work on this one item setting the goal (number of "clicks") higher each time until you reach your goal and have things working the way you want them.
4. Chances are you won't achieve 100%; but you will see an improvement rather rapidly in the number of "perfect shots" you are able to achieve. You will also start to see those "near misses" become X's.

Move on to the "Next Item" once you have achieved your realistic goal. Simply follow the steps above to work on the next item or to improve on some other aspect of your shot that is not quite what you want. Always make your goals measurable and achievable. Always document them in your journal.

Other Uses/Techniques for that "Hand Tally Counter"

Many shooters use some sort of counter to count points down, which during a tournament might not be a bad idea as long as you don't focus on that negative aspect of scoring! However, using that Hand Tally Counter or other (*see photo next page*) can be a real boon to your practice sessions; especially when you use it to count positive

things and not negative things (examples of negative things are: points dropped, X's down, bad shots, and the like).

Here are some suggestions on how to use the Hand Tally Counter to support positive reinforcement and to give you something that can add spice to your shooting sessions:

1. Use a Hand Tally Counter to count if your focus doesn't leave the X-ring. Every time you aren't caught during a shot shifting focus back and forth from the scope to the target and back, you get to click the counter.
2. Use a Hand Tally Counter to count every shot that doesn't touch the next scoring line. On a field round, this could be the 4-ring "identity line," it could be those that don't touch the white at all out of the 5-ring (or the black on the hunter face). For FITA-style faces, you could count the solid "golds" or the solid 10's that don't touch the next scoring line. The French call those "grands dix."
3. Use a Hand Tally Counter to keep track of low or high arrows (one at a time—either high or low—for a full practice session). This is especially useful if you have noted a trend that when you miss, you tend to miss either high or low. A short term goal would be to reduce those high or low misses. However, you need a baseline to measure this and to avoid simply flailing about guessing. If you have actual numbers to track, it makes it easy to see improvements.
4. Use a Hand Tally Counter to keep track of any shots you execute where your sight appears not to leave the X-ring more than twice. If it does that more than twice, it is a "let down and start over" (religiously) and no click is made on the counter. In other words, once off the center, put it back; twice off the center, and it is a let down and start over.
5. Use a Hand Tally Counter to keep track of those shots where your release hand didn't tighten up (a top priority problem to work on!).

Use your ingenuity, but always, during a practice session, if you use the Hand Tally Counter, use it for positive things and never for bad things.

Summary

In this chapter, I addressed what I've found to be lacking in most compound archers today, namely any sort of plan or even a clear reason as to what they are trying to achieve during a practice session. Most archers come onto the range, get out their bows, shoot ten practice arrows (some will practice for a half-hour or more, thinking they need that many practice shots to loosen up), shoot a scoring round, and then fold it up and go home. They don't keep a journal; they don't document how they felt, or what errors they were making during that session. Most archers have in mind that they are going to shoot a certain number of arrows and "try" to simulate tournament conditions every time they practice. Practice for them is always about score and nothing else seems to matter. Little do these archers realize that without some sort of plan to work on a specific element of their form or shot sequence that is breaking down, they will never achieve any steady progress or consistency leading towards moving up the leader board. Still others will come in and start a scoring round practice session, and when they miss, they stop scoring and go into "practice mode." This is a huge mistake! You have now subconsciously taught yourself that even during a scoring session, that if you miss, you can just up and quit, practice a bit, and then "start from there," or worse yet start a new round over. You don't get "Annie, Annie overs" in a tournament or league. In most venues, you don't get to buy a "Mulligan" or do-over. Always finish what you start; never quit during a scoring round no matter how bad it gets. Quitting during a bad non-scoring practice session isn't a bad idea, however. Why practice doing it wrong?

I strongly recommend keeping a journal and indicated what things to mention in it before and after each shooting session or tournament. In addition, I addressed the importance of listing items to work on, prioritizing them, and then picking just one item to work on at a time and having a means to track your success on that item. I emphasized that writing positives in that journal are extremely important and that finding something positive to write down and remember from even a poor session or scoring round is paramount. If you focus on the negatives and write down the negatives, then those are what will wreck your psyche. I've been there and done it; it is a poor mental management practice (pun intended).

The purchase of an inexpensive Hand Tally Counter can really help in measuring those goals you set before each practice session. The questions remain:

- Will you have a Practice Plan in mind before you go to the range for your next shooting session?
- Will you prioritize your shooting problems and work on one item at a time?

What I am asking is: do you want to improve your odds of success by choosing to develop a plan and measuring how far along you are in achieving the goals in that plan?

Finally, which is the only arrow you can control? What is the goal you have for shooting this arrow? If you say, "Hit the X-ring," you are then putting the cart before the horse and thinking into the future instead of into the present. A better goal is to "execute this shot with proper back tension," because if you do, then the chances of that X-ring hit increase exponentially. If you embrace ProActive Archery with a plan and goal in mind, and you keep tabs on your progress toward having a "one arrow at a time mentality," then controlling that one arrow and forgetting about everything else will become easier and easier. After all, you have now learned a quick way to make practicing fun and meaningful and can measure and track your progress with something simple.

There is more to come in subsequent chapters of this book.

Tom Dorigatti

24

Do You Stretch or Exercise?

Part of becoming ProActive with your archery is to leave as few stones unturned as possible as you strive to move up the leader board and hopefully onto the podium. Some of this has to come after your arrival at the shooting venue but before you have even shot the first arrow. No, this isn't about mental imagery, or Zen meditation, or framing the proper mind-set. I am talking about a simple point saving and "settling down" methodology that most shooters never think about, especially just prior to beginning a tournament. Most shooters have come to the conclusion that the only way to get "warmed up" for shooting is to get on practice bales for a half hour or so, and that without this amount of "practice" before their allotted shooting time, that they aren't ready to shoot. Many openly state, "I need 30 or 40 shots before I'm "loosened up" and cry the blues when there isn't line time given to their "warm up."

I believe that "warm up" is necessary, but you don't have to shoot the bow to get that "warm-up" and/or stretching out but, if you don't think about it ProActively, you can do more harm than good for your score! First, if the warm up/"practice" doesn't go well, many shooters start changing things; a bad mistake! Second, if the practice goes well, most shooters fail to realize that they've taken what may well be the best 30 or 40 shots of the day . . . and wasted them on practice. Third, that extra half hour to hour's shooting of those 30 or 40 or more arrows has taken a toll on you and you go into the early stages of the competition partially fatigued. Remember, during tournament situations, you are running a bit higher on adrenaline than normal; and you do not want to burn this stuff more than necessary; you certainly don't want to be gulled into shooting 50-100% more arrows than are required for the day. If you think you "need" all that practice/warm up before you are ready, you should be ProActive enough to use it to check your equipment, period, and not as a life-line to "be ready" to shoot for score. In my opinion, it isn't wise to burn up your best shots of the day and all that energy on the practice bales and take all those chances. If you are practicing ProActively, then you are practicing by warming up the muscles in an entirely different fashion and are ready to go for score without any practice arrows being shot out of the bow, and use the practice ends/targets to simply settle your psyche and get into your competitive mode.

Certainly, if you fail to stretch out and warm up muscles, joints, and tendons that by itself can easily result in not only poor performances, but also in a serious or even career-ending injury. Having been an exercise fanatic for many years, I've learned from experience that if I fail to warm-up my muscles and stretch them out prior to any of the many types of aerobic and exercise routines I do, I perform very poorly at the beginning, tend to cramp up, and have much more muscle soreness after the routine is over. This holds true in my archery. My warm-up regimen only includes shooting arrows out of the bow for the "official" practice ends or "official" practice arrows. I won't burn myself up or out on a practice bale, for many reasons. As this section develops you will see the reasoning behind this practice.

With regard to archery, I've found a series of very simple exercises that can be done quickly while waiting to start shooting for a tournament or practice session, either indoors or out. The intent of this chapter is not to sell any of the products mentioned. Nor is my intent to make an issue out of any particular warm-up or stretching regimen as being the only one(s) that work. With my involvement in distance running, competitive racquetball, hunting, aerobic exercising, and long distance road bicycling, I have found that many of the same stretching exercises I use in those endeavors were easily and readily applied to my archery. I feel strongly that much of my success in the past with competitive archery has been more from a fitness standpoint than it was ever from a "talent" standpoint. I strongly believe that fitness and stamina play a major role in success on the shooting line indoors and even more so when shooting outdoors. You depend upon your legs (more than you think). Your "core" is also extremely important and being aerobic fit should be an obvious advantage. High "resting" heart rates from lack of good cardiovascular and aerobic conditioning are not good for any shooting sport.

What to Do *Before* Shooting

TheraBand® Exercises Many of you know about "TheraBand®" stretching exercise routines, and I have a home-made band that I use all the time. This is not an endorsement for the TheraBand®, but rather only to make you aware of their easy availability and usefulness. "When used properly they help improve strength, range of motion and flexibility of the muscles. They can also help restore muscle and joint mobility, plus they are portable and versatile with virtually unlimited uses. Different resistance levels are determined by the thickness of the band. Each thickness is color coded so it is easy to monitor your progress from one level to the next. TheraBand® resistive exercise bands are endorsed by the American Physical Therapy Association." (Source *www.yogaaccessories.com/TheraBandsIndividual.asp*)

Morin Trainer This is an excellent device that you can use to warm up with, but it isn't something you can take out on the field course with you. Great device and, in my opinion, well worth the money. If you have room in your bow case, it would be

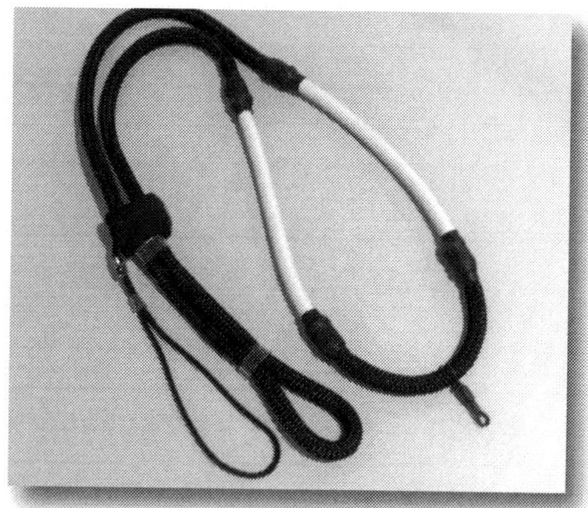

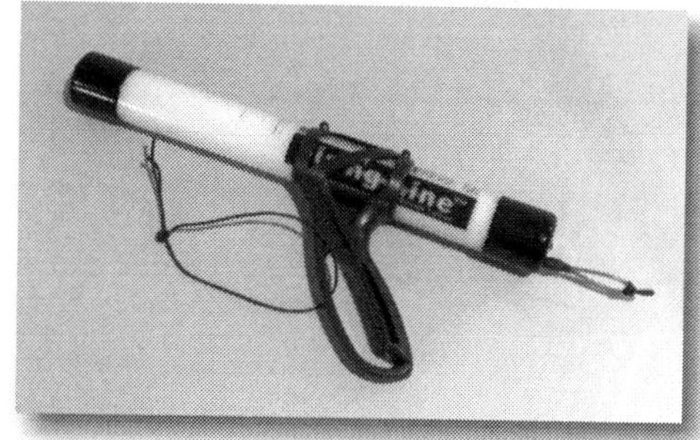

The Morin Trainer (left) and the Saunders Firing Line Simulator (above)

ideal to take with you to events, using it instead of the practice bales to "get warm." Just don't overdo it with the trainer and "shoot yourself out." At least with the Morin Trainer, you won't have any negative affects on your mental game by seeing arrows not going into the middle.

Saunders Firing Line Simulator This product is also a good one to use for prepping prior to a tournament round. Once again, however, it is too large and cumbersome to take with you onto a field range.

So, if the above devices aren't "good" to carry with you, how can you warm-up without the use of any mechanical system or device? Simple. The good "old-fashioned" way: exercise by using your body for resistance!

In keeping with my promise, I'm not going to provide you a series of step-by-step photos, diagrams and schematics concerning how to do these exercises. You've seen these before. The question comes down to whether or not you bother to "loosen up" properly without getting into the mode of "I must shoot for 20 or 30 minutes before I can be ready to score" syndrome. Once again, if you are practicing that you need to shoot that long or XYZ arrows before you are "ready to score," then, in my opinion, you are probably using a less than ProActive approach with regard to this process. Taking a ProActive approach isn't complicated, nor is it intensive enough to strain muscles or tire you out before you make it to the shooting line. You certainly won't have thrown off your mental game because some shots weren't in the middle, and you certainly won't have shot most of the best arrows of the day into the practice bales. Nothing is stopping you from doing these as a daily relaxation routine either!

Here are some "body resistance" exercises you can use:

Head Roll Rotate your head to the right for one count, feeling the stretch up the left side of your neck. Next, rotate your head back for one count, stretching your chin to the ceiling and letting your mouth open.

Rotate your head to the left for one count, and finally, drop your head to your chest for one count. Do five repetitions; more if you feel that necessary.

Shoulder Lift This exercise can be done to help loosen up your shoulders and neck prior to lifting your bow. Lift your right shoulder up toward your ear for one count. Then lift your left shoulder up for one count and lower your right shoulder. Repeat this for 5 to 10 repetitions; more reps if you think it necessary or it feels so good that a few more really helps settle those shoulders for you.

Side Stretch Open your arms to the side (T-Form!) and then lift them until they are over your head. Reach your right arm as far upward toward the ceiling/sky as you can for one count. Feel the stretch up your right side. Relax and then repeat this with the left arm. Repeat from right arm to left arm for 5 to 10 repetitions. A variation of this exercise is to grab the wrist of the raised arm with the opposing arm and gently lean and stretch to the opposing side of the fully raised arm, and hold for three counts as you feel the entire side of your body stretch. Five repetitions for each side work well for me. It feels so good stretching out the lats and other torso muscles. Beware; this can be habit forming!

Side Stretch Variation This exercise is a variant of the Side Stretch (*above*) that really helps to loosen up the arm and side muscles. Raise your left arm above your head and then bend it so that the forearm crosses the top of your head. Grab the left arm with your right hand to hold it in place on your head, and then simply raise the left elbow to feel the stretch of the muscles in your upper arm and left side. Hold the upper stretch for a 5-count. Repeat with the right side. Three repetitions on each side are enough to start with; more if you feel the need to stretch a bit longer.

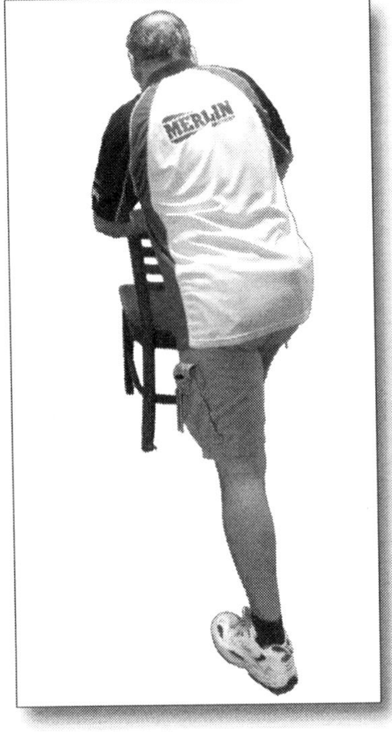

Calf–Achilles Stretch This exercise really helps a lot if you do this prior to shooting a field round or even prior to getting to the shooting line for an indoor event. Normally people don't think about their calves and Achilles tendons when shooting archery. However, I've found, especially with my left knee problem, that if I do this exercise prior to shooting, I am much more comfortable standing on the line or walking a field course. My legs remain loose, and I avoid problems with "burning calves" when climbing hills.

Here is how it is done: lean against a wall, or pole, or car with your left leg in front of the right and your arms forward. Keep your right leg straight and the left foot on the floor; then bend the left leg and lean forward by moving your hips toward the wall. Keep the right foot flat on the floor! Hold this position for 15 counts and feel the stretch, then repeat it for the left leg for 15 counts. Hint If you cannot keep the straight leg's foot flat on the floor, you probably have it too far back and should move it close to the other foot. Another thing that really helps is to relax the 'bent knee" so you better feel the stretch of the calf and Achilles on that straight leg.

Toe Touches Oh, how we hated this exercise when we were in PE class, right? You know, you put your feet at just narrower than shoulder width apart (archery stance, huh?), then slowly bend forward from your waist, letting your back and shoulders relax as you stretch toward your toes. Reach down as far as you can and hold for 15 counts. The key to this exercise is to not bounce up and down, and don't try to put your palms on the floor! It is a slow stretch exercise. I normally do about 15 repetitions of this slow stretch, but with a wrinkle: when I straighten back up from the bend, I lean backwards by putting my hands on my hips and slow stretching my back for a slow 5-count. Try not to bend your knees very much. At first you will bend your knees a lot, but as you gain flexibility, you'll be amazed at how much this will help you.

T-Formation Arm Rotations This is probably the most useful exercise I have run across for "loosening up" while waiting to shoot a field tournament or waiting for my line on an indoor event to start. It is simple, easy to do, and worth every second of time. Here's how: stand erect with your shoulders down and arms at your sides. Raise both arms to the "T-form" while keeping your shoulders down and your neck and head relaxed. Extend your arms and hold the "T-form." Then, rotate both arms in a clockwise rotation in small circles (4-6 inches) for 10 counts. Stop, and then reverse the rotation of both arms to the counter-clockwise rotation in small circles for 10 counts. Your arms will start to tire, so let them down to your sides, shake them loose, and then repeat this again. Two reps for me seem adequate. Then, following the same procedure, use larger circles (12″ or more) for the same exercises, and, if you want, flex your wrists at the same time. This feels surprisingly good and makes picking up that bow for the first time that day much easier. Your shoulders and arms loosen up nicely

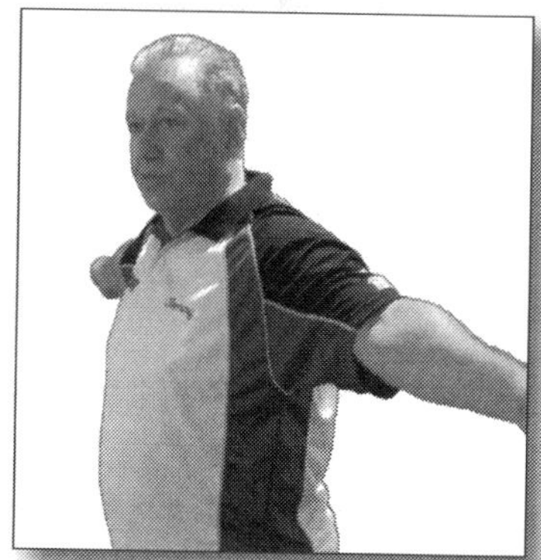

Cross-Armed Swings This is another exercise that really helps loosen up and stretch your shoulders and arm muscles. It is very relaxing and you don't really think you're doing much; however, the benefits show up soon enough. Here's how—bring both arms towards the centerline of your body, one arm under the other. Stretch them past the center-line of your body, left arm to the right side of your body, right arm to the left to feel the stretch. Then, open your arms back up to the T-formation mentioned above and rotate your arms behind you to feel the stretch and hold for two counts. When you come back across your body centerline in front, reverse which arm crossed on top and repeat. I've found that 5 or 10 repetitions of this, while feeling a slow and steady stretch, works wonders in loosening me up prior to even thinking about pulling the bow. I normally do two sets of 10 repetitions on each arm.

Warning Always, always, always, if something starts to hurt when exercising, stop doing the exercise. You are either overdoing it, doing it wrong, or are aggravating an existing injury.

First Practice End and First Target for Score Technique

One last thing that has really helped me is not an exercise *per se*, but it is a final little thing that could make a difference at the very beginning of your tournament round. It is simple and is done twice during the first practice end, and also once during the first scoring end. Here's it is: Draw back your bow and anchor. Settle in and aim at the target, but without your finger on the trigger and without any intention of shooting that arrow. Hold the position and stretch, aiming the entire time, and then let the shot down. Repeat one more time for the practice end or target. For the first scoring target, I choose to do this only once and only if I find myself more jittery than normal. This added stretching and breathing seems to work really well to relieve competition butterflies. If you need to settle down more, there is nothing wrong with doing this twice on that first scoring target. Just remember the "let down" rule per arrow or the shooting clock (if there is one) and don't let yourself get carried away.

Between Shooting Sessions or If Time Permits before a Tournament

Hamstring Stretch I learned this variation of the popular stretching exercise while in rehabilitation therapy after my heart surgery. I don't have great knee flexibility, so they modified this for me by having me doing it with both legs straight out in front of me about half-shoulder width apart. While sitting on the floor with both legs extended, simply stretch toward your toes with both arms extended as far as you can go. Do not bounce and stretch. I do five repetitions of this. Then, I repeat the same exercise by extending one arm at a time to the opposing toe, straighten up and then reach with the other arm to the opposing toe. I do three sets of five repetitions of this exercise.

Knee Bends Deep knee bends are difficult and a person must be careful with them. However, shallower knee bends when used in unison with the arms was an integral part of my rehab therapy and I found that they really helped me with my other activities, including archery. Here's how—start with your feet about shoulder width apart, begin to squat down while at the same time bending and raising both arms up to head

Deep Knee Bends—Here I am holding hand weights to increase the load.

height (not beyond). I was told not to even go to 90 degree bends in my knees. Do two sets of 10 reps to start with. As you get better at it, you can add 1 pound weights to your hands to add some "spice and burn" to this workout routine. This sounds silly, but at home, I've modified this and use my Morin Trainer by drawing the Morin to anchor when upright, hold it until I hit the bottom of the knee bends and let it down at that point. Feels good. I'd never do this with a bow in my hand and I certainly wouldn't do this out on the range. First off, I don't think it is safe to do it with a bow in your hand, and secondly, people would think I've gone daft!

Running, Cycling, Walking Of course, any fitness regimen should involve a variety of different types of activity to build or maintain your fitness level. Everyone has their favorites, and I certainly cannot list them all. Any of a variety of the above, indoors or outdoors, can provide any number of outlets for stress and let you have fun while actually doing something away from archery that will help your archery.

I cannot stress enough the importance of good and sensible aerobic training and how it can help with archery. If you are more aerobically fit, your heart rate and breathing rate are lower and your lung capacity is increased; all good things for competitive archery! I have admitted that I'm a fanatic when it comes to long distance road cycling and racquetball, so those are my choices for aerobic and cardio workouts, along with Nordic Tracking and a new addition to my arsenal, the new ProForm *Generation 2 Tour de France* cycling simulator. This has allowed me to get as close to real cycling conditions indoors when the weather is too lousy outdoors to get out onto a bicycle. So, if you live in an area that is too hot, too cold, or too wet to exercise aerobically outdoors comfortably, there are such alternatives.

Summary

A good pre-shooting stretching and warm-up regimen, in my opinion, can have a huge impact on how well you start out and also on how well you hold up during the rigors of an archery tournament.

It almost goes without saying that physical, cardiovascular and aerobic conditioning can be very important to your success on a field or 3-D course. What is indeed sad is that I see very, very few shooters do anything as far as warming up or stretching prior to shooting. They just walk in, set up their bows and equipment, walk up to the shooting line, and start shooting arrows. I guess they figure that shooting arrows is the only way to "get their muscles going" or something. Many of today's shooters have come to count upon shooting arrows, either for some pre-determined quantity of arrows, or an amount of time. If they don't get that, then they have it in their heads that they cannot be "ready to shoot for score" and that "warm-up" is needed or else. It shouldn't be that way, and with ProActive tournament preparation, and a set of exercises that accomplish the same thing and more, coupled with a practice regimen of shooting first arrow is for score during scoring practice rounds, a person shouldn't "need" all those practice shots to get ready to go for real in a tournament.

As I stated earlier, I've managed over the years to place higher than my talent should have allowed me to, simply because I was more physically and aerobically fit and sometimes more confident than my competition. I strongly feel that because of my regimen including exercises described above, I've not only saved myself from injury, but I've enhanced my capabilities and I do know for a fact, I've even prolonged my life.

You have nothing to lose by trying some or all of the above stretching and warm-up exercises and routines: nothing to lose and much to gain. Always be careful to not over-stretch or to over-repeat any of the above routines. Too much of a good thing can have negative effects as well.

Be safe, be fit, and enjoy archery to the fullest.

Tom Dorigatti

25

Your Personal Shot Sequence

I am sure you have read countless articles about a having a shot sequence, following a shot sequence, and even competing while using a shot sequence. However, there is seldom of any mention of how to figure out your shot sequence or what goes into setting your shot sequence. Amd is this really how the pros have their uncanny ability to do the same thing in nearly exactly the same manner, shot after shot, and round after round? All you seem to hear or read is that as long as you do everything the same exact way every single time, even if it is "wrong," you will be competitive and shoot great scores or you will be able to easily bring down any game that comes within your range. Once again, the "how" to go about it is lost in the translation; the emphasis always being placed on the "what" to do part of it.

Sometimes, this is even all contradicted with the advice "don't think about it, just let it happen." That is fine and good for those who have been at this for years and everything is pretty much automated. What about those who don't have all this stuff automated and really don't know whether or not they have any sort of ProActive approach to how they go about shooting each and every arrow with as close to the same sequence each and every time? What about those who are trying to learn their own process? What about those who are having to make some changes and need to reorganize things?

There is an order of things that have to be accomplished. Obviously, you can't draw the bow back without hooking up the release first. Obviously, you can't draw the bow back without setting your bow hand into the bow. You can't hook up the release before addressing the target, er, well, I mean, you can, but then what happens next? I'm not going to list anyone's opinions or details of 12 (or 4, or 9, or 10) steps of a shot sequence; you can read that in other books and from different sources.

This chapter is intended to help you to put together your own personal shot sequence based upon what your tendencies are, where you tend to unconsciously make "changes" to the way you do things, and what critical things you tend to forget that throw off your concentration or focus and ruin your scoring potential. Thus I offer you a means for you to figure things out as they apply to your situation and get yourself better organized, "One Bite of the Elephant at a Time."

How to Begin Isolating Your Personal Shot Sequence

All of you do indeed have a shot sequence, but I'm willing to wager that very few of you, especially those of you who are beginning-to-intermediate archers, have any idea as to what you actually do when executing any given shot. My reason for saying this is simple: very few beginners or intermediate shooters are shooting perfect 300 indoor scores, or 300 scores with greater than 45 X-ring hits. Therefore, it should be pretty evident that you need work, and the starting point isn't in just more practice. It should also be obvious that you are inconsistent as to what order or manner you are accomplishing each shot; otherwise, you'd be getting 300 scores more frequently and with more X-ring hits. Something is changing from shot to shot, and it is up to you to isolate it. The solution is practicing and learning to shoot each shot with exactly the same sequence of events performed for every single shot you take. As I have stated, your objective can't be a future event, such as "I want to hit the X-ring with this shot," but rather it should be in the execution of that shot with proper form, and let the X-ring take care of itself. You can only control the present, but if your present isn't controlled, then obviously, you are defeated before you even start. Even negative thoughts or a lack of confidence can disrupt the entire process. This I know from first-hand experience. If you aren't practicing being consistent in repeating your correct shot sequence, just when is that supposed to happen? The path to consistency is through your shot sequence and is right there for the taking; all you have to do is go sit down and take the time to find it!

Writing Down What You Do

It may sound silly, but about the only way you can isolate your shot sequence is to write it down. Using someone else's shot sequence is likely not to work for you. Sure, it gives you a great basis as a start, so that is good, but the bad is that the "how they do it" isn't in that shot sequence. You have to learn that for yourself. That is to say, you must write down every single thing that you do when you prepare to shoot an arrow; from when you step up to the shooting line or stake, right on through to when you hear the impact of the arrow on the target. It is essential that you don't miss even what may seem as a miniscule, inconsequential item in this entire process. I have given you some tools to establish your correct body positioning and stance. I've given you other tools to help make sure you and your equipment are set up properly. I've given you the tools to help you isolate and quickly correct your equipment setup when something moves or gets knocked out of whack. We are now going to organize these events allowing you correct yourself when something in your shot gets out of whack, always keeping you focused on your shot process. Something to help you slow down, think things through, and stay focused on the job

An archer's best friend—a cheap notebook in which eveything can be written down.

at hand and not allow the outside influences to make you nervous. Remember, you can only think of one thing at a time out there, so if you can keep yourself on task, that last miss, or that shooter next you talking to himself on the line won't enter your world, since you are in a "zone" and a world of your own.

Remember this very important thing: the top echelon shooters have their shot sequences "automated" from countless hours of practice, modification, analysis, and still more practice in doing exactly the same thing in the same order, time after time after time until it does indeed become "automatic." It didn't come to them as if by magic as they stood on the line flinging arrows and trying this and trying that. The "trying this" and "trying that" are exactly what beginner level and many intermediate and even some "upper level" shooters do at every practice session. In the first chapter of this book, I listed 20 things shooters change with their equipment or setups "on the fly." That chapter came first, because I needed that emphasis as a springboard to what the philosophy about being a ProActive archer is all about. Well, most of us do exactly the same thing with how we set up and execute our shots as well. We change this and then we change that to the point that our shooting sequence becomes haphazard and a "what did I do wrong" approach (instead of, "I know what I did right, and I also know that I messed up on this specific item").

Here's a scenario: you are shooting and you shoot an arrow out high and to the left for the third or fourth time. You already start to think, "Well that didn't work, so I better try this with my bow hand, and this with my release hand, and this with my bow arm, and be more careful about my aiming, and. . . ." Sound familiar? Yes, you have now put four or more other "things to do" into your thought process all at once and lost your focus. If you have a shot sequence written down or memorized, the correct approach is not to analyze all of the past shot or to dwell on it. The right approach is to go back through your mental or written checklist, review it in you mind, and then, execute the next shot correctly, or at least as close to correctly as you can. You need to focus on what is right to do and not on what you are doing wrong. If you adopt this method, you won't have to think about four or five things all at once as you try the next shot; you are doing it one step at a time. And, if you don't know which step you erred on, because you are disorganized and simply go through the motions, how can you correct it? Are you beginning to see my rationale about having a written shot sequence?

An Example of a Beginning Shot Sequence

Quite probability, the easiest way to help you through this process is to give you an example of what I'm talking about. I'll describe a shot sequence that one of my students and I put together and, yes, the basic steps are all covered and in order, but in that shooter's own words and in words that make sense to that shooter and might seem like nonsense to somebody else. I've heard people tell my students just that! I'll proceed to break it down into a manageable list, one that isn't cumbersome and confusing to you when you are on the shooting line trying to concentrate. Comments will only be made based upon observations or, if necessary, to further explain that particular item.

An Example of a Complete Shot Sequence (Beginner Level)

1. *Get correct shooting stance.* I see even mid-level archers who do not have the same shooting stance from end to end, and sometimes they even change their stance from shot to shot. Changing your stance changes your alignment, and has a huge impact on your consistency. From the beginning, I was always taught to keep my feet still unless I was sure that I had not assumed the proper stance. In my opinion, this should be the first step in everyone's personal shot sequence. If you are having problems with this, I previously outlined how to make sure you had a proper stance each and every time you step to the line. This involves placing a sheet of poster paper or butcher paper on the shooting line, and marking the shooting line on the paper for proper re-positioning. Then, once you have your proper stance, you simply use a permanent marker to mark the position of your feet by outlining them onto the poster or butcher paper. Then, for a month or so, at every practice session, you put down the paper onto the shooting line, and then step into position with your feet as previously marked. You will have "memorized" that foot position in short order and will also have a reference for future use, in case the old habit creeps back in. Remember, your draw length is tuned to your stance, and your stance is tuned to your draw length. If you change draw length or stance, then you need to mark your new foot position on your "paper" and memorize it again.
2. *Withdraw correct arrow from the quiver.* I teach my students to number their arrows and to shoot their arrows in a prescribed order. The number of the arrow matches the particular target face (if you are using the 5-spot NFAA or 3-spot Vegas faces, for example). This also lets you analyze later on, while scoring your arrows, if a particular arrow is acting up or whether "you" are acting up on a particular arrow during an end.
3. *Load arrow onto bowstring in correct orientation.* With many of today's arrow rests, loading the arrow in the wrong orientation won't matter much. However, with some "shoot around" arrow rests, loading the arrow in the wrong orientation can cause a miss down range. Some top professionals have their arrow rests set up so that even with the wrong orientation, they will still hit the X-ring at 20 yards. However, beginners and intermediates are not pros. That is why this item is in a beginner's checklist.
4. *Be sure arrow nock is between the knots on the D-loop.* Sound silly? Well, I've seen this happen to shooters on the line more often than you can imagine! (My editor tells me he did it at the NFAA Outdoor Nationals.) So, when starting out, it isn't a bad idea to get this one written down. It will become a matter of habit to do it correctly in short order. You will only mess this up once, but why take the risk of having it happen? Be ProActive about it, prevent it ahead of time.
5. *Locate correct target.* Believe it or not, archers often shoot at the wrong target, especially under tournament pressure. It is impossible to not get rattled if you shoot the wrong target! By matching step #2 (above) to this step, it helps you to keep your concentration and prevent shooting the wrong target face or putting two shots into the same target face, etc.

6. *Load release onto D-loop*, or connect release to bow string.
7. *Put slight pressure on bowstring with release.* Make sure to set the angle of your release hand at this point and not to change it when you hit anchor! Moving around the release hand angle at full draw takes time, and makes it very difficult to replicate. It is tough enough to do at release hookup, but impossible if you are gyrating around as you are trying to acquire the target and take care of other business at full draw. The fewer changes and movements you make during the draw and anchor, the better!
8. *Place bow hand into position on grip of bow.* Way too many shooters spend an inordinate amount of time at this step, only to change it later! Too much fuss is being made by beginner-to-intermediate shooters concerning "exacting" bow hand placement (more to come on this).
9. *Raise bow arm to target level.* Regarding this item, "skying" the bow is becoming too commonplace these days as more and more beginners get hooked on high poundage for more speed. "Skying" the bow is not only a problem that can cause injury to joints and muscles; it usually leads to those muscles being in the wrong positions for what we want to do. It also is a safety problem as well. Many lights have been shot out, ceiling tiles ruined, and even building sprinkler heads shot off because of this practice by inexperienced shooters. Many ranges will not allow "skying" of the bow.
10. *Pre-aim at the correct target.* If you have followed step #5, you already know which spot you should be shooting at.
11. *Position your draw elbow up.* Once again, if you are over-bowed the tendency is to draw the bow by twisting at the hips, lowering the drawing elbow to the side of your body and forcing your arms and body to draw the bow back to its full draw position and then struggle to move it into your full draw position and find your anchor. This places a huge strain on the rotator cuff of the bow shoulder, the shoulders, lower back, and even the neck muscles. It is a harbinger of a serious injury. Once again, more movement and fidgeting around means that replication of the same thing over and over again is less likely to occur.
12. *Take a breath, let it out.* Many shooters use this step to relax themselves and also to provide oxygen with which to draw the bow. Many also do this along with Step #1; nothing wrong with that, however, between this step and step #1, a lot has happened, so you need oxygen!
13. *Avoid "Re-setting" the Grip.* This step is a final check to step 8 above. I stated that most shooters actually set their grip just before drawing the bow. I learned about grip from an "old school" archer of PAA fame, Denise Libby. I was having problems shooting left and right with my Golden Eagle recurve bow and finger tab. Denise shook hands with me one evening and her hand was . . . all gooey. She also ran her hand around the grip of my Golden Eagle Recurve bow! Then, she told me to go ahead and shoot. I told her I couldn't shoot with this slime on my bow hand because the bow would come back and hit me in the face. She told me not to worry about it and just shoot. I shot several arrows with this "gooey" set up

and to my amazement, the arrows were going right down the middle, and the bow was extremely comfortable in my hand to boot! Denise then told me that with the "Vaseline grip drill" that I would quickly learn to just let the bow settle into what is a natural fit for the bow to my hand and not worry about it. She said that the bow grip, if I just let it work by itself, would find that "sweet spot" every single time. The very next league night, I shot my first indoor 300 with fingers on the string, and believe me, left and right arrows were not a problem! Since then, I've always just let the bow seek its own natural position, not being overly concerned with my "grip" of the bow. It is akin to "letting it float, and shooting the shot." Set it once (step 8), check here in step 13, and if it has moved, let it down and start over! Set it and forget it, unless you have knowingly changed it; this is about your last chance for recovery, so be ProActive about it.

14. *Drop your shoulders.* This step is often missed, especially with beginners and intermediate shooters that are struggling with either too long of a draw length, too much poundage, or both. This critical step is one that can really cause problems with alignment, sight picture, steadiness, confidence, and of course the point of impact of the arrow. Some drop their shoulders and are able to keep them down during step #8 or step #12. If so, then fine; otherwise, I teach my students to make sure those shoulders are down and that bone on bone alignments are in place and that their bow shoulder is not up and back towards their chin or extended too far towards the target, or sagged in towards the shooter. If it isn't right, start over.
15. *Smoothly draw the bow to full draw/the stops.* You shouldn't just jerk the bow back quickly, but rather draw it smoothly and deliberately, never taking your eye off the correct target. Many shooters will have problems with this step if they are overbowed or are shooting either too weak of a launcher blade or too narrow of a launcher blade for the diameter and/or mass of the shaft they are trying to shoot. Anytime the arrow falls off the rest while trying to draw the bow, your concentration is broken, and you should start over. Anytime this becomes a constant problem, you need to analyze why you are having this problem and correct it . . . immediately. Normally it is from being over bowed, or having a launcher blade that is too narrow or too weak for your arrow shaft selection, or a pinched nock, or a combination of these things. This will destroy your focus if it becomes a constant problem!
16. *Move the bow string to you with minimum movement of your head, neck, and shoulders and release hand.* I can't emphasize this one enough. Keeping your head and eyes still goes a long, long way to making you consistent and able to duplicate everything from shot to shot. Some head movement may be inevitable, but bobbing your head/chin up or down or moving your head inwards or outwards to reach the string takes time, and when it comes to shot execution, taking too much time will result in a poorly executed shot. I preach, "Bring the string to you, don't you go chasing the string."
17. *Settle into your anchor firmly and solidly.* One problem for most beginner-to-intermediate shooters is the "anchor." As I wrote in Chapter 14, there are many

shooters who are convinced that today's cams are designed with "hard stops" and that means that they are drawing back the bow to the same spot every single time. My data indicate that this is far from the truth. And consistency of your "to anchor draw length" is probably directly related to your score; especially when it comes to X-counts. Outdoors, variation in "to anchor draw length" is very troubling; especially if the bow's draw length setting is too long for the shooter in question. I've seen archers who vary their "to anchor draw length" by as much a ¾″ from shot to shot, or end to end, or from beginning of the round to the end of the round as they tire. These people are shocked when I prove it to them. They cannot believe that those "hard stops" aren't automatically solving this problem for them! The real problem is getting into the hard stops fairly consistently, but due to alignment variations and you becoming tense, you are "leaking away" or losing tension to the point you cannot hold steady at all. Obviously this is a critical step. The most critical aspect of proper shooting form is achieving correct draw length. The sooner you master getting exactly to your draw length shot to shot, end to end, and round to round, the sooner your scores are going to come up and be more consistent.

18. *Center the scope into the peep sight.* The key here is that you already have your head in the correct position, and that your anchor and peep height are accommodated to each other. If you have to move your chin up or down, or if you have to fish for your anchor to get to your peep, you need to move your peep until you don't have to do that. Misaligning the scope housing with the hole in the peep sight can cause serious misses at distance. Indoors, it can "kill" your X-count and even cost you a 300 score. Watch out for bobbing the release aid hand, changing the angle of your release hand, and moving around to "hit anchor." This will cause you to be moving your head and chin at the same time. The procedure should be to accomplish this with little to no moving around or gyrating.
19. *Level up the bubble.* Many indoor shooters don't pay any attention to their bubble at all, and many do very well that way. However, since many shooters also shoot outdoors, I'm sure that those shooters are very cognizant of their bubble positioning no matter whether they are shooting indoors or outdoors. Yes, if you do the same thing every time, then it will have the same effect every time. However, with regard to the bubble, what you get away with indoors (being off level) will not serve you well outdoors past 20 yards! Why practice two different sequences and give yourself the chance to confuse which one you are using?
20. *Set your breath.* Most shooters will take a deep breath and let half of it out at this point.
21. *Take up the slack/go to the trigger/release aid body.* What is meant here is, through the learning process, to get the right amount of pressure onto the trigger of the release (take up the slack), and get "on" the trigger (or release aid body), but only firm enough to insure you are in contact with said trigger/body and not tending to punch it or being tentative with it. This is a learned process, and it is a tough part of the shot sequence. Apprehension, fear of missing, tightening up the release hand, pushing with the bow arm too much or too little, raising the draw-

ing elbow, elbow too low, too steep of a release hand angle, stiff pinky and/or thumb, will all cause problems with this step. Nobody can teach you the "how" of this part. You must learn how much pressure you can apply to the trigger or release to be comfortable with it not firing too early or too late.

22. *Continue your "pinch."* Notice that I did not say "start your pinch." If you are "starting" your pinch at this point, then obviously you have stopped it sometime during the process. This means that you really didn't have the proper full draw body position and now you have to re-establish the positioning and dynamics. This shot is wasted; you might as well let down and start over! The "tension" (back tension) or pulling should never completely stop during any drawing cycle. This is really a continuous effort. Starting or stopping the "pull/push" is problematical for most shooters because you get into "calibrating" and trying to make sure that the sight is dead center instead of "letting it float, trusting your form, and shooting the shot." I personally struggle with this particular element of my shot sequence every single arrow. Sometimes I execute it correctly, and it is nothing but "X." If I miss this step, or make a haphazard effort at it, then I'll shoot 5's and often lots of 4's. This step, at least for me, is more critical than step #17. However, keep in mind that I have shot for many years, so many of the steps above are second nature for me now. (This is a hint as to where we are going after this list is completed. Read on.)
23. *Let it float/don't force it.* This is pretty much self-explanatory. However, if, during this step you start to tighten up or the sight won't settle, or the sight is bobbing all over the place, then you have messed up long before you got to this step. Let down and start over! A rule of thumb I give to my beginners and intermediates is that if your dot comes out of the bull's-eye for the third time, let the shot down. For more advanced shooters, the rule of thumb is if it comes out of the X-ring for the third time, let down and start over. This step is very, very difficult to master and be religious about, especially under tournament pressure or when people are waiting on you during a practice session. I struggle with "forcing it" myself, so you aren't alone, my friends!
24. *Keep your chin steady.* Many shooters tend to let their chins sag when a shot is taking too long. At this point, once the chin comes down or even rises, everything else falls out of whack and the shot is a lost cause. Let down and start over.
25. *Finish the shot.* What is meant by this step is that the bow arm stays up until you hear the impact of the arrow. I teach that the shot isn't over until the arrow is in the target. Other variants used that are based upon this theme are "same contact point with release hand," or "bow directly towards the target." Remember, as Dean Pridgen says, "Followthrough; the last thing to happen, but the first thing to go."
26. *Remain focused/restart for next shot.*
27. *Run the next shot's shot sequence through your mind.* This step is important to accomplish every single shot, every single time. First off, it keeps you focused on the positives. It allows you to shake off that last shot, forget about it, and get focused on the only shot you can control, that being the one that you are now

loading up in your bow. If you are using the placard, then read it through entirely between each shot, and at the same time, visualize exactly how you are going to execute this next shot. Remember, it is the only shot you are in control of at this time. This also keeps you focused on your job and gets your mind away from the past and into the present. You can only control the present when it comes to shot execution, so re-establish this contact now. Besides, if you are reading your checklist or running it consciously through your mind, you won't hear that person next you to saying "Oh, Crap!" (or worse).

28. *Think no negative thoughts.* I cannot stress this enough. Anything negative that enters your mind should prompt a complete restart of any shot sequence. If you even think "miss" or "wrong" or "isn't right" then this should prompt a complete re-starting of the shot sequence, no matter where your happen to be during that shot sequence. Stop now!

What's Next?

By now you are saying to yourself "I'll never have time between shots to go through all of this stuff!" You are absolutely correct in saying that. However, now that you have it written down on paper, you simply need to go back through it and, on a separate paper or on your computer, ask yourself two questions as you read each step of your shot sequence:

A. Do I already do this every time without having to really think about it? (It's automated already).
B. Does this item ever cause me to miss or shoot a bad shot because I tend to forget to do it?

If you answered "yes" to A and "no" to Question B, then you don't need to put it on your "new" list. If, on the other hand, you answered "no" to Question A and "yes" to Question B, then you need to keep the item on your new shot sequence list and highlight it in red. You might be doing it every time in your mind, but the effect of not doing it causes you to miss, so you are probably "off and on" with the item.

This is a simple process. Be aware, however, that beginners will have longer lists, typically of about 10-15 key items. An intermediate shooter might have about the same number of items, but they are likely more sophisticated or refined than those on a beginner's list. I recommend that an upper level shooter keep their checklist down to eight items or less. In addition, if you have found a discrepancy not on your shot sequence, or you are learning a new release aid or making a form change, then those critical items will need to be incorporated into a new checklist. If you are, say, not having bow hand positioning problems, then why put it on the checklist? If you aren't having problems keeping your chin in position, then why have that on your checklist. You'll understand more as we progress.

Example of a Pared Down List for a Beginning Shooter

Here's an example of a "pared down" shot sequence list for a beginning shooter or one who has not used a written checklist before, but opted to trust their memory. This is one possible checklist as a result of asking and answering the two questions for each of the 28 steps above.

1. Correct Shooting Stance.
2. Correct Arrow/Nock Orientation/D-loop?
3. Correct Target
4. Hook Up/Bow Hand, Settle Grip
5. Pre-Aim
6. Elbow Up, Shoulders Down
7. Breathe
8. Draw String to Me
9. Solid Anchor/Stops
10. Center Scope/Level up/Focus
11. Take up Slack
12. Continue Pinch
13. Chin Steady/Relax
14. Finish Shot

This checklist was developed by asking the two questions for each item of the master list and then using only the "Key Words" and combining related steps together. This list is a little long, but again, it is intended to help a beginner who is just learning his/her shot sequence. Thus, they need the extra support and prompting so that they are more easily accommodated into doing the same things in the same order, every single time.

You will notice that this shot sequence is down from 28 steps to only 14. You will also notice that "aim, aim, aim" is not part of this checklist. The reason for this is that step #23 handles this just fine. I try to teach my students to concentrate on "Letting it Float and Shooting the Shot" rather than aiming. In my opinion, "aiming" or "aim hard" brings on calibrating, and calibrating brings on freezing or being tentative in shooting the shot and as a result, the entire shot sequence breaks down too quickly. Besides that, what is "aiming" anyway? If you ask ten people what aiming is, you will likely get ten different answers! Notice also that the checklist does not contain any negatives. This is a "can do" list and not a "don't do" list. Remember, anything negative that enters your mind during a shot will cause you to end up in a miss. You certainly don't want to have your checklist countering this philosophy.

How Do You Get this Up Front and Personal?

If you have done this for yourself, you now have your shot sequence pared down to a more manageable level and your "Key Words" contained therein. It is a simple process to type it up, size it, print it out, and then place it where it is directly visible to you without having to hunt and for it or cause a lot of movement on the shooting line (so as to avoid disrupting the shooters next to you). Here's how I accomplish this:

Assuming you have access to a computer:

1. Make a Text Box in MS Word (or other word processor) that is 2.0 inches wide by 3.0 inches long.
2. Then, by numbering your items, simply make a list inside the text box, using a

font size you can easily read.

3. Put those critical items you tend to make mistakes on in red on the list, the others can go in black or blue. My personal checklist is down to seven items (I'm learning three new elements that have come up and causing me problems since my change over to left-handed shooting), so my card is only 1½″x 2½″.
4. Put double sided tape on the back of your check list.
5. Cut out your check-list from the paper/tape combination
6. Cover your checklist with writeable clear cello tape to prevent it from washing out.
7. You can make a "placard" out of the material used for blister packs. Release aids, nocks, vanes, etc will come in a blister pack large enough to accommodate the size you need. Just cut out a piece to match the size of your Text Box cut-out.
8. Place your checklist onto the blister pack plastic material
9. Attach the checklist to your bow riser with Velcro. Attach it so that it is in plain view for you to read between shots and so that you don't have to move around to see it or get at it. Make sure that it isn't in your sight window or view when you are aiming at the target.

Sample Beginner's Checklist and What it Looks Like in Bow-ready Form

1. Correct Shooting Stance.
2. **Correct Arrow/Nock Orientation/D-loop**
3. Correct Target
4 **Hook up/ Bow hand**
5 **Pre-Aim**
6 Elbow UP, Shoulders Down
7 **Breathe, Settle Grip**
8 Draw String to You
9 Solid Anchor/stops
10 **Center scope/Level up/Focus**
11 Take up Slack
12 Continue Pinch
13 Chin Steady/Relax
14 Finish Shot

(This is in "red.")

My Present Personal Checklist

1. **Stance**
2. Set Release angle
3. Center Peep
4. Rotate Elbow
5. Maintain Contact
6. RELAX
7. Chin Up
8. RELAX

(This is in "red.")

A Student's Personal Check-List

1. Proper Stance
2. Correct Arrow
3. Correct Target
4. Thumb Contact
5. Chin Steady
6. Pull / Contact
7. 2X off = Let down
8. Bow Arm Up

(This is in "red.")

Summary

We have discussed the importance of getting organized and writing down your shot sequence. You should start with writing down everything you do in the process of shooting an arrow. (This really has to be "everything," because what will happen if you leave something out?) Then, after itemizing this shot sequence checklist, you ask the following two questions:

1. Do I already do this every time without having to really think about it? (It's automated already).
2. Does this item cause me to miss or shoot a bad shot because I tend to forget to do it?

- If you answer yes to "A" and "no" to question "B", then delete it from your "new" list.
- If you answer No to question A and yes to question B, then you need to keep the item on your new shot sequence list and highlight it in red. You might be doing it every time in your mind, but the effect of not doing it causes you to miss, so you are probably off and on with the item.

Be aware that beginners will have longer checklists (about 10-15 key items). Intermediate shooters will have about the same number of items, but they will be more sophisticated than those of a beginner. I recommend that an upper level shooter keep their checklist down to eight items or fewer. In addition, if you have found a discrepancy that is not on your shot sequence or you are learning a new release aid or form change, then those critical items will need to be incorporated into a new checklist.

I then took an example 28 item list and pared it down to 14 "critical" items that beginning shooter needed to complete in order every time in order to complete a perfect or nearly perfect shot. I outlined how to make the "Checklist Placard" on a computer so that you could cut it out, apply it to a piece of blister pack plastic, and then attach it to your riser with Velcro, placed it so that you could read it between shots before you start the next shot. This constant reviewing of your shot sequence will quickly get it ingrained into your mind so that it will more quickly become part of your shot sequence without you really having to think about it. If you need it, then read it, if you are having problems refocusing between shots, then pull it out and read it from start to finish between each shot; it will help you to settle down and stay focused on the job at hand. It will also help you to quickly discover the "goof up" you may have just committed but have yet to figure out!

I also emphasized the importance of having a proper shooting stance and being consistent with adopting it. We discussed reiterated the importance of being as close as possible to the same exact "to anchor draw length" and its potential effect on consistency and accuracy, especially outdoors. I pointed out that a common error is made by drawing the string of the bow in a direction other than to the shooter's full draw position. In addition, the shooter should keep his/her head/chin position as movement free as possible, especially when coming in to anchor and during the completion of the "pinch" (back tension).

You were provided with three sample Shooter's Checklists, among them my own current personal checklist that I'm using at the time of writing this chapter. Be advised that my personal checklist is, as is yours, not cast in stone and is indeed a Work In Progress, with the positive being the emphasis on "Progress."

Shot sequences can and do change. What is good about this ProActive approach to having a written and visible shooter's check list is that it can be updated quickly and easily. It is visible to you any time you want it. If you find something that has crept into your form that isn't on the check list, or if something that is on the check list is out of date and no longer needs to be there, you simply add the new item or get rid of the old.

The placard is inexpensive to make, is light, and can be positioned in such a fashion that you can have it readily available to help you keep on track, shooting one good shot at a time. It can and will help to keep you focused on your game and help you to forget about a bad shot, get it out of your mind and allow you to focus on the next one.

You can only think of one thing at a time. Thinking through your shot sequence is thinking form. Thinking form will allow you to focus on only form and to "let it float and shoot the shot." If you trust the shot, then it happens by itself. It will happen by itself, if you repeat the steps on your check-list exactly the same way every time, from shot to shot, end to end, and round to round.

If you've never given any thought to what your shot sequence is, then perhaps it is time you give this method a try. If you are having shooting problems, I think you will find that by following the above program, you will begin to improve and better understand what it is that you do correctly, and what it is that sometimes you get out of sequence or perhaps rush by or forget to complete it at all. If you use this method and things are going well, you may well remove the Placard from your bow's riser. However, it would be wise to retain that checklist for use "when" (not if) your shooting takes a down turn. You will most likely get yourself right back on track in minutes by breaking out this checklist, reattaching it to your riser, and reading it between each and every shot. You will most likely say to yourself "Holy cow, I let that one slide, and

I can now fix it."

This is yet another piece of "ProActive Archery" at work.

26

Your Personal Shot Sequence—Practicing What You Preach

This statement from the previous chapter bears repeating:

"You, I am sure, have read countless articles about a having a shot sequence, following a shot sequence, and even competing while using a shot sequence. However, there is seldom of any mention of how to figure out your shot sequence or what goes into getting your shot sequence. You probably also ask yourself, is this really how the pros have this uncanny ability to do the same thing in nearly exactly the same manner, shot after shot, and round after round? All you seem to hear or read is that as long as you do everything the same exact way every single time, even if it is "wrong," you will be competitive and shoot great scores or you will be able to easily bring down any game that comes within your range. Once again, the "how" to go about it is lost in the translation; the emphasis always being placed on the "what" to do part of it."

This chapter expands upon the previous chapter to give you guidance and insight into making your shot sequence work for you and not against you.

A Word of Caution Some shooters will scoff at the idea of you having a checklist/placard mounted on your bow while you are shooting. Typically these are more experienced archers who have already mastered their shot sequences, and can repeat them without much forethought. In other words, they already have this "thing" mastered and automated. They run their mental checklist out of habit more than out of conscious forethought. This is fine . . . for them. They have the experience. However, let me caution you that many of them will eventually have something creep into their shot sequence that will give them great difficulty in tracking down, simply because they won't have anything written anywhere to help them figure out what has wormed its way into their form. I see this routinely, and often it occurs to those who scoff at me and my students when they see these placards appear from time to time. Yes, you have it, this checklist and placard checklist is more "ProActive Archery" at work!

In the form of general support for this approach, let me quote George Ryals IV, a top professional archer and instructor. George says in a posting on Archery Live's forum, "Occupying your "urge to control" with a regimented task list that is simple and very straight forward will free your automatic process to run the important stuff in the background." Bingo! There you have it. I hope this chapter will allow you to build your shot sequence and occupy your "urge to control" by using that regimented task list, thus freeing up your automatic process to run the important automated stuff in the background. What you have to find out and figure out is what you already have under subconscious control, and work on only those items that you need to get automated. It is next to impossible to do this without a checklist of some sort. Remember, your mind can only focus consciously on one thing at a time.

I will add here, again, that aiming is not the answer! I discourage my students to put "aim" into their conscious checklists. There isn't really a solid or even a well documented definition of what "aiming" really is, certainly not one that will work with the conscious or subconscious mind. So, why incorporate an unknown into your personal shot sequence checklist?

A Closer Look at My Current Personal Shot Sequence

If you have read the previous chapters, you know about my background and forced change to left-handed shooting. Obviously that change also forced me to adopt a completely new shot sequence. A lot of what used to be automated and subconscious no longer was "automatic." Think about it: I used to close my left eye while shooting and that was an ingrained automatic process. Now, however, I had to learn to close my right eye, only to find out that my right eye wants to open and mess with me, causing double vision and all sorts of maladies. I only recently discovered that I can simply remove my glasses and now, for the first time in my archery career, I'm shooting with both eyes open! However, for months, "Right Eye Shut" was on that checklist!

Here is my current shot sequence checklist as it stands right now, along with a better explanation of why each item is even in the checklist:

1. ***Stance*** In Chapters 17 & 18 I discussed how to find your personal stance and body alignment through the use of a floor template that you use religiously until the stance becomes second nature. Remember, however, that "the stance is tuned to the draw length and the draw length is tuned to the stance." It doesn't take very much variation in foot position to change your body alignment and subsequently the impact point on the target. As distance increases, this slight variation in stance can and will show up more and more with regard to arrow impact points.

Thus, it is my opinion that all shots must start with the proper shooting platform. I also have, over the years watched innumerable archers, and many of those who aren't top finishers, who don't pay much attention to their stance on the shooting line. I watch many a mid-level or even higher level shooter take up a different shooting stance each time they get on the line. Worse yet, I see many archers who move their feet between shots, either because they move while using their binoculars, or they simple shuffle their feet to load the bow! Thus, often times, not only are they not assuming the same stance from end to end, but many change their stance from arrow to arrow!

My body shape and flexibility have changed dramatically as I have gotten older and also as a result of my open-heart surgery of twelve years ago. As a result, I've had to assume a different stance from what I have been accustomed to. In addition, the left side of my body is doing things differently from what they were automated to for 25 years! If I don't think about this item when I get onto the shooting line, I will naturally fall back into the much more open stance that I used to shoot for so many years. For me, the result of not making sure of this seemingly little item as I start my shot sequence is a shot that falls out of the X-ring to the right; and quite commonly, even a 4 out the right side of the bull's eye. If I keep my stance correct, then I don't have to deal with right side misses. The obvious motivation is then "Stance."

2. ***Set Release Angle*** I also tend to flatten out my release hand while I'm going through my pinching motion to activate the release. This results in my anchor rising, the drawing elbow coming up, my chin coming down, and my scope floating right out the bottom left part of the bull's-eye, and even worse if the process is allowed to continue. If I don't make sure of this, then a miss is inevitable on the low side or low left side of the bull's-eye. In addition, the shot doesn't trigger quickly and I struggle to get the shot to break. I've never been able to master a higher anchor, nor can I successfully fully rotate my release hand to the straight vertical position and use the side of my cheek as another contact point. I previously discussed the release angle and how you need to find your own positioning to insure you don't have a tight release hand and arm. Doing this forces my already high drawing elbow even higher and exaggerates the aforementioned problems with chin, hand positioning, and the aperture dropping out the bottom. Maintaining the "Set Release Angle" from the very beginning is easy to accomplish as long as I mentally check it off. This, I've found out, is much easier to maintain as I start to draw the bow and it also keeps other motions to a minimum and pretty much insures that my head, chin, and neck stay in place and I can draw the string to me instead of me going to the string! I am currently close to taking this item off the list, because I'm not having much of a problem with forgetting to keep it in line.

It is amazing how easy it is to tell at this point whether or not I've got a good shot going. Correcting this takes time and movement. Thus, if it isn't right from this step, then it isn't going to get any better and I should let down and start over.

3. ***Center the Peep*** It may seem odd to you that I don't say, "Center the scope." The reason for this is to help me pay more attention to the peep sight and keep my head in position. Peep height is way more critical than a lot of shooters are willing to admit. For me, when I set up item #2 above, it is only a quick check to keep the *peep* centered with regard to the scope housing. It reinforces "drawing the peep to me," and not "moving me to the peep." It is a matter of head positioning and not bow positioning and definitely not bow-hand positioning. This is a momentary item that is accomplished at the same time as I'm settling the scope onto the correct bull's eye.

4. ***Rotate Elbow*** This particular item is, at present, giving me the most problems. This is a result of having set up my draw length way short in the beginning and having to break that bad habit by actually sacrificing months of intentionally setting too long of a draw length in order to teach me what it feels like to have the elbow in proper position. Yes! It appears to be a step backwards and quite radical, but it worked. Now, if steps 1-3 are done correctly, but I forget to rotate that drawing elbow and keep

that elbow down, then things fall apart quickly. My elbow continues to rise, my anchor shifts, my chin comes down, and the sight drops out of the bottom of the bull's-eye. However, if I rotate the elbow and then avoid raising it any further, then the shot will break quickly and cleanly, because I'm in proper full draw position for the proper execution of back tension. This item alone is responsible for probably 95% of the 4's I shoot, and probably the vast majority of the missed X's as well. If this item isn't correct, then the next item won't work out either. This is yet another "caution" point in the sequence. If this step is done correctly, then Steps 5 and 6 come easy. If the elbow rotation and height aren't correct, I can pick it up by how the sight is settling. The key here is to let down and start over when it isn't right. This, of course, is also easier said than done, but it is the key to shooting high scores. There is no good that can come from shooting bad shots "any way." If you can't let down and start over, you cannot become a top echelon shooter. Period. You really don't capitalize on many points from a "bad shot, but good result" mentality. It only festers as a source of more "bad shots."

5. ***Maintain Contact*** This is with regard to the holding the release aid. I'm shooting a Carter Only triggerless release, so the comments relate to this release aid or other "rotational" releases. (Even though the Evolution Plus isn't a "rotational release aid," this is even more critical with that release aid.) With my Carter *Only*, I pull back the release with a lot of first finger pressure. I have done away with the thumb post because it was causing too much movement and also it was causing a lot of tension in the release hand and forearm. When I removed the thumb post, most of what was tense became relaxed. Once I hit anchor and continue through to this step, it is a simpler process to transfer the tension and relax my release hand and forearm and allow the tendons to relax, stretch, and the back muscles to give the release the minute rotation it needs to trigger the shot. The big thing here is that I must have good finger contact on the release aid; especially the middle finger and ring finger; otherwise I'm not going to get the release to rotate. Also, without that finger contact with the release, I can "pinch" my shoulder blades together; I can rotate my elbow all I want to; and the release still won't rotate. The reason is that I haven't any contact on the outside of the release to get it to move. If I'm pulling all first finger and have nothing else going, then the release cannot rotate because I'm not doing anything to counter the pull on the first finger. How can the release angle then change to get the gate to trip? Letting go with the first finger of the release is a way of cheating the release, and will result in a shot that will impact way low and left. "Wristing" the release is yet another way of cheating it, and will result in wild misses that are scattered all over the place. The problem here is that I never learned how to "wrist off" a triggerless release, and I obviously see no reason to learn that. Squeezing the release fingers is yet another way of cheating the release, but that results in impact points all over the compass and lots of inconsistency because then the release hand is tightening up and so are the forearm and upper arm muscles, and not the rhomboids which are really supposed to be providing that tiny bit of pressure needed to correctly trigger that release aid. So squeezing off the release is like punching it, and I don't know how to punch a release

aid either, and obviously, once again, I'm not really interested in learning how.

6. ***Relax*** This item is also critical after I've accomplished #5 above. If I tense up my release hand after I "Maintain Contact," then this step becomes much more difficult. I have a tendency to tighten up the back of my hand, then my forearm, and this is transmitted to my elbow and shoulder as well. The result is that I am involving way too many of the wrong muscles, and the rhomboids cannot effectively work for the execution of the shot. My sight picture becomes very unstable. In addition, I'm working backwards and having to watch for Step 4, since the elbow will come up when my forearm muscles tighten up. An "un-relaxed" shot is a missed X, and most of the time a 4 waiting to happen.

For me, if I can't get this step working, I must let down and start over. It is a simple process of just letting the back of the hand relax and acting like I'm holding a bucket. The muscles will relax and the rhomboids will be able to do their job. Once again, many missed X's and missed 5's are the result of not relaxing and "letting it happen."

7. ***Hold chin up***. This has to be happening continuously during the shot. However, I have a tendency to drop my chin while accomplishing steps #5 and #6. This checklist item is simply my way of telling me to finish the shot. I don't have trouble with dropping the bow arm or peeking. I do, however have problems with keeping my chin up (literally and figuratively).

8. ***Relax*** Once again, during this process, relaxing is a key element. This step is here, for now, due to me having to force a longer draw length to allow me to learn to get my draw elbow around. Now that I "know" my elbow positioning, I'm shortening up my draw length and still keeping the elbow in line. That, of course, means some more imminent changes in my list. I've told you that the shot sequence list isn't ever cast in stone. Little things come up, nuances develop, and/or you forget something along the way and soon you have a new score robbing habit. You have to fix things when they get broken or forgotten one step at a time.

For me to shoot consistently and to shoot a high X-count, the items above must be accomplished in the order I have them listed. If I get any item out of sequence, then the entire shot will break down. Either the shot will fire pre-maturely, or the shot will not break cleanly, if at all.

Items You Will Note Are Missing

There are countless items that you might incorporate into your own personal shot sequence checklist. You have probably already noted that there are two very obvious items that you likely have in your checklist that are completely absent from mine.

Grip Foremost among these is "Grip," am I correct? Here is my philosophy on "grip" steps. Since I learned this from my coach, Denise Libby (the Vaseline grip trick), I've always just let the bow seek its natural sweet spot for my hand. I'm not saying for you all to go out and lube up your bow grips with Vaseline as she did for me, however, I am saying that, if you let it, the bow will find its own sweet spot in your hand without you really having to think about it. Of course, this is also assuming that you don't grab the bow in too deep past the life-line or have loads of riser contact on the outside portion of your bow hand. If you do, then you will have to correct your bow hand form to reduce your tendency to torque the bow due to having too much hand in the bow. There is a new item out on the market called the "True Shot Coach." This small device is designed to teach you proper hand placement without having to read about it or be "walked through it." See the photos below of this inexpensive and handy device (it can be purchased through their website, where you can also read the instructions and learn even more about correct bow hand positioning and how to easily achieve it and understand how it works (*www.dontchokearchery.com/instructions*).

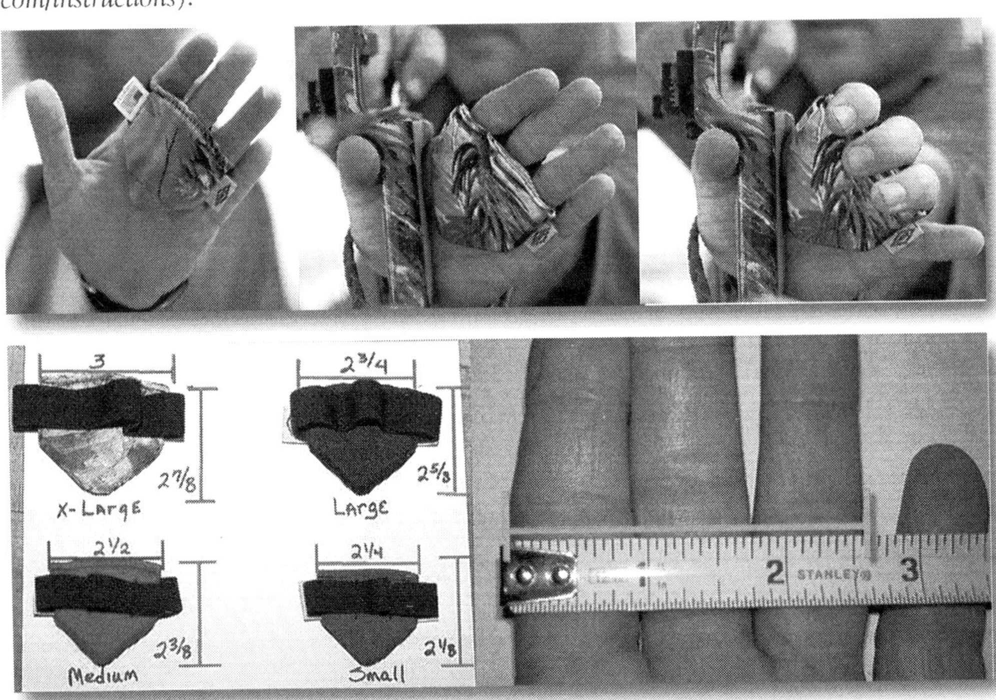

(Top) The True Shot Coach guides your hand into proper position on your bow while blocking incorrect postions. (Bottom) The TSC comes in four sizes normed to the combined width of your top three fingers.

Aim In the last chapter I discussed why "aim" isn't a part of my shot sequence checklist nor is "aim" a part of the checklist for any of my students. "Aim" means too many things to too many people, and all the meanings are different. Aiming is nearly indefinable. Aiming to one person may mean trying to hold the dot of the scope on the cross of the X (next to impossible to do for any more than a second or two), while for another person, "aiming" might mean to let the dot float and allow your eyes to do the work. For one person it might mean having the target fuzzy and the focus on the scope. Yet for another person, it might be to have the scope fuzzy and the X of the X-ring their main point of focus. Some stare at the X and let it happen; some stare at the dot and let the dot find its way to the X. I know others who aim at the color break and not at the center of the bull's-eye. I know still others who almost totally cover the gold or the white with a huge dot in their scope so that they don't get distracted by off-center arrow holes. I know others who favor huge/small circles; more who use larger circles, reticles; you name it and people have likely tried it. Others don't know what to do, so couldn't ever incorporate "aim" into their checklist, because they really don't know how they aim; they just let it happen all by itself. It sounds like that last sentence makes the most sense of all. Our eyes and mind naturally make things concentric and if we just let them "do their thing," we don't have to think "Aim" or "Aim Hard," it will simply happen if we just let it. Those who don't want to cobble up their brain to figure out "how" they aim, just try to remember to let it happen without forcing the issue. In a nutshell, is any one of these the "only right way to aim"? I don't think so, but the last one makes the most sense to me. Now, if I could just do that every time . . . that is why "Aim" is something I leave off of my checklist/shot sequence.

Follow Through Yes, "follow through" is also apparently missing from my personal checklist. I don't have a tendency to drop the bow, nor do I have a tendency to "peek." I also don't know how to punch a release aid and certainly don't want to learn how to do that, either. In reality, I do have "follow through" in my checklist as my last item, "Hold Chin Up." If I accomplish that little task, then I am going to see the arrow impact the target through my scope and/or in my unaided vision more often than not, because my head and eyes will remain still and I'll pick up the arrow as it strikes the X-ring or close to it. Keeping my chin up helps me to maintain and finish my shot and is more meaningful to me than "follow through." "Follow through" involves a lot of interpretation and can involve more than one thing.

Summary

My current checklist has only eight major items, likely soon to be down to only six; all of which are critical for me in that they must be accomplished in that order for every single shot. Each has a point of no return, and therein lies the difficulty with them. If you don't follow the checklist or you allow yourself to get sloppy with it by disregarding the danger signals and trying to recover a poor shot, then you need to take stock of your dedication to perfecting your own shot sequence.

You can only think of one thing at a time. Thinking through your shot sequence is thinking form. Thinking form will allow you to focus on only form which allows you to "let it float and shoot the shot." If you trust your shot, it happens by itself. It will happen by itself, if you repeat the steps on your checklist exactly the same way, every time, from shot to shot, end to end, and round to round.

I have one last comment about this personal shot sequence checklist. It is only as good as your willingness to work at it one step at a time. If you try to work on seven or eight things at a time, or change more than one thing at a time, how can you ever figure out which one is the real culprit and which of the others (if not all) are only secondary. To solve a problem, you have to get at the source. This can only be accomplished through examining one variable at a time, changing it if it is a problem, letting it become assimilated, and then re-checking things to see if you need to work on another variable. It is, indeed variations in how we accomplish each and every shot that make our arrows impact at different points.

All of these "corrections" have to be integrated into your form, with the goal of actually ridding yourself of the written checklist and using it only when/if you start to shoot poorly or are having unexplained problems with missing.

The greatest feeling is a shot with your focus is on the X, your scope is centered, your release is crisp and a surprise, and the shot breaks, all at the same time. You then see the arrow dive into the X-ring because your full focus was on "letting it happen." When you reach this point and you are seeing your arrows "dive" a majority of the time, you have arrived!

Tom Dorigatti

27

Determining *Your* Shot Timing and Rhythm

When have you ever heard of someone telling you to do what it is you are already doing? Usually, when working on your form or shot sequence, the recommendations are to change something, adjust something in your form or on the bow, or something else to move you out of your comfort zone. The technique described below is different; time consuming yes, but the results you will obtain will be worth every minute you spend on it. What is better is that for once, there is nothing to "change."

I used this technique very successfully in the mid-1980s. It improved my shooting immensely. It is not for those of non-committing personality, nor is it necessarily the only way to go about getting what you want. What this is, however, is something that will work; but only if you take the time and make the commitment long enough to allow it to work. I have since shared this technique with several other shooters. In every case the shooter has shown a marked improvement, without having changed a thing. Well, that is to say, nothing major was changed. They simply continued to do what they already were doing, only with a new understanding of exactly what was already working!

I'm a type "A" personality, which is not necessarily a type who deals well with top level competition; at least not without a lot of effort. I'm also a perfectionist and deal a lot with the blacks and whites of issues. During my changeover from shooting left-handed to right-handed, it became apparent to me that while I was hitting a lot of Xs and 5s, the quantity of 4s that I was shooting, along with the low 50's on X-counts were very troubling. I also noted that some shots were going off easily and others were coming off with greater difficulty. Then an idea hit me one afternoon during a practice scoring round and I decided to pursue it. If there is a challenge and data to be found, I'm all for it; after all, I am a science major, and scientists just love gathering "data" and "facts."

My misses weren't consistently in any one place, but I had noted that obviously the quick shots were a bit questionable, but more solid in the white, and those shots I didn't let down but should have were almost always the 4's or worse; those that were borderline could be anywhere. I felt that I really needed to isolate a rhythm and see if there was a definable "window of opportunity" for my "good shots" rather than doing it by how it feels alone. Once I got into it, what I was doing was so obvious that I was appalled that I hadn't thought of it before! My first decision was that I probably didn't need to change anything at all; my misses were occasional and I was shooting better than I had ever shot up to that that time. I simply needed to find out what already worked and figure out a way of doing that as often as possible.

As with any research, one first needs to state the problem, form a hypothesis, and then gather data. This is simple enough (follow the scientific method). *Problem* "What is the timing that produces the most X-ring hits for me"? *Hypothesis* "Finding the shot timing that produces the best results for me will result in more consistent scores and higher X-ring hits." Since I didn't have a video camera at the time, I needed to develop a manual system for gathering the data.

Equipment Needed

1. Stop watch
2. Assistant/Timer (my wife was the official timer)
3. Shot recording document (see figure below)
4. Ten full rounds of shooting normally and gathering "normal shot sequence data"
5. Standard method of ascertaining the "shot timing" so that data was consistently gathered
6. MS *Excel* or other spreadsheet program (or manual system) to compile and sort the data

Gathering the Data

Figure #1 (right) shows a small sample of the miniature target that I made for data recording. The full sized version has a 5-spot (or a 3-spot Vegas face) for each end of a complete round. For the initial determination of what timing was producing the most X-ring hits, I decided to gather data for 10 full rounds of normal shooting (600 scoring shots). Here is an explanation of the data recorded:

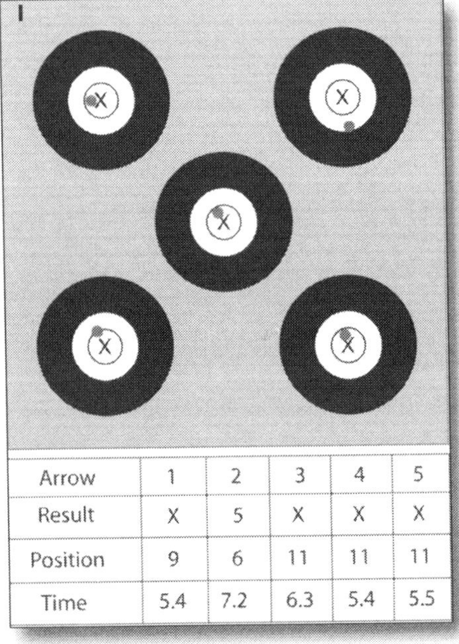

Arrow	1	2	3	4	5
Result	X	5	X	X	X
Position	9	6	11	11	11
Time	5.4	7.2	6.3	5.4	5.5

- Arrow 1, 2, 3, 4, 5 Arrow number for each end.
- Res Record of the result. For data purposes, I used X, 5, 4, 0 just like scores are recorded in order of the arrows shot for each end. Recording your order of shots and their times and impact points is very important!
- Pos Record of the position of the hit in a "clock" position, such as 2 O'clock, 10 O'clock, etc.
- Time Record of the time in seconds (to the nearest 0.1s) that it took for the shot

to break. You need to adopt a standard start time for this data, so that the timer knows when to start the stopwatch. For me, since I come in from the top of the bulls eye, my wife started the stopwatch when my stabilizer stopped moving and my finger went to my release's trigger. This indicated that I had acquired the Bull's-eye in my shot sequence. It doesn't matter what you use for a standard start time, as long at it is consistent. The stopwatch was stopped when the shot broke. The "timer" then recorded the time on the form.

- Record "hits" on each spot of each target face. This is very simple to do, and provides a visual reference you need as well as the other data. You can see your results quickly for each end of that round. (That is what the gray dots on Figure #1 represent.)
- My "job" was to shoot normally and try not to skew the data by rushing shots, intentionally counting or doing anything out of the ordinary. Once an end was completed, I took the data form and placed a "dot" with a pencil on each spot on the tracking target in order, along with recording the Result (Res) and Position (Pos). I ignored the time even though it was recorded. I had my scoring round to complete and besides those 5 shots or even 30 shots wasn't going to tell me much from the "raw" data anyway. My sequence of shots is top left, top right, center, bottom left, and bottom right. That is how the shot numbers in each end were numbered and recorded. Consistency in data gathering is the key, since you want consistent data. Remember you are not to change anything during the 10 rounds of data gathering! You are to just shoot the shots and then make the dots on the miniature targets along with recording result and position.

Compiling the Data

You can use whatever means you choose to compile the data. Initially, I used "VisiCalc" and then converted to "Symphony" and long since converted over to MS *Excel* for data grouping and sorting. Simply make a column for each main data field for your database. This allows you to group and sort the data in a variety of ways. You will find that shot timing is not the only piece of information you gather from this. I'll address more on that later. Figure #2 below is an example of the fields I initially used. You might be able to generate even more with a little ingenuity!

Figure #2

After each shooting session, it is a simple thing to copy the data into your spread-

End #	Arrow #	Res	Pos.	Time
1	1	X	9	5
1	2	5	6	7

sheet from your data sheet. *Note* I avoided the tendency to sort the data after the completion of each round. I felt that the last thing I should do was to try to sneak a peek at the data and possibly end up skewing the results. I had decided to analyze 600 shots worth of data, so to analyze it before completion is unscientific and a violation of the protocol.

Analyzing the Data

Since the original intent was to find my best shot timing (defined as that which produced the most X-ring hits), the initial sort was by "Res," then by Time, then by arrow number. This will group all of the X's, 5's, 4's, etc together, along with the other sorts. In my data, after the 10 complete rounds, what I found was quite shocking. I found that over the course of the 600 shots that I was never missing the X-ring if the shots were breaking between 5 to 6.5 seconds! However, if the shots went over 7 seconds, I was missing the X nearly every time and shooting low 5's or even some 4's. If the time was over 8 seconds, I was shooting few fives and mostly 4's (this was expected, and now proven.). I now had upper limits, lower limits, and an optimal range to work with. Of course, there were occasional X's at 8 seconds too, but they were rare and definitely not consistent. If shots went off early, which there were not very many of those, I also didn't miss the bull's-eye (all were 5's), but the X-counts were not very good.

The Next Step in the Process

Now that I was armed with some truly great information about my shot sequence I had to maximize the number of shots that would break in 5 or 6 seconds. This is where my type "A" personality came into play. Remember, I said I didn't radically change anything; I merely capitalized upon what was already there but that I didn't know about for sure? The next ten full rounds were shot by having my Timer say "Stop!" out loud once more than 6 seconds had expired. The reason for the 6 seconds instead of 6.5 is I needed some "lead time." For example, if she said "Stop!" at six seconds, then I was at nearly 7 seconds before the "stop" process was initiated.

My job was to attempt to shoot the shot "normally" and not exceed that six second interval. The first round, I heard "Stop!" quite a bit and religiously stopped the shot sequence and let down. To not do so was again, violating protocol and defeating the purpose of the entire program. The second round, I heard "Stop!" less frequently. By the tenth round, I wasn't hearing "Stop!" but once or twice for the entire round. I was amazed at how well I got with the program so that I could shoot arrows in correct rhythm and avoid hearing the word "Stop!" About the only thing to avoid is counting or bouncing on the trigger (or release) in a counting fashion rather than executing shots correctly. It is not difficult at all, if you put your mind to it. I was making a game of this and having a lot of fun doing so. Of course, anytime you are getting results like this, you become elated and most of all confident!

The Results

1. I was able, in only ten indoor rounds, to capture the information of the shot timing/rhythm that was producing results for me.
2. The subsequent ten rounds of using the "Stop!" routine allowed me to make certain that I was shooting only good, solid shots that were producing positive results (thus avoiding bad shots).

3. I found that I was not only working with a consistent shooting rhythm, but my confidence was soaring, because nearly all the results were positive, and I was having fun doing it.
4. After shooting an additional five rounds by myself, I found that my X-count was up from the low 50s (out of 60) to the 57 to 59 range with a few 60X rounds thrown in.
5. After those five rounds by myself, I had my Timer recheck my newfound consistency by timing me for five more rounds. My average for those five rounds was 58.6 Xs per round, with no 4s and nearly all shots completely inside the 5-ring. In other words, my performance on X-ring hits was at 97.7%, and my performance for 5-ring hits was at 100%.
6. This timing became integrated into my shot routine, and held me there for over eight years. Even to this day, I subconsciously know when I've exceeded that limit and will detect a "shimmy" if the shot doesn't break. This exhibits how powerful the sub-conscious mind can become when something of this nature becomes automated . . . but breaks down over time. *A Personal Note* At the present time I know that my "timing" has changed significantly and I have to find it again. However, I have some other issues to deal with that are, as yet, not consistent enough for me to undertake this very high level of analysis.
7. That following summer, I found that the same timing sequence was working outdoors as well. I started the outdoor season by shooting over 550 (out of 560 points possible) Field Rounds for the first time ever.
8. Several very close friends who I worked with using this same program have shot their first 60X indoor rounds and are averaging 58X to 59X on their rounds. Some others have shot Personal Bests soon afterwards. Their Vegas target timing works out the same for them, as it did for me as well. They also do "checkups" occasionally to help them isolate tendencies or changes.

Limitations

As with any data, there are limitations. These are the ones I've noticed:

1. If you change bows, % letoff, or you change draw weight, you can end up with a slightly different rhythm.
2. Changes in health, age, or injury can result in changes to this rhythm.
3. You will need to take "checkups" every now and again to keep yourself on track.
4. You should keep up the database and enter data every now and again and check things for changes. That is not to say that if your scores and/or X-count go down that this is the first place to look. You will certainly see the changes in your X-count right off, and you should suspect a change in rhythm as a potential source of that. You are better off checking out your shot sequence and "check list" before resorting to this advanced technique. To find out if it is your rhythm, check your shot timing and analyze the data; but only after checking out your shot sequence first.
5. This takes time and dedication. It is not for those unwilling to learn the truth

about themselves. If you gather the data cleanly and honestly, you will have a wealth of information; if not, then as the adage goes, "garbage in, garbage out." Don't ever try to make yourself look good on the paper; if you cheat on this data gathering or try to skew the data, then you are wasting your time.

6. Just because you see some pros who "hold forever" doesn't mean that this is right for you. In fact, chances are it is not a thing for you to emulate. Keep in mind that the longer you hold, the more time you give your entire process to break down. The longer you hold, the worse things going "off" get and the less likely you are to make a good, solid, X-ring eating shot.

Added Benefits

If you were to sit down and ponder them, you could easily list many. Some of the more obvious ones deserve mention:

1. Building your confidence . . . because the results are yours and are going to give you something positive to work from for a change. Remember I said at the beginning: "When have you ever, in this sport, heard of someone telling you to do what it is you are already doing?" This isn't asking you to change a thing, since you already are doing the right thing, but didn't know what that right thing is. Now you do know, so you can work on that item and clean up your act.
2. Finding out other tendencies in your shooting . . . such as: (all you have to do is use a different sort criterium/criteria)
   a. Do I tend to lag on the fouth or fifth shot of an end?
   b. Which target face do I miss the most on? Top left? Top Right? Middle? Bottom Left? Bottom Right?
   c. Which end do I miss the X the most on? The 5-ring?
   d. Is my #3 arrow at fault or is it my shot timing? There are ways to further isolate such data.
   e. How do I do at the target change from top to bottom or bottom to top? Tendencies in impact point?
   f. Do I tend to miss the X low? Do I miss the X high? Where are the bulk of my 5-ring hits?
3. Learn how to deal with your own idiosyncrasies, and how to adapt them to your benefit.
4. Shooting your form and timing and not trying someone else's will make a monumental difference to you. You are now really shooting your game as it fits you and your psyche and ability.
5. Ability to see the results simultaneously instead of seeing shot after shot and trying to remember them. You have solid data and this is no longer an "I think" situation.

Summary

We all have our own natural shooting rhythm. Yours might not be the 5 to 6.5 seconds that mine was at that time. It could be shorter; it could be longer. The range of your window of opportunity may well be a lot wider than mine. I feel I have a very, very limited window of opportunity, and it may well be even shorter now! I'll have to find out about that when/if I can get my other issues corrected and automated.

Realize, however, that only you can determine which shooting rhythm is right for you. If you don't know it now, then isn't it about time you found out? Use of this system may not be as cut and dried for you as it was for me. One thing I do strongly believe, however, is that if you try this or even a videotape version from which you can get at the data, you will show positive improvement and good results. You will be able to isolate tendencies you never knew you had. You will find your X-counts going up and your performance and confidence levels on the rise as well.

How would you like to perform at the 98% level consistently for several years, and have a simple means of a checkup to find the source? Doesn't it beat guessing or just shooting round after round in the same rut? The best part of this is that you really aren't changing anything, but rather finding out what works best and making it work for you. It is there the right now and you all you have to do is to finally go out and find it.

Tom Dorigatti

28

Proactive Preparation For Indoor Tournaments

While there are numerous methods you can use to prepare for tournaments, there are few people who do much else other than form perfection and trying to hit the center. Many critical and point robbing details get set aside in an effort to bring scores and X-counts up. During any tournament those at the top of the leader boards were those who came to the tournament prepared and well-practiced and versed in their capabilities and that of their equipment. Here I address indoor tournaments and in the following chapter I offer some insights and tips to assist you in preparing for those less than perfect sets of conditions that arise in outdoor tournament settings.

You aren't going to find magic bullets in either chapter. I'm not going to talk about stabilization, weight and balance, holding weight, peak weight, arrow selection, point weights, arrow rests, cable guards, quick-disconnect angles or other items of that nature. Once again, there are volumes of words, suggestions and recommendations concerning all the above mentioned things so repeating them is unnecessary. What you are going to get are some different insights and tips to assist you in preparing for those less than perfect sets of conditions that arise in tournament settings both indoors and outdoors. Things are not always perfect no matter where you go to practice or compete. Being ProActive involves preparing for the inevitable and knowing in advance how you deal with those variables, how you best adapt to those variables, and exactly what you will do to make those adaptations. If you've not properly prepared, then you are putting yourself behind the 8-ball before you even start. You always hear people complaining that "the lighting is so dark; I've got the wrong sized aperture in my peep," or "These lanes are so narrow, not like I'm used to shooting in; I'm worried the person next to me will bump me," or "I'm shooting next to a lefty today; I don't like that at all." Another good one is, "Crap, I'm starting on the top target. I hate starting on the top target." I could continue to list the things I hear, and maybe even you say, but I think you get my point by now. You know those conditions will come up, so why not sit back and figure out ahead of time how you are going to deal with them? All of the above and more can be dealt with, if you just practice ProActively.

Tips on Preparing to Compete Indoors

Most shooters claim that they practice indoors "like they would shoot a tournament." Do they really practice what they preach? Here are some tips to help you rid yourself of some of the early point robbers and target change jitters.

1. *Check your strings, nocking point, D-loop condition, peep height, arrow rest, sight extension, scope, rod and lens, brace height,* ATA, *and cam timing before shooting.* Do it again when you get to the venue. Play it safe! Cams should be marked so that you can tell at a glance if a cable or string has stretched, or something was jarred out of position during the trip to the venue (vibrations in airplanes are notorious for loosening small screws, etc.). You should have all the important details written down and marked on your bow or bow square so that you have a consistent reference. If you are not checking your bow or don't have things marked, you are inviting disaster at the worst time and a lot of frustration if/when something does happen. You do have your Master Bow Configuration Table with you, don't you?
2. *Routinely change your arrow nocks.* If you do not, then perhaps you should set up a routine cycle of changing your nocks. They are the most overlooked piece of equipment you have. They do crack and they do bend. It is too late to discover this 5 or 6 ends into a tournament. Especially when dropping one X will take you out of the shoot offs and missing two X's will likely take you off the podium.

   Check all your arrows before and after each practice session and after each end during the event. With the advent of all-carbon arrows, this is especially important. Even if you didn't have arrow strikes, those all-carbon arrows can and will fail. This is for peace of mind as much as anything. A loose vane or feather can have an effect on arrow impact.
3. *Do not move your feet during the end at any time!* I've said it before; I'll say it again. Many archers I see shooting indoors move their feet between arrows, either to spot with binoculars or just out of nervousness. Most don't even realize they're doing this. I've even seen some shooters shift across their lane back and forth as they shoot the left side or the right side of their target face. One thing I was taught from the very beginning was to never move my feet once I have established your positioning. I recommend you do the same. Moving your feet changes your body positioning that you've worked on and practiced. Moving your feet changes your body angle and changing your body angle changes the all important shooting triangle. So, once you get set in your shooting lane, stay put. I also recommend that if possible, you look at the floor and make a mental note of any marks you can use to realign yourself the next time up. If you don't feel comfortable, get comfortable and then stay there!
4. *Always shoot the same pattern on the five-spot face.* If you aren't starting at the top row of target faces and coming down, then you are actually overworking your muscles during the end. I teach and recommend letting gravity be your friend instead of your enemy. This way, as you tire during the end of five arrows, instead of you having to exert extra effort to hold the bow higher to get to the top row of faces on your 5-spot target, you let gravity help you out . . . by shooting the bot-

tom row last during your end. A recommended pattern is a "Z" or "Reverse Z."

5. *When you shoot the top target assignment, bend at the waist instead of raising your bow arm higher*. Be careful here. If you are a short person, there could be implications similar to shooting a steep uphill target outdoors. So practice shooting those top target assignments and don't take them for granted. If you "don't like shooting the top target" then emphasize starting on that top target a bit more often during practice and learn to like it. Obviously, you will be assigned a top target to start with during competitive events; it is unavoidable. During practice sessions, at least alternate starting and finishing on the top target. Write this in your journal so that you remember to change on the next practice and scoring practice round scheduled. Do not avoid this, and do not shoot an entire round with your target at the same level. Some ranges are way too high with their top target assignments, and if you aren't prepared, this can really rob you and hurt your concentration, so prepare for it by practicing placing your high targets a bit higher than normal. Same goes with the bottom targets. Get used to shooting those closer to the floor.
6. *Make sure that you do not practice on the same shooting lane twice in a row*. Lighting differs in every range and across them as well. There can be subtle differences in the lighting that can and will "throw off your windage" and possibly even elevation slightly. I've seen instances of a full turn in windage from one side of an indoor range to the other.
7. *Do not always shoot two practice ends, or shoot blank bale before you start a session for score*. This is not necessarily the best practice, since at most tournaments you won't get "blank bale" practice shots. Sure, you can waste your official practice end by blank baling it, but I personally don't think this is the best of decisions. What happens if you are late and miss those "normal" two practice ends? You had best be prepared. The best way for this is to practice by starting scoring with the first shot, after stretching out (string method, Morin Trainer?).

   Another way to do this, if you are bent on "practice ends" is to draw back the bow, hold, and let down two or three times before you launch that first arrow. As I mentioned before, I have used the technique of drawing back the bow the first two times during the first practice ends with no intention of shooting that arrow. Then I shoot as normal. Come time for that first scoring end, well, the quiver quivers, so I help alleviate butterflies by intentionally drawing back the bow, aiming, holding and letting down at least once, if not twice. If you have ProActively practiced this and it is incorporated into your pacing, you can even do this in a tournament situation, since you do have some time for letdowns. Remember the let-down rule if you do this in a tournament or if you are being clocked. Be sure to time yourself in practice to see if you have the time to do this comfortably. This will be uncomfortable at first when you start doing this during practice and, of course, your practice scores might suffer a tad for a short time. However, they will come around, and you will be better for it. Tournament practice ends then become a bonus instead of a pre-requisite for you to "get ready."

   Let every one else have to "get ready" by shooting a ton of arrows ahead of time and tire themselves out, or better yet, psyche themselves out if that one half to one hour of shooting arrows doesn't go well. You spend that time relaxed and fully confident in your abilities to shoot from the get go. You remain fresh and ready to go from the get go. You have checked out your equipment ahead of time (marks, measurements, "Master Bow Configuration Table"). Your goal is to shoot your first arrow easily, and continue to take it slow and easy for all 60 shots and then make that last arrow just as easy as the first. It is all about one shot 60 times; not about 60 shots one time each, and having the stamina to handle perhaps many more than that just as easily. ProActive practice develops this level of skill and confidence.

8. *Shoot the Vegas target in the correct order, not 2-1-3, or 1-3-2 or 3-2-1, etc.* This is where the gravity issue discussed earlier could possibly hurt you. Until recently, most local places I've shot require you to shoot the Vegas face in the correct sequence, but it is becoming less common to force that issue. During the shoot downs at Vegas, if you make it, you are also required to shoot them in order. If you have formed the habit with the Vegas face by shooting them out of order, then in a shoot-off, you will be changing your routine. Any change in routine will upset your rhythm. Therefore, I recommend that you always practice shooting the Vegas face 1-2-3 . . . every time.
9. *Number your arrows.* If not, how do you know if a particular arrow is striking in a different spot or not? Just like the target faces on the Vegas or 5-spot, I feel that each arrow should be assigned a "spot" to shoot at. This keeps you on routine and thinking about keeping that routine. If you are thinking shot sequence and routine, then you don't have time to "get nervous." If you have an arrow that is going a particular direction, you will know it and can put it in the penalty box. Know your arrows like you know yourself and the rest of your equipment. Any doubt about the arrow → penalty box, period.

   Track your scores and your impact points. During practice sessions, especially scoring rounds, I feel it is imperative to track each shot you shoot and mark its impact point. You are looking for tendencies you might have, impact points of particular arrows or shots during the end, etc. Everyone has patterns, and if you have a particular pattern or problem area, you won't know it if you don't track it.
10. *Practice letting down on bad shots.* Can you tell yourself "Stop!" when you've lost it, or do you just try to recover what is clearly not a good shot? Once you've tightened up, or even thought about letting down, the shot should come down immediately. You should never try to recover a shot. This is much easier said than done and I will admit that I don't practice this one as religiously as I should. You should know when you hit anchor if it is right, and if at a later time it isn't right, you should know that too and Stop!, let down, and start the sequence completely over. You should never accept "less than perfect" shots, if your sight leaves the bull's-eye, think Stop! Let down, and start over. My coaches have preached that to me over and over again; I'm repeating what they've told me, because it is that important. If a shot isn't right, don't accept it, because you will never recover it

once it is "lost" during the shot and aiming cycle. Don't forget that there are times when a "good shot = bad result" and learn to accept this.

11. *Know your own rhythm.* That is to say, know enough about your shooting tendencies to know for sure how long of a holding time will nearly guarantee you an X? Everyone has this rhythm (see Chapter 27). It varies from person to person, and can vary with the peak weight or letoff of the bow (with a heavier holding weight normally resulting in a shorter "break time" for the shot). If this limit is exceeded, a missed X or worse is virtually a guarantee. If you watch the top pro shooters, they have a rhythm that is within a second every single time. Some have established a longer rhythm than others, but they know their limits, and the word Stop! hits them and they obey it religiously. Put the odds in your favor and don't push the envelope beyond your limits. Under no circumstances change your rhythm and rush things during a competitive event. So what if you are the last one on the shooting line? You have your 4 minutes or whatever for your end, so use them if you have to. Also, don't change your rhythm to slow down very much either. If you know a shot isn't right, then wait and don't rush it, but don't overdo the "slowing down." Stay within your practiced rhythm and your game, not somebody else's.

12. *Practice with some noise in the background and with people talking within earshot.* This includes screaming kids or extra-ordinary banging and clanging. Personally, I find headphones on me when I'm shooting to be a major distraction, but I welcome noise in the background during practice. In addition, more and more venues are prohibiting the use of any listening devices of any kind on the shooting line during practice and during scoring, so get rid of your mp3 player, *iPod*, etc. while practicing. You are liable to get upset when (not if) they tell you to put those headphones away. The reason I can handle most noises may come from the fact that for many years, we shot in the basement of a bowling alley and there was an indoor rifle range in the other half of the basement. Try shooting a recurve bow and clicker under those circumstances and you'll understand. We had bowling balls banging right above our heads along with dust falling in our face and hair, and then the sound of .22 rim-fire rifles going off all the time while we are trying to shoot. Those of us with clickers quickly learned to feel the clicker in the riser when it went off because we couldn't hear it!

    Practice shooting with people around so that shooting in front of onlookers won't bother you. Shoot with newbies on the line; shoot with experts, and mix it up. Make it a point to get on the shooting line next to the best shooters in your area. Never practice alone, off in a corner by yourself, especially if you are scoring a practice round. There are times when it is best to be completely alone; especially when you are working on a problem area. The last thing you need is for somebody to come up to "offer help" or say, "do you know your bow hand is shaking." However, you should learn to deal with the inevitability of somebody making a comment. I haven't and it is costing me dearly because of this.

13. *Practice with added pressure.* Get with some friends during practice rounds and

shoot for sodas or quarters or "signed ones." (*Note* A "signed one" is a $1 or $5 bill that is given to the winner of the "match" and has your signature on it. The winner keeps this until you beat him/or her in a match, and then they signe it and you keep it until they beat you in a match.) This will help enormously for you to get used to pressure and besides, it is fun and all of you will be better as a result of it. Challenge the top shooters to shoot against you with a "handicap" (to make it not quite even—make yourself stretch) for a quarter or a dollar, a signed one, or a soda. They will welcome the challenge, too. You may pay off for awhile, but sooner or later, you will find yourself not needing the handicap or being spotted points. You'll be the better for it. Have a "shoot down round" at the end of league. Everyone who wants in puts down a dollar. Shoot two ends and the lowest X-count total goes to the pine (sits down). Then shoot two more ends and lowest inside out X-count sits down. If a tie, then the higher two stay. Then, when you get down to the final two people, shoot one end, inside out X-s only are counted. If still tied, then one arrow at a time, inside out only counts and first to miss the inside out X loses. This is a hoot and some people come on strong while others falter.

14. *Run a mental checklist and imagine each shot in your mind.* Or, use your shot sequence placard or laminated checklist you have and completely read it between shots. If you don't do this, you need to. I have at times placed a placard either on my bow or in my quiver with my shot sequence listed on it. I read it between every single arrow and visualize the shot before doing it. It doesn't take long, and if you are thinking about the shot, you don't have time to get nervous. Remember, if it doesn't feel right at the beginning, stop. If you tighten up or the thought of "miss" enters your mind, stop and start over. You cannot recover from such a lapse and a miss is imminent. Be ProActive and don't take chances.
15. *Getting the release to trip.* If you are struggling getting your release off, you speed it up, right? Absolutely not! The reason you are struggling is that you aren't committing to the shot. You are not executing. Most likely (not a guarantee, but in most cases) the more correct thing to do is to slow the release down, or increase the trigger tension. This forces you to get with your program and execute the shot. I know of numerous cases where shooters have won tournaments after struggling and using a backup release that is set a bit slower or with more tension. Some shooters make a practice of having several releases, each one set at a different speed/tension in their release bag and they don't know which one they are pulling out to shoot each shot. It made them execute. Never change the release setting during a scoring round and especially not during a tournament. If that thing was firing correctly during your last practice session or even during the first half of today's round, then you have changed, not it, and if you change that release you are going to pay a dear price. I frequently see people changing the speed of their release at the slightest inkling that it is harder to fire. They are like a puppy chasing its tail and likely to never find or learn that sweet spot. If you are thinking about how the release is tripping or not tripping, then you are violating your first

step, aren't you? You definitely are not executing the shot with proper back tension today, because you are having troubles getting the release to trip. Correct yourself, not the release aid; *it* didn't change.

Owning This

Take out a piece of paper and write a list of every weakness you have and every irritating thing that bothers you during indoor tournaments. Using the techniques provided in the tips above or using your own ingenuity, come up with ways to deal with these. Write these down in your practice journal and incorporate them into your tournament preparation routine.

Whenever a new irritation comes up (we didn't used to have to deal with cell phones going off on the line, for example), add it to the list and figure out a way to deal with it.

Summary

What I have addressed in this chapter are some key elements of indoor practice and working with your personal system and rhythm. There are other methods not mentioned, and not all the methods above may work for you. If you are ProActive and use your ingenuity, I'm sure you can think of more things to help you become ProActive and prepare for the less than desirable conditions you are going to run up against during a competition. If you don't try them and know how you react and what they do to you, you'll never learn to deal with them. What I have outlined above does work for me and has worked for many shooters I've helped over the years. Many of them came on quickly to beat me and continue to do so. I was, and continue to be, very happy for them. Most of them shot personal bests after they established their shooting rhythm and religiously stuck with it for only a short time.

It is one thing to be able to tell it like it is. It is yet another thing to be able to actually do it. The one thing I know for sure is that while I personally cannot perform at the level I was so used to, I certainly remember how I got there; I haven't gone brain dead. Remember, it is the little things that are overlooked or skipped that are the real score robbers. Once you are at the middle to top level in your skills, the difference may well be one of those items listed above.

In the next chapter, I will discuss practicing ProActively for outdoor shooting, both field and target and 3-D as well. Items coming include wind shooting, uphill and downhill shooting, preloading the shot, practicing "Kentucky windage," and many other little score savers often overlooked because too many shooters are too busy trying to hit the center of the center every time, under only ideal conditions that rarely exist during an outdoor tournament.

Tom Dorigatti

29

ProActive Equipment Preparation For Outdoor Performance

There are numerous methods used to prepare for outdoor field or target rounds. The most common method is to practice the course, arrow after arrow, often in the same order every time, trying to shoot as close to a perfect score as you can accomplish. This is normally done under the best conditions and weather. Problems arise when shooters take their indoor setup outdoors and attempt to shoot their 20 yard setup and use it at longer distances. Other problems arise with methodologies involved in long distance tuning and especially in the methodology used to obtain sight settings for the various distances involved in all outdoor rounds. Many shooters simply increase the poundage of their bow to a certain, pre-selected point and then spend as little time tuning and sighting in that setup as they can so they can get to "real practice." After all, there is a tournament around the corner and you have to get ready for it in a rush, correct? Little thought is given to the nuances and differences in the equipment and setup that must be attended to. This is a recipe for, if not disaster, close to it.

This chapter addresses outdoor equipment preparations; those little things that can and will translate into some added points to your outdoor scores; specifically the bow, the arrows, and that pesky piece of plastic, the nock. I will deal with other nuances in subsequent chapters. You aren't going to get a course in walk back tuning, nor will you get a course in French tuning or the bare-shaft method of tuning. What you are going to read about are some pointers about techniques and ProActively that can save you many lost points. For outdoor shooting, because the distances are often changing and the average distance being shot is more than double of what you do indoors, the entire "system" is far less tolerant of things not quite right or out of kilter. Once again, in order to be ProActive, you must anticipate what to do "when," not "if," these occur and make sure that you check everything first. If anything is out of spec (compared to your Master Bow Configuration Table and your markings on the bow itself), then fix it. If it is worn, replace it. If it is out of line, realign it. If it is loose, tighten it. So many people, rather than take the time now, will keep putting it off, only to have a failure at the most inopportune time (as in out on the course). Some of what you are going to read is repeated elsewhere in this book. As I have said I can't assume you are reading the whole book and you should get what the title of this chapter promises . . . here.

Your Bow

Most shooters claim that they practice for field tournaments "like they would shoot a field tournament." Do they really practice what they are preaching? How often do you really check out that bow completely before leaving the car or even drawing it back for the first time? It has been in the bow case, you likely are in a hurry, to get started, correct? Daylight is wasting away, and you don't have time for that. Such are ordinary "practice plans."

Here are some tips to help rid yourself of some of the often overlooked aspects of outdoor equipment setup which will progressively eat away at your potential to achieve higher scores when shooting outdoors in ideal conditions and do worse under those less than ideal conditions you often encounter. So, tag along with me as we review some of these critical, if not imperative items.

Another Personal Story I had been shooting pretty well of late. I keep close tabs on the condition of my strings, cables, and D-loop. The harness had, at the time, several thousand shots on it, and as always, I checked the positions of the cams and such items as part of my pre-session equipment checks. I had noticed that each session for a couple of weeks, I was having to move my sight down a few clicks at a time, but figured it was "me" because of having to work on getting my elbow around. When I don't get "elbow around," I shoot low shots. So, during this practice session, out of what appeared to be nowhere, I couldn't hit the bull's-eye consistently no matter what. Good Shots = Bad Results were running rampant, and heaven forbid if I had a bad shot; that result was really, really bad. After a few ends of this, I finally decided to dig deeper into the equipment checks. Since the misses were pretty much wild low and wild high, I had an inkling of where to look. Do you know where you should start looking? Read on and I'll tell you what I discovered in my deeper check over.

Check your strings, nocking point, D-loop condition, peep height, arrow rest, sight extension setting, scope tightness and rod condition, lens tightness, brace height, axle to axle length. If the bow is set up with a lanyard for a fall away arrow rest, check the condition and positioning of the lanyard. You would be surprised at how overlooking any of these simple items will destroy your score and confidence and have you going in circles trying to figure "what went wrong" when they become the sources of lost points.

1. *Cams should be marked* so that you can tell at a glance if a cable or string has stretched or something was jarred out of position during transport. You should have all the important details written down and with you, as well as marked on your bow or bow square so that you have a consistent reference. If you are not checking your bow or don't have things marked, you are inviting disaster at the worst time, and asking for a lot of frustration. Using an equipment time out is stressful, and it will be even more stressful when you haven't a clue where to put whatever has moved back where it belongs! Most shooters simply chalk up the

day unnecessarily.

2. *Check the bolts on your sight mounting block* (the part that bolts to the side of the riser). You have "marked" the positions of those bolts, haven't you? Previously I described a true story about what happens if those screws come loose. You can chase your sight settings for several targets before you find the culprit. The time to check this is before you start . . . every time. In addition, while you are checking that sight mounting block, it is a good idea to make sure you mounted your sight extension into the correct slot. If you mount your sight extension wrong, then your sight settings are going to be off and obviously so will your score. This one has been a very common occurrence and the people I've seen make this mistake have gone on a long ways before discovering the source. Even worse, I know of a few people who lost in shoot-offs because they got hurried and didn't get their sight extended correctly and, of course, didn't check it until it was way too late.
3. *Check the bolts that mount your limb pockets to the riser.* Havoc can be created if those limbs shift around on the end of the riser. You have marked these, no?
4. *If your bow has modular cams, check the bolts on the modules.* Cam bolts have an uncanny way of working loose (at the wrong time, always the wrong time). As you may recall, because these are such small screws, I personally never use blue LocTite® on them. I've found that snugging them up without reefing down on them works and by marking them, I can tell at a glance if they've worked loose or not. If you crank them too tight, then you create another problem, because dissimilar metals are involved and getting them too tight, well, when you try to loosen them up, you will be lucky to get them loose at all. One of these coming loose while you are shooting will play havoc with your impact points and you won't find the cause until it is so loose it is rattling. Then, you might not be able to get the other bolt loose to help get things lined back up and snugged down. Remember what I said about having Allen wrenches in good or new condition?
5. *Check the marks on your limb bolts to make sure the limb bolts haven't moved.* While most of today's bows have some sort of locking mechanism for the limb bolts, it is always a good idea to mark your limb bolt positions so you can tell at a glance if they've moved. In addition, when/if you do move the limb bolts, it is much easier to keep track of exactly how far you have moved them should the Allen wrench slip out of the Allen bolt socket while adjusting them. My personal technique is to mark them parallel with the riser, with the marks facing each other at the limb butt end of each limb. In spite of the limb pocket locks on my bow, I keep an eye on those limb bolts. It only takes a glance to confirm if they're in proper alignment or not.
6. *Tie in that peep sight securely.* Mark and write down your peep height. You do realize that if that peep moves even slightly, you are going to have problems shooting high or low, correct? Do you remember the story about my experience at the field tournament? Had my peep been tied in more securely, it would have made it more difficult to move. However, had I not had it previously measured and marked, I would have lost a lot more points than just the loss on that single arrow! Being

ProActive saved the round and the tournament, and I've never forgotten that, and I never will. In addition, knowing where you started, should you have to move that peep for a "quick adjustment" to finish a round, you can put it right back later and resolve the real source of the issue. I'll discuss later on in the book a technique often used for those cases of "low-itis" or "high-itis" that can befuddle you from time to time. It beats moving the sight's indicator pointer and fouling everything up. It is easy to mark your bow square from the top of the arrow nock to a positive reference on the peep sight and also to write that measurement down. It only takes a few seconds and will save your score and some frustration in the event you start shooting high or low. When that happens, the first thing I always check is peep height.

7. *Check the marked arrow rest position.* Once again, I remind you of my lost opportunity for a perfect 280 half on a field round; simply because one screw on a questionably designed launcher came loose. Today's arrow rests are a lot more solid, but they are still prone to shifting. So, by being ProActive and having indicator marks and measurements, you can check these before the beginning of the round and save yourself some grief. Most people, simply tune in their arrow rest, and trust the bolts and screws to hold it in place. Then when something comes loose there is a mad scramble to figure out just exactly where that arrow rest was positioned before. You might get away with it indoors where a small movement might keep you in the bull's-eye. Outdoors, however, at distance there are huge effects, and it doesn't take much to throw your arrow off into the 4-ring or worse. Techniques of marking that arrow rest were outlined in Chapters 5, 8 & 9. If you've marked the arrow rest bracket's positioning right on the riser in a contrasting color and marked the bolt position, it is an easy visual double-check before you even start the round.
8. *Check your D-loop.* I've witnessed more D-loop failures of varying degrees than you would ever believe. If you are ProActive, you take care of and replace a frayed or weakened D-loop before it fails. You don't try to make it last just one more round. You also have the starting length for that D-loop written down. If you are really ProActive, you have a spare pre-fabricated D-loop or two in your quiver. You know exactly how long that loop opening is and can cinch it up to that length when you replace it in the field. In addition, you also have the D-loop position on the bow string marked and set up so that, when you replace the loop "one knot at a time" you are confident that it will be in exactly the same position as the one you replaced. There is no reason you cannot replace a D-loop in the field and not continue to shoot your score without missing a beat. Yes, you should use an equipment time out, but you won't need 15 minutes' time to replace it, but why not get the two practice ends after replacing it to make dead certain you did the job correctly? The length of that D-loop opening, if varied by more than 1/16″ can cause a significant change in your anchor point, so you can ill afford to get it wrong. Know that opening size and adhere to it.

Your Arrows

There is one more thing to remember about a bow tune. In nearly all cases, a 20 yard tune is just that, a 20 yard tune. Most archers today use different arrow sizes for indoors and outdoors. However, a ProActive technique for indoors would be to take several different sizes/diameters of arrows and tune them at 30 or preferably 40 yards. Find out which of them gives you the tightest and most consistent groups at 40 yards and go with those for indoors at 20 yards. If you can get a fat shaft to group tightly at 40 yards, then that shaft is going to make shooting consistently with it at 20 yards a chip shot. Realize, however, that even if you are using correctly spined arrows indoors at 20 yards, chances are you will have to tune them differently at distance to maximize their performance. You may have to move your arrow rest in or out slightly, or up or down slightly to get the best performance. You may well even have to move the poundage slightly up or down to improve grouping. Don't be afraid to change the poundage up or down to see if you can find a better "sweet spot" than the one you are set at for indoors. Normally, a setup that is tuned for distance will be a real "X-killer" at 20 yards! Seize that opportunity.

Group shoot your dozen arrows. I prefer not to use the same set of arrows for practice and for tournaments, but both sets are group tuned and marked. For outdoors, I mark my arrows in batches of four arrows each (for four arrow ends). One of my techniques is to mark the arrows that group together the tightest from 50 through 65 yards as "11, 12, 13, and 14." Those that group not quite as well, but still hold good at 35-59 yards are numbered "21, 22, 23, 24." Those that hold up well at closer yardages of 15-32 yards are numbered "31, 32, 33, 34." Finally those that are marginal at distance (but still hit close with the others at distance) are my 'bunny' and short distance arrows and numbered "41, 42, 43, and 44." The first number designates the "status" of the arrow while the second number tells me the order in which I shoot the arrow.

1. *The point being made here is that if you get an entire dozen arrows to group all together at long distance, and then count yourself lucky.* It isn't normal that all of them will go into the same hole outdoors, and I don't have a "Hooter Shooter" shooting machine to play with to get the arrows set, if possible, by rotating their nocks. Of course, nock orientation is critical, even with fall away rests. It is my experience, however, that no matter how well a set of arrows might "match," when it comes to the system I'm using, there are always some that just don't cut the mustard, so those get culled out. I never use arrows 41-44 to shoot long distances . . . unless those entire dozen arrows all shoot tightly together (not a common occurrence). I won't shoot my "11-14" arrows at 15 yard or 20 yard targets either; those are my prime special stock and are only for long distances. Why take the chances of damaging or robin-hooding one of your best arrows on a 15 or 20 yarder? Save those primo specials for where you need all the help you can get, and use them only in those designated distances. You cannot do this, however, if you don't group your arrows by shooting them at long distance, cull out those that won't cut it and then label the arrows accordingly. This seemingly small piece of being ProActive can

really add points to your score and your confidence in your equipment!

2. *There can, and likely will, be arrows in the same dozen that won't group at any distance with the others and my have to be re-fletched, retried, or even discarded.* In addition, when shooting your score, any arrow that goes away from the group on any target should be checked; anything can happen at any time, so be ProActive and check things before they become more of a problem.
3. *Psychological boosts are simple.* These techniques are subconscious or even subliminal things to keep you on balance and give you a boost after you've shot and scored your arrows on a target. Personally, I never allow someone else to pull my arrows from the target. I don't like the idea of someone else pulling, especially with the advent of nock inserts and bushings that can be moved with a simple twist of the wrist, be it intentional or otherwise. That is the first issue. The second issue is that I have a technique I picked up many years ago to always walk away from any target with the most positive thing I can come away with to help me psychologically for the next target. While most shooters pull their arrows and then maybe check their nocks, spin them, and place them one by one into their quiver, they will normally pull all of them at once, and not in any particular order either. Being ProActive like I am, I use a completely different technique: I pull the arrows, not in the order I shot them, but from the lowest scoring arrow sequentially to the highest scoring arrow last (including X-ring hits). I want to save the best for last . . . and I never pull the worst arrow or the big miss last, ever. Many shooters will pull the missed arrow last so they can "check it out." They have, in my opinion, psychologically upset themselves, because now as they move to the next target their entire thought process is negative and the thoughts are about the miss and not the best thing that happened on that target. Recall that I recommended that you do everything you can to pull a "positive" from every scoring end? Well, what better way to complete this process than saving your best for last and having the last thing you see and think is that nice gorgeous highest scoring arrow as opposed to that crappy one? By pulling the worst scoring arrow first, even if I know it wasn't a poor shot, it goes into the penalty box. The highest scoring arrow and the others naturally go into their proper slots in my quiver. Group 2's move out of Group 2 and into Group 1 before any from Group 3 get there and the penalty box arrow, unless I know for sure something is wrong with it, will obviously go back to the rotation long before I ever promote a Group 4 arrow to Group 1 status!
4. *If you can afford it, have at least two separate sets (or more) of arrows; one for practice (and yes, those are grouped together and numbered too) and one set (at least) of your "tournament special" arrows, which you have shot to make sure they are scoring worthy.* Maintain consistency in numbering and labeling in each set so you don't end up losing you sanity over which is which. While you do have to "practice" with your prime tournament arrows, don't make it a habit to always shoot your practice scores with those prime tournament arrows. Test them, and then reserve them for the big shows. (Never go into battle with an untested weapon.)

5. *Check all your arrows before and after each practice session.* With the advent of all carbon arrows, this is especially important and is even more important when you are shooting outdoors. Even if you didn't have any arrow glance-offs, those carbon arrows can, and will, fail. In addition you don't know if the side of the shaft hit something inside the bale and nicked or slightly crushed a wall. If you shoot one of those arrows, you could get severely injured. We've all seen pictures of people that have had serious injuries as a result of a carbon arrow shattering upon release and impaling itself through their bow hand, correct? Checking those arrows isn't only for nocks, etc; it is for safety and piece of mind. A loose vane or feather can and will have an effect upon arrow impact points. Either end of the vane can be nipped loose. Heaven help you if it is the trailing edge that comes loose and you don't see it. A loose vane or feather will not fly right, and will not impact with the other arrows. It is too late when a "flier" that nets you a "4" or worse is found to only have a loose vane on it because you didn't check it in advance. Again and again, become ProActive and head it off at the pass while you can do something about it. Sooner rather than later.

Nocks and Nock Fit

Yes, I know, here I go again. But, outdoors, this piece of equipment is so very critical that what I recommend bears repeating. And, don't skip this, because I'm not repeating things verbatim and I'm offering up some more "tips" in addition to those in Chapter 13. No teacher ever gives away all their secrets all at once; that would be boring.

1. *Routinely check and change your arrow nocks.* Are you ProActive about this and change your nocks before they become problems? If you do not want to check them after every shot, then at least set up a regular schedule to replace old with new. I gave you the alarming fact of the amount of G-force imparted to the end of the arrow to accelerate it from zero to 240 mph in only 20″ of forward movement. This should have alarmed you enough to make you realize just how much stress is placed upon arrow nocks and explained why pin nocks have become so popular. Nocks do crack, they do fatigue, and they do bend. It is too late to discover a bent nock or a cracked nock when you have shot a 4 or worse that resulted from a simple oversight, or worse yet, poor preventive maintenance practices. This is one of those "pay me now, or pay me later" situations. The latter part comes with a penalty, that penalty being points lost irrecoverably on your score card.
2. *Create a consistent nock orientation.* One thing that is overlooked by many shooters is the orientation of the arrow nock with regard to how the arrow sits on the arrow rest. The arrow nocks must be aligned exactly the same to the vanes or feathers going over or through the arrow rest. With shoot-around or shoot-through arrow rests, this is very, very critical. No, you do not need to have total and absolute vane clearance to get perfect grouping. What you must have, if you do have contact, is consistent contact with that arrow rest. With some arrow rests it is impossible to get total vane or feather clearance anyway. What many shooters try to accomplish is to get total vane clearance by going to the narrowest launcher blade possible.

What they fail to take into account is that if they don't have perfect form, they are then minimizing the arrow guidance needed to launch a clean shot consistently. If that blade is too narrow, then they will have problems drawing the bow back without it falling off the rest (not good). They will also have unexplained flyers on strong or weak shots. One small mistake, with too narrow of a blade and you get a "skidder" or an arrow that just doesn't follow the same path on the arrow rest due to your inconsistency. It isn't the arrow rest to blame, but rather our frailties as human beings in not being as perfect as we may think we are. I avoid super narrow blades, especially with fat shafts. I see many, many shooters using a launcher blade intended for *X-10*'s or *Nanos*, or other super small diameter shafts, and those shooters are trying to use them with 25, 26, or 27 diameter shafts and wondering why they get "skidders" and occasional (and sometimes frequent) wild fliers. Interestingly, when you point out the problem, they get defensive and say, "Well I powder tested them, and I don't have any vane contact; if I use a wider blade I get a little contact, so I have to have the clearance." Okay, that's fine, I guess, if that is what you want.

Prime cases in point are the Springy arrow rest and the wider launcher blades. It is impossible to get zero contact with a Springy rest. It is, along with the launcher blades a "shoot around" arrow rest. Contact is inevitable. So, what you must have is consistent contact; that being the same orientation of that/those bottom vanes set exactly the same on every arrow in your arsenal, with no exceptions. When I was using the *Springy* rest, and I will add that the first and actually most of all my personal best scores came while shooting this style of arrow rest, including 60X 300s, and mid to higher (557) field and hunter scores, I placed the nocks onto the arrows without any glue (or once Uni-nocks came along, would set them close). I shot the arrows, and those that went into the middle and were solid shots were set aside, and used as Master patterns for the rest of the arrow sets. Then, I would take the remainder of the set and rotate the nocks to match the Masters, and try those arrows again. Those that went in the middle like the Masters were set aside. I would repeat this until all the arrows were "set." Then, before doing anything else, I scribed a scratch on the shaft taper or Uni-bushing that matched the mould line on both sides of the arrow nock. Then, I would proceed to glue on the nocks and align the mould lines with the scribed line. When Uni-bushings came along, then I was done with nock alignment at that point and could, until a nock was broken, bent, cracked or due for change. You too, can do this by becoming ProActive and setting yourself up with a means of getting your arrow nock alignment back as close to exact as humanely possible. Note Personally this is the main reason why I use very low temperature hot melt glue rather than "plumber's tape" or plastic food wrap to help hold Uni- or pin nock bushings into the shaft. It is too easy for the "unglued" bushings to move around or to get moved. If the bushing moves, then even if your nock mould lines are aligned to the bushing's scratches, the scratches are not where they were before the bushing moved/got moved.

I find it hard to believe, but there isn't a really reliable and consistent nock-alignment tool on the market today. In my opinion, the best one out there was/is the old (ancient) Saunders unit. You can find one, once in awhile on eBay, but they are few and far between. There are other tools available (*see Chapter 13*), but they don't do the job as accurately as the one built in the 1970's. In my opinion, nock rotation is still important even for today's fall away arrow rests. Whatever the tool, in order to make a nock change in the field, you will still need to be ProActive and come up with some way of aligning the new nock in the correct orientation.

a. *Nock Orientation for Fall-Away Arrow Rests* Even with the advent of fall-away rests there can be vane contact with the arrow shelf or even the cabling due to misalignment or inconsistent alignment of your arrow nocks. The fall-aways don't address contact with the cables or arrow shelf when using larger feathers or higher profile vanes. They don't address the potential contact of the controlling lanyards that run from the up or down cable to the arrow rest itself. I see many, many shooters shooting their fall-away rests with higher and higher profile vanes or feathers and they have the index vane pointing downwards. In my opinion, this increases the odds of having contact with the launcher arm or even the launcher support arm or even the arrow shelf simply because you have reduced the clearance by the height of that feather or vane. The only way to accommodate this is to speed up the fall of the rest, and when you do that, you reduce the guidance the arrow rest provides the arrow, and when you reduce the guidance, then you really can foul things up due not to the bow, but due to the human elements involved with the loosing of the arrow. While nock rotation being perfect is a bit less critical with a fall-away rest, there are still potential problems that can be avoided if you just take the time to think things through. More speed of the fall is not better with regard to fall away arrow rests. Since the rest is falling away in a downward movement, in my opinion, it just doesn't make sense to have any vane, which in many cases is ⅜″ or more in height, oriented downward and increasing the chances of contact at the wrong time. If this vane isn't the same on every arrow, and does have contact, then you have inconsistent contact and, as a result, inconsistent impact points. This potential source of contact is being overlooked by a lot of shooters. Being ProActive means heading things off at the pass so that they are less likely to be a problem in the first place.

3. *Check the fit of the nock on the center serving.* Another overlooked item is how your nocks fit onto the string. Nocks that fit too tightly or too loosely will not shoot the same and will impact differently from the other arrows in the set that have correctly fitting nocks on them. One way to deal with is to check all the nocks when you buy a package for correct nock fit and group them accordingly. I toss out nocks that fit way too tightly or way too loosely. There will be come in every pack that just don't meet muster.

a. *Replacing a Nock* This is simple. You have the location index already marked, so you simply put on the new nock, align the mould lines to the indicator lines on the bushing and all is okay. Well, not quite yet. There is one more thing, that is, of course, the fit of the new nock on the bow string. When you have replaced a nock on an arrow that means that the new nock has not yet been fired out of the bow. Well, I recommend and also follow the rule to at least pre-stretch that nock some so that it is somewhat better than a brand new, untested nock. When I replace an individual nock (I don't do this if I'm replacing all of the nocks in that set of arrows), I make it a procedure to push it on and pull it off of the bow string 25 times minimum before I shoot the arrow (someplace other than the nocking point so that area doesn't get unnecessarily worn). I then recheck the alignment, and the arrow is now deemed ready to shoot. The reasoning is that since the other arrows have been already shot numerous times, those nocks are "broken in" or worn to the point that they fit properly, whereas that new nock isn't ready yet. It just pays to try to get a little more consistency. A lost point in score is a point lost forever. When it can be minimized, a ProActive archer will opt to do so.

b. *Replacing the center serving on your bow string.* When replacing your bow string's center serving, make sure to wrap your serving in the same direction as it was before you replaced it. If you don't do this correctly, your peep sight will rotate something terrible and in the wrong direction, and you will end up doing the serving over. Chances are, if you do this correctly, you won't totally lose your peep rotation. You might have to remove the peep and rotate it 180 degrees, but that will be about all you'll have to do. Don't forget nock fit. Adjust the tension on the serving tool so that your nocks fit correctly. A little tension goes a long ways, so you can do this as you move down towards the actual location of the nock on the string. Now you know yet another reason why I recommend that the top of the serving be at least 2″ to 2½″ above where the nock goes onto the string. It gives me room to test for and ensure correct nock fit and also that it lowers the odds of the serving slipping on the bowstring itself, because there is a lot of support to resist the upwards pressure you place on the arrow and arrow nocking point when you shoot the bow with a release aid. If you want to get fancy, you could use a caliper to measure it and write it down. I don't normally go to this extreme, but hey, it is your bow. If it has been awhile since you've replaced the nocks in your arrows, now might well be the time to replace them and fit the serving to the new nocks, saving you having problems with nock fit. You can then kill two birds with one stone.

c. *Also, before you remove the old serving, mark its location on the bowstring, both top and bottom, before you remove it.* It is obvious that you will measure and write down your finished D-loop length, the D-loop location, and the peep height (on your Master Bow Configuration Table). You want to get this length of serving as close as possible to what it was originally. So, take the time to do it right. The rest of the procedure in duplicating the setup is in Chapters 10-13.

The Answer (To the Where to Look Puzzle)

So, after reading all of the above, have you figured out what went wrong and caused the radical change in the grouping of my arrows (see Another Personal Story above)? I said I had an inkling of where to look because I was paying attention to the impact points of those misses. I said I was having extreme highs and lows on bad shots and highs and lows on good shots. That suggested to me to look into . . . my nocking point! I shoot a bow that has perfect nock travel, so my arrow nock's center and thus the arrow are aligned through the arrow rest mounting holes and thus the D-loop on the string is set so that the center of the arrow nock is in the center of the D-loop. So, since the old rule of thumb of "high and low, nocking point down" still applies, all I had to do was check that the center mould line of my arrow nock was still in the center of the D-loop. Well, I'll be snaggle-toothed that I had a second indicator, too. The D-loop was deformed slightly upwards and when I checked the mould line alignment, the bottom of the nock was where that "line" fell in relationship to the center of the D-loop. I know for a fact that several thousand shots ago, I had centered that D-loop correctly. The only thing that could have happened is that the D-loop moved up the string (even though I tie it in above it) and/or the serving had slowly been creeping up the string.

Either way, this is what I did to correct this. First, I re-centered the D-loop in to the proper pulling position. Then, I loosened the lanyard on my fallaway rest (Hamskea *Versa-Rest*) to allow the arrow rest to go to the full "up" position. Then, it was a simple task of moving the arrow rest so that the properly centered D-loop and the tip of the arrow matched what the tuned measurement was supposed to be. Simple tasks—took less than two minutes. Sight setting came back to where it belonged and groups immediately tightened up. Lesson learned? Yes. Just because you think you have 2″ plus of serving above the arrow nock/D-loop and you've tied in the D-loop doesn't mean that after several thousand shots that upward pressure doesn't gradually move that D-loop and the tied in portion of the serving upwards on the string!

There are some additional things learned as well: I learned that with this particular bow, there is a "sweet spot" range where the bow will operate even if it is slightly out of whack; it will still shoot well as long as you are within that range, but heaven help you once it hits its "upper control limit." I'm no longer a good enough shooter to pick up on very minor changes, but I sure picked up on things when that range of the sweet spot went out of limits for the bow-arrow combination with regard to nocking point. It pays to check nocking point height more accurately and more often; tied in D-loop or not. I now check the centering of the mould line vs. D-loop positioning before each practice session. ProActive archery: if something can move, it will move (eventually), be prepared for it.

Summary

Some key elements to equipment preparation for the outdoor season were discussed in this chapter. This is more critical than it is for an indoor setup because of the variations in distance and the longer distances involved. Special attention to the details outlined in this chapter along with other details you might think of yourself can really help to improve your scoring simply because you have taken the time to get your equipment as consistent and fool-proof as you possibly can. There are other methods than those mentioned, and not all the methods recommended will be new to everyone. If you don't use them and you don't try them, then you'll never know what a difference can really be made by paying attention and becoming more ProActive.

What I have outlined above does work for me; otherwise it wouldn't be here. It has also worked for most all of the shooters I have helped over the years Remember, it is the little things that are overlooked, forgotten, or skipped over that are the real score robbers. Once you are at a mid- to higher-echelon level of skill, the difference could well lie in something listed above that you hadn't thought about or don't practice at all. If you aren't winning, you might want to ask yourself if the difference is in what the other guys are doing and you are not. Or, if the other guys are just better, can you close the gap between you and them by being better prepared?

The next chapter will delve into practicing ProActively for outdoor field and target shooting. It has implications for 3-D shooting and hunting, too. Items coming up include: wind shooting, footing, "Kentucky windage" and "bubbling" for shooting in the wind, along with dealing with other score robbers. You can practice and learn how you and your system will respond to the inevitable poor conditions relating to the above, and more instead of always practicing under ideal conditions and getting yourself tied up in chasing the elusive 280 half or 560 perfect round under those conditions, when in reality, ideal conditions are seldom if ever found. So, it is better to prepare for the inevitable ahead of time.

Tom Dorigatti

30

Proactive Practice For Outdoor Performance, Pt I

(Footing, Shooting the Angles, and the Wind)

This chapter deals with some more aspects of outdoor tournament preparation, those little things that, if prepared for in advance by becoming ProActive, can and will translate into some added points to your scores. These practice techniques address the need to prepare for competition in all terrains and weather, specifically what to do about poor footing, shooting uphill, downhill, and sidehill targets, and dealing with the wind. Some items will be repeated from previous chapters simply because they are considered critical, deserve the added emphasis, and I can't be sure you have read the previous chapters, so everything on this topic needs to be here, too.

So, you have been shooting pretty well of late. You are shooting an unfamiliar field course and you come up on this 50 yarder on your first 14 target unit of the day. Your group is shooting two abreast an each target and you have the left side of the shooting stake to shoot from. The stakes are set on a rather steep sidehill slope and when you stand at the stake, you quickly notice that there is no level position to shoot from. Your toes are pointing severely uphill. You note that the target bale itself, while level, is also slightly uphill and also is on the steep slope that falls from high left to low right. What are you going to do here? How are you going to shoot this target? How are you going to stand in that awkward "toes up" stance with the slope of the hill into your body, at an uphill target and still be able to execute each shot with proper back tension? You've all had such situations before if you've shot any field rounds at all, so . . . how do you handle this? I might add that watching your opponent won't help much, since he is a lefty, and you are shooting this target right-handed; uh, oh . . . two completely different approaches to shooting this target; ouch. If you have been ProActive and practiced for this inevitability, this is not really all that tough, since you've practiced this and know exactly how this situation affects you and your form, you know what to try to accomplish (besides "shooting 5's") and you also how you are going to have to go about it because you already have a plan. If you haven't done this before, or you are not versed in this situation, you are going to really have some issues with this target! There are lots of things to consider, but let's talk about the major issue you will have to deal with first.

Shooting with Less than Optimal Footing

Most shooters claim that they practice for field tournaments "like they would shoot a tournament." Most shooters don't really practice this, they just say it. Here are some tips to help you practice overlooked aspects of outdoor shooting that eat away at your potential to achieve higher scores when under less than ideal conditions.

1. *Shoes* Tennis shoes might be fine on flat, target-style courses out on a flat field. In fact, it seems that many shooters wear open-toed sandals or tennis shoes while competing in these events. Then, under the hot sun on the shooting line, they find their balance has changed and their feet get tired and sore. Their scores suffer as a result.

   The type of shoes you wear impacts your shooting especially when it comes to longer rounds shot outdoors. With the exception of 3-D venues, most outdoor rounds range from 60 arrows for an International Round to 112 arrows on a NFAA Field or Hunter round, to 144 arrows for a full FITA round. You would be wise to select a comfortable shoe that cushions your feet and provides a forward balance (slightly higher heels to move your weight forward some) so that you are not shooting on your heels and putting strains on your calves and upper legs. When shooting a field or 3-D course on uneven terrain or muddy conditions, tennis shoes are not the way to go. A good ankle supporting hiking boot or walking shoe is much better suited to the task. One other bit of advice—I've found over the years that it is best not to wear the same shoes going to and from a tournament. The change of foot gear provides a welcome relief to those tired and warm feet; especially after the round is done! Having a change of socks available doesn't hurt either. Your body, mind, and feet will thank you for it!
2. *Uneven Footing* It is a given that, sooner or later, you will have uneven footing on any field or 3-D course you shoot. Some courses are more difficult than others. So, how can you prepare for this if your course isn't set up with any targets with uneven or sloped footing? How can you train to handle the situations of toes pointing uphill, toes pointing downhill, front foot way below back foot, front foot way above back foot, or otherwise being forced to move weight to the front foot or back foot or having to bend one knee or the other to get comfortable? I will tell you that if you haven't ProActively practiced the above techniques, your score and attitude are going to suffer when you do run up against them. I have seen many competitors "performing construction" at national tournaments by literally digging out either in front of or behind a shooting stake for a firm front foot plant. This does work, but before long, you find yourself adapting to someone else's preferred footing instead of your own and having to make even more changes. In addition, this constant construction work is tough on the legs, feet, and calves and will tire you out quickly! If you haven't practiced the techniques, you have no other alternative.

   The solution to practicing these various footing conditions is very simple, and only involves a little ingenuity and a piece of ⅝″ or ¾″ plywood about two feet square (or less), and a couple of pieces of 2x4s or 4x4s or even 2x6's (better yet).

You construct an "incline board" like those used at work-out centers for calf and shin splint stretches, because basically that is what this is. Do you have kids in the neighborhood who have made ramps for practicing bicycle or skateboard jumps? Now you know what I'm talking about.

You can then practice your footing in any direction you want and just about any degree of severity you want on any target on your course. In fact, you do not need to even be outdoors to work on this. You can practice this at your local indoor range; or, if you have a target in your basement or garage, you can do it there too. Simply place one end of the plywood on the ground or floor, and then, by using the 2x4s (or whatever) at varying distances from the opposite end, change the elevation angle and, voila, an instant hill. Put your front foot on the ground and your back foot on the plywood to simulate a lower front foot stance in varying degrees. Reverse this and simulate your back foot being lower than your front foot. Move the plywood and stand on it with toes pointing uphill or downhill to simulate toes up and toes down to any angle you choose. While it won't provide you with the body angle of having the target above or below you, this simulation will, even on flat ground, provide you with much needed information of how you are affected by this change in your normal footing, and how far it throws you off and in which direction. You must learn this and practice it and then learn how uphill and downhill targets change your bow arm angle and how that affects your shot, also when coupled with the footing problem. As I have said over and over—once you have established comfortable footing, never move your feet between shots at the same shooting position. This is even more critical for field shooting than it is for indoors or target shooting. *Another Tip* I recommend that you avoid ever putting your ankles together for footing. Standing with your ankles together is probably the most unstable stance you can use when shooting indoors, let alone outdoors where things really get dicey. Yeah, I know, you've seen a few shooters of note doing exactly that from time to time, blah, and blah. Remember, the more stable your stance, the more stable your platform and balance and the more stable your platform and balance, the more stable your body; and on and on. Why would you want to destabilize yourself if you don't have to? Scoring isn't about emulating somebody else; scoring is all about putting yourself into the position that works best and most consistently for you.

3. *Uphill, Downhill, and Side-Hill Targets* With the advent of handheld computers, clinometers, "cut-charts," and now angle compensating rangefinders, uphill and downhill corrections for angle are much easier than they were in the past. However, any shooter who depends completely on these instruments for giving them the "answers" to shooting uphill and downhill, without practicing, is in for a big disappointment. The computer doesn't solve the entire problem for you. Those instruments can give you all the "yardages" and the angles, but one huge thing they cannot give you is the shot process for a shot at that odd angle. You can crunch out all those numbers you want, but when it comes right down to it, those "numbers" won't shoot the bow; you have to do that part of it all by your-

self. Here are some tips on "hill shooting:"

a. *Draw Length* if any of you have seen the video "Straight Talk from the Pros," the one thing that comes through loud and clear is the importance of draw length. In a nutshell, "draw length is the most critical aspect of accurate and consistent shooting." Most compound archers are shooting too long of a draw length, and many by two inches or more! It is well known by most good field and target shooters that in order to shoot consistently on any roving field course, your draw length must be set near perfectly. It is better to be slightly short than too long. Most people don't notice their too long draw length on level ground, but give them a target that is steeper than a few degrees up or down or on a side-hill, and the problems really start for them. While they might get by on one shot under those situations, it is next to impossible for them to get by with all four shots consistently enough to score well. Many blame the uphill and downhill nature of the shot for their woes when, in reality, a simple draw length adjustment would gain them a lot of points. So, how can you know if your draw length is causing you difficulty on hilly courses? How can you "practice" to really find out? What can you do to insure you are indeed coming to the same "to anchor draw length" each and every time?

I set you up for this back in Chapter 14, I just didn't tell you that this was coming. I always tell my students that what I sometimes say now might not mean anything to them just then, but I don't talk just to hear myself talk and there are reasons for everything I try to teach them. Read on, you are now going to have some fun.

How can you tell if your draw length might be causing you difficulty because of the hills? First off, in Chapter 14, I recommended the "Triple Tape System" for which you place small pieces of masking tape on your cables and when you practice and shoot, you make sure you match them up when at full draw? I told you that if you do this religiously, you won't depend upon those supposed hard stops, and will soon reduce your variation in your actual draw length to little or nothing. I also told you that each 0.05 of an inch harder into the stops is going to increase your holding weight by one pound.

What I didn't tell you back then was when you are shooting uphill, you tend to draw the bow longer; when shooting downhill, you tend to come in short. How long or how short your tendencies are depends upon the severity of the slope and . . . your footing! Oh, my; no more standing nice and flat all the time at one distance; we have a new animal here, don't we? Those hard stops can be of help, if you use the things and practice them. Those tapes will be a huge help; especially for a beginner to mid-level shooter. Will it take a 550 shooter to 560? Not necessarily, since those people already have most all of this figured out. You've read, I am sure, about bending at the waist to keep your upper body full draw position consistent and, absolutely, you need to do that! But, you won't do that correctly without practicing it! If you have a local range that has a lot of ups and downs, you have an advantage, use that advantage. If your local range is flat, you can practice various footings (toes up and toes down and front foot low, front foot high), but it is tough to practice working on the uphill and downhill body angles . . . or is it? On your outdoor course, yes. But who ever said you cannot simulate that body angle stuff indoors or in your basement or garage? Think about this a bit. Who says you have to shoot full distance at your basement or garage target? Who says you have to always shoot 20 or 30 yards at your indoor range? Ever heard of trigonometry? No, I'm not suggesting you start a series of calculations and play trig and solve problems or dig out your clinometer. That is just a hint to get you thinking.

Simulating Shooting Angles Here's a technique to help you ProActively simulate and practice your body positioning and such (especially with triggerless release aids) for uphill and downhill shooting without having to have a hilly course or even set foot outdoors. True, there isn't a replacement for the "real thing" but having something to deal with it is better than having nothing. This will help you immensely in getting used to how to acquire the same to anchor draw length and to bend at the waist and still be consistent with that crucially important to anchor draw length.

- First off, always match up those triple tapes; it has to become almost a religious step of your outdoor shot routine until it is mastered under all course conditions.
- Step up to your shooting bale at a very short distance that will not let your main stabilizer hit the bale when the shot breaks.
- Start out at shoulder level and shoot a bunch of shots horizontally across the bale (don't shoot for groups, please; you will trash your arrows). I suggest shooting four arrows, since that simulates shooting an end on a Field/Hunter round.
- Shoot several more ends intentionally coming in at shoulder level and bending at the waist to bring the bow down, but this time you are aiming on your bale about 6″ lower than last time. Repeat this, making sure to come to level, then bend at the waist so you are now shooting 8-10″ lower into the bale. Continue this coming to anchor at shoulder level, matching your triple (or double tapes), shooting several arrow ends horizontally across the bale, each time going lower and lower. Here you are simulating shooting downhill targets with a level stance and coming to full draw and the same to anchor draw length, but each time, the severity of the downhill gets more and more. You are so close to the bale that you can do this and not worry about trashing or losing arrows.
- Now shoot dead level again, coming into the tapes, then for the next sequence, you will bend at the waist to raise your bow up about 4-6″, shoot four shots, and repeat doing this, raising your impact point each time. Move your practice butt up if necessary.
- If you really want to get fancy, bring in your incline board and work that into this drill. You won't get the feel for where your impact point on the target will be, but, with a little ingenuity, you can put up reduced size spots and get a

general idea of how this messes with your aiming. However the feel for how this angling of the body and how you respond to it, and that it isn't such a big deal to come to the same full to anchor draw length time and again, will boost your confidence and give you the ability to deal with such issues without hardly thinking about them.

One last thing before I go on. You might possibly end up with a slight decrease in your bow's set draw length in order to handle this set of outdoor circumstances. (If you do change it, document and date it in your Master Bow Configuration Table. In my case, I shot about ⅛″ shorter draw length for outdoors than I did indoors, which wouldn't seem like much; but trust me, it is; especially for hilly field courses. You won't know this until you fully check things out, however. Obviously, you should use any and all opportunities to seek out and shoot hilly courses as much as you can. The more the better, and the better you'll get at handling your footing, body positioning, and "to anchor draw length" under those inevitable conditions.

b. *Reading Targets* So, we are still on that 50 yard target, but now you have practiced your footing and body positioning and getting your "to anchor draw length" down to a fine art. It is time now to pay more attention to what is around you. The targets do talk to you, but you have to watch closely and pay attention because you might learn something. Never think that you will always "cut" the yardage on downhill shots and "add" to the yardage on uphill shots. If the angle uphill is steep enough, you can have many situations where you must deduct yardage on the target, or you will shoot right out the top of the spot or possibly even miss the target entirely! It is a good practice to always "read" the target with your binoculars when you get to the shooting stake. Look for telltale signs concerning how previous shooters have been hitting this target. Pay attention to the caliber of shooters that are ahead of you on the course; this also can give you important information. Field shooting is a lot about paying attention to what is around you. Often this reading of the tendencies of the targets will save you many points over the course of the round. Just because a target "looks" only to be uphill doesn't mean that it necessarily "shoots" that way. There are loads of other variables, including one that people are never really quite sure of—the yardage markers being slightly or occasionally measured incorrectly. Sure, the rangefinder and clinometer can help you out, but, I've seen many targets that sure seem to defy physics, gravity, and even common sense, and believe me, I've seen and shot a lot of them over the years.

Some uphill and/or downhill targets not only shoot for an "add" or a "cut," but for some reason, they also tend to shoot a little left or right. If you don't "read" the target for that, even proper execution will probably not net you a 5-ring hit. In addition, if you haven't practiced and/or don't know your tendencies for footing on those types of shots; you are not in a good position to figure out just what to do. I can tell you right now, without looking, that the 50 yard target I described starting this chapter will have most of the misses and even the bulk of the 5-ring hits . . . on the right side of the target face, and likely a tad high to boot. Why? Read on.

c. *Sidehill Shooting* Much like uphill and downhill shooting, sidehill footing can be practiced on any target by using the incline board previously described. You can practice positioning your body up close and personal as well, even on level ground or in your basement or garage or indoor range. What you cannot practice is the distance; unfortunately, simulations cannot do everything. The actual shooting of a sidehill target involves more than just the leaning forward into or leaning backward into the slope of the hill and pre-loading the bubble (more on that in a minute), but if you know your footing changes and how they affect you, you are much better prepared to handle the other issues.

- *Pre-loading the Bubble* Another important compensation is to "pre-load" your sight's bubble into the hill before you come to full draw. If you don't do this pre-loading, then chances are your shot will impact on the downhill side of the bull's-eye and low due to your tendency to fall down the hill with your shot. If you level up the bubble first, like you normally do on level ground, then you have already unloaded the bow to the downhill side. I would recommend that, after reading the target to see all those holes on the down hill side, and to check for the high and low impacts, that you pre-load a "full bubble" (entire bubble just outside the bounding line) into the hill, and when you reach anchor, then level up the bubble and shoot a strong shot. More often than not, unless you shoot a weak shot or didn't pre-load the bow into the hill, your windage should be right on. This will work whether your toes are pointed uphill or downhill. However, a word of caution: you need to know your tendencies with regards to toe up or toe down footings! This might force you to "give" a little bubble one side or the other to compensate, and this comes from that "p" word—Practice, and be ProActive about it; learn this stuff in advance.

d. *Practicing those "Cuts" and "Adds" Practicing "cuts" and "adds" is also easy enough to do.* What I've found to be the most successful thing is to take the time and quit practicing "dead on" targets occasionally and to find out what a 'click', or a half-yard, or a full yard actually does to my impact point. In other words, where does my equipment shoot if I intentionally set the sight off of the sight setting for that yardage? This is a critical thing to know on any target when field shooting. Cut chart or no cut chart, if those arrow holes in the target are telling you a story, then you'd better know how that affects you and don't worry about the other guys in your group. Their bows won't shoot the same as yours, and they are going to react differently to the circumstances than you do. Do not depend upon them to tell you what they shot it for, or if they do, use that information coupled with your gut feeling and experience to help make a better adjustment. If you are using a "cut chart" or a clinometer and cut chart, do those holes agree with that cut chart or not? If you haven't practiced by mis-setting your sight so that you know your impact points from an intentionally misset sight, then you are again left wondering what to do. And doubt breeds more misses and lost points. So, simply go out and learn what your impact points for ½ yard short and long, 1 yard short and long, 1½ yards short and long, and 2 yards short and long. Those will really save your bacon when you are out on the course trying to decide about a "cut" or an "add." Once again knowing your equipment and your tendencies to this degree are pretty much imperative if you are ever going to excel at field shooting.

Back to that 50 yard target: So, I have discussed most of the items concerning the draw length issue, the uphill down hill issues, the sidehill issues. I've given you some tools and practice drills to master your "to anchor draw length" consistency and to work on bending at the waist with regard to shooting uphill and downhill. I've given you a tool that you can build to help you practice different foot alignments and positions, simulating uneven ground. I also emphasized the importance of you knowing your tendencies on all those things and how you and your equipment reacts to them. You know the importance of paying attention to what is going on around you and how to "read" the target face and to take stock of those ahead of you and their prowess, along with that of those in your shooting group. So, okay. Now what? We know that the 50 yarder is uphill and the slope runs from high on your left to low on your right. You know to expect, when you look at the target that most of the holes are going to be on the right side of the bullseye or target face. Next, you need to pay close attention to the elevation of those holes, too. Why? Because, even with a rangefinder, the target may or may not be shooting what the range indicates either. I know, a yard is a yard, is a yard. However, I've known targets to not shoot the yardage, too.

And then, you have the human element too. You see, I know that most shooters are right-handed and we have an uphill/sidehill shot of this nature, that those holes would be a little on the high side, too. Why? Because even with the yardage being correct, that is the tendency of most shooters in this situation! How do I know this? First, that is my own tendency, and secondly I've seen lots of it so I go upon experience too. I already know what to watch for, by how much and where those holes are versus my tendencies give me a lot more information. If those holes are only an inch or two at 2 o'clock, then I know to either "bubble over" a hair more into the hill and aim a tad low, or to "bubble over" a hair more into the hill after correcting my sight one half yard short, at 49.5 yards, aim dead on, and shoot a strong shot. Now, watch out here . . . because, left-handed shooters have a different shot because they are leaning back into the hill with their toes down, so they could be shooting to the downhill side and a tad low. That is one more reason to pay attention to how many lefties you see out on the course! If your first shot doesn't go well and you know you shot it correctly, then make an adjustment; don't sit on it and shoot all four of them out there. It is easy to over-compensate too, but, you have the advantage over the lefties in this scenario; it is much easier to lean the front of your body into a hill than it is to have your toes down and your body falling away from the hill and having to lean backwards into the hill! Thus, those lefties will tend to shoot farther to the right on this scenario than a right handed shooter—another good thing to know.

Shooting the Angles with The Bubble

You have probably noticed that I have only briefly mentioned the notorious aperture bubble in talking about pre-loading sidehill shots. That was by design, because the "bubble technique" is a hotly debated item as to "how and how not," and "when and when not," to bubble a shot. While indoors, the bubble isn't considered much of a factor in shooting perfect 300s, but I think you will find that it is a factor for many shooters in shooting high X-counts indoors. However, outdoors is another story. If you cannot hold your bubble centered up and you cannot "control" how you bubble up, then you are in for some trying times on just about any field course! Put in a light wind and oh, boy can this really get dicey in a hurry.

1. *Get Your Bubble Leveled Up in All Sight Axes* There are many different methods of leveling up the bubble, and I won't go into them. I've tried several of them over the years, and must admit that for me, there isn't one that works any better than another. Whichever method you choose to use, then make sure you are consistent with it, and check the bubble leveling often. Sights are notorious when it comes to their bubble leveling changing or moving around. They are not locked into one position, nor do they necessarily stay in the scope solidly either. Today, there are several jigs on the market that make leveling your axes a bunch easier. These products do indeed work and they work well, but they don't come cheap. Once again, be ProActive about setting these axes on your sight, and then be ProActive in marking the bolt positions so you can tell at a glance when something comes loose. Years ago, we didn't have such devices, so we learned pretty much by trial and error and I must say we didn't do so badly on it. I shot many perfect 560 rounds on the old NFAA Field and Hunter targets (5-3 scoring), but I've never shot 560 on the post 1976 NFAA field or hunter rounds (5-4-3 scoring), but did accomplish 557 Fields and 556 Hunters. Not too shabby for manual "shot in" sight settings using the "doorjamb method" of leveling the sight, and a "hook or crook" method of re-placement of the bubble into the scope body with epoxy. The products for leveling come from Hamskea Archery, Zenith Archery, Brite-Site Pro Tuner, Sur-Loc, and several others. Some claim the only way to level the 3rd axis is at full draw, while others claim otherwise. However, I will tell you that if you fail to line up your 3rd axis and you run into a hilly field course, you could be in for a long, long day!
2. *Practice "Bubbling" on Targets under Level and Calm Conditions* Most shooters again, practice round after round with everything peachy keen and under ideal conditions. Then, when the chips are down and those ideal conditions are nowhere in sight, they are ill-prepared to handle the environmental changes and, well, they lose. Remember what I told you a bit ago about knowing your equipment and how it shoots by shooting targets while intentionally mis-setting your sight? This allows you to learn how your impact points are affected in half yard

sight setting intervals so that when you see those multiple arrow holes 1″, 2″, or 3″ high or low, you know how your sight needs adjusting to accommodate that. It also helps if, after that first shot, you realize you "missed your cut" and need to make an adjustment. How much? You first evaluate your shot. Was it strong? Was it weak? Were you aiming a tad high or low? If you know you shot a good one, take stock of that and adjust again for that high or low impact point. Be ProActive, pay attention, and don't be hesitant to re-set.

a. *How to Practice Bubbling* Just like intentionally shooting with your sight set to the wrong yardage to learn from that, you should also practice under level and calm conditions so that you learn how much left and right your impact point moves if you give it ¼, ½, ¾ or a full bubble in either direction. This is extremely important information when you couple it with your learned tendencies for toe up or toe down (sidehill shooting). Practice "bubbling" at all yardages so that you know the affect it has on your impact point. This will be another useful tool in your arsenal, believe me. I've seen so many shooters more talented than me who simply could not figure out how much bubble to give or quite what to do because things just weren't like they had practiced over and over. The end result is that I placed higher than they did because I was prepared and simply knew myself, my equipment, and shooting techniques better than they did.

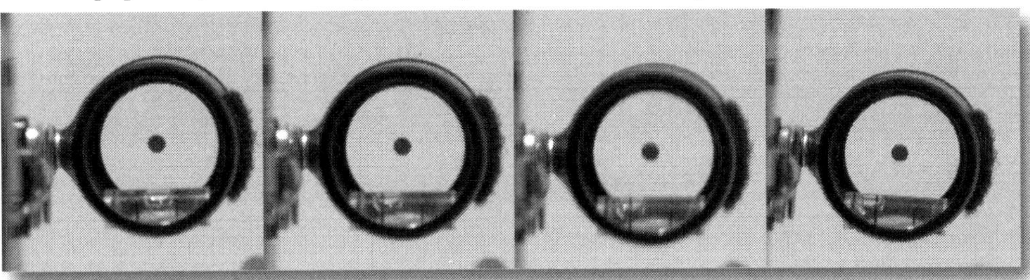

(Left) Here the bubble is "centered up." (Center-Left) Top limb is tilted to the right enough to get one quarter of the bubble to the left of the line (arrow will go to the right). (Center-Right) This is half of a bubble. (Right) This is three quarters of a bubble. Note This scope didn't allow a "full bubble" with the edge of bubble lined up with left hand mark. Bubbles going the other way will cause arrows to impact to the left.

b. *Natural Cant* If you are one of those shooters who has a "natural cant" built into your form, then that is fine, but you sure need to make sure that it is set right and that the bubble is set to that natural cant in all axes. I know some shooters who spend the time to level everything up perfectly and then either knock the top of their sight bar out of level either to the left or right, depending upon their natural tendency to cant their bow! They know what they are doing, and know how to re-set their windage for it and carry on. This is fine, but you really have to know yourself and what you are doing if you are going to use this technique.

c. *Fourth Axis* Recently, there has been much discussion concerning the fourth axis and a new device for setting it properly. If you do change your sight extension during a round or from indoors to field to target or FITA, then I highly recommend that you make sure that the 4th axis is properly aligned. I, for one, do not change sight extensions, so I do not set the 4th axis or bother with it.

Shooting In the Wind

Oh, yes, I always save the best for last! The nemesis of many a fine shooter—shooting in the wind. Let me dispense with the "PA" word here and get to the point. As far along as you are in this chapter, you already know I'm going to say, "Take the time to practice in the wind any chance that you get." If you don't practice in it, then how can you ever expect to shoot well in it? So there, I've said it and now on to techniques and the good stuff.

1. *Wind Shooting Techniques* There is constant debate concerning whether to "bubble it" in the wind or to aim off center when shooting in the wind. There are many successful shooters out there that can do either, but I think you will find that there are more successful shooters out there that choose when and where to do either or both.

   a. *"Bubbling" to Shoot in the Wind* The rule of thumb when bubbling in the wind is to "cant the top limb into the wind." The question is how much bubble to give it. This is simple, if you have practiced bubbling in the calm and level and know how far your impact point moves left or right based upon how much bubble you give the shot! If you haven't practiced in the calm, then you are clueless as to how much bubble to give it when the wind is already blowing. You can see the impact points by reading the target, or how that first arrow went nuts on you. But if you don't know the impact point distance-to-bubble ratio, you are lost and it becomes a guessing game. ProActive archers don't have to "guess" very often, they have practiced for as many of the variables as they can, and know themselves and their equipment stone cold.

      The technique involves aiming dead center on the Bull's-eye, canting the top limb into the wind to a certain amount of "bubble," and shooting a strong, controlled shot. This technique is very effective, even in moderate wind conditions. The key is to not get flustered or upset and to accept the fact that your bow arm is going to move a little and that are going to miss some shots. Those who accept this and shoot strong shots are those who will score the best. Those who whine and cry and say things like, "I'd be shooting so much better if the wind weren't blowing" are giving you points. If you've worked on your game, then you have a huge advantage, don't waste the opportunity by joining the whiners.

   b. *Aiming Off the Target Based on Arrow Drift* Many shooters choose to use this method because they haven't learned or don't necessarily accept the bubbling methodology. Others use "aiming off" when the wind is blowing hard. Once you have determined how bad the drift is and if it is consistent, then aiming off isn't all that hard. You just have to remember that a day of this may mean three or four days of hard work to break that bad habit of aiming off center again! Often times, the wind is so bad that you don't have enough "bubble" to cover the wind, so you are forced to shoot with the aiming off technique. Yes, I'll say it once more. If you haven't practiced the aiming off technique, then you are going to have serious problems when using it in the wind. You also have to know when to not bother with bubbling and to simply shoot a strong bow arm with a strong shot.

Aiming off can be practiced in no wind conditions by deliberately mis-setting your windage and/or elevation settings. Mis-set your sight, shoot on target and then pick a spot to bring your arrows back on center. After several successful shots, change your sight settings for a different "wind" direction and strength.

2. *Cautions Regarding Both Techniques*
   a. You need to make sure which side the wind is blowing from, not only at the shooting line but at the target as well. The wind can be blowing from multiple directions and often is! Reading the target on a field course and watching those flags on an outdoor target course are necessary when the wind is blowing.
   b. *You also need to pay close attention which way the wind is pushing your bow arm.* If it is pushing your bow arm away from your release arm, then expect the release (especially a back tension model) to be going off more quickly and expect also (for a right-handed shooter) a slight push to the left for your impact point. This can affect how much "bubble" you give the shot. If the wind is pushing your bow arm towards your release arm (caving you in), then you will get a "softer" shot and the release will take a little longer to fire. You will tend to collapse on these shots. You have to know how to compensate for this as well. Practicing in the wind is a must. Keeping a solid bow arm follow through is also imperative. You won't get away with a sloppy bow arm in the wind, but it is amazing how many well-shot arrows go into the center, even when you thought you were pushed out of the bull's-eye by the wind. One sneaky little trick when your release is hesitating to trip in a wind that is caving you in is to slowly and steadily draw in a deep breath to expand your chest and help assist that drawing elbow around just a nudge! We "clicker slaves" used to do this on those windy days when the wind was caving us in and the clicker was hanging on the edge; it is something to keep in mind; it works, folks!
   c. *The "aiming off" technique should be used with caution.* This is because all this time you have been shooting with your sight centered up on the bull's-eye. Well, now, on this occasion, you are aiming off-center. So, your subconscious mind gets crossed up and now tells you that something is out of line. The first thing you do is, just as, or actually just before or during the shot break, you jerk the bow over to center, and tend to throw the arrow out the opposite side! I've seen this happen often, and when I've used the aiming off technique, this is my most notorious tendency. Now you know why I mentioned earlier that I don't do this with the bubble technique, so I use the bubble whenever possible to keep my mind squared up. Of course, there is always the possibility and probability that sometimes the amount of wind lets up or changes so you miss anyways. Well, that is part of wind shooting and why, when shooting in the wind, you are going to miss some shots.
3. *When should you draw the bow?* You will see most shooters wait to start their draw cycle until the wind is dying down (they listen for it or watch the flags or what-

ever). In my opinion, I think this causes more problems than it solves. In my experience and watching many fine wind shooters, most will wait until the wind peaks and then draw their bows to anchor. By the time they've settled into anchor and moved towards the bull's-eye, the wind is dying off and they get more time to get off a solid shot. I, too, had much more success waiting for the wind to peak to start drawing my bow and then settling in. It seems I have fewer letdowns and have better control of my shot. I also have fewer problems with the wind expanding me or caving me in. You will certainly get caught sooner or later and misjudge, but drawing while the wind is peaking seems to be the better option, because your odds of it backing off are better. Always check out those flags or trees at the target, they can tell you a lot. It isn't all about how the wind is blowing you around; what is going on at the target can sometimes be different. This is yet other reason to pay attention closely to what is going on around you. Shoot your "A" game if you can. After all, you have been ProActive; you know how to handle shooting in the wind better than most of your opponents. You have been out learning your technique, while they have avoided shooting in the wind like the plague.

3. *Shooting directly into the wind or with the wind If the wind is blowing at you or away from you, you can expect changes in the height of your impact point, similar to shooting uphill or downhill.* Also, be aware that if the wind is blowing into your face, your eyes will get watery, and you might even have the sensation of a teary-eyed strain on your eye behind the peep sight. The wind will get between your eye ball and your glasses, if you wear them, and could cause some teary eyes, blurred vision, and floaters. If there is a lot of pollen in the air and you are using a clarifier or verifier in your peep sight, this could also be very problematical. This isn't like shooting indoors; you have to be very aware of a lot more variables and changes that are going to occur; many under less than ideal conditions. Also, if you wear contact lenses be prepared for dust and grime. If the humidity is low your contacts can be dehydrated by a facing wind. If the humidity is high, glasses can "steam up" and salty sweat can run down into your eyes. Then there are the sweat bees and other biting insects. Use caution when applying bug spray and if it is windy, be courteous to those around you, your overspray can be blown right onto them and their equipment, and they won't be happy pilgrims if that oily stuff gets onto their peeps and scopes!

A Sample Evaluation Process

Now, let's have a little fun and evaluate a situation. I think it is important to give you a situation and my take on how I'd handle it when the wind starts to blow. As I've stated, there are different schools of thought as whether to "bubble it" or to simply aim off center to cover the wind drift. For me, it depends upon wind speed and whether or not the wind is really gusty or has unpredictable patterns. I prefer to "bubble it" and aim dead center as much as possible as that is how I learned to shoot outdoors in the wind. I started shooting in Wyoming, so wind was a given I learned to accept. It normally didn't start blowing until around 10:30 in the morning, and then worked its way up in velocity as it warmed up. Warm air rises, and wind is caused by air movement from an area of higher pressure to an area of lower pressure. Our outdoor ranges were on Casper Mountain a few thousand feet or so above the city of Casper. The ranges were at the head of a long, long series of draws, so that wind funneled right up the mountain from below and then later in the day went back the other direction. But, this is not about meteorology, this is about why to this very day I opt to bubble and aim dead center.

Most all of us want to aim in the middle or as close as we can get it there, correct? Okay, now let's say the wind is blowing from right to left and the arrow holes are way more on the left side of the target. You should read the target and determine how far that wind has been drifting the arrows. If you are on a target course, you have the flags on the butts, and you can even look to see those on both sides of you for how the wind drift is affecting their impact points. You aren't watching the scores, you are checking impact points and amount of wind drift; nothing else. This gives you a basis to make an evaluation of the wind's effect. So, for example, for me, if those holes are 1-2″ out the left side, then at 50 yards, that means about ¼ bubble with the top limb into the wind, and aim dead center. However, I'm not finished with my evaluation; it isn't done. I could aim at the right edge and catch the bull easily, but I won't do it that way. Why? What inevitably happens is that as that shot sequence develops, I'm going to sub-consciously move my sight over to center, usually as a quick movement, and in all likelihood, the arrow will go out the other direction because of that movement. Sure, you can concentrate on not doing that; but odds are, my automated sub-conscious was going to beat me to the punch. Remember those arrow holes out on the other side of the bullseye I mentioned? Now you know where those arrow holes came from. But we are still not done. Evaluate that wind; is it even, and are the gusts pretty consistent between high and low velocity? Are there moments of calm? If there are moments of calm, then you could end up bubbling, then the wind quits and you end up going out the other side of the spot. Those are the breaks and a risk you have to take.

If you are shooting in the wind, the first thing you have to accept is the fact you are going to miss. The key parts of the evaluation at this point are wind direction and the degree of gusting. This will help me make a final decision on aiming center and with how much bubble to use, or if I have to use the alternative and to aim off and hope, or if the wind isn't blowing all that bad and I can shoot it "dead on," hold center, and shoot a strong shot executed with proper back tension in spite of the wind.

In this right to left scenario, however, shooting right-handed, the wind is going to push my bow and bow arm to the left while I'm aiming, so I will be trying to stop it in order to neutralize it, correct? Well, sort of. However, one more thing few think about is the fact that the wind is going to make your release, especially a triggerless release trigger a hair faster because it is helping in opening you up with regard to the shooter's triangle! So, for you right-handed archers shooting off of back tension (even with thumb triggers) and those of you shooting trip-gate releases, pay attention to this! You can use this to your advantage or if you ignore it, it can be a curse. A lot of trip-gate shooters will opt for switch to a trigger release if it gets windy. This is okay, but once again, many do this out of fear of missing and because they probably haven't really practiced and learned to shoot in the wind or how to bubble, and all those other nuances. If you have practiced with this sort of release change, then fine, if you haven't, then here you are changing something in the middle of a tournament; it could pan out, or it could be a disaster.

I've given you my take on this "wind situational analysis" in order to help you do the same. Others may go about it differently but, at least, you have one take on the situation to help you apply to others and learn how to think your way through inevitable windy shooting conditions.

Summary

To be ProActive, you must make yourself as consistent and foolproof as you possibly can. This applies to practice and preparation to compete outdoors. In this chapter I addressed what you can do to prepare for suboptimal footing (downhill, uphill and sidehill footing) combined with uphill, downhill, and sidehill shooting (shooting the angles) and how to deal with wind while you are shooting. There are other methods available and you can try something new, but you cannot develop new things if you don't try them, so you will never know what works for you and what doesn't. What I have outlined above does work for me and works for many other shooters. Once you are at the middle-to-top level in your skills, the differences to get to the next level or to a podium finish may well be much of the above for you to pick up on and develop into your shooting repertoire.

We constantly hear that practice doesn't make perfect, but perfect practice does make perfect. In my opinion, improved field shooting requires imperfect practice; that is, practicing for the imperfect settings and conditions that are going to show up during tournaments so that you know how each affects you personally. You have to know what and how much you have to do to correct for your tendencies under those less than perfect conditions that will occur sooner or later and way more often than we crave or practice for.

Shooting in the rain, shooting in varying lighting conditions, and practice regimens for field shooting outdoors as will be covered in subsequent chapters. We'll be getting there.

Tom Dorigatti

31

Proactive Practice For Outdoor Performance, Pt II

(Rain and Lighting)

This chapter deals even more with outdoor preparations (see previous chapters), specifically concerning shooting in the rain and preparing for various lighting conditions. Shooting in the rain is one of those situations that most archers try to avoid. They won't prepare for it, because they don't plan on shooting in the rain and if rain is forecast, they stay home or go to the indoor range. However, this doesn't do a lot for them when they get caught out on the course in rain and the shoot continues, getting both them and their equipment wet. Your competition is not likely to have prepared for drastic differences in lighting conditions either. Thus, the choice is to either bag it for the day, or continue on, likely not happy and grumbling to themselves. You, on the other hand, have done your homework and ProActively prepared for this inevitability. You, because of this, are going to be many points ahead of your competition. Why? Being a ProActive archer you are physically and mentally prepared to handle the conditions. Unlike most of your competitors, you have done this so many times before as part of your practice regimen that it is second nature; you don't like it, but you certainly aren't a stranger to it. In addition, you have taken the time to ProActively prepare your equipment as well, and have supplies with you that will alleviate a lot of the irritating things that are going to really bother other shooters. Many of my recommendations may seem like common sense, but it is surprising how many don't do them. Foul weather coming isn't an "if;" it is a "when." In this chapter you'll get some handy tips about preparing for and shooting in the rain and poor lighting conditions.

Preparing for the Rain

Most shooters claim that they practice for outdoor tournaments "like they would shoot a tournament." Most shooters don't really do that, especially when it comes to precipitation; they just don't go out in the rain and practice, so when they find themselves in a situation where they don't really know how to react or what to do or how to do it. The following tips will well help, in fact, unless you are in a heavy downpour, you can actually end up shooting a better score, because rain will make you concentrate even more—if you have prepared yourself for it.

A True Story As I often have throughout this book, I have a story for you. This one relates directly to shooting in the rain and under the changing lighting conditions that occur during a rainstorm.

Many years ago, I was shooting in a steady rain at a tournament. At the time, I was using a home-made rope spike release that had parachute cord as the rope (this was before the Stanislawski and sear-type trigger releases came out). As the conditions got wetter and wetter, I started to notice that my release was going off better and better all the time. I had prepared the bowstring (as I will describe later in this chapter), so I wasn't really having problems with low impact points. My shots were going off better and better all the time, while my competitors were having problems shooting low. I got lucky and managed to win that tournament. The next time I shot, the release aid wasn't going off as easily and was just not the same. Then it hit me that the rope was dry. I got out my canteen, and soaked the release rope with water. Immediately, the shots came off cleaner and my groups tightened up considerably. So, for the next year or so, until I switched to a Stanislawski release and then a trigger release, I shot practice and tournaments with a soaking wet release rope! So much for the "rain" killing a release aid.

Did I mention a good attitude helps?
Photo by Claudia Stevenson

Of course, today, we no longer have to worry about wet release ropes . . . or do we? Not so fast. Those D-loops most of us use get wet in rainy conditions, and then when they dry out, they shrink, and ⅛″ shrinkage can severely affect your grouping and "feel."

So, what does this tell you? I obviously wasn't the most talented shooter out there that wet and soggy day, but I was the most prepared. I shot the highest score for the day because of this and learned something from it. I had been ProActive in making sure I knew how to shoot in the rain and dark lighting. I had my equipment weatherproofed, excepting one piece I had overlooked, and I was lucky it turned out that the release worked better when wet. I often wonder if using string wax on that rope would have worked, or would it have just made it sticky? I think that it would have been the latter. I do know that I was not the one losing yardage as time went on, but my competitors were getting flustered about how their equipment and they were performing. I also know that while I was correcting some for the rain, I wasn't having the drastic changes my competitors were. I was just as wet as they were. I also know that they "lost" the dots out of their scopes, but I had found that out while practicing in the rain, came up with a positive solution, and eliminated that problem. I did mention "weather-proofing" my equipment. What is this about?

String and Cable Preparation Most shooters purchase their strings and cables, put them on the bow, twist them up or otherwise tune them, and then go out shooting. If waxed at all, they only wax those portions of the string that look "fuzzy" or roughed up. They also will rub wax into their bowstring, usually using a piece of leather or something else, don't you? Oh, oh, this can be a huge mistake, folks. I'll discuss this more later.

I assume most of you have seen the huge splash when it is raining and you release an arrow. The water splatters everywhere, including onto you. In addition, rainwater is absorbed into your center serving material, (even *Halo* can absorb some water) thus increasing the weight of your bowstring, thus causing low impact points that only gets worse as the distance increases and the serving absorbs even more water. Over the years, I have learned from experience that waxing the end servings of the entire harness system, and the center serving of the bowstring (even if Halo serving) can be a real point saver when shooting in the rain. It is like weather-proofing almost all of your entire string. I know that this one item has put me into much higher places on the leader board many times and has helped me win many times because more talented shooters hadn't taken the precaution. This one thing alone has given me added points above other, more talented shooters time and time again.

Simply placing the wax on the end-servings, etc. doesn't finish the job; it is only the start. Many people burnish the wax into the string using pressure and a piece of leather. While this works, you also run the risk of overheating the string material and, worse, also are forcing any dirt and grit deeper into the material. Subsequently the grit acts like sandpaper and breaks the string material down on the inside. A safer method is to use high quality bow string wax or the synthetic types. Before starting to wax, take a piece of serving thread and tie it around the bowstring using a half-knot (see photos below). Don't pull the knot really tight, but get it tight enough that you can work it back and forth while moving upwards or downwards the length of the string before you begin to place the new fresh wax onto the bowstring and cables. This will remove excess wax and grime accumulation without pushing that grime into the material. This is akin to cleaning the material first before adding more wax into the system. Now, using the wax dispenser to dispense a small quantity of wax onto the

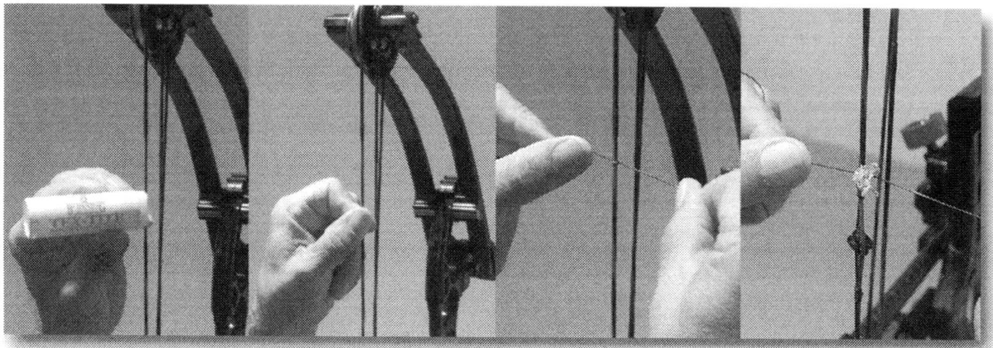

string, you finish up by rubbing the wax up and down the string quickly and lightly with your fingers. You want to warm the wax and by using your fingers you can feel the heat and stop before it gets too hot. Today's materials are very heat sensitive, and if you rub too hard with a piece of leather or other material, you will stretch the material and/or cause damage to the fibers. Any stretching of the cables or bow string changes things on your set up drastically. Remember, 1⁄16″ change in the length of a cable is a ton of change! Finish this up by using a new piece of serving material with a half-knot and work it down the string in a back and forth motion (firmly, but lightly) to remove the excess wax. You want a smooth finish on the entire length of the strings and cables. Then, move to the end servings and do the same thing for the exposed portions of the end servings of the bowstring and cables. I choose to never remove the bowstring or the cables from the pegs on the cams or the axles to re-wax that portion of the cables/string. I either put my bow into my crank board and draw it back and lightly place the bow wax onto the servings, or, I put the bow in a press, and pull the string and cables from the cams laterally without removing them from the pegs and then lightly re-work them . . . but only occasionally. Most of the time, I simply weather-proof the string and cables up to where they roll into the cams, because I don't like the wax build-up in the string groove in the cams themselves.

Removing the string from the pegs on the cams can result in you losing your peep rotation and, in addition, your "fine tune" of your draw length. Removal of the cable(s) from the pegs or axles can result in losing your "cam synchronization", draw length, and also your cam lean adjustments. I prefer to put enough wax on the end servings to make it a smooth surface (fill the grooves between strands) but always remove the excess with the half-knotted serving thread to get the smooth finish and weather-proofing desired. This includes any "Y-splits" and the servings involved in those, and the lanyard on a fall away arrow rest.

D-loop or Release Rope Preparation Because D-loops get wet in rainy conditions, and then when they dry out, they shrink, and 1⁄8″ shrinkage can severely affect your grouping and "feel," I propose that if the weather calls for rain, wax down your D-loop, using the same technique as for a bowstring. You could, if you have that finished loop opening length documented in your Master Bow Configuration Table remove the bottom knot of the d-loop, wax the material, remove the excess and then re-tie the bottom knot and stretch the loop tight to its previous finished length. If you are piddling with that d-loop, always put a nock on the string against the other knot before tying the waxed knot back in place. Then remove the other end, do the same, and tie the knot back. If you only do one end at a time, you won't lose anything. Also, an added benefit to this is that the D-loop seems to 'grab' the bowstring better if it is waxed like that before tying the knot(s). In my opinion, it is not wise to ever remove both ends of the D-loop unless you have no other alternative, such as when you require a new center serving or completely new D-loop due to wear. Changing a D-loop only requires that the new loop be of the same starting length as the old one and be placed in the same position, so a D-loop change should be done one end at a time. Spare loops should already be a part of your "emergency kit." You can then simply tighten the D-loop to the same length opening that it was before you started. Even if you don't do it this way, you can still at least put wax onto the part of the D-loop that isn't knotted and clean off the excess wax. This will waterproof that part quite well. You can then simply rub some wax on the knots and work it into the material with your fingers and get the job done quite effectively.

If you are using a release rope around the string, the same problem exists, so I also would wax the release rope material occasionally, but especially when the weather calls for rain. I've not seen a waxed rope cause problems, but I have seen a wet rope cause problems, mostly from shrinkage after being wetted in the rain and then drying out. If you haven't waxed either your D-loop or release rope and it gets soaked, it is going to shrink when it is finally dry, and so you need to know ahead of time the exact length of that D-loop or release rope.

One last item with regard to releases is to allow the release to fully air dry after shooting it in the rain. Then, once it is air dried, blow it out quickly with short spurts of canned air like you would use on a computer keyboard. Last, use a dry, or quality silicone, spray to lube the release and it should be fine. A few release aid manufacturers will void the warranty if you open the release case by yourself, so use caution before opening up the release to clean, dry, or lubricate it as does *Tri-Flow*. I've found that electrical contact cleaners such as *LPS I* or *LPS II* work really well. One product to avoid is *WD-40*, since that product attracts dirt and grime and isn't what I'd ever recommend for lubrication on any part on my bows or release aids.

Arrow Preparation Most of us use vanes outdoors, so there is minimal concern for the fletching becoming water soaked, right? Again, not so fast with that conclusion! Many shooters will draw the arrow out of the quiver, place it on the string, draw and shoot and watch their scopes get splattered with a gush of water, along with seeing a low hit. A good technique is to take the arrow from the quiver, grab it by the point end, and give the arrow a swift shake. This gets a lot of the water off the arrow and the fletching. In the couple of seconds it takes you to shoot, you shouldn't accumulate anywhere near as much water on your shaft and fletches. In a downpour, this technique really helps. The people at that tournament looked at me like I was crazy, but it wasn't long before they saw the light and started doing that with their arrows too, ha. Also, a light coat of wax on the arrows is a good thing to do anyways. It removes grime and helps prolong the finish of the shaft. Even using a silicone rub commercially available for coating arrows to help pull them out of bales is a big help in the weather. You still need to get the water off the shafts and fletches before trying to shoot it, however. That can be the difference between a bulls-eye and a low miss; especially at distance.

I know some shooters who carry a large Baggie in their quivers and when it starts to rain, they whip it out, open it up and drop it over their arrows in their quiver. This keeps much of the arrows drier while waiting to shoot, simply shake off any excess water when you pull, quiver your arrows and lift the Baggie up off of the other arrows in your quiver to drop it down over the one's you just pulled.

Bow, Sight, & Scope Preparation If the weather forecast calls for rain, it is a good idea to "pre-lube" the axles on the bow and give the bow a good coat of wax several days beforehand. It is a good idea to coat your scope lens with some sort of "fog-preventive" material as well, since the scope will be getting wet when shooting in the rain. Personally, I don't use a plastic bag to cover my scope because it holds in moisture and increases the fogging. I would recommend a better option of using one of the commercial covers now available. Another item I always carry with me when shooting in the rain is a small piece of chamois (*left*). I use about a six inch square, and routinely wipe down the limbs cams, sight, rest, and every couple of targets, my quiver, and even the arrows. I wring it out, and put it back into my quiver pouch, and then a few targets later, do the wipe down again. Doing this keeps water accumulating on the limbs, etc. and just makes things easier. Many camera companies make lens brushes and blotters for camera lenses. One or two of these units is a worthwhile investment. You have to be careful you don't scratch up the lens or remove your "dot" out of the scope.

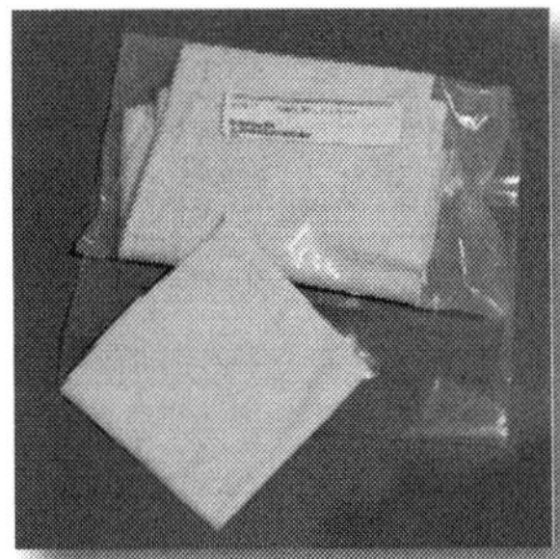

One last piece of rain gear I carry is a scope shield (*see photo below*). I have made these for my scopes since the mid 1970's and always have one on hand; not only for the rain, but also the inevitable glare on some targets when you are shooting into the sun or you are in the bright sun and shooting at a target that is in the trees. You can make one yourself, but you can get these at a decent price, in a size that will fit your scope housing and stay on with a small piece of Velcro. This makes it removable when you don't want it around. The types pictured are those from Specialty Archery Products. It is a good idea to practice with the scope shield in place so that you know how it works and what it does to your sight picture due to the shielding. When shooting outdoors, it isn't a case of "if" you have rain or glare, it is a case of "when" you are going to have rain and glare. A ProActive archer prepares for the inevitable.

Scope shields can be purchased or you can make them out of an old plastic film can or a scrap from a plastic report cover and some Velcro.

After Shooting in the Rain

When you get home after shooting in the rain, never put the bow into a hot, dry environment nor an overly cool, moist environment; it needs air to dry itself out. Never use a hair dryer to dry off your bow, and don't put it near a radiator or source of heat either. Also, don't leave the bow in the bow case to dry. I would recommend you wipe the bow down with a chamois as best as you can, then allow it to air dry overnight or longer. Then, the next day, re-lube the axles, give the bow and accessories another wax job, check the D-loop or release rope lengths, check for rust and take care of it right away. Then, it is a good time to go shooting to help you get over the ill effects and "bad habits" you might have started to develop while shooting in the wet conditions.

Personal Preparation Many shooters never go out and practice in the rain, and if they get caught in it during a practice session, they leave as soon as possible. In my opinion, as I have expressed during this entire series of chapters, practicing in such conditions is the only way you will ever know how it affects you. If you are practiced in those conditions, then you are better prepared than most of your competition. They will just complain and won't know how either they or their equipment is going to perform. Your competitors likely won't have weather-proofed their strings, cables, D-loop, etc, so they are going to chase their sight settings more and more as the rain goes on while you, on the other hand, won't have anywhere near the ill effects, will you?

Rain Coat or No Raincoat? This is personal preference. Personally, I've tried both, and prefer to go without the added bulk of a raincoat, due to the fact that the sleeves are notorious for sticking out, and also they are fitted poorly in the chest region. Both of these will either create the potential for string contact, or force you to use an armguard and chest protector. If you haven't practiced with these items, then again, you aren't prepared physically, or mentally. Another disadvantage is that the rain gear is notorious for creating a sweaty environment, and you can end up wetter from sweat than you can by just shooting in the rain. There is good quality raingear out there now that doesn't cause the perspiration problem. It is expensive, but worth the consideration. Just make sure it fits snuggly, and that you practice shooting with it on; if you don't, you'll pay a price in lost points on the range. Then, in an emergency, there is the old "garbage bag rain coat." I've used those before in heavy cold downpours. You simply cut holes through the bottom of the garbage bag for your head, and in the sides to get your arms through and pull it over your body. I didn't like shooting in them, but they did provide some relief from a cold downpour! If you know in advance about a rain storm coming, then Woolrich clothing is nice to have with you or even a lightweight cycling rain jacket is really a plus to have. They fit snugly around the arms and torso, since they are designed to give a cyclist as little wind resistance as possible. These are far and above better than raincoats such as golfers use!

Footwear There are many fine types of light and waterproof footwear out there. However, one thing I would not recommend is to wear heavy rubber overshoes with only socks on inside them, or "barn boots." I've been on courses where some shooting positions were in mud puddles because of the rain, and when people wearing barn boots stepped into the puddles, their boots got stuck in the mud and they pulled their feet right out of the boots and were forced to put their stocking feet right into the puddle. Then, for the rest of the day, they had wet feet and ended up with terrible blisters and severe discomfort. Wet and tired feet are not going to cut it, and in addition, you could end up with a case of trench foot and be incapacitated for quite some time afterwards. Rubber overshoes are a better option since you are in your shooting shoes and you have the foot protection provided by your socks as well. Laced up "duck" boots are a much, much better option, since they have good insides to them, and you won't be pulling your feet out of them should a mud puddle catch you. In addition, they'll keep your feet cozy, dry, and warm. The other major concern with footwear is the tread on the shoes. If you know it is going to rain, it is not a great idea to wear shoes that don't have good traction. Never wear tennis or deck shoes. I tend to wear a Vibram© type sole on my shoes for field shooting as a matter of habit if I'm going to be on ranges with uphill, downhill, and sidehill shots. When it is wet and muddy, it is very easy to slip and fall trying to negotiate the hills and steps. I've seen some severe injuries as a result of this. In addition, I've seen shooters have to quit shooting because they fell and broke their sights, stabilizers, V-bars, and even a limb on their bow. Footwear is serious business if you are going to have to negotiate a range during or after a rain. In addition, the lugs on the Vibram© type soles are great "construction shoes" should you have to dig yourself out a flatter standing position at a shooting stake so as to get better footing.

Varying Lighting Conditions

Indoors or out when the light changes or you end up shooting from sun into shade or the reverse, are you prepared?

Glare from overhead lights or side-lighting, or even subtle differences of lighting on a target can affect your impact point from range to range and even from lane to lane in the same range. Indoors, I have had to adjust windage as much as a full turn when shooting from one side of the range to the other! At one particular indoor range, I've had occasions where I've adjusted windage more than that. Outdoors, the lighting conditions are ever-changing and ProActive shooters need to be prepared for this. Most of the tips below are common sense, but many shooters don't bother, and those few points between first place and being way down the ladder—are yours for the taking.

Cleanliness Keep your scope lens, your glasses, and, if you are using one, your clarifier peep clean. In certain lighting conditions, any of the above being dirty or coated with dust can obstruct your ability to see the target picture clearly, if at all. As far as clarifier peeps outdoors, I don't use one, due to the many experiences I've had with not being able to see the targets at all due to glare, dust, and in some cases pollen that got stuck to the lens in the peep. It pays to clean your lenses with some sort of fog dissipating cleaner as well.

Headgear Always bring along a hat, visor, or cap when shooting outdoors. This can make the difference between being able to see your target picture clearly or not at all. Some venues do allow the use of umbrellas to shade shooters from glare. However, field shooters normally shade each other with only a cap or hat, placing it between the shooter's eyes/peep and the sun. FITA allows the shading item to be no larger than a legal-sized envelope. In field and target shooting, shielding shooters from the wind by using a golf umbrella is disallowed; in World Archery (WA was formerly FITA)/USAA competition, it is strictly prohibited.

Coloration & Size of Reticles The color and size of your dot or circle in your scope can also affect how you see the target in different lighting conditions. I choose to make my own dots and circles out of red bumper reflective tape, and have since the mid-1970s. (I will show you how later in this book.) I have tried other products and have always migrated back to the reflective tape since I've never had occasion in any lighting where I couldn't at least see the dot or circle in my scope. Certain colors work well on certain targets for different people, but choose your dot color wisely when shooting outdoors. In my opinion, green is a color to avoid outdoors, unless it is a fiber optic, and yellow, in my opinion is almost as bad. Since a lot of the reflections outdoors are green, it is easy for things to get "lost" in the scope due to those reflections.

Practice Seek out and find places to practice where you have to shoot while standing in the sun with the target in the shade. You have got to know in advance how you can best deal with this situation, because it is going to happen sooner or later. Not only can this affect the clarity with which you see the target and sight picture, but it can affect your elevation and windage slightly as well. The same goes for situations where the sun is directly in front of you or coming in at an angle that blurs your peep sight. Sometimes you can simply put on your cap and move the bill of the cap to the side, or tilt it back or forward to get the shading you need. One other thing that you can do is adjust the tilt of the scope itself to help reduce the glare. However, if you do this, you must practice this technique so that you know if it affects your sight marks. On most of today's scopes a few degrees of tilt on the scope may well not affect your impact point or the viewed shape of the target perceptibly.

Scope Shield This is an item, mentioned before (see the photo) that can be purchased from several sources or, using Velcro, you can make them out of old 35 mm film canisters, taped together. I always carry one on an unfamiliar range or a range where I know there are glare problems. When you need it, you simply stick it on the top of the scope, shoot the target, and then remove it. This handy item also can help in the rain as well. Honestly, I would say, "never leave home without a scope shield" because it is inevitable, you will need a scope shield when shooting outdoors.

Summary

Some key elements of ProActive preparation for the varying conditions of weather and lighting were addressed in this chapter. Special attention to these and, of course, other details can help to improve your scoring simply because you have taken the time to prepare yourself and your equipment for operation under unfavorable conditions and then practiced for when those situations occur. You must make yourself as consistent and foolproof as you possibly can.

Preparing both you and your equipment for rain and glare from the sun or uneven lighting indoors can only make you better prepared for when they do pop up. Working through all of these situations and preparing for them gives practice a purpose and certainly variety from just trying to hit the center shot after shot.

I will shift gears in the next few chapters show you how you can make your practice regimen meaningful, beneficial, and fun. In addition, there will be some routines in there that will help you avoid the boredom of doing the same thing day in and day out. With these suggestions and a little ingenuity, you can enjoy practicing more, learn something by doing it, and gain points as a result of the pleasures in learning about yourself and your equipment in the process.

Section 5

Getting More Accurate Sight Settings

I have covered many topics about becoming a ProActive archer—how to prepare yourself and your equipment for the inevitable difficulties that seem to prevail at competitive events. You now know how to document things. You know how to keep a journal. You know how to make a string and cable change so that it doesn't involve a complete re-tuning of your entire setup. You have been given suggestions on how to simulate and prepare for poor weather conditions, poor footing, and shooting at uphill, downhill, and sidehill targets. I've recommended that you intentionally set your sight for the wrong distances in half yard increments so you learn how much your impact points change. I suggested you learn to use your scope's bubble in preparation for shooting in the wind. You have been given some suggestions on how to make your practice sessions more invigorating and less tedious and boring.

In this Section, Chapters 32 through 36, we'll take a look at how to get your sight settings as accurately as your capabilities allow and, as you might expect, that won't be a "close is good enough" endeavor. I'll detail three systems you can use to get near perfect sight settings including printed out accurate sight tapes. In Chapter 36, I'll outline a process that I use to acquire the best set of sight settings I'm capable of, cross-checking them, printing out my settings, and mounting a placard to my sight extension with the list taped to it.

I'll also provide you with methods that will provide you with a redundant system of "back-ups" for when your sight tape on your sight bar isn't quite right, or gets damaged up by weather or abuse (or sabotage!). After all, a ProActive archer never goes out to practice for score or to a competitive event, especially outdoors, without a backup system for his/her critical sight settings. I have seen people out on the course with no backup system, and even several without any sight tapes of any kind on their sight bar, opting rather to trust an electronic device and application to stay up and running for them. I've seen the units fail, too.

Tom Dorigatti

32

Obtaining More Reliable Sight Settings

To whet your appetite about sight marks, a short history about how we used to obtain our sight marks is in order: In the past, before the advent of calculator-based and computer-based sight settings and sight tape generators, we had to rely upon actually "shooting in" each and every sight mark. We quickly found out the obvious: the better your sight marks, the better your chances of shooting a high score. With today's technology and computer-generated sight tapes, a lot of the work is no longer necessary to get accurate sight marks. However, the computer adage "garbage in, garbage out" holds true for sight settings you get from the computer. In this chapter, I will discuss some techniques to assist you, newbies and old-timers alike, in obtaining more reliable sight settings based upon your ability level. It still comes down to getting those initial marks as close to being perfect as is possible in order that the computer-generated sight tapes are as accurate as they can be. After all, you are the one aiming the bow and shooting the arrows. The bow only follows the guidance you give it, so can you really blame any of those erroneous sight marks on the computer or the bow?

Techniques for Getting More Reliable Sight Marks

While all this sounds like it can get very complicated, it is simple enough if you just think it through in a step-by-step fashion and take it for what it is: gathering data; and the more accurate the data, the better the output. It just takes a ProActive approach to get marks that work. Realize, of course, that you can still shoot in every single sight mark you need and, as much as some shooters hate it, it is absolutely essential to get sight marks for shooting 3-D's for IBO or ASA by shooting spots and that means shooting spots accurately and consistently. Getting accurate and precise sight marks by shooting them in is time consuming, and can be prone to inaccuracies. It is still a reliable method, if you have the time.

Over the years, people have devised all sorts of methods for getting more reliable marks. These range from:

- Shooting a Bunny/Birdie target at 40, 50, and 60, or even 80 yards. I've found that for me, using a smaller face, especially a Bunny/Birdie target at 50 yards doesn't allow me to shoot my shot and I pay way too much attention to trying to force the sight on the spot instead of relaxing and shooting. I never get reliable marks using this method, and always get frustrated because I'm not relaxed while shooting.

- Accepting nothing but inner X-ring hits before a mark is accepted as a "good" sight mark.
- Sighting in intentionally high or low based upon how you tend to hold or aim.
- Sighting in intentionally high to "cover" when you start to fatigue and tend to be dropping your bow arm.
- Having a completely different sight and sight marks for each course that you shoot on a regular basis. (I have actually shot with archers who did this very thing!) They go out and sight in on a specific course ahead of time and use a specific sight and scope for only that course. I knew one person that had 8 sights and scopes, each sighted in for a specific field course that he shot during the outdoor season, plus another sight for indoor shooting, and one more for 3-D shooting! Sad part is that it didn't really help him all that much.

The technique outlined below may well be the one that can really help you to get good sight marks that you enter into your computer program or mark onto your sight bar as close to perfect as you can get them.

The Horizontal Tape Technique for Shooting in Sight Marks This technique is one that really works and is the best of any I've found. What isn't so obvious to most shooters is that the real emphasis of getting your input sight marks is on the vertical; that is, you are trying to determine the up and down impact point of your arrows and get it down to the absolute minimum in order to count that "number" as your mark for that distance. As you may know, a horizontal piece of tape across the target or a piece of cardboard or poster paper is used for "creep tuning" (tuning the cam timing) your bow for arrow impact point control. During any normal sighting in process, we tend to try (over try?) for the tightest groups possible, leading us to tighten up and not "shoot the shot" relaxed and without effort. We want even more Xs so that we think we are verifying our sight marks, correct? We hear "shoot the shot" so much these days and yet, when we are sighting in for vertical control, we try for tight groups aiming at a small circular point, and do not "shoot the shot." As a result, we end up with less than desirable results. Most shooters will call a sight setting good if their arrows are in the X-ring at their selected distance for a "setting." Is that really good enough? Since the X-ring is one half the height of the 5-ring, wouldn't it be better if you had them all well within the X-ring? Well, that sounds good, but in reality, you are aiming at a circle, aren't you?

The horizontal tape system will take shooting for super tight groups out of the drill and allow you to concentrate solely on the vertical impact point of your shots. You will find that you can relax and shoot your shot and that your concentration is really on the vertical control of the shot; exactly what you are really after while obtaining sight settings.

A Tip Regarding Peep Height For outdoor shooting, in order to help keep your anchor from floating, I think it is extremely important to lower your peep height slightly. This will allow you to shoot without a "floating" anchor at the farther targets.

In case you didn't know, when you set up for longer targets, the bow is held higher (the sight aperture is lower), and the peep stays in front of your eye (always), so your anchor point is necessarily lower. If you set your peep like you do for indoor shooting, with your most comfortable anchor at 18m/20yards, when you are trying to score at 80 years, your anchor touch point may be clean off of your face, i.e. floating. Not a recipe for accurate shooting.

Since on a field course the average distance is about 45 yards, I personally prefer to set my peep height at 50 yards so that I'm using my most solid anchor at that distance. Yes, this makes your anchor for the 20 yarder and the bunny "tight," but considering that most of your shots are actually longer than 30 yards, it makes better sense to take advantage of a solid, repeatable anchor that is under control at distances longer than 25-30 yards. So, I strongly recommend that you lower the peep to accommodate a 50 yard anchor, and you will find your consistency at all distances will improve. Write this distance down (in your Master Bow Configuration Table, of course), along with your normal 20 yard indoor peep height measurement. Now you are ready to go out and get sight settings for whatever program you use. It is essential that you know that peep height anyways, so get it right at this time and you shouldn't have to mess with it again. By the way, my peep height setting between what I use for indoors at 20 yards and what I use for field shooting is right at 2mm lower for outdoors than indoors. It is 3mm lower for 70 meters, and 4 mm lower for 90 meters; it has worked that way for me for years. I do not recommend you use a different peep height on field courses, however, since there are so many distance changes involved. If you are a FITA shooter and shoot compound, then have a peep height setting for 90 and 70 meters, and then for 50 and 30 meters, since so many arrows are shot at each distance before moving to the next. On field courses, you don't shoot more than four arrows in a row at any one distance before changing distances, so you can see why moving the peep for each distance shot would be a real hassle. Besides that, your sight settings in the computer will not work out by doing this anyway.

Horizontal Tape Sighting In Procedure This technique is quite simple. The hardest part is selecting which width of tape to use at the distances you plan on using for your two main sight settings (or more if you so choose).

1. Based upon how well you can hold on the vertical, use a horizontal piece of tape (black, red, orange, or any good contrasting color) across the back side of a target face or cardboard. I used the front side of the faces in my photos for illustration purposes.

   I recommend doing this first at 20 yards then 30 yards, and then at 65 yards instead of 60. Do not use a tape width too narrow and force yourself beyond your abilities. For me, I find that ¾″ wide tape at 30 yards and 1½″ or 2″ wide tape at 65 yards is about my limit these days. Both of these widths are still smaller than the vertical height of the X-ring on target faces used at those distances. Use whatever you are comfortable with as a width and go for it. If you can't hold steady and relax, then widen the tape slightly. For illustrative purposes, I shot an end at 20

yards on a "blue face" and one arrow at a ½″ wide tape (*see Photo 1 above*).

Then, I refined my sight setting by shooting at the horizontal tape until I got the elevation control I was after. The "new" sight setting (*see Photo 2*) differed by 6 clicks from the "group" in Photo 1. Which of the two would you prefer to have for your sight setting?

2. Shoot six or seven arrows by aiming at and along the horizontal line. Do not try for groups. After all, you are trying to determine just the vertical placement of your shots. Throw out the bad shots. This allows you to concentrate neither on the groups nor the spot, but on one plane, the vertical plane, and you aren't worried about the left and right at this point in time. Shoot several ends at each distance to verify them. Bad shots don't count and the more shots you accomplish at each setting of the sight, the more verification you have. One other benefit of this is that you are going to quickly learn how much a "click or two" moves your arrow impact point. This is very valuable information, so pay attention to it.

   Photos 3 and 4 (*below*) were taken for clarity using a 35-yard field face and a ¾″ wide tape. The group in Photo 4 is within the confines of the bull's-eye on a normal 30-yard face, and many would accept this as a good setting. In Photo 4, however, I had tweaked the sight setting to get control over my vertical impact point. Again, the difference was 6 clicks on my sight bar and then I was hitting the horizontal line consistently (*see Photo 4*). Photo 5 gives an even better view after

further tweaking for vertical alignment. Remember that when shooting the horizontal line, it matters not which size face you are shooting, since the line is the key and not the spot on the target. Imagine the error involved if you would have used the setting for those arrows shot on the target face instead of the horizontal line! With my bow, the height of the bull's-eye at 30 yards is plus or minus 12 clicks, or a full height/width of 24 clicks on my 20 click sight! If you do this and select either the lower or higher "click count" and plugged that into your computer program, your sight tape would have been very inaccurate and you'd be at a loss to figure out why.

a. Once you can keep six out of six either close along that tape width, or better yet within the confines of that tape width, then give or take a click or two on the sight to verify it. You may be surprised as to what a few clicks will do. If you like to "cover yourself" by sighting in slightly high, then use some extra clicks, know how much this is, and go for it. Consistency is the key here, but you have reduced your margin of error immensely by using this method.

b. Mark this number down (including the number of clicks between lines on the sight's fixed tape) and then move to the 65 yard distance and the width of horizontal tape you've selected for this.

c. The tape widths you select should be smaller than the height of the X-ring on the 30 yard and the 65 yard face.

d. Once you have these numbers marked down as accurately as you can get them, it is time to go back and use a regular target face and triple check those impact heights.

e. What you will find at first is a bit of focus difference, and you may swing some shots left and right. However, you should find that your impact points are most likely going to be better than what you've gotten in the past by just aiming at the bull's-eye and using a rough estimate of "group tightness" to get those marks.

f. Use these newly ascertained marks, including the tenths (or hundredths if you are on a 20 click sight system) to input into your computer program.

g. Go back one last time and check those 30 and 65 yard "marks" by shooting that horizontal tape. Be sure to count clicks and set the sight exactly; otherwise you're guessing again and inducing error into things.

Caution Make absolutely certain that your peep height and sight radius distances are as perfect as you can get them as well. If you employ this method above, you should find, with some practice that the sight marks you get will probably be the most accurate set of sight marks you've ever had. Remember above that you moved your peep down for outdoor field shooting in order to accommodate and minimize the float of your anchor at longer distances past about 30 yards. No not move the peep during your sighting in process; otherwise you will have to sight back in again and also generate a new sight tape!

Other Precautions Some other things that can radically affect your sight tape accuracy are simple things, but often overlooked:

1. Watch what kind of paper you use for running your computerized sight tapes. Copy paper is easily stretched when you put on double stick tape or put clear markable transparent tape over the top. Always press the double stick tape *straight down* onto the back of the printout, do not roll it on. Always press the transparent tape onto the face of the sight tape, do not roll it on.
   a. Many people have gone to using Avery labels or even photo paper to run their sight tapes onto. This is good, since those tend to have less stretch in them and are easier to trim and place onto the sight bar. However, this paper is thicker and can cause problems with your indicator/pointer pin on the side of your sight bar. If you move the indicator pin or it slips, then you can ruin the tape.
2. Before the new sight tape is placed onto the sight bar, have your sight pre-set at a given distance (don't forget those tenths or clicks, they are critical). I tend to leave my sight set at 65 yards. Then set the new tape dead on (use a magnifying glass) to that indicator pin at that distance matches the tape's sight mark. After that, once the tape is in place, move the sight using the scribed numbers to set it at 30 yards using those tenths again) and then look at the new sight tape and make sure the needle on your sight is on the 30 yard mark on the new tape. If it isn't, then you've either stretched your tape or you've not set your tenths correctly on your first setup to get the tape on the sight bar. Everything you set on the on the printed tape, should match the scribed numbers that you used for generating the tape. If they don't, then you've set your sight tape incorrectly on the bar or made some other error.
3. Always run a complete printout of your sight settings and carry it in your quiver. I make a placard for this purpose and it is my backup; in fact, 95% of the time, I'm using the etched in marks on my vertical sight bar instead of the generated sight tape! I use the placard to set my sight rather than a generated sight tape, but I still have a generated tape on the bow if I need it. You never know when it might rain or the sight tape on your sight bar might come loose or you lose the placard. This way, you can use the fixed scale of the sight to set your sight based upon the spare sight settings table you have with you. Whichever way you choose be ProActive about it and prepare for the inevitable.

Don't take the risk! I also know that some use their smart phones or other electronics to "store" their sight settings. Some people don't even have a sight tape on their sight, or a printed out set of sight marks with them; opting to store everything on their handheld device. Some even use their computers to generate a sight setting on the spot while out on the course. This isn't all bad; it is time consuming, but I guess it works. However, be very, very cognizant of the fact that if your "computer's" battery runs low, you drop your unit, or it otherwise won't operate, that the computer or electronic failure is not considered an "equipment failure" and you will not be afforded a 15 or 45 minute repair time and two practice ends to get things back into line. You will be expected to continue without the "assistance" of your electronics. The same goes for any other electronics you use out on the course. If they "fail" it is not considered real equipment so you don't have the option of declaring an equipment failure and must continue on. Be ProActive about this and make sure you carry spare batteries with you or that the unit is fully charged before going out on the course, or both. It wouldn't hurt to also have that printed sight tape on your bow sight and in addition a placard with your sight settings written down on it, laminated and carried in your quiver.

Summary

I have discussed just how critical using those "tenths" or "hundredths" are in obtaining reliable sight marks. We have also listed some of the disadvantages of using the whole bull's-eye or entire X-ring as being "good enough" to mark a sight setting as being reliable. In addition, we addressed the disadvantages of trying to use a very small target as an aiming reference to get sight settings because it would force us out of "shooting the shot" and into tightening up in order to force tighter groups.

I discussed in detail the Horizontal Tape Method for obtaining vertical impact points of your arrows as a more reliable means for getting those sight marks for computer sight tape input. I also discussed the use of a "placard" as either a primary or backup reference for setting your sight, should one of the other become obliterated. Look at those photos again and decide for yourself if you think it is worth the effort to sight in using this method or not. You have nothing to lose by trying it, right?

Of course, it still falls upon you to judge your own capabilities and your desire for obtaining the most accurate sight marks you can get. It still comes down to how well you are able to shoot consistently from shot to shot and how well you measure up the items on the bow. It still depends upon how accurately you input the information into your computerized sight tape generation programs. Just like anything else, you will only get out of this system what you are able to put into it. Becoming ProActive while obtaining sight settings will reap huge benefits out on the course.

Tom Dorigatti

33

A Basic System for Accurate Sight Settings

A Short History of Getting Sight Marks

When I first started competitive shooting in the late 1960s, the only means we had of getting our sight marks for shooting field or hunter rounds was to "shoot them in." This meant that we would shoot numerous arrows at each distance used on the round until we thought the mark was as good as it was going to get and then mark and label it on a piece of adhesive tape or something of that nature with a fine-tipped pen or pencil. Since the target face at the time allowed for some margin of error, we shooters also allowed for a margin of error in our sight marks. The better shooters would try to sight in on the "dot," while the less skillful shooters would sight in trying to accommodate as close to the "dot" as they could get a grouping of arrows, and if they erred, it was better on the high side than on the low side. The bows then were recurve bows and the arrows heavier, so shooting low normally meant that you were likely to get a 3 instead of a 5 (on the old NFAA "5-3" targets), so we covered ourselves by trying to sight in slightly above the "dot." It quickly became apparent during any tournament who had reliable sight marks and who hadn't quite worked them out yet or who hadn't yet come up with a reliable method of getting more accurate sight settings, or both.

Then people started using release aids, compound bows, and the NFAA outdoor target was changed in 1976 (to the "modern" (5-4-3) targets we use now). Suddenly, the reliability and repeatability of those sight marks became critical and very important. We shooters started spending much more time on our "shot in" sight marks. We devised ways of cross-checking these marks, even resorting to using dividers to make sure the gaps were increasing every five-yard increment. Then we started breaking those five-yard increments down by dividing that distance into equal segments for the one-yard increments. It was a simple skill, dividing a line segment into equal parts, something we learned in geometry and could actually apply to our archery. I would well imagine that most of you have forgotten how to divide any line segment into equal parts, no?

The Age of Computerized Sight Tapes

Over the past few years, there have been a series of computer programs developed that basically do the same things as the calculator-based system of the 1980s, but the computer-based systems do it much better. Now, an archer can input data from their bows, a chronographed speed, and several other pieces of information. The computer will then generate a sight tape, in the format of your choosing that can be placed right onto the sight bar. Sounds just great, doesn't it? However, "garbage in, garbage out" always applies. You must be aware that any bad data or poor measurements also generate a bad sight tape. Rounding off your numbers by failing to count "clicks" can really skew your sight marks and throw off the entire tape!

As a shooter, then, you must figure out your capabilities and just how accurate you want your sight settings to be. Of course, you are thinking, "I want my sight marks to be as perfect as possible." This depends entirely upon you, your capabilities, and the technique(s) you use to get those initial measurements and sight setting inputs (discussed in the previous chapter if you haven't read it). I have previously discussed how to measure up the bow for all your specifications and how to duplicate things as closely as possible. Now, I will discuss different techniques that you can use to get those all important "data input" sight marks. What you got away with at 20 yards indoors, you aren't going to get away with once the distances get out past 25 yards.

In addition, this chapter should help you to prepare and mount a reliable sight settings placard as well as preparing a backup set of sight settings to carry with you on the course. Most people prefer to have a sight tape mounted on the vertical bar and there certainly isn't anything wrong with that. However, I'll show you another way of getting the same thing, as either a primary or a backup system, that virtually guarantees that you have two or even three sets of sight marks with you at all times, even if you use a Palm *Pilot* or other electronic application for your sight settings.

It is obviously up to you to choose your primary system; but I hope you come away from these chapters with a much better insight into just how important a backup/cross-check system can be. I continue to insist that "close enough for government work" is an attitude to avoid if you are hoping to get good enough to win. "Close enough" doesn't cut it for the top echelon shooters, because those with the best and most accurate sight marks, along with the best preparation and mastery of shot execution are those on the winner's podium. A lousy or hastily prepared set of sight marks won't do you much good, no matter how talented you might be. What happens if you punch in the wrong numbers into your electronic device and you don't catch the error? The best shot on the planet cannot recover from that error. Keep in mind that the guys winning are doing this and if you don't, you are just spotting them points they don't need to beat you right now.

Before we begin, I recall an appropriate line from the movie "The Ghost and the Darkness" with Michael Douglas (Remington) and Val Kilmer (Patterson). Patterson had just missed a golden opportunity to bag one of two man-eating lions, because his weapon had failed to fire, and the lion got away. Remington then asks Patterson what happened, and Patterson said that his gun didn't fire. Remington was told that the gun didn't belong to Patterson but was borrowed from the doctor. Remington then said something like, "You went out into battle with an untested weapon? You never go into battle with an untested weapon." This same idea applies to archery and your sight settings! You will not believe the number of times I've seen other competitors come to a competitive event with a "new" set of sight settings or a "new" sight tape on their bows without having completely checked it out before getting there. They have, in essence, "gone into battle with an untested weapon." Of course, you also know that many shooters will move the indicator pointer on their sight, move their peep, or make adjustments out on the practice range, which are all huge no-nos for ProActive archers.

Some Sighting Scenarios

So, here are a couple of scenarios for you to ponder as we go through this process. These scenarios have occurred to me (but obviously, since I'm now ProActive, none have happened in years), and I know of many other archers who have had the same problems.

- You are out on a field course, and you notice that you are shooting high on most everything from 45 yards in, but are shooting pretty much dead on for everything from 48 yards out. What do you suppose is incorrect here?
- Your close range and your long range sight settings on your printed sight tape are "off", but the ones in the mid-yardages seem to be perfectly fine. You are shooting low on the close targets, and high on the long targets. You know the "numbers" that you put into your computer are good. What could be the source of this problem? (I know many of you have experienced this scenario, especially with the advent of the computer generated sight tapes, or even the selection of a sight tape from a series of pre-printed tapes that you match up a couple of yardages and the select the closest one of the pre-printed ones to use as your very own to mount onto your sight bar.)
- You have a couple of programs that you are using for your sight tapes and bow data. However, while they agree really close on the sight tape and yardage numbers, they differ quite a bit with regard to arrow spine match, and also calculated arrow speeds, even though you've entered the same bow set-up data into those programs. This bothers the delights out of you, and leaves you with the dilemma of trying to figure out why. Even worse is that the tapes match so closely that you can't decipher "why" the speeds and spines out of the two systems are so very different.

I won't promote any particular sight tape/bow setup program over another, but in the last chapter of this section, I will outline my preferences and why I chose that option over the others. I also will address only the three particular programs that I have and have used and, thus, am most familiar with: The Calculator Method from the early 1980's (that I still use today), *Archer's Advantage*, and finally, *On-Target 2*. I know that there are others available, but I'm not familiar with those, so I'm not prepared to discuss them. I also don't have a need to investigate them as a better option for personal use, and to do so is also beyond the scope of this book.

I might also add that I still have a lot to learn about *Archer's Advantage* and *OT2* along with their nuances and differences. I don't have all the answers and I don't think anyone does. What I will offer you are some basic guidelines and techniques to help you get better numbers out of the three systems so that the sight tapes and yardage cards you do print out are as accurate as you can make them. There likely are things that I'm missing at this juncture, which is why I work with all three and then compare results, because it is the results that are most important.

If you look very, very closely, you are going to note some "discrepancies" between the two computer program results (see the "print screens"). I've noted this and investigated them a great many times. However, the important thing is that despite the discrepancies spit out, the sight tapes themselves match up closely regardless, and that, my friends is the most important part.

Yes, the spine matches between the two programs do differ, but, that isn't my point of focus for doing the work. My focus is in getting those sight tapes; even though, for me, the printed tape is only a backup system.

Killian Chek-It Products Sight Marks Calculator

In the 1980s, Killian *Chek-it* products, I believe, came up with an aluminum self-adhesive sight tape, scribed with numbers, that you could place on the front of the then popular Killian *Chek-it* sights, or that you could trim down and stick onto the sides or fronts of other brands of bow sights. Along with this scribed tape came a set of "calculations" that were used to obtain all your sight settings in one-yard increments from 15 yards through 80 yards. The key here was that you needed to get good 20 yard and 65 yard sight marks first. Then, you would use the gap between the 20 and the 65 as a "constant" in order to calculate the rest of your sight marks. This system was quite accurate and I used it for many years. In fact, it was this "calculator based system" that I used when I was shooting the best scores of my life. Of course, the accuracy of this system depended entirely on the accuracy of what you entered as your 20 and your 65 yard marks. It quickly became apparent out on the course which of the two sight marks was "off" and you quickly learned which it was, and by about how much, too.

What does this have to do with today's archery? Actually, it has a lot to do with it. Many shooters still don't have a computer or won't invest into a Palm *Pilot*, tablet, or whatever. Many shooters don't bother to take the time to get really accurate sight settings, and if they do, then they go out and get two "reasonably" good marks to enter into their computer program, which is fine, if that is what they want to do. The problems arise however, in that unless they have a Palm *Pilot*, tablet, or other such devices with them on the course, they can't get the

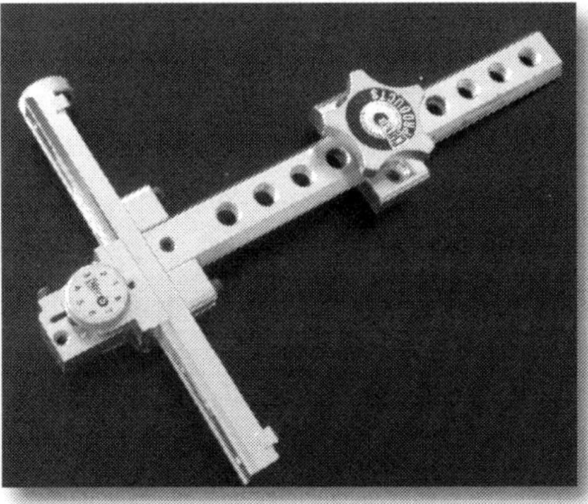

A later model Killian Chek-it sight.

rest of their marks so that they have something to cross-check when they get home after the sighting in session. They also have no means on hand for printing out the tape to mount onto the sight bar. We'll discuss that in Chapters 34-36.

As I said earlier, this little known calculator-based application works, and you can, once you've shot only two distances, those being 20 and 65 yards, calculate the rest of your sight settings in less than 10 minutes. Then you can go out on the course and shoot any distance you want up to 80 yards and make the necessary cross-checks and "fill-ins" to get the other distances you want to plug into your computer program at home, such as *On Target 2*. You don't waste an entire shooting session for two sight marks, and you get to enjoy the rest of the day on the range.

I figured I'd offer up something really useful and accurate for you to have available so you can enjoy a sighting in session, get accurate results for comparisons once you do use your computer based system, and not have to rush home to print out a sight tape, nor do you have to even own a computer or one of the fancy programs. All you need is a hand-held calculator. Then with the Calculations Table (see below), your calculator, a pencil and a few minutes' time to get your 20 and 65 yard marks, you can then calculate the rest of your marks and get them written down on the Calculations Table.

Sight Settings Calculations Table

A=20 Yd Setting:						BOV	A=20 Yd Setting:						
C=65 Yd Setting:						SuperNova	C=65 Yd Setting:						
B= Difference, C-A:							B= Difference, C-A:						
15 Yds	-B	X	0.0588	+	A		44 yds	B	X	0.4936	+	A	
20 Yds	A	X	1.0000	+	0		45 yds	B	X	0.5176	•	A	
21 yds	B	X	0.0720	+	A		46 yds	B	X	0.5415	+	A	
22 yds	B	X	0.0742	+	A		47 yds	B	X	0.5654	•	A	
23 Yds	B	X	0.0764	+	A		48 yds	B	X	0.5893	+	A	
24 Yds	B	X	0.0786	+	A		49 yds	B	X	0.6132	•	A	
25 Yds	B	X	0.0804	+	A		50 yds	B	X	0.6373	+	A	
26 Yds	B	X	0.0996	+	A		51 yds	B	X	0.6616	•	A	
27 Yds	B	X	0.1188	+	A		52 yds	B	X	0.6859	+	A	
28 Yds	B	X	0.1380	+	A		53 yds	B	X	0.7102	•	A	
29 Yds	B	X	0.1572	+	A		54 yds	B	X	0.7345	+	A	
30 Yds	B	X	0.1765	+	A		55 yds	B	X	0.7588	•	A	
31 Yds	B	X	0.1981	+	A		56 yds	B	X	0.7831	+	A	
32 Yds	B	X	0.2197	+	A		57 yds	B	X	0.8074	•	A	
33 Yds	B	X	0.2413	+	A		58 yds	B	X	0.8317	+	A	
34 Yds	B	X	0.2629	+	A		59 yds	B	X	0.8560	•	A	
35 Yds	B	X	0.2843	+	A		60 yds	B	X	0.8804	+	A	
36 Yds	B	X	0.3070	+	A		61 yds	B	X	0.9047	•	A	
37 Yds	B	X	0.3297	+	A		62 yds	B	X	0.9290	+	A	
38 Yds	B	X	0.3524	+	A		63 yds	B	X	0.9533	+	A	
39 Yds	B	X	0.3751	+	A		64 yds	B	X	0.9776	+	A	
40 Yds	B	X	0.3980	+	A		65 yds	C	X	1.0000	+	0	
41 Yds	B	X	0.4219	+	A		70 yds	B	X	1.1275	+	A	
42 Yds	B	X	0.4458	+	A		80 yds	B	X	1.3920	+	A	
43 Yds	B	X	0.4697	+	A								

The Calculator-Based Method for Field/Hunter and 3-D Sight Marks

1. Enter in your 20 and your 65 yard sight settings into the Table, and then figure the "gap" (the difference between them, per the Calculation Table, C – A = B). Be sure to include the "Clicks" (on a 10 click sight 10 clicks equals one line on the fixed scale so one click = 0.1 of one of those lines, on a 20 click sight 20 clicks equals one line on the fixed scale so one click = 0.05. If your sight doesn't have clicks, at the very least, you need to count quarter turns (0.25), and do not round up or round down, use those "clicks" or fractions of a turn instead! It is a common mistake to simply round up or to round down to "keep things simple." You don't want to do this, since it can really throw off your sight marks. Remember 0.5 is equivalent to 10 clicks on a 20-click sight bar, 0.25 is equivalent to 5 clicks and, at longer distances 5 clicks is huge! You can even eyeball things to the nearest 0.25 if you simply read the scale carefully.
2. Using the difference between your 20 and 65 yard sight marks (C – A = B) and "the Multiplier," calculate your sight settings (see the table again). Once again, do not round up or round down to whole numbers, keep the tenths or even hundredths. (See the example calculation below.) You can, if you have a 20 click sight, simply convert the 10ths to "clicks" and write those down later if you want, since ⅒th = 2 clicks. For example 31.8 = 31 + 16 clicks. I could write 31+16 or, as in the case in the photo, simply double the decimal and count clicks. (The sample placard pictured is in decimal, and not "click" form, since that requires a conversion and extra typing). Yes, you have to count "clicks," but you will be doing that with most of today's sights anyways. *Caution* Please note that on the 15 yard setting, you start with a negative number (–B)! This is the only setting that is negative and if you don't follow instructions, your 15 yard setting will be way out of line. It should stand out like a sore thumb if you make this mistake, but some people believe the calculator and don't have a "probable number" in their heads before starting to compare with what the calculator produces. Also note that I have MS *Excel*, my spreadsheet program, set to display only one decimal point for purposes of this article, but it can be set to any number of decimals that I would prefer. (It also doesn't round those numbers, all the digits are still there, the setting is just for how many it shows you.)

   Sample Calculation Let's go through a sample calculation. This is based upon the "numbers" depicted in the table above. *Note* In the photo, you see only two decimals as I have *Excel* set to "two-decimals."

   Data A = 20 yd setting = 22.50
   C = 65 yd setting = 55.90
   therefore B = C – A = 33.40

   Using these numbers, the other marks are calculated as follows:

   15 yd –33.40 x 0.0588 = –1.9639 + 22.50 = 20.536
   25 yd 33.40 x 0.0804 = 2.6853 + 22.50 = 25.185
   30 yd 33.40 x 0.1765 = 5.8951 + 22.50 = 28.3951
   50 yd 33.40 x 0.6373 = 21.2858 + 22.50 = 43.786

65 yd 33.40 x 1.0000 = 33.4000 + 22.50 = 55.90
(Obviously, since this is "C", your 65 yd setting).
80 yd 33.40 x 1.3920 = 46.4928 + 22.50 = 68.9928

3. If you have automated this into Microsoft *Excel* like I have, your numbers can be set up with formulae to automatically go into the Sight Settings Table. If not, you can type them in by hand or write them in. *Note* You will see in the photo of the placard (*see bottom of next page*) that my system has the yardages color-coded. The red numbers depict those settings that are used on the Hunter round (normally shot from the red colored stakes); while the Field Yardages are those in black (field stakes are normally white with black numbers). This, once again, is another means to help me be ProActive and to help reduce the chances of not setting my sight correctly.

I use this system as my primary system for ascertaining the sight settings to enter into my two computer-based programs. Use of the Calculator Based System, allows me to be out on the course and get a reasonably reliable base-line set of sight marks that I can use to compare to the results of the computer-based programs and catch obvious errors quickly This also allows me to immediately test shoot what I calculate out on the range, so that the next trip out on the range is really the final check on what is likely to be a very, very reliable set of sight marks. This also allows me to actually cross-check the other two programs to make sure I haven't entered or done something wrong along the way. Always remember "garbage in = garbage out."

shaft size:		1914	tom
15 Yds	20.54	44 yds	38.99
20 Yds	22.50	45 yds	39.79
21 yds	24.90	46 yds	40.59
22 yds	24.98	47 yds	41.38
23 Yds	25.05	48 yds	42.18
24 Yds	25.13	49 yds	42.98
25 Yds	25.19	50 yds	43.79
26 Yds	25.83	51 yds	44.60
27 Yds	26.47	52 yds	45.41
28 Yds	27.11	53 yds	46.22
29 Yds	27.75	54 yds	47.03
30 Yds	28.40	55 yds	47.84
31 Yds	29.12	56 yds	48.66
32 Yds	29.84	57 yds	49.47
33 Yds	30.56	58 yds	50.28
34 Yds	31.28	59 yds	51.09
35 Yds	32.00	60 yds	51.91
36 Yds	32.75	61 yds	52.72
37 Yds	33.51	62 yds	53.53
38 Yds	34.27	63 yds	54.34
39 Yds	35.03	64 yds	55.15
40 Yds	35.79	65 yds	55.90
41 Yds	36.59	70 yds	60.15
42 Yds	37.39	80 yds	68.99
43 Yds	38.19		

Weaknesses of Calculator Based System

There are some weaknesses in this system, however:

- You still have to shoot in all of the bunny/birdie target settings. (20, 25, 30, 35 feet, and 11 yards).
- You still have to shoot in the 14 yard setting.
- If your 20-yarder isn't dead on, then all the marks up through 45 yards are either high or low.
- If your 65 yard mark is wrong, then everything from 48 through the 80 or beyond is wrong too. Obviously, one does the calculations and then "shoots in" to test those sight settings to be certain. This calculation system is a huge time saver. By getting just two good sight settings, you can come very close with the remainder in short order and it only takes a bit of tweaking to have some really good marks.
- The biggest mistake you can make using this system is to round up or down instead of including the tenths and hundredths for each reading. For example, if your 20 yard mark is really 30.4 for a given distance, but you rounded it down to 30, then every other sight setting you calculated is in error, and this gets worse as the distance increases or decreases away from this bogus entry. The other thing

that doesn't help is that the original Killian *Chek-it* sight, for example, does not have "clicks" for adjusting the elevation or the windage, so you have to use quarter turns (= 0.25 of a unit on the fixed scale) if your sight doesn't have clicks. However, with experience, you quickly get pretty good at setting your sight including those tenths just by reading between the lines on the scale.

- Many good shooters err or intentionally sight in on the "high side" because when they get tired, they tend to shoot low and, also, with most bows, a soft shot will likely go low as opposed to high, thus you cover your bases.

This system or modifications of it has helped many archers to improve the reliability of their sight marks. The same "garbage in, garbage out" principle applies, only this time, if you use what the calculator says to use and it is off, you now know where to start looking and don't have to spend inordinate amounts of time chasing down the bad mark. You can calculate the entire set of marks, in one-yard increments in less than 10 minutes.

Another disadvantage of this system was that the only means of using your sight settings was to have either a placard that you made to mount on your sight extension bar or, by consulting a table that you carried in your pocket or quiver. Since originally, none of the commercial sights had scribed numbers on one side of the sight bar and a place to put a printed tape on the other as all do today, many shooters used the printed form and simply wrote down their settings on that, and then, using double stick tape, they mounted that to their upper limb. This caused many shooters to incorrectly set their sights due to either transposing numbers, or reading a number wrong in the first place. Most shooters also laminated the complete calculation sheet (which I still do today, by the way) so that they had it and also carried a calculator in their quivers at all times. It was easy to pull this out to reference while setting your sight, but you can probably see that there has got to be a better way, can't you?

Quick Solution to This Problem Since it was so easy for a person to make a mistake setting their sights by either forgetting the numbers or by transposing numbers (example: "was that setting 32.1, or was it 31.2?") I quickly figured out that you need to have your "numbers" right in front of you for immediate cross-check. My solution is to make a placard to mount within easy view of my sight's scribed numbers. This placard only has the settings used on the field and hunter rounds, and those are color-coded (it

	field		1914	tom
B	21.8	S	41	36.6
10	20.1	P	44	39.0
11	19.9	R	45	39.8
14	20.0	N	48	42.2
15	20.5	O	50	43.8
17	20.8	V	52	45.4
19	21.4	A	53	46.2
20	22.5		55	47.8
23	25.05	1	58	50.3
25	25.2	9	59	51.1
28	27.1	1	60	51.9
30	28.4	4	61	52.7
32	29.8		64	55.2
35	32.0	8	65	55.9
36	32.8	1	70	60.2
40	35.8	0	80	69.0

	3-D		1914	tom
10	21.80		41	36.59
15	20.54		42	37.39
17	20.80		43	38.19
20	22.50		44	38.99
23	25.05		45	39.79
25	25.19		46	40.59
28	27.11		47	41.38
30	28.40		48	42.18
32	29.84		49	42.98
35	32.00		50	43.79
36	32.75		51	44.60
37	33.51		52	45.41
38	34.27		53	46.22
39	35.03		54	47.03
40	35.79		55	47.84

is hard to see in black and white but you can see from the shades of grey in the table (*below left*) that these were different colors).

I print the placard the exact size of the plastic mount I made to go onto my sight extension bar so that all I have to do is cut it out and place it upon. I have one placard for field/hunter rounds, and another for my 3-D set up. In addition, I have a set of settings that has all yardages on it that I print-out, fold, and laminate (*see photo above*). The laminated placard has transparent tape over it so that it can be written on with a ball-point pen or a pencil. I prefer pencil, because then I can re-use the Calculations Table over and over again simply by erasing the old numbers. This allows me to calculate my settings and record them quickly and have them handy when I need them. I can also get those sight settings that have to be "shot in" (because the Calculator Based Method doesn't have the multipliers for those settings).

I mention again that I color-code my settings on the placard to draw my eyes to the correct setting, be it for field rounds or for hunter rounds, thereby nearly eliminating the chances of me using a wrong sight setting. I must say that in all these years, I have yet to make an error on the sight setting I wanted because that placard is right there next to the sight bar for quick and accurate comparisons and cross-checks (see the table opposite page, below left again).

A laminated full set of marks can be used as a back up to the placard and also for use on the NFAA Animal Round, or for getting exact yardage settings for a "cut," should I choose to do that. Either way I have a backup in the event that my placard gets lost or damaged (not likely, but it could happen). You will also note that there is an open space on the right side between the two columns of settings. I use this gap area to write down any changes after I've made the placard and go out to re-check things and find any discrepancies.

My third backup is, I repeat, a filled out copy of the full "Sight Settings Calculations Table" (*see three pages above*) which I keep in my bow case along with a calculator. This way, should any conceivable problem develop, I can recalculate a reasonably accurate set of sight marks with the use of the calculator and table.

I've had many an occasion where a fellow shooter had messed up his sight tape or had it get wet and got obliterated. Rather than them quitting because they didn't have a backup system, I simply went back with them and we shot in a 20 and 65 yard setting, ran the calculations and wrote down the numbers, and the shooter was back on the course shooting in no time, with a reasonably accurate set of sight marks to boot! I will address using *Archer's Advantage* and *On Target 2* in the next chapters and how to convert them to the placard system along with creating printed sight tapes and "cut charts."

A third disadvantage to the Calculator Method, is that you must "shoot-in" your Bunny/Birdie target settings, and also the 14, 17, and finally, the 19 yard sight setting, since the calculator system only goes down to 15 yards. This is a simple process, and once finished, you simply type in those values and make a final placard. Naturally, if you are going to use the Calculator Method, you must check the settings ahead of time, make final corrections, and then print out your final placard. Good sight settings are your bread and butter, so you must become as ProActive as possible with regard to them.

After all these years, I've become a proponent of using a placard as my primary means of setting my sight with the printed sight yardage tape being a backup. That is not to say that I think everyone should use the placard system, however.

None of the additions to your sight (the Velcro and the placard) weigh all that much. They aren't going to throw off the balance of your bow or interfere with your sight bar or extension bar. They are out of the way as far as shootability of the bow goes. In addition, by having the placard right next to your sight's "scribed and unmovable scale" on your sight bar, you are going to minimize the chances of incorrectly setting your sight. Nor will you ever worry about a sight tape becoming damaged, worn, unreadable, or at worst coming off completely and leaving you in a frustrated pickle. I have heard that some years back a top archer had his sight tape come off his vertical sight bar at the NFAA National Marked 3-D/Redding Trail Shoot, and it obviously cost him dearly.

After all, the placard is set up with the settings you'll need on the course, and you have backups in your quiver should you need them. Sure, you can have the "sight tape" correctly mounted on the other side of your vertical sight bar; and in addition, you can have a Calculator Based Method table with multipliers, along with a calculator in your quiver. I know way too many shooters who have had sight setting problems, sight tape problems, and some who even relied on their Palm *Pilots* or other electronic systems for their sight settings only to have them fail. What is going to happen when your batteries die or when the unit simply fails to operate? Again, please note that it is not considered an equipment failure if an electronic device breaks down.

Making and Mounting the Sight Placard to your Vertical Sight Bar

I set-up my MS *Excel* spreadsheet to make the printout match the size of the plastic placard mount to the sight extension bar. When it is mounted, I have the orientation so that I'm reading the numbers off the placard and matching them to the numbers on the adjacent vertical sight bar.

Even though I have a sight tape on the other side of the sight bar, I opt for the placard as my primary, since I've become so used to it over the years. I have also found it easier to read the sight settings placard and the scribed numbers on the sight bar than it is to read the sight tape on the other side of the sight bar. You will notice from the photos, that all my placards and settings are printed on a single page (see photo opposite/top right). It is then a simple process to cut them out, and following the steps below, to prepare the printouts for mounting on the placard base, to waterproof the placard (and also setting it up so that I can write corrections on it; you must be ProActive with this).

Equipment Needed

1. Sharp hobby knife.
2. Roll of transparent tape, ¾″ wide. I prefer the writeable type of tape as opposed to cellophane tape.

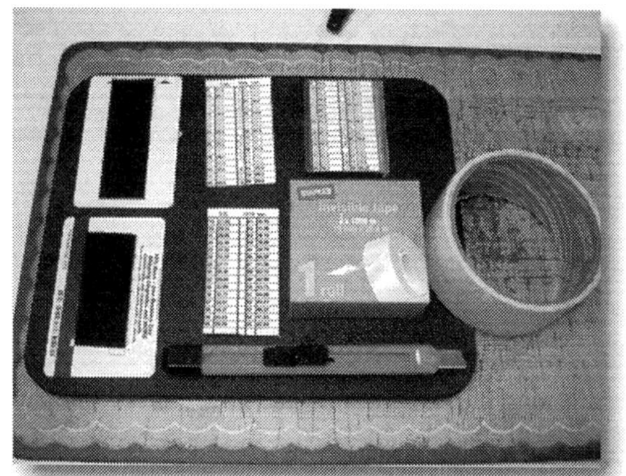

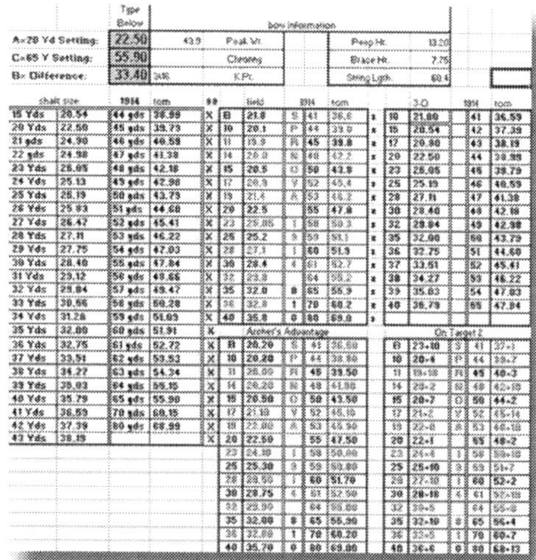

	Type Below	bow information			
A=20 Yd Setting:	22.50	43.9	Peak Wt.	Peep Ht.	13.20
C=65 Y Setting:	55.90		Cheoreg	Brace Ht.	7.75
B= Difference:	33.40	3x8	K.Pt.	String Lgth.	60.4

shaft size		1914	tom	
15 Yds	20.54	44 yds	38.99	X
20 Yds	22.50	45 yds	39.73	X
21 yds	24.90	46 yds	40.59	X
22 yds	24.98	47 yds	41.38	X
23 Yds	26.05	48 yds	42.18	X
24 Yds	25.13	49 yds	42.98	X
25 Yds	26.19	50 yds	43.79	X
26 Yds	25.83	51 yds	44.60	X
27 Yds	26.47	52 yds	45.41	X
28 Yds	27.11	53 yds	46.22	X
29 Yds	27.75	54 yds	47.03	X
30 Yds	28.40	55 yds	47.84	X
31 Yds	29.12	56 yds	48.66	X
32 Yds	29.84	57 yds	49.47	X
33 Yds	30.56	58 yds	50.28	X
34 Yds	31.28	59 yds	51.09	X
35 Yds	32.00	60 yds	51.91	X
36 Yds	32.75	61 yds	52.72	X
37 Yds	33.51	62 yds	53.53	X
38 Yds	34.27	63 yds	54.34	X
39 Yds	35.03	64 yds	55.15	X
40 Yds	35.79	65 yds	55.90	X
41 Yds	36.59	70 yds	60.15	X
42 Yds	37.39	80 yds	68.99	X
43 Yds	38.19			X

field			1914	tom
B	21.8	S	41	36.6
10	20.1	P	44	33.9
11	19.9	R	45	39.8
14	20.8	N	48	42.2
15	20.5	O	50	43.8
17	20.9	Y	52	45.4
19	21.4	A	53	46.2
20	22.5		55	47.8
23	23.85	T	58	50.3
25	25.2	9	59	50.1
28	27.1	1	60	51.9
30	28.4	4	61	52.7
32	29.9		64	55.2
35	32.0	8	65	55.9
36	32.8	1	70	60.2
40	35.8	0	80	69.8

3-D			1914	tom
10	21.00		41	36.59
15	20.54		42	37.39
17	20.90		43	38.19
20	22.50		44	38.99
23	26.05		45	39.79
25	25.19		46	40.59
28	27.11		47	41.38
30	28.40		48	42.18
32	29.84		49	42.98
35	32.00		50	43.79
36	32.75		51	44.60
37	33.51		52	45.41
38	34.27		53	46.22
39	35.03		54	47.03
40	35.79		55	47.84

Archer's Advantage				
B	20.20	S	41	36.60
10	20.20	P	44	38.90
11	20.00	R	45	39.50
14	20.20	N	48	41.90
15	20.50	O	50	43.50
17	21.10	Y	52	45.10
19	22.00	A	53	45.90
20	22.50		55	47.50
23	24.30	T	58	50.00
25	25.30	9	59	50.80
28	28.50	1	60	51.70
30	28.75	4	61	52.50
32	29.90		64	55.00
35	32.00	8	65	55.90
36	32.80	1	70	60.20
40	35.70	0	80	69.00

On Target 2				
B	23+00	S	41	37+1
10	20+4	P	44	39+7
11	19+10	R	45	40+3
14	20+2	N	48	42+10
15	20+7	O	50	44+2
17	21+2	Y	52	45+14
19	22+8	A	53	46+10
20	22+1		55	48+2
23	24+4	T	58	50+10
25	25+10	9	59	51+7
28	27+10	1	60	52+2
30	28+10	4	61	52+10
32	30+5		64	55+8
35	32+10	8	65	56+4
36	33+5	1	70	60+7
40	36+6	0	80	68+13

3. Card stock paper or cutting board to protect your desk or table top from being cut up by your hobby knife. I use an old Masonite placemat or a smooth surface cutting board. If you use wood, there is a tendency to press the knife too hard and then the knife follows a course of its own; sometimes right into your finger! I've found that a hard surface and a sharp knife prevent stretching of the paper as you cut out the sight tape.
4. Strips of Velcro material to mount onto your sight extension bar and to the back of the Sight Settings Placard.
5. Roll of thin double-stick tape I prefer at least 1½″ wide double stick tape. The stuff I get is called "carpet tape" and it has a backing which makes it easy to handle (*see photo right*).

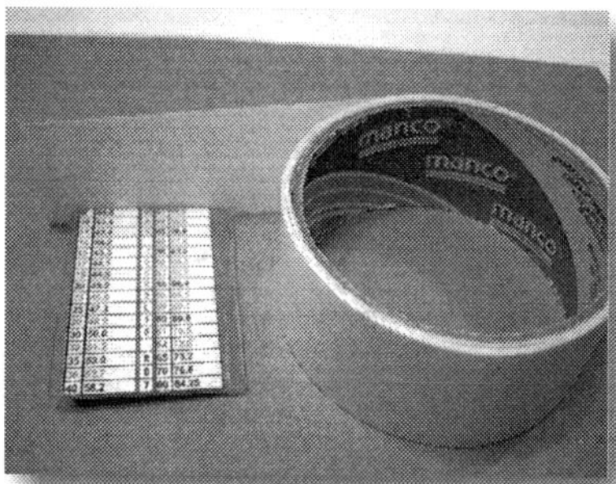

6. Printed sight placard on plain paper, or Avery label paper, or photo paper
7. Thin plastic Placard cut to the size of a credit card.
8. Tweezers or forceps These can help you to get the backing layer off the tape printed on a label and to position the tape initially on the sight bar.
9. Straight edge to use in getting a straight and clean cut on the printed sight settings placard.

Procedure

1. Select which sight settings placard you want to cut out. (In this example, the one labeled "calc.")
2. Turn over your printout (printed side down) and then, using thin double stick tape put double stick tape on the back side of the placard. Obviously, If the printout is wider than your tape, you'll need to use more than one piece.
3. Cut out the sight settings table placard.
4. If you haven't made a plastic or metal placard, you can now cut one out of either thin aluminum or Plexiglas, or use a flat piece of plastic from a blister pack con-

tainer. *Tip* An expired plastic "gift card," or expired membership card works perfectly for this purpose (*see the photo previous page top left*). Make this a little bit larger so it sticks out past all four sides of your sight settings table. This will allow you to waterproof the table a little better.

5. Remove the backing from the double stick tape and simply mount the sight settings table to the placard base you just made.
6. Using one or two strips of Velcro, mount one part of the Velcro to the back side of the placard and the other side of the Velcro to either your sight extension bar of the side of the riser that is on the same side of the sight extension as the scribed scale on your vertical sight bar.

Tip Due to the fact that there isn't a lot of contact area on my sight extension bar, in order to make things hold better on my Axcel bow sights, I wrap the non-looped part of the Velcro completely around the sight extension bar and overlapped it on the side away from where the placard mounts. This gives a very secure mounting that won't slip or come loose. You can use your ingenuity to come up with something that holds the sight settings placard securely. It hardly weighs anything at all, so it isn't a big problem to get it to stay put on the sight extension bar.

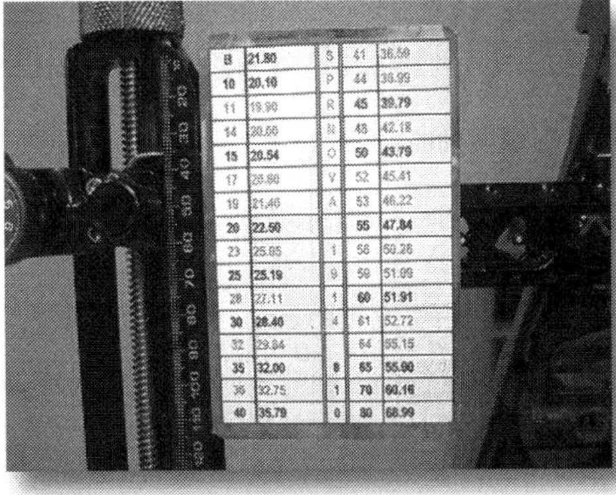

Question What about when you have to sight in again? You might be curious as to how to handle when you change equipment, arrows, or whatever and have to sight in again. This is simple and why the open space is on the right side of each setting line. That open space, when you waterproof the sight settings placard, has plenty of room for you to record your new settings for 20 and 65 yards, and more if you so choose. You can then simply pull out your calculator and Sight Settings Calculation Table, perform the calculations, and then write in the new sight settings so that you can check them out while still on the range (*see photo at right*). When you get home, run your *Excel* spreadsheet, it fills in your new placard for you or do the calculations with a hand-held calculator, and you cross-check your pencil copy. You then cut out the new settings table, and mount it right on top of the old one (unless you want to peel the old one off); waterproof it and you are ready to go.

I also use the Placard System if I'm using either *Archer's Advantage* sight marks or *On-Target 2* sight marks. It is a simple matter of going in to my *Excel* program and typing in the sight settings from either program in the appropriate boxes, printing out the page, cutting out the new sight settings table, and mounting it to the placard.

Summary

I hope that you have now gotten a taste of how easy, yet how complex getting a reliable set of sight marks for your bow set up can be. For those of you that cannot afford to, or those of you that don't want to, use electronics on the course, you now know that there is a quick, simple, and quite accurate Calculator Based Method for getting reliable sight settings while in the field and that you don't have to shoot in every single mark.

Yes, there are computer-based applications that offer much the same benefits. Since *Archer's Advantage* and *On Target 2* are the two I have the most experience with, I'm going to address them one at a time in the next two Chapters and also tell you about some of the nuances I've discovered with regard to these two systems (see Chapters 34-36).

I will not be discussing all the in's and out's of either program, since I'm really far from an expert on either of them. I am simply going to relate to you what I've learned from my experiences with these two particular means of getting reliable sight tapes, individual yardage sight settings, and "cut charts" and also offer some hints and techniques I've learned through those experiences. I will also tell you what one offers compared to the other, but won't attempt to sway you one way or the other. Fair enough? I want to once again remind you that when using any program of this nature, that "garbage in = garbage out" and the reliability is only as good as the information fed into the system. The more careful you are with regard to your measurements, the better those sight marks and/or sight tapes are going to be.

I also hope that you realize that when it comes to this area, it is so very critical that becoming ProActive and covering those bases are not something to be slighted or approached haphazardly. It is imperative that this be done right, checked and checked again. It isn't rocket science; it isn't life or death. However a simple oversight can quickly drag what could be a good score down into the doldrums from a simple thing such as incorrectly mounting a sight tape, or "going into battle with an untested weapon."

Tom Dorigatti

34

Sight Settings with Archer's Advantage

In this chapter, we'll take a look at *Archer's Advantage*, a computer program used to get accurate settings and to print out accurate sight tapes. I'll provide you with methods including a redundant system of "backups" for when your sight tape on your sight bar isn't quite right, or gets messed up by weather or abuse. After all, a ProActive archer never goes out on a course or to a competitive event, especially outdoors without a backup system for your critical sight settings, do you?

In addition, this will help you to prepare and mount a reliable sight tape and to also prepare a hand-carried backup set of sight settings to carry with you on the course. Most people prefer to have a sight tape mounted on the vertical bar, and there isn't anything wrong with that. However, I'll show you another way of getting the same thing, as either a primary or a backup system, that virtually guarantees that you have two or even three sets of sight marks with you and available at all times, even if you use a tablet or Palm *Pilot* for your sight settings.

It is entirely up to you to choose your primary system, but I hope you come away from this chapter with a much better insight into just how important a backup/cross-check system can become. In addition, I hope to clarify that "close enough" is something to avoid if you are getting your sight settings for Field, Hunter or Animal rounds, or even for 3-D shooting. "Close enough" won't cut it for the top echelon shooters, because those with the best and most accurate sight marks, along with the best mastery of shot execution are those on the winner's podium. A lousy set of sight marks won't do you much good, no matter how talented you might be.

I will mostly address generating that accurate sight tape from *Archer's Advantage*, and then how to more accurately mount that sight tape onto the sight bar so that your mounting process doesn't foul up a perfectly good sight tape and make it inaccurate. There will be some repetition from previous chapters, but I think that it saves me from referring to previous sections, and saves you flipping back and forth among the pages of this book.

Some Sighting Scenarios

So, here are a couple of scenarios for you to ponder as we go through this process.

These scenarios have occurred to me (but obviously, since I'm now ProActive, none have happened in years), and I know of many other archers who have had the same problems. (The first three are the same as in the previous chapter.)

- You are out on a field course, and you notice that you are shooting high on most everything from 45 yards in, but are shooting pretty much dead on for everything from 48 yards out. What do you suppose is incorrect here?
- Your close range and your long range sight settings on your printed sight tape are "off", but the ones in the mid-yardages seem to be perfectly fine. You are shooting low on the close targets, and high on the long targets. You know the "numbers" that you put into your computer are good. What could be the source of this problem? (I know many of you have experienced this scenario, especially with the advent of the computer generated sight tapes, or even the selection of a sight tape from a series of pre-printed tapes that you match up a couple of yardages and the select the closest one of the pre-printed ones to use as your very own to mount onto your sight bar.)
- You have a couple of programs that you are using for your sight tapes and bow data. However, while they agree really close on the sight tape and yardage numbers, they differ quite a bit with regard to arrow spine match, and also calculated arrow speeds, even though you've entered the same bow set-up data into those programs. This bothers the delights out of you, and leaves you with the dilemma of trying to figure out why. Even worse is that the tapes match so closely that you can't decipher "why" the speeds and spines out of the two systems are so very different.
- You are using a sight tape on your vertical bar. You are also using a "tape magnifier" on the side of the sight bar so that you can see your sight tape better. You are constantly having problems with inconsistencies with regard to the impact points on the target, and when you check your setting, it appears to be set okay, but upon another check, it isn't set okay. What could be the problem here? You were careful when you set the sight tape on the bar, so why one time are you shooting high with a setting and the next time you are shooting low with a setting, and the next, "right on"?

I might also add that I still have a lot to learn about *Archer's Advantage* especially with regard to its nuances/differences. I don't have all the answers; and personally, I don't think anyone does. What I will offer you are some basic guidelines and techniques to help you get better numbers out of the system so that the sight tapes and yardage cards you do print out are as accurately done as you can possibly get them. There likely are things that I'm missing at this juncture, which is why I work with all three systems and then compare results.

There are some "discrepancies" between the two computer program results. I've noted this and investigated many times. The important thing is that despite the discrepancies in the numbers spit out, the sight tapes themselves match up closely none the less, and that is the most important thing.

Of course, you also know that many shooters will move their sight's indicator pointer, move their peep, or make adjustments out on the practice range, all of which invalidate their sight tapes and are all huge no-no's for ProActive archers. In my opinion, moving the peep height up or down "slightly" is a better option for correcting consistent high or low errors than moving your indicator pointer!

An Overview of Archer's Advantage

This program is Windows-based and is very user friendly. You can find it on-line at *www.archersadvantage.com.* This program provides the following (per its advertising):

1. Prints Sight Tapes
2. Has a Shaft Selection Section
3. Uphill & Downhill Adjustments (cut chart)
4. Prints Scaled Targets for shooting at any distance selected.
5. Graphic display of arrow trajectory
6. Provides a comprehensive shooting log (journal) (Something close to the "Master Bow Configuration Table," but not quite as detailed. You can use ingenuity to get more information in there, but remember, you can't take the computer with you, or at least you don't normally have it in your bow-case, unless you have a Palm Pilot. Or something of that sort. Personally, I don't have those electronic devices; thus my details are in my written journal and on my "Master Bow Configuration Table".)
7. Spine Converter Routine.
8. Software Updates can be performed from within the program once you've installed it and registered your software.
9. Very detailed series of Help and FAQs are readily accessible.

In addition, the Palm Version of *Archer's Advantage* provides the following:

1. Fast & accurate sight settings for those using a sliding sight.
2. You can easily re-sight in on the range if you want to in order to compensate for changing conditions.
3. You can adjust for Uphill & Downhill Shots.
4. You can keep your score and count your X's for a variety of scoring rounds.
5. You can track arrow holes, by arrow number for up to 6 arrows per end.

Many of the above five items have been covered in previous chapters of this book, so obviously, I won't repeat them here. This software simply allows you to have this information in one place; but once again, "garbage in = garbage out," so the information is only as good as the archer providing the data input to the system.

Using Archer's Advantage

Here are some tips concerning *Archer's Advantage* that are extremely important:

1. *Read the Help Tutorials* The first thing you should do is read the help tutorials. You will save yourself a lot of grief in trying to figure things out if you do this.
2. *Be sure to set up your bow configuration first.* The measurements should be close to what your bow setup is at the time. Make use of your "Master Bow Configuration Table" to get these numbers. (You should know by now that I won't have you do something for nothing.)

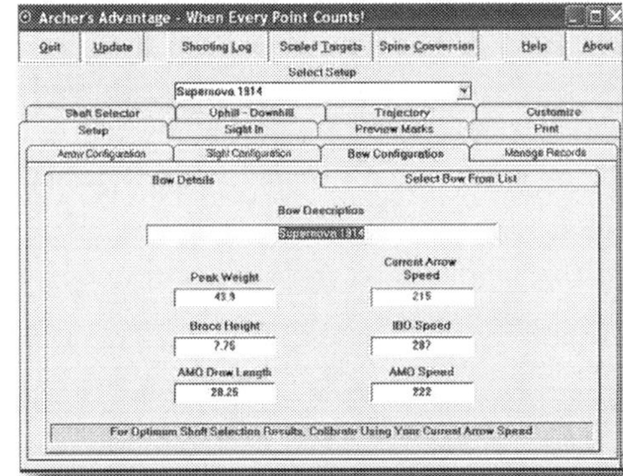

3. *Archer's Advantage* does recommend shooting the bow through a chronograph. Otherwise, you can use the selection tab and get information on just about any bow. Archer's Advantage does go on to say: "The Chronograph Speed method provides reasonably accurate sight settings for typical 3-D shooting. However, for optimum results I always recommend sighting in by getting two sight marks as shown in the Calculate Speed Method." (*Note* My experience with chronographs is that there is no known standard, so you have no means to tell whether your chronograph is "spot on," or is reading fast or slow, or by how much it is off. In other words, the chronograph is a good guide, but I take all chronograph speed readings with a grain of salt. Personally, I don't opt for the Chronograph Speed Method, even for 3-D sight settings. It might do in a pinch to get you onto the paper or the animal, but don't expect accurate sight tapes or marks).
4. Put in your arrow configuration. Doesn't have to be the exact arrow you think you need, but if you have an arrow you are using, then put in the information for that arrow as accurately as possible. This will really help you later. Note Don't make the mistake of measuring your arrow from the end of the point to the bottom of the nock slot. When *Archer's Advantage* says, "Arrow length" that means "Shaft length" and doesn't include the nock bushing (if you have one) and the plastic portion beyond the edge of the shaft to the bottom of the nock slot. That extra ½″ to ¾″ makes a huge difference on "spine selections."
5. Set up your sight configuration. The biggest errors to avoid here are in how you go about measuring your sight length and peep height. Having these incorrectly measured and entered can really mess up your closer distance sight marks. *Archer's Advantage* recommends the following (*see screen shot at right*):

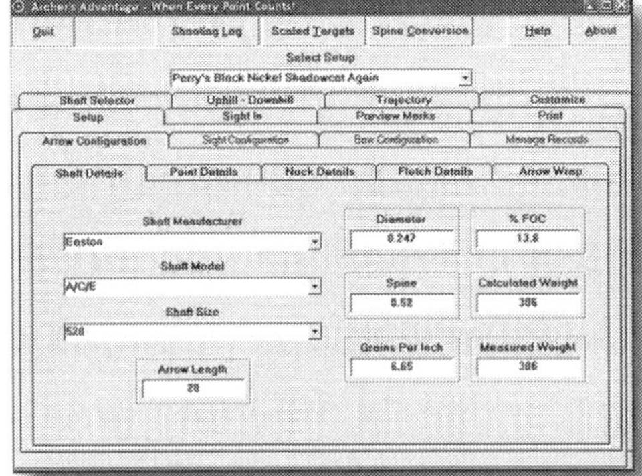

   - *Scale Types* are generally defined by two parameters, Number of Marks per Inch and Number of Clicks per Turn.

     If you have a Sur-loc sight, you simply select it on the sight configuration. If not, you can easily measure the "number of marks per inch" on your fixed scale with calipers, and then "count clicks" between each full number. This allows Archer's Advantage to translate sight settings into your particular sight's parameters.
   - *Sight Length* is measured at full draw from your peep sight center to your Aperture/Scope dot/ring to the nearest ¼″. If you do not use a peep sight, meas-

ure your Sight Length from your Aiming Eye to your Aperture/Scope. I recommend, however that you do this to the nearest ⅛″. If you have a "crank board," then use this to get this and also the following measurement. Take more than one measurement to be sure that they are accurate. As previously, I've recommended that you take 3-5 measurements and toss out any "fliers" and then average the closest ones.

- *Peep Height* This one is commonly done incorrectly and, if you do, you'll wonder why your short distance marks are off. *Archer's Advantage* recommends the following (as does *On Target 2*): "Measure Peep Height from the center of your Peep, at full draw, straight down to the center of your arrow shaft to the nearest ¼″. If you do not use a Peep Sight, measure the distance between your aiming eye and the center of the Arrow Shaft." Once again, note that it is from the center of the peep to the center of the arrow and not to the top of the arrow. Also, measure this to the nearest ⅛″ or better. Personally, I don't think ¼″ is close enough.

6. *Sighting In* I've managed to keep the data from many years of using the 20 yard and the 65 yard sight settings as my "standard" for field/outdoor shooting. I will get into more about this when I discuss the *On Target 2* program, and it will be explained more thoroughly there. Within *Archer's Advantage* there are three ways to acquire sight settings: (a) Calculate Speed, (b) Chronograph Speed, and (c) Build Bow Speed. Although Archer's Advantage recommends that you shoot your bow through a chronograph, it doesn't use this directly (unless you tell it to) for sight tapes. It uses it to calibrate *Archer's Advantage* to your particular bow to the extent that it differs from the "standard data" from manufacturer's specifications for your setup.

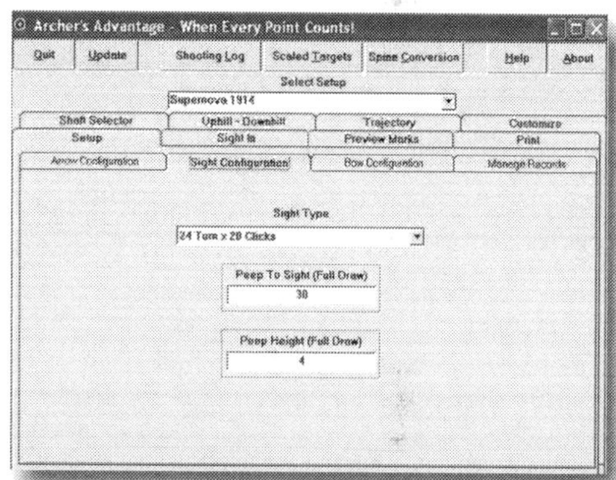

Since *Archer's Advantage* recommends the "Calculate Speed" method as being the most accurate, that is the only one I will discuss. You can generate a "quick and dirty" sight tape to get you started if you use the Bow Chronograph speed, however. Such a tape might get you at least onto the target so you could refine your settings from there. I think I offer a better option (see Chapter 33), however.

Calculate Speed You will note from the Sight In Screen (see screen shot below), that Archer's Advantage uses two distances along with their corresponding sight setting numbers gotten off the permanent scale on your sight bar. However there is one very critical step to do before performing the data entry and it has to do with the bow sight itself and that is Zeroing the Indicator Pin/Pointer. Once you do this, it is not advisable to readjust the indicator pointer pin afterwards; because if you move that indicator pointer pin, then you have messed up all of your sight settings and will have to start over and generate a new sight tape!

Here's what *Archer's Advantage* has to say about this zeroing: "Many target sights have a calibrated knob at the top of the sight. This knob can be used to read sight settings accurately without having to squint to read the precise position of your pointer. The following describes how to read sight settings accurately from a Sure Loc sight:

1. *Before sighting in, do the following:*
   - Rotate Knob at Top of Sight all the way to Zero. The knob has numbers on it, so align the "0" on the knob to the mark on the top of the vertical sight bar frame.
   - Move Pointer on Sure Loc Scale so that it evenly divides a line on the Scale. Note I recommend that you use a magnifying glass to accomplish this. It is very hard to see if you are centered on a line or not and you could be off by 4-5 clicks. And do watch the angle at which you "read" from and be consistent with it.
   - This completes calibrating your Pointer to your Knob (Zeroing The Pointer)
2. To read your sight setting, determine which two lines the pointer rests between (*e.g.* between 15 & 16).
3. Now look at the position of the Knob on top of your sight.
   - If your knob is sitting on 5, then your sight setting is 15.50
   - If your knob is sitting on the Click between 5 & 6, then your sight setting is 15.55
   - If your knob is sitting on 1, then your sight setting is 15.10
   - If your knob is sitting on the Click between 0 & 1, then your sight setting is 15.05

   Then:
4. *Get 20 and 65 yard sight settings.* I would recommend at this point you read, or re-read or review Chapter 32 concerning how to achieve the most accurate "shot in" sight settings. As I mentioned there, you are not after groups at this point in time, you need to minimize only the vertical aspects of your arrow impact point. Thus, shooting at a horizontal line is much easier to manage than trying to concentrate on getting circular groups. Furthermore, it will stop you from accepting an "X-ring' height distribution and thinking it "close enough" for a sight setting for that distance.

   The farther apart these two settings, the better, but don't exceed your capabilities! Only you know your limitations. I have used 20 and 65 yards for many years and those two have proven to work out extremely well for me when only using two settings. I also double check *Archer's Advantage* with my Calculator method. ProActive archery always involves a systems that can be verified, that is checked for accuracy.
5. *Input two "ranges" and "sight settings."* Once you have these two sight settings, then put the Range 1 and the Distance 1, then the Range 2 and Distance 2 settings into the Archer's Advantage Sight in Tab (*see photo*).
6. *Click on "Calculate Speed."* Do not fail to do this! Archer's Advantage will then use this information to prepare your sight tape "numbers." If you fail to "calculate speed," then you will get a tape based upon erroneous information or one from a

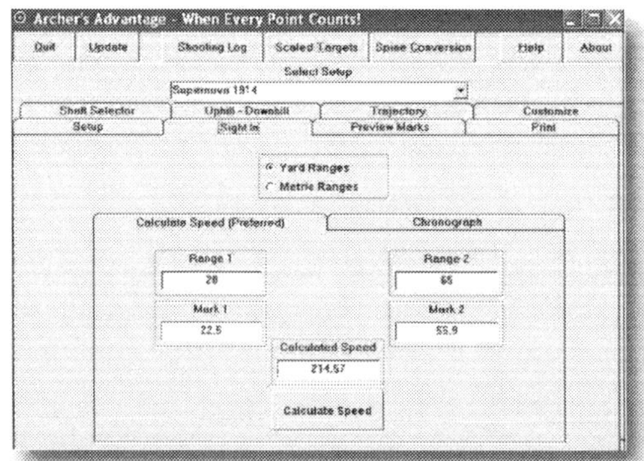

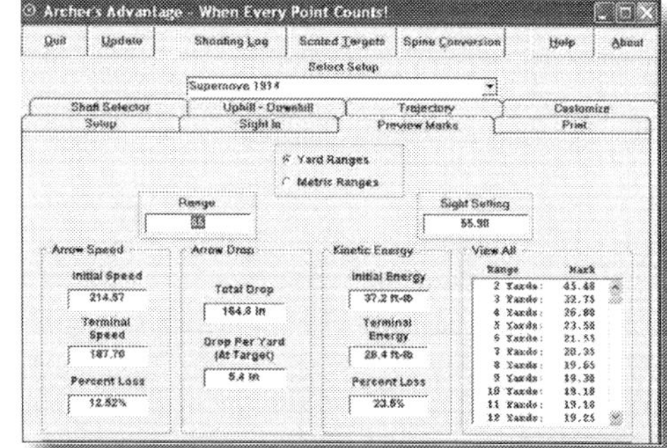

previous bow's information.

7. *Setting up your Sight Tape* Click on the "Preview Marks Tab." From this screen you can perform a quick check of individual sight marks from 2 through 150 yards (or meters, if you select that option).

Next, you should click on the "Customize Tab", and then click on the "Tape Layout" Tab to set up the layout of your printed sight tape (see photo). My preferences are depicted in the photo, but are as follows:

- Max Range: I select 90 yards, but if you want, then you could do 80 or 100, or whatever.
- Orientation: Top to Bottom
- Number Range: 10, 20, 30. Unfortunately, Archer's Advantage only prints the even numbers for each 10 yard increment; that is 10, 20, 30, 40, etc. It does not offer the option to print odd numbers, like 25, 35, 45, 55, etc. That is yet another reason to "color code" the lines on the sight tape when using *Archer's Advantage.*
- Line Width: I prefer narrow lines, but Medium works well, too. I avoid wide lines because then the lines are wider than my pointer or the magnifier indicator line and makes reading the tape more difficult.
- Font Type: I use Times New Roman, but there are other choices.
- Font size: I use Large Font, but if you have good eyes, you can use something smaller.
- Line Spacing: I always use one yard increments.
- Justification: Since for me, the indicator pointer is on the right side, then I justify the numbers to "Left Justify" so that I have only lines on the right side where the indicator pointer is located.
- Line Weight: I select "Light," once again due to the width of my Indicator pointer or the magnifier indicator line.
- Line Colors: Once again, being a

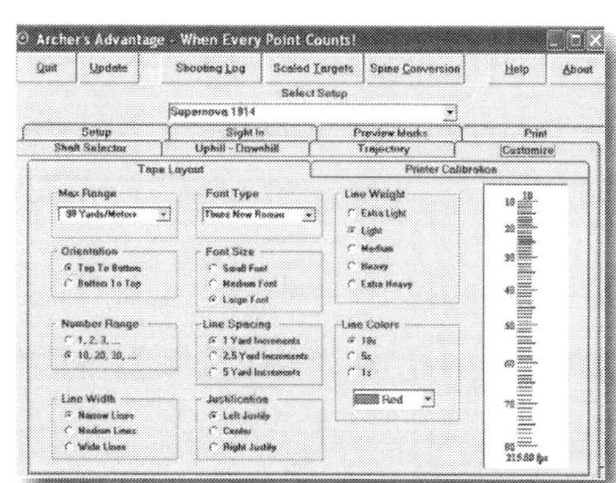

ProActive archer, I take advantage of color-coding things at every opportunity. Thus, my personal selections are as follows: 10's = Red; 5's = Blue and 1's = Black.

8. *Printer Calibration in Archer's Advantage* Now you might think you can just print out your tape, correct? You could . . . but if you really want to be sure that you have the best tape possible, you really should next select the "Printer Calibration" Tab and generate a Printer Calibration Tape

   As per *Archer's Advantage* instructions, not all printers provide enough accuracy to print a reliable sight tape without using the printer calibration feature. To calibrate your printer:

   - First print either an "Inch Calibration Scale" or a "Metric Calibration Scale." If you select an Inch Calibration Scale, the printed scale should have exactly 100 marks in a 4 inch span. If you select Metric Calibration Scale, the printed scale should have exactly 100 marks in a 10 centimeter span.

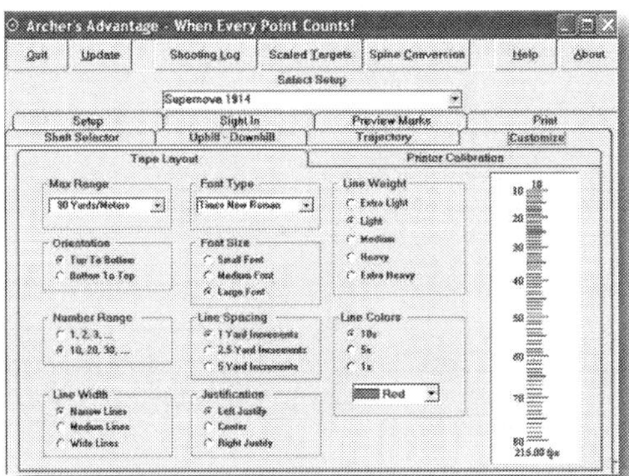

   - Use a pair of calipers or precision scale, to measure the number of marks in the Specified Span (4 inches or 10 centimeters).
   - Record the number of marks, to the nearest 10th of a mark in the Specified Span.
   - Enter this recorded value as Calibration Scale Value and then . . .

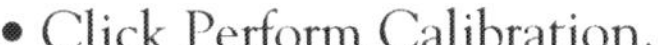

   - Click Perform Calibration.
   - Print out the Calibration Scale again and verify that the Scale is the proper length.

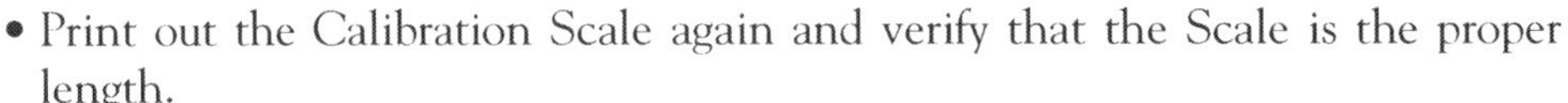

9. *Printing Your Sight Tape* You are now ready to print out your sight tape from *Archer's Advantage*. I'm not going to put in an image of the Print Tape screen, because the items on this screen are self-explanatory. I will, however tell you what your printed output off this screen will contain, one thing at a time. You will get the following on your paper when you select "Sight Tapes" (*see screen shot below*):

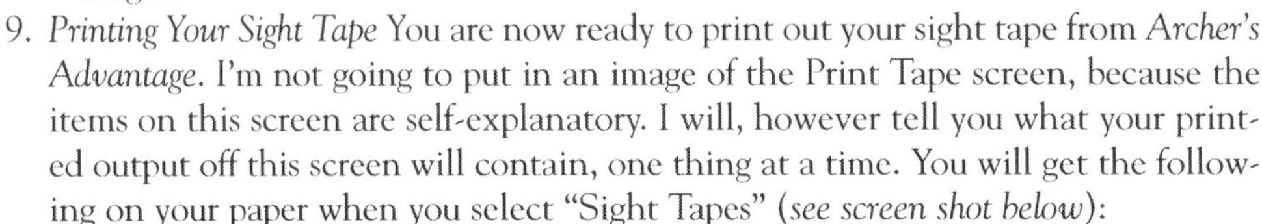

   - Your sight information including: the Clicks per turn, the Sight Length in Inches, and the Peep Height in Inches.
   - Your Arrow Specifications including: shaft length in inches, shaft diameter in hundredths of inches, arrow weight in grains, and your fletch length in inches.
   - Six sight tapes. You will have two with heavy outlining that represent the *Archer's Advantage* Calculated Speed. You will also have a sight tape generated for 1 foot per second and two feet per second slower and also for one foot per second and two feet per second faster than that which your sight settings say your bow is sighted in for in *Archer's Advantage.*
   - In addition, you will have a "Short Range Conversions Table" that will tell you where to set your sight for distances of 6 feet up through 36 feet. This table will

only be as good as how well you have measured your sight length and peep sight height, so it pays big dividends to cross check this table by actually shooting at several of the distances.

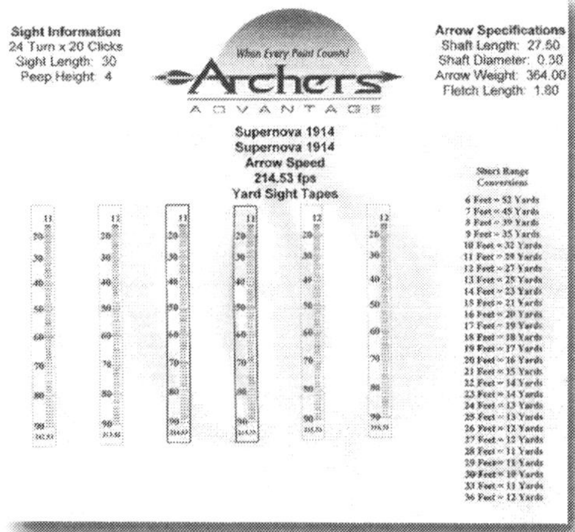

If you select the "Sight Marks Tab," you can get a print-out of your sight settings from 2 yards up through 150 yards. If you select the "Down Range Statistics" Tab to print, you will receive a print-out depicting your Range, Terminal Speed, Arrow Drop, and Arrow Drop per yard, and the Kinetic Energy. I personally haven't used that information, so I don't bother to print it out.

Getting a "Cut Chart" from Archer's Advantage

In order to get a printout of a "Cut Chart" you need to Select the "Uphill-Downhill" Tab and then click on "Print Cut Chart." This chart prints Uphill Yard Ranges from 20 yards through 100 yards in 5-yard increments and degrees of incline in 5 degree increments. It does the same with Downhill Yard Ranges. This table prints out in landscape format and can be folded in half length-wise and laminated. As it comes from Archer's Advantage, the "Cut Chart" is a bit large and hard to handle, since it fills a normal 8½″ x 11″ piece of paper. Don't fret, you also have the option to Export the "Cut Chart" to *Excel*, where you can manipulate it to whatever size you want.

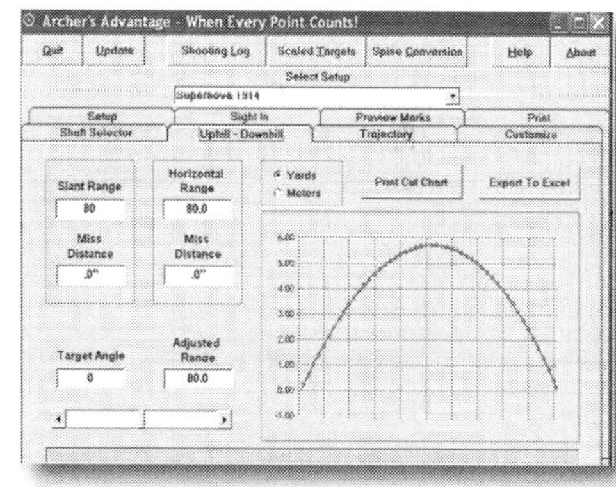

Now, all you have left to do is to cut out your sight tape selection and prepare it for mounting onto your sight bar. This step is not as "cut and dried" as most shooters think that it may be. A ProActive archer takes steps to minimize as many chances for error as possible, and when it comes to mounting a sight tape, there are potential pitfalls to avoid.

Mounting the Printed Sight Tape

We are finally ready to mount your sight tape onto your vertical sight bar. Do you remember the scenario in which you are shooting low on the close ones, dead on in the middle, and high on the long ones? Well, that was caused by stretching the tape while mounting it. Another scenario involving a "stretched sight tape" is that some shooters tend to mount the tape by mating the tape to the sight indicator pointer when with the sight set at only 20 yards. Then, the settings at the top end of the stretched sight tape are dead on and as you shoot progressively longer distances, you begin to shoot higher and higher and higher. I'm sure that you have heard many a shooter gripe that the "programs" are not generating accurate sight tapes for them. I will show you how to virtually eliminate this problem by once again, being ProActive.

It doesn't matter whether the sight tape is printed out from *Archer's Advantage*, *On Target 2*, *TAP*, or any other sight tape printing program, the mounting procedure should be the same. This should also partially explain why personally, I prefer the placard system that uses the scribed and unmovable "numbers" on my vertical sight bar as my primary sight setting procedure and the printed sight tape as the 3rd alternate (should I lose my placard or backup printout). I'll discuss this issue last, because the placard system isn't without its problems.

Before going into detail on how to more properly mount your tape, let me give you a few other things to watch for and avoid.

- If you are going to use "photo paper" to print your sight tapes on, be sure to allow for the thicker paper! You are going to need some extra space between the sight bar and the indicator pointer for that thick paper. In addition, since my method of configuring newly printed sight tapes for mounting involves three additional layers besides the printer paper itself, you also need to accommodate the angle of your indicator pointer to handle this extra thickness. The last thing you need to have happen is for your indicator pointer or, worse, your slider on the sight bar to catch on the printed sight tape and rip it right off of the sight bar. I've seen this happen more than once.
- Be sure to clean the area where you will be mounting the sight tape on your sight bar with alcohol and to allow it to dry.
- Avoid putting your fingers onto that area of the sight bar during the mounting process. The oils in your fingerprints can weaken or even prevent the adhesive from sticking. You don't want your sight tape slipping and sliding around on the sight bar.
- I recommend that you accurately pre-set the sight at 40 or 50 yards before you mount the sight tape. (I mean you count those "clicks" or read the "zeroed" wheel and get it exactly right.) The main reason is that most of the shots during a field or hunter round are around the 40-50 yard ranges, so I feel it is essential to make darned sure that this area of the tape is mounted properly. The margin for error is less at these and longer yardages, so make them right. Secondly, this helps to reduce the chances of the sight tape being stretched since you have less surface area to work with on a longitudinal axis (if you properly install it, that is).
- I strongly recommend that you use a magnifying glass or some magnifier to pre-set the sight and also when you align the new sight tape to the vertical bar. The print is small as it is, so it is easy to misalign the tape yardage with your indicator pointer, and especially easy to misalign the tape if you have a magnifier on the sight bar. Again, it is worth repeating: Watch the angle at which you place the magnifying glass in relation to the site bar/site tape. If you change your reading angle, you induce inaccuracies and inconsistencies.

- Before you start, make sure that the sight tape itself won't be too wide or too long for your vertical sight bar. You will not believe the number of shooters that print out the sight tape only to find it doesn't fit on their sight bar! It is easy to go back in and re-set the length/width of the sight tape and re-print it, so take that time now. Trim it if necessary, but get it right.
- When you align the sight tape, make sure that part of the tip of the indicator pointer will at least reach to the end/tip of all of the yardage lines on the tape, not in direct contact with the tape but rather in alignment with it. Having to bridge a gap between the end of the indicator pointer and the end of the yardage lines is a source of error.
- Make sure you allow the ink time to dry before you start the mounting process. If you don't, you may smear the lines and make them unreadable. If you are using picture quality paper, the drying time is longer than for ordinary paper.
- Wash and dry your hands thoroughly before you start this process.
- Make sure you have adequate lighting to assist you in tape placement.
- Take your bow sight off of the bow and lay it down so it is horizontal. Trying to mount your sight tape with the sight in a vertical position can really create problems for you.

Items Needed to Mount Your Sight Tape

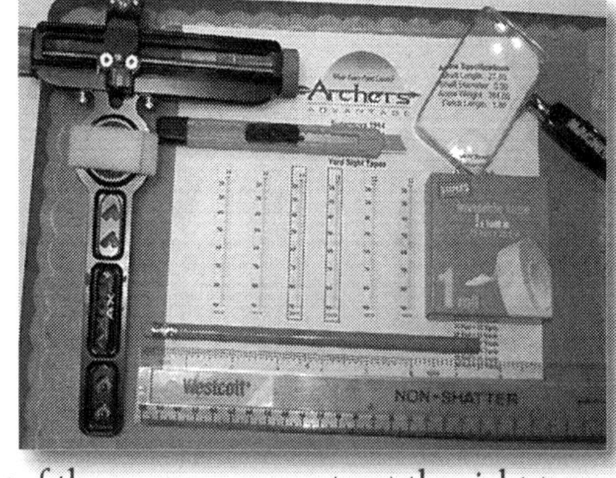

1. Sharp hobby knife
2. Roll of transparent tape, ¾″ wide.
3. Card stock paper or cutting board to protect your desk or table top from being cut up by your hobby knife. I use an old Masonite placemat or a smooth surface cutting board. If you use wood, there is a tendency to press the knife too hard and then the knife follows a course of its own; sometimes right into your finger! I've found that a hard surface and a sharp knife prevent stretching of the paper as you cut out the sight tape.
4. Roll of thin double-stick tape. I prefer at least 1½″ wide double stick tape. The stuff I get is called "carpet tape" and it has a backing which makes it easy to handle (*see photo below right*). This is not needed if you use Avery labels with the stick-em already in place.

5. Printed sight tape on plain paper, or Avery label, or photo paper.
6. Pencil with rubber eraser.
7. Tweezers or forceps. These can help you to get the backing layer off the tape printed on a label and to position the tape initially on the sight bar.
8. Straight edge to use in getting a straight and clean

cut on the sight tape.

Preparing and Trimming the Sight Tape

1. Cut a piece of double stick tape that is about ¼-½″ longer than your sight tape and a lot wider. You will trim it up later.
2. Turn the sight tape printouts face down on your cutting board.
3. Carefully align one sticky side of the double stick tape so that it will cover one or two of the sight tapes you intend to use.
4. Press your double stick straight down onto the sight tape paper. Do not pull the paper or the double stick tape. Press it straight down onto the paper.
5. Using the tip of the pencil eraser and not your fingers, gently press the tip of the pencil eraser straight down onto the double-stick tape much like a blotter. Do *not* "rub" it into place on the tape paper.
6. Turn the sight tape/double-stick combo back over to the printed side up.
7. Cut a piece of transparent tape that is about ¼-½″ longer than the sight tape.
8. Place the transparent tape straight down over the printed side of the sight tape. Once again, do *not* pull the tape down, don't "rub it" from top to bottom or bottom to top. Straight down without moving the sight tape paper.
9. Using the tip of the pencil eraser, press it like a blotter straight down for the entire length and width of the sight tape you want to use.
10. Using a solid straight edge, carefully align the straight edge with one edge of the sight tape you want to use and then carefully cut out your sight tapes, one edge at a time.

Step by Step: Mounting the Sight Tape

Before we begin the process of mounting that sight tape to your sight bar, it is important to outline some items that are indeed problematical when mounting the sight tape, and even carry over to you when you go to set your bow sight out on the range.

Once you have your sight tape completed by following the steps above, if needed trim it up to make that it fits your sight bar. It is a good idea, one last time, to check the sight tape prior to removal of the backing layer on the reverse side of your sight tape. If you press it down onto the bar only to find out it doesn't fit, you've just wasted your new sight tape and your time. After checking your new sight tape for proper fit, then do the following:

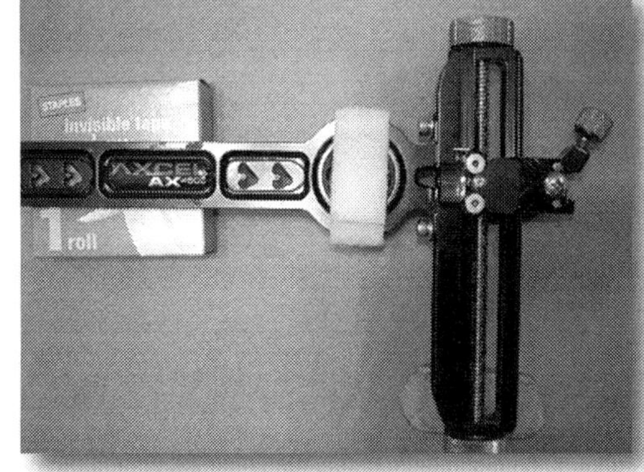

1. Make absolutely sure you have your bow sight set "exactly" onto the yardage you've decided to use to mount your sight tape. Once again, I use 40, 45, or 50 yards. I do mean exactly, as in right down to the "click count." If you've been ProActive you have it already set, but a final check is a good idea.
2. Slide your sight tape under the indicator pin and/or magnifier to make sure

that the indicator pin won't catch or drag on the sight tape. This one last final check is important, since you don't want that indicator pointer or magnifier or any part of the sight slide mechanism to be in contact with that new sight tape. Adjust things as necessary to insure that you have clearances, but be careful about that indicator pointer!

3. Decide whether you are going to use the magnifier or the unmagnified indicator pointer as your reference for placing the tape. On many sights, these are not the same point of reference (*see magnifier photos*).
4. Carefully remove the backing from the reverse side of the sight tape (the double sided tape backing).
7. Keeping your visual frame of reference so that you are looking straight down at the indicator pointer or magnifier, place the yardage line for the distance your sight bar is set at directly onto the sight bar. Make sure that you also position the tape parallel to vertical bar from top to bottom. Once you press this on, the only way to change it is to remove the tape and start over with a new one.
8. Do not rub onto the sight tape with your fingers (which could stretch the tape), but use the pencil eraser like a blotter. By pressing straight down a "blot" at a time, press the sight tape straight down onto the sight bar, all the while keeping the tape flat and aligned as you move along the tape, from the middle towards each end.
9. Once you are certain that most of the tape is pressed down, recheck that your preset setting is in proper alignment, and then you can move the sight block out of the way so you can get at the indicator pointer/magnifier area of the tape to make it finally secure.
10. Once you have the entire sight tape pressed down and it is straight and solidly mounted, then use the tip of the eraser to "blot down" the edges of the sight tape to the sight bar on both sides.
11. The last step is to make one last final seal by placing another layer of transparent tape over the top of the entire sight tape and extending that beyond the ends of the sight tape by ¼″ to ½″, and then use the sharp knife to trim the sides. This last step just helps to give a little more insurance that the sight tape is weatherproof and also that it won't slip or come off of the sight bar.

If you have been careful and followed the steps, you should now have a mounted sight tape that has not been stretched or otherwise misaligned with the indicator pointer. The sight block/pointer will be clearing your new sight tape without any interference. The last and important thing to do is to go out on the range and double check your new sight settings tape to make sure it is indeed accurate. After all you would not go into battle with an untested weapon, would you?

Final Check for a Stretched Sight Tape Check one last time by setting your sight to 20 yards using your sight tape. Check this against the proper numbers on the scribed side of the sight (including the clicks), and then check the tape similarly at several other distances along the entire length of the sight tape. Make certain that all the sight tape settings match what the numbers are supposed to be on the scribed scale of the bow sight. This is your final check that you haven't accidentally stretched that tape while mounting it to the sight bar. Of course, always remind yourself to make sure you keep your head to sight alignment when you make your sight setting, always keeping in mind that a magnifier, if mis-used can magnify your setting error, and it isn't the tape that is to blame, but your own eyes, coupled with the magnifying lens! For those of you not using a tape magnifier, you, too, must be aware that you can mis-set your sight by not keeping your head angle the same with regard to the indicator pointer and sight tape, too!

Comments Regarding Using a Magnifier of any Kind

- If you don't have a magnifier added to your sight bar, consider getting one if you have difficulties seeing your yardages/lines on the tape. If you don't want to use one of those, you can purchase some magnifying glasses made for tying flies that clip to the brim of your hat; they don't cost much and work really well for setting your sight.
- If you do have a magnifier on your sight bar, they aren't without some potential pitfalls. I feel it is also essential to make some kind of "indicator" mark on where the red line (or blue line) on the magnifier intersects with something you can use as a reference. If you don't line up the magnifier's line correctly, you can easily mis-set your sight by quite a bit. If you don't get proper alignment, then you are going to have a significant error. (This is called a parallax error.) On my particular magnifier, I can mis-set the sight by one full number either way (40 clicks range possible) simply based upon how my eyes are positioned relative to the sight bar/sight tape/magnifier/red line combination! That amounts to a huge miss! Remember the beginning scenarios, when I mentioned the inconsistency of setting your sight and not knowing why? Well, here is the likely source of that particular error and inconsistency with the "same" (only obviously different) sight setting. It isn't the sight tape, and obviously it isn't the yardage on the course, it is way simpler than that. The problem is that most people don't even think about this, magnifier or not! Since for me, the use of the sight tape/magnifier is my third option, I rarely have to deal with it, but if I do have to deal with it, then I have ProActively prepared the sight to be used safely. I still do have to deal with it if I use the scribed side of the sight bar and align the indicator pointer to it by using a fly tier's magnifying glass or even my regular prescription glasses to set my sight.

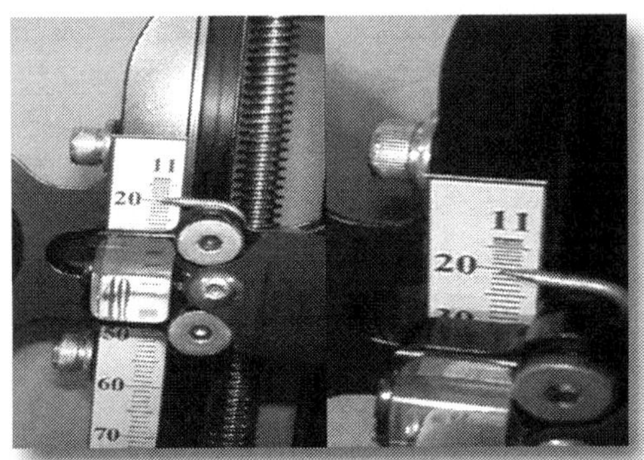

If you don't look square on to your scale you may get parallax reading errors like these. All of these are the same sight viewed at different angles.

Parallax errors are still in play anytime you align one object with another with your eyes (*see photos*). The photos clearly demonstrate how easy it is to mis-set your sight this way. Most people aren't even aware of this problem and how it is accentuated when you use a magnifier. Put bluntly, a "magnifier, if mis-used, magnifies any error you may create."

- Even if you don't have a magnifier installed on your sight, it is still essential that you make sure your eyes are in the same position relative to the yardage on the tape and the point of the indicator pointer every time you set your sight. If you change your head angle, then you begging for a mistake to be made setting the sight. Take your time to look at the pointer tip from the same head position each time you use the tape. Also, don't fall into the trap of moving your indicator pointer pin to adjust your sight settings. Moving the peep slightly is, in my opinion, the better option; never move that indicator pointer.

Summary

I do not profess to be the "expert" when it concerns all of the features, nuances, and corrections in *Archer's Advantage*. What I have shared are my experiences with being successful in getting accurate sight tapes out of the system without having to apply any of the corrections and arrays of different features within the program.

So, there you have it. I've given you a quick seminar on how to effectively utilize two systems in unison in order to gather all your sight settings in one shooting session and use one with the other to get as accurate of a sight tape as you are capable of. Once again, I've outlined what I consider to be the simplest method of doing this that is ProActive and gives me the best chances of not only saving time and money, but also gives me backup systems that are handy and easily retrievable.

The next chapter is all about *On Target 2*, in which you will see that I utilize all three of the systems and at its conclusion, I will give you information on how to utilize the three systems together as a group of checks and balances.

35

Sight Settings with On Target 2

Since some of you may have skipped over the previous two chapters, and rather than frequently referring you back to those chapters, it is much easier to simply repeat the information here.

In this chapter, we'll take a look at another software program, *On Target 2* (or *Software for Archers*) that you can use to get your sight settings and print out accurate sight tapes. I'll provide you with methods to create a redundant system of "back-ups" for when your sight tape on your sight bar isn't quite right, or gets messed up by weather or abuse. After all, a ProActive archers never go out on a course or to a competitive event, especially outdoors, without a backup system for their critical sight settings.

In addition, I will help you to prepare and mount a reliable sight tape and to also prepare a backup list of sight settings to carry with you on the course. Most people prefer to have a sight tape mounted on their sight/vertical bar, and there isn't anything wrong with that. However, I'll show you another way of getting the same thing, as either a primary or a backup system, that virtually guarantees that you have two or even three sets of sight marks with you at all times, even if you use a tablet or an old Palm *Pilot* for your sight settings. It is up to you which to choose as your primary system; but I hope you come away from this chapter with a much better insight into just how important a backup/cross-check system can become. In addition, I hope to clarify that "close enough for government work" is something to avoid if you are getting your sight settings. "Close enough" doesn't cut it for top echelon shooters, because those with the best and most accurate sight marks, along with the best mastery of shot execution are those on the winner's podium. A lousy set of sight marks won't do you much good, no matter how talented you are.

To be clear, this chapter will deal mostly with generating that accurate sight tape from *On Target 2* and also how to more accurately mount the sight tape, should you choose to use it onto the sight bar so that your mounting process doesn't foul up a perfectly good sight tape and make it inaccurate because of improper mounting techniques.

Some Sighting Scenarios

So, here are a couple of scenarios for you to ponder as we go through this process:

These scenarios have occurred with me, and I know of many other archers that have had the same problems.

- You are out on a field course, and you notice that you are shooting high on most everything from 45 yards in, but are shooting pretty much dead on for everything from 48 yards out. What do you suppose is incorrect here?
- Your close range and your long range sight settings on your printed sight tape are "off", but the ones in the mid-yardages seem to be perfectly fine. You are shooting low on the close targets, and high on the long targets. You know the "numbers" that you put into your computer are good. What could be the source of this problem? (I know many of you have experienced this scenario, especially with the advent of the computer generated sight tapes, or even the selection of a sight tape from a series of pre-printed tapes that you match up a couple of yardages and the select the closest one of the pre-printed ones to use as your very own to mount onto your sight bar.)
- You have a couple of programs that you are using for your sight tapes and bow data. However, while they agree really close on the sight tape and yardage numbers, they differ quite a bit with regard to arrow spine match, and also calculated arrow speeds, even though you've entered the same bow set-up data into those programs. This bothers the delights out of you, and leaves you with the dilemma of trying to figure out why. Even worse is that the tapes match so closely that you can't decipher "why" the speeds and spines out of the two systems are so very different.
- You are using a sight tape on your vertical bar. You are also using a "tape magnifier" on the side of the sight bar so that you can see your sight tape better. You are constantly having problems with inconsistencies with regard to the impact points on the target, and when you check your setting, it appears to be set okay, but upon another check, it isn't set okay. What could be the problem here? You were careful when you set the sight tape on the bar, so why one time are you shooting high with a setting and the next time you are shooting low with a setting, and the next, "right on"?

I am not promoting any particular sight tape/bow set-up program, but I will outline my preference and why I chose that option over the others. I also will only deal with the three options that I have and, thus, am most familiar with: "The Calculator Method from the early 1980's (see Chapter 33), *Archer's Advantage* (see Chapter 34), and finally, *On Target 2* (OT2) in this chapter. I know that there are others, however, I'm not at all familiar with those. I also don't have a need to investigate them as better options for my own use as I am happy with the accuracy and quality of these three.

I might also add that I still have a lot to learn about OT2 along with its nuances. I don't have all the answers and, personally, I don't think anyone does. What I am offering you are some basic guidelines and techniques to help you get better numbers out of the three systems so that the sight tapes and yardage cards you do print out are as accurately done as you can possibly get them. There likely are things that I'm missing at this juncture, which is why I work with all three data input/output devices and then compare results.

If you take the time to scrutinize the pictures within the three chapters, you are going to note some minor "discrepancies" between the two computer program print screens' results. I've noted this and investigated it, however, the important thing is that despite the discrepancies in the results spit out, the sight tapes themselves match up closely regardless, and that, my friends is the most important part. By being careful I have, so far, been able to avoid having to use any of the special correction factors that are available in these sophisticated software programs.

The arrow spine recommendations between the two programs do differ, but, that isn't my point of focus for doing this work. My focus is in getting those sight tapes, even though, for me, the printed tape is only a backup system.

On Target 2 from Pinwheel Software

This Windows-based software program is quite similar to *Archer's Advantage*, but has several additional items, along with quite a bit more sophistication. While it isn't quite as user friendly as *Archer's Advantage*, it does offer a lot of extras and "checking" capabilities and options, once you understand how to use the utilities. It has a larger learning curve, but the basics are easily accommodated. You can also purchase OT2 on-line from *www.pinwheelsoftware.com*.

You can also purchase two other products, "Shaft Selector Plus," and "Tapes and Charts" if you don't want the full-blown version. The version I have contains all three in one package. The software is also available from Lancaster's Archery and several other distributors, if you want a copy on DVD.

Once again, I'm not going to give you a full blown course in how to run and operate *On Target 2* software. I will give you some tips and some pitfalls to avoid, though. I will tell you what this software offers that the others don't, but the promotion stops there. The choice is yours and yours alone.

The Basics of OT2 The basic inputs and outputs for this program are the same as they are for *Archer's Advantage*. *On Target 2*, however, differs in many respects:

1. First off, once you have entered all your specifications for your equipment through the Equipment "Database Selections" Screen (*see screen shot below*), you press the "Apply" tab by each selection which automatically transfers your selections to the My Setup Tab. If you move your cursor over each item and then hold your cursor over that selection, a yellow bar pops up that tells you what the selection is and what it will do.

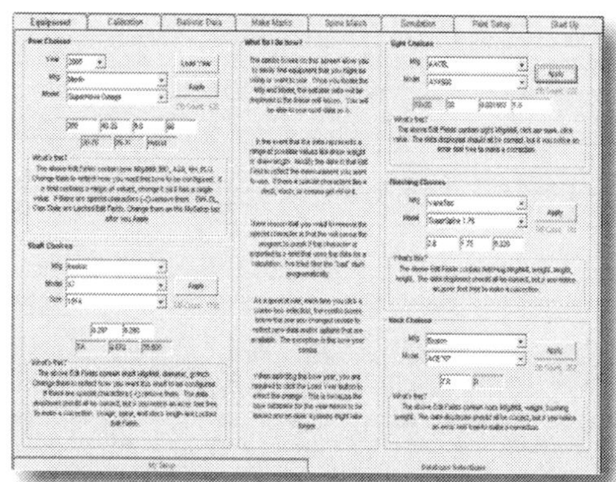

2. Select the "My Setup Tab" to further specify your particular set up. If you move and hold your cursor over each item, it will tell you what that selec-

tion means and how it will work. For example, if you move and hold your cursor over "Peep Height," you will see a popup that will say, "Height of peep above arrow centerline (measured from peep center to arrow center at full draw)." If you hover over "Sight Radius," you will see a popup that says "Distance from peep to sight lens/pins (measured at full draw)." If you want the system to perform calculations or activate, you press the "equals sign" (=) wherever it is offered.

Tip On this screen, under "Complete Arrow," it is wise for you to weigh your completed arrow and enter that data (in grains, to nearest tenth of a grain). However, let OT2 take care of the Velocity Calculation from your sight settings input and leave it at the "Manual" selection. Just a small "trick" I learned that allows OT2 to do its thing more easily, without overriding a setting.

3. Under "Bow Specs," which is for your equipment specifications, simply enter in your data that you have already measured and placed in your "Master Bow Configuration Record."
4. You should measure your Percent Letoff and put it into the appropriate box. I have a special 60% module on my Merlin *SuperNova*, so I entered that there instead of the default 65-70% from the Database screen. I also own an Easton Digital Scale that will give me my peak and holding weights. Once again, being ProActive, I never take just one reading from this scale. I take five readings and toss ant "ringers," then average the other readings.
5. Make sure to check on your cam style; sometimes this doesn't necessarily pop up correctly. This affects your arrow spine match a great deal. Spine match isn't a focus of this chapter, but is still important. 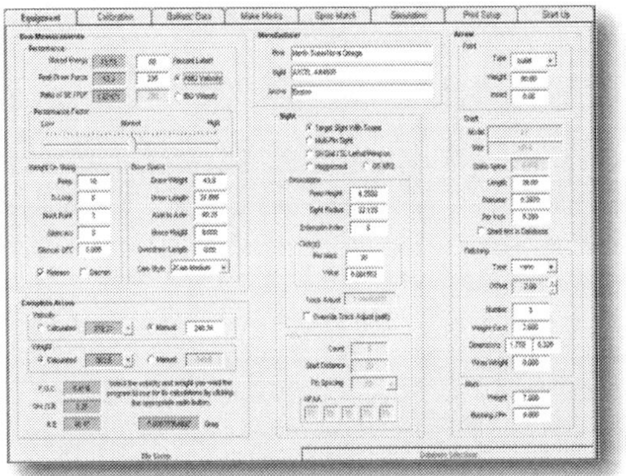
6. Put in point weight and point style, but if you change it later to find another arrow, that isn't a big deal. It is a big deal, however once you start to generate a sight tape!
7. Double check your shaft length, point weight, and other data and enter those on this screen. You can change them on the Spine Match screen later, but it is a good idea to put the initial measurements here. Make sure that you measure your shaft length that only includes the shaft material! Do not measure your arrow length from the bottom of the nock slot to the end of the arrow shaft/bushing. This throws off your spine match by quite a bit.
8. Once completed with this, it is a good idea to now save this information for the bow into a User Configuration file (see screen shot above). This is accomplished by clicking on File, then Save User Record, naming the file something you can identify later. Tip I simply use the Make and Model of the bow, along with the arrow size I'm shooting (*Example* Merlin *Supernova* – 1914), and then press the "Save" button. Your configuration is now saved as a OT2 User Configuration

record under OT2. When you go back into *On Target 2* the next time, you can then load this configuration record and your information for the particular setup will be displayed. You then simply save any changes or if you've made a major change, then save it with a different file name (I add the date in the format 032812, for mm/dd/yy) and the old one is still available to you to go back to! Once again, being ProActive, you should never set yourself up to lose your starting point. You never know when you'll need that information!

Spine Match This screen is obviously used to find an arrow spine match for your bow/set up. There is a wide variety of selections. Once again, if you hover over the name of a selection, a yellow bar will pop up to tell you what that represents. Tip If you hover over "Shaft length" you will see that OT2 reminds you that it means: "Shaft length (Shaft material only)." It is a common mistake to use some other length. The normal thing to think is that you go from the end of the shaft to the bottom of the nock slot to measure the length of the arrow. This is not the case with OT2, and that difference will dramatically affect your arrow spine matches! Of course, you can make changes and select a different arrow, change the arrow length, point weight etc.

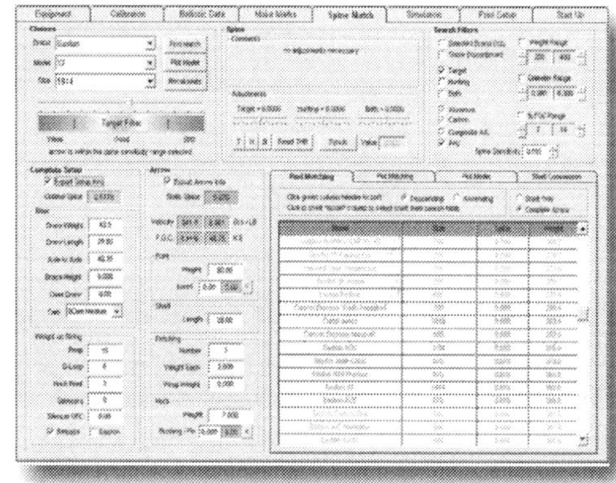

Any time you make changes on the screen, you should go back up under "Choices" in the upper left and click on "Recalculate" and then "Find Match" to trigger new spine recommendations.

Calibration Screen Now we are going to get to the "meat" of OT2's ability to generate good sight tapes. You have a lot of choices to make here, and it is up to you to decide what works the best for you. I'm going to show you what works the best for me, possibly even better than the other two systems discussed (in Ch. 33-34). You will note in the screen shot (*below right*) that most all of the boxes are "greened out." This is due to the item(s) I've selected to use for calculating those numbers on the sight tape generation.

Determine Velocity You will note that I've selected "Sight Scale Marks" in this area. I do that for a very specific reason. If you are a "pin shooter" you would use pin gap. I don't use "Chronograph" because as I previously discussed in the chapter about *Archer's Advantage*, I don't have a known standard with which to ensure that the shop chronograph is really correct or not. However, OT2 has the means to calculate the arrow speed of my equipment based

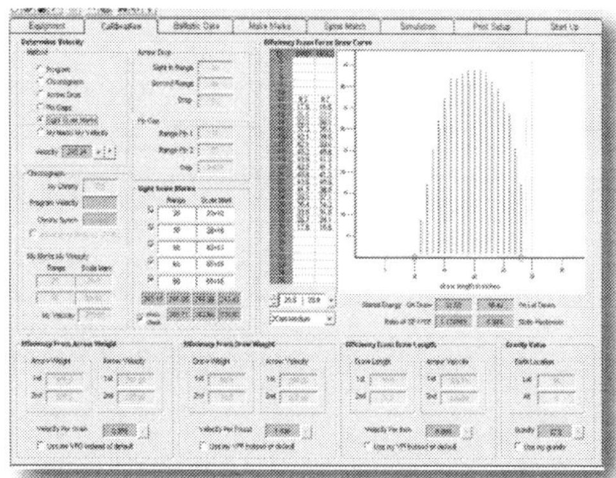

upon the sight settings data I have entered, and I consider this better than any chronograph speed I could enter into the system.

Sight Scale Marks The boxes in this area of the screen are white because of the selection in the "Determine Velocity" area. You can go with as few as two or as many as five sight settings. I'm a sound believer in giving as much data as possible, so if OT2 will allow me to spread five sight settings of my choosing, I'm going for the settings with a maximum distance spread that I shoot the best at. Thus you will quickly note that I've entered five sight settings: 20, 30, 50, 65, and 80 yards. You should also note that I have checked the "Cross-Check" box in this area. (Remember my personal standard distances of 20 and 65 yards from Chapter 33? Notice that I continue this standardization so apples are compared to apples among the three cross-checks I use).

Pressing the "Cross-Check" box will, when I press the "=" under "Determine Velocity," give me a cross check by comparing among the sight settings entered, calculating velocities for those comparisons. A "?" will appear while OT2 is performing those velocity checks, so give it some time to finish.

Take note (*see screen shot*), that the results of those comparisons are in the seven boxes under "Sight Scale Marks" and that they are close and also, for the longer distances, show a slowing of the arrow, which is what you should expect. OT2 will generate and display the velocity in the "Determine Velocity" area and send that number to the Calibration Screen automatically. In addition, OT2 displays the calculated comparison velocities against one another and allows you to see if you have a "ringer" that is throwing off the calculations. In this particular case, it appears that I have a pretty good set of sight marks. My sight settings were dead on when I went out to check them. The sight settings were as good as I could get them based upon my capabilities at the time and the fact that I was using the "horizontal tape method" discussed in Chapter 32 to get them. This way, if you have a ringer, you can see this, print out the tape if you want, or, using the placard, simply go out and recheck the ringer sight mark for sure, and then get back into OT2, open your User File for that setup, make the correction(s), re-calculate, and re-generate a new sight tape.

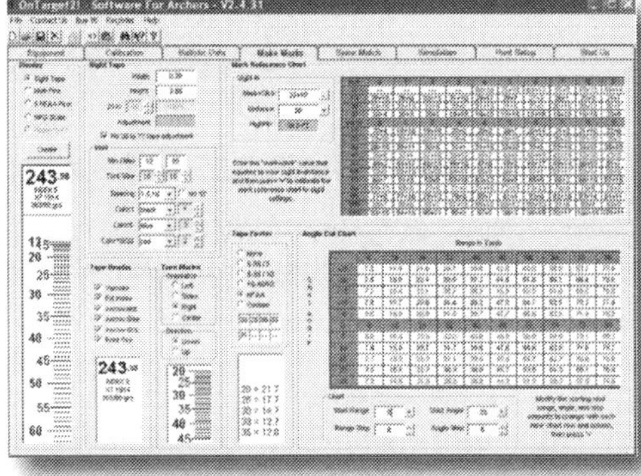

I never go out on a course to shoot a score, and obviously never go to a competitive event, without my sight tape or placard having been checked in advance for accuracy. A ProActive archer never "goes into battle with an untested set of sight marks," nor do they move their indicator pointer or try to change sight marks in the practice area! I see this all the time and just shake my head about it. I'm sure you've seen this too, or might even be guilty of said offense.

When you press the button with the " ^ " symbol, you will export that calculated velocity to the Equipment Tab, thus saving you the trouble of remembering to do this.

Efficiency from Force Draw Curve OT2 automatically creates a force draw curve for your bow based upon the data you provided and the cam style selected.

Remainder of Information (*Bottom of the Screen*) I don't make any changes to the bottom part of the screen, since I don't understand what that is all about, and obviously don't know how it will impact the final generation of sight tapes and other data. I find the "Gravity Data" enticing, however, and maybe some day, I'll play with that one! Here in Illinois, we are at a high altitude of 744 feet above sea level, so I seriously doubt that it would pose a problem. However, at 6,000+ feet altitude and 46 degrees N. Latitude, one never knows.

Make Marks Screen We are now ready to generate our sight tapes, Sight Marks Reference Chart, and the Angle Cut Chart. This is done through the Make Marks Screen in OT2. Once again, hovering over any area of selection will tell you what that is going to do and what it means. There are a lot of things you can do in this screen prior to printing your sight tapes and the other charts. Here are a few things I've learned to do to make my sight tapes and printouts more to my liking and to help me become more ProActive and avoid some common mistakes.

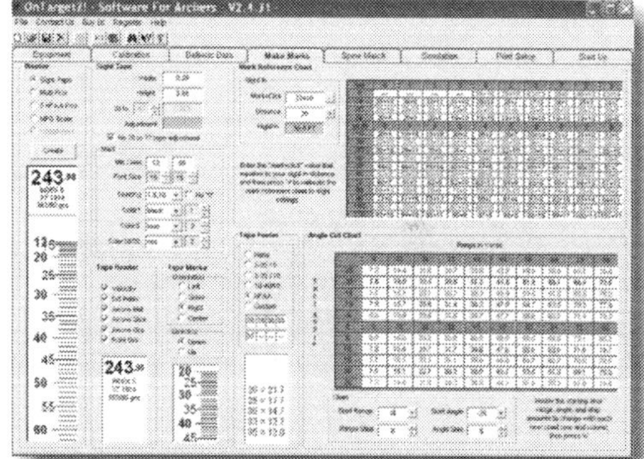

Reminder Anytime you make a change of your selections below, you need to press "Create" under the Display portion in the upper left portion of the Make Marks screen. This allows you to see what you have just done to the appearance of your sight tape. It is not a bad idea to press the "Create" button and check this each time before you go on to the next item.

An Example of the Selection Process for Sight Tape Generation

a. *Width & Length* I've set this for a width of 0.2929 inches and length of 2.55 inches based upon my Axcel 4500 sight bar width and length. If you have a shorter sight bar, then make sure you list that as the length, or go back into the Equipment Tab, "Database Selection" and select the correct sight so that it gets into the database properly. I also cross-check those dimensions and make adjustments if I have to. Notice that I checked the "No 20 to ?? Tape Adjustment" box. The bow sight has a standard scale on it, so if your sight is in the database, you shouldn't have to make any adjustments here.

b. *Mark: Min/Max* I change this to 15 min, and 85 max. If you try to put in 10 Min, you will get a truncated set of marks above the 20 yard setting.

c. *Font Size* A point size of 15 works for my eyes. You can play with this however you want.

d. *Spacing* I always use 1, 5, 10 with the Zeroes in place. If you use the "no "0" setting", then you'll only have 1, 2, 3, etc, printing onto the sight tape, which in my opinion isn't adequate. I like having the real numbers right in front of me.

e. *Color 1, 5, 10/20* Once again I opt for color-coding (Black, Blue, Red) for those yardage lines and major/minor increments on my sight tape, just like I do on my placards. It is important to mention here, that unlike Archer's Advantage, when you set up your colored sight tape in OT2, both the numbers for the yardages will print at 15, 20, 25, 30, 35, etc. In addition, the "odds" of 15, 25, 35, etc are indented to help you pickup your sight settings more easily as you read the tape. This is extremely handy and one of the many features I really like about On Target 2 (see Photo 5, lower left corner).

f. *Tape Header* In OT2, you can select your tape header information. I utilize this so that I have the reminders that really do help things along. The "Extension Index" is helpful if you are one who removes your sight from the bow during transport. That is the "hole" setting of your extension bar. The Axcel sight "holes" are numbered, and this Index tells me I'm set up in Hole #5 with my sight extension. The rest of the header tells me the arrow size, weight, and point weight of my arrow. You can remove any or all of those selection boxes. By un-clicking those which you don't want or need you will simply remove that information from the top of the tape

g. *Tape Marks: Orientation* Once again, I've selected "right" because of the location of my indicator pointer and magnifier. Obviously, since the numbers on my sight bar increase as the distance increases, the selected direction is down. When you make this selection, don't forget to press that "Create" button in the upper left portion so that you see what you have just done to your sight tape presentation.

h. *Tape Footer* You will note that I decided upon "NFAA." The reason is simple: OT2 will give me my sight settings for the Bunny target distances at the bottom of my sight tape! These distances are for 20, 25, 30, 33, and 35 feet and are very handy to have right in front of you. Since I cannot get the sight tape to generate those settings closer than 12 yards, it is very handy, and saves having to dig out the other table from my quiver, if I've decided to use the sight tape system. Be aware, however, that these are only going to be as accurate as you were in obtaining your peep height and sight distance in the setup screens (Garbage In = Garbage Out!). It is essential that you cross-check these marks well before going out on a scoring session or tournament. You should note that on the OT2 sight tape, those are the settings in yards for each of those distances for the bunny targets.

i. *Mark Reference Chart* If you aren't using "clicks," you can press the button with the "." on it and toggle the yardage chart from "+" over to Decimals and back. I don't make any other changes here. Photo 5 depicts "clicks," which is what I would recommend you use if your particular sight has "clicks" you can count as you set your sight past a "main number." Remember, if you've moved your indicator pointer, then you have lost the exactness and must trust your eyes and counts rather than the numbers.

j. *Angle Cut Chart* This is obviously your Cut Chart Table. However, you can change the increments for your cut chart. I've opted to use a Start Range of 0 yards and a Range Step of 8 yards, along with 5 degrees of angle and plus or minus 25 degrees maximum. This covers more information for my cut chart and doesn't waste room by giving me information I won't ever use, since "0" yards doesn't apply. Notice that now, instead of 0 and 100 yards for the table, I have from 8 through 80 yards in 8-yard increments. This table is easily interpolated and provides me with better data should I decide to use the cut chart to help with my "gut feeling" on a hilly course. Since I shoot almost exclusively Field and Hunter Rounds and don't have a need for 90 and 100 yards on the cut chart, I thought it best to maximize the cuts and eliminate anything past 80 yards. This along with your distance marks prints out and all you have to do is cut them out, fold the sheet in half, and then laminate it. This is about the size of a 3x5 index card. It gives you your "backup" sight marks and your cut chart all in one item!

Printing the Sight Tape and Tables

So now, after you have pressed the "Create" button on the "Make Marks Tab" and confirmed that you like what you see with regard to sight tape, yardage chart and cut chart, you are finally ready to generate your sight tape and Tables from *On Target 2.*

The Print Setup Tab gives you three choices: Sight Tape and Charts to Plain Paper, Sight Tapes to Plain Paper or Labels, and even the option to print Target Cards to Plain Paper or Labels for 3-D targets. If you select the print to labels options, there is a listing of compatible labels available. On the Print Target Cards tab, you can select which brand of 3-D targets you would like to print a card of and print those in color if you so choose.

For my print-outs I opted for the "Sight Tape and Charts to Plain Paper Option" (*see screen shot*), since that gives me print-outs of the Sight Tapes, the Cut Chart, and the Sight Settings Table, all on one sheet of paper. It is then a simple matter of preparing the sight tapes and charts for mounting and/or lamination. I find the sizes of the charts very handy, since they can be mounted back to back and then laminated for waterproofing. This way, one side of the card has your Cut Chart, while the other side has a complete list of sight settings as a backup in case your sight tape gets rendered useless.

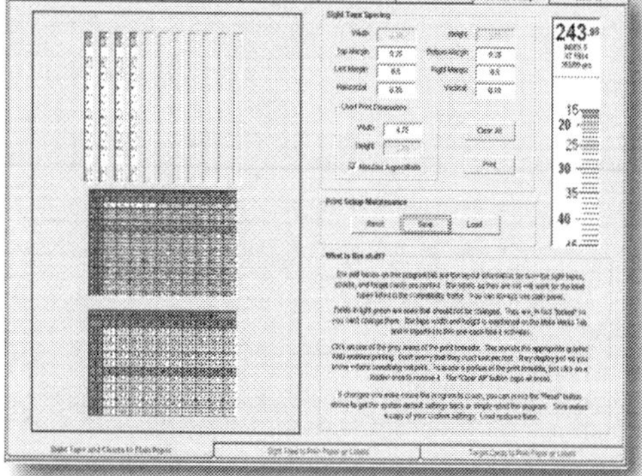

When it comes to sight settings, you should never leave yourself hanging out there with only one set of marks and no backup system. This includes relying on a Palm Pilot, tablet, or other electronic system. If those batteries fail, or the system goes down, you aren't given an "equipment failure" for electronics, so you would be done for the day. A ProActive archer always does what they can to be ahead of the game for when something goes awry.

Note that a complete explanation of what to do is in the lower right corner of the screen. I choose not to make any changes in the upper portion of the screen. It is a simple process to decide how many tapes you want to print out and then click on the gray area to get a tape to the paper. You then click on the two larger boxes to get the Cut Chart and the Yardages Table onto the printout. After that, click on "Save" to save that information. Then click on "Print" and your Page will print out on your printer. While they may not look pretty on screen, your printouts will turn out just fine.

When you have completed your printing, you need to save the User File on OT2 by clicking on "File," then click on "User Record," name the file or select the same user file, and then click on the Save button. Then you can exit OT2 and start to prepare your sight tapes and charts for mounting.

The OT2 Target Cards Option Some very handy items you can get from OT2, if you are a 3-D shooter, are the Target Cards for 3-D Animals. You will have to keep your Cards Updated, and those updates will have to be done manually, but this capability comes with *On Target 2*. Or you can buy just the Target cards program if that is all you want.

To get these cards, click on the "Print Setup Tab," then click on the far right lower tab, "Target Cards to Plain Paper or Labels" and begin making your selections. There is a listing of compatible Avery Labels in the upper right portion of the screen or, as it says, you can print up to 6 animals at a time by selecting them. In this screen shot, I selected MacKenzie Color, and then under model, I selected the animal I wanted, then clicked on an empty space in the left side of the screen to transfer that animal to the print-out. Once you have finished selecting all six animals to fill the screen, select the "Print Button" and wait for the printing to be completed. Then press the "Clear" button and repeat the process. You also have the option for NFAA and FITA faces for indoors and for outdoors as well as Rineharts and Deltas in both B&W and color. It is then easy to cut them out and laminate them to make your own set of Animal placards.

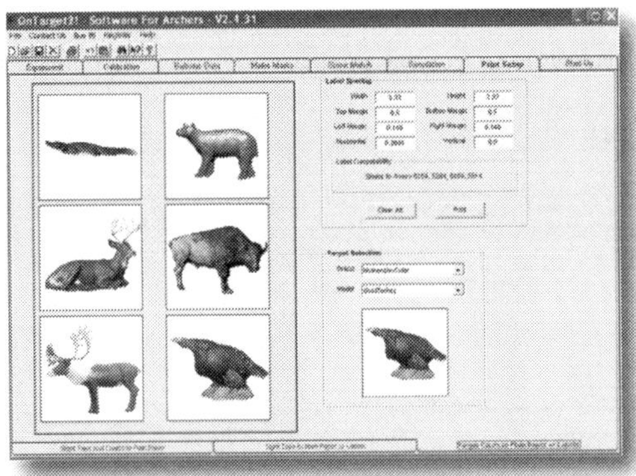

Preparing & Mounting the Printed Sight Tape to Your Sight Bar

For those of you who skipped the previous chapter about Archer's Advantage, what follows is a repeat of what was given in that chapter. Chapter 33 discussed the making of the "Placard" for the Calculator-based system, but you can also make a placard for your *Archer's Advantage* sight settings or your OT2 sight settings and use the scribed numbers instead of the sight tape; or you can elect to have both available, plus the printout and cut chart, for a "three-way system" should something happen to the sight tape. Later on, pay very special attention when we talk about errors easily made while setting the sight for any given distance while out on the course! A simple process of setting your sight can get complicated if you aren't aware of the problems and don't ProActively prepare for alleviating those potential errors.

We are finally ready to mount your sight tape onto your vertical sight bar. Do you remember the scenario in which you are shooting low on the close ones, dead on in the middle, and high on the long ones? Well, that was likely caused by stretching the tape while you were in the process of mounting it. Another scenario involving a "stretched sight tape" is that some shooters tend to mount the tape by mating the tape to the sight indicator pointer when with the sight set at only 20 yards. Then, the settings at the top end of the stretched sight tape are dead on and as you shoot progressively longer distances, you begin to shoot higher and higher and higher. I'm sure that you have heard many a shooter gripe that the "programs" are not generating accurate sight tapes for them. I will show you how to virtually eliminate this problem by once again, being ProActive.

It doesn't matter whether the sight tape is printed out from *Archer's Advantage*, *On Target 2*, *TAP*, or any other sight tape printing program, the mounting procedure should be the same. This should also partially explain why personally, I prefer the placard system that uses the scribed and unmovable "numbers" on my vertical sight bar as my primary sight setting procedure and the printed sight tape as the 3rd alternate (should I lose my placard or backup printout). I'll discuss this issue last, because the placard system isn't without its problems.

Before going into detail on how to more properly mount your tape, let me give you a few other things to watch for and avoid.

- If you are going to use "photo paper" to print your sight tapes on, be sure to allow for the thicker paper! You are going to need some extra space between the sight bar and the indicator pointer for that thick paper. In addition, since my method of configuring newly printed sight tapes for mounting involves three additional layers besides the printer paper itself, you also need to accommodate the angle of your indicator pointer to handle this extra thickness. The last thing you need to have happen is for your indicator pointer or, worse, your slider on the sight bar to catch on the printed sight tape and rip it right off of the sight bar. I've seen this happen more than once.
- Be sure to clean the area where you will be mounting the sight tape on your sight bar with alcohol and to allow it to dry.
- Avoid putting your fingers onto that area of the sight bar during the mounting process. The oils in your fingerprints can weaken or even prevent the adhesive from sticking. You don't want your sight tape slipping and sliding around on the sight bar.
- I recommend that you accurately pre-set the sight at 40 or 50 yards before you mount the sight tape. (I mean that you take the time to count those "clicks" or read the "zeroed" wheel and get it exactly right.) The main reason is that most of the shots during a field or hunter round are around the 40-50 yard ranges, so I feel it is essential to make darned sure that this area of the tape is mounted properly.

The margin for error is less at these and longer yardages, so make them right. Secondly, this helps to reduce the chances of the sight tape being stretched since you have less surface area to work with on a longitudinal axis (if you properly install it, that is).

- I strongly recommend that you use a magnifying glass or some magnifier to pre-set the sight and also when you align the new sight tape to the vertical bar. The print is small as it is, so it is easy to misalign the tape yardage with your indicator pointer, and especially easy to misalign the tape if you have a magnifier on the sight bar.
- Before you start, make sure that the sight tape itself won't be too wide or too long for your vertical sight bar. You will not believe the number of shooters that print out the sight tape only to find it doesn't fit on their sight bar! It is easy to go back in and re-set the length/width of the sight tape and re-print it, so take that time now. Trim it if necessary, but get it right.
- When you align the sight tape, make sure that part of the tip of the indicator pointer will at least reach to the end/tip of all of the yardage lines on the tape, in contact with the tape but rather in alignment with it. Having to bridge a gap between the end of the indicator pointer and the end of the yardage lines is a source of error.
- Make sure you allow the ink time to dry before you start the mounting process. If you don't, you may smear the lines and make them unreadable. If you are using picture quality paper, the drying time is longer than for ordinary paper.
- Wash and dry your hands thoroughly before you start this process.
- Make sure you have adequate lighting to assist you in tape placement.
- Take your bow sight off of the bow and lay it down so it is horizontal. Trying to mount your sight tape with the sight in a vertical position can really create problems for you.

Items Needed to Mount Your Sight Tape

1. a sharp hobby knife
2. a roll of transparent tape, ½″ wide.
3. cardstock paper or cutting board to protect your desk or table top from being cut up by your hobby knife. I use an old Masonite placemat or a smooth surface cutting board. If you use wood, there is a tendency to press the knife too hard and then the knife follows a course of its own; sometimes right into your finger! I've found that a hard surface and a sharp knife prevent stretching of the paper as you cut out the sight tape.

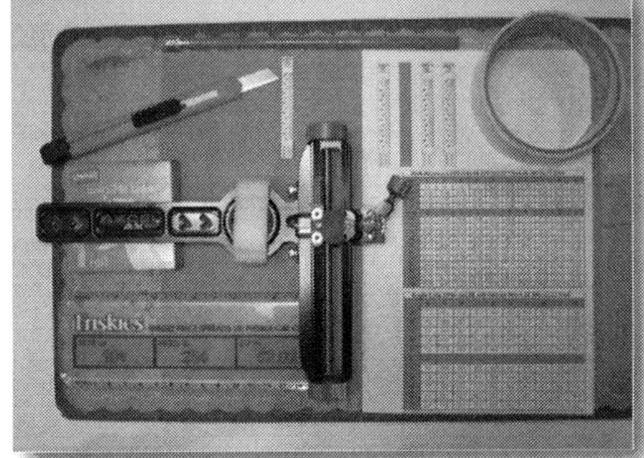

4. a roll of thin double-stick tape. I prefer at least 1½″ wide double stick tape.

The stuff I get is called "carpet tape" and it has a backing which makes it easy to handle (see photo). This is not needed if you use Avery labels with the stick-em already in place.

5. your printed sight tape on plain paper, or Avery label, or photo paper.
6. a pencil with rubber eraser.
7. tweezers or forceps. These can help you to get the backing layer off the tape printed on a label and to position the tape initially on the sight bar.
8. a straight edge to use in getting a straight and clean cut on the sight tape.

Preparing and Trimming the Sight Tape

1. Cut a piece of double stick tape that is about ¼″ to ½″ longer than your sight tape.
2. Turn the sight tape printouts face down on your cutting board.
3. Carefully align one sticky side of the double stick tape so that it will cover one or two of the sight tapes you intend to use.
4. Press your double stick straight down onto the sight tape paper. Do not pull the paper or the double stick tape. Press it straight down onto the paper.
5. Using the tip of the pencil eraser and not your fingers, gently press the tip of the pencil eraser straight down onto the double-stick tape much like a blotter. Do not "rub" it into place on the tape paper.
6. Turn the sight tape/double-stick combo back over to the printed side up.
7. Cut a piece of transparent tape that is about ¼″ to ½″ longer than the sight tape.
8. Place the transparent tape straight down over the printed side of the sight tape. Once again, do *not* pull the tape down, don't "rub it" from top to bottom or bottom to top. Straight down without moving the sight tape paper.
9. Using the tip of the pencil eraser, press it like a blotter straight down for the entire length and width of the sight tape you want to use.
10. Using a solid straight edge, carefully align the straight edge with one edge of the sight tape you want to use and then carefully cut out your sight tapes, one edge at a time.

Step by Step: Mounting the Sight Tape

Before we begin the process of mounting that sight tape to your sight bar, it is important to outline some items that are indeed problematical when mounting the sight tape, and even carry over to you when you go to set your bow sight out on the range.

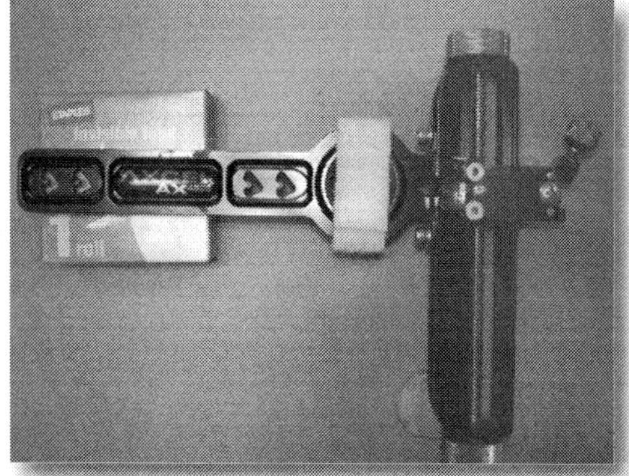

The photos for this procedure are for clarity's sake. I didn't take the time to actually set the bow sight to the proper scale setting for 40 or 50 yards. However, you will note in the pictures that I'm demonstrating using the indicator pointer as the reference for mounting the sight tape on the 40 yard setting. So, here's how to go about mounting your sight tape:

1. Make absolutely sure you have your bow sight set "exactly" onto the yardage you've decided to use to mount your sight tape. Once again, I use 40, 45, or 50 yards. I do mean exactly, as in right down to the "click count." If you've been ProActive you have it already set, but a final check is a good idea.
2. Slide your sight tape under the indicator pin and/or magnifier to make sure that the indicator pin won't catch or drag on the sight tape. This one last final check is important, since you don't want that indicator pointer or magnifier or any part of the sight slide mechanism to be in contact with that new sight tape. Adjust things as necessary to insure that you have clearances, but be careful about that indicator pointer!
3. Decide whether you are going to use the magnifier or the unmagnified indicator pointer as your reference for placing the tape. On many sights, these are not the same point of reference (*see magnifier photo*).
4. I've found it to be very difficult to mount a sight tape if the sight is on the bow, so, remove the sight from the bow and then lay the sight down horizontally on a desk or table top.
5 Position the sight itself in the same "positioning" that you will use when setting the sight. This doubles up as a cross-check for your frame of reference when setting the sight. However, by having the sight by itself, this makes things more stable for positioning the sight tape on the bar.
6. Carefully remove the backing from the reverse side of the sight tape (the double sided tape backing).
7. Keeping your visual frame of reference so that you are looking straight down at the indicator pointer or magnifier, place the yardage line for the distance your sight bar is set at directly onto the sight bar. Make sure that you also position the tape parallel to vertical bar from top to bottom. Once you press this on, the only way to change it is to remove the tape and start over with a new one.
8. Do not rub onto the sight tape with your fingers (which could stretch the tape), but use the pencil eraser like a blotter. By pressing straight down a "blot" at a time, press the sight tape straight down onto the sight bar, all the while keeping the tape flat and aligned as you move along the tape, from the middle towards each end.
9. Once you are certain that most of the tape is pressed down, recheck that your preset setting is in proper alignment, and then you can move the sight block out of the way so you can get at the indicator pointer/magnifier area of the tape to make it finally secure.
10. Once you have the entire sight tape pressed down and it is straight and solidly mounted, then use the tip of the eraser to "blot down" the edges of the sight tape to the sight bar on both sides.
11. The last step is to make one last final seal by placing another layer of transparent tape over the top of the entire sight tape and extending that beyond the ends of the sight tape by ¼″ to ½″, and then use the sharp knife to trim the sides. This last

step just helps to give a little more insurance that the sight tape is weatherproof and also that it won't slip or come off of the sight bar.

If you have been careful and followed the steps, you should now have a mounted sight tape that has not been stretched or otherwise misaligned with the indicator pointer. The sight block/pointer will be clearing your new sight tape without any interference. The last and important thing to do is to go out on the range and double check your new sight settings tape to make sure it is indeed accurate. After all you would not go into battle with an untested weapon, would you?

Final Check for a Stretched Sight Tape Check one last time by setting your sight to 20 yards using your sight tape. Check this against the proper numbers on the scribed side of the sight (including the clicks), and then check the tape similarly at several other distances along the entire length of the sight tape. Make certain that all the sight tape settings match what the numbers are supposed to be on the scribed scale of the bow sight. This is your final check that you haven't accidentally stretched that tape while mounting it to the sight bar. Of course, always remind yourself to make sure you keep your head to sight alignment when you make your sight setting, always keeping in mind that a magnifier, if mis-used can magnify your setting error, and it isn't the tape that is to blame, but your own eyes, coupled with the magnifying lens! For those of you not using a tape magnifier, you, too, must be aware that you can mis-set your sight by not keeping your head angle the same with regard to the indicator pointer and sight tape, too!

Regarding Using a Magnifier of any Kind

- If you don't have a magnifier added to your sight bar, consider getting one if you have difficulties seeing your yardages/lines on the tape. If you don't want to use one of those, you can purchase some magnifying glasses made for tying flies that clip to the brim of your hat; they don't cost much and work really well for setting your sight.
- If you do have a magnifier on your sight bar, they aren't without some potential pitfalls. I feel it is also essential to make some kind of "indicator" mark on where the red line (or blue line) on the magnifier intersects with something you can use as a reference. If you don't line up the magnifier's line correctly, you can easily mis-set your sight by quite a bit. If you don't get proper alignment, then you are going to have a significant error. (This is called a parallax error.) On my particular magnifier, I can mis-set the sight by one full number either way (40 clicks' range possible) simply based upon how my eyes are positioned relative to the sight bar/sight tape/magnifier/red line combination! That amounts to a huge miss! Remember the beginning scenarios, when I mentioned the inconsistency of setting your sight and not knowing why? Well, here is the likely source of that particular error and inconsistency with the "same" (only obviously different) sight setting. It isn't the sight tape, and obviously it isn't the yardage on the course, it is way simpler than that. The problem is that most people don't even think about this, magnifier or not! Since for me, the use of the sight tape/magnifier is my third

If you don't look square on to your scale you may get parallax reading errors like these. All of these are the same sight viewed at different angles.

option, I rarely have to deal with it, but if I do have to deal with it, then I have ProActively prepared the sight to be used safely. I still do have to deal with it if I use the scribed side of the sight bar and align the indicator pointer to it by using a fly tier's magnifying glass or even my regular prescription glasses to set my sight. Parallax errors are still in play anytime you align one object with another with your eyes (*see photos above*). The photos clearly demonstrate how easy it is to mis-set your sight this way. Most people aren't even aware of this problem and how it is accentuated when you use a magnifier. Put bluntly, a "magnifier, if mis-used, magnifies any error you may create."

- Even if you don't have a magnifier installed on your sight, it is still essential that you make sure your eyes are in the same position relative to the yardage on the tape and the point of the indicator pointer every time you set your sight. If you change your head angle, then you begging for a mistake to be made setting the sight. Take your time to look at the pointer tip from the same head position each time you use the tape. Also, don't fall into the trap of moving your indicator to adjust your sight settings. Moving the peep slightly is, in my opinion, the better option; never move that indicator pointer.

Preparing the "Yardage Chart" and the "Cut Chart"

On Target 2 has a nice feature for the "Yardage Chart" and the "Cut Chart" that gives you the option of printing them both out at the same time that you print out your sight tapes. Personally, I take advantage of this option and print them both out (*see screen shots below*). What is nice about these is that you can cut them out as a unit, fold the printout in half and then laminate it. This gives you a two-sided document that is waterproof and gives you everything you need for a backup system and for those downhill and uphill shots where a "cut" may well be needed. The printout will be a

feet	0	1	2	3	4	5	6	7	8	9
0	***	***	***	***	94+10	75+19	63+13	55+0	48+13	43+14
10	38+19	36+0	33+11	31+10	29+17	28+7	27+2	26+1	25+3	24+7
20	23+18	22+19	22+9	22+0	21+13	21+6	21+0	20+15	20+12	20+7
30	20+4	20+3	20+1	19+18	19+16	19+18	19+18	19+18	19+19	20+0
yards	0	1	2	3	4	5	6	7	8	9
10	20+4	19+18	19+18	20+0	20+2	20+7	20+14	21+2	21+10	22+0
20	22+10	23+1	23+13	24+4	24+17	25+10	26+2	26+15	27+10	28+3
30	28+18	29+11	30+5	31+1	31+15	32+10	33+5	33+19	34+15	35+10
40	36+6	37+1	37+18	38+12	39+7	40+3	40+18	41+14	42+10	43+5
50	44+2	44+17	45+14	46+10	47+5	48+2	48+17	49+14	50+10	51+7
60	52+2	52+19	53+15	54+11	55+8	56+4	57+1	57+17	58+14	59+9
70	60+7	61+3	62+0	62+16	63+13	64+9	65+6	66+2	66+19	67+15
80	68+13	69+8	70+6	71+2	71+19	72+15	73+13	74+9	75+6	76+2
90	77+0	77+16	78+13	79+9	80+7	81+4	82+0	82+18	83+14	84+11
100	85+7	86+5	87+1	87+19	88+16	89+12	90+10	91+6	92+4	93+0
110	93+18	94+15	95+11	96+9	97+5	98+3	98+19	99+17	100+14	101+1

	8	16	24	32	40	48	56	64	72	80
-25	7.2	14.4	21.6	28.7	35.8	42.8	49.8	56.8	63.7	70.6
-20	7.5	15.0	22.4	29.8	37.2	44.5	51.8	59.1	66.4	73.6
-15	7.7	15.4	23.1	30.7	38.3	45.9	53.5	61.0	68.5	76.0
-10	7.9	15.7	23.6	31.4	39.2	47.0	54.7	62.5	70.2	77.9
-5	8.0	15.9	23.9	31.8	39.7	47.7	55.6	63.5	71.4	79.2
0	8	16	24	32	40	48	56	64	72	80
5	8.0	16.0	23.9	32.0	40.0	48.0	56.0	64.0	72.1	80.2
10	7.9	15.8	23.7	31.7	39.6	47.6	55.6	63.6	71.6	79.7
15	7.7	15.5	23.3	31.1	39.0	46.8	54.7	62.7	70.6	78.6
20	7.5	15.1	22.7	30.3	38.0	45.7	53.5	61.3	69.1	76.9
25	7.3	14.6	21.9	29.3	36.8	44.2	51.8	59.3	67.0	74.6

feet	0	1	2	3	4	5	6	7	8	9
0	~~~	~~~	~~~	~~~	94+10	75+19	63+13	55+0	48+13	43+14
10	38+19	36+0	33+11	31+10	29+17	28+7	27+2	26+1	25+3	24+7
20	23+10	22+19	22+9	22+0	21+13	21+6	21+0	20+15	20+12	20+7
30	20+4	20+3	20+1	19+18	19+18	19+18	19+18	19+18	19+19	20+0
yards	0	1	2	3	4	5	6	7	8	9
10	20+4	19+18	19+18	20+0	20+2	20+7	20+14	21+2	21+10	22+0
20	22+10	23+1	23+13	24+4	24+17	25+10	26+2	26+15	27+10	28+3
30	28+18	29+11	30+5	31+1	31+15	32+10	33+5	33+19	34+15	35+10
40	36+6	37+1	37+18	38+12	39+7	40+3	40+18	41+14	42+10	43+5
50	44+2	44+17	45+14	46+10	47+5	48+2	48+17	49+14	50+10	51+7
60	52+2	52+19	53+15	54+11	55+8	56+4	57+1	57+17	58+14	59+9
70	60+7	61+3	62+0	62+16	63+13	64+9	65+6	66+2	66+19	67+15
80	68+13	69+8	70+6	71+2	71+19	72+15	73+13	74+9	75+6	76+2
90	77+0	77+16	78+13	79+9	80+7	81+4	82+0	82+18	83+14	84+11
100	85+7	86+5	87+1	87+19	88+16	89+12	90+10	91+6	92+4	93+0
110	93+18	94+15	95+11	96+9	97+5	98+3	98+19	99+17	100+14	101+1

	8	16	24	32	40	48	56	64	72	80
-25	7.2	14.4	21.8	28.7	35.8	42.8	49.8	56.8	63.7	70.6
-20	7.5	15.0	22.4	29.8	37.2	44.5	51.8	59.1	66.4	73.6
-15	7.7	15.4	23.1	30.7	38.3	45.9	53.5	61.0	68.5	76.0
-10	7.9	15.7	23.6	31.4	39.2	47.0	54.7	62.5	70.2	77.9
-5	8.0	15.9	23.9	31.8	39.7	47.7	55.6	63.5	71.4	79.2
0	8	16	24	32	40	48	56	64	72	80
5	8.0	16.0	23.9	32.0	40.0	48.0	56.0	64.0	72.1	80.2
10	7.9	15.8	23.7	31.7	39.6	47.6	55.6	63.6	71.6	79.7
15	7.7	15.5	23.3	31.1	39.0	46.8	54.7	62.7	70.6	78.6
20	7.5	15.1	22.7	30.3	38.0	45.7	53.5	61.3	69.1	76.9
25	7.3	14.6	21.9	29.3	36.8	44.2	51.8	59.3	67.0	74.6

bit larger than a standard 4x6 index card, but, if you so chose, you could scan it into your computer as a picture and size it accordingly without losing hardly any detail.

Summary

I do not profess to be the expert when it concerns all of the features, nuances, and corrections that can be had in using *On Target 2*. What I have given you are tips based upon my experience with successfully getting accurate sight tapes out of the system without having to apply any of the corrections and arrays of different features within the program. I don't think any of those corrections would make me more accurate, since I simply cannot hold my bow that steady anymore and lack the skills of the top professional archers of today.

So, there you have it. I've given you a quick seminar on how to effectively utilize two systems in unison in order to gather all your sight settings in one shooting session and use one with the other to get as accurate a sight tape as you are capable of. I've outlined what I consider to be the simplest method of doing this that is ProActive and gives you the best chance of not only saving time and money, but also provides you backup systems that are handy and easily retrievable. If you've taken the time to read all three of these chapters, I've provided you information on how to utilize three systems together as a group of checks and balances.

Remember to go out on the range afterwards and check your sight marks, because as I've said, a ProActive archer never "goes into battle with an untested weapon."

36

My Personal Process to Get Perfect Sight Settings

I'm sure that after reading the last three chapters, you are asking yourself why on Earth would I use all three systems to get my sight settings? Why not just choose one and stick with it? The main answer is that it is all about data gathering and accuracy and, shocking though it may be—these programs give different results from the same data! A couple of clicks when shooting up close may not matter much, but those same couple of clicks at long distance can make a big difference in your final score.

In Chapter 32 I offered up what I consider a better method of getting my main distance sight settings for entry into the Calculator Based system, along with getting those that I routinely use for entry into *On Target Two* and *Archer's Advantage*. (I used the same 20 and 65 yard settings as a standard of comparison.) That sight mark determination process involves shooting at a horizontal tape across either a target or a blank piece of cardboard/poster paper. I mentioned that vertical impact points are more important than horizontal when determining elevation sight settings.

Chapter 33 was about the Calculator Based System I've used since the early 1980's. It involves getting accurate 20 and 65 yard marks, and then, using a "Calculations Table" to calculate sight settings out to 80 yards. I then demonstrated how to perform the calculations including "automating" them by using a simple MS *Excel* spreadsheet. Keep this spreadsheet in mind as we progress through this chapter. It will be brought up again.

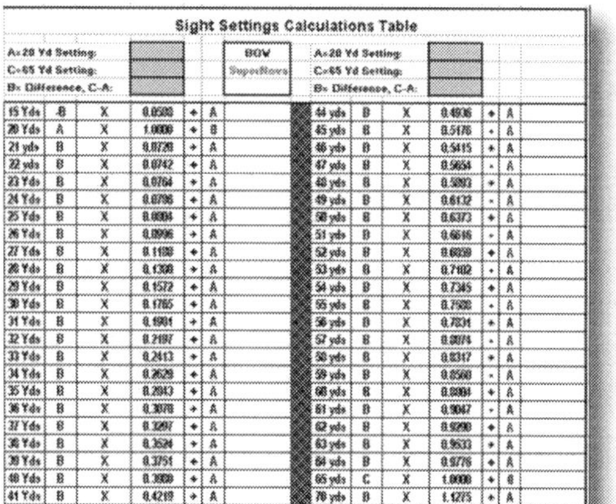
Sight Settings Calculations Table

A=20 Yd Setting:
C=65 Yd Setting:
B= Difference, C-A:

BOW
SuperBows

15 Yds	-B	X	0.0503	+	A
20 Yds	A	X	1.0000	+	B
21 yds	B	X	0.0720	+	A
22 yds	B	X	0.0742	+	A
23 Yds	B	X	0.0764	+	A
24 Yds	B	X	0.0786	+	A
25 Yds	B	X	0.0804	+	A
26 Yds	B	X	0.0996	+	A
27 Yds	B	X	0.1180	+	A
28 Yds	B	X	0.1380	+	A
29 Yds	B	X	0.1572	+	A
30 Yds	B	X	0.1765	+	A
31 Yds	B	X	0.1981	+	A
32 Yds	B	X	0.2197	+	A
33 Yds	B	X	0.2413	+	A
34 Yds	B	X	0.2629	+	A
35 Yds	B	X	0.2843	+	A
36 Yds	B	X	0.3070	+	A
37 Yds	B	X	0.3297	+	A
38 Yds	B	X	0.3524	+	A
39 Yds	B	X	0.3751	+	A
40 Yds	B	X	0.3980	+	A
41 Yds	B	X	0.4219	+	A
42 Yds	B	X	0.4458	+	A
43 Yds	B	X	0.4697	+	A

A=20 Yd Setting:
C=65 Yd Setting:
B= Difference, C-A:

44 yds	B	X	0.4936	+	A
45 yds	B	X	0.5176	+	A
46 yds	B	X	0.5415	+	A
47 yds	B	X	0.5654	+	A
48 yds	B	X	0.5893	+	A
49 yds	B	X	0.6132	+	A
50 yds	B	X	0.6373	+	A
51 yds	B	X	0.6616	+	A
52 yds	B	X	0.6859	+	A
53 yds	B	X	0.7102	+	A
54 yds	B	X	0.7345	+	A
55 yds	B	X	0.7588	+	A
56 yds	B	X	0.7831	+	A
57 yds	B	X	0.8074	+	A
58 yds	B	X	0.8317	+	A
59 yds	B	X	0.8560	+	A
60 yds	B	X	0.8804	+	A
61 yds	B	X	0.9047	+	A
62 yds	B	X	0.9290	+	A
63 yds	B	X	0.9533	+	A
64 yds	B	X	0.9776	+	A
65 yds	C	X	1.0000	+	B
70 yds	B	X	1.1275	+	A
80 yds	B	X	1.3920	+	A

Remember this?

Chapter 34 addressed the use of *Archer's Advantage* software as another means of obtaining and printing out sight settings tables, sight tapes, and cut charts. This system calculates settings out to 150 yards based upon the two sight setting entries you place into the system. Of course, my standard is to shoot in 20 and 65 yards and then let *Archer's Advantage* calculate my sight marks from those two input distances. The lines on the tapes can be color coded, but the yardages are only labeled as 1, 2, 3, 4, etc; or 10, 20, 30, 40, etc. In addition we went through how to prepare your finished sight tape for mounting and how to mount the sight tape to your vertical bar without stretching the paper. I also demonstrated how easy it is to misread your sight settings if you don't place the indicator pointer or magnifier in the same relationship to your eye each time. The photos showed clearly how a "magnifier can magnify a sight setting error" even though the sight tape is correct!

Chapter 35 focused upon using *On Target 2* software as the third means of obtaining and printing out sight settings tables, sight tapes, and also the means of printing out Targets and 3-D animals. I mentioned that *On Target 2* allows you to input five distances and also provides a means of a cross checking between and among those five distances by calculate arrow speeds based upon your sight marks. Its sight tapes can be color-coded and you can also have the option to print yardage numbers as multiples of five: 15, 20, 25, 30, 35, etc, which is a very nice option to have. I repeated how to go about preparing a sight tape for mounting and how to mount the sight tape on your vertical bar without stretching the paper. I also demonstrated how easy it is to misread your sight tapes if you don't place the indicator pointer or magnifier in the same relationship to your eye each time you set your sight.

This chapter will detail my personal process to ensure I have the most accurate sight settings possible.

My Process

Here is an outline of how I use the processes I've detailed in the past three chapters.

1. The Calculator Based Method works very well, but does have limitations (explained in Chapter 33). You can compare the placards created from the three different systems and they aren't all that far apart, which is why the Calculator Method is first in this series of Chapters about getting sight settings. It is fast and easy and doesn't need a computer and can be done at the range.

   I can go to the outdoor range, get a 20 and 65 yard setting, calculate the others, shoot in the bunny target distances and the other yard settings not covered on the Calculations Table and have them recorded on a blank or old placard in pencil without ever leaving the range (see Photo 1 above). I can even shoot a round or two to confirm those calculated sight marks and refine them while I'm out on the course and recalculate if necessary. The scribed numbers on the sight bar don't change. You will remember that once I've zeroed the indicator pointer, I don't move it again. In the old days when the sights didn't have the "clicks" system on them, it wasn't a huge deal to move the pointer if you were consis-

	field	1914		tom
B	21.8	S	41	36.6
10	20.1	P	44	39.0
11	19.9	R	45	39.8
14	20.0	N	48	42.2
15	20.5	O	50	43.8
17	20.8	V	52	45.4
19	21.4	A	53	46.2
20	22.5		55	47.8
23	25.05	1	58	50.3
25	25.2	9	59	51.1
28	27.1	1	60	51.9
30	28.4	4	61	52.7
32	29.8		64	55.2
35	32.0	8	65	55.9
36	32.8	1	70	60.2
40	35.8	0	80	69.0

tently hitting high or low. You could normally correct that slight error by getting "on" with your mark and then simply move the pointer. I have always preferred to bump the peep sight slightly up or down, however, as long as it wasn't anything large, that is.

2. I can then go home, plug the pretty well confirmed sight marks into *Archer's Advantage*, checking the numbers I'm going to use for entry into OT2 the sight marks tables and tapes.
3. I then compare the "outputs" of the two systems, making notes of any "ringers" (normally these are the shorter distances not covered by the Calculator Method and a few tenths on the 70 and 80 yard marks), and then mount a placard of the most trusted. Note that I didn't say that I mounted a sight tape. You can see in Photo 3 the "combined" print out of placards for all three systems in decimal format. Note how close the sight settings are among the three systems. Even though the speeds that are calculated by AA and OT2 are only 0.16 foot per second different, you can see differences among the sight settings calculated by each program. Please also note that for the Calculator Based Method and the *Archer's Advantage* system, the 20 and 65 yard settings are the same. However, in spite of the same number being entered into OT2 for that 65 yard mark, you see a difference: the Calculator Based Method and OT2 both say 55.90 (that is what they were given), while OT2, by comparing sight settings among five different settings has adjusted the setting to 56.20. This is only six clicks different, but at the lower draw weight I now shoot, and at that distance, it is an indicator that perhaps my data is slightly incorrect. You can see this comparison in the screen shot below.

You can enter five distances in *On Target 2* instead of just two in *Archer's Advantage*. It also gives me the option of having five-yard increment numbers printed onto the tape (25, 35, 45, 55 yards). In addition, *On Target 2* allows me to toggle between decimals and "clicks" for my sight settings, while both the

	field	1914		tom	Archer's Advantage					On Target 2				
B	21.8	S	41	36.6	B	20.20	S	41	36.50	B	23.50	S	41	37.05
10	20.1	P	44	39.0	10	20.20	P	44	38.80	10	20.20	P	44	39.35
11	19.9	R	45	39.8	11	20.00	R	45	39.50	11	19.90	R	45	40.15
14	20.0	N	48	42.2	14	20.20	N	48	41.90	14	20.10	N	48	42.50
15	20.5	O	50	43.8	15	20.50	O	50	43.50	15	20.35	O	50	44.10
17	20.8	V	52	45.4	17	21.10	V	52	45.10	17	21.10	V	52	45.70
19	21.4	A	53	46.2	19	22.00	A	53	45.90	19	22.00	A	53	46.50
20	22.5		55	47.8	20	22.50		55	47.50	20	22.50		55	48.10
23	25.05	1	58	50.3	23	24.10	1	58	50.00	23	24.20	1	58	50.50
25	25.2	9	59	51.1	25	25.30	9	59	50.80	25	25.50	9	59	51.35
28	27.1	1	60	51.9	28	28.50	1	60	51.70	28	27.50	1	60	52.10
30	28.4	4	61	52.7	30	28.75	4	61	52.50	30	28.90	4	61	52.95
32	29.8		64	55.2	32	29.90		64	55.00	32	30.25		64	55.40
35	32.0	8	65	55.9	35	32.00	8	65	55.90	35	32.50	8	65	56.20
36	32.8	1	70	60.2	36	32.80	1	70	60.20	36	33.25	1	70	60.35
40	35.8	0	80	69.0	40	35.70	0	80	69.00	40	36.30	0	80	68.65

Calculator System and *Archer's Advantage* generate all settings in decimal format.

4. For the next couple of days, I go to the range with the "most trusted" placard mounted and shoot a couple of full rounds and make note of anything that doesn't come in correctly (rare, but it sometimes happens). I still have my Calculator Based Method placard with me, along with the Calculations Table. In addition, I have the 3x5 Sight Settings and Cut Chart printout from *On Target 2* with me as well. Remember that I stated that *On Target 2* allows you to toggle between decimal and "clicks" print out formats? The photo below represents the print-out for the placard from OT2, but instead of decimals, it has the "clicks" entered in and I don't have to do any mental work. I simply count the clicks from the main number down (or subtract the number of clicks from "20" and move up).

On Target 2

B	23•10	S	41	37•1
10	20•4	P	44	39•7
11	19•18	R	45	40•3
14	20•2	N	48	42•10
15	20•7	O	50	44•2
17	21•2	V	52	45•14
19	22•0	A	53	46•10
20	22•1		55	48•2
23	24•4	1	58	50•10
25	25•10	9	59	51•7
28	27•10	1	60	52•2
30	28•18	4	61	52•19
32	30•5		64	55•8
35	32•10	8	65	56•4
36	33•5	1	70	60•7
40	36•6	0	80	68•13

I won't mount that sight tape until I'm sure the "numbers" are correct or, at least, as good as I can get them! I use my placards to check everything because printing and mounting a placard less fuss than mounting a sight tape. ProActive archery comes into play, and I don't waste the effort for a printed sight tape until I know my results are what they need to be.

Plus the placard system is really handy for jotting down settings that aren't quite right, and if necessary, you can go back into your sight tape generating program and tweak those settings a nudge (most times at this juncture I don't need any tweaks, or if I do, it is only a few clicks) to get an even better tape. As you can see from the placard photos, I have space to the right to allow me to pencil in any changes to those settings if need be. That becomes my input document for the next iteration of settings.

The first yardages to be checked are the easiest, and also they are the ones that are not included in the Calculator Based System; those being the settings for the Bunny/Birdie target. I use the ones that *Archer's Advantage* and *On Target 2* tell me they should be, and if they aren't right, then I make note of the correct settings on the placard.

As careful as I am with regard to measuring peep height and sight radius, there is a potential that the 20´, 25´, 30´, 11 yard, and 35´ settings could be wrong. Some people are able to use the same setting for all four distances. From years of experience, I have found that I don't have very good luck by "aiming off" to the top or bottom of the spot. Thus, I still shoot them in and then refine them as needed.

Note the "B" on my sight setting placard (*see first photos*); the "B" setting (stands for "Bunny/Birdie") is for the 20 foot and 25 foot shots, while the "10" is for the 35 and 30 foot shots. I then shoot in the 11, 14, 17 & 19 yard settings and then, once I've finished getting the calculator based settings out on the range, I come home and generate the settings tables from both *Archer's Advantage* and *On Target 2* for a final confirmation. This actually simplifies the process because I am able to get very solid settings out on the range.

5. At my leisure, I then print out the sight tapes, update the placard to the one that is as perfect as I can get it, print and mount the new and final placard.

Did you note the "810" at the bottom of the center column on the placards? That is code for the month and day of the placard! Yes, there is a system to all this. Are you surprised? Note that the bow name and arrow size are in that same column! I have redundant systems for a very solid reason: you won't catch me out on the course with a bad set of sight settings trying to shoot a score, nor will you catch me without back-ups in place for the placard and sight tape. I must have learned that from my military service where most all aircraft systems were redundant, along with always having more than one back-up plan for when a mission turns crazy. I also have backup "plans" because Murphy always seems to rear his ugly mug at the wrong time.

You will obviously be making your own choices as to which program or sight tape system you use. For me, the reasons that I use *On Target 2* for the printed sight tape are simply because:

1. Being able to use five shot-in sight marks is very advantageous in that it that points out errors between them (by calculating arrows speeds based on pairs of those marks). I expect a reduction in bow speed as the distance increases, so if I have a speed increase between 50 and 80 yards, there likely is a problem with the longer setting.
2. *On Target 2* prints out sight tapes with labels in five-yard increments: 25, 35, 45, 55, etc. while AA doesn't have this capability. See the photo below for a comparison of the two sight tapes. Both are easy to read, but I simply like the numbers printing out for each five yards for another visual cue to help avoid incorrectly setting my sight. The photo shows the differences in appearance more clearly. *On Target 2*'s sight tape is on the left, and *Archer's Advantage*'s sight tape is on the right.
3. I use the placard system as my primary sight marks and the printed tape is only a third backup. I have a blank "Sight Settings Calculations Sheet" prepared and ready for 20 and 65 yard sight settings to compute any settings I need right on the spot. I have the *On Target 2* Cut Chart and the *On Target 2* Sight Settings table for yardages not on my placard, and, last, I also have the printed sight tape (*see photo next page*).
4. I like the sizes of the printouts for the Cut Chart and Individual Sight Marks Tables out of *On Target 2*. I simply cut those Tables out, fold them in half, which makes for one double sided 3x5 card, laminate that, and put it into my quiver.

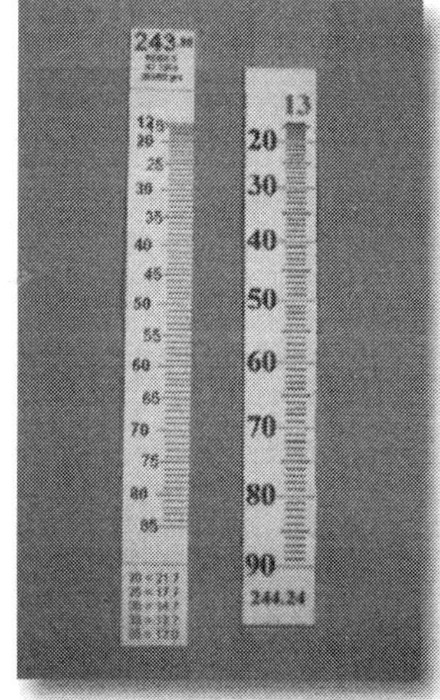

You are probably thinking that this is overkill and a lot

of extra work for nothing. In reality, it really involves a system of cross checks, and takes less time to do than to describe. This is a sure fire way of making sure that everything has been tested and retested so you go into battle with a tested and proven weapon.

feet	0	1	2	3	4	5	6	7	8	9
0	---	---	---	---	94+10	75+18	63+13	55+0	48+13	43+14
10	38+19	36+0	33+11	31+10	29+17	28+7	27+2	26+1	25+3	24+7
20	23+10	22+19	22+9	22+0	21+13	21+6	21+0	20+15	20+12	20+7
30	20+4	20+3	20+1	19+18	19+18	19+18	19+18	19+18	19+19	20+0
yards	0	1	2	3	4	5	6	7	8	9
10	20+4	19+18	19+18	20+0	20+2	20+7	20+14	21+2	21+10	22+0
20	22+10	23+1	23+13	24+4	24+17	25+10	26+2	26+15	27+10	28+3
30	28+18	29+11	30+5	31+1	31+15	32+10	33+5	33+19	34+15	35+10
40	36+6	37+1	37+16	38+12	39+7	40+3	40+18	41+14	42+10	43+5
50	44+2	44+17	45+14	46+10	47+5	48+2	48+17	49+14	50+10	51+7
60	52+2	52+19	53+15	54+11	55+8	56+4	57+1	57+17	58+14	59+9
70	60+7	61+3	62+0	62+16	63+13	64+8	65+6	66+2	66+19	67+15
80	68+13	69+8	70+6	71+2	71+19	72+15	73+13	74+9	75+6	76+2
90	77+0	77+16	78+13	79+9	80+7	81+4	82+0	82+18	83+14	84+11
100	85+7	86+5	87+1	87+19	88+15	89+12	90+10	91+6	92+4	93+0
110	93+18	94+15	95+11	96+8	97+5	98+3	98+19	99+17	100+14	101+11

	8	16	24	32	40	48	56	64	72	80
-25	7.2	14.4	21.6	28.7	35.8	42.8	49.8	56.8	63.7	70.6
-20	7.5	15.0	22.4	29.8	37.2	44.5	51.8	59.1	66.4	73.8
-15	7.7	15.4	23.1	30.7	38.3	45.9	53.5	61.0	68.5	76.0
-10	7.9	15.7	23.6	31.4	39.2	47.0	54.7	62.5	70.2	77.9
-5	8.0	15.9	23.9	31.8	39.7	47.7	55.6	63.5	71.4	79.2
0	8	16	24	32	40	48	56	64	72	80
5	8.0	16.0	23.9	32.0	40.0	48.0	56.0	64.0	72.1	80.2
10	7.9	15.8	23.7	31.7	39.6	47.6	55.6	63.6	71.6	79.7
15	7.7	15.5	23.3	31.1	39.0	46.8	54.7	62.7	70.6	78.5
20	7.5	15.1	22.7	30.3	38.0	45.7	53.5	61.3	69.1	76.9
25	7.3	14.6	21.9	29.3	36.8	44.2	51.6	59.3	67.0	74.6

Making and Mounting the Placard to the Sight Extension Bar

If you haven't read about how to make a Placard yet, this time I am sending you back to Chapter 33 instead of repeating it here. The placard sits right next to your sight bar so you can see both easily at the same time, minimizing mistakes.

How to Set up an Excel Spreadsheet to Do Most of the Work for You

Automating these processes with an MS Excel Spreadsheet is easily done, so that once you enter in your 20 and 65 yard sight settings, all the placards and other sight marks (via the Calculator Based Method) will be automatically completed. Since there aren't any links to of from Archer's Advantage or On Target 2 to do this directly, you'll have to type your settings into those placards manually, which only takes a few minutes.

The key things are making sure you enter the formulas correctly and that you set up the column widths and row heights correctly so that the print-outs will fit onto the credit card sized o(r smaller, if you prefer) placards. This isn't complicated, and once you have it done it the first time, you won't have to do it again unless you change the sizing of the placards.

Items Needed

1. Microsoft *Excel* or similar spreadsheet software.
2. calculator for calculating formula entries (for checking purposes).
3. Calculation Based Sight Settings Calculations Table (see Photo 9), which doesn't have to be completed; you only need the multipliers in order to enter those into the *Excel* Spreadsheet as part of each formula.
4. *Archer's Advantage* Sight Settings Print-out
5. *On Target 2* Sight Settings Table
6. color Printer
7. printer paper.

How to Prepare the MS Excel Spreadsheet I'm not going to detail each and every step of preparing the Excel spreadsheet; to do so would take many pages of print-screens and instructions. I will provide the "basics" and a listing of Column Widths and Row Heights that are set up for my Hewlett-Packard Inkjet printers (works the same for both of my printers. Are you surprised that I have two printers? By now, you shouldn't be!). I will then provide you with a couple of examples of formula entries that will save you a lot of time in trying to figure out how to do them and how to continue working the same basic formula, but with only one "number" different in each formula you type into *Excel.*

This is a process that will save you hours of work after the initial set up of your spreadsheet. I will be referring to the following screen shots.

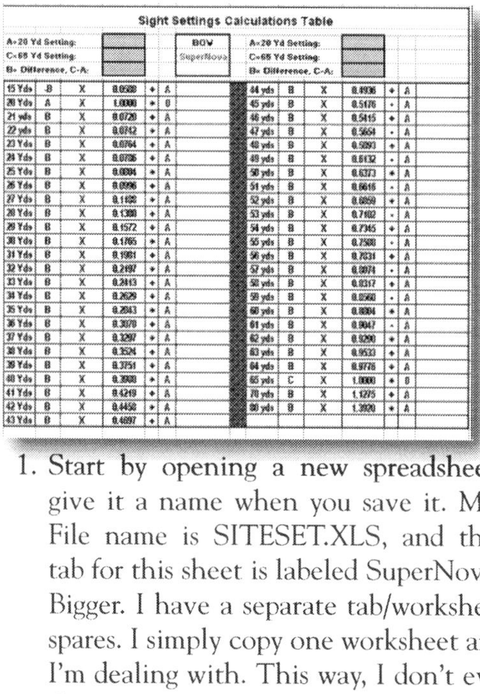

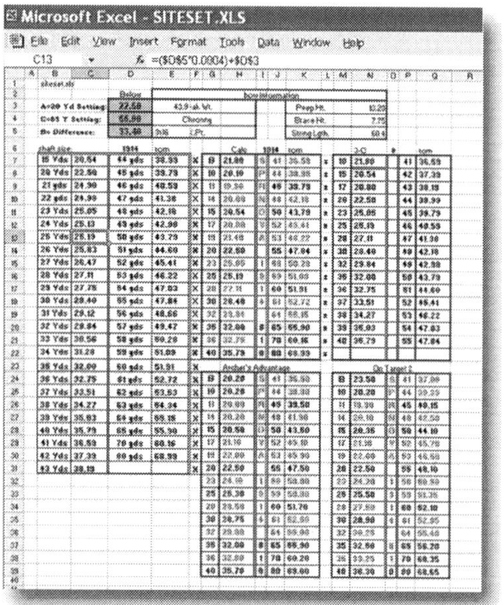

1. Start by opening a new spreadsheet give it a name when you save it. My File name is SITESET.XLS, and the tab for this sheet is labeled SuperNova Bigger. I have a separate tab/worksheet in Excel for each bow I have and a few spares. I simply copy one worksheet and then re-name the tab to the specific bow I'm dealing with. This way, I don't ever have to re-type any formulas or do anything tedious! There is nothing wrong with using your first worksheet as the template, copy it to a new Tab and re-name the tab.
2. Click on "File," then Page Setup; leave the orientation as Portrait.
3. To set the margins click on the Margins tab in Page Setup and set the margins as follows: Top: 1; Bottom 1; Left: 0.25; Right 0.25. Header: 0.25; Footer: 0.25. Then click "OK."
4. Set the font style and size for the spreadsheet as follows: Arial Narrow, Size: 10. You can do this for the entire spreadsheet by clicking the block above Row 1 and to the left of Column A. This selects the entire spreadsheet for font sizing. Then you simply select "Arial Narrow" from the drop down list and "10" from the font size drop down list.
5. Set the column widths in pixels as follows (see Photo 10): Column A–24; Col. B–60; Col C–66; Col D–78; Col E–66; Col F–22; Col G–33; Col H–64; Col I–21; Col J–33; Col K–64; Col L–22; Col M–33; Col N–64; Col O–21; Col P–33; and Col Q–64. You can do each column, one at a time by selecting the column, holding down the left mouse button and dragging the width until you get the width

pixels you want and let off the left mouse button.

6. Set the row heights as follows, using the same procedure, but this time selecting rows by using the clicking the left mouse and dragging it down for the rows you want to be the same height: Row 1–18; Row 2–37 pixels; Rows 3, 4, & 5–22 pixels; Row 6–28 pixels; Rows 7 through 39–22 pixels in height. Again, you can do each row one at a time.

You have now completed the Orientation, Page setup, Column Widths, Row Heights, and font sizing for the entire spread sheet. Next, you have to start typing in the information as depicted in the last screen shot.

- Column A is blank.
- Cell B1 is your <filename>, mine is "siteset.xls." It tells you the name of the file.
- Cell D2 Type in "Type Below." This is a reminder that you type in whatever your sight settings are for your 20 and 65 yard settings. You will not type numbers into Cell D5, since that has a "formula" entered into it. To set it so that "Type Below" appears as depicted in Photo 10, click on "Format", then "Cells...," then "Alignment," and then under Text Control, click on the Wrap text box, and click on "OK."
- Cell B3 Type in "A=20yd Setting"
- Cell B4 Type in "C=65 Y Setting"
- Cell B5: Type in "B = Difference." In cell D5, type in the following formula (formulas in MS *Excel* always begin with an equal sign, "="). Note It is important that you type in the formulas as depicted. So, in Cell D5, type in the formula: =$D$4–$D$3 then press "Enter" or click on the green arrow that appears, so that the formula is completed. You never type anything into Cell D5 again from this point forward! If you do, you erase your formula and will have to do it over. The dollar signs make that a specific cell reference that won't change should you move things around. If you want to make the type boldface, you simply select the cell you want bold type for and then click on the "B" button on the toolbar.

For the other cells in Rows 3, 4, & 5, you can type in whatever you want, or leave that area blank, your choices or use your ingenuity; this is your spreadsheet.

Inputting the Yardages into the Spreadsheet Now we get into the real "meat" of the spreadsheet. I recommend that you do Columns B, D, F, G, H, I (if you want, or leave Column I blank (it is a filler space); then Columns J, L, M, O, and P, since none of those have formulas in them.

7. You can either type in the numbers one at a time, or if the numbers sequence in order, you can use the AutoFill feature of MS *Excel.* For example: in Cell B7, you type in 15 yds and press the Enter key and the cursor moves down to cell B8. You then type in 20 yd press enter and the cursor goes to Cell B9. Type in 21 yd into cell B9 and press Enter. Then, move the cursor onto Cell B8 and click on it. Keeping the left mouse button depressed drag down to highlight both cells B8 & B9. Once they are highlighted, then you will see a box in the lower right corner of Cell B9. Move your cursor over onto the box until it makes a bold "+" sign.

Once you have that, you can then press and hold the left mouse button and drag it straight down row B until you have highlighted through cell B31 and the let up on the left mouse button. Excel will "automatically fill in" all you need from Cell B9 on thru Cell B31 for you! It even tells you, with a yellow bar, what is going into each cell. If you make a mistake, you can always "undo" (CTRLS) the previous action.

8. Move over to Cell D7, only this time type in "44," for 44 yd, into cell D7, 45 into cell D8, and then auto-fill down to cell D30.
9. For Cells F7 – F31, type in "X" for F7 and F8, and auto-fill down thru cell F31, and X's will be filled in for you.
10. Starting in Cell G7, you'll type in a "B", then in G8 a "10" and then follow the sequence as depicted. The same goes for the rest of Rows G, I, J, L M, O, & P, from rows 7 through 39.
11. To "Color Code" your data, simply select the cells you want to color the same and then hold down the CTRL key and select the next cells that you want the same color. When you have selected all the cells you want in that color (in this case, it would be light blue, since black is the default), you can then click on the box in the tool bar that has a big "A" with a black bar under it and a drop arrow box to the right. Click on the drop arrow box, and select the light blue. Then all those cells you have selected will appear and print in light blue. You can now do the same for rows H, K, N, & Q, only this time you will highlight those that are depicted in red and then once you have them selected, click on that big "A" with the bar under it and down arrow to the right, select the color Red, and you are done. It is no big deal to do these one at a time. There are other ways, but it requires way more key strokes, and this isn't complicated. If you make a mistake in color of font, you can fix it later. Once again, you can do this one cell at a time, if you so choose.

Typing In the Formulas You are now ready to start typing in your formulas. The "multipliers" are obtained from the Sight Settings Calculations Table (*see previous screen shot on left*). Once you have typed in a couple of formulas, you will get into the swing of it, and it moves along quickly. We will fill out the individual sight settings portion of the spreadsheet first.

12. Below are several examples of the formula that you will be typing into each cell up through 25 yards; after that, you should know how to go it on your own. We will fill in the individual yardage area cells C7 through C31, and then D7 through D30 first, since those are all yard by yard for all sight settings needed on a field or animal round (excluding those exceptions discussed in Chapter 33). Again, once your formulas are entered, you never have to type anything into these cells again.

    If what you type into Cell D3 and D4 changes, once you press the enter key, then cell D5 will automatically change, and you will get a resultant calculation for the tables, excepting those for *Archer's Advantage* and *On Target 2* (those have to be done manually). So, you type in two numbers and the entire spreadsheet of tables (except AA and OT2) change to the "new numbers" automatically; how's that for slick and easy?

- Select Cell C7, and type in the following EXACTLY (you don't have to capitalize the "D" in the formula, I do it for clarity and emphasis' sake): =$D$3-($D$5*0.0588) and press enter. This is for the 15 yard calculation, and the multiplier comes from your Sight Settings Calculations Table. The cursor should be now on Cell C8
- Select Cell C8, and type in exactly: $D$3 ; You are telling Excel to take what is in Cell D3 and put that same number into Cell D8. (Your 20 yard sight setting). Press enter and the cursor moves to Cell C9.
- Select Cell C9 and type in exactly: =($D$5*0.072)+$D$3 This is telling Excel to take B (difference between your 20 and 65 yard settings), multiply that result times 0.0720, and then add A (your 20 yard setting) to it for the final result. Easy, isn't it? *Tip* Spaces are not allowed in formulas!
- Select Cell C10 and type in exactly: =($D$5*0.0764)+$D$3 and press enter. You cursor should go to cell C11
- If not, Select Cell C11 and type in exactly: =($D$5*0.0554)+$D$3 and press Enter. The cursor should move to Cell C12.
- If not, select Cell C12 and type in exactly: =($D$5*0.0786)+$D$3 and then press Enter. Your cursor should move to Cell C13, if not
- Select Cell C13 and type in exactly: =($D$5* 0.0804)+$D$3 and press enter.
- Select Cell C14, and continue on typing in the formula for each distance, using the multiplier for that distance from your Calculations Table (Pic #9). YES! There is a quick way of doing this, but for me to explain that would take more pages of explanation and it can get tricky for someone new to Excel. You could auto fill the formulas starting with Cell C9 and auto-fill down to Cell C31. Then you go in and simply change the multiplier for each distance. That would be quicker, since the only part of the formula that is different is that multiplier after the * in each formula. If you feel brave, then you can do it that way. I find, however in having taught many people this, they almost always prefer to do this one by one.
- Then, you move over to Column E to do those formulas:
- Select Cell E7 and type in exactly: =($D$5*0.4936)+$D$3 and press enter.
- Continue that sequence down Column E until you are done with the 80 yard setting. This completes the individual distance table, and gives you the quick reference for use on the range, and in addition, a cross-check of your formula typing in Cells H7 through H22; Cells K7 through K22, Cells N7 through N22, and Cells Q7 through Q22. If you choose to copy/paste the formulas over from the individual settings table this will work, since you have a permanent reference to those cells (that is what those "$" signs in the formulas do for you!). You just have to be very, very careful that you copy the formula you want into the correct cell on the other two tables. It is quicker than typing those formulas three times!

Copy/Pasting Formulas from Individual Yardages to Field/Hunter and 3-D Placards Here's an example of how to copy/paste those formulas more easily once you are done with the individual yardage calculations table. I'll demonstrate how to copy your formula for your 35 yard sight setting over to the placards in only a few clicks of the mouse.

- You start this by first right clicking on Cell C23 to select it (Cell C23 contains the formula for your 35 yard sight setting). Next, left click your mouse on "Copy". Then, simply move over to cell H20 (which is your 35 yard setting on the placard), right click on it and then left click on "Paste". Your formula from C23 for 35 yards is now copied over to Cell H20 which is the 35 yard setting on your sight settings placard. To get that formula over to your 3-D settings placard, you then Right click your mouse on cell N16 (35 yards on your 3-D settings placard), and then right click 'Paste', and the formula is copied from Cell C23 to Cell N16 also. Again, you can do those two repetitions of "pasting", but once you change something, then your pasting days are over until next time.
- You then simply follow the same pattern by selecting each yardage on each placard and copy/paste the formula from the main Excel Yardages table over to your placards until you have all the formulas copied over.

  Note Never type any numbers into columns C, E, K, L, N, or Q. Should you do so, you will erase your formula in that cell and unless you have a backup (discussed a bit later on), you will lose your information and have to re-enter it. If you mistakenly type into one of those columns, you can undo the past actions, by clicking the undo button on the toolbar, or by clicking on "Edit", then "Undo". Now you know why you should print out and save a copy of the "Calculator Based Calculations Table" as well as making a tab in your spreadsheet for another back-up.

Archer's Advantage and OT2 Placards Data Entry I don't want to get so fancy as to link up an *Excel* import from *Archer's Advantage* to this spreadsheet, which could be done, but I figure it is quicker and easier to simply type in the sight setting numbers manually. So, using your *Archer's Advantage* printout of individual yardages, you simply type them into the *Archer's Advantage* placard in sequence in Cells H24-H39; and then K24-K29.

Then, you do the same for your Placard for OT2 by using the Yardage Table Printout from OT2 and type those settings into Cells N24-N39; and Q24-Q39. The columns are set wide enough so that you can choose to either use the Decimal System or the "clicks" system. I've used both, and either of them works just fine.

Formatting your Placards for Color Coding The last thing you have to do is to Color Code your Yardages on your three Sight Settings placards; those being the Calculations Placard, the *Archer's Advantage* placard, and the OT2 placard. Getting colors into cells was explained above for doing the individual yards. It is the same procedure for doing the red coloration for the sight settings used on the Hunter Round outdoors. You can both select each cell individually and "color" them by clicking on the drop down arrow next to the big "A" with the bar under it, or you can select a cell, hold down the "CTRL" key and left click on each cell that you would like to have the contents to have that color. When you have selected all those cells you want to print in "RED", then you click on that drop down box next to the big "A" with the bar under it and all those cells will then be displayed in red. Black is the default color, so this is a "rule by exception" situation. There is no need to color code the 3-D placard, so I just leave the print color as the default black.

A *Tip—Make a Custom Footer* Here's a tip on locating your computer's file location from a printout. I've taught this for many years and it is worth the time to do it for most all of your important things. I recommend the use of a custom "footer" at the bottom of each page. Here's how to create a custom footer:

1. Click on "File", then click on "Page Setup...."
2. Click on the "Header/Footer Tab"
3. Click on "Custom Footer" Button
4. Under left section, you can select the following: There are five sets of buttons above the white boxes. The fourth set over from the left are file locator buttons. I recommend that you, unless you specifically know what you are doing, at least click on the first two buttons to the right of the button that looks like a clock. This will at least allow you to find the path of the current file on your hard drive. If you want to, press the third button over as well, but you don't have to do that.
5. Highlight all that information that is now in the "Left Section Box", and then click on the "A" button on the far left.
6. Click on "8" which makes the font size 8 instead of the larger 10 default. You could manually type in a "6" if you want an even smaller font sizing.
7. Press the TAB key twice and you should move over to the Right Section.
8. Click on the button that has an 8/7 on it. This puts the date automatically into your footer.
9. Press the space bar and click on the button that looks like a clock. This automatically puts in the time into your footer.
10. High light everything in the right section box, and follow steps 5 & 6 above only for the Right Section Box.
11. Click on "OK"
12. Click on "OK" again.

You now have an automated footer that gives you the path to your file, and also the date and time of that last printout. You know not only know where to find it, but you also know from looking in the lower right corner exactly which printout is the most current one too.

Saving your Spreadsheet It is extremely important that you save your work if you haven't already done so several times already. I recommend that you save your work in a special folder you can find later, like a sub-folder named "Sight Settings" you keep in a folder named "Archery." Obviously you can name your file anything you want to call it, you just don't want to misfile it and lose it.

Caution If you click on just "save" you are going save that file wherever a file was last saved, like in with your taxes or household expenses. It would be like opening a drawer in one of many file cabinets and just tossing it in there with the hope you'd remember where you put it. This is not the best way to go when you've put all the work into something, so . . .

1. First click on "File", then Click on "Save as..."
2. Then select which directory and folder you want it saved into, give this file a unique name.
3. Then make sure of the file type, and
4. Press OK to save that file exactly where you want it contained in your folder system.
5. You can, if you so choose even save this to your desktop so it is readily handy like your OT2 or AA programs and other handy stuff are. Then to open it, you simply double click the icon created and your spreadsheet is opened.
6. To be ProActive, always save into two locations, that is, make a backup! In my opinion you should always save your work into at least two different locations. One copy should be saved onto your hard drive, and a backup could be saved onto a thumb drive or external hard drive. Once again, as with anything archery, anything with computers isn't an "if" it is going to happen; it is a when it will happen. I would hate to even think what I'd do when (not "if") my hard drive failed and I didn't have an adequate backup of my work. That would be catastrophic. I have had hard drives fail, but I've never lost major amounts of work because of not having a set of backups. Being ProActive with computer work is also a commonsense practice.

Printing out the Spreadsheet Now that you have saved your work and if you have done things correctly with regard to the column widths and row heights, then this should all print out on one page. You can do a Print Preview by clicking on the box on the toolbar that looks like a magnifying glass or you can click on "File," then "Print Preview." You will get a reasonable facsimile of what the printout will look like and whether or not it is one page or two (ooops).

To print out the spreadsheet, you simply click on the printer button on the toolbar or click on "File," then "Print...," then select your print options, quality, and number of copies, and then click "OK." Print out a couple of copies so you can check the sizes of the placards and also the accuracy of how you typed in your formulas and other settings. If things print okay and you are happy, then things are good. You can finish up your placards etc. If not, then you need to adjust column widths, row heights, correct spelling errors, or errors in your formulas, re-save your work and print it out again. *Tip* Always keep a "hard copy" of your work. This is another redundant backup, but when something happens, you always have a hard copy to fall back upon. This is yet another reason to have an automated footer at the bottom of each printed page (including the date and time printed); you know for sure which one is the most current! That time stamp is a very valuable asset when you are working on corrections! This lets you know exactly which print-out is the most current.

Making another TAB in the Excel Spreadsheet There is one last thing before you are finished, however. I'll now teach you how to make a "second copy" of that worksheet in this very same spreadsheet and is saved right along with it. This is in case you mess something up on your "main" copy or if you change bows but want to keep the original settings. In other words doing this provides a spare template. You did notice I named the example worksheet tab "SuperNova 1914?" This is clearly distinctive, telling me specifically which bow and shaft size that the "tab" represents. I also have other tabs in this worksheet for other bows I've owned, including my more current bow, the Merlin *Excalibur EX-40* (a tab is named for that one, too). It is a simple process to "copy" the entire worksheet to another tab! All you have to do is:

1. Double click on the gray bar at the bottom of the page that says, in all likelihood, "Sheet 1," type in a Name (such as the name of the bow (e.g. "Supernova 1914"), and press Enter. It is now re-named "Supernova 1914" for example.
2. Left click on that Tab you just named, hold down the "CTRL" key, and drag your mouse over in between that Tab and "Sheet2" and let go of the mouse button. You will now have a Tab Named, for Example "Supernova 1914 (2).
3. You then simply right click on that tab, select "rename" and call it as "Spare" or whatever you want to call it, and you now have a perfect copy of that worksheet all right there ready for you. You don't lose your first one, and you can make new copies within the worksheet for another bow's sight settings, or for a friend's bow anytime you want.

I told you would only have to type in all those formulas once! Pretty slick, huh?

Summary

I know these processes seem complex but combining these three separate systems allows me to get the most accurate set of sight marks I can. Once you have things organized and a spreadsheet built, it only takes a few minutes to generate new placards. I normally only have to make a maximum of two trips to the range; the first to get the initial sight settings using the Calculator Based Method and the second to verify the marks for the final time before printing a sight tape, which is for me, a backup system. It is so much easier today than it was back in the 1980's when I started using the Calculator Based Method to obtaining sight settings. We had no other "backup" besides shooting in our marks. Now, with software programs like *Archer's Advantage* and *On Target 2* to help us do this job, getting those cross checks is so very simple. The important things with regard to obtaining your sight settings are:

1. First, don't put blind faith into group shooting, just because all your arrows hit in the confines of the "X" or "5-ring" doesn't mean that that sight setting is good enough.
2. Use whatever systems you have to check the others.
3. Garbage In = Garbage Out: the sight settings you get out of your software systems are only as good as the measurements you put into them.
4. Always make the "sight tape sandwich" first by placing the double stick tape to the back of the sight tape or placard, then putting on transparent tape over the sight tape or placard without stretching the paper .
5. Trim the sight tape to size, but check the dimensions so it fits on the sight bar first.
6. Make sure that the sight tape will fit under the indicator pointer and/or magnifier, and doesn't contact the slider mechanism. Not clearing any of those could ruin a tape.

7. When mounting a sight tape, always be sure that you aren't stretching the paper or moving it while mounting it.
8. When lining up a sight tape, make sure you have the bow sight set exactly to a selected yardage mark based upon the etched settings on the vertical sight bar, and then carefully match up the sight tape yardage to the exact yardage the bow sight is set for.
9. Count those clicks, they are extremely important!
10. Watch your head angle and alignment with the indicator pointer when reading your tape. If you are using a magnifier, the magnifier will magnify any head or eye alignment error you may be making.
11. Always check all of your sight settings by setting the yardage on the scribed side of the sight bar and then going to the sight tape and making sure all of the tape indications match the settings. If anything is off, it is likely to be the tape alignment (unless you forget to count clicks).
12. Never go into battle with an untested weapon. Never go into a tournament with a brand new sight tape that hasn't been checked out with at least a couple of scoring rounds.

I hope that the MS *Excel* explanations, while fairly basic, give you enough information so as not to preclude you even trying to automate your calculations. In MS Excel, there are countless ways to do any one thing. What I've recommended seems to work the easiest for me. A series of "print screens" really gets complex and confusing, and takes up way more space than necessary. That is why you only see one in this entire chapter.

There is much information to convey and all of it is important. I hope that you have now gotten a taste of how easy, yet how complex, getting a reliable set of sight marks for your bow set up can be. I also hope that you realize that when it comes to getting reliable sight marks, it is so very critical you approach it ProActively; it is imperative that this be done right, checked, and checked again. A simple oversight can quickly drag down what could have been a good score.

Section 6

Attitude & Mental Game

This section deals with "scouting." In all sports and even in the working world, people scout or scope things out in a constant search for the means to do something better and more efficiently. Some corporations call these "best practices." In athletics, scouting reports and game films are a vital part of game for competitive preparation. Why should archery be any different? What you are going to find in this section is not only about scouting top shooters and how to do this with a purpose and a methodology, that is ProActively, but also how to scout for a coach, plus I will offer up some perspectives from the other side of the coin, that is how coaches can scout prospective students. This section may well change your perspective on how to evaluate a top notch person, be he/she a professional archer or a coach.

Since archery coaches are not on the public payroll, things operate differently; but yet, they also have a lot of things in common to the public or even private school sectors. The chapters "Student Selects Coach" (Chapter 38), and "Coach Selects Student" (Chapter 39) are very important for any of you who are looking at getting coached and trying to find the right coach for you. I think they will also be of interest to archery coaches who may be reading this book.

The concluding chapter, "Are You Up to the Challenge" offers a better insight into how something like a release aid and your attitude and mental approach to learning to use it can and will make all the difference in your performance. The chapter isn't just about pull through release aids; there is more to it than that. Consider how you would approach any other piece of equipment after reading it. Enjoy this section as we delve into "scouting," "ProActive Emulation," and both sides of the coin when it comes to selecting a coach and having a coach select you.

Tom Dorigatti

37

Emulating a Pro ProActively

As a group, we archers are always seeking that magic, that cure for all that ails us, a magic potion that will vault us to the top of the leader board. We watch professional archers and make attempts, typically futile attempts, to exactly copy that paragon of archery skill, from their equipment right on through to even wearing the same types of shoes and clothing! Of course, we can see what they are doing, but cannot pick their brains to get at how they do it. And, frankly, many of them cannot explain the "how," they just know that is what they are doing. Their technique has become so automated that they really don't think about it anymore; it just happens! We have previously discussed automating your shot sequence in Chapters 25 & 26. In this chapter we are going to discover how to go about finding one or two top archers who might provide a template to follow. While it is impossible to do exactly what those top archers are doing, with proper "scouting" you can at least figure out not only the what they are doing, but maybe even get a handle on the "how," too. Your powers of observation, the use of inductive and deductive reasoning, and yes, ProActive archery all come into play if you go about this in an organized fashion. If, on the other hand, you do what everybody else does, just go watch a top Professional shooter, the first thing people do is get caught up on his or her score and how many X's they shoot. You will find yourself not watching the archer and their shot sequence, but rather you end up watching where their arrows go. Don't do what "they" do; try this instead.

So What Does This Have To Do with Emulating a Top Archer?

We all need a base from which to operate. We all started out in this game with a lack of knowledge about what to do and especially how to do it. We all ended up copying someone else by either watching them or getting help from them. This is a given. Then, we watched better shooters and asked more questions and read more and more about the "what to do," because the "what to do" was readily available. What was missing was the "how to do" what it is you were supposed to do.

In the past few years, many top shooters have realized that to become better shooters themselves, they needed to have more archers to compete with who shoot as well or better than they do. We all knew, or at least we should have known, that those top archers would never give up all of their "secrets." Believe me when I tell you that they are much more open now than they were even a short ten years ago! It used to be that in order to get the inside scoop you had to pay your dues and become part of the in-crowd, and even then the information you needed would come around indirectly and in little bits and pieces. Today article after article, including interviews with top professionals, that address equipment setups, form issues, how they set off their release, set up their scopes, stabilization, mental game, coaching, philosophy, and more are available. Naturally, what follows is that many, many shooters wanting to improve their games immediately start making changes in their form and execution to pattern them as closely as possible to these model archery behaviors. Little thought is given to any sort of rationale for making these changes. What thought there is seems to be: "If he/she does it this way with this setup, then that is what I will do." Herein lays a potential disaster if this isn't thought through in advance.

Stories It is fitting to relate to you a couple of stories (yes, true ones!) to demonstrate just how far this can be carried. If my memory serves me correctly, back in the mid 1970's, Jack Lancaster was a top professional shooter (*see photo*), especially when it came to field shooting outdoors. His "form" was radically different from archers shooting today; but back then, compound bows had low let offs (28-35%), they were very long axle to axle in length (56″ wasn't uncommon), and we didn't yet have trigger releases. Most of the bow grips were "high wristed," so obviously most of us shot high wristed. For some reason, the term "California high wrist grip" comes to mind. As a result, most all shooters tended to lean back at the waist and shot with a high bow shoulder, a low anchor, a dropped chin, and thus, a lower drawing elbow than what we deem "acceptable" today (*see photo again*).

However, I digress with this story, since it has really nothing to do with "form," but it does have a lot to do with the lengths that shooters will go to if they think a top professional archer is "on to something" that might be making the difference! People will latch onto anything as you will quickly see. I think Jack won the NFAA Outdoor Nationals and, during that tournament, he had placed a piece of knitting yarn, about a foot to foot and a half long onto the end of his main stabilizer. Since Jack won the National Championship with that item as part of his set up, it wasn't but a matter of a few weeks, and the "knitting yarn" found its way onto more archers' stabilizers than you could count, including my own. Did that piece of knitting yarn or piece of Dacron B-50 really help and make the difference with Jack shooting all those 560's (old NFAA "5-3" targets)? Probably not, since he had shot more than his fair share of 560's before that. We will never know for sure if he did this simply for the fun of it or if it really was "the separator," but I certainly doubt it made all the difference between him winning and coming in second! The effect however, was practically instantaneous, much like so many little things we see today that are likely more hype than help. I will admit, however, that you never saw so many variants in the lengths and colors and styles of knitting yarn on stabilizers; it was quite colorful out there on the field courses. The funnier part of this is that, at least where I was in Ohio, all of our field courses were mostly in the trees and out of the wind anyway! Useless trivia? Not necessarily. Take the time to reflect on this and relate it to some of the gadgetry being marketed these days.

The above reminds me of another story, but I can't remember the name of the pro shooter who started it all. Lots of pros were shooting "concho-style" releases like Jack Lancaster was shooting, since those seemed, to be a bit easier to shoot and master than "ledge style" releases. In fact, Jack shot exceedingly well with a concho style release aid with release rope around the bow string. You held onto the rope with your thumb and the loop was held in place on a rivet (for a solid holding spot). The archer then drew the bow back, anchored, and then gradually let up pressure on the thumb and the rope would let loose and fire the shot. Maintenance of adequate back tension was the key to this, and many shooters had great difficulty avoiding creeping and just letting the thumb off the rivet all at once. It happened that a couple of pros got the idea to remove the flat, round plastic or metal plate off the back of the concho and replace it with…a drilled golf ball! It wasn't long that many, many amateur shooters had golf-balls on the back end of their concho style releases. Some used Titleist golf balls, some used Wilsons while still others used some other brand or whatever was easiest to find. Can't imagine it made a big, if any, difference in their technique.

A "Concho-style" Release Aid

Isn't it amazing how something like this gets started as people grasp at any straw to find or buy perfect scores? I like to tell my students that they can't purchase that magic box of perfect 60X 300's because I have first "dibs" on it and I have ordered a gross of them. The main problem for them is that they have been on back order since 1974!

Keep these stories in mind as we progress through this section. Also keep in mind the first chapter of this book, "Things Archers Change 'On the Fly' (and Shouldn't)."

The focus of this chapter is how to take a ProActive approach in selecting a professional archer or top echelon amateur to emulate through the use of an organized and comparative approach. There is way more to any pro's setup and shooting "style" than what meets the eye. Everything is done for a reason and what may fit them could be way off-base for you! Thus, as you are reading this chapter, you should also be making a list of those form and execution elements that you already know are negatively affecting your performance, and then put them on your own "Scouter's Checklist." I might add that this same checklist can be used if you are a coach and evaluating students.

What Is In This for Me?

I know you are already asking this question. The answer to "what is in this for me" are: first, you can save yourself a lot of wasted time and effort. In addition, it naturally follows that you can also save a lot of money in the form of unneeded equipment/gadget purchases. This sport is no longer a "poor man's sport." The prices of everything are not insubstantial, and it doesn't take long to spend $1,000 or more on gadgets and gimmicks, most of which won't help you at all. How many of you have already changed over to a different release aid because you saw a friend or saw a pro who got a new release and shot a super score with it? How about the same with a scope? What about that new-fangled stabilizer, or down angled stabilizer coupler? Should you get that new tournament sight? How about those new arrows? Are you getting the message? What is in it for you, when it comes to emulating a professional or amateur top echelon shooter, is a practical and organized approach to scout out the situation before you get into changing anything or adding to your equipment inventory. You can avoid chasing your tail, making expensive and time consuming mistakes only to not gain a thing or even possibly lose ground.

How to Scout a Pro

Few people I know take a methodical approach when they are watching pros shoot. Normally, when people watch pros shoot, they are mesmerized by how the top archers "shoot like a machine." These archers shoot arrow after arrow into the X-ring. You watch them draw back their bow, anchor, and then turn your attention to their target to see where the arrow hits. Then, you move on to the next pro and repeat the process. You ask, "What is he/she doing that makes them so close to perfection?" The real question should be: "How are they getting so close to perfection?" Most of this "what" and a lot of the "how" can be answered through the organized and planned approach to scouting I'm about to outline for you.

If you are intent on emulating a pro, doesn't it make better sense to really watch a pro who has close to your own body build? If your build puts you into a position of having to shoot a closed stance, wouldn't it be better to watch a pro with a similar body shape to yours who also shoots with a closed stance? If you shoot with a high drawing elbow, wouldn't it be better to scout out pros who tend to shoot a higher elbow rather than force yourself to change to shooting a lower elbow position? Wouldn't it be better to watch a pro who shoots the same type of release aid that you have chosen to learn to shoot? Isn't it better to watch a pro who is shooting a bow that is close to the same length as yours? Isn't it better to watch a pro who is left-handed if you are left-handed or right-handed if you are right-handed? Don't forget that if you are a short-draw length person, it might not be so bad to watch top echelon female archers, too.

What follows is a start at a ProActive means of scouting a pro for potential incorporation of some of his/her techniques into your own form and execution. You may then begin to see patterns in your own shooting in the comparison and from them make up a ProActive plan, a plan with great images in your mind and some data to support it.

What You Need to Have

You will need the following:

1. *A reasonably easy to operate and "silent" stopwatch.* It need not be expensive, since

you will only record times to ±0.1 second. Try to make sure that it doesn't have a loud "beeper" on it; one without any beeper would be even better. You would be amazed at how well people can hear something like the beeper on a stop watch, and on a shooting line this can be very, very irritating indeed.

2. A *good set of binoculars* for checking the impact points of the arrows in the target. You need to be close to your shooter in order to observe things, but you will also need a view of his/her target face as well. Remember, these observations are to be unobtrusive and not offer any distractions to any of the competitors. Since it could be very distracting to your shooter if he knows his every move is being watched, I personally would not ask for permission to watch him ahead of time. In fact, I highly recommend that you be very discreet about it so as not to throw off his/her concentration by being a pest.
3. A *pencil* (so you can erase if necessary)
4. *Your own version of the "Scouter's Checklist"* that is outlined in this chapter. It will, of course, be made up of those key elements you feel are most important to you. Some of the items you will only have to observe a few times during a round, others you will want to make special note of and really watch them closely. During the "Shot Phase" you will be documenting timing and shot placement during the round (or rounds) of scoring. With proper use of the checklist, you may well be able to find that "glitch" or error the archer made that could have caused a miss. You won't be in a position to analyze a missed "baby X," however, since you cannot see your shooter's sight picture through his or her scope. However, I will describe a means of determining where that shot may well have gone before you even look at your shooter's target! It is all in observing and learning your shooter well enough to predict the impact point without looking at the target. How is that for being fun and offering a challenge! With this way to watch an archery tournament, it doesn't have to be boring (like watching grass grow, like watching paint dry, etc.). I think that you will find, once you have organized the suggested items into a list of items most important to you and your shooting, you will have a more enjoyable time watching and will have a means of learning something instead of watching only to forget most everything you saw.

Yet Another Story Here is a story concerning how quickly you can learn a shooter's tendencies by observing things closely. Once you have adopted an organized checklist of things to watch, you will be amazed at how quickly you pick up on little inconsistencies that have large impacts on that particular shooter's shot results. This ultimately helps you to understand your own tendencies. Once you begin to accomplish these sorts of things, you will never observe another archer in the same light as before you learned these techniques.

We have several shooters in my area who can shoot 60X 300's on the indoor NFAA face quite regularly. I have been watching one particular archer a lot; mostly because he shoots a triggerless, grip gate release like I do, and he is darned good at it. I've watched him shoot X after X and watched him shoot 60X 300's many times. However, over the course of several weeks, that "X-count" was dropping; not terribly, but it was dropping. So I used my little checklist and checked things out, one at a time, systematically. I had been having problems with my release hand, so my top priority in watching him was "how" he works his release hand, since his release hand position is similar to mine. It only took about two ends into the round and I picked up on one inconsistency, and I could tell if he was going to shoot an "X" or if he'd shoot a solid "5" simply by watching this one little thing! During the course of the next couple of weeks, I was never wrong with this "call." You are asking in suspense, "What was this one little element?" When he anchored and continued his "pull," if his release hand thumb was relaxed, the shot broke one to two seconds quicker than if that thumb was tight and flexed (Relaxed thumb = "X," Tight and flexed thumb = Solid "5" low right). Since I rarely offer up advice unless asked, and I don't have a clue as to whether he/she was working on any particular item, I choose not to say anything to the shooter, but I did continue to watch. Well, low and behold, he somehow must have picked up on the tight release hand. He started relaxing that thumb more and his shots broke more quickly and fluidly, and he shot yet another 60X and several 59X rounds too. However, to this day, if I watch him shoot and see that thumb tighten up and he continues the shot, he is not going to hit the "X;" he will shoot a solid "5" low right, and I don't even have to look at his target to know it.

There is a lot of power in organized and systematic observation. Since that time that shooter asked if I saw anything and I relayed this information to him. He told me he thought he was tightening up his release hand and had been working on it. So, my keeping the observations to myself didn't hurt him; he had already isolated the problem on his own and was working on it. Had I said something, it could have upset his practice plan and made him self-conscious about it; much like the story I related to you concerning the comment "Look at that guy, he is shaking so bad that they should get him off the shooting line before he hurts somebody." Becoming self conscious or trying to "stop" doing something can make matters worse instead of improving them. This is yet one more reason to be very discreet when "scouting." (It is a basic rule of coaching archery that one never offers unsolicited advice.)

The "Scouter's Checklist"

I have developed what I call a "Scouter's Checklist." It contains many, but not necessarily all, items to watch for when observing a professional or top echelon amateur archer who you may be interested in emulating. While I've come up with a system to lessen the volume of information, I leave it to you to develop your own shorthand for completing the checklist in an understandable fashion. You must realize, however, that an adequate scouting job isn't made from watching your selected model archer just shoot an arrow or an end or even two. You cannot watch everything at once; thus I would recommend that if you really want to adequately check out a particular shooter, you closely watch them for at least one, if not two full rounds or more. The more information you have, the easier it will be to put together your "report" and pick out key elements for you to tackle at a later date. For most of the checklist, to save time and maximize your ability to watch rather than record, some parts of this checklist are

Scouters' Checklist

Archer ______________________ Date ____________ Event __________

Style ______________________________

1. *Bow Brand* Hoyt, PSE, Martin, Elite, Mathews, Alpine, Merlin, BowTech; (Other) __________________
2. *Axle to Axle (estimate)* Short ATA (35″ or less), Medium ATA (36″-39″), Long ATA (>39″)
3. *Handedness of Bow* Right Handed/ Left Handed (RH or LH)
4. *Cam Style* Single, Dual, Hybrid, Binary, (Other) _________
5. *Arrows* All-Carbon, Aluminum, Aluminum-Carbon—Large Diameter, Smaller Diameter
6. *Arrow Length* Long (lots of arrow overhang), Short (little to no arrow overhang)
7. *Arrow Rest* (Fall Away Type) Limb Driver, Trophy Taker; Mathews, Fuse; (Launcher Type) Pro Tuner, GKF/Spott-Hogg, Hamskea (Other) __________
8. *Arrow Rest Mounting* Close in, Over the Wrist
9. *Release Aid* Wrist Strap, Hand Held Thumb Trigger, Hand-held Triggerless, Hand-Held Poundage Trip (Evolution+, Stan?)
10. *Bow Sling* Bow Sling (bushing mount), Wrist sling, Finger Sling (leather), Finger Sling (rope)
11. *Stabilization* Multi-rod; Single rod (flexible, thin); Single rod (stiff, thick); B-Stinger, Doinker
12. *Stabilizer Length* Very Long (34″+), Medium (28″– 33″), Short (<28″)
13. *Stabilizer Tip Weight* Heavy, Medium, Light
14. *Side Weighting* Single side weight rod (close in); Side weight rod (wide angle); V-bars (narrow), V-bars (wide); V-bars (forward); V-bars (downwards, narrow); V-bars (downward, wide)
15. *Additional Mass* Counter weight (straight back); Riser weight (upper), Riser weight (lower)
16. *Peep Sight* Tru-Peep; Hooded Peep, Other _____
17. *Scope Housing Diameter* (Large / Small) *Scope Aperture* (Dot / Circle)
18. *Sight* Copper John/Ants; Axcel; Spot-Hogg; Sur-Loc; Shibuya, (Other) _____
19. *Sight Extension Bar* Long (far out) / Medium / Short (close in)
20. *String Attachments* D-loop (Short / Long); Kisser Button
21. *Eyeglasses & Blinders* Glasses; No Glasses; Off-eye (is Open / is Closed / has blinder)
22. *Hat or Cap* Shoots with hat or cap or none
23. *Shoes* Tennis Shoes; Walking Shoes; Boots; Loafers; Crocs; Sandals, (Other) ____________________

set up as "circle the option" or "fill in the blank" formats.

The Archer's Equipment The following can be circled or checked off during the practice ends. Remember, this is not the time to talk with the competitors or ask them questions. They are preparing for competition, and most will not be willing to discuss such items with you. You must also make yourself as unobtrusive as possible and "keep your distance" so as not to distract or in any way interfere with your subject pro.

Once the practice ends are over, and you've documented the above items, it is time to get down to some serious, but again, unobtrusive and non-interfering observations. Here are some things that you need to document for several scoring shots and ends. This is a puzzle you will be putting together, piece by piece. You cannot possibly cover all the items listed for every single shot during the round. However, some of them need be observed on a per shot basis, others only need to be checked occasionally for consistency. For some I have included sample abbreviations to assist in your "short-hand" documentation.

Archer's Physical Characteristics

1. *Body Type/Build* — Tall / Medium / Short and Slender / Medium / Stocky
2. *Shoulders* — Wide Shoulders, Normal, Narrow Shoulders
3. *Arms* — Long / Medium / Short
4. *Hands & Fingers* — Big hands (stubby fingers or long fingers); Medium hands, Small hands (stubby fingers or long fingers)
5. *Upper Body* — Barrel Chested / Normal Upper body / Slender Upper body
6. *Legs* — Long (slender or well muscled); Medium (slender or well muscled), Short (slender or well muscled)

Shot Preparation and Shot Sequencing

1. ***Stance 1*** The stance a shooter takes in addressing the shooting line is a more critical aspect of their shooting than most realize. Remember "The draw length is tuned to the stance, and the stance is tuned to the draw length." Body shape, upper and lower body flexibility, upper arm length vs. forearm length, position of the anchor, and head positioning can all affect how an archer aligns their stance. In addition, slight adjustments in the stance can and will reduce or eliminate tendencies to shoot left or right. Basically there are three main types of stances used with variations.
   a. *Square Stance* Both feet are even with each other and parallel to the shooting line: Symbol "|"
   b. *Open Stance* The front, or left foot (right-handed archer) is back (to the left when observing the shooter from behind the shooting line), from the right foot: Symbol "\". I also use abbreviations: SO = Slightly Open; MO = Moderately Open; WO = Wide Open.
   c. *Closed Stance* The front, or left foot (right handed shooter) is forward (to the right when observing the shooter from behind the shooting line) in relation to the back or right foot. Symbol = "/" Abbreviations for the Closed Stance could

be SC = Slightly Closed; MC = Moderately Closed; WC = Wide Closed

2. ***Stance 2*** The other part of the stance is how far apart the shooter's feet are. Once again, this can vary widely from shooter to shooter, and depends upon things such as body build, width of shoulders, how low- or high-wristed the shooter grips the bow, the person's weight, adjustment for comfort in the lower back, curvature of the spine, and whether or not the shooter places more or less weight on one leg than the other! The rule of thumb is to have the feet no wider than shoulder width apart, but you will see many variants of this, from people who shoot wider than that, to people that put their ankles together while shooting. However, you need to take note of this. A person can adjust the width of their stance to help them reduce high and low misses! Possible abbreviations: SW = Shoulder Width; IS = Inside Shoulders; AT = Ankles Together; OS = Outside Shoulders; VW = Very Wide
3. ***Bow Positioning when Loading Arrows*** Some archers set the end of the stabilizer on the floor in front of them. Others will place the bottom limb on their upper leg, while others will use a bow holster to cradle the bottom limb. This little detail can be important because some practices give the bow arm some sort of break between shots to reduce fatigue. Still others will hold the bow at or near eye level to load their arrow. However, experienced shooters will never tilt their bow sideways (toward horizontal) to load their arrow, since this would interfere with archers on both sides of them. If they are shooting a bow with a "shoot through" riser, then some shooters load the arrow through the front of the bow and back to the string, while others will load the arrow by sliding the arrow forward through the riser. In addition, depending upon how they start their shot sequence, it can be used to help configure their hand position into the grip as they begin their shot sequence. This normally will not vary from shot to shot, so if you document it once, it will usually suffice. You will find that this routine is performed time and time again without variation. Abbreviations: BH = Bow Holster; SF = Stabilizer on Floor; BC = Bottom Cam on upper leg; BHE = Bow Horizontal at Eye Level; STB = Shoot Through Back loading; STF = Shoot Through Forward loading
4. ***Setting the Grip*** Most shooters set their grip after they've hooked up the release to the bowstring and have a small amount of pressure on the string. This ties closely into #3 above. Some variants of this include:
   a. Setting the grip with lower cam on leg
   b. Setting the grip with bow supported by release on the bowstring
   c. Setting the grip with bow out in front and in "pre-aim position"

Every shooter's shot sequence varies, but every good shooter has a regimen and sequence of steps that doesn't vary from shot to shot. They all have very specific checkpoints in the initial stages of the shot from the loading of an arrow onto the string, right on through to "pre-aiming" or "pre-drawing." At that point, they then enter into more critical aspects of their shot sequence. The list below contains elements that you really need to watch closely for the entire round of observations. It will allow you to glean a lot more details about your selected shooter and how he/she goes about their business. One thing you are likely not to see is that the upper echelon shooters will not change their bow hand position from when they set it before drawing the bow until the arrow is in the target. Same goes with that release hand angle; they won't be "searching for it" and bobbing around once they hit their anchor point. Most, but not all, will be drawing the string to them and won't go out leaning toward the string. There are exceptions, but they are few and far between.

The Shot

During this phase of your observations, you are going to need that stopwatch mentioned earlier, and a pair of binoculars. This is where your observations should really start to pay benefits. It is also where the fun of predicting shot impact points really comes into play. Your shooter has set his grip and begins to draw back the bow. Watch him/her closely, because this is where things start to come undone and can really go wrong! He/she won't make a mistake often, nor will the same mistake likely be made twice in a row. Here are the factors to observe:

1. ***Pre-Aiming***
   a. Draws bow straight back to anchor, bow hardly moves.
   b. Draws bow back above the level of the target and comes down into the bull's-eye. (How far? Safe or Unsafe? (you be the judge!)).
   c. Draws bow back below the target and comes up into the bull's-eye.
   d. Draws bow left or right of bull's-eye and comes into it from left or right.
2. ***Drawing the Bow I***
   a. Draws straight back in a smooth, continuous motion with medium speed
   b. Draws back rapidly
   c. Draws with high elbow; draws with lower elbow; draws with really low elbow (circle one)
3. ***Drawing the Bow II***
   a. Draws bow with nearly locked bow-arm
   b. Draws bow in a "push-pull" mode with a bent bow arm and then straightens/relaxes bow arm once at anchor
4. ***At Anchor***
   a. Draws bow to anchor, very little or no head movement
   b. Draws to stops, then moves drawing hand into anchor and moves head into alignment
   c. Draws bow to anchor, movement of drawing hand into solid anchoring position, either from above or from below the jawbone
5. ***Anchor Point***
   a. Drawing Hand
      1. Drawing hand: under jawbone or behind jawbone (circle one)
      2. Back of drawing hand: straight up or beyond vertical; or at approx 45 degree angle; or level (circle one)
      3. Drawing hand: Lots of first finger pressure or even pressure with all drawing fingers (circle one)

b. Anchor Contact points
  1. String in corner of mouth and tip of nose
  2. String in front of corner of mouth (more centered on chin) and tip of nose
  3. String in corner of mouth and on side of nose
  4. String in front of corner of mouth and on side of nose
  5. String behind corner of mouth and on tip of nose
  6. String behind corner of mouth and deep into face beyond tip of nose

6. ***Head position***
   a. Chin is level
   b. Chin is tilted downwards
   c. Chins is tilted upwards slightly
7. ***Bow Arm & Bow Shoulder***
   a. Shoulder down, bow arm appears to be completely locked or extended beyond locked position (double jointed)
   b. Shoulder down, relaxed, bow arm slightly bent (unlocked)
   c. Shoulder down, relaxed, bow arm bent well (unlocked)
   d. Shoulder up, bow arm appears to be completely locked or extended beyond locked position (double jointed)
   e. Shoulder up, bow arm slightly bent (unlocked)
   f. Shoulder up, bow arm bent well (unlocked)
8. ***Drawing Elbow***
   a. Drawing elbow high (elbow at ear level or higher)
   b. Drawing elbow level with arrow (below or even with ear lobe)
   c. Drawing elbow below line of arrow (maybe slight bend in wrist)
9. ***Body Alignment from Side*** (line through navel and aiming eye)
   a. is vertical
   b. is leaning back slightly
   c. is leaning back lots
   d. is leaning forward towards target
10. ***Body Alignment from Behind*** (looking toward target)
   a. Drawing elbow to right of line of arrow (right handed shooter)
   b. Drawing elbow even with the arrow.
   c. Drawing elbow to the left (beyond the line of the arrow, right-handed shooter)
11. ***Bow Grip*** (This can be hard to see.)
   a. Grip very relaxed no finger contact with riser
   b. Grip very relaxed; first finger and thumb are in contact with each other
   c. Grip relaxed, first finger only touching front of riser
   d. Grip relaxed, but fingers splayed or "open hand" with no finger contact with the riser
   e. Closed grip with several fingers in contact with riser
   f. Grip 45 degrees or in "hand-shake" position, no contact beyond "life-line"
   g. Hand deep into riser, but fingers not in contact with riser
   h. *Bow Hand Thumb* This item is very, very important and gives you a really clear indicator of just how relaxed or tight the bow hand really is when at full draw.

Thumb pointed at target? Thumb flexed upwards? Thumb flexed downwards? Thumb straight out away from riser.

I need to relate a short story about this very item. I was watching a complete video of a World Cup series of one-on-one matches. I watched the semi-finals and finals of the Women's Compound division. I was specifically watching the bow hand positions of both ladies. The winner had the thumb on the bow hand consistently pointed at the target the entire match. The first match was won handily by this particular shooter. During the Finals for the gold medal, things started unraveling after the first end for this same shooter. What to you supposed I picked up on? You got it! Suddenly, out of nowhere, the tension became very evident in her bow hand and that thumb started pointing straight up while she was at full draw. I obviously couldn't see her sight picture, but the positioning of her thumb told the story. Her bow hand/arm had tightened up. Unfortunately, this continued the entire match from the second end onwards, and she didn't win the gold medal this time. I knew she wasn't going to win simply by seeing a little thing such as her thumb on her bow hand which wasn't the same as it was in the previous match.

12. ***Bow Cant*** (or lack thereof) Many shooters use a natural cant and don't regard the bubble. Others have a natural cant but the bubble is set to read "true" with this cant. Typically, you only need to look at the top limb and see which way it leans.
    a. Top limb to right
    b. Top limb to left.
    c. No apparent canting of the bow.
13. ***Shot Timing*** A great many professional shooters are rhythmic; that is to say that from the time they acquire the X-ring in their scope and contact the trigger or continue (not start, since top shooters do not start and stop pulling the bow during the shot sequence) their "pinch," the timing from that point until the shot breaks is quite repeatable and will happen within 1-2 seconds of the same amount of time, shot after shot after shot. Some are able to hold longer than others. This "timing" however is not haphazard, and is a practiced routine arrived at through constant analysis of how long they have a "window of opportunity" to shoot the most X's. There are some shooters, however, who seem to have no "rhythm" as to how long they hold, but there are very few. Establishing your shooting rhythm has been covered (Chapters 25 & 26) in this book. It is simple to do, but does require a lot of testing to determine your best timing" and then more practice to insure you are in your "window of opportunity" as often as possible when the shot breaks. Some of the better shooters also "take the opportunity," that is to say, they don't exactly punch off the shot, but they know how to take the opportunity when it best presents itself by doing the closest thing to punching. I think that Dave Cousins and Tim Gillingham are two of the best in the world at "taking the opportunity" when it is there. Some call it a "controlled punch," others call it a "micro punch." I much prefer to call this learning how to "take the opportunity."

For this part of your observation, you will need a stopwatch. In addition, you must select a starting point that is as recognizable as possible, so that you start your stopwatch at the same point in the shooter's shot sequence. I like to start my stopwatch when the shooter locks in their shoulder/elbow and they contact the trigger to continue their "pinch." It is the easiest, most consistent point at which to start the timing. Of course, you stop the watch when the shot breaks. Record the time to the tenth of a second, then look at the target and determine the impact point. This is a very important measurement to establish, since you can quickly determine if a shooter should be letting down and how disciplined they are from this "normal time window" alone. You can also eventually predict an outer ten or a miss from this measurement.

It is best to track shot timing for as many shots and ends as you possibly can. It is simple to record "time in sec," score, and impact position. Below is a sample table that you can make up for each end of a round. Then, all you have to do is fill out the table for each shot. It only takes seconds, and you can analyze it later concerning impact points and timing. Ultimately, if you use this for yourself, you can determine your own personal best "shot timing" that gives you the highest probability of shooting an X. My particular window of opportunity for a guaranteed X-ring at 20 yards is 5-6 seconds. I won't miss an X if the shot breaks during those two seconds. Any longer than that and it is anyone's game. (Again, this was covered in Chapters 25 & 26.)

Shot Timing and Impact Table

Res = Result of shot, i.e., X, 10, 9, 8, etc. or *X, 5, 4, etc.*
Pos = Clock position of the shot. 1, 2, or 6, 7, 9, 10....11, 12 o'clock.
Time = Time in seconds (to the tenth) from the consistent start of your clock until the shot breaks.

	1	2	3	4	5
Res	X	X	5	X	5
Pos	1	9	3	1	7
Time	4.3	5.3	6.1	5.7	8.1

You can make up your own table for each end of the round, as depicted above. This will give you a complete set of data for that round, and you can also have the shooter's score and X-count (other than line calls), and if the archer is tending to shoot mostly high, low, left, right, etc. This can then be analyzed to see which "timing" gave them the most X's during that round. For my "Shot Timing Program" that I developed several years ago, I have a mini-target made up for each end and I record a dot on each spot of the multi-spot target for the arrow impact point. Obviously, you can also use this same item to analyze your own shooting and shooting tendencies.

14. ***The "Break" of the Shot*** There are three main areas to watch for when the shot "breaks." First and foremost is the action/reaction of the release hand to the shot and where it ends up as a result. A top shooter's release hand will rarely come forward, forward and down, or out away from their face when the shot breaks. Top

shooters will also rarely have a "dead release."

a. *Release hand reaction*

1. Release hand comes straight back and slightly downward with a consistent contact point after the shot.
2. Release hand comes straight back and around and behind the drawing shoulder.
3. Release hand is explosive with a lot of "recoil" and the drawing elbow comes down below shoulder level.

b. *Reaction of the bow as the shot breaks* Most often, top echelon shooters will drive the bow directly towards the target and then, for right-handed shooters, it will naturally also break to the left and down as the followthrough continues. However, this latter phase happens after the arrow is well out of the bow.

c. *Watch the tip of the stabilizer* If you are paying very close attention and you use something in the background with which you "line up" the tip of the front stabilizer, you can learn to "call" the shot before you even look at the target face, after only a few observations! It is a simple matter of getting into a position to observe and line up the tip of the stabilizer with something in the background. You can then begin to see those little "quirks" that all shooters have (some shooters call this "English" applied just as the shot breaks). But, too much "English" and a shot becomes a miss. Some shooters are, however, pretty good at those last, split-second corrections. Thus, observe several shots by watching the stabilizer. You are going to learn something.

Caution Obviously, you cannot be watching the shot reaction and also doing the "timing" and also watching the release hand reaction at the same time. Thus, you need to decide which you are going to watch and then document what you see. On occasion, you will also pick up that the top limb might "break" quickly to the left or to the right just as the shot breaks. Obviously, this in response to the sight being left or right of what the shooter wants to have.

d. *Reaction of the head and eyes* The third thing to watch for is the reaction of the shooter's head position and especially his/her eyes as the shot breaks. Most top echelon shooters will have literally zero head or eye movement when their shot breaks. That includes blinking. However, you will find many shooters who will blink during their shot sequence! Some will blink only once or twice, others maybe more. Blinking when the shot breaks is a reaction which can cost a shooter dearly, if the blink hits at the wrong time. (An eye blink takes about 300-400 milliseconds of time; a shot takes only about 20 milliseconds. Ed.) From this comes the adage "stare a hole or burn a hole into the middle of the X with your eye and don't let it or your head move until the arrow is in the target." I know of a couple of top pros who have a series of "blinks" while at full draw. What is striking about this is that those people blink exactly the same number of times at precisely the same interval and well before the shot breaks. I figure it is perhaps that they are setting their contacts or using the blinks to moisturize their eyes so they don't "fuzz out" later in the shot sequence.

e. *Time taken between shots and time remaining at the conclusion of the shooting end* These two aspects will vary widely between shooters. Of course, the "standard' is that all arrows in any given end must be shot before the expiration of the allotted time and, by NFAA rules, archers cannot "let-down" any one shot more than three times (or get a zero on that shot). It is a simple thing to record the number of seconds between when the shooter releases one shot and when he/she starts the next shot sequence by hooking up the release aid. You may be surprised at the results of these observations. There are "games" being played on the line with this, so it is one thing to pay attention to. If a shooter is having problems with his third shot, you may well see him or her take a few seconds longer between the second and third shots to allow muscle recovery and take stock of the situation. Also, shooters are very cognizant of their time remaining to complete an end. Most all of them have practiced their routine to allow for so many seconds remaining just in case they need a letdown or two during any given end.

Summary

I'm sure that there are other elements that you can think of to watch when observing a professional archer. I have covered a lot of territory and the information provided is lengthy: however, much of its intended purpose is to make the point to you that any top echelon archer has worked long and hard to develop their shooting prowess, consistency, confidence, and mental game and that more than just a casual observation is needed to winkle out their "secrets."

Some key items worth considering include:

1. I recommend that you select a top echelon amateur or pro who has a body build similar to yours.
2. If you are left-handed, then I would recommend that you first try to find another lefty to observe.
3. Make your own "Scouter's Checklist" from the above items and then add other items that you find important to you.
4. You cannot possibly cover all of these items in observing any shooter for only a few shots. Developing a shot sequence takes time, and if you are trying to incorporate elements from someone you want to emulate, you need documented information about those elements in written form (otherwise you will forget the information). Then you need to prioritize those items and if need be incorporate them one at a time. Don't go making changes "on the fly" without some sort of practice plan in place. If you change more than one thing at a time, you'll never know for sure which worked and which didn't work and you'll end up spinning your wheels, wasting time and effort, and then having to go back to square one without ever knowing what you did or didn't do correctly.
5. Body positioning, head positioning, type of stance and stance width, and arm alignment are all critical aspects that should definitely be incorporated into your checklist.

6. Shot timing is a key element in all this. Many shooters are "rhythm shooters" and you will find that their shooting rhythm doesn't vary much. Some shooters shoot very quickly, with little rest between shots, while others shoot more slowly and deliberately. Above, you were given a sample table to use for each end of observation rounds. You can also choose to incorporate a facsimile target for each end so you can record impact points upon it. I recommended that you use the same point of the shot sequence, preferably when the shooter goes to the "trigger" or continues their "pinch" to engage the shot, to start your timing sequence.
7. What a shooter does during the aiming process isn't hard to observe, excepting you cannot see the shooter's sight picture. I recommend that you get into a position whereby you can line up the tip of the stabilizer with something in the background and superimpose the stabilizer on that item. Then, it is a simple case of watching that stabilizer and which direction it is moving during the aiming process, the break of the shot, and the followthrough.
8. What happens with regard to the release hand and the direction of its travel when the shot breaks is a critical key to whether it was a good, solid shot or a sloppy one. Most top echelon shooters have a certain reaction of their release hand to the explosion of the shot and they repeat this action to near perfection every single time. Often times, you can pick this up, but only if you have watched them enough to pick up the differences. This also relates and follows through (pun intended) to item #7!
9. Watching the head positioning and eyes of the shooter can tell you a lot about the shooter's focus as well. Eye blinking prior to a shot can be very consistent, or it can be a clue to the shooter having problems focusing or a loss of concentration. Very few top echelon shooters will have any head or eye movement during their shot and that includes what happens at the explosion of the shot—their head and the aiming eye will not move.
10. Timing between shots is normally consistent. However during your observations, it could pay you to know what your selected shooter is doing with regard to time between each shot and time remaining when his/her last shot is in the target. Timing between shots is a key element and a significant problem area for mid-level archers (most tend to shoot too fast). It also pays to note, however, that some of the best top professional shooters will shoot very fast indeed. They learn to take (not punch) the shot at the moment of the best opportunity. Top shooters also have limits beyond which they will not go; if it isn't right, they will let down and start over.
11. Watch the thumbs on both the release bow hands. There is a world of knowledge to be gained there. You can instantly tell if a shooter is tightening up at either or both ends simply by watching their thumbs. Some may be "all thumbs" and be really tight when they start out, and out of nowhere, come time to score, those thumbs are loose and relaxed. Others, you will quickly find will start to flag their thumbs and with that, their scores and/or "X-counts" go down the tubes. This is an apparent little thing that turns out to be big.

Top professionals and top echelon shooters have worked on all of the above items until they have become pretty much automated for them. It has taken many hours of concentrated practice to work out a system whereby they can repeat nearly exactly the same process time and time again with little to no variance in that routine.

To watch a professional archer shoot can be mesmerizing and at the same time make you really appreciate what it must be like to shoot like a machine. If you are striving for this perfection, then you should definitely observe a top professional who is similar in body build, shoots the same hand as you do, with hopefully the same release aid (or at least the same style) as you do. If you are barrel chested, emulating the stance and alignment of a tall and slender shooter will be exceptionally difficult to do. In addition, if you are an older shooter, you may well not have the flexibility or build to get that same type of body positioning and alignment as a younger pro you might want to emulate. In fact you might not be able to get the same alignment that you had when you were younger!

I have given you some tools and questions to answer as you build your own "Scouter's Checklist" so that you can carry on a quality observation of a selected professional or top echelon amateur shooter. You have the tools to work with; the rest if up to you as to whether you want to spend the time really learning something.

The last thing to add here is that videotaping your selected shooter can be useful, but you still need to have those written notes, timing data, and visual observations to complete the entire picture. I don't recommend that you videotape a pro at a competitive event for any length of time. They would pick up on this and it could disrupt them. Out of courtesy to them, don't do that. Use your written checklist for this process instead.

The next step would then be to videotape yourself, and . . . yes . . . perform the "Scouter's Checklist" on yourself from your own video! If you watch yourself for the sake of watching yourself, and you don't have a plan, you are spinning your wheels. Better yet, you may well choose to have a close friend complete a "Scouter's Checklist" on your shooting in exchange for you doing one on him/her. You can eat an elephant by taking one bite at a time and by using what is contained in this article you have a meaningful and valuable means of enjoying an archery tournament. This will be well worth your time and effort.

Tom Dorigatti

38

Student Selects Coach

There has been quite a bit of discussion in the archery literature and in online forums about how a student should select an archery coach. However, you probably don't realize that coaches, too, also have a process that he/she goes through in selecting students. There is a tendency for students to look for a coach who is local, has a good reputation, and has reasonable fees for lessons. Most also figure that a top level archer, since he/she knows how to shoot so well, will automatically make a good teacher/coach.

On the coach's side of the table, nothing is ever said about selecting students whose goals, needs, and personality characteristics match the coach's teaching style and philosophy. Being a profession educator, I had to learn to see both sides of this coin in order to become more effective. Educators have to learn how to teach, just as students have to be taught how to learn. This doesn't all come about by osmosis. Believe it or not, teachers and coaches are learners too, and they never stop learning.

I am a retired professional educator, with an Associate's Degree in Secondary Education, and a BA Degree in Secondary Education and Biological Sciences with minors in Physical Science and French. I also hold a Master's Degree in Teaching and Leadership. In addition, I have been an Air Force officer, an in-flight Instructor Navigator/Evaluator in Standardization-Evaluation, and a professional Quality Assurance/Sanitation Control Manager. I have been a certified trainer in many aspects of computer software applications, especially Microsoft *Office*, bringing "newbies" up to speed on how to use those and other various software applications. I've developed training programs and various devices to organize office work, quality assurance laboratory data and reports and budgeting data. And, over the past 45 years, I have worked with innumerable fellow archers as a coach. In all of the above, I have had direct interaction with many different personality types which required me to assess how my personality would or would not mesh with those of my "trainees." I learned from experience that using the wrong type of training program or the wrong approach would spell many hours of lost time and frustration on both my part as the trainer and on the part of the trainees. Do I make mistakes? Absolutely. Do I "connect" with all my students? Absolutely not. But I certainly give that my best effort, since a connection is so very important. Some think that students can and will learn in spite of their teacher(s). While this may be the case in some instances; it is not the norm, and is not acceptable in today's educational environments. With regard to archery, not having a connection with an archery student simply won't work. Don't forget that this is a two way street; the student has a responsibility to connect to their coach just as the coach has the responsibility to connect to his/her student(s).

By now, you may be thinking: "So what does this all have to do with archery"? Or "What is in this for me?"

So What Does this Have to Do with Archery?

Nearly all of us, at one point or another during our archery career, has taken some "coaching," be it formal or informal. In other words, we have all had pointers or constructive suggestions given to us at one time or another. Some of the comments or pointers we asked for, while others had been volunteered to us from a casual observer. In fact, I would wager that all of us have probably had more of the "volunteered" types of tips and pointers than those that we asked for. I would also wager that many of those tips and pointers, although they may have started out being constructive, ended up being more destructive than helpful.

You probably accept the notion that coaching can help to make you a better shooter. Good coaching can determine whether or not you move up the leader board. Good coaching can save you lots of money over the long run, but many archers are very hesitant to commit to coaching sessions or seminars because of various barriers, like "they are too expensive," yet those same archers don't hesitate to purchase the latest and greatest trinket or gadget in an attempt to buy better scores. Then, what normally happens is that "magic bullet" doesn't work out and it either gets tossed in a drawer or gets sold; most times at a substantial loss.

Even if you do subscribe to getting coached, as too many chefs spoil the soup, too many "coaches" spoil the archer. Listening to advice from too many sources will ultimately lead to frustration and confusion, with too many changes being made to too many things at once, and a near total loss of focus on your game and what you are trying to accomplish. "Changing Things on the Fly" was discussed at length in the very first chapter of this book, followed by "Eating the Elephant" one bite at a time. If you haven't read those I recommend you do so now.

What Is In This For Me?

I would also wager that very, very few of the tips and pointers you have gotten came from someone who is a "coach," be it a coach with a shingle/certificate or just a high echelon shooter who offers advice. In this light, I expect that you have been overwhelmed with conflicting advice from several "coaches" or persons oh, so willing to help you with what ails your shooting. I'll also venture to guess that at times, you didn't know who to believe, what to believe, and ultimately, ended up not understanding anything about what it was "they" wanted you to do or how to go about doing it. You got "do this and do that" recommendations and "oh, no, not quite that way, but you are close" assessments of your efforts. You probably received a lot of "don't do this" or "don't do that", or "Why can't you do . . . ?" Worse yet, you also probably received a long list of things that needed to be changed in their rush to "help" you out? Am I correct on this?

You ended up having several "coaches," but you weren't sure which one had suggested what, and none of them told you the "how to do" what was suggested. He/she only told you the "what to do" part of it; leaving you to struggle aimlessly trying to figure it out for yourself; almost always leading you into more difficulties rather than helping to solve your problem.

What is in this is the difference between mastering things *one step at a time* or being confused, disorganized, and frustrated by too many things coming at you from several directions. Being able to separate the good advice from the "do it this way because Joe (or Sally) Top Gun does it and look at all the tournaments he/she has won" advice can be an insurmountable task. Couple that with different pieces of advice for correcting multiple things being thrust at you all at once and you are destined to spiral down into mediocrity. This can and will destroy your self-image and confidence; sometimes beyond repair. Remember I mentioned the comment "This guy is shaking so bad that he should be taken off the shooting line before he hurts somebody?" Well, that is about as low as it gets, but I've heard "helpers" ridicule the person they are trying to help in close to the same manner. If a shooter is in a slump or having difficulties, the last thing he/she needs is negativity.

A Story—A Coaching Scenario From Way Back

This story is from an impromptu coaching session I received back in my recurve/finger shooting days, circa 1973. I was shooting an indoor league and while not shooting any 300's at the time with my Golden Eagle recurve bow, I wasn't doing all that badly either. I had shot several 297's and 298's but couldn't seem to get to the 299 or 300 level even once. I was having problems with lateral shots across the bull's-eye and couldn't figure it out. I had made comments about this right after having shot a 298 league score. Denise Libby, of PAA fame, was shooting in that same league along with Vic Leach, Kevin and Roger Erlandson, and Jim Yochum. Denise heard my comments about those danged left and right arrows. She came up to me to "congratulate me" on my 298 and extended her hand for a hand-shake; or so I thought that was what this was all about. When I shook hands with her, her hand was all slick and slimy, so I pulled my hand away wondering what was going on. That being said, she grabbed my bow, picked it up (Denise was left-handed) and drew it back. Now realize that she had just shook my hand (using her right hand), and now she is drawing my bow back (again with her right hand). I'm still trying to figure out just what is only my hand when she says, "Hey, Tom, why don't you try and shoot your bow? I want to check something." I remember telling her that I needed to wipe off my hand and dry it up. She said that she didn't want me to wipe my hand off but that I should draw and shoot the bow just like it is right now. I hadn't yet made the connection until she said "just like it is right now." I then recall telling her that I couldn't shoot a "slicked up bow and bow hand because the bow would come right back and smack me in the face." She told me not to worry about it, to just draw the bow back and settle the shot and let 'er rip. So, trusting her as I did, I drew back the bow, settled in, let the sight settle, drew through the clicker and let the shot go. The arrow went dead center and it was effortless. I shot a couple of more ends before she told me that she had placed Vaseline on my hand and bow handle. She then replenished the Vaseline on the bow and told me to shoot some more. I only shot a half round, but never had any arrows even come close to missing left or right! She told me to shoot a couple of practice rounds by using the Vaseline on the bow handle and to just let the bow settle into its natural position, the position it would find all by itself. She said that she had noticed that I was taking way too much time and movement trying to "force my bow hand into the bow" rather than letting it find its own sweet spot. I followed her instructions, and shot two consecutive 300's the next two practice sessions, and shot a 299 in league the following week in addition to that. In fact, I went to an indoor tournament a few weeks later and shot my first ever 300 in competitions. Had this impromptu coaching session not taken place, I likely would have never figured out this small but nagging problem. Since that time, I've not spent much time at all trying to gyrate my hand position around, but rather I try to let the bow seek its natural fit to me. Don't get me wrong, however, letting the bow settle to its natural position is not the same thing as the story I told you about the "magic thumb." Those are related, but not related. It is all about getting consistency by simply *letting* it happen; not *making* it happen. The tight thumbs issues are manifestations of this and are very common in archers.

Student Selects Coach

I might as well restate now that it is very common for a student to select an archery coach based upon the coach's prowess with a bow and arrow. Students figure that since said shooter can *shoot* very well and place high in tournaments that he/she must know how to *teach* others how to do what it is he/she does so well. I will tell you right now that this is not always the case, especially with regard to getting you to the top level of this game. I've found over the years that while most of the top shooters are very good at telling you the "what to do" side of things, when asked "how he/she does it," many are at a loss to give you that most important piece of the puzzle.

Another common approach is for archers to select someone who shoots on the same range and who has been shooting a bow for a long, long time. This "coach" offers you free advice, is very friendly, and also is easy going and doesn't push you hard at all. He/she makes your interactions into tutoring sessions which offer a lot of "what to do" suggestions, but don't provide "how to do" what it is you are supposed to do. They often give orders instead of offering suggestions or solutions. Often you are going to find several of these folks at your local range. Each of them tells you "what to do" in a different manner, which isn't always bad, however they will have you doing several things during a session and will be coming at you from different directions, all at the same time. You will hear, "Well, yes, Bill does it that way, but that doesn't work for me, so try it this way." The next thing you know, a change is made away from what Bill had you do and the next time you see Bill, he is upset with you because you went out and asked Ava. Ava changed what Bill was working on with you and now, neither of them understands what you want, and you aren't sure that either of them knew how to get you to make the change in the first place. They are both going to be upset because you went away from their advice.

Notice that this chapter is titled "Student Selects Coach" not "Student Selects Coach*es*." If there is one message I will hammer on in this chapter it is that students need to work with a, meaning one, coach and not multiple coaches at any one time. One of the things that will turn a "coach" away from a student in a heartbeat is when that student goes to someone else and changes are made undoing what the first coach has been working on for however long. When said student comes to the first coach and says, "Bill said I should try it this way, and it seems to be working better. What do you think?" It is a near guarantee that you will lose that first coach quickly and probably many subsequent "coaches" as well. For some reason students in archery seem to think their coaches won't notice a change or a digression from the plan. Of course the other "coaches" don't even know the original coach had a plan and for sure don't know what said plan is.

So, how does a student select a coach? So you your decision on knowledge, potential archery students should observe a coach in action. Some things to look for are:

1. Does the coach appear to be organized?
2. Does the coach appear to have a "plan" when working with his/her students, or is he/she offering advice on several things all at once in a helter-skelter fashion?
3. Is the coach a "screamer" or does he/she work with the student on an amicable basis?
4. Does the coach convey his/her expectations of what is going to be done?
5. Is the coach hands-on, that is does the coach demonstrate to the students what he would like to see done?
6. Does the coach allow time for the student to assimilate what has been asked of the student?
7. Does the coach allow input from the student as to how to accomplish the task?
8. Does the coach allow the student some options concerning the change or changes being asked for?
9. Are the coach's fees reasonable?
10. Is the coach available for you to ask questions or get additional comments or coaching sessions?
11. Is the coach friendly, but firm?
12. Is the coach suggestive and offer up alternative solutions to a problem?
13. What credentials does the coach have? Is he/she a "Certified Archery Instructor?" Is this person a "Certified Professional Educator?" Is this person a top echelon shooter with lots of local, state, regional, or national titles?
14. Does this person come highly recommended from knowledgeable fellow archers?

Clashing Personalities

Some other things to do when selecting your coach include: trying to talk extensively with a potential coach to see what type of personality he/she has. Does his/her personality type mesh with yours? What is your personality type? You have undoubtedly read about personality types and their success levels in archery. I'm not a psychologist, however, so I'm going to include a table below that describes one system that splits people into two groups based on some simple personality traits. It pays to be familiar with this if you want to become a better shooter and not only understand yourself, but also your competition and your coach as well. If you haven't read something similar before, I think you will find it most interesting.

What basic characteristics make up each of these personalities?

Type A	Type B
Impatient	Patient
Has trouble relaxing	Relaxes easily
Aggressive	Easy-going, mellow
Has a "short fuse"	May avoid confrontation
May get upset over small things	Not quick to anger
Competitive, achievement-oriented	
Time urgency (interrupts others, becomes frustrated while waiting in line)	

It is also possible to have a mix of these characteristics, which is classified as Type AB personality.

Most good teachers will, as they learn to teach, swing to both sides of the pendulum in order to become more proficient at working with their students. Even though said teacher might be a Type A personality, they may need to behave as a Type B when doing so is the way to benefit a student or get a needed connection. Then, of course there are times when being competitive, achievement oriented and time urgent must come into play in order to get the tasks accomplished in an organized, orderly, and timely fashion. There are even times when the teacher must switch from being mellow, to becoming aggressive, and great teachers know how do get the best out of both sides of this coin. You can, if you think about it relate this directly to your shooting as well.

Personality Tests on the Internet

There are several free personality tests out on the web that you can use to learn more about your personality type. Go to the following URL for one that I found most interesting and easy to use: *http://stress.about.com/library/Type_A_quiz/bl_Type_A_quiz.htm*

Space limitations and my lack of expertise prohibit me from going into further detail concerning personality traits and types. However, I also think that you will find the reading at the following website to be interesting and rewarding in helping you find out more about yourself and your personality type. It may well help you in how to deal with yourself and others as it relates to your archery, your professional life, and your relations with other people and your family. All of the above will have a direct affect on how well you can perform at a competitive level and how well you will or will not work with your selected coach! Remember, this is your money that you are going to be paying this coach, so pick wisely and intelligently.

http://www.personalitypage.com/portraits.html

Summary

Since the "What to Do" aspects of archery are so openly discussed (over and over and over again), I have become more and more cognizant of trying to teach from a "How to Do It" aspect of the game. This is an important approach for both students and coaches, and I've incorporated ProActive archery into the entire scheme of things.

Making it to the winner's circle requires that the finer points of form and shot execution be mastered and programmed. It is extremely difficult for an archer, especially one who is just entering the game of archery, to find the resources to get started properly. The cost of equipment must be born and with coaches being hard to find and also needing to be paid, it is easy to just learn from more experienced archers.

On the other hand, if you are learning improper technique, this can lead to injuries and also frustratingly slow progress in acquiring proficiency. "Free advice," while often times helpful, can become confusing and even frustrating for any student of the game (and worth every penny).

Trying to find a coach is easier these days than it was even in the recent past, however, the key is in finding the right coach and then the coach also making sure that he/she has the right student. I have offered my insights in the hope of getting both the potential archery student and the potential coach some firm ground on which to stand to make the experience more beneficial.

The key lies in both parties selecting one another based more upon a proper fit of styles, schedules, costs, and having a methodology of things to consider in the selection and screening process should help.

I highly recommend that even if you are not an archery coach, you read the following Chapter, "Coach Selects Student." This too will be very valuable on your quest to become a "ProActive Archer."

Tom Dorigatti

39

Coach Selects Student

It goes without saying that once you have selected a potential coach your coach will not be signing on until he/she has also "selected" you. Good coaches will be going through an analysis of you as to whether or not you and he/she are a fit. The coach will be asking much the same questions as I listed in Chapter 38, "Student Selects Coach."

In addition, any teacher or coach would like to have the attributes described below in his/her selected students. You must realize that archery coaches are not public school teachers being paid taxpayer dollars. The student has their choice of coach and the coach has a choice of which student(s) he chooses to take on in his classes. This is a two-way street. Yes, it is your money that is being spent, but you are purchasing the coaches' time and the coach has expectations as to what he is getting as a student.

Again, I'm not a high level archery coach. However, like any reasonably good professional educator, I had to first learn how to teach in order that I could teach how to learn! I had to realize early on that there is a definite difference between a teacher with 42 years experience and a teacher with one year's experience 42 times.

I'm going to list the attributes that any teacher or coach would really want to have in a student. This seems to me to be the easiest way to get across the point I'm trying to drive home to not only potential archery students, but also to archery coaches. See how many of these you match up to:

In selecting a student, I personally would recommend the following:

1. A visit to the student's home shooting range and a long observation of the potential student in the process of shooting. This should be non-verbal and the potential coach should be taking notes, either mentally or in writing as to what the student may need with regard to a coaching technique or style, form flaws, personality, confidence, mental game, etc.
2. Offer help only when asked for, and then perform an assessment. During my preparation of this chapter, my editor, Steve Ruis mentioned an important element concerning a good coach. Steve Ruis said, and I quote: "When good coaches are asked for advice (good coaches never offer without being asked except under special circumstances) they simply say they would have to do an assessment first. I often will

say something like "I think we would want to look at your stance and bow hand and release techniques, but I will need to do an assessment first." Olympic Coach Al Henderson would watch a student shoot for quite a while in silence, sometimes more than one lesson. Then he would ask "What do you think your problems are?" and that would begin the discussions and the relationship."

. . . Another Story

I had occasion one year while I was competing at Vegas to receive some coaching. My brother had asked Frank Pearson to do an assessment of me during the first day of the Vegas tournament. When I finished the round that day, Frank came up to me and asked if I had the time to sit and talk about what he observed. Frank, at the time, was one who also had the philosophy of taking things one step at a time. He told me about the one main item (and only one) that he had consistently observed during my shooting. He told me to focus on this one thing for the next day, but he did this in such a positive manner that it really stuck with me both as a "learner" in this situation, but also had an impact on me as a professional educator and archery coach. In addition to this main "negative," he also came up with numerous positives so that I didn't feel he was being super critical about everything. I didn't feel at all overwhelmed by a list of things that were out of whack. He gave me one main thing, and added only one other one that related to it for me to work on.

. . . Lessons Learned and Practiced

One thing to always remember as an educator/coach/evaluator is that no matter how bad things are, you must, absolutely must, find as many positives and/or things your students are doing correctly as you find they are not quite doing up to snuff. If you unload on them with all the things they are doing wrong, that is a boatload of negatives, and you will lose them from the very beginning, and it will be very tough to get them back. Mix your recommendations for changes (always sound like negatives) with things done well (always sound like positives). You must also remember that you can give way too many positive strokes, too and end up sounding insincere. Remember that no matter how bad a shooter appears, find something positive to start with, and also end with something positive. Allow the student to connect with you by even asking them, "What do you feel you are doing the best?" It will go a long way toward this thing called "connection." The word "wrong" has a much worse effect on a student than the word "incorrect," however phrases like "You need some work on. . . ." or "Let's see if we can perhaps make a correction to this. . . ." go a lot further than either "wrong" or "incorrect." There is such a fine line between turning on a student to what you would like to have them accomplish and "turning them off" for a session or maybe losing them forever. Of course, for you students reading this, once again this is a two-way street, "I can't. . . .", or "I don't like this. . . .", "This isn't going to work. . . ." or the worst: "Whatever!" are all complete turn offs to your coach and will tend to move them, understandably, to the "Type A" side of the personality spectrum.

3. I highly recommend that coaches write and print out a "Student Interview Checklist" and fill it out as you interview each potential student. I also recommend that you give a copy of the checklist to the student as well. It is up to you as to whether or not you give them this copy before or after the interview. Some instructors don't want the student(s) reading ahead of them and not focusing on the question at hand, while others want the students to know what is coming next. I think it best to have the copy ready and, if the student is reacting well and focusing then give them the copy; otherwise, hold off. However, if parents are involved, then obviously, I would give the parents a copy of the "Student Interview Checklist" so they can follow along. Here is my list:
   a. What are your goals with regard to archery?
   b. What are your favorite types of shooting (3-D, hunting, indoors, outdoors, etc.)?
   c. What level of competence to you expect to achieve as a result of being coached?
   d. Do you have any other "advisors" that you speak with regularly? (Try to keep names out of this, but if they have been already professionally coached, it can help a lot to know the names of those coaches).
   e. What is your personality type? At this point, give them the links to the website mentioned in Chapter 38, so that they can find out for themselves.
      http://stress.about.com/library/Type_A_quiz/bl_Type_A_quiz.htm
      and *http://www.personalitypage.com/portraits.html*
   f. Tell the student exactly where you are coming from with regard to practicing, other "advisors," making changes without prior notice to the coach, etc.
   g. Discuss briefly where you think the student is with their level of competence in archery right now, and a brief idea with where you are going to start. You will probably need to evaluate the student to do this. (Having an "evaluation session" as an audition, so to speak, is a good way to feel a student out.)
   h. Discuss the costs of coaching including equipment upgrades, etc.
   i. Discuss the availability and frequency of the coaching sessions.
   j. Discuss that there may be a written and oral competitive plan and a written and oral "practice plan" put in place to organize the student's progress.
   k. Discuss with the student that an immediate increase in scores and a sharp move up the leader board may not happen. Be sure that the student fully understands that there may well be some peaks and valleys in the process.
   l. Discuss with the student the importance of the 21-day rule of thumb; that is that any change of habit takes at least 21 days of effort to incorporate the change. Things will not be happening overnight.
   m. If you, the coach, so choose make up a "coaching contract" that outlines behavioral responsibilities for the student, a release from liability should the student injure themselves, etc. I do not have the expertise to write such a contract, but if you are a new coach, there are sources out on the web for such items. You may well incorporate a Behavioral Contract as part of this if the student is a youngster. Today's students are used to Behavior Contracts in school,

so they are pretty much used to the idea.

n.Go over the list below: "My ideal archery student would . . ."

My Ideal Archery Student Would . . .

An ideal archery student has a certain set of attitudes and behaviors. No one student would have all or even most of these but each is worth exploring or emulating. These also, not surprisingly, apply to coaches as well.

My ideal archery student would (these are in no particular order):

1. Seldom, if ever use the words "I can't", I won't, "This isn't going to work", or "Whatever!" Those are a sure-fire ways to lose a coach!
2. Seldom, if ever, when the coach observes something and relates to the student what the coach saw, should the student say, "No, I didn't do that."
3. Always "Fess up when you mess up." That is to say, when there is a mistake made or a failure to communicate properly, own up to it and get on with the business at hand.
4. Never hold a grudge. What is done is done; it is over. If it isn't, discuss it until it is. Try not to repeat the same circumstances again.

An Aside—Yes, Yet Another Story

My students were always surprised when after they were "corrected" for inappropriate behavior or not complying with class procedures, I didn't continue on with "the look," or "stay angry with them." (Yes, I said "with them," because they were probably angry at the same time.) If they had to be removed from class, they would be so flabbergasted upon their return to class I would say "hello" to them as if nothing had happened. Try as I may, even though they were told at the beginning that "what is done is done; it is over, learn from our mistakes, and let's move on," they still had a puzzled look on their face. It was even more interesting when they would, should they have a birthday or special occasion, get a birthday or special occasion card personalized for them and directly from me. It was like, "I just got kicked out of your class and you are still giving me a card?" Why certainly . . . what is done is done; don't repeat that behavior. It was the behavior that needed correcting, not the person.

5. If another "coach" gives you advice, bring it to your coach for discussion before you do anything about it. Accepting "help" from another person is one thing, but utilizing that help and making changes that result in lost time or regression is nearly unforgivable.
6. Realize that there are going to be misunderstandings. Resolve them immediately and don't linger on them.
7. Never be a "screamer." Never belittle a coach or embarrass them publicly (the same goes for students). If you are approaching a boiling point, ask for a break. Go get a soda, go to the restroom or go outside and get a breath of fresh air. Don't let this blow up into a major confrontation or even a minor one. A simple, "Wow that is sure a lot more than I expected" can defuse things quickly.

8. Like a coach, always find something positive, and address any negatives including something positive. No matter how bad it gets, there is always something that the coach or student is doing right.
9. Try to learn (teach) from a positive standpoint. It isn't, "you are doing this wrong" but rather, "I think it might go better for you if you would try to do it this way."
10. Students, if you are having difficulty understanding a concept, ask questions in a positive manner. Don't say, "This isn't going to work", but rather ask if there might be a different way of doing the same thing. Or, you could simply ask, "If I tried it this way, would that be a possibility of getting it done?"
11. Avoid emotional outbursts. Before frustrations can build to such a level as to cause such an outburst they need to be stated and addressed. Never walk away or pout openly. Asking for a break versus simply walking off are going to be interpreted in two entirely different ways, especially if there is a body language or facial expression or other non-verbal communications involved.
12. Always be up front and honest concerning practicing between sessions. If you didn't practice a new concept, simply say so. Doing so will save lots of time and expense. Feeding your coach false information doesn't help him/her help you—it hurts.
13. Always make sure you agree to what the rate being charged is. Then be sure to pay on time and not fall behind.
14. Keep the rate of pay between you and the coach private. This is a must. It is business between coach and student and is not open for public scrutiny.
15. Understand that different levels of student may well be charged different rates. Many good coaches don't charge every single student exactly the same rate. There are simply too many other variables involved for any coach to set a "standard rate."
16. Always ask your coach in advance whether other parties can be involved in one of your coaching sessions. (Can I bring my cousin; he's visiting from out of town?) Never try to get a friend in on a coaching session for free. Friends and relatives observing can also be more of a hindrance than a help due to distractions and the tendency of the student to show off for their friends. Not a good idea. Parents are one thing, but friends are yet another.
17. Always call ahead if you have to cancel a coaching session. Again, this is another two-way street.
18. Always be respectful of a person's "free time" and don't invade it.
19. If a coach feels physical contact is necessary, they should advise you that they need such and should be able to explain why. This is very, very critical in today's society, especially in a public place. Onlookers can and will get the wrong idea over misinterpreted touching.
20. Always turn off cell phones, *iPods*, and other electronic communications gear during coaching sessions. If this is not possible (single parents with sick children won't want to be out of contact, for example) discuss the use of such devices and the circumstances under which they will be used. Never start your coaching session with earplugs in your ears or electronics in plain sight.

21. Remain focused on the task at hand and give your full and undivided attention.
22. Always keep your language appropriate and avoid the use of vernacular or street talk.
23. When asked for an assessment of how you feel or how a shot felt, or what you did or didn't see, be totally honest; never answer such a question based upon what you think the coach wants to hear.
24. Give honest effort without bias towards what you think the coach has in mind. If you don't understand, ask.
25. Not try to jump ahead of the "program." If you think you could make faster progress, discuss it with your coach in advance.
26. Tell your coach immediately if something being tried causes pain or undue stress. Never try to tough it out by being silent about this sort of thing.
27. Avoid second-guessing your coach and his/her recommendations. If you have a problem with something the coach is asking you to do, find a way to ask why without being sarcastic. Same goes for the coach; a good coach is never belittles or is sarcastic toward a student.
28. Advise your coach of any muscle soreness or major health issues you are experiencing.
29. Advise your coach when you are tired, frustrated, or cannot concentrate.
30. Make eye contact at all times when your coach is trying to relay information to you.
31. Tell your coach when you think that "what so-and-so told you to do seems better." Once again, being diplomatic and polite is always the best approach, for both the student and the coach.
32. Tell your coach that you read something about you are working on. Ask for his/her opinion. Ask if the advice you read applies to you.
33. Do not make a change back to an "old" form element because the new form element "wasn't working for you." Remember the "21 day rule of thumb" on learning something new.
34. Do not make changes to your equipment setup without checking in with your coach first. This is especially important with regard to bow and/or release aid adjustments, footing, stance, etc. Those are set for specific reasons, and while a change could be appropriate, don't try to change it on the fly.
35. Always make an assessment of what is working with your coach and how his/her teaching style is impacting your learning. Your coach, on the other hand, should be constantly assessing how his/her teaching style is impacting each and every student's learning.
36. Take the personality test above to find out your personality traits. This helps learners realize what their tendencies are with regard to the shooting process and how their personality meshes or doesn't mesh with competitive archery. If you think that the results would help the coach to get to know you better, you might share those important elements with him/her. You don't have to give your life's story, but knowing each other better up front is better than constant discovery.

Summary

While the lists above is long, it is hoped that both archery students and archery coaches will quickly realize that "being coached" and "coaching" are not simple processes. Most times "getting coached" is not a short term project, but rather a long term work in progress. These WIP's are likely not going to follow an exactly predictable path. There will be ups and downs and even diversions. Plans will be written and changed and changed again in order to accomplish goals and objectives. If done properly and with both parties fully cognizant of their responsibilities in this process, both will have positive and fulfilling experiences.

Tom Dorigatti

40

Are You Up to the Challenge?

The New "Pull Through" Style of Release Aid

The new "pull through" or tension activated release aids such as the Carter *Evolution+*, the Carter *Revolution+* and the new Stanislawski *Element* are quickly becoming staples in the arsenal of serious compound archers. At the same time, however, many archers are using them but for a very short time before giving up on them. These archers claim "the release is changing on me all the time" or "this release doesn't work at all for me." As you may know, I did extensive testing concerning the first statement above (see *Archery Focus* magazine, Vol. 12, No. 6, 2008) and the data clearly indicate that the release itself doesn't change. As far as the second statement goes, that "this release doesn't work at all for me," is believable, albeit not a foregone conclusion. However, for the purposes of this book, the data and opinions are not the focus.

The intent of this chapter is neither to refute nor support the "doesn't work at all" theory. The intent is to offer some tips and guidelines along with more facts concerning "the learning curve" of this type of release aid. Most professional archers cannot fathom the problems faced by archers who aren't in the upper echelon. Most "ordinary" archers cannot understand how the pros can pick up just about any release aid, set it, and shoot perfect scores as if perfect scores were easy. These gifted archers do

understand the "what to do" part of this. However, most cannot relate the "how to do it" part of this operation, which is the very thing developing or mid-level shooters need. I intend to fill that void.

I'm going to revisit some items contained in articles that I wrote for Archery Focus magazine about tension activated release aids and add some additional interesting things I've found since doing that research. I've learned a great deal more of the "how to."

Some call me the king of fiddle, but it is by fiddling and learning that is keeping me shooting, so what the heck? I'm having fun doing it, and maybe, just maybe, what I've learned (the hard way) will make it easier for those of you who are trying to learn from the beginning. I do know that there are several archers who I've helped get started on this style of release aid who are shooting personal best score after personal best scores. Several others wouldn't be shooting today if they hadn't elected to go the route of the tension activated release aids.

I won't be focusing on specific brands and models of tension release activated release aids. What I will definitely do, however, is to offer up suggestions, based upon the experiences of mid-level shooters, to help you shorten your learning curve with this most interesting and challenging type of release. The techniques discussed do work, but like anything else, there is more than one way of doing things. Typically you may try a technique and not have success and then try another and have it be the one you're looking for.

Now if you are wondering "Why is this chapter about release aids in the section on 'Attitude & Mental Game' instead of the 'Equipment' section?" The answer is contained in quoted claims: "These archers claim 'the release is changing on me all the time' or 'this release doesn't work at all for me.'" In my line of thinking, those comments bring up a problem, not really with the equipment per se, but more to do with the archers attitude/mental game. If you have a poor attitude toward, or a lack of confidence in any piece of gear, it affects your mental game and subsequently your performance. So, I'm taking this particular piece of equipment to demonstrate how a simple adjustment to attitude and mental game can turn things around. I think you will come out of this chapter with a better means to evaluate many other aspects of equipment, setup, and other archery-related elements. However, as the title of this chapter asks: Are *you* up to the challenge?

To get started we need to talk about the subtleties involved in using tension activated release aids. Many archers go into this with some skepticism (bordering on negativity) because they've heard horror stories from others who have had difficulties with this type of release aid and gave up on them. Most of these folks haven't really checked out the opposition, so to speak, and have gone into this with neither an open mind nor a clear understanding of what these releases require in the way of form, attitude, and alignment adjustments. These archers also have, more than likely, lacked a clear, organized plan of attack. Like so many other things, they'll make changes "on the fly" (see Chapter 1), and violate the rule of "one thing at a time." Worse yet, many won't work with this new fangled thing for very long, then go to a competition ill-prepared, and thus be "going into battle with an untested weapon." Last, most of them went into this figuring that if it doesn't work, they can always "go back to the old way that worked." Basically, they are defeated before they even start with their attitude and mental game being responsible and not their "new toy."

To avoid this trap, here is some background information that affects how these releases work.

Hard Cams and Hybrid Cam Bows

Draw Length and Draw Length Control I cannot emphasize enough how critical draw length and draw length control are to successfully shooting this particular type of release aid. In my opinion, you cannot spend enough time getting your draw length correct and your control of this aspect of your form down. As discussed in earlier chapters (see Chapters 14-18), the "to anchor draw length" is, in my opinion, the most important aspect of shooting this type of release consistently and I've written before and proved with data and pictures that hard stops are not really hard (see Chapter 14). With this type of release, you need to be as close as is humanly possible to the exact same spot against those stops every time you pull the bow to anchor. If you pull too hard one time, the release is going to trip early; if you pull a bit softer the next (the tiniest bit), then the shot is going to take longer for you to make the poundage to trip the release. Here is more about draw length control:

- A tiny bit short on draw length is better than any bit too long. I've found that it is much easier to get the proper "to anchor" draw length consistent by being just a tad short. I don't mean ¼″ either; we are talking much less than that!
- Use of "cable tapes" will help you get things going. Put the tapes on your cables in such a position that they come to match up at peep level when you are at full draw. This allows you to just give them a glance and go to the shot sequence. After a few hundred shots, you will be amazed at how you will have reduced the range in your to anchor draw length from ¼″ to ½″ down to ⅛″ or less! This or even less than ⅛″ is what you must have to be successful and consistent with this style of release aid! This is all due to paying close attention to this detail and doing it religiously to the point it becomes second nature. In my opinion, you cannot shoot this release consistently by "feel" alone (the "feel" of how hard you are against those stops or the wall). Close isn't good enough with these release aids.
- Cam synchronization (timing) is a part of draw length control and the feel of the release at anchor. On a hybrid cam bow, the wall is spongy if the cams are out of synch. This really creates problems with steadiness and draw length control. You will need to creep tune those hybrid cam bows for sure to get that mushy feeling out of them.
- Positioning of your bow shoulder has a huge impact upon draw length control (as well as on pulling ability). I've found that you cannot get away with any shoulder float if you expect to be consistent with such a release and its trip time. If you come into anchor and let your shoulder rise up, you have already come in short. You have also already tightened the wrong muscles across to the other side, raised

your drawing elbow too high, and it will translate into the tightening up of the drawing forearm muscles. At this point, you aren't pulling anymore and will tend to push with the bow arm, raising the shoulder more and tightening up more. You will swear you are pulling your guts out, but what you are doing is pushing your shoulder up which is shortening things up, not relaxing them out. You are going nowhere and going nowhere fast. If you don't let down, you are in for a huge miss.

- Finger placement on the release itself is also part of the "to anchor" draw length control. Pick a finger depth with all the fingers on the release and stick with it. You cannot go deep with your fingers one time and not so deep the next. This directly impacts your to anchor draw length and impacts that pressure you have on the wall of the cam. I think finger placement is one of the biggest things overlooked by archers when using these releases.
- Letting up with the first finger (or any fingers, for that matter) when you let off the safety. This again, drastically changes many things, but the first amongst them is your to-anchor draw length. You might think that it is only ⅛″ or so, but you lose that ⅛″, and you now have ¼″ to make up for that you have lost at the beginning of the shot! I struggle with this when shooting this type of release aid.
- Coming off the safety slowly and carefully. This is costing you time. I also guarantee (through my own experience) that all the time you are coming off that safety you are also losing tension and will have to make up all of that time and effort to get the release to trip. This is akin to starting and stopping your tension or "starting your pinch." The pulling cannot stop; not even for an instant. Get off that safety as quickly and with as little movement as possible, immediately after getting to your to anchor draw length.
- Having the release fire as soon as you let off the trigger. This is a big concern of many newbie and even experienced tension release archers. What happens after a premature release is that the next shot probably won't go off easily, if at all. Then your next thought is to change the release setting. My recommendation: Don't do it! Leave it alone or, if you do change the setting, increase the tension very, very slightly. What you did was to just draw in ever so slightly tighter into the wall. You weren't paying attention and that is all. Don't nurse your way off the safety. Get off the safety as quickly and smoothly as possible. This release style is "set it and forget it." I have a few students who haven't touched the setting on their tension releases in over two years now, and counting. I also know several back tension release shooters who haven't changed the position of their "half moon" on that style of release in many years; some as long as 10 years or more. Why change was has worked nearly perfectly for so very, very long and you have been successful with?

Hand Positioning at Anchor

Hand positioning will affect your to anchor draw length quite a bit. I recommend that you use this style of release with a bit more first finger pressure and avoid any rotation of the release at the pinky end. By having more first finger pressure, you insure that your loop is at the proper point on the release hook, giving you full mechanical advantage. If you "roll or rotate" the pinky end of the release aid away from the bow, you place the loop too close to the body of the release and lose a lot of your mechanical advantage. This makes you come in short making you feel like you have to pull that much further to get the bow to the weight needed to trip the release.

- Hand positioning with the Carter *Revolution+*, which has a little finger controlled safety, however, is quite different. (I don't know of any other tension release out there that has the safety at the pinky end of the release aid, so I'm mentioning it specifically.) The trip gate on the Carter *Revolution+* is in the opposite direction, thus you don't necessarily want to pull the *Revolution+* with first finger pressure, since that would reduce your mechanical advantage. In addition, my own experience tells me that engaging its safety with your pinky finger, while pulling with more first finger pressure, is a sure-fire way to acquire a fat lip, an arrow into the wall or off the bales, and some embarrassment.
- Hand positioning with respect to your jaw bone can make the difference between the release firing or not firing, no matter how hard you pull.

People who anchor more on the side of their face or those who anchor with a "pinky finger up" orientation won't normally have this problem. The problem that they have is rotation of the pinky either to a more vertical position or bringing the pinky down to level as they "pull" to get the poundage needed to trip the release. As the attitude of the release changes, they are engaging forearm and hand muscles and lose engagement in their back muscles. This costs them in time and effort.

If you simply learn to set the release hand angle at the stage of your shot sequence where you engage the release onto the string, put slight pressure on the release, set that release hand angle, and then set the bow hand position, you are going to be much better off. Once that hand angle is set, it is best that you don't bounce around and change this position once you get to anchor. Doing so costs you time, and also makes it very tough to replicate.

Tip You can learn to feel whether or not your pinky finger is up too much to the vertical or down too far to the horizontal. It is quick and easy once you think about it. All you have to do is, without drawing the bow; place your release hand at your normal anchor position. Then, rotate your pinky upwards to the vertical upwards position. You will feel the muscles in your forearm tighten and also those across your pulling shoulder. Now, let back down, and start over only this time rotate your pinky to straight and level or slightly below. Once again you will feel different forearm and shoulder muscles tighten up. Now, simply come to your normal anchor and rotate your pinky up or down until you feel little to no tension in those forearm muscles or muscles across the top of the shoulder. That, my friends is your personal most relaxed release hand rotation, the one you should be looking for. (There is no advantage to tension in your release hand, just the opposite.) Each person needs to find his/her own hand angle positioning with regard to the angle of the pinky finger, since everyone's anatomy is slightly different and, frankly, emulating someone else's release hand angle is a haphazard means of going about this. That relaxed release hand, wrist, forearm, upper arm, and drawing shoulder are key elements of shooting any release aid, but are even more critical with tension style release aids. Master your hand position, and you will be well on your way to improvement no matter which style of release you are shooting!

Not All Hand Positions Are Good What about people (like me) who shoot a pretty level hand position? Well, this one is the real drawback for using these release aids. The hardest thing to get around is when you anchor under your jawbone with a flat hand (pinky parallel to the ground) and remove your thumb from the safety, you inadvertently re-engage that safety ever so slightly because it is touching the side of your neck! I caught myself doing this some time ago and this item has been exceedingly difficult for me to accommodate. In addition, with your release hand more horizontal, the tendency is to rotate your draw elbow around, thereby causing the release body to rotate. Rotation of the release body will not trip this style of release aid, so rotation of the release hand or release body is to be avoided.

Yet Another "True Story" I didn't discover this solution to the problem (neck engagement of the safety). It comes from a "newbie" tension release archer of only a few days, Glen Gaul. He doesn't shoot flat handed, but he was watching me shoot and I told him that the last arrow didn't go off easy because I had the safety ever so slightly touching my neck. Glen says, "Why don't you try what I've done to mine?" He showed me that he had changed out the small friction peg with a larger round barrel normally used on thumb-trigger models. He said it gave him a better feel and made his tension release match his outdoor backup thumb trigger release even closer. I tried this, and voilà, it worked! Having that extra diameter there allows me to sense it much sooner and avoid that re-engagement of the safety when at anchor.

Drawing Elbow Positioning

Most of those I work with end up with a slightly higher elbow position shooting a tension style release aid. Some of this is due to some using a slightly shorter draw length once they have accommodated the throat length of this style of release aid. Others use a slightly longer draw length and still end up learning that the drawing elbow needs to be a touch higher to allow the shoulder and back muscles to work in the correct plane. The other items include:

1. The fact that they quickly learn that they cannot rotate the release body to trip the release; something they are accustomed to doing with a thumb trigger release aid (the amount of rotation is only slight with a thumb trigger, but people think they are moving the release aid a long distance. Many trip gate shooters however like to have a lot of handle rotation to help keep the element of surprise and avoid "wristing off" the release or cheating on it. With the elbow up, they are finding it easier to pull straight back and slightly downwards, not swinging their draw elbow around to help engage a thumb on the trigger.
2. To keep the release positioning more consistent it is easier to raise your elbow very slightly, which helps you to draw straight back instead of the "around your head" type of drawing that you had to do with a thumb trigger or most trip gate

releases. In actuality the rotation is more around and down with the elbow due to the physics related to how our shoulder and rhomboid muscles do their work.

3. It also helps to keep you from moving the pinky positioning downwards to level, because if you do, you will immediately feel the twisting motion in the forearm and know it isn't right. You did take the time to try the exercise in the "Tip" above, didn't you?

   Bringing the elbow around and into line as you hit your anchor. This, of course, must be done without rotating the release frame at the same time! Having to do this is a result of the tad shorter draw length. It is, in my opinion an essential thing to get under control. The tendency one has once they learn that they cannot rotate the release is to forget to get the drawing elbow around and thus make it next to impossible to engage their back muscles and lift the scapula to "lock them" into proper position. If you don't bring that drawing elbow around, it is impossible not to use arm muscles to hold back the bow; your sight picture is going to be shaky, your bow arm will tighten up, and you won't get this type of release aid to trip consistently, if at all. This is yet another place to check to make sure your drawing elbow has come around into line (but not past the line of the arrow). Sometimes this might mean bringing your front foot forward very slightly to get your shoulder alignment corrected. Do you remember the "blind bale" stance alignment exercise from a past article? This comes into play once again if you change to a tension style of release. It is easy to do, and even easier to integrate into your shot sequence.

Soft Cam and Twin Cam "Wheelie" Bows

During my learning stage, I decided to give this type of release a try on a soft-stopped twin cam "wheelie" bow. Those of you who have never shot a "wheelie" bow probably cannot even fathom the smoothness and ease of draw of such a bow. Nor can you appreciate the lower let-offs of 55% or less. Here is my personal take on shooting a twin cam bow with soft stops and a long valley with a tension style of release aid.

1. All of the items discussed above apply to the twin cam bow, but you must have even tighter tolerances and precision for "all the above."
2. One would think that it would help if you set the poundage of the release tripping closer to the holding weight so that when you come out of the valley, the release would trip before you go too deep past the "wall." I found just the opposite, like so many other release settings! I initially thought that I would have to set the release about two pounds over holding weight. I had installed cable tapes and was drawing the bow very consistently, or so I thought. But, some of the time, the release tripped as soon as I let off the safety, and others, the release wouldn't trip at all! Most of these were from inconsistencies I noted above. However, a large part of it was also the fear of the thing going off too early. Thus, the biggest culprit? The trip weight was set way too light. I have the most success with the twin cam by setting the trip weight at five to six pounds over the holding weight!
3. Cam timing is critical when you are pulling back past the valley this far. On my

particular bow, I was pulling against the cables on a shoot thru system. The creep tune had to be right on in order to get any consistency at all out of the bow.

4. To anchor draw length is extremely hard to duplicate! I have draw tapes on the bow, but the valley is so long that it is very easy to vary that "to anchor" draw length by ¼″ or more. I started shortening up the draw length in half twists on each of the four cables until I got the most stable sight picture. I shortened it some more until the bow was shaky and then lengthened it a half twist and left it there. Even at this setting, adjusting the bow so I can get release consistency is a really tough thing to do.
5. Coming off the safety too slowly. I can't emphasize how many misses or let-downs this has cost me and others. Set the tension so you can get off the safety without letting up on anything. Do it smoothly and quickly with as little movement as possible.
6. Conclusion about shooting a twin cam long-valley bow with the tension style release aids: I'm not a professional level archer. However, I'm a very experienced twin cam "wheelie bow" shooter. I shot all of my personal best scores with this type of bow when I was in my prime. Shooting this bow is like going home to a long-lost family. However, my initial hypothesis that shooting this kind of bow with the tension style of release would be a walk in the park was totally incorrect! While the bow "tuned up" just fine and aims just fine, getting the tension releases to trip in any semblance of consistency is beyond my homely capability. I can take any of my other Carter releases, my old Stans, and even my *FailSafe II* and shoot just fine with this wheelie bow. However, after several weeks of shooting the bow with the tension style releases, I became convinced that unless you have heavy mettle and have form that is utter perfection, this type of release is not going to be an effective release with a twin cam bow with a soft wall or long valley.

Summary

In this chapter, I've reviewed what I've found to be the main stumbling blocks in getting yourself to shooting the new tension style of release aids and get them working for you and you working with them instead of against them. The key elements are:

1. Draw length and draw length consistency, including absolute control of the to-anchor draw length
2. Cam Timing/Synchronization
3. Shoulder Positioning
4. Finger positioning on the release aid. With the majority of the tension releases, more first finger is better and gives more mechanical advantage. However, with the Carter Revolution+, pulling with all fingers and very little if any increased pressure in the first finger is recommended, because the Revolution+ has the safety on the pinky side of the release aid.
5. Letting up with first finger (or any finger) once you disengage the safety.
6. Hand positioning at anchor. A "pinky up" orientation gives clearance for the safe-

ty to not brush up against your neck. If shooting a "flat hand" anchor, then try replacing the small friction post with a "thumb barrel," it will give you a hint that you are too close and you'll avoid a lot of let-downs and forcing of shots.

7. Drawing elbow positioning. You'll end up with a slightly higher elbow. Don't forget, as part of the new sequence to bring the drawing elbow into line, but without changing the angle of that release.
8. Unless you have great mettle and perfect form, trying to shoot a twin cam bow with soft stops and long valley is a trial and tribulation. The tension style of release aid isn't designed to shoot with this type of cam system, in my opinion.

My experiences and those of my students, along with an extensive study and data collection I did on this style of release aids clearly show that the release aid is not what is changing from shot to shot. The archer's variations, things that change from shot to shot (even minor ones), have to be worked out with perseverance and practice, seeking perfection. This takes a commitment, but one that is worth every minute of your time. I'm seeing people who I've worked with come off the range on cloud nine. They are shooting better and better and coming up with personal best after personal best scores. Several are still in the game today only because of this commitment and successes with the tension release aids, and more are trying them all the time. Certainly many give up on them and sell them dirty cheap or even give them away. Most have accepted the challenge and taken the time, and now they "are up to the challenge."

These people made the adjustment, and they also had and continue to have their attitude and mental game worked into shooting this style of release aid. The attitude & mental game aspects from this chapter can and should be applied to other aspects of your equipment or form adjustments as well. You attitude and mental approach to any change in style or equipment can and will make or break that experiment. If you approach any change, no matter how small, with your attitude and mental game out of whack you have already lost more than half the battle. You won't have the mettle to continue on because in reality you have given up before you even started. I remember being told by archery legend Dean Pridgen; "If you ever walk up to the shooting stake or go to shoot an arrow and any doubt enters your mind, or you think the word "miss," you must learn to stop immediately, let down, clear your head, and start all over." He didn't add to what he said but I will: "If you step up to the line or approach an equipment or form change with the wrong attitude or mental game, then you must stop, re-focus and start over. You are not 'up to the challenge' for that shot/change at that time, so don't even try it."

Section 7

Making Archery Fun (Again)

In this section, you will see some things from previous sections and chapters repeated. I have no means of knowing which chapters you have read or will read in this book. I also have no means of knowing which order you will opt to read the sections and chapters. So, forgive the repetition. Hey, ProActive archers know when to skip over things!

Making archery fun, in my humble opinion, has a lot to do with being ProActive about your archery. You already know you can and may well now suffer from slumps, from boredom, and even suffer near complete burn-out. Some of you have heard top shooters say that there isn't a challenge to some of the rounds, especially the indoor rounds. So, why not take the time to figure out some preventive measures you can take to alleviate this situation before you have a problem? Why not become ProActive and creative and put some challenge and fun back into the game by varying things up while still accomplishing the goals of any practice session? By reading this section and embracing the message, you will be able to revitalize yourself by varying your practice regimens while also varying the types of rounds and target faces you use to practice on. There is much out there to relieve the monotony of practice but still allowing you to accomplish your goals. So, read on, enjoy, and take a spin through a different perspective concerning practicing and participating in your archery. As the cartoon character Foghorn Leghorn always said, "Pay attention, yuhIf you don't look square on to your scale you may get parallax reading errors like these. All of these are the same sight viewed at different angles.442

might learn sumpthin."

Tom Dorigatti

41

Making Practice Fun

There is something to be said about the fact that nearly all shooters want to "win" and often have lofty goals of winning a league or winning a State Indoor Title, then a Sectional Title, and then the National Indoor, or the Vegas Shoot, or whatever. Unfortunately they also often lose sight of the fact that all of this isn't going to come about over night, or even in a year; in fact these lofty goals may be unreachable but for a select few archers. So, why set such lofty goals so soon? Here's my take on this "winning" focus. Let's say you go to a tournament with the goal to win your division. That may be a reasonable goal, provided you know your scores have been at that level. You should remember a couple of things, however. If your scores haven't been at that level of expertise before you arrive at the tournament, then they aren't likely to climb to that level at the tournament. In other words: if you don't have your "A" game before-hand, it isn't likely to magically appear at the tournament. However, there is another way to look at this. Going to a tournament with a goal is a good idea, but that goal should be to shoot a better score than you shot at your last competition. If you do that, then you have accomplished your goal, and you are a winner. You really have nobody to beat but yourself; if you can do that, then you are well on your way to vastly improving your position on the overall leader board. If you come out of that tournament with a personal best, you win even bigger. And if that score takes a medal or trophy, then that is even better; but you are still the real winner. Beating your best score at a tournament and achieving a personal best score tells you that you are still getting better.

Some go to competitions with the goal to shoot a higher score than a friend, or the "top dog" in their area. You have to be careful with this kind of goal: if your friend or the top dog has an off day and you beat them, what have you really accomplished? You obviously got them on a bad day, which is good for you, I guess. However, where was your score with relation to how you shoot? If your score was also down or the same and their scores were down and worse than yours, then you really won nothing, since you didn't show any improvement in yourself. You haven't really beaten your friend or the top dog until they have shot as well as they can shoot and you have outscored them, plain and simple. Always remember: there are those who haven't been beat and there are those who are going to get beat; we all end up in the second category sooner or later; some much sooner than later.

The Long Indoor Season

The woes of long indoor seasons, especially in the higher northern latitudes are something nearly all of us have problems dealing with. The most common practice regimen in use is to practice the rounds in the same order over and over again. It isn't long before we all begin to suffer from boredom. Most limit the choice of target faces to practice on to two: the Vegas Target face and the NFAA 5-spot or single spot face. Let's talk a bit about the real life scenarios of the two main types of archers I'm most familiar with. I've been in both categories and also have dealt with more problems concerning indoor boredom that I ever have while shooting outdoors.

For Bowhunters Many shooters put up their target rigs come late August or even earlier and start on their hunting routines. You focus your efforts on your hunting and hunting set up and you spend less and less time, if any, practicing your form and shot sequence. You have it figured that getting a trophy White-tail comes first, and you can always "get your form back" in a few weeks once your hunting season is over. You avoid shooting in leagues that start up in the fall because you don't want to give up even one evening a week to shoot spots. Many shooters fall into this trap, and if you are a top echelon shooter, you can normally get away with this . . . or can you? Some of the top professionals do this and don't seem to ever show any ill effects from it. However, all of you aren't professional archers, so you find yourself struggling once you start shooting your target rigs again. Actually, your "burn out" will simply start later than those who continued to shoot their target rigs while you were hunting.

You don't get serious about "spot/paper shooting" until deer season is completely over, and this could be mid January in some places. That gives you no time to get ready for the early tournaments, such as Presley's, Iowa, Kansas City, or Lancaster's. It also gives you very little time to get ready for the Vegas shoot that is in early February. Thus, you try to cram your training and practice into a period of less than four weeks, if that much. Remember something here: competitive target shooters will come to Vegas with no fewer than six competitive events under their belts; their equipment has been tournament tested, their form is already honed and at a high level of automation, and their mental game is spot on because they've never stopped preparing. They are ready!

I'm not telling you to give up bowhunting. What I am saying that if you also want to be serious about competitions, then you must become ProActive and formulate a plan to allow you to do both: Get in your hunting time plus work on your form and mental game, along with getting that indoor set up tested and prepared for battle. Only a few shooters can shoot nothing but their hunting bows for three months, shooting only a few arrows a week, and go into a competitive event ready to compete with the best in their style.

So, with all this, you force yourself into a helter-skelter approach of thinking you have to practice for score every time you shoot. This can be unnerving and become laborious and end up actually taking you out of your own game before it even begins. So, hitch up your wagon, and let's delve into ProActively "Practicing with a Plan" and how to begin planning for more meaningful and less boring practice sessions.

For Non-Bowhunters If you aren't a hunter, then when you first start out in the fall, if you have been shooting outdoor field and hunter rounds, things are great indoors to start with, because the bull's-eye looks like it is the size of a basketball, and your initial scores usually reflect this. You likely have been shooting a lot of 4X-20's on the 20 yard field or hunter targets most of the summer. The Blue Face is a piece of cake, in that event, right? At least it is a piece of cake for the first few weeks until you start getting bored with it, that is. It isn't long before your scores flatten out and your X-count drops. You lose the prime form that you had worked on all summer in order to shoot long distances and fall back into a rut of "20 yard form." Monotony sets in and saps the fun from practice: you go to the range to practice. You shoot 10 official practice arrows, and then you shoot 60 arrows for score and go home. The next thing to happen is that you will go to the range to practice, start a scoring session, and when you miss the spot (some do this if they miss an "X"), you quit scoring then and there and either shoot a few more arrows anyway, or you fold things up and go home. This is a huge mistake; but I see shooters do this a lot. You have just taught yourself something that you shouldn't; that being that "if I miss, I can just quit, shoot a few arrows and either start over or I can just let it go and go home." Once you start a scoring round, you should always finish a scoring round . . . no matter what. You started something, finish it and learn to take the good with the bad. I know you are thinking, "Won't I teach myself a bad habit if I continue to score when I'm shooting poorly?" My reply to this is, "No, you are teaching yourself a much worse bad habit by quitting. The next thing you know, your attitude and mental game become conditioned to the "I'll just quit" syndrome and you'll find yourself giving up during a competitive event, too. Is that what you really want? What happened to, "I will execute this shot with proper back tension? What happened to your written practice plan (see Chapter 23)?

Next, normally in December or January, you switch to the Vegas target which, once again, adds a new challenge, being a bit more difficult from a scoring standpoint. This too, soon gets boring and you start to try too hard to hit those baby X's. You start shooting in the past and future and forget to shoot in the present. You try forcing the issue and complaining that you aren't doing so well. Your frustration level goes up, then you find yourself getting either bored or disgusted and don't want to practice that very much either. With all this, you have forced yourself into thinking you have to practice for score every time you shoot. This can be unnerving and will become laborious and end up taking you out of your own game before it even begins.

The next thing you know, you find yourself shooting your league scores and maybe, just maybe, another practice score once or twice a week. Suddenly you are only shooting scoring rounds and don't schedule or perform any sort of form maintenance practice to work on elements of form or execution. You no longer have a plan other than to "get it over with" so you can go home. You have lost your good attitude and, with it, your mental game. You are now in the mode of going through the motions and thinking, "Man, I'll sure be glad when we can get outdoors!" You find yourself with a host of problems concerning focus, attitude and your mental game, asking yourself, "How did I get here? I was doing so well a month ago."

Do any of the above situations sound like what you go through? There is no real reason to become bored while shooting indoors. A little ProActive ingenuity and varying your practice regimens will go a long ways to alleviating indoor boredom. You can start by becoming more involved with your practice and also your scoring sessions by planning and incorporating various events and playing little games while you are practicing, either by yourself, or with a practice partner. Who ever said that practice had to be a thing you do by yourself?

What I will suggest in the rest of this chapter are some techniques that should not only take the boredom out of your indoor practice regimen, but also contribute to raising your "comfort level" on each competitive round and for each practice session. These will naturally fall over into your scoring sessions; not only for your leagues, but also for your other competitive events. If you haven't already done so, it might not be a bad idea to read (or re-read) Chapter 23, "Do You Practice with a Plan?" So, let's kick this in gear, and let's delve into ProActively "Making Archery Fun" and how to begin planning for more meaningful and less boring practice sessions.

Alleviating Boredom Indoors

The indoor season is long. It is also difficult to maintain concentration for the length of a round when you have to shoot five arrows in four minutes for the NFAA face or three arrows in 2.5 minutes or less. Add to this that you also have to adjust to having a "tight" lane on the shooting line. Most shooting lanes are 24″ wide but many shooting lanes are substantially less than this, so you have to get used to accommodating everything you do within these boundaries.

The target's spot is rather large, just over 3″ in diameter and, for most shooters, a perfect 300 score is quite obtainable; however shooting a 60X 300 on the NFAA face or a perfect 30X round on the Vegas face are very elusive for most. Unfortunately, in today's competitive events, it isn't so much about the perfect 300 score, it is all about that X-Count, because at the highest levels of competition, you obviously cannot miss the 300 score, and to make matters worse, now you can ill afford to miss the X-ring more than two or three times if you want to stand any chance of winning an event. In the Professional ranks, you cannot miss the X at all if you expect to even get into a shoot-off with several other archers. All of this adds to a shooter's difficulties: wanting to excel and when they don't, then frustration sets in, and along with it a pressure to try to "figure out everything all at once" so they can be ready for their next tournament or league night.

Nearly all shooters change up their practice routines among three common methods, mostly because volumes have been written about them. I added another method in Chapter 18, called the "Blind Bale Method." I'll mention this again, but with a wrinkle in it this go-around.

Methods 1-3 The first common method is to shoot two ends for "warm up," then shoot a scoring round of 60 or 30 arrows and go home. The second method in common use and commonly taught is to use the "10-yard" routine on a reduced size target, and scoring the round in the same manner. The third common method is to shoot one or two practice ends on "blank bale" to re-familiarize yourself with proper shooting technique and redevelop your muscle memory, thereby attempting to automate the shot process and then go to the target to see how to score. A variant is to shoot two or three arrows blank bale, then two on the target, and then back to blank bale, switching back and forth to try to "memorize" the feel.

There is nothing wrong with these methods. In the long run, however, each one of them can and will lead to boredom, and if things don't go well, to frustration because of not getting things "perfect" and "working right" at full distance. Shooters often fail to realize that, in order to improve, a new comfort zone must be established, which is one of the main intents to having you practice up close and work your way back to full yardage after you reach a certain comfort level.

Setting Plans, Goals and Benchmarks Before we even start this, however, I really think you should begin this indoor season with a written plan and establish a series of written goals that fit into this written plan. Yes, I know it is time consuming to sit down and write goals and plans or plans and goals; but if you don't, you will soon find yourself in the same old rut as you have had for past indoor seasons and accomplishing little, if any, real improvement. Why would you want to knowingly continue to do the same old thing the same old way and expect different results? That is exactly what is going to happen if you go into this year's indoor season on the same beaten path that has failed you every other indoor season in your career. Realize that you can only control the present and can only control the arrow that is on your bowstring right now. Remember thinking the shot process with "I will execute this shot with proper back tension." You will then shoot one shot sixty times instead of 60 different shots one time each.

Yes, I'm saying that you need to sit down and write yourself a letter to define exactly what it is you want to do differently. Write down exactly what, at that moment, you think your most pressing problem areas are and then prioritize them. Then under each of those perceived problems, write down a plan to attack them, one at a time, establishing time frames to complete that work, and set goals for what you expect to do. Remember that a goal must be achievable and it must be measurable so you have to have a standard of comparison. The goal must also be realistic. If you have a personal best of 290 with 35 X's, don't be for setting a goal such as, "I will shoot a 60X 300 on or before January 31," because that isn't realistic. If you set your goals too lofty and fail to achieve them, it isn't long until you give up and then abandon that goal.

There is nothing wrong with setting short term goals that lead up to a long-term goal, creating a ladder to success. Once you have those baby steps for improvement written, then you should continue and write a calendar of events that you intend upon competing in for this coming season. Why do I not have you setting your schedule first, and then making a plan to fit the schedule of events? The reason to take a look at the calendar last is to get you to go back and check the plan and your goals to see just how realistic you were in your first assessment. Always keep in mind that anything new normally takes at least 21 days of practicing that way to become incorporated into your form and/or shot sequence. Also, under pressure you are likely to regress to the old method. Also remember that there are going to be some highs and some lows during the learning/memorizing process. You will have good days and you will have not so good days. Avoid changing something when you have a bad day. One thing at a time, one step at a time, rush jobs are not part of your plan.

By setting the calendar last and then going back to the goals, you can do a better job of fitting and prioritizing the items into a more reasonable plan. Most people tend to shoot for the moon the first time through and, then, once you see your calendar, you should be able to come back to reality. Obviously, if you think you have to make major changes, like adjusting your bow hand position and the angle of your release hand and to change your draw length and anchor, and your first tournament is in 45 days, you aren't going to be even close to getting all that accomplished effectively. So, you set your priorities, one step at a time, and accept the fact that in 45 days, you will go to that tournament with the goal of having your draw length and new anchor point established and well practiced (those two are closely related, and one affects the other, so they can be combined) and be working on your bow hand position and release hand positioning in your shot sequence, since bow hand position and then release hand position follow in sequence. You must realize that often times a different draw length may well mean your anchor point can stay the same! The draw length change, if needed, is more for elbow positioning, or bow shoulder and body alignment, and your anchor point isn't affected at all!

Thus, after about 21 days you should have a good handle on that new draw length and anchor (assuming you don't up and change it every day). You'll also have some practice rounds to show what is working or not working. If your draw length is good and you can see improvement by looking at the pictures, scores, and data, then you now have 24 days to work on your bow hand and release hand positioning (realizing that placement of the bow hand can be radically affected by the draw length). So, without pressing yourself beyond your means, in 45 days you could, with diligent practice and by not changing things during every practice or scoring session, be well on your way to accommodating a new draw length and anchor (if the anchor change is really needed).

Plans and goals need to be evaluated and adjusted on a regular basis. Write down your successes and non-successes, but whatever you do, don't dwell on negatives. Dwell on the positives. Set your goals accordingly.

Write down your goal for each and every practice session and make a plan: For example: "Tonight, my plan is to attempt to come into my "to anchor draw length" with a relaxed setup on every shot. If not, I'm going to stop, let down and start over. My goal is for no more than 10 let downs out of 60 times drawing the bow." Use your tally counter to count how many let downs you have that evening. If you don't make goal of 50/60 being right, then say so, but write down how many let downs you did have, it makes the next session easier to evaluate. If you had 15 let downs last time, then your goal for this time becomes no more than 12 let downs. You have to be tough about this and not even think about trying to "recover" it if it isn't right. This takes time and diligence, but even something as simple as a relaxed to anchor draw length/anchor is measurable, isn't it? You also must write this down in your journal so that you can track your progress. If you are diligent about this, it is just like form and shot sequence items; keeping that journal with its plans, goals and benchmarks in it becomes a habit.

Making Your Practice Sessions More Fun

Here are some suggestions that will allow you to liven up your practice routines and also build your confidence and also to help establish a new comfort zone.

1. *Use a Variant of the "10-yard" Practice Routine* Most of us are not shooting 60X 300 on a full size face at 20 yards. To me, it then doesn't make any sense to cut the distance in half and also to cut the size of the target in half! What have you gained to help yourself in this instance? Yes, you supposedly get the same sight picture, but if you aren't steady at 20 and a full-sized face, then you sure won't be steady at half-distance and a half-sized face. Try this suggestion instead. Play a challenge game with yourself. Shoot a full-sized target face at 10 yards until you shoot five 60X rounds in a row (you can set your own goal, but not less than three 60X full rounds in a row). If you are so inclined, challenge yourself to shoot the 60X rounds "inside out" (arrows touching the line from the inside are out!). Once you have done this, then you "graduate" to 12 or 15 yards, again at a full-sized face until you can shoot five 60X rounds in a row. Then graduate to 15 or 17 yards and repeat the process. In my opinion, you are creating a comfort zone and can learn to relax your way into it as you increase the distance on the correct target. You build confidence, and you still teach yourself to relax during the shooting process because you aren't forcing yourself to aim tighter by using a reduced size face. The idea here is to build confidence without over-stressing yourself and creating frustrations. You might be thinking, "I can do this the first night out." Oh, really? You won't know until you try it, will you?
2. *Alternate Blank Bale and Target Shooting* Another great technique that really helps is to shoot two shots at a blank bale, then one shot at the target, trying to duplicate on the third shot the feeling you get when you don't aim at a target. If you don't make a strong shot, then you shoot another two shots on the blank bale and then try again to duplicate that feeling when aiming at a target. Once you can shoot two arrows blank bales and one into a target, then you can graduate to one arrow blank bale and one in the target. Next step is to shoot one blank bale and two into the target and so on. You can score this as well but, of course, the lengths of your practice sessions will change. However, you are teaching yourself a couple of things: first, you are teaching yourself to duplicate the strong shots that you normally get when not aiming at a target; secondly, you are also building your stamina. I have found over the years that most shooters do not have the stamina needed for a successful tournament. Normally a shooter will shoot two practice ends and a full round and then hang it up and go home. If they continue the session, they don't score. It has been my experience in both indoors and outdoors

that if I practice for at least double the number of shots that I would shoot in a tournament that I tend to shoot much stronger shots during the tournament action. I also have less "pit in the bottom of my stomach" nervousness and I never fatigue halfway through a round as most shooters tend to do.

3. *"Blind Bale" Shooting* I hope that you recall the "Blind Bale" technique that I developed and discussed in Chapter 18. This is where you put up a clean single spot target face and shoot it at full distance for score, only with your eyes closed. The rules are simple: You are allowed to come to full draw, settle your sight on the bull's-eye, and then close both eyes completely and finish the shot. By finishing the shot, I don't mean punch it off as soon as your eyes close! I mean finishing your shot sequence properly. Any arrows shot that go off the instant you close your eyes don't count; you don't shoot that fast when you shoot with your eyes open, so you can't do that now; it would totally defeat the purpose of the exercise. The advantage of this technique is that it allows you to work on the entire shot sequence from target acquisition all the way through the followthrough, since you won't open your eyes again until you hear the arrow impact the target. The game is to shoot all five arrows each end for score, for at least one full game of 20 arrows, or preferably, no less than one half of a round, again for score. You should take pictures of your arrows in the target after each end is completed. Can you shoot a perfect 100 point game? Can you shoot a perfect half round? Honestly, this is doubtful. However, I know that you can eventually learn to shoot perfect 25's with your eyes closed! I like to tell my students that if "I can do it, then there is no doubt in my mind that you can do it, since I'd never ask you to do something I cannot do myself."

   You will quickly find that you will stop concentrating on controlling your shot. You will also start to feel those little nuances that you are pulling off (pun intended) during your shot sequence, too. You'll be able to correct those nuances, because without your eyes to constantly correct for your errors, those errors will be magnified and made more noticeable. If you know where you are tending to move around without your eyes, then you can learn to get the "balance" back in your form and shot sequence to correct those errors. You will be surprised at the challenge and the fun involved in this simple little practice routine. You can mix it up by shooting blind bale for a game, then one or two games of normal shooting. Always shoot blind bale for score, take pictures, and you will be planning a practice session, recording the results, establishing goals and benchmarks and measuring the results! Some people I know have had to go to the 5-spot face, because they got their shot sequence and form down so well that they were breaking nocks and ruining arrows if they used the single spot face.

   If you want to really have some fun and an even bigger challenge, then take a 20 yard field or hunter face and shoot four arrows per target and shoot for score using the "Blind Bale Method." Can you shoot 20's on the field or hunter face with your eyes closed? Your author can. Not every end, but I can do it. I can also consistently shoot very good groups, too; they might not all be 5's, but I get solid groups and can learn from those.

4. *Shoot Against Better Shooters for . . . Something* Find someone who shoots better than you and shoot against them for a soda, or a quarter, or a dollar . . . something. Try to put pressure on yourself to compete with the best. Most good shooters will do this and many will "spot you" a few points as a handicap. This not only helps you to get used to competition pressure, but it helps them too, since they can't let up and still win. You will find that you will operate and shoot better in the long haul. Always try to shoot on the line and next to the better shooters whenever you can, practice or not. What better way to get used to "pressure?"
5. *Count "Clicks"* By "counting clicks" I'm not talking about setting your bow sight; so just what is a "click," then? I mentioned earlier in the book that it is an interesting and fun thing to do during any practice session or practice scoring session to have a hand operated Hand Tally Counter with you (*see photo*). Sometimes I use mine to count how many points down I am on a practice round. Sometimes I use it to keep track of X-count during a round. Sometimes, when I'm working on not accepting anything that doesn't feel right when I hit anchor, then I use the counter to keep track of my let downs, since most times those are the lowest things I keep track of as part of a goal. You do remember that I said that your goals must be achievable and also be measurable and also that you needed to track your progress? Well, in comes the Hand Tally Counter. I've not seen but a very, very few shooters ever incorporate something like this into their practice or goal tracking routine; trusting things rather to their memory, which I guess is okay . . . but when I get into some serious practicing sessions and or practice scoring rounds, I want to know what the final outcome is at the conclusion of those sessions. I know how many arrows I attempted to shoot and, by using the Hand Tally Counter, I know how I'm tracking my goal for that session plus setting a benchmark from which to challenge myself against at the next session.

One of the best and most positive uses I've come up with for using the Hand Tally Counter is to keep track of "Perfect Shots." It helps to keep me on track in trying to "execute this shot with proper back tension." Once again, if you have a plan, and you have a goal set for the session, you really need to track your results and not be guessing at how you are doing. Here is a quick review of the only 4 outcomes or result of any single shot you make: The first two qualify for a "click" while the last two obviously don't:

a. *Good shot, good result.* This one gets a "click" on the Hand Tally Counter. I often say to myself that if I could execute this type of shot 120 times, I'd be National Champion, it feels sooooo goooood! You've shot these types of shots, so you know what I'm talking about. These are like great golf shots; all it takes is a few to bring you back the next time to get more of them.

b. *Good shot, bad result.* This one also gets a "click" on the Hand Tally Counter. In my experience, this type of shot normally results in a slightly high or high right arrow, and sometimes even a "4" (Remember, I shoot left-handed).However since it was properly executed, it merits a click as such. I like to think of these shots as "if I could execute 60 of these in a row, then I'd get to move my sight because I wouldn't have to worry about covering those "great shots" by masking an error with the sight setting".

c. *Bad shot, good result.* I know that on this type of shot that I got super lucky and ginched or gunched it in there somehow. Positively does not merit a "Click" on the Hand Tally Counter in any way, shape, or form. This is one that you simply confess to yourself that you "messed up, so fess up" and try not to do that again. You don't ever want to catch yourself counting on these to make or break your scores!

d. *Bad shot, bad result.* I like to think of these as "Hey, you got what you deserved, so work on reducing these."

There are other uses that you can make of this Hand Tally Counter to help put the fun back into the game by manufacturing your own challenges as you work on your form, your shot sequence, or keeping track of improvements. I don't recommend however that you keep track of negative things (even how many points you are down can have a negative effect on you), but rather figure out things that you only get to "click" when you do them right, or they are a good thing. I have had loads of fun conjuring up all sorts of little games and goals to set by utilizing this handy little device!

You can purchase a "Hand Tally Counter" for under $5 most anywhere. One website is: *http://hand-counters.com/* or you can get them at this website for a little more money: *http://www.tallycounterstore.com/Default.asp*

Shoot Different Rounds or Even Make up your Own Practice Rounds

1. *Horizontal Line or Vertical Line Round* You may recall that in Chapter 32, "Methods for Obtaining More Reliable Sight Settings," I discussed using a strip of masking or contrasting color tape horizontally across the target and use that to gauge your vertical impact point distribution for obtaining really accurate sight settings. In addition, the "horizontal tape" can be used during a "Creep Tuning" process.

   I've also found that the use of a pieces of horizontal tape across a piece of poster paper can make for some fun and help to teach you how to control your aiming on the horizontal plane and, if you use a piece of tape vertically on the paper, a vertical plane as well. This can be especially useful if you are having problems with your sight dropping out of the X-ring or bull's-eye during aiming. You can even place several horizontal (or vertical) pieces of tape across the piece of paper or poster board. This helps you placing shots to avoid trashing arrows while aiming at a single spot target. All you have to do is work on holding your horizontal aiming where you want it to be and learn how to control that. If you are having problems with lefts and rights as far as aiming, or even as far as impact points, you can work on it in this manner. Instead of having a 1″ round or 3″

round "circle" to swim all over, you now work on your vertical hold on a ¾″ or 1″ horizontal or vertical piece of tape and simply shoot at a different point on the tape for each shot. You will only be moving left or right or up or down a few inches for each shot of the end. You can even make a "scoring round" out of this, giving yourself a 5 for hitting the tape and a 4 if within 1″ of the tape, etc. Another variant, if you have trouble with low arrows, is a "penalty" of two points if you shoot out of the tape more than ½″ low. Remember, the tolerance should be the size of the X-ring, but the tape should be less than the width of the X-ring in order to make this effective. You can still shoot a "300," only to do it you have to hit the horizontal tape all 60 times! Are you up to this challenge? Try it, you might like it as something to break the boredom and learn something in the process.

2. *Shoot a "Modified Freeman Round" using the NFAA 5-spot face.* The "Freeman Round" was a very fun indoor round many years ago. Unfortunately the green Freeman Target faces are no longer available, so we have to improvise by using the NFAA 5-spot target face. The old "Freeman Round" consisted of three ends of five arrows shot at 10 yards; four ends of five arrows at 15 yards, and five ends of five arrows at 20 yards. The old green Freeman target face was a single spot face and the spot was smaller than the NFAA spot is today. In addition, the Freeman target didn't have an X-ring. What it did have was a ring outside the white spot that counted as a 5 as long as you didn't go outside of that ring. So you could "miss" the spot on the Freeman face and still get 5 points. You couldn't miss the spot by much, but at least there was a margin for error. I was so interesting to watch even the top shooters get complacent and shoot a 4 at 10 yards on this face. The fun of it was in breaking the boredom by moving around and getting to shoot some different distances for a change, and also in setting the goal of not touching the green with any shot for the round. Some went with the goal of not touching the green with any arrows at 10 and 15 yards. The goal wasn't in "shooting clean," rather it was almost like shooting "clicks" at 10 and 15 yards and keeping the arrows "inside out" at those distances.

   I mentioned a *Modified* Freeman Round didn't I? Since the correct target face isn't available today, I've improvised things a little bit. You put up a normal NFAA 5-spot face (we don't want to be trashing $12 arrows by shooting a single spot face!). You shoot:

   - Three ends of five arrows each at 10 yards. However, at 10 yards, only X's count as 5's, anything outside the X-ring is a 4 for the white, and a 3 for the dark blue.
   - Four ends of five arrows each at 15 yards. However at 15 yards, you still count the X as 5 points, and the rest of the white as 4 and the dark blue as a 3.
   - Five ends of five arrows at 20 yards with "normal" NFAA scoring, where the X and the white are 5 points and the dark blue is a 4.

3. *Shoot a 20 yard Field or Hunter Round* This is something few will attempt during indoor season. I think it is mostly because you get all caught up in getting ready for league shooting or the "next" indoor tournament. In my opinion, you are missing a great opportunity in keeping your skills honed than you get from shooting 5-spot

targets every time, or shooting the 3-spot Vegas face when you are in a hurry. Getting ready for a league or tournament can really tax and frustrate you. Eventually you are so taxed, frustrated, and bored, you lose your edge. So, take some time out once in a while and do this. Use two target faces, either two hunter faces or two field faces or one of each face. The round I've made up consists of ten ends of four arrows per end at the 20 yard field or hunter target face. The scoring is the standard field/hunter round scoring of 5 points for the bullseye, 4 points for the white on the field face, and to the first line on the hunter face, and 3 points for anything outside of this. This makes for a perfect score of 200 points. You can count "X's" if you want; most shooters count their X's. Your primary goal should be to shoot a perfect "200" on this round. It may be tougher than you think! Potential "sub-goals" include: Shooting a 200 "inside out" (no arrow touching the opposing color) or you can set goals on your X-count. A good starting point for X's on this round is to shoot 50% X's and then adjust your goal from there. You might even ignore the "200" and simply establish a goal to hit 20 X's and when you make that, go for 25 X's, then 30 X's and so forth. This is quite challenging, and when you go back to the NFAA 5-spot face, you'll think you are shooting at a basketball again. You'll be revitalized and into having fun; trust me. You could even improvise and include some ends at 15 yards, 17 yards, and 19 yards, 20 yards and even 23 yards if you want to. There are all sorts of variants you can use with these two target faces. Just a little improvisation is all that is necessary to break things up and relieve the monotony and still not cost you anything as far as preparedness goes.

4. *Shoot a 20 Yard Group IV NFAA Animal Round* "What, shoot a NFAA Animal Round indoors? You have got to be kidding me." C'mon, lighten up! Realize you are in the process of trying to relieve some monotony and still provide yourself challenges while shooting indoors. Secondly, the maximum distance for the NFAA Group IV animals is 20 yards. This is no walk in the park, for sure. There are eight different animals in the Group IV selection of NFAA Targets. These animals do have kill zones clearly defined and there is a small ring in the center of each "kill-zone" that is not visible from 20 yards. The modifications you make to this are that you dump normal Animal Round scoring, that is you don't shoot just one arrow and score a 20 or an 18 or whatever. That wouldn't be much fun indoors. What you do is to make a series of "rounds" out of this. You have eight different animal faces, so you have the opportunity to shoot eight different rounds to complete a circuit. The animals are: Prairie Dog; Grouse: Squirrel; Rabbit; Duck; Crow; Muskrat, and Woodchuck (*see at right*).

   The kill zones are clearly defined and are indeed visible from the shooting line. The problems are that the orientation of the kill zone differs from animal to animal; some are vertical, some are horizontal, and some are diagonal left, and some are diagonal right. Most all of them have very little room between the edge of the kill zone and a complete miss off the animal, especially the Muskrat and Prairie Dog. In addition, these targets throw off your "centering of the scope housing on the target" as well. The additional aiming challenge is that there isn't a

The NFAA Group IV Animal Target Faces

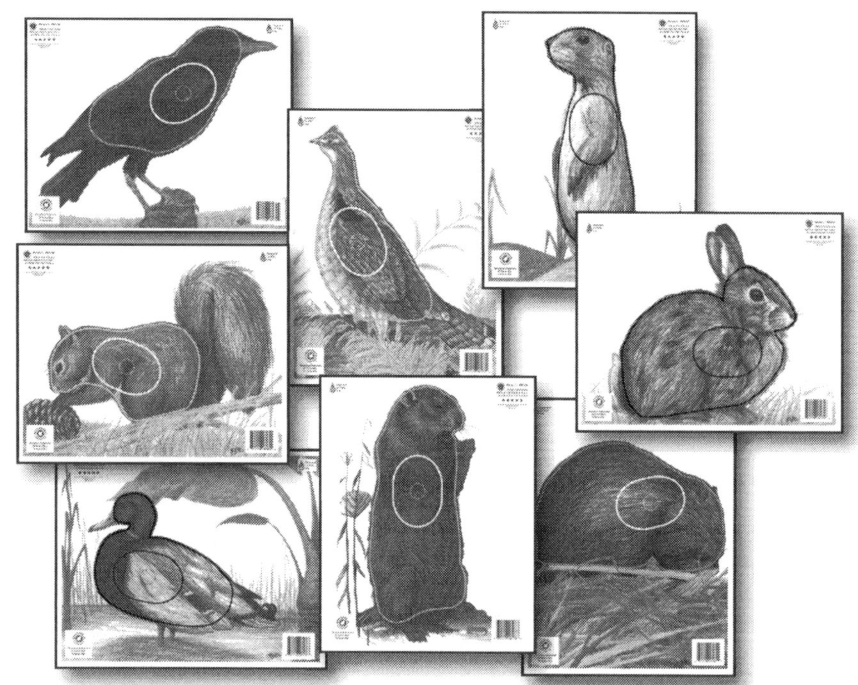

Images Courtesy of Maple Leaf Press

well defined clear aiming spot in the middle of the kill. Yes there is that circle, but you can't see it from the shooting line, and you do not want to put "aiming dots" on the animals like they do outdoors. That takes the real fun out of it, for sure. The round is easy. You get two target faces of the same animal. You can line them up horizontally, vertically, or however you want them on your side of the bale. You shoot four arrows per end for 10 ends, or a total of 40 shots. You can shoot all four arrows at one animal if you want to, or you can shoot two and two, or even three and one; that is all up to you. Scoring is 5 points for the kill zone, and 3 points for a "wound;" touch the line for higher value. The maximum score is 200 points; but wait! What about that circle in the middle? How much is it worth? Here in comes the challenge and the fun. The circle in the middle which you cannot see is worth a bonus point or 6 points for hitting it! Your first goal is to shoot a perfect 200; this goes without saying. The better goal, and the more fun one, is to see how far over 200 you can shoot on this tougher than it looks round. Again, no fair putting a colored dot in the middle; shoot the targets as they are. Don't shoot the same animal for two consecutive rounds. Keep track of your score and number of 6's and establish new goals each new round. It will take you eight sessions to complete a circuit. Can you shoot over 200 every week (not necessarily likely you will), and/or how far over 200 will you be? Which animal(s) will drive you crazy because you can't hit them like you think you should? I might add that that "wascally wabbit" is a score killer, too! This is great fun and will give you a real shot in the arm because of the challenge and also making you learn to center up when there isn't a "center" to "center up" on. There is also the added benefit of teaching you how to aim steady even if you don't have a well-defined spot to hold onto; that is, learning how to "let it float and shoot the shot."

5. *Shoot a 20 Yard Indoor Flint Round* This round was a very popular indoor round many years ago. It hasn't been used much of late, and I think that the round isn't even contained in the listing of the "Official NFAA Rounds" in the NFAA Handbook. However, it is an easy round to shoot. You need four NFAA "bunny/birdie" targets, and either one or two 35cm (20 yard) NFAA field faces. (If you want, Hunter faces can be substituted, it is your round, right?) Once again, you shoot four arrows per end and can either shoot a 7-target set, for 28 shots, or you can shoot the 7-target set twice around for a 14-target set. If you shoot the 7-target set, then a perfect score is 140; if a 14-target set, then a perfect score is 280. Here are the target numbers, distances shot, and the size of the target face shot at each "station". Naturally, this is marked distance, but it is fairly easy to use hash-marked lines on the floor of any indoor range and number the stations accordingly.
   Target #1: 50 feet, 4 arrows, 35 cm (20 yard) target face
   Target #2: 20 feet, 4 arrows, 20 cm (Bunny/Birdie) target face
   Target #3: 60 feet, 4 arrows, 35 cm (20 yard) target face
   Target #4: 45 feet, 4 arrows, 20 cm (Bunny/Birdie) target face
   Target #5: 40 feet, 4 arrows, 35 cm (20 yard) target face
   Target #6: 30 feet, 4 arrows, 20 cm (Bunny/Birdie) target face
   Target #7, Walkup, one arrow each at 60, 50, 40, 30 feet, 35cm (20 Yard) target face.

   Scoring is standard NFAA field and hunter round scoring: 5 for the X-ring and middle spot; 4 for the next ring, and 3 for the outer ring. Touching the line scores the higher value. Total possible score is 140 points per 7-target set. The same order is followed for each subsequent set.

   On the Bunny/Birdie faces, you can opt to use standard NFAA procedure for shooting the Bunny targets outdoors; that is one arrow in each target shot either from top to bottom or bottom to top, or, you can be easy and simply make sure that you shoot one arrow into each of the vertical row (any order).

   Are you up to the challenge to see if you can shoot a perfect 140 or 280 on this round?

Summary

I addressed setting goals and objectives along with establishing benchmarks from which you can make those goals and objectives realistic, achievable, and measurable.

You can accomplish nearly all of these during a long indoor season by using the suggested practice routines of:

- Use a Variant of the "10-yard Practice Routine"
- Alternate Blank Bale and Target Shooting
- "Blind Bale" shooting
- Shoot Against Better Shooters for "Something"

- Counting "Clicks"

In addition to the measures above, you can also incorporate different rounds into your practice. I outlined five different rounds and, with a little ingenuity, you can modify these to make them more fun or more challenging, or even invent your own. Some of the "rounds" are obviously not something published anywhere else, but I've have success with them in the past; especially when I feel the doldrums coming on and need a shot in the arm. You'd be amazed at how a few sessions on any of these can help to rekindle your interest in shooting indoors, or at least break the routine and still offer you a big challenge. Those improvised rounds are:

- Horizontal Line or Vertical Line Round
- "Modified Freeman Round" using the NFAA 5-spot face
- 20 yard Field or Hunter Round
- 20 Yard Group IV NFAA Animal Round
- 20 Yard Indoor Flint Round

I'm sure that if you use your imagination and ingenuity, you can even come up with some challenging variants of the above by using 3-spot or even a single spot Vegas faces or even other targets

So, there you have it, how you can make indoor practice fun. ProActive archers not only try to take care of problems before they happen and has a backup plan in place for when things do go wrong, ProActive archers performs preventive maintenance and don't wait for something to fail before they take action; ProActive archers also perform preventive maintenance on their form, shot sequence, attitude, and mental game; and ProActive archers always have written practice plans and has written goals, objectives and benchmarks in order to measure and track progress towards said goals and objectives.

And ProActive archers try to have fun when doing it!

Tom Dorigatti

42

Making Outdoor Practice Fun

This chapter could have been in the section on Tournament Preparation or the section on Attitude & Mental Game, but it ended up here because this is a better fit. Making archery fun is a different animal, and while it is related to both the above mentioned topics, it belongs in this section because by placing it here, it will not be glossed over or ignored. Most shooters today think that "Practice" has to be serious stuff, and that you have to "Practice" all the time. They think, especially during outdoor seasons, that there isn't time for preventive maintenance on form, shot sequence, attitude, and mental game. For some, this is because of a shorter outdoor season with fewer outdoor competitions. They feel rushed because we all need scoring rounds under our belts and can't take time away from that to do what some might call "playing games." They forget that in this rush to get ready, things might go better if they went about it in a more relaxed manner, especially if they want to be successful at automating things and avoid over-thinking and over analyzing their every move. Some top professionals have stated that they shoot every single arrow, practice or otherwise for score. You have to remember that these particular people have most everything in their form and shot sequence mastered after years of work, practice, and adjustment. They don't need the extensive work we mere mortals need; they are competing nearly every weekend and in some cases, they are actually shooting archery as their primary means of employment! Nearly all of us, on the other hand, don't have this level of mastery, nor do we have the luxury of having archery as our job.

In addition to the pressure to "get up to speed" outdoors, there is tournament pressure, but if you have learned to be ProActive about your preparation and attitude/mental game, then even shooting in tournaments can become less arduous and . . . more fun. If you watch top professionals closely, you will see that almost all of them are having a great time out there. You will also quickly realize that while they want to win, they also want their competition to be shooting well. Why? The better the competition shoots, the more likely they are to step it up a notch in order to keep with them and not embarrass themselves by falling apart. This is one case in archery where more is actually better!

Once on the line to shoot their end, they are all business, but when off the line, most all of them are unwinding, refocusing, and getting themselves to think about something else for a few moments. Yes, they may well take a few moments to analyze a few things, but they too need some time to mellow out.

The length of the outdoor season, especially in the higher northern or lower southern latitudes well above the Tropic of Cancer or below the Tropic of Capricorn, tends to be quite short. This is the focus of this chapter, as it is something nearly all of us have problems dealing with. It seems that we are always in a rush to: get those sight settings, and shoot so many practice rounds, and get it over with so we can be ready for hunting season. Cramming all of this into a short, four month "season" . . . Whew! I'm getting tired just thinking about it!

There are numerous methods in use to practice for outdoor rounds. The most common method is to shoot practice rounds in the same order time over and over again, looking for "perfect scores." If you limit your choice of target faces to practice on to two—the field face and the hunter face—which is typical for field archers, it isn't long before those doing this begin to suffer from boredom or frustration. But really, what you choose to do with those is entirely up to you. You can either settle into boredom or you can spice things up and make every single practice and/or practice scoring session more than just work on "score" and, while doing such, fail to work on the other things that will lead to better scores. You won't gain much on a field course by shooting the same course in the same order, session after session. You might gain on your stamina, but will you be ProActively making gains on even more important things?

One More "True Story" I recall a State Field Tournament that I attended several years ago. I had shot well all spring and summer, and was at or near the top of my field game. Even back then, I practiced and shot ProActively. I always practiced with a plan. I always had goals to achieve in every practice and scoring session. I practiced what I have preached in this book, and it paid off. My main goal for this tournament wasn't to win it. That isn't to say that I wouldn't have liked to win it. As it was, I knew from past experience that in order to win it, I'd have to shoot two solid days of scores that were close to my personal best of 557/560. I had not been shooting that high for the past month, so, I felt that setting too lofty of a goal would be setting myself up for failure. I backed off and set my goal to simply make it onto the Bale #1 (Top bale) for the start of the second day; that being to be in the top four shooters after day 1. There were over 200 people at that State Tournament and a good share of the competitors were in AA Men's Freestyle Unlimited. My goal wasn't unrealistic because I had not placed below third in any event I'd competed in that summer. To make a long story short, I did indeed make my goal of being on the Top Bale for the start of the second day; in fact, I was in third place at the start of the day. We were assigned one of the tougher courses on Day 2 and our only practice target was the 70 yard walk-up (We were only given one practice target each day at this tournament.) Of course, this meant that we would finish our scoring round on the same target, the longest target on the hunter round. This was an uphill 70 yard walk-up target with a downhill slope to the right (toes down attitude for a right-handed shooter). Keep that in mind.

We all started out pretty well on Target 1; actually; we all started off with a big bang. There were many X's, and 20's were mounting up quickly. As time went on and the targets went by, fewer and fewer arrows were falling outside of the 5-ring. We finished up the first 14 with each of us getting better as time went on. We had all faltered a bit in the middle targets of that first half, but things were getting better for all of us.

We went into the second 14 targets neck and neck, and everyone was having a great time. Like I said, the better I shot, the better they shot and vice-versa. We were all having a good time calling each others' shots, calling them as we saw them and basically we were honestly cheering each other on in an effort to keep each other going. We all wanted to win, but the only way to do that was to keep relaxed, keep focused, and to keep having fun. We all knew that if we started thinking "score" and quit thinking "one arrow at a time," that we'd lose focus and relaxation and cease having fun; all of which are quick ways to blow a good score.

We got to the last target, #28; that 70 yard uphill with the down slope to the right (toes down for us right handed shooters; I was still shooting right handed at the time) I was telling you about. It all came down to this one last target. I was only 3 points down for the second 14 targets and I knew couldn't catch the leader even if I shot a "20" on the target, since he hadn't given any of us any openings. The leader was still "clean" for the half. He hadn't missed on the past 13 targets or more and in addition he had shot a higher score than me on the first 14 of the day. Obviously, I couldn't catch the leader, even if I shot a "20."

Oh, I haven't mentioned my goal for the day, have I? My goal had initially been, that since I had made Bale #1, I stood a chance at winning the whole shooting match so, yes, my primary goal was to win the event. However, my secondary goal (as always) was to avoid being "bottom man" out of the group of four shooters; I didn't want to be dead last in this group of four shooters. So, I didn't know it at the time, but I was indeed dead last in the group when we got to that target in spite of only being two points down on the last 13 targets. In a group like this, a 271 first half wasn't cutting the mustard.

Thus I knew that I had better shoot at least a "19" on this target. I also knew that I hadn't missed a shot on my first arrow on any target that day. (You will recall my practice technique of shooting until I missed, and then I had to go pull the arrows and come back and shoot 12 consecutive shots in a row from that stake without missing before I could move on. From that I had learned to always make that first shot count.) This really gave me the confidence that, if I took the time to read the target, remembered how I shot it during the practice, and paid attention to my shot sequence, I would easily get that "5" on the 70 yard shot and it wouldn't be all that tough from there on.

We were shooting two abreast on the target because the lane wasn't wide enough to all four of us to shoot at once. I performed my "scouting/reading" view of the target with my binoculars and noted that most of the arrow holes were a tad high and to the right about 2″ out at 2 o'clock. Two of the other guys never glassed the target, but the #1 man, the one who had shot the 13 targets "clean" was glassing it just like I was. He and I were shooting together as a twosome. He shot his first arrow, and it was high, but looked like it was in the bull, but barely. None of us could make the distinction because that arrow was so close. I knew then that he had "cut" the target and allowed some bubble (as he should have), but maybe, just maybe not quite enough cut. So, I "cut" my shot a little bit more than my gut feeling, bubbled it as I normally would for this type of target and took the shot. I got that first arrow solidly in there for an X. The other two guys shot their arrows, one getting a 4 out at 2 o'clock; while the other guy got a 5 at 2 o'clock.

We stepped up to the 65 yard shot, and once again, the "leader" shot his arrow and hit his first arrow at 12 o'clock. Once again, by appearances it looked "in", but none of us could tell for sure. Both of those were going to be close for him. I knew that I tended to shoot low when I got tired and was sighted in a tad high for that reason; so I didn't want to take the chance of a soft shot and shoot out the bottom by over cutting it. At my low draw weight and this distance, I rarely snuck in a low edger; they were almost always just out. I managed to shoot another solid 5, just below the X-ring on my second shot. I think the other two both shot 4's up in that 2 o'clock area. I do know that they had given me an opening and I'd better capitalize on it.

We stepped up to the next shooting stake and the leader pin-wheeled his shot for an X. I "bumped" my shot a little bit, shot a pretty clean arrow and hit one of his high arrows, fortunately on the bottom side, so I know I have a 5 by benefit of hitting his arrows. If his were out, they weren't out by much, so I had confidence that I only needed one more for my 20 on this target. So be it; fairly good shot, but good result.

On the last shot, the leader shot another solid X, and so did I. I knew that I had a solid 20 on this and a 277 half for last 14 target unit, which made me very, very happy. So, there sat the leader with a potentially perfect half; if those two high ones are in, that is. When we get up to the target to score, however, the two high arrows are just out of the 5-ring, barely, but they are indeed clearly just out. He therefore shoots a 278 half. I shot a 277 half; one of the others also has a 277 half, and the bottom man for that half has a 276. Four people on that target and the low man has a 276/280 on a half-hunter round. I'd never been in a group of four shooters who shot a half such as this. So we, as a group had shot 224 arrows that second 14 targets and of those 224 arrows, we scored 5 or better on 212 of them. Can you imagine shooting 276 out of 280 for 14 targets and come in the low man on the totem pole in the group for that half? Heck, 277 was only good for a tie for second on that half!

While I didn't make my primary goal of winning that tournament, I did at least make the goal of not being the bottom man on my bale, so I was happy with that. I did not, however even make third place for the event. There was another shooter on the bale behind us who had shot two points better than me overall, so he got third place and I eked out a fourth place finish.

The memory of that day and that particular round is getting fuzzy, but I'll never forget how much fun it was shooting with people of such high caliber; shooting with people who encouraged and helped one another along and had a ton of fun doing it. Sure, we provided each other with a boost. There wasn't any trash talking; there wasn't any of "I'll whup your butt today" kind of stuff. This was a competition and while everyone wanted to win, we knew well that we'd best stay with the group and soak up the karma that was there while it was there. I had several poorly executed shots the first 14 targets that day, and those cost me dearly; which they will at this level of competition. However, I'll never forget that 277 half either, because the three misses on that second half were silly errors; they were on easier yardages (like shooting a "19" on a bunny/birdie target, for example), and I didn't execute a good solid shot on any of the missed shots. For the day, I had a few that were those "bad shot, good result" types, but obviously cleaned up my act on the second half.

The lesson in this story is simple: by being ProActive in my practice and learning my equipment and how I tended to react to different body positions, I had averted problems on that course. I knew how to read targets, and I knew my impact points. I don't know how many points I saved that day because of knowing how to read a target and apply what I read to set my sight for how my equipment shot and how I reacted to those situations. I didn't miss on a first arrow on any of the 28 targets; while others in the group had done so. Two of the three other guys on my bale weren't as well prepared, and when the chips were down, they paid a price; likely due to fatigue and not taking the time to read those targets like they should have been doing. I hadn't made my primary goal, but I did make the secondary goal; I wasn't "low man" for the day in my shooting group.

Outdoor Practice Routines

For outdoor practicing, I have noticed over the years that most shooters will start on the first target of whichever half of the field range they decide to shoot. Most will shoot at the same time of day, in the same order, round after round. They prefer to try to "get their scores up" by practicing the same thing over and over and over again. Most all of them also only shoot 14 targets and go home. There are dangers in this. Here are just a few:

1. *You will soon memorize the target sequence.* This is extremely dangerous to your concentration level, and in my opinion leads to you "pre-setting" your sight for the next target out of habit. This can result in you losing that edge in a tournament on a strange course and mis-setting your sight out of habit. For example, if the 55 yarder on your course is followed by the 35-fan, there is a probability that you will come off a 55 yarder in a tournament, and without thinking, set your sight for 35 yards. I have seen this happen to shooters many times.
2. *You will get lackadaisical about your shooting and just go through the motions.*
3. *You will tend to shrug off some targets because you know the "easy ones" are coming up.* This is bad because in a tournament on a strange course, you will subconsciously set yourself up for this. To shoot at the 540 level or higher, you can't afford to have a couple of bad targets and try to "make up" the difference. At that level, you must score 20s on every target up through the 45 yard targets and snap a couple of 20s on the longer ones too. You won't "make up" if you miss on anything under 45 yards. Remember this for later.
4. *You aren't pressuring yourself at all.* This is home and you'll be very comfortable

with that, because you know when the 80 yarder is coming and when the bunny/birdie target is coming, too. Not good.

5. *By only practicing 14 targets, you are setting yourself up to only have stamina and concentration for 14 targets.* Come tournament time, you are out of your element and only conditioned for shooting 14 targets. You will start to falter after about 18 targets or so and fatigue and lost concentration will start to work in and your scores on the last 8 to 10 targets are going to suffer badly. As you start to struggle, then the physical starts to wear on the mental game, and before long, you've lost your attitude and your mental game.

Fun Things to Spice up your Outdoor Practice Sessions So, here are some fun things to do to make your field practice much more worthwhile. You can combine some of these, or you can just pick one for a particular practice session and use a different one the next time.

1. *Never start on the same target for any two sessions in a row.* Always vary which target you start on. You never know which target you will start on in a tournament away from home (unless it is some local shoot), so why would you ever want to always start on a 35 fan every time? The first thing that will happen at a major shoot is that you will have to start scoring on a 50 or 65, or heaven help, the 80 yarder and you are forced right out of your comfort zone on the first scoring target. If you don't think this upsets you psychologically, think again. In addition, I can tell you from experience, the "outsiders" almost always get assigned a tough target to start on for score. Happens all the time. So learn to anticipate this by becoming ProActive. Make sure you start your scoring on tougher targets as you get closer to tournament day.
2. *Never shoot top target the entire time or bottom target all the time.* It is too easy to get into a rut if you always practice by starting on the top or always on the bottom target. I have even alternated bottom and top target as I go through a practice round just to keep me concentrating and making sure that I tell myself which target I'm supposed to shoot. If you tell yourself every time, you then form a habit of telling yourself which target you are supposed to shoot every time and it may well save you from the score killer of shooting the wrong target! The same goes on the fan targets; you should vary the way you shoot them, and keep yourself honest. You won't always necessarily shoot left to right or right to left on a fan target in a tournament, so don't practice it that way either.
3. *Always start scoring without any "practice arrows."* Learn to be ready to go from scratch and without practice. I didn't say to not draw the bow back several times, did I? I always draw the bow back, hold, and let down two times on the first target for score anyways. It settles me down and stretches the muscles in as well as helping me rid myself of some butterflies. Start your practice sessions with a draw back/let down routine and remove yourself from depending upon practice targets to bail you out. I hear the excuse so often, "I need a few shots to get loosened up and then I'm fine." Well, if you practice needing a few shots to "loosen up" then you establish a habit of needing a few shots to "loosen up" before you can score

well. I am of the opinion that a person needs to learn to make the first shot count, regardless. Just remember that there is a "let down rule," so don't overdo those let downs on that first scoring target.

4. *Shoot all four arrows from the farthest stake.* How well can you do on an 80 yarder when all four shots are taken from the 80 yard stake? How about the 45 walk up, with all four from the longest stake? Don't do this every practice round, but it is a good technique to put a bit more pressure on you on those walkups, especially during hunter rounds. This technique helped me enormously when I was at the top of my game. It is time consuming, and sometimes can be frustrating, but it sure does teach you to "make the first shot count."
5. *Shoot the normal sequence until you miss.* This technique is extremely valuable to "Type A" personalities, like me. The game I played is simple: I would pick a target to start on as mentioned above. I got no practice arrows, but did the stretch out and let down as I have mentioned. Then, I would shoot normally and score normally until I missed. The rule was, however, that when I missed, I would have to put the bow down, walk to the target, pull all my arrows and then walk back to the stake I missed from. I would have to shoot six in a row from that distance into the Bull's eye. If I missed, I would have to go get the arrows again. If I shot six in a row, then I moved to the next stake or target and continued on until I missed again. Each miss resulted in my having to shoot six in a row into the bull before I could move on. (Sometimes, if the miss was on a close target, then the rule was 12 in a row before I could move on). Some days, I didn't get many full targets shot, and some days when I elected to use this technique I would get lots of targets shot. The best part about this is that I taught myself to shoot to try to make every shot count and every shot into the bull's-eye. A person gets tired of shooting only one or two and having to go get the arrows and try again! I think that this technique actually helped me the most of anything I tried to improve my game. I quickly learned to try to make every shot count, and my misses became smaller and fewer, and my x-counts came up drastically.
6. *Set a goal for 25% X-ring hits.* This is a good starting goal to try to improve your psyche and build some confidence. If you can shoot 25% X-rings right away, then move the goal to average 35% or 40% Xs for the round. Then go for 50% Xs. I found that, if I was concentrating on the above, and my X-ring count was solid, so were my scores. It doesn't take a rocket scientist to figure out why. Of course, you must keep records of this so that you have those benchmarks to go from. If you play this "X-ring" game and concentrate on trying for even one more "X" this time as opposed to what you shot last time, you wouldn't believe how much this can help you.
7. *Shoot an occasional Hunter Round from the Field Stakes or a Field Round from the Hunter Stakes.* This one is a ton of fun to do. Makes the Hunter round more of a challenge, and gives you a boost shooting the field targets from the closer stakes. It is not only a way to break the monotony and keep you from getting careless about setting your sight but also to keep you paying attention to which stake you

are shooting from instead of going through the motions on your "memorized" course.

8. *Shoot a "Double 14" while walking the course only once.* This one gives you more stamina and concentration on which target on multiple target bales you are supposed to shoot. You shoot four arrows from one stake on the multiple target bales, and then move to the other side and shoot four more arrows. The first four at the bottom target face, and second four at the top target. For Walk-ups, you can either shoot two arrows from each stake (be careful, however, you don't want to make this a habit!) and walk up; or better yet, shoot one arrow from each stake, walk back to the longest stake and shoot the target again in sequence as you should; one arrow from each stake. Same goes with the fans.
9. *Shoot an arrow from every distance stake on the target* (excluding the Animal, Youth, and Cub stakes). So what if you shoot arrows from the "wrong stake"? You can couple this with shooting until you miss, or anything you want; it is your practice. I like to do this to help build stamina and to keep me setting my sight and then checking my sight settings as I get to the stake. Some targets you might shoot eight arrows on, while others you could shoot five arrows from. It is also a great way of keeping tabs on all of your sight settings and making corrections to them if need be. (The placard system I use has open space on the placard to write down corrections.)
10. *Shoot all four shots from the longest stake (of any kind) on the target.* This is a variation of #4 in which you shoot the target from the longest stake presented, be it either hunter or field that is the longest stake at that particular target? Some courses will set a 28 fan on the same target number as a 25 yarder, some stick the 53 Walkup on the same target number as the 55 yard Field target. Imagine if the hunter face is up and you shoot it from the 55 yard field stake instead? The point here is to challenge yourself as much as possible.
11. *Intentionally mis-set your bow sight.* I mentioned learning your impact points by intentionally mis-setting your bow sight by 1 yard, 2 yards, etc. in Chapters 28-31. Here is your opportunity to make sure you do just that! The story at the beginning of this chapter relates to this. I would never have shot that nice of a half-round had it not been from knowing my equipment stone cold and how, by reading the target, to set my sight based upon the "read" of the target. I know how much to adjust my sight for to cover those "arrow holes" that are out there 1″, 2″, 3″. I know how much "bubble" to give my shot depending upon how far left or right the read shows the holes to be. I know how much I have to correct myself for toes up or toes down; or front foot higher or lower, or rear foot higher or lower. I know how I react to uphill and downhill shots; it isn't quite all about making the right cut from your cut chart. That helps, but if you don't know your "personal" correction for those angles, then the best cut chart won't do you much good.
12. *Practice with a slant board to simulate those toes up, toes down, one foot higher than the other, and any other odd-ball stances and body positioning you will eventually find on any field course at any time.*

13. *Practice "bubbling" intentionally on calm days* or in the trees out of the wind so that you know exactly how far your impact point changes for ¼, ½, ¾, and a full bubble on both sides. You need to learn those impact points from bubbling. It won't help if you don't do this and then you get to the tournament on a windy day and you need to bubble, but are clueless as to how much for any given drift of your arrow.
14. Practice in the wind; Practice in the rain. If you don't, then when it is windy and when it is rainy, you'll be down with the rest of the people that refuse to go out and practice anytime the weather isn't perfect; which is the majority of shooters. You need to learn how to deal with wind in your face, wind from behind you, and especially wind from the left and right sides. All of these affect your shot and your body's reaction from trying to slow down the aiming movement. You need to learn how to figure out the wind. Many shooters wait for the wind to start to calm and then they quickly draw back and rush their shot. My opinion and experience is to draw up when the wind has gusted, since it is going to ebb soon and then you are already at full draw and nearly settled when that down turn in wind velocity comes around. Sure, you might not time it exactly right, but waiting for the wind to go down before you being your drawing of the bow is, in my opinion not the wiser of the two choices. Practice in the rain? Yes. Review Chapters 30 and 31 on how to prepare for this and then get out and do it. Yes, it can be "fun" because if you are ProActive about it, you will be telling yourself that it gives you an advantage over your competitors that aren't ProActive; they won't be out practicing in the wind and/or the rain. Not only with their loss of confidence hurt them, but their lack of preparedness gives you even more points.

Summary

I have outlined several practice regimens and games you can play to help you increase your comfort level and improve your outdoor scoring potential. These and others have helped many shooters that I have worked with and shot with over the years. In addition to not being lulled into a false sense of proficiency by shooting your home range over and over they same way each time, if you play little games and offer yourself small challenges, then these can be built upon to make your practice sessions rewarding and beneficial. Like the adage goes, "Practice doesn't make perfect, perfect practice makes perfect." However, there is another side to the "perfect practice" part of it. People tend to think "perfection" as a score which is just fine; most of the time. However, you don't get perfection outdoors when it comes to the conditions on the range or conditions with regard to weather, course conditions, and such. So, in order to learn how you react to these things that will occur, you have to practice for the imperfect by intentionally setting yourself with imperfect sight settings and/or imperfect footing and/or imperfect bubbling. If you don't, then you are clueless when this happens, and there goes all that "perfect practice" under "perfect conditions" and you join the rest of your group in being lost, with a poor attitude, failed mental game and, of course, a poor score. If you only practice by having everything just so, then you aren't practicing reality; at least not for outdoor shooting. I like to relate this to my profession, teaching, and to teaching experience—there are many teachers who have 30 years experience; unfortunately, some of them only have one year's experience, repeated 30 times.

Tom Dorigatti

43

Making Target Rounds Fun

The multi-colored target face has been utilized for centuries. You've seen it in the movies, the ones that most often come to mind are the famous "archery tournament" scenes in the Robin Hood movies where there is the plan to capture Robin Hood by hosting an archery tournament whereby the winner gets a golden (or in some versions, a silver) arrow.

Even today, the round "matt," "butt," or "boss" is still used for "target rounds" as is the multi-colored target face. Are you aware that there are over 100 different rounds and variants that can be shot while utilizing this target face? Here in the United States, the most popular round utilizing this target face is the American 900 Round. Secondly is the FITA round. In Olympic competition, the full FITA round is no longer shot, even if just to rank the archers to place them in the now familiar a series of elimination rounds (match/face to face competitions at 70 meters).

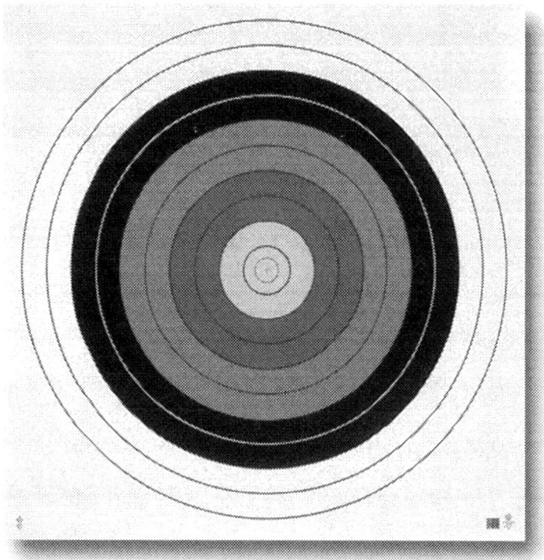

You know the colors, right? From the outside: two rings each of white, black, blue, red, and "gold."

Since this particular type of target face is so different from what has been previously discussed (NFAA/IFAA target faces), and the rounds being shot on this type of target face also differ in mental and physical approaches, I felt it best to devote some space to give you some tips and pointers concerning getting prepared to compete on an open field and the large multi-colored target face and, of course, making it fun! Since most events in the USA are centered on the 122 cm face and the 900 round, I'll address this and its iterations specifically. Keep in mind that preparation for the FITA round; the 50 meter elimination rounds for the USAA (formerly the NAA) and the "World Cup" competitions are quite similar. The full FITA round, in my opinion is by far the most difficult to prepare for both from a number of arrows being shot standpoint a distance standpoint and an endurance standpoint as well.

Listing all the rules for all of the rounds in each association is well beyond the scope of this chapter. The rules for the rounds can be found on the NFAA, the USAA's, and the WA (formerly FITA) websites. (Keep in mind that rounds shot internationally are in meters while ours are in yards.) Rather than take up loads of space talking about each association and their rounds, I've opted to go with the rounds listed in the official NFAA rule book. As I said earlier, there are over 100 different shooting rounds that utilize this type of target face.

The NFAA lists only five of these types of rounds in their rule book: the 900 Round, the 810 Round, the 600 Round, and the Classic 600 round, as well as the Lake of the Woods Round. The differences are mostly in the distances shot, the scoring, and/or number of arrows shot on the 122 cm target face, while the Classic 600 round uses the 92 cm target face "patch" whereby each shooter has their own target face to shoot at on the bale. This patch only covers the area out to the 6-ring, so arrows outside of the "blue" score a "0". The Lake of the Woods round uses different sizes of target faces based upon the distances being shot; the target face getting smaller as the distance decreases.

So let's discuss the particulars of these few rounds. I will be talking NFAA, but will interject the small differences with regard to USAA/WA events where appropriate.

The NFAA 900 Round

This round, also called the American Round, is most commonly used for State Target events nationwide. Many states use a two-day format, while others have this event as a one-day event. I've personally competed in both the single day and multiple day formats, and frankly, I prefer the single day format because it is economically more feasible and normally tends to draw more competitors as well.

- The NFAA maximum poundage is 80 pounds (peak) and maximum arrow speed is 300 feet per second with a 3% variance allowed due to chronograph error. In USAA/WA competitions, the maximum bow draw weight is 60 pounds (peak).
- The shooting distances are: 60, 50, and 40 yards.
- Archers shoot 30 arrows from each distance. Six ends of five arrows per end. Often at the 40 yard distance a switch is made to three arrow ends to avoid damaged arrows. For USAA/WA competitions, every shooter's arrows must have their name on them. This is not required in the NFAA.
- There is a five minute time limit to shoot the 6-arrow end. USAA/WA have a 4 minute time limit for 6 arrows.
- Scoring is 10 for the inner gold, 9 for the outer gold, 8 and 7 for the red area, 6 and 5 for the blue area, 4 and 3 for the black area, and 2 and 1 for the white. The arrow needs to only touch the line to score a higher value. Normally there is double scoring and the arrows holes are marked on the target face as after they are all scored and before pulling the arrows.
- In some events, there is a shooting line for each distance. In others, the target butts are moved forward closer to a static shooting line after each distance's shooting requirements are fulfilled.

- Shooters are allowed optical devices on the line with them as long as they don't interfere with other shooters on that line or space.
- Shooters are not allowed any aids to screen from the wind, rain or the sun at any time, with the exception of being able to have someone shield their sighting mechanism from glare (which doesn't happen often). In the event this shield is used, it cannot be larger than a legal sized envelope. Most often a ball-cap or hat is used for this purpose and is held by another shooter and not by a spectator. Umbrellas on the shooting line are not permitted.
- The courses are supposed to be laid out in a South to North direction, with allowances of up to 45% due to land layout and/or safety concerns.
- Most times, there are flags placed on the top of each target butt, but I've competed in events that only had flags on the two butts at either end of the line of target bales. I've also shot events where there weren't any flags at all to use for wind direction indications.
- Sometimes the shooting lane for each bale is clearly marked, but I've also shot events where they were only marked on the shooting line; or not marked at all.
- Normally, only four shooters are assigned to a shooting bale, and only two shoot at a time on the shooting line. Once the first shooters have completed their 6 (or 3) arrow end, then the whistle blows and the next line is up to shoot their ends. I don't recall ever competing in an event where all four shooters assigned the bale were on the line at the same time.

The NFAA 810 Round

When I first started archery back in the late 1960's, this was a very common round to shoot for State Target events and local competitions on this target face. As release aids and compounds took over, the 810 round became "too easy" for the shooters, so it has all but been abandoned in favor of the 900 round.

The 810 round has the same rules, number of arrows shot, and shooting distances as the 900 round. I won't bore you with giving those details again. The difference is in the scoring of the arrows. This round uses only the "colors" to determine the score of each arrow; once again, touching the line gives the arrow the higher score. For this round then, the entire gold is "9" points, the entire red is "7" points, the entire blue is "5" points, the entire black is "5" points, and then entire white (excepting the petticoat or outer area outside the circle of the outer-most rings) is scored as "1" point. (This is the original/traditional scoring system.) Thus 90 arrows all in the gold would score a maximum of 90 x 9 = 810 points above; I mentioned something about this round becoming "too easy" for the compound/release shooters, didn't I? With regard to this, I need to relate a story to you once again. I could put this story closer to the discussion on preparing for this type of event, but it is more appropriate right here as I briefly discuss this "easy" 810 round.

Yet Another True Story A few years back, a local shooter, Vic Wunderle, had qualified for the United States Olympic Team. Our club decided to hold a benefit shoot to generate some funds to help pay for Vic's expenses. We decided that since most all of our shooters in the area were shooting compounds and releases that we would make the round more "interesting" and to draw more people by making it an 810 round instead of the 900 round. This took away the " tens" and thus made it less intimidating to newbie archers and bowhunters/3-Ders. Another motive behind it was to give everyone who attended a chance at a much better score because they wouldn't have to be in the center of the center to score maximum value on each shot. We had great attendance that day, with lots of archers coming out of the woodwork to support Vic and to watch him shoot. Sally Wunderle, Vic's sister, also attended the tournament as did several state champions from different shooting divisions from the 900 round shot only a few weeks before. As is typical, the weather was hot and there was some wind blowing (but at least it wasn't raining). So, on with the shooting. When we finished up the 60 yard distance, only two shooters were still "clean" with a total score of 270 . . . Vic and Sally! So much for shooting at a basketball sized bullseye 9″ in diameter at only 60 yards being "easy," huh! When we finished up the 50 yard scoring, only two shooters were still "totally clean" with perfect 540 scores (obviously, the same two), but several of us had cleaned up our acts and managed to shoot perfect 270 scores at 50 yards. Then came the 40 yard distance, where we shot only three arrows per end before going up to score. Sally had one "burp" and just barely missed the gold, while Vic continued to pound the middle of the middle time and time again, just like he had all day long. It came down to whether or not Vic could end up being the only shooter to shoot a perfect 810 for the day. Now, you must recall that Vic Wunderle shoots Olympic style, that is, a recurve bow, fingers on the string, no peep sight, and no scope, but rather a simple open aperture. How is it then, that the compound archers couldn't stay with Vic and also shoot a perfect 810 on this very easy round? Sally had an 808 (having had only that one burp), and I think the next best score was 804 or something. Even our best of the best couldn't muster a perfect 810 on this "easy" round and target. I mean, c'mon, a 9″ circle at only 60 yards and people are missing it and shooting out into the red or the blue while using compounds and release aids? What makes it worse was that many of us also managed to shoot an arrow or two out of the gold . . . at 40 yards, too! Of course, you also must realize that we were competing with two "Masters" of the FITA style multi-colored target face, in both Vic and Sally Wunderle. Vic competes in Olympic style, while Sally competed in Compound style on a National and World level. Both of them held many national and world titles at one time or another.

So, how is it that this "finger shooter" showed up all those compound/release shooters then? It obviously wasn't all about the supposed advantage the compounders have over the Olympic-style shooters. What it was about is preparation, attitude, and focus on the task at hand. I must also mention that Vic Wunderle went on to win the Silver Medal in the 2000 Olympics and has since won many other events as well. He continues to be a force in the United States and world Olympic-style shooting scene. Of late, however, Brady Ellison has over-shadowed nearly all of his competitors with his uncanny shooting abilities. As of this writing, Brady Ellison is favored to win the Olympic Gold Medal in the 2012 Olympic Games in London. (Compound bows are not allowed in Olympic archery competition. Brady, like Vic, started out as a compound archer but made the switch to be able to compete for Olympic medals.)

The NFAA 600 Round

This round differs only in the number of arrows shot per end and the number shot for the round. All other details are the same. For this round, five arrows are shot per end; four ends per distance, for a total of only 60 arrows. The time limit is four minutes for the five arrow end. I know of a few states that have adopted this round for their State Target event instead of the 90-arrow 900 Round.

The NFAA Classic 600 Round

This round is quite different from the others. It got its start at the old Atlantic City Classic that was, until recently, an indoor event. Now, since the building of the NFAA Archery Headquarters and Easton Facility in Yankton, SD, this event is being shot outdoors.

The rules for this round are the same as for the 600 round except that instead of shooting the 122 cm face at 60, 50, and 40 yards, the archers shoot a 92 cm target face. The distance for the round starts at 40 yards, then moves back to 50 yards, and you finish up at 60 yards. In addition, each shooter has their own target face to shoot at, which is a "patch" that has the scoring rings out only to the 6-ring.

The Lake of the Woods Round

This round was very popular back in the 1970's and 1980's. We don't see it much anymore, but when we do, people really enjoy the format immensely.

- 20 targets per full round, 10 targets per half. This is designed for recreational facilities or public parks.
- Shot at progressive distances 20 through 65 yards in 5-yard increments. Each distance has its own target face(s).
- Multi-color FITA faces are used.
- Three arrows per end for the 20 targets in the round for a total of 60 arrows. 2½ minute time limit per end. Of course, for the NFAA, the "three let-down rule" applies.
- Four target faces on each butt for 20, 25, & 30 yards. 40 cm target faces arranged in a square.
- For 35, 40, 45, and 50 yards, the 60 cm target faces are used, one target face per bale.
- For 55, 60, and 65 yards, the 80 cm. target faces are used, one target face per bale.
- Shooting lanes on the line are 30″ in width.
- The shooting line is static, but the bales themselves are staggered to the different distances involved.
- The shooting distance for each bale is marked on the bale and clearly visible to the shooters on the line. The bale is marked with the distance and the target number (#1-10, or #1-20)
- If you start on the left side the first ten targets, you will start on the right side for

the second half. Same goes for top versus bottom target. If you shot top-left the first half, you will shoot bottom right the second 10 targets for those bales set up with multiple faces.

- The two closest to the marker at the start will shoot the bottom targets and the two farthest from the marker will shoot top targets for the first half.
- You are allowed to shoot the 20 yard target as "practice" once for each half before going to the 20 yard scoring target and then progress in order, 20, 25, 30, etc.
- Scoring is 5 points for the entire gold, 4 for the red, 3 for the blue, 2 for the black, and 1 for the white for a total possible score of 300 points. I have seen some variants of this to score the targets 10, 9, 8, 7, etc, which would make the total possible score of 600 points. Touching the line scores the higher value.

So, there you have it, a brief synopsis of the "target rounds" currently shot mostly in the United States. I reinforce the fact that the United States and Britain shoot most of their rounds in yards, while the other countries almost always shoot their distances in meters. In addition, as I mentioned earlier, the USA doesn't utilize the vast array of variant rounds devised for this style of target face. With all the other types of rounds and competitive archery events in the United States, having more and more variants would really tend to confuse people. It has been a very, very long time since I've seen or participated in a York Round, a round that was very popular, but demanding. In fact, I don't know for sure whether or not there are any York round events in the United States anymore.

So why am I writing so much about the outdoor multi-colored target rounds? I've told you that I won't talk about something for nothing, haven't I? So, now that you know a bit about the different rounds that use this humongous large bull's-eye it is time to get into the point of this chapter. Most compound archers think the target face can't be that intimidating; the thing is huge—4 feet in diameter, with a 9″ diameter gold ring? How can you miss? Well, we do miss and we miss a lot on this style of target face, much of which is from a preparation and attitude standpoint.

You will see some repetition of things from many previous chapters, but it is better to repeat those things rather than reference them and then have you flipping pages back to those chapters which are referenced. Besides, how am I to know if you bothered to read those chapters?

One More True Story

Not too long ago, I knew a very good shooter who was exceptionally talented at field shooting. For this person to shoot a score below 550 was rare. However, this person also hated to shoot indoors and hated the 900 round or any round associated with the multi-colored face, especially outdoors. We were finally able to convince this fellow to compete in a 900 round that was coming up at our range. The first comment was, "I sure don't see any point in going out there to shoot at a basketball-sized spot at only 60 yards and then sneak up on it. It isn't worth the time and I seriously think I could shoot a 900 or very close to it; the target is just too big and easy." It took us some doing, but we finally got this archer to attend the 900 round. The tournament begins out in an open field, on a clear, hot, and windy day. This shooter hadn't spent any time at all shooting on the FITA target face and to our knowledge hadn't been out on our field shooting at those target butts. We allowed the courtesy 45 minutes of practice and two practice ends for everyone at 60 yards before starting to score. We weren't at all surprised to see this archer shooting a lot of 9's and an occasional 8 as the practice continued (a rude awakening, perhaps?). The archer in question didn't have a lot to say, but one of the comments eventually uttered was, "I never prepared for this. The target looks so easy, but it is way tougher than I ever thought it was going to be. This constant wind and hot sun is wearing me down, too." He didn't win this particular tournament, but shot pretty well for the round once his mental game was refocused and he figured things out as the round progressed. Since that time, however, this person does compete in 900 Rounds and has learned to prepare and to do very well on this venue. In fact I've seen him shoot 894 or better several times on the round. Additionally his indoor scores have also gone up and 60X rounds have pretty much become routine and this fine archer has become quite the all-around shooter.

Do you see how the story above has been related to you? ProActive archery can and will help you. Lack of preparation or not being ProActive and strong mentally can and will lower your scores and, obviously, your position on the leader board.

Unique Aspects of Preparing For and Shooting Target Events

Shooting out in the open is one of the prime considerations that must be considered. Obviously, you are not going to have any shade while you are on the shooting line. In order to accommodate this, you must consider several things:

1. *Your Clothing* I don't recommend you wear dark or tight fitting clothing. Light colors and loose fitting shirts and slacks (or shorts) are highly recommended. Do you think that this might have been some of the reasoning behind the "all white" in times past for the NAA/FITA events (as well as tidiness and neatness)?
2. *Your Footwear* I see lots of people shooting in flip-flops or sandals. This is okay . . . if you have been out in the sun a lot and your feet are tanned and accustomed to this. If you are doing this for the first time and your feet aren't "tanned," then you are going to have problems with sunburn (take care of that with sunscreen). Also, if you haven't been accustomed to wearing flip-flops or sandals, I can guarantee you that your feet are going to get sore and tired over the course of the round. You cannot concentrate and maintain your shooting platform if your feet and legs are sore and hurting you. Shooting in tennis shoes is also not what I consider the best option either. While they are somewhat comfortable, they tend to put your weight balance too far back. We need to have a bit more of our weight distributed towards the toes of our feet rather than flat (flip-flops or sandals), or back (like tennis shoes). Thus, I personally opt for either walking shoes or shoes with a heel on them that helps get my body weight centered more forward. I also make it a point, especially for this type of event that involves a lot of walking to change into my shooting shoes before I go into the competition and then to change out of those shoes after the event is over. What relief this is, especially

after the competition is over. Nice cool, comfortable shoes and clean dry socks after the event is such a relief! Don't forget your socks. There are moisture wicking socks that really help with the "hot-foot syndrome" and can additionally prevent sore, tired, blistered feet.

3. *Head Gear* I see only a few shooters outdoors on a 900 or FITA round without head-gear. Those are normally the ones who don't fare well as the sun beats down on them. At a minimum, a good quality billed cap is a must, in my opinion. Some people also use a bandana under the cap as an extension to shield the backs of their necks from the sun.
4. *Hydration* Staying hydrated is essential. While you are out in the hot sun, you are perspiring and losing water at a high rate. If you don't hydrate, you are running the risk of cramping, disorientation, extreme fatigue, and even heat stroke. A rule of thumb is to drink at least 4-6 ounces of water between scoring ends. It isn't a bad idea to have some sports drink with you too. Soda isn't really adequate for you and can actually increase thirst as well. Also be aware that if you are super thirsty and super hot, drinking down ice cold water in a hurry is not the thing to do either. As a long distance road cyclist, past runner, and racquetball player, I know the value of and requirements for proper hydration. Even with this knowledge, however, I do tend to put off hydration during rides and especially during target archery events. After all, I'm in the shade between ends while I'm waiting my turn, so I shouldn't need so much water, should I? Wrong.
5. *Food Intake* I see many shooters not eating anything while they are participating in a target event. Not a good idea! You are burning calories and need energy to keep your body fueled. You should consider taking some energy bars with you or even some chocolate bars. If they give you a break between distances, get some food, an energy drink, and some water into your system. In addition, some of the sports nutritional products are a huge help in re-charging your system. Many of them have great taste and provide 100 to 200 calories of the "right stuff" to keep your electrolyte and nutritional needs satiated during this activity. Never short yourself on hydration and food intake, especially during this type of archery event!
6. *Sun Screen* Even if you are tanned and have been outdoors a lot, you really need to consider using sunscreen on your arms, legs (if you are wearing shorts), feet (if you opt for flip-flops or sandals), face, and neck. Don't forget to use some sort of lip balm or sun screen lip balm on your lips too. Getting sunburned is not good and you could pay for this lack of care during the round, and more so after the round. Sun blistered lips, arms, face, feet, and legs are not fun at any time! Plus long-term effects, such as skin cancer, are not to be scoffed at.
7. *Something to Sit On* Bring some kind of comfortable stool or folding chair to sit on and take a load off your feet and body between ends. Standing up in the heat all day like this is not good and it will wear on your legs and stamina in a hurry, even if you are under the shaded canopy (if there is one available or you brought one). I never recommend sitting on the grass. First it is a long ways down and much

harder to get up from (you run the risk of cramping up, which is not any fun at all), but more importantly, you never know what kinds of bugs or creepy crawlers are traipsing around down there; anything from ticks, chiggers, fire ants, to ground wasps can be down there. Don't take the chance; don't sit in the grass.

8. *Something for Your Bow to "Sit On"* Yes, you should consider something to place your bow onto or into so it isn't simply lying on the ground, pretty much invisible and likely to get stepped upon by someone who isn't paying attention. There are all sorts of bow stands available for you to choose from. I've even used an old arrow and prop my bow up using the arrow against a part of my sight extension (behind the scope) or riser just to keep it propped up. However, if it is raining, it is a good idea to find something that keeps that bottom limb out of the mud.
9. *Acclimating Yourself to the Elements* All too often, we tend to be shooting our merry old way on field courses, knowing full well there is a 900 or a FITA round coming up. We continue to shoot in the shade of a tree up until the very last minute. We haven't been out in the sun; we haven't been out on a flat, open field; we haven't bothered to shoot or become accustomed to the target face (more on this later). In other words, we have "failed to prepare" and we have failed to become "ProActive," both of which are asking for a less than desirable performance at the target event. All athletes acclimate themselves to the conditions that they will be facing during their competitions; they prepare for this well in advance. Why do we archers tend not to prepare in the same manner? If you haven't been shooting out in hot sun, on a windy, flat, hard field surface, out in the rain, or whatever, then how can you expect to know how those conditions are going to affect you? Shooting field courses which are under a canopy of trees, even if on the same property, is not preparing you for the hugely different conditions you are going to experience on the target field! You cannot prepare your mental game and your body for this if you don't go out there and get it done! You know about the event, so get out there several times before the event, and if possible at the hottest part of the day so you get acclimated to the sun and heat. Your body will respond positively, but only if it is already acclimated to the conditions. This also affects your mental attitude as well, so be ProActive and prepare yourself in advance for the inevitable.
10. *Your Optics* First off, you do not have to have a spotting scope and tripod, but they are entirely within the rules should you choose to use them on the line. Personally, I don't use a spotting scope when shooting target rounds. However, should I decide to shoot a full FITA round, then I would opt to bring out my spotting scope and tripod for that. I've found that the 11 power binoculars I use for field shooting do just fine for me during 900 rounds, so I use those. And, I'm used to having them over my shoulder for long periods, but even so, being out in the hot sun and shifting those binocular straps around my neck to my eyes and back down to my shoulder does have an impact on my fatigue level and comfort.

    Here is something else to consider and keep in mind while using optics under bright conditions for extended periods. I also find that anything less than 8 power is inadequate for 900 Rounds. You must get used to a "flock" of arrows in the gold background and get used to memorizing arrow positioning in an effort to try to sort out your arrows from the others in the same area of the target. Often times, you and your line partner can "call" for each other, but that has become less common over the years. There is a rule on verbal coaching, so calling each other's arrows is pushing that rule a bit (not normally enforced, but it is there). The really important thing to consider is the brightness of being out in the open and the huge potential for eye strain and fatigue if you over use your optics! Eye strain and fatigue can be a real headache (figuratively and literally) if you aren't careful. This can also cause vertigo and dizziness, among the dangers of headache and burning sensations. So, when using your optics use them as necessary and for as short of a time "in the glass" as possible. Give your eyes a break or they will break you.

One last thing to say about glassing your target and/or looking for your arrows in the target. Always keep this in mind concerning the four possibilities on the result of any single shot. You are going to have all four happen to you during the course of the round. Be cautious about allowing a "good shot, bad result" to fluster you and force you into an "I can't buy an X today" mentality. This will wear you down and you will lose focus in a heartbeat. You should have been training yourself to pretty much know where your shots are going and to use the optics as a means of verification or to look for patterns in case you are doing something differently and need to move the sight. Like anything else, you must keep on top of things and not use anything to excess or to the point of having it break your confidence or concentration. Of course, in windy conditions you will tend to use the optics more than under calm conditions, because you need to know how this is affecting your impact point. Use your optics with discretion and discretion is always the better part of valor.

ProActively Practicing for a 900 Round Tournament

I have written about conditioning and acclimating your body as ProActively preparing for a outdoor target round. Now we need to talk about preparing your mental game and equipment knowledge in order to eek out every last point on the scorecard.

From my experience, those who think a 900 round is a cake walk because of the huge target face are in for a very rude awakening and a kick in the humility butt (like the guy in the story above)! Normally it happens to those who are ill-prepared, unpracticed, and taking things for granted. Those who don't know about wind, rain, lighting and other shooting conditions and the effects they have upon their shooting. They also haven't prepared themselves for the large differences in their sight picture and holding patterns as opposed to having a well defined aiming spot. (The 5-ring on NFAA field targets started out as a small aiming dot in a much larger 5-ring.) The FITA face is a completely different animal from a 3-D target, and differs hugely from Field and Hunter target faces too. After all, you have this huge gold spot down there, only 60 yards away for 30 shots; and you move in from there! So, not so fast, sports fans!

The 900 Round target face, or any of the outdoor multi-colored faces take some getting used to. Very few people can just waltz out there on the field for a 900 Round and start pounding 10's like there is no tomorrow and keep them there. Let's talk more about this 'getting used to' situation. Yes much of this comes from what I've mentioned before, but there is more to this venue than meets the eye of the casual or inexperienced observer.

Centering Up I think I have spoken many times about "let it float and shoot the shot." Nothing could be closer to the truth when it comes to centering up on the large gold area on the 900 round's target face. You have a 9″ gold area, and most of the time, from the shooting line, you cannot see the "ten-ring" let alone the X-ring through your scope. What you have to hit consistently is the 4½″ 10-ring that is in the middle area of this huge gold blob. Those who try to man-handle their bows to force a solid hold are already in the process of changing the methodology in which they shoot. Remember that any time you try to force an issue, it usually forces things in a direction that isn't a path you wish to follow.

So, what can you do about this issue of centering up? Lessons can be learned from Olympic-style shooters. First, they have no scopes or peep sights, so what they see through their sight aperture is very small and ill-defined. However, many are not using a drop or up pin; they are using a small aperture ring and trust the rule of concentricity (our eyes are naturally built to concentrically align circles upon circles, if we let them do it) to take care of "centering up." Secondly, Olympic style archers are not trained to dilly dally around, forcing getting their aperture centered and holding it there for several seconds in an effort to get perfect alignment. Olympic-style shooters don't have the time or the strength to "piddle," they literally let it float and shoot the shot. Always realize that the longer it takes you to line up and execute, the less likely you are to hit the center of the center.

- You might need a larger aiming dot in your scope or a larger ring instead of the dot in the scope. You might well need a smaller one too, but for me, I see less movement if I select a larger dot size when aiming on a larger area like this. This is much of the reason why I've made my own dots and circles for all these years. I have all sizes readily available and can shoot and test the sizing out and select that which gives me the most relaxed aiming pattern. Then once the 900 Round competition is over, I simply go back to my selected field shooting dot or hole size that has been working for me.
- You might need a different color than you are used to with regard to the dot or the ring. I've almost always used the red bumper reflective tape that I cut out myself because of this issue. It works on every type of target face I've ever shot; indoors or outdoors, in poor lighting and in bright lighting. I've never had a situation where I could not see this type of dot or circle regardless of the conditions. I have had situations where I couldn't clearly see the target, but I've always been able to see the dot or circle in my scope. Obviously, gold or yellow wouldn't be the wisest choice of color, since what you are aiming at is that color.
- You might, but I don't, decide to move your sight in or out depending upon which setting makes it easier to aim with. However, remember that when you do this,

your "Field/Hunter sight settings" will be wrong and you'll have to accommodate this when sighting in.

- Don't force it. If you try to force your dot or circle to center up, you aren't staring a hole into the middle of the middle and you are rather directing the shot by using the wrong muscles instead of letting your eyes and brain do the work for you. You are in for a long day if you try to force your aperture to sit still in the middle of that large area.

Arrow Selection I've always used my field arrows for 900 Rounds and not had much of a problem there. However, with today's modern arrows, I'm finding that a little more FOC (front of center) with having more tip weight really helps the arrow when the wind comes up. Shooting high speed/lightweight and low FOC 3-D arrows isn't necessarily the thing to use on rounds out in the open like this. Larger diameter and heavier arrows are also not the wisest of choices. First off, they will have a lot more wind drift when the wind blows; secondly, neither your fellow shooters nor you are going to be very happy concerning the "kiss-offs" you and they will get off those big arrows. Lighter arrows bleed speed much faster than a heavier arrow, but the heavy arrow is more about the "pile" or tip weight (FOC) to help keep the arrow on line. The old rule of thumb was, "Weak or light arrow in the calm, stiff or heavier arrow in the wind." With this in mind, most shooters today are indeed selecting smaller diameter carbon arrows to shoot FITA and 900 rounds. Several companies have started making smaller diameter carbon arrow shafts and these, when coupled with 100-125 grain points make an exceptional outdoor arrow for shooting at distance and also for shooting up close; especially in the wind. In some venues overseas, the target bosses are extremely hard, so shooters have to use very expensive Tungsten arrow points so that their arrows aren't damaged in those tough target bosses. Carbon arrows or aluminum carbon arrows are today's choice of arrows, and aluminum arrows are pretty much out of favor. Once again, for distance shooting, the general consensus is that, if you are going to be "off spine," then opt to the stiffer and not the weaker one.

Vanes or Feathers? Most archers are shooting vanes on their arrows. However, the vanes are not the higher profile vanes preferred by hunters. They are also not using Spin-Wing vanes because the speed tends to bleed off much quicker and the arrows "balloon" or "die" much past 40 yards. Some vanes as long as 3″, but most are 2″ and under. Helical fletching is common, but angled straight fletch is more commonly used in order to get clearance of the vanes off the arrow rest. While feathers are lighter and perhaps less critical, they become a real liability in unfavorable weather and wind conditions and are easily damaged, thus I don't see many people shooting with feathers on FITA or 900 Rounds.

Arrow Rests There are myriad arrow rests in use. I see mostly launcher blade or "fall away" arrow rests, and most shooters who are using launchers are using the narrowest blade they can get by with because of the small diameter of their arrows (there isn't much room between vanes on these tiny shafts). However, if you cannot draw your bow smoothly with a super narrow blade or have lots of flyers or let downs, then it is worth your time and trouble to tune in a wider launcher blade. This comes down to personal preference and what has been proved to be the best and most consistent for you.

Draw Weight The USA Archery limit is 60 pounds maximum peak weight. While the NFAA permits 80 pounds maximum and 300 feet per second arrow speeds, not many shooters have the prowess or stamina to shoot more than 90 arrows for the round, doing so by shooting six arrows in four minutes or less at that high of a draw weight. Heavier poundage (roughly above 60#) plus being out in the sun and elements drains them of energy and they tire quickly. You have to decide upon the poundage you want to shoot and then get the setup properly tuned so that you and the equipment mesh together.

Release Aids If you are a release shooter, you often hear bad news stories about shooting a 900 or a FITA round in the wind with trip-gate releases, or with pressure activated releases. More and more shooters are indeed shooting trip gate releases on these rounds and in these venues. Some are even trying pressure activated release aids (Carter *Evolution*, *Revolution*, or Stan *Element*). A few are shooting index finger release aids and do very well with them. However, it seems that the majority are shooting thumb trigger releases.

Stabilization We can go around and around about stabilization. Most bows being built today are not built with the same initial balance points as they were just a few short years ago. Heavily reflexed risers through much of the riser's weight out in front of the bow hand, so today's bows almost all require some sort of back weighting to get them to react the way a person prefers. That being said, there are some shooters who have a lot of stabilizer tip weight and a lot of weight on their back stabilizers as well. This all boils down to personal preference and a lot of time spent trying different balance points and finding what you can document gives you the best stable holding pattern and gives you the most consistent and proven results. You cannot do this in a day, a week, or a month. It takes time and commitment. Overloading your bow with weights so your bow arm fatigues quickly is not a recipe for stability or accuracy.

Anticipating Difficulties

I have so far addressed archer and equipment, now for some tips on getting the ProActive practice accomplished so that when things go awry you are already prepared to handle difficult situations.

Wind I have previously discussed practicing in the wind and intentionally shooting with your bubble canted ¼, ½, ¾, and full bubble left and right. It is very important that on this target face you also take the time to learn when under calm conditions how far the "bubbling" affects your impact points left and right. You won't get the same perception as you do on a Field or Hunter face, so it pays to learn this on the "basketball sized gold ring" you'll be aiming at during your competitive rounds. Do this on calm days, and then when you have windy days, you put this into practice proving it under fire during practice. Some other things about wind that most people don't think about until it is too late:

- You are going to miss the bull's-eye when it is windy. You have to get into the mindset that you are not going to shoot a 900 that day or any other day when the wind is blowing; especially if it is gusting and changing on you all the time.

- Keep an eye on the flags, just because the wind is hitting you in the face when you are at full draw (wind from the right for a right-handed shooter) doesn't mean that the wind is blowing in the same direction 60 yards down range. Keep an eye on those flags. They give them to you as a resource, so use them. Keep an eye on how the targets are "reading," that is, how far off the holes in the targets are? You know that other people are compensating, but, for you how much is that difference in relation to how much bubble you give your set up? They likely aren't shooting the same point weight, arrow size, etc as you are. They likely aren't shooting the same arrow speed as you. Many of them are likely not prepared for shooting in the wind or don't know how. There are going to be those whose arrow holes can give you a picture of what is going on, if you pay attention. You don't watch their score; you simply look at how much windage variance they are getting.
- There is continuing debate over whether to "hold off" the center or to "bubble it" by putting the top limb into the wind by enough bubble to allow for that "windage" and then aiming dead center. Personally, unless the wind is really strong and gusting, I prefer to aim dead on and shoot a strong shot. Often times, just shooting the strong shot will produce good results without having to make any corrections whatsoever. However, if a strong shot isn't doing it then "bubbling it" is my next option. Here is one reason why I don't prefer to aim off center: for months, no, for years, you have trained yourself to aim centered up, correct? If you try to aim off center, then, your mind is going to see this and at the last instant, you are going to push the sight over to get to center and the end result will be a shot clean out over to the other side (from the wind). You are conditioned to center up, so give yourself every opportunity to remain that way. If you have decided to "aim off," then you had better be practicing that, and practicing that a lot so that you always have control of where you want to aim, and can keep the sight there regardless of the wind. You determine how much the wind is moving your arrows, and then you aim at a point opposite and through the center to compensate for that drift (if you are drifting 3" to the right, aim 3" to the left, etc.). And get used to the idea that sooner or later, and likely several times during the round, you will loose an arrow just as the wind quits or just as it gusts, and your "correction" will be all for naught, and you'll hit right where you were aiming or where your bubble says you were corrected to. Oh, well, good shot, bad result.
- Look, feel, listen and stay focused. I'm not saying that you should be thinking wind, wind, and wind. What I am saying is that you should pay attention to the rhythm of the wind and whether gusts, if there are any, are quick to subside or do they hang on for more than a few seconds. How long is the "normal lull" between gusts? I see most shooters waiting until they hear or see a gust tailing off and then they quickly draw their bows and try to get off the shot before the next gust hits. Think about this. You have now put yourself into the position of rushing your shot based upon a preconceived notion that if you hurry, you can get it in before

it the wind rises again. It is never a good idea to rush your shot. In my opinion, unless it is a day when the wind is simply howling, it is wiser to draw back your bow as the gust is about to peak, settle in, and normally by the time you have settled in, that gust has subsided and you have plenty of time to execute the shot before the next gust of wind comes up. Once again, if that wind is just plain strong and continuous then all bets are off and you just have to do what you have to do. I've had occasions where I have held off out in the petticoat and a few where I was nearly aiming over at the next butt over (well, not quite that bad, but it certainly seemed that bad).

- Don't complain about the wind. You can't do anything about it; you cannot control it, so don't allow it to control you. However, since you have been ProActively practicing in the wind, this isn't any big deal to you. Let it bother your competition, while you stay focused and shoot your "wind game," allowing your opposition to continue to give you points and get frustrated.
- Wind and back tension release aids. As I wrote earlier, many shooters will change over from a back tension or tension activated release aid to a thumb trigger release the second the wind starts to blow. Some do quite well this way; for a while. There are some who practice with back tension or tension activated release aids and shoot competitions only with thumb trigger release aids. I am not talking about those archers. I'm talking about those who violate the rule against "changing things on the fly." Here are some things to keep in mind when shooting in the wind with back tension release aids.
  1. Concentrate more on keeping strong and letting the sight float rather than how much your sight is moving around. Every time the sight moves, archers tend to let up on their back tension. This tendency can be overcome with more practice while shooting in the wind, so never pass up the opportunity to shoot under windy conditions.
  2. You can move your feet ever so slightly to help proper execution of back tension based upon which side the wind is coming from. (I mentioned this in one of my stories concerning Darrel Pace using golf tees for his foot positioning during a warm up for a FITA event.)
     a. For a right handed archer, if the wind is blowing from right to left, the wind is pushing your bow arm out and away from your line to the target (opening you up, or giving you more bow arm push); thus, the shot will tend to break easier as long as you maintain back tension. If you know this, it helps you and won't surprise you at all; other than the shot breaking a tad easier, that is. You can close your stance ever so slightly to help offset this expected situation.
     b. For a right handed archer, if the wind is blowing left to right, then it is forcing the bow arm toward the center-line of the body and making it feel like a weak shot, so the shot is going to be a bit tougher to get to break. You are trying to aim to the left, but the wind if trying to force a weak shot with bow arm to the right. If you know this, you can use this to help you set up for a stronger shot. You can even open your stance ever so slightly to help keep you more strong-

ly aligned; but be careful when doing this if you haven't practiced it.

c. If the wind is blowing directly from the target towards you, then your arrows tend to shoot lower slightly, depending upon wind velocity. If the wind is coming from directly behind you, then your arrows will tend to shoot slightly higher. Pay attention to the wind flags, pay attention to the arrow patterns on your target and those adjacent to yours. Reading the targets, especially if better shooters are on them, can tell you a lot about how you can compensate based upon your setup.

Rain Shooting in the rain can bé downright miserable. If there is lightning, the tournament committee is going to get you off the range and into some shelter other than trees, however, the tournament will go on during a plain rainstorm. Be ProActive and set up your equipment for shooting under damp or rainy conditions. This puts you yet another step or two ahead of your competitors. Here again are some things to think about.

- If you have practiced in a rain jacket, then by all means go ahead and use one. If you haven't, then I would resist the temptation to start using one now. Once you are wet, you are wet, and sometimes raincoats/jackets can get you more wet inside the jacket that you would be if you hadn't bothered to wear it.
- Your foot gear should be prepared for rain; especially if rain is forecast.
- Your bowstrings and cables should be weather resistant. Once again, being ProActive and having that taken care of in advance is going to save you points on the rainy day. End servings from the cams toward the center serving, the center servings, cable stop servings, and other exposed string surfaces can easily be sealed/weather resistant with simple bow string wax. This will help prevent the rain from soaking the servings and making your bow string weigh heavier, slowing down your bow and causing you to shoot low and lower as the water accumulates in the servings.
- Carry a small piece (6″x6″) of chamois with you in your quiver. Use this to wipe down your limbs, riser, sight, and arrows between ends or even between shots. This is very handy in dabbing out water from your scope lens too. You will see people using Zip-loc bags over their scopes and fletches between targets, too. The only problem with this is the potential fogging up the scope lens.
- If rain is forecast, consider taking out your clarifier from your peep sight and get set up with a peep sight without any lens in it. Clarifier peeps can be a real pain when rain gets into them. You will want to blow out the rain, and then the clarifier gets fogged up and you have to wait for it to clear. You only have four minutes for five or six shots. You can't stand around waiting for scopes and lenses to de-fog before you can shoot.
- When you withdraw an arrow from your quiver, grasp it by the point end and give it a rapid shake to remove water from the shaft and the vanes. Then load it up and start your shot sequence.
- Watch your optics; they too will fog up or get rain drops on them. This is yet another use for that piece of chamois cloth, as well as drying off your glasses if you wear them to shoot in.

- Carry a plastic bag with you in your quiver so that you can place the score-cards into that instead of having them exposed to the rain. Carry a pen as well as a pencil so that if the cards get damp, you can still write scores onto the cards. If rain is forecast, it is not the best idea to bring a water soluble pen or marker to write scores with!

General Tips

- Always carry at least six extra arrows in your quiver to the line with you. Often times your arrows are going to get beat up. You aren't going to be given time to hold up the line and go back to your car to get another arrow if you only have six in your quiver and one becomes damaged. Carry a full dozen "marked and tested" arrows with you.
- Carry several extra arrow nocks of the same color you are using. Also carry a nock aligning tool.
- Carry a spare, pre-cut and pre-melted D-loop with you in your quiver. A D-loop can be changed in only minutes if you have been ProActive about marking it and making a duplicate D-loop that can be quickly put on. This need not be a 45 minute fiasco where you have to sight in again and go through the devil to fix this. You should be able to put on a new D-loop and be back up and shooting in the bull's-eye within five minutes, max. This definitely should never be a day ending event for you just because a D-loop goes bad.
- Carry extra launcher blades with you in your quiver. A launcher blade change should also not be a day ending event.
- Always have a spare release aid of the same style and size as your primary release.
- If you are a finger shooter, always carry a spare shooting tab with you.
- Never move the indicator pointer pin on your bow sight to compensate for your sight settings suddenly going off on you. Count clicks or move the peep sight slightly to cover this. If that doesn't work, check the bolts on your sight mount to make sure they didn't loosen up. If that doesn't fix the problem, check to make sure your second axis hasn't come loose. If that came loose, then your scope will follow gravity and you'll be shooting high. Keep an eye on things and check the variables before you indiscriminately start fiddling with sight or sight settings. Of course, you have been ProActive and marked your cam positions and cable positions, right?

Summary

So, there you have it. We have discussed many things that relate directly to the shooting and preparation for a 900 Round outdoors. All of the items discussed are important; otherwise I wouldn't mention them in this chapter. Some highlights are:

- *Get yourself physically and mentally acclimated for the 900 Round venue.* You will be shooting out in the open, and if you aren't used to it, you are going to really end up suffering in the middle of the event. If you haven't prepared for shooting in the hot sun, then it might not be a bad idea to pass on this event until you are prepared.

- *Hydrate properly at all times*. When you feel thirsty, it is already too late. 4-6 ounces of water and/or energy drinks after every end or two could be enough, but could be a minimum. Be careful that you don't over hydrate. This, too, is dangerous. Be careful when drinking really cold water if you are really hot and thirsty; the sudden surge of cold water can cause all sorts of problems.
- *Eat something during the round.* Energy bars, chocolate bars, some protein, even the energy supplements that contain necessary electrolytes are going to really help you. Don't short yourself on how important this is.
- *Wear proper head gear, clothing, and foot gear.*
- *Make sure you wear sunscreen on exposed skin.* If you are wearing sandals, flip-flops, shorts, etc. for the first time, whatever you do, do not skimp on putting on sunscreen. You are out in the open and you are going to get sunburned unless you protect yourself.
- *Wear some type of protective lip balm.* You are likely to get dry lips, too, so protect them. You won't be sorry you took this ProActive step in self-protection.
- *Bring something to sit on.* Standing for long periods out in the open or even under a canopy will drain your legs of strength. It just isn't the same as shooting a field tournament where you are in the shade most of the time.
- *Don't sit in the grass.* You never know what is lurking down there. Anything from ticks to millipedes to ground wasps, fire ants, and other creepy crawlers. Those bites are not fun, especially if they are in the "most sensitive areas" of your body.
- *Bring something for your bow to sit on, too.* If it is rainy, then make sure you have something to keep that bottom cam out of the grass/mud.
- *Prepare for how you react to shooting in the wind.* Know how much bubble to give for a miss 3″ to the left/right or 6″ to the left/right. Also know how many clicks to give your sight for 2″ high or low, etc. This only comes from intentionally practicing under ideal conditions so that you learn these corrections for your set up and shooting patterns when (not if) the wind starts to blow.
- *Know and learn the secrets of how you react in windy conditions when shooting with a back tension or tension activated release aid.* Wind from left to right or right to left will affect how easy or hard the release will trip.
- *Shooting directly into or directly with the wind does affect your impact points.* You need to know at the first get-go, how many clicks it takes to "cover" this difference based upon the conditions/impact points on your target with your arrows and set up.
- *Never be caught short on arrows or spare nocks.* Also be ProActive and carry extra pre-cut and melted D-loops with you. You should know how long that D-loop opening is for your setup. You should be well practiced in changing a D-loop out on the line and have confidence that you can do this in under five minutes and continue to shoot without any adjustments to the sight or bow.
- *Learn and know what to check for when things happen with regard to changes in impact points.* You have to learn whether it is you or it is the bow or other equipment. Be ProActive and have things marked, measured, and written down.

Oh, and if you are wondering where the "fun" is in all of this, the biggest challenge we have as archers is boredom. Mixing up the rounds and targets we shoot is one way to increase the challenges and variety in our schedules. Shooting at something really big rather than something tiny with its inherent challenges of avoiding over aiming, etc. is a good way to learn how to "let it float" and "shoot your shot." If you don't have a goal to win the event, have some fun by shooting a 900 Round with just the goal of "letting it float" and finishing each shot to see what happens. It can be fun and you can learn something at the same time. For a matter of fact, you should try sometime to see if you can shoot even close to "900" with the target set at only 30 yards! It might be more of a challenge than you think!

Tom Dorigatti

44

An Incentive Program to Boost Participation

"Target archery is seeing how far away you can get and still hit the bull's eye. Bowhunting is seeing how close you can get and never miss your mark!"
Unknown

But you must be patient and careful;
nor should you expect to become an accomplished archer
without long and severe training.
Maurice Thompson, The Witchery of Archery, 1879,(pp. 153-154)

Okay, ProActive archers: why do you think I am including a pair of chapters about "Working with an Incentive Program to Boost Participation?" Basically, it is because there are too few archers who put something back into our sport. Rather they opt to stay in the background and enjoy the goings on. What "they" don't realize is that boredom sets in, shooters get tired of the same old stuff with the same old shooting buddies, and before long you not only don't have new blood coming into your club or range, but even many of the old timers go on to pursue something else, leaving "them" shooting by themselves and having an even more difficult battle with the doldrums. I strongly feel that fully ProActive archers need to contribute back to the sport and do whatever they can to provide others with a "raison d'être" (French for "reason for being").

You, even as a ProActive archer, can only do so much to keep yourself going; we are all social animals, and we need to be among others. Thus, if you show some motivation and come up with "new ideas" to keep things fun and interesting, then the chances are your motivation and positive attitude will help to keep other shooters motivated and this will in the end result in keeping ranges going.

Without archers doing this most ranges, indoors and outdoors, come to the point of no return sooner or later. Every archer really owes it to the sport to do something about this. So, in this chapter I'm going to provide you with some easy to do ideas to help give other shooters a shot in the arm and to motivate them to do better; or at least to come to the range and join in the fun. It isn't all about winning or "getting ready for competition," because a constant load of always being serious and preparing for tournaments gets pretty old in a hurry too; when you are doing this by yourself all the time, then you are not receiving any "line training" or being pushed by anyone but yourself. You have the ideas given in the last two chapters. Now let's adapt those ideas to the group of shooters and not just an individual's perspective. Makes sense, doesn't it?

We will talk about indoor archery leagues and promotion in the next chapter, once again getting a ProActive archer involved directly instead of from the outside looking in and soaking up the benefits.

Getting Them Going on Field Courses and Outdoor Ranges

Getting your "merry men and women" out on the courses to practice and shoot is an age-old problem for most archery clubs and indoor ranges, especially those oriented towards field/paper shooting. While competition leagues are a partial answer, they only serve to get shooters together once a week. Then there are problems with absenteeism and makeup scores, vacations, and the fact that many beginners think that they aren't good enough to shoot with the rest of the archers. Thus, rather than feeling embarrassed or having to commit to something for the summer, they pass up the opportunity to shoot a field league (or and indoor league).

Shooting a field or hunter course fulfills the aspects and requirements of the quotes at the beginning of this chapter. You, target shooters as well as you bowhunters will get numerous opportunities to fulfill the requirements of your particular niche in the game of archery, since field shooting provides archers with shots varying in distance from 20 feet up to and including 80 yards. The target size and the size of the highest scoring ring vary with the distance as well. Four arrows are shot at each target on the 28 target marked distance field and/or hunter target course. Scoring is 5 points for the X-ring and "spot," four points for shots within the next scoring ring, and 3 points for the outside scoring ring, for a total possible score of 20 points per target and 560 points per round.

Many years ago, I developed a simple, non-competitive system in an attempt to motivate all shooters in the club, regardless of skill level, to practice and to turn in scores. This system has proven itself, time and time again, to give shooters who just like to get out and shoot a challenge and something to shoot for as well. It offers a non-competitive opportunity for participants to compete only with themselves at their own skill level and to be able to track their progress with little to no hassle. All they have to do is to go out and shoot when they want to, complete a 14-target round, put their score for each target on a scorecard, date and total the score, and turn it in. Add to this the setting of goals, benchmarks, and additional games such as those mentioned in Chapter 41, they (and you) should be able to see that they (and you) can have an outdoor season that provides challenges and opportunities galore with little chance of getting bored with it.

A common question asked at this point in every discussion of this system is: "How can we be sure the shooter isn't 'fudging' his/her score?" (All the world hates sandbaggers!) The answer is simple: "Who cares?" It will be very obvious if a shooter turns in a 270 score for the incentive system and then goes to a tournament or into a league and shoots a 230, won't it? This is not for anyone else's satisfaction but that of the individual shooter and to get people participating. Everyone is a "winner" and the only ones to lose are those who don't or won't participate. How many scores you shoot each week is entirely up to you, and if you don't shoot a score, there isn't a penalty for it. There isn't a meeting or shooting time, there isn't a schedule, and there isn't a handicap to figure out. There are no "games" to win or to lose. Everyone who participates is a winner in many, many ways. In the five clubs I've used this system in since the 1970s, it has never failed to boost shooter participation, range usage, and shooter scores as well. In one particular club, we had only 40 active shooters, and during the first outdoor season from April through August, those 40 shooters turned in over 1,400 scores! Yes, you read it right, 1,400 scores turned in for only 40 participants in five months! Now that is obviously a huge boost in participation and course utilization, is it not? I'll tell you for certain, we didn't hear anything like, "The range isn't being utilized, so why spend the money maintaining it?"

The Participation System in Detail

Items Required

1. A 14 or 28 target field course (or hunter course). Most courses are staked for both the field and hunter rounds.
2. Field and/or Hunter target faces per the NFAA/IFAA specifications.
3. Score cards to handle 28 targets.
4. Mail box (or some type of box) with a padlock for the shooter to place completed scores into
5. Spare scorecards adjacent to the locked box.
6. A 3-ring binder for master copy of each participating archer's scores
7. "Shooting Club" Poster Boards or simply the Club Newsletter can be used to post the "Shooter Clubs" and its members.
8. Secretary to maintain #5, #6, and #7 above for each shooter. If that means you, trust me, it isn't a hard thing to do and isn't all that time consuming! You are trying to generate more competitors by getting fellow archers to improve their games; you have a lot to gain from this, and frankly, little to lose!

The Rules The rules are kept simple. It is only necessary for each shooter to:

1. Write their complete name, the date, and the round being shot onto the scorecard.
2. Shoot 14 targets (or 28 targets) and add up their total score and X-count for each 14 target unit shot. The shooter must shoot the correct shooting stakes and write down the scores just like they are done in a tournament. Only official club scorecards or official tournament scores are acceptable.
3. Total up the scores and Xs, sign the card, and then place the scorecard in the lockbox (a mail box with a padlock works just fine).
4. Any score cards not totaled up will not be counted. It isn't the job of the secre-

tary to total up score cards, so this should be made very clear.

5. It is best if two shooters shoot together, but it is not mandatory. If two shooters shoot together, then signatures should be on the scorecards for each shooter. Once again, make it clear that we aren't getting into this "padded scores thing," shooters are only hurting them by padding their scores.
6. Tournament scores count in this incentive system. Simply turn in a copy of your tournament score properly signed along with the date, the type of round (field or hunter) and where it was shot.

The Binder Setup You can set up the 3-ring binder any way you choose. I've found that the easiest way is arranging the shooters alphabetically (last name first) with the archer's name in the upper right corner of the sheet. Items entered onto the individual archer's sheet include: date, round shot, total score, and total X's (*see figure below*). I strongly recommend that every shooter participating has their own scores record and that every score that each shooter turns in be recorded on a sheet similar to the one below. All columns are self-explanatory with the exception of the "Present Club," which will be explained later.

Sample Shooter Record Sheet

Incentive System Shooter Record, 2011

Archer's Name ______________________________

Date	Round (F, H)	Total Score	Total X's	Present "Club"
6/1	Field (or F)	250	19	250
6/5	F	254	18	
6/6	F	256	20	255
6/12	H	259	20	
. . .				

The Key to the System The "key" to the entire system is the "Shooter Club." Every shooter who turns in a score above 200 for 14 targets becomes a member of a shooter club that is based upon a 14 target score. The most successful shooter club plateaus over the years is: 200, 210, 220, 230, 240, 250, 255, 260, 265, 270, 272, 274, 276, 278, Perfect. The reason I use 14 target scores is because the majority of shooters will come and shoot 14 targets but won't participate if you want them to shoot a minimum of 28 targets. A full 28 targets is considered by many as a marathon, especially newbies. You don't want to discourage participation by requiring full rounds to qualify for a score to count. I did find that later on, the shooters were indeed shooting more than 14 targets per visit, and turning in two scorecards, but let them make their own decisions.

Shooter Club Rules Once you attain a given "club" level, you cannot go backwards and pick up a shooter club you missed at a lower level. You can only try to move up to the next level. You can continue to shoot and turn in as many scores as you so choose. Each score will be recorded on your personal scoring record. As a result of your improvement, you can skip shooter clubs. For example, you have shot a score of 256. A few weeks later you turn in a score of 266. You are now a member of the "265" club and have skipped the "260" club and cannot go back to become a member of the 260 club. Or, if the secretary so chooses, if you "skip over" a club, they can automatically include you in that club. It doesn't really matter all that much.

Shooter Club Listing Posters The secretary should make up these posters so that the shooters can be aware of who else is in their respective shooter's club. These can be made out of regular paper and enclosed in plastic, or they can be made of poster board with each shooter club on its own poster sheet. That is to say, you need a separate poster for each of the shooter clubs from 200 right on up to the Perfect Club. These can all be done ahead of time, or can be made as shooters "join" each sequential shooter club. The names should be listed as each shooter gets into each shooting club. That way, you don't have to make up new sheets all the time, but rather just continue your sheets as they occur. (See the sample below). This can also be modified to simply place into the Club Newsletter or onto the Club's website for viewing; just use your ingenuity!

Sample Shooter Club Poster

Skybow Bowmwn 200 Club Members

Shooter Name	Date	Score	X Count
Alcorn, Jim	4/1	205	6
Ferry, Alice	4/8	200	8
Zalcorn, Harvey	4/8	209	11
. . .			

Helpful Hints The secretary or manager should make it a point to keep the scores up to date, at least on a weekly basis. Be absolutely certain to keep the Shooter Club Posters up to date and that they are neatly and completely done. By keeping those posters or listings up to date, everyone gets to see how everyone else is doing and they find the added incentive to try to make the next higher club level; either from a personal challenge standpoint, or to try to catch up to their buddies. Also make certain that every score, if it is added up and properly completed, is entered onto each shooter's personal score record and kept in the 3-ring binder. It is imperative you have a hard copy of those scores. It is also a good idea to keep the original score cards to fall back on, just in case questions arise. In all the years I have done this, I haven't had any questions arise, but I kept those original scorecards in the club house anyway.

Awards Awards aren't necessary, but are a nice touch if your club has an annual banquet. Awards can provide a finishing touch to your incentive system. The club can decide on what, if anything, to provide for the awards. Some things that have been done include:

- embroidered patches made for each shooting club so that shooters can put them on their shooting shirts or mount them in a frame,
- making pin-on buttons with the club logo on the border and the shooting club score in the middle (or vice-versa),
- certificates for the highest shooting club attained during the year for each shoot-

er (*see photo*),

- NFAA style patches; and
- Engraved metal bars with holes in them for chaining them together in a stacked fashion similar to the NFAA 20-pin system.

It is a good idea to give a shooting club award for each and every "club" each shooter attains during each year. This little thing can really provide a year-end banquet with some festivity! It is the culmination of the Incentive System for that year, and will allow the club to have further gains the following year, since word gets around in a hurry. You can even give them out at the annual Election of Officers Meeting as a means of getting people to come to the meeting! This works better for this than you can imagine.

If desired, the club can also make up "X-count" clubs, starting at say, Five Xs per round and going up to Fifty X or even more! This is easily accommodated, as it is part of the recorded data anyway.

Summary

What better way to promote your field range and club than to provide a non-competitive, non-hostile, pressure-free means of accomplishing the three goals reflected in the open quotations for as many shooters as want to participate? I have yet to see this system fail to radically increase the use of the courses and to improve the scores of all the participants. You all now have a personal reason to shoot and participate without the pressure of a tournament environment!

Remember that if you, as a ProActive archer, want to continue to advance and improve your level of expertise, you really do need a place to shoot, and other archers to shoot with. Without others around, you can't very easily establish a benchmark as to how you are really progressing in comparison to others; finding this out at only the bigger events isn't exactly being ProActive about your competitive level. So, once again, become ProActive and head off a downward trend by getting out there and giving back to the sport and your local area clubs and ranges.

45

Indoor Incentive Programs to Boost Participation

The definition of "target panic" reminds me of what has been described as "an old Chinese poem:"

"If archer shoots just for fun he has all his skill.
If he shoots for score, his hands tremble
And his breath is uneasy.
If he shoots for a golden price, he becomes mad and blind.
His skill was not lessened, but the vision of the target changed him."
Dan – fiondel@fastrans.net (Source: http://archery.mysaga.net/quotes.html)

As times have changed and people's free time has dwindled setting up indoor leagues that demand everyone's presence only on league nights is a thing of the past. Today, people work on rotational shifts; some are forced to work overtime; others are involved in more activities than they can keep up with. There are additional work obligations, the kids have expanded school activities as well as extra-curricular activities (football, basketball, wrestling, dancing classes, concerts, recitals) . . . I think you get the message. Thus, a range that is trying to force everyone to be present at a specific time, is losing out as well as are the shooters, because so few archers can participate . . . unless there is a very liberal make-up policy, or that accommodations are made to allow them to shoot during the day instead of evenings. In addition, more and more shooters are feeling intimidated by the top shooters, so they aren't so open to competing in leagues against them, no matter what handicap is employed. It used to be that three- and four-person teams could easily be accommodated. That too has changed and I'm finding that two-person teams are much easier to get people involved and committed to, and in addition, it is easier for the shooters themselves to coordinate with only the two of them to get their scores accomplished. We've also found that allowing people to pick their own partner works much better than forcing things by drawing a top gun against a beginner, and working toward the middle.

Enter the ProActive Archer(s) This is the second of a pair of chapters on the theme of "Working with an Incentive Program to Boost Participation." In my opinion, there are too few archers today who put something back into our sport. Rather they opt to stay in the background and enjoy the goings on. What "they" don't realize is, as I have mentioned, that boredom sets in, shooters get tired of the same old stuff with the same old shooting buddies, and before long you not only don't have new blood coming into the range, but even many of the old timers go on to pursue something else, leaving them shooting by themselves and having an even more difficult battle with the doldrums. I strongly feel that fully ProActive archers need to contribute back to the sport and do whatever they can to provide others with a "raison d'être" (reason for being).

You as a ProActive archer can only do so much to keep yourself going; we are a social animal, and we have a need to be among others. Thus, if you show some motivation and come up with "new ideas" to keep things fun and interesting, then the chances are that your motivation and positive attitude will rub off and help to keep the shooters motivated and this will help result in keeping the ranges going.

Without archers doing this, most ranges, indoors and outdoors, come to the point of no return sooner or later. Every archer really owes it to the sport to do something about this. So, in this chapter I'm going to provide you with some easy to do ideas to help give other shooters a shot in the arm and to motivate them to do better; or at least to come to the range and join in the fun. It isn't all about winning or "getting ready for competition," because a constant load of always being serious and preparing for tournaments gets pretty old in a hurry too; when you are doing this by yourself all the time, then you are not receiving any "line training" or being pushed by anyone but yourself. You have the ideas given in the last two chapters. Now let's adapt those ideas to the group of shooters and not just an individual's perspective. Makes sense, doesn't it?

We will talk about Indoor Archery Promotion in this chapter, once again getting a ProActive archer involved directly instead of from the outside looking in and soaking up the benefits. What I'm presenting isn't anything new, I'm simply using some items from Chapter 41 and adjusting them for group activities. They can be used for informal get togethers among a group of shooters just for the challenges, or they can actually be readily adapted to a different kind of league once the winter season standard NFAA and Vegas target leagues are completed. The versatility available is huge. All that is needed is someone to take the bull by the horns and as the Nike commercial says, "Just do it!"

Getting Them Going on the Indoor Range

Getting your "merry men and women" to the indoor range to practice and shoot is an age-old problem for most archery clubs and indoor ranges, especially those oriented towards target/paper shooting. While leagues are a partial answer, they only serve to get shooters together once a week. There are problems with absenteeism and makeup scores, vacations, and the fact that many beginners think that they aren't good enough to shoot with the rest of the archers. Thus, rather than feel embarrassed or having to commit to something for the summer, they pass up the opportunity to shoot an indoor league that takes up a lot of time, especially in the spring, summer, and fall.

Shooting indoors fulfills the aspects and requirements of the beginning quote to this chapter. You, the target shooter as well as you the bow hunter will get numerous opportunities to fulfill the requirements of your particular niche in the game of indoor archery. Since most indoor venues are set for a maximum of 20 yards, you won't be able to incorporate much in the way of longer distance shooting; but you don't really have to do this anyway.

The Outdoor System Adapted for Indoors Think about how easy it would be to use the outdoor system from the previous chapter for indoors as well! It will generate interest among new shooters to come in and shoot and earn their place on the "Wall of Honor." (One thing about most indoor ranges is that they have plenty of wall space available for the "Club Placards" described.) So, while this may be a tad repetitious, keep thinking about how easily this can fit into an indoor situation including NFAA rounds as well as Vegas 300 and 450 rounds. I haven't tried it full scale for indoors for many years; mostly because for several years, we didn't have an indoor range close enough. Now, we have an indoor range, but the participation level is pretty good on the leagues year round, so I haven't felt the need. This system might fit for your indoor range situation, however; so read on. I will be offering some very successful options for other types of indoor leagues later on.

Many years ago, I developed a simple, non-competitive system in an attempt to motivate all shooters in the club, regardless of skill level, to practice and to turn in scores on the outdoor course. This system has proven itself, time and time again. It gives you, the shooters who just like to get out and shoot for yourself a challenge and something to shoot for as well. It offers a non-competitive opportunity for you to compete only with yourself at your skill level and to be able to track your progress with little to no hassle. All you have to do is to go out and shoot when you want to, complete a round, put your score for each target on a scorecard, date and total the score, and turn it in. Add to this the setting of goals, benchmarks and the additional games discussed in Chapter 41, you should be able to clearly see that you can have an outdoor season that will provide you with challenges and opportunities galore with little chance of getting bored with it.

A common question asked at this point in every discussion of this system is: "How can we be sure the shooter isn't "fudging" his/her scores?" The answer is simple: "Who cares?" It will be very, very obvious if a shooter turns in a 270 score for the incentive system and then goes to a tournament or for league and shoots a 230, won't it? This is not for anyone else's satisfaction but that of the individual shooter and to get people participating. Everyone is a "winner" and the only ones to lose are those that don't or won't participate, for whatever reason. How many scores you shoot each week is entirely up to you, and if you don't shoot a score, there isn't a penalty for it. There isn't a meeting or shooting time, there isn't a schedule, and there isn't a handicap to figure out. There are no 'games' to win or to lose. Everyone that participates is a winner in many, many ways. In the five clubs I've used this system in since the 1970s; it has never failed to boost shooter participation and range usage as well as shooter scores. In one particular club, we had only 40 active shooters, and during the first outdoor season from April through August, those 40 shooters turned in over 1,400 scores! Yes, you read it right, 1,400 scores turned in for only 40 participants in five months! Now that is obviously a huge boost in participation and course utilization, is it not? I'll tell you for certain, we didn't hear any of this stuff about, "The range isn't being utilized, so why spend the money maintaining it?"

It works outdoors (*see previous chapter*) and it works indoors.

The System in Detail for Indoors

Items Required

1. A 20 yard Indoor Range and, if the range is not the club's," coordination with its proprietor to collect the shooters' range fees and mark the scorecards as "PAID" before placing them in the box (see #5 below).
2. NFAA Blue Face Targets, Vegas single spot or 3-spot Targets.
3. Score cards to handle 12 ends of 5 arrows per end
4. Score cards to handle 10 ends of 3 arrows per end, or 15 ends of 3 arrows per end.
5. A mail box (or some type of box) with a padlock for the shooters to deposit completed scorecards. Or at least somewhere where the scorecards after being marked "Paid" are placed.
6. Spare scorecards adjacent to the locked box.
7. A 3-ring binder for master copies of each participating archer's scores
8. "Shooting Club" Poster Boards "Shooter Clubs" and its members.
9. Secretary to maintain #3 through #7 above for each shooter. If that means you, trust me, it isn't a hard thing to do and isn't all that time consuming! You are trying to generate more competitors by getting fellow archers to improve their game; you have a lot to gain from this, and frankly, little to lose!

Rules The rules are kept simple. It is only necessary for the shooter to:

1. Place their complete name, the date, and the round being shot onto the scorecard.
2. Shoot what ever round, be it Vegas 300, Vegas 450, or NFAA 300 or NFAA 360 round and add up their total score and X-count for each round shot. The shooter must shoot the correct full round(s) and write down the scores just like they are done in a tournament. Only official club/range scorecards or official tournament scores are acceptable.
3. Total up the scores and Xs, sign the card, and then place the scorecard in the lockbox (a mail box with a padlock works just fine).
4. Any score cards not totaled up will not be counted. It isn't the job of the secretary to total up score cards, so this should be made very clear.
5. It is best if two shooters or more shoot together, but it is not mandatory. If two shooters shoot together, then signatures should be on the scorecards for each shooter. Once again, make it clear that we aren't getting into this "padded scores thing"; the shooter is only hurting them by padding their scores.
6. Tournament scores count in this incentive system. Simply turn in a copy of your

tournament score properly signed along with the date, the type of round (field or hunter) and where it was shot.

The Binder Setup You can set up the 3-ring binder any way you choose. I've found that the easiest way is aligning the shooters alphabetically by last name first, with the archer's name in the upper right corner of the sheet. Items entered onto the individual archer's sheet include: date, round shot, total score, and total Xs (*see example below*). I strongly recommend that every shooter participating has their own scores record and that every score that each shooter turns in be recorded on a sheet similar to the one below. All columns are self-explanatory with the exception of the "Present Club," which will be explained later.

Sample Shooter Record Sheet

Incentive System Shooter Record, 2011

Archer's Name ____________________________

Date	Round (V3,V45,N)	Total Score	Total X's	Present "Club"
6/1	N	290	19	290
6/5	V3	254	11	250 V3
6/6	N	296	20	295
6/12	V3	259	20	255 V3

. . .

(V3 = Vegas 300; V45 = Vegas 450; N = NFAA 300) You can make up your own coding; it is your book.)

The Key to the System The "key" to the entire system is the "Shooter Club." Every shooter who turns in a score above 200 for the round becomes a member of a shooter club that is based upon that qualifying score for the shooter club. The most successful shooter club setup that I've determined over the years is as follows: 200, 210, 220, 230, 240, 250, 255, 260, 265, 270, 275, 280, 285, 290, 295, 299(Almost Club), Perfect. Of course, once again, you can design your "Club" cutoffs anywhere you so choose. For Vegas rounds I've used every two points from 290 and up, excepting the 299(Almost Club).

Shooter Club Rules Once you attain a given "club" level, you cannot go backwards and pick up a shooter club you missed at a lower level. You can only try to move up to the next level. You can continue to shoot and turn in as many scores as you so choose. Each score will be recorded on your personal scoring record. As a result of your improvement, you can skip shooter clubs. For example, you have shot a score of 256. A few weeks later you turn in a score of 266. You are now a member of the "265" club and have skipped the "260" club and cannot go back to become a member of the 260 club. Or, if the secretary so chooses, if you "skip over" a club, they can automatically include you in that club. It doesn't really matter all that much. People like seeing their names and then comparing with their friends to see how much each has to improve to keep up with or to pass their buddies! This works, let me tell you. It doesn't cost anything but time to keep up with things, but the value added is really there for the taking.

Shooter Club Listing Posters The secretary should make up these posters so that the shooters can be aware of who else is in their respective shooter's club. These can be made out of regular paper and enclosed in plastic, or they can be made of poster board with each shooter club on its own poster sheet. That is to say, you need a separate poster for each of the shooter clubs from 200 right on up to the Perfect Club. These can all be done ahead of time, or can be made as shooters "join" each sequential shooter club. The names should be listed as each shooter gets into each shooting club. That way, you don't have to make up new sheets all the time, but rather just continue your sheets as they occur (*see the sample below*). This can also be modified to simply place into the Club Newsletter or onto the Club's website for viewing; just use your ingenuity!

Sample Shooter Club Poster

Skybow Bowmwn 200 Club Members

Shooter Name	Date	Score	X Count
Alcorn, Jim	4/1	205	6
Ferry, Alice	4/8	200	8
Zalcorn, Harvey	4/8	209	11
. . .			

A shooter's name only appears once in each club; you don't list them again for another score or scores in the same "Club." Make sure you keep individual records for each shooter; it isn't hard to do.

Helpful Hints The secretary or manager should make it a point to keep the scores up to date, at least on a weekly basis. Be absolutely certain to keep the Shooter Club Posters up to date and that they are neatly and completely done. By keeping those posters or listings up to date, everyone gets to see how everyone else is doing and they find the added incentive to try to make the next higher club level; either from a personal challenge standpoint, or to try to catch up to their buddies. Also make certain that every score, if it is added up and properly completed, is entered onto each shooter's personal score record and kept in the 3-ring binder. It is imperative you have a hard copy of those scores. It is also a good idea to keep the original score cards to fall back on, just in case questions arise. In all the years I have done this, I haven't had any questions arise, but I kept those original scorecards in the club house anyway.

Awards Awards aren't necessary, but are a nice touch if your club has an annual banquet. The rewards provide the finishing touches to the incentive system. The club can decide on any number of things to do for the awards. Some things that have been done include:

- embroidered patches made for each shooting club so that shooters can put them on their shooting shirts or mount them in a frame
- making pin-on buttons with the club logo on the border and the shooting club score in the middle (or vice-versa)
- certificates for the highest shooting club attained during the year for each shooter (*see photo*)

- NFAA style patches, and
- Engraved metal bars with holes in them for chaining them together in a stacked fashion similar to the NFAA 20-pin system.

It is a good idea to give a shooting club award for each and every "club" each shooter attains during each year. This little thing can really provide a year-end banquet with some festivity! It is the culmination of the Incentive System for that year, and will allow the club to have further gains the following year, since word gets around in a hurry. You can even give them out at the annual Election of Officers Meeting as a means of getting people to come to the meeting! This works better for this than you can imagine. You can also give those out at a League Banquet or Indoor "end of season" get together. Given advance notice, people will show up for these sorts of things, and they are like kids with new toys when receiving those Certificates.

If desired, the club can also make up "X-count" clubs, starting at say, Five Xs per round and going up to the 60 X Club! This is easily accommodated, and is part of the recorded data anyway.

The Different Rounds You Can Use for Incentive or for Leagues

Standard Vegas 300, Vegas 330, NFAA 300, and NFAA 360 Rounds Most everywhere, these are the Standard Rounds being used for indoor archery leagues. In some areas of the country, the Vegas face is the only one shot up until the Vegas shoot is over; then the NFAA blue face is the one shot the most in preparation for the NFAA Indoor Nationals. With the advent of the Presley's Midwest Open, the Iowa Pro-Am, and the Kansas City Shoot Out, among others, there is more emphasis being placed on the Vegas 330 and NFAA 360 rounds, so some ranges are using those rounds for their "Fall Indoor Leagues" in an effort to help their shooters prepare for those events. Then, come January, the Vegas 300 and NFAA 300 rounds begin to show. This is fine and good, and what the ranges likely should be doing; especially when sharing the range space with indoor 3-D leagues that also start in January and run until April.

You can spice up those leagues with league banquets and achievement certificates, so that everyone participating, and not just the winners get something for their efforts

A couple of other things to spice thing up during league night that have been successful include:

- Drawing an "End Number" at the beginning of the second practice end.

This tells everyone that there will be a "Victim" drawn during that end of tonight's/today's league round. Prior to stepping to the line for that end, the "Lane Number" (not a name, but a lane number such as 10 Top, or 12 Bottom) is drawn randomly out of a hat. This is this session's "Victim." The rules are simple: If the victim can muster a "25" on this end, then said victim gets a free soda. If said victim can shoot a 5X-25, then everyone on that bale wins a free soda. I've witnessed many top echelon shooters come unglued when they've become the "Victim" with all eyes upon them, watching their every arrow . . . and the grief they take from those on the bale with them if they don't shoot that 5X- 25.

- Shooting for quarters for each end. Top shooters have to shoot "inside out X's" while others shoot for regular X's, and those with handicaps over "10" (290 average or below), shoot for the "5-ring" (counts as an "X" for them). Winner of each end takes those quarters for that end. In event of a tie, the quarters carry over and those tied shoot for those quarters. You need somebody to keep track of this, so it can be cumbersome, but it is fun.
- Money shoot down round after the completion of the night's scoring. Everyone who wants to puts in a dollar. Then two ends are shot with normal scoring. The lowest two shooters in score are out (including X-count). Then two more ends are shot, and bottom two go. Then, one end is shot, but the X-ring is all that counts and nothing else. Even if a Miss is a 4 and that person shoots 4 X's and another shoots a 25 with 4X's, the X's prevail and that 4 means nothing. Then we shoot another end counting only X's. Once we get down to two shooters remaining, then we shoot two ends of "inside out X's" only. Nothing counts but inside out X's. If tied, then we go arrow for arrow, inside out, first to miss is out. If they both miss the inside out X, then the shoot off continues arrow for arrow until one hits the inside out and the other doesn't. The winner takes all the dollars. This is normally very short and sweet and doesn't take long, but it sure is fun for everyone. Those who went to the pine can continue to shoot, but they aren't shooting for any of the dollars.
- Same as immediately above, but back them up to 22 or 25 yards (if you have room in the range). This really spices things up in a hurry!

Modified "Freeman Bowman" Indoor Round This round is something new I just threw together recently for a League Banquet in an effort to shoot something different. Old green Freeman Bowman targets aren't available anymore, so I had to improvise. It was a hit with the shooters, so we are likely to be using it this summer for a 4-6 week two-man team indoor league. Here is how I've modified the round:

It is a 60 arrow round consisting of 12 ends of five arrows per end. Total possible score is 300. Target face is the NFAA 5-spot target (everyone shoots the 5-spot target for this round).

- Three ends of five arrows each shot from 10 yards. Scoring: the X-ring counts as 5 points, the rest of the white counts as 4 points and the outer blue counts as 3 points. You can toughen it up by having them go "inside out" on the X-ring for the 5 points; but I found that it wasn't necessary; the shooters created their own damage.

- Then four ends of five arrows each shot from 15 yards. Scoring: the same.
- Then five ends of five arrows shot from 20 yards. Normal NFAA scoring. X-ring and white = 5 points; dark blue = 4 points.

The round actually goes a bit faster, but the shooters really enjoy moving around and doing something different. Using only the X for 5-points at 10 and 15 yards adds some challenge to the round, and we aren't busting up any arrows either. Of course this can be played with 2-, 3- or even 4-person teams, and handicapped if you want. We just shot it for the trial, but it has been asked for as a league item later on.

Field and Hunter 20 yard Indoor Round This round uses the Standard NFAA 35 cm (20 yard) Field and Hunter Faces. This one was also very successful and we had a lot of shooters come in one or two evenings a week just to beat the heat and still have the opportunity to shoot their field and hunter faces. Many of them found it quite challenging to see if they could shoot Ten 20's in a row at 20 yards or not. Some could, most couldn't, or at least didn't, that is. Here's the round:

- Create two person teams.
- Shoot four arrows per end for 10 ends (40 arrows) for the round using a single target face just like we do outdoors.
- Distance is all from 20 yards, normal NFAA scoring of 5, 4, and 3 with the total possible for round being 200 points. The handicap is based upon a perfect score of 200, 80% of the difference between your average of the best two out of the last three shot and 200.
- We rotate target faces each week, for four cycles on each target face: Field, Hunter, Field, Hunter, Field, Hunter, Field, Hunter.
- Awards are Highest Score Achieved Certificate for the Hunter and the Field Rounds (*see photo*).

20 Yard Indoor NFAA Group IV Animal League This is yet another improvised Indoor Round that has proven very successful with the shooters. This round really provides a challenge to everyone, top echelon shooters and beginners alike. We use the Group IV NFAA Animal Target faces. Note that the maximum distance for use of these targets is indeed 20 yards and they are all shot at maximum distance. In addition, I recommend against placing any aiming dots on the animal faces. Not providing aiming dots adds to the challenge.

League Duration Since there are eight NFAA Group IV animals, the league duration is set at 8 weeks, and we only run this during the spring or early summer. It provides a break from the monotony of shooting "spots" all the time. We've been at it since November, so it is time for something really different.

Teams We use two-person teams, but you can set up anything you want.

Target Faces All targets are Group IV NFAA animals, however, target faces are rotated each week; that is to say that each week, everyone shoots a different animal. The wrinkle here is that nobody knows which animal will be shot for that week until they arrive to shoot league. We draw the name of the animal out of a hat, and that is what we all shoot that night.

Number of Target Faces Everyone is given two target faces of the same animal. It is their choice how to arrange the targets on their quarter of the bale. They cannot overlap scoring areas or animals.

Numbers of Arrows We shoot four arrows per end for 10 ends. It is the shooter's individual choice how many to shoot into each of their two target faces. Some elect to shoot all four arrows into one, others do two and two, some will see how tight things are, and maybe shoot 3 and 1. Doesn't matter as long as you keep them in your two target faces. We did have some arrow destruction, so you could modify this to shoot only two arrows per end, score, and pull. It simply means that you have 20 ends of 2 arrows each and doesn't really take much longer.

Scoring This is where it gets fun. Scoring is "5" points for the Vitals, 3 points for a Non-Vital hit, and "6" points for the nailing the circle in the middle of the Vitals (it is invisible from the shooting line).

Handicap Total possible for handicapping purposes is "200" points. Yes, we know that it isn't long before people are well over '200' and don't have any handicap. That is what every shooter was striving for...no handicap. I tell them at the beginning how this works and that they don't have to "try" for those 6's. The reply I get is that if there is a *bonus* involved, then they are going for as many of the bonus points as they can get. Nobody has yet to "clean" this round regardless of animal for a "perfect" 240! It is tougher than it looks!

Awards Once again, certificates work just fine for the highest score achieved and which of the eight animals that the highest score was achieved upon.

Rotating Target Faces from Week to Week Another wrinkle that I've used very successfully is to rotate target faces from week to week. You can have a 60 arrow round, but you have to modify the scoring to accommodate this. This league is intended to draw in more newbies and can be a separate league from your normal ones that you do.

- NFAA blue face, normal scoring for 300 points, then the following week:
- Vegas Face 60 arrows (20 ends 3 arrows per end), but scoring the entire gold as 5 points the red as 4 points.
- Field Face, 15 ends of 4 arrows per end, normal scoring of 5-4-3.
- Hunter Face, 15 ends of 4 arrows per end, normal scoring of 5-4-3.
- Repeat the cycle one or two more times, making it a 8 or 12 week league.

Handicapping Since everyone is on the same or nearly the same footing, handicaps are based on the average of best two of the last three rounds shot, regardless of target face, subtracted from 300 and then the shooter gets 80% of that for their next round's handicap. The system works just fine.

Beginner's League, NFAA Blue Face Most ranges have a lot of newbies coming in who are intimidated at the thought of even trying to compete with those people with long stabilizers, telescopic sights (Oh, my!), release aids, and carbon shafts. I don't blame them. They don't understand handicap systems, they don't know the people, they don't know how to score, and all sorts of scary things. It is one of the jobs of a ProActive archer to think ahead and try to get new people into the fold and to try to prevent this fear of shooting around people. So, I came up with this idea. We have had one go around at it, and while we didn't have tons of shooters, the word is out, so we hope to do better as time goes on.

Since these people are so new to shooting, I knew that handling a full 60 arrow round on the blue face was going to be really hard for them. So here's how we did this:

Duration The league was for 12 weeks.

Teams We created two-person teams. If at signup a person didn't already have a partner, we found them one. This worked out really well.

Schedule You can use any scheduling software to do this. However, for a 12 week league, you might have some teams shoot against others twice while others might only see them once, or even some might see them three times . . . it all depends upon how many teams you have. Total games won was what was used to determine the winners.

Round Durations

- For four weeks, the beginners only shot one half round, or 6 ends of 5 arrows each. Handicaps were based upon a 150 possible score.
- For the next four weeks, the beginners shot 45 arrows, or nine ends of 5 arrows each. Handicaps were based upon a possible score of 225.
- The last four weeks, everyone shot a full NFAA round of 12 ends of 5 arrows each, for a total possible score each week of 300 points.

Awards We had an awards banquet with awards for the 1st, 2nd, and 3rd Place teams. We also gave Achievement Certificates to every participant. I'm sure you can come up with even more ideas to help get more new people involved and to help promote archery in your area

Summary

What better way to promote your indoor range than to provide a non-competitive, non-hostile, pressure-free means of accomplishing the things reflected in the open quotations for as many shooters as want to participate? Yes, I know that we hope we don't end up with everyone having "target panic," but I think the point is well taken;

if they don't shoot, then we don't have a range to in which to shoot. We need to promote participation and if we can't do it all by leagues, then we improvise. I have yet to see this system fail to radically increase the use of the range and to improve the scores of all the participants. You all now have a personal reason to shoot and participate without the pressure of a tournament environment!

Remember, if you, as a ProActive archer want to continue to advance and improve your level of expertise, you really do need a place to shoot, and other archers to shoot with. Without others around, you can't very easily establish a benchmark as to how you are really progressing in comparison to others; finding this out at only the bigger events isn't exactly being ProActive about your competitive level. So, once again, become ProActive and head off a down-ward trend by getting out there and giving back to the sport and the local area clubs and ranges.

For the past four chapters, I've discussed things that a ProActive archer can do to get more meaningful fun out of practice sessions, both indoors and outdoors, I mentioned how you, as a ProActive archer, may embrace some responsibility to further help your own cause to improve by helping others to also have more involvement and fun with their archery. I mentioned that both indoors and outdoors, everyone reaches a saturation point; either from sheer boredom from the constant repetition of shooting or from frustration due to your not improving as quickly as you think you should. I offered up ways to spice up your outdoor practice sessions. I then offered up several means to spice up your indoor shooting in addition to making your private practice sessions less boring and more meaningful.

I also outlined several outdoor and indoor incentive programs/innovative shooting rounds to provide more challenges and also alleviate the monotony. It goes without saying that we as archers all know that target archery isn't getting the involvement and interest that it once had. Becoming ProActive and trying to fend off further reduction in participation levels is, in my opinion, one of our jobs as not only ProActive archers, but even those who are only participating for the fun of slinging arrows at the target, regardless of how well they fare. Without promotions and without people getting newcomers into the sport, outdoor and indoor ranges will continue to come and go because of a lack of growth due to the lack of promotion.

I hope that the preceding chapters have given you some ideas to follow up on to give you and your fellow archers in your area some ways to help improve things for everyone.

In conclusion, if you recall, I said earlier that a ProActive archer should give back something to the sport. The following quote is quite notable in this regard, and you can relate "clinics" to leagues and fun things for people to do with their archery.

> "*My dad has always taught me these words: care and share. That's why we put on clinics. The only thing I can do is try to give back. If it works, it works.*"
> Tiger Woods
> American Professional Golfer

Section 8

Making Your Own "Stuff"

This section is special to me and I hope you enjoy it as I delve into what seems to be among the most favorite endeavors we archers undertake; that being customizing some common items, or even improvising and making your own "stuff" from scratch.

When I first started archery, almost everyone I was around was into creating their own things. I've made my own peep sites out of black plexiglas, long before the advent of the hooded Pa-Peeps or Fletcher Tru-Peeps. I made my own feather rests replete with a cut off nock ear as a pressure point, mounted to a leather pad that was adhered to the sight window. In fact, I shot many scores over 500 on the old NFAA field and hunter faces (5-3 scoring) with a home made sight aperture, a home-made stabilizer, and one of my home-made, custom built double feather arrow rests! I've made (and still have) my own rope-spike release aids, but before that, I was in to making my own ledge-style release aids out of Plexiglas, too.

Anything from the custom finger slings and dots & circles discussed in the next two chapters, right on through the shot-timing sequences (using *VisiCalc* and then MS *Excel*), the placard system for having your most frequently used sight settings, on through to using a horizontal tape across the target face for getting more accurate sight settings are things I tinkered up.

Of course, how can we forget that very refined set-up for learning muscle memory for your "to anchor draw length" I called the "Triple Tape System?" Even though it is over 40 years old, it still works very well today.

So, it should by now go without saying, because you know it to be true, "Archers are always on the prowl to have our equipment custom fitted to us." Often, this means purchasing items and then tearing them apart or otherwise modifying them to fit. Even a $150 release aid we will carve into to get it to feel right on up through grinding on a bow's grip or riser to get that elusive perfect fit, or jockeying with the strings and cables to find a better sweet-spot than the "specs" call for on a particular bow. We are tinkerers, we are inventors, and we are improvisers to the nth degree. There is simply no denying it. You cannot be a "real" archer unless you tinker, now can you? So, read on and get some more insights into a couple of more things to tinker with; both of which are extremely useful and can/will add points to your game. It is sometimes the little details that create the bigger benefits—once the basics are mastered and your form is set and all but automated.

Tom Dorigatti

46

Making Your Own Custom Finger Slings

For those who use wrist slings, these can be purchased and then adjusted to length very easily, or a person can make their own to get them to proper length. In the case of finger slings, however, purchasing them, while a very viable option, usually leaves the archer with a sling that is either too long or too short. After purchasing them, the temptation is to tear them apart and try to figure out how adjust them and to get them back together again. You can make your own slings out of parachute cord or nylon rope.

Presented here is how to make your own custom-fit and comfortable finger slings out of either leather or rubber. Once you have established your finger sizes and the length of sling needed, you can make one in less than 10 minutes time and have fun doing it. Each sling will last for a couple of years of hard shooting. In addition, it won't "catch" on the bow like some of the others do. You can tweak their length or width in a matter of a few minutes without destroying the sling in the process.

Sound interesting?

Background

You might be thinking "I really don't need a sling, since the bow doesn't come out of my hand and I have good control over it. Besides, a sling gets in my way and can cause problems when I'm out hunting." The other thought I hear, especially since the advent of the "dead in the hand" bow technology is, "My bow is dead in the hand; there isn't any recoil, so I don't need a sling."

My reply is really quite simple: "A ProActive archer doesn't wait until the bow comes flying out of their hand due to not having a bow sling fitted to prevent it." Remember, ProActive archers are never "reactive," they take measures to prevent bad things from happening. Sooner or later, when you do have your bow fly out of your hand because you didn't like or thought you didn't need a sling, you will, if lucky, only be replacing the bottom cam. It could be worse, however as in having to replace the scope, the bow sight, the extension bar, the stabilizer, and potentially even the bottom (or both) limbs! Bows are not designed to be thrown or dropped like that; even though some people do, in a tantrum, throw their equipment. (I call that "gravel tuning.")

In addition, you might think you don't grab the bow when the shot breaks, but if you don't grab at the bow or hold it somehow, then it shouldn't stay in your hand when the shot breaks. I've yet to see a person not using a sling that wasn't gripping the bow, especially those starting out with an open hand who then grab the bow just before they launch the shot. (Starting with an open bow hand primes the reflex to close the hand.) So, what kind of surprise shot is that? Easy answer, it is not a "surprise shot," but rather a punched shot or worse. So, if you have a problem with spending $5-$20 on a "store bought" sling, then I'm about to show you how to make one that might cost you 10-20 minutes of time and less than $0.50.

You don't have to make a sling out of leather or rubber as described below; nylon rope will work fine, too. It is really almost the same procedure, excepting you make loops with the rope and tie them off to fit your thumb and whichever finger you like having this type of bow sling placed upon. You can even use Tygon tubing in short sections to make a "sliders" so you can tighten and loosen the sling from your thumb and finger. Yes, they make slings you can buy, but nearly all of them are too long or too short and need to be fitted anyway. Many top shooters use finger slings of the type I'm describing. Some make their own while others purchase them and then perform the custom fit to get the length just right; too tight and it creates problems, too long and the bow comes out of the hand too far, and the arrow rest will come down and hit you on the top of your bow hand. When that happens, before long you end up trying to "catch" the bow before it does that to your hand. This is a bad habit, no?

You can even make a sling out of release rope or nylon rope and put it through holes in the riser and then custom fit that length so the bow stays in your hand and isn't too loose or too tight. There are other slings available for purchase that come pre-made and which allow a full range of adjustment in length so that you don't have to hook up and un-hook to get yourself detached from the bow. Many bowhunters and 3-D shooters use these types of "slip in" slings. They do the job very nicely and will not allow the bow to come out of your hand and to hit the ground or the floor.

What I'm saying here is simply this: without a bow sling on your bow, you are risking all of your money, because it is going to come flying out of you hand sooner or later. I cannot understand why anyone would take the chance with a $350 to $1200 bow, and another $400-$600 worth of accessories which can be protected using a simple $0.50 to $10 item, something that will also increase your accuracy and consistency as well. It is sure a small price to pay to protect that huge investment.

Items Required

Here's what you need to make your "insurance policy" and how to do it in a matter of a few minutes (*see photo*).

1. Rubber O-rings purchased from a local hardware store—two sizes, custom fit to the thumb and either pointer or middle finger.
2. Thin and narrow leather strips cut to width; or rubber strips cut to width. I have used tennis/racquetball leather or rubber wrap grip "tape" for over 25 years for use in making the slings. I find this much more comfortable than commercial leather such as that used in purchased leather finger slings. The rubber material I use is

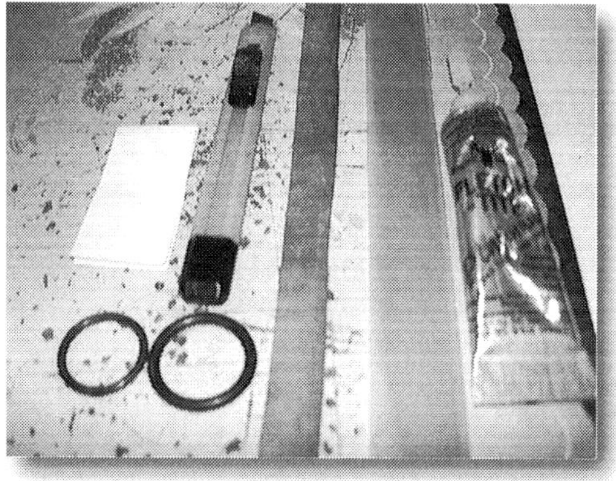

Ektelon® Vision Power Wrap, but there are several other brands out there that will work just fine.

3. Measuring instrument for cutting length and width of the material
4. Sharp hobby knife or sheet-rock cutter
5. Double Stick Tape
6. Serving Thread
7. Fletching glue

Preparation

1. *Selecting O-ring Sizes* O-rings can be purchased for pennies at a local hardware store. By using two different sizes, one for your thumb, and the other for either your pointer finger or middle finger, you will find that the comfort and security of the finger sling will improve greatly over a pre-made item. Try both the "thin" style and also the "regular" style O-rings to decide which is more comfortable for you. There is a difference in comfort and also how long they will hold up. I've never had a failure of either type, however.
2. *Leather or Rubber Racquet Grip Tape?* I have used leather racquet grip tape for many years. Normally, the leather ones will last two to three years before needing replacement. The rubber grip wraps come in many colors. They are inexpensive and from one grip tape, you can make upwards of 10 or more slings, depending upon the length you need. In addition, the rubber does give an additional soft "cushion" for you when the bow is shot. It will depend upon whether or not you like the cushion and stretch of the rubber one, or the solid feel of the leather one.
3. *Cutting the Material to Length* This, to me is the best part of making the slings. You can customize the length of them pretty much on the go. If the sling is too long, then the bow tends to fly too far out of your hand and you could have problems with the arrow rest coming down and hitting you on the hand. If it is too short, then it hangs up on you and you will find that any hand action at all is then imparted to the bow, thus causing even more problems with your shot process and accuracy. I feel that proper fit of the sling is similar to proper fit of the draw length, but not quite as critical as the draw length. For my preferences, to allow for the overlap and tying off the O-rings, I start with an unfinished length of 6½". For my hand size and bow grip thickness, this allows for about ¾" of play between my relaxed hand and the riser when the sling is in place. If your bow's grip is small, then the sling starting length will obviously be shorter. You will clearly see a difference in comfort and the reaction of the sling by taking the time to get the length right. ***Caution*** Be sure to use a very sharp cutting tool, such as a hobby knife or a sheet-rock cutter. The leather is thin and cuts easily, but a dull cutter can be dangerous. The rubber material really requires a very sharp instrument. It is easily cut, as well, but offers more resistance to being cut. You may need more or less, but always start long, finish it off, and don't trim until you have the length you want.

4. Cutting the leather or rubber strips to width. I have found that the narrower width, about ⅜″, seems to work better and there is more comfort and less interference with the fingers and bow positioning when compared to wider widths. I have gone down to ¼″ width and had zero problems with it. Pick your width and see how you like it. I haven't seen any difference in the service life of the slings due to a difference in width (*see next photo*).

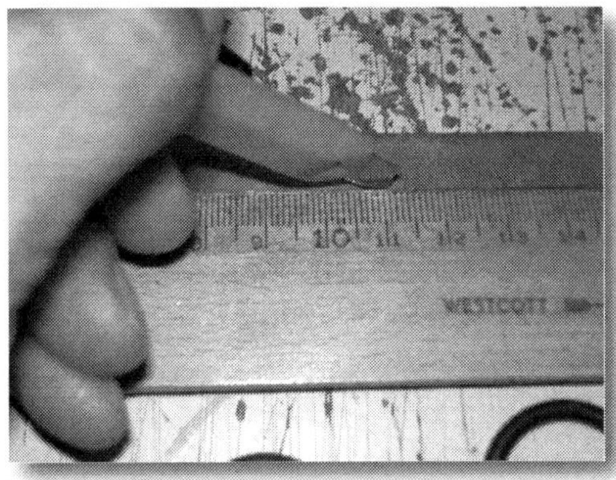

Putting the Pieces Together

1. The first step, now that you have the length and width as you want them, is to install a piece of double stick tape onto one end of the strip of leather/rubber. The purpose of the double stick tape is to hold the end in place while you tie it off. Of course, if you are using leather and you have access to a sewing machine, you could use the machine to sew in the end over the O-ring. If you are using rubber, it works best to do one end at a time. (*see photos below*) With leather, you can match up the length you want and double stick both ends at once.
2. Once you have the end of the leather or rubber over the O-ring, you can now tie off the end. I use normal soft center serving thread, 0.021″ or 0.025″ diameter. Don't use a thin, hard serving such as Halo if you are making rubber finger slings. You run the risk of cutting into the rubber when you tighten your knots. In addition, the hard serving material will also wear into the bow's riser and mark it up. I start the tying off close to the O-ring, but leaving room for the O-ring to spin freely. If you use a "double" half knot, or a surgeon's tie off for the first knotting, your tightness will be maintained; otherwise, the knot can slip. What you then do is to use a half-knot on alternating sides and place adjacent knots side by side, alternating sides of the sling from "clean side" to "cut side." Move towards the center of the sling with the knots for about ¼″. This is very similar to tying in a

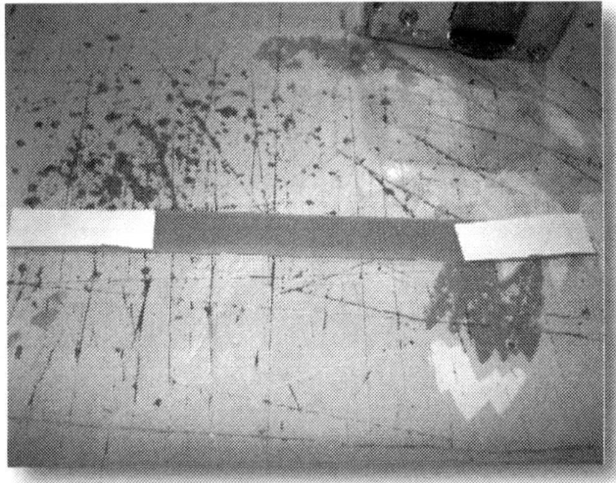

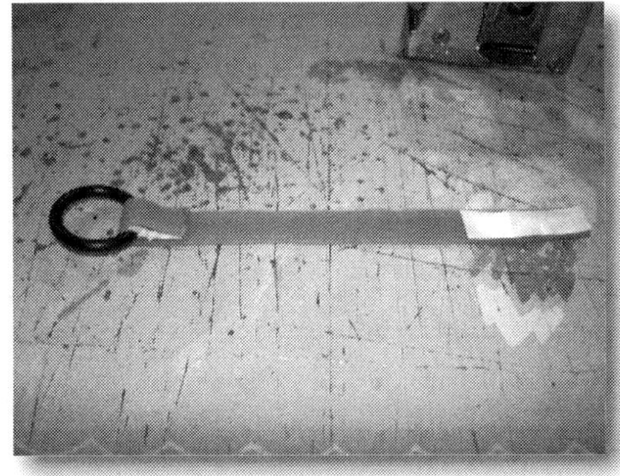

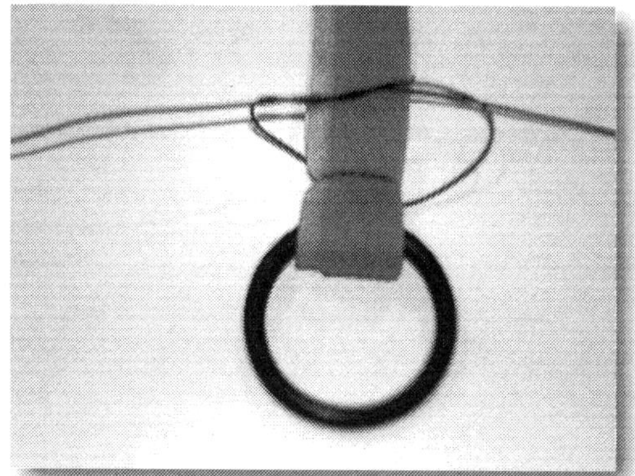

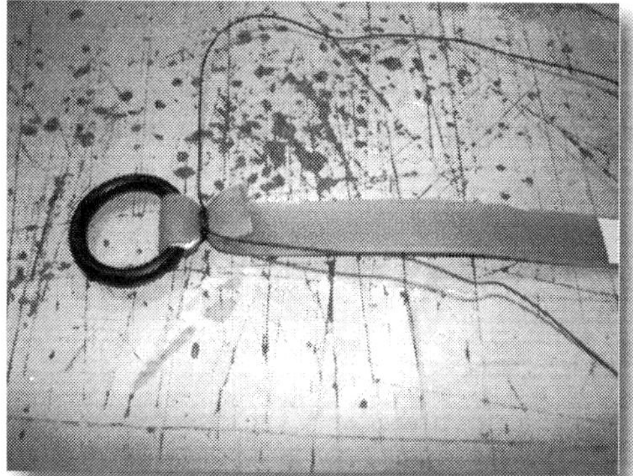

nocking point locator on your bow string; that is, it uses the same process of alternating the knots. Just be sure to pull each knot tight before tying the next on the opposite side. Then, go back on top of the original knots with a double half-knot to hold the knot tight, and alternate half knots back up and over what you've already tied (*see photos below*).

Note Always tie off the final square knot of the leather on the "rough surface side." You want the smooth, uninterrupted surface to be the one facing the bow. Same goes with the rubber grip tape. The rough surface is the side where the "cut-end" should be. This allows for a slip-free point in case of contact with the bow on the shot, and prevents the sling from potentially "hanging up" on the bow during a shot.

3. Once you have both O-rings tied off and knotted, check for length, re-size as necessary, then melt the ends of the serving thread and immediately touch the knots lightly to flatten the ends to prevent slippage (*see photos below*).
4. Use fletching glue to seal the thread by applying some around the entire circumference of the serving thread and also to seal the serving thread knots on both ends of the sling. Wipe off any excess glue, and then allow the glue to dry. You have now completed your "Custom Fitted and Comfortable Bow Sling."

Summary

I chose to highlight making your own slings with the "finger-sling" style because they

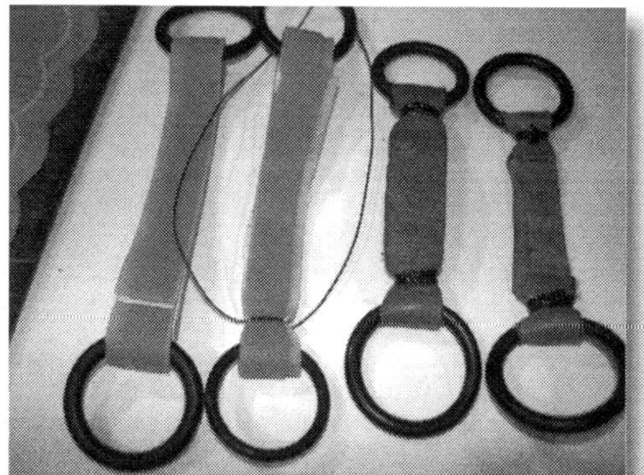

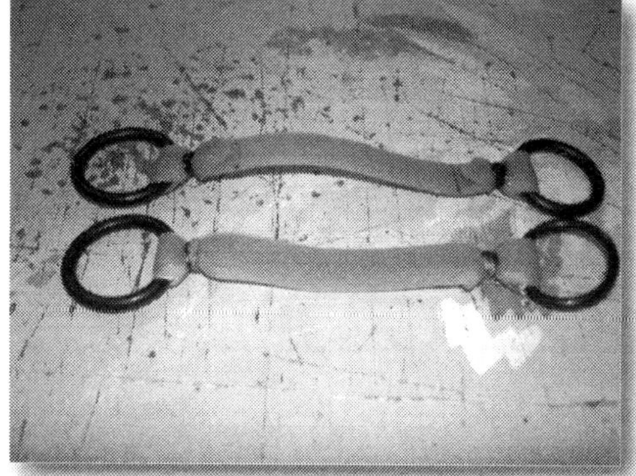

are so popular with target shooters. You can, make your own bow slings from ski tow rope. In addition you can make them by weaving together different colors or ⅛″ or $^{3}/_{16}$″ nylon cord, or you can even make an adjustable "wrist sling" with ski tow rope that has a loop for your wrist in one end and a clip hook with the clip removed on the other end. You then place your wrist thru the loop, wrap the loose end around the riser, and "hook up" the hook to your wrist. This style of wrist sling was very popular many years back and does the job very well. The more popular bow slings are those that use leather or rubber attachments that go behind the main stabilizer, and stay on the bow all the time. You simply slip your wrist under the wrist sling, set it to the proper length, and you can get into and out of the bow quite easily.

Custom fitted and comfortable slings are not difficult to make. They are definitely not expensive, and in addition, they also don't take very long to complete. They are durable and last a long time. If you lose one, you aren't really out any money and it isn't something to get excited about. After all, you have so thoroughly enjoyed making them that you have made several spares, right (*see photo*)?

I offer you a means to custom fit your finger sling in length, width, and finger size in a very inexpensive fashion. If you want the solid feel of leather, then that material is readily available from any store selling tennis racquets or racquetball racquets in the form of grip wrapping materials. This type of leather is thin, pliable, and absorbs sweat easily without shrinkage or turning hard when it dries. If you prefer rubber grip tape, then it is offered in a variety of colors or even in a "clear" version. The O-rings don't interfere with the bow, since they are very soft and pliable, and they also won't rub your fingers raw or come loose on you, yet they stretch and give, offering more comfort. One other advantage is that while you need two hands to put the finger sling on, you will eventually learn to slide your thumb right out of the sling without using the other hand. I'd recommend you try both the leather style and the rubber style to see which you prefer. This still remains as an individual preference, as does the style of finger sling you choose to make and use, be it the style offered up in this article, a parachute cord finger sling, or even one of the several styles of wrist slings. However, it never hurts one to try the alternatives and go with whatever you like the best and that is most comfortable for you.

Shooting your bow without a sling or retainer of some type is taking a very high risk of having the bow come out of your hand and getting damaged, if not destroyed when it hits the ground. It isn't a case of if the bow comes flying out of your hand, it is the case of when it finally happens. It comes down to the old "Mr. Goodwrench" advertisement from years past concerning preventive maintenance, "You can pay me a little now, or pay me a lot later."

Tom Dorigatti

47

Making Your Own Custom Dots & Circles

Archers have always needed to customize something in their equipment setup. Arguably, among those ranked as most important is being able to customize what you are seeing as a sight picture while you are aiming and "centered up" on a target face. There are a few manufacturers that offer limited sizes of "dots and circles" for application to scopes and some scope manufacturers even include a batch of dots and circles when you purchase a scope from them. In addition, there are options available for clarifiers and verifiers, both of which serve a great purpose in clearing up or enlarging what you see through your scope while aiming. However, in many instances having higher magnification and adding a clarifier or verifier can add to the problems of getting your view through the scope just the right size in order for you to be comfortable. Too small and you either cannot see clearly, or you can't find your "dot." Too large and the "dot" or circle covers too much or not enough of the bull's-eye. So, with all these options, how can you come up with just the right size dot or circle that fits you and your aiming style? How can you do it inexpensively and have a multitude of options available to you and not be limited by what you buy? I now provide you with an easy, inexpensive, and nearly unlimited option . . . making your own.

Some Background

When I first started competitive shooting in the late 1960's, a magnifying telescopic lens (a "scope") was not available. However, prisms of varying degrees were available, though rudimentary at best. Even the prisms had "dots" on them so that a person could have a reference point with which to aim. Most of the people I was associated with, however, opted for just a simple up pin or drop pin with a bubble mounted in them. Later on a couple of manufacturers started making a loop aperture (with no lens) and the option of having a drop or up pin within the aperture. These pins had a fluorescent coating on them and were very visible in just about any lighting conditions indoors or out. Without a lens, they provided no magnification whatsoever. These are still being used today by many FITA Olympic-style or recurve bow shooters, only without the option of having the "bubble," since bubbles are illegal in their competitions. Even when magnifying lenses got added, they were not of the best optical quality, and we had many instances where we couldn't see the target if we were standing out in the sun and the target was in the shade, for example. So, many of us carried a spare sight block with a sight pin aperture mounted in it for those instances where we couldn't see through our scopes. We would simply change from the scope to the aperture and shoot without magnification. I recall well that by being ProActive with regard to this visual problem helped me to keep my scores up and also to win several tournaments that I would not have won had I not carried that particular insurance policy with me. While I haven't had to go to such lengths in years, it is still a viable option for shooting in really poor lighting conditions. You will read, later on, however how I found a means to not have to worry much about not being able to see my dot.

It was sometime around 1973 or 1974, when a few manufacturers, including Killian, started making "scopes" (telescopic sights). The diameters were around ¾ inch to one inch, and magnifications were in diopters such as 0.25 to 1.25. Each increase in 0.25 diopters (power) was supposedly representative of a "power." I found that the Killian *Chek-it* 1.0 or 1.25 was way too blurry to see much with, so I opted for the 0.75. The lens glass was rather soft and very easily scratched. What was worse was that many of the dots on the scopes were made of water soluble paints. You soon found out that in a rainstorm, when you tried to wipe out the water from your scope, the dot came off with it as well! The remedy was that several of the scope manufacturers put a ground indentation into the center of the lens so that all was not lost if your dot washed out.

I had the "disappearing dot" problem only once, and my remedy at the time was to use a toothpick and fluorescent pink model paint and to paint on the dot into the middle of the scope. Sometimes, however, the dot wasn't quite round, and most times, it wasn't the right size either. The remedy I came up with was to punch a hole into a piece of tape of a selected diameter with a leather punch. I then stuck the tape onto the lens, centered the hole over the indent in the center of the lens and filled the hole with fluorescent (usually pink) paint and then let it dry. When I peeled off the tape, I had a nice round, highly visible dot on the center of my scope that wouldn't wash off.

The Custom Dot is Born

Then, one day, when I was fiddling around with my car and putting on some reflective bumper tape, the idea hit me. I figured out that by using a flattened drill bit as a punch, you could cut out a perfect dot of any size you wanted and stick it to a lens in an instant. You could always have several more of the same size cut out and available with you, and could replace them anytime you wanted. The "fluorescent reflective bumper tape dot" was born. I soon discovered that depending upon the target; I needed a different size dot to be able to see what I wanted to with regard to my sight picture. If the dot was too small, then I tended to see a lot of motion and would chase it around trying to force it to center up. If it was too large, then I would try to look around it to see the X-ring. For the indoor blue face, I used a bit larger dot. For outdoors, I went down in dot size for Field and Hunter face shooting, but up in dot size on the American Round FITA face. However, under all circumstances and lighting conditions, the fluorescent bumper tape meant that I could always see the dot in my scope even if I couldn't see the target clearly at all, such as shooting in the rain or foggy conditions outdoors, and under poor lighting conditions indoors. I'm lucky in that I don't like a crystal clear view of the target; I prefer a slightly soft image, but I do need to have my dot in my scope clearly visible as a reference.

So I began experimenting. By varying dot sizes I was able to find just the right dot size that fit how I was aiming and also which target I was shooting on at the time. I found that, for me, the size of the dot could vary from the beginning of the indoor or outdoor season to the end, as I got more used to the face and distances involved. I found that indoors, a larger dot, but not overly large, was better for me than moving my sight extension in or out. The same occurred outdoors. I didn't mess with my sight extension; I simply changed my dot size to accommodate what I was seeing and how I was shooting. I could make up a range of dot sizes in 1/64th inch increments and go out to find the one that worked best for me. I would simply peel off the old dot, and remove one from the card of dots I had made and try them out at whatever yardage, 50 was good, until I had the one that worked the best for me. I always had spares, and always seemed to have the right size that someone else needed as well!

Then, in the early 1980's, or thereabouts, Stanislawski came out with a scope that was ¾″ in diameter and had a bright fluorescent insert in it that you could also clearly see in any lighting conditions (*see photo*) The bubble was mounted right below the scope, and the outer diameter fit well into the *Pa-Peep* opening I was using, so I converted to the Stan scope. Later on, the Stan scope was modified to let more light enter the housing and the dot was even easier to see. Even if the insert came out, which it did sometimes, you still had the hole in the scope that was clearly visible, and you could shoot with that "hole" in your scope, stare at the X-ring and still shoot really well. One of the best scores I had shot up to that time on a Hunter Round was shot when that fluorescent dot somehow fell out of that scope and I was staring through that hole in the scope in order to aim for the middle! It was if "letting it float and shooting the shot" became somehow automatic, or something, at least for that day and some time to follow. I had a good thing going, so I figured I'd milk it for what it was worth.

Around 1984, I purchased, on a whim, a scope called the "Magna-Sight." This scope was of a much larger diameter than the Stan scope and also had a ground in dot in the center of the lens. It was clearer in the 6X than the Stan, but of course, much heavier as well. I had learned that bending the scope rod to allow the bubble to remain "level" for uphill, downhill, and flat shots was asking for the rod to break. So, I cut out the original bubble that was epoxied in, remove the old epoxy, laid a bed of fresh epoxy, mounted the bubble so it was level for the 2nd axis first, and then simply moved one end of the bubble forward or back as I inclined the bow for uphill and downhill simulation, and set the bubble so it was level all the way through that arc. We didn't call this the "3rd axis" back then, but knew that we had better do this if we wanted better scores on hilly courses. By cutting down the depth of the scope, also cut the weight of the scope housing which helped prevent scope rod breakage, while also letting in even more light. With the *Magna-Sites* (*see photo above*), I went back to using my "bumper tape" dots and still use them in all my scopes to this day, unless I'm using the new *True Spot* "Double Lens" system.

Followed by the Custom Circle

During the winter of 1986, I noticed that many shooters had started shooting with circles in the center of their scopes. Most were using circles they had purchased from some company (the name slips my mind now), and were fiddling with their sight extensions to try to get just the right view of the spot through the lens and not have too big or too little of a "halo" around the spot. It was then that the idea hit me that I could not only customize dots, but I could customize the outer part of the circle and the inside "hole" that I was looking through. I started experimenting with an outer circle size of ⅜″ and an inner circle opening the size of a 1714 arrow. It was simple, because I could use a ⅜″ bushing as the outer cut-out and then a piece of 1714 shaft for the hole in the middle. As the winter progressed, I started cutting down the diameter of the inner hole and was able to get it set so that I could just see beyond the X-ring. Of course, that was then, and this is now, and I can no longer go that small on the hole size! I still use this system to this day, with a few added twists. With the *Magna-Sight*, there is a ground dot in the center of the lens. I tried centering the "circle" in the scope lens, but that dot was taking away from me letting the bullseye center up in the hole. Thus, I had to move the center of the "hole" down just enough to cover the etched in dot. This was indeed off of optical center, but, apparently it didn't hurt me very much, because I suffered absolutely no loss in score once I made the sight correction and got used to the idea. I also found it helped me to keep my bubble level because the bubble was closer to the center of the area I was aiming with.

Some Tips I have found over the years that I tend to look around any circle that has a narrow boundary between the hole and the outer edge of the circle. So, to circumvent this, I use a ½″ bushing for the outer part, and then custom fit the hole size I need for each power lens I might want to shoot. Getting the hole centered is a problem sometimes, so I have to make many of them to get several that are almost perfectly centered up. Not to worry, however, since I tend to always look over the top . . . I put the wide side up. Then I don't worry about the fact that the outer boundaries aren't even. I'm using the *hole* to center up on the target and the outer edge only serves to keep me looking through the hole instead of over the top of it. Again, I must have a wide boundary in order to stop me from looking over the top of the entire circle.

I have also found that a 2613 or 2712 shaft works real well for the outer portion for lower power scopes of say 2X to 4X, because I use a much smaller hole than for the higher power scopes. I never change my sight extension; only the hole size. I've also found out that for people new to shooting with circles, it is far better to start out with a large (and I do mean large) hole, shoot several rounds so that you just let things float and allow your eyes to do the work, and then gradually (and I do mean gradually, since 1⁄32″ makes a huge difference in hole size) work the hole size down as you become progressively better at letting your eyes do the work and stop trying to force the "hole" to stay centered. I do think that one of the main reasons many scope dot shooters have major problems when they try to shoot with circles is that they start out with way too small of a circle to begin with; they can't seem to keep that hole centered, and then they are forcing it, tensing up, and generally don't get a steady sight picture at all. Many will also try to shoot a small hole with a larger diopter (power) scope, and really struggle trying to hold it steady and let the eyes do the work. It is a matter of commitment and finding the right-sized hole that works for you. Some shooters like a bigger halo around the bulls-eye, while others want to see a very small area outside the line of the "X-ring" on the NFAA Face. This all becomes personal preference, and trial and error is the only way you can get this right.

Using a Fluorescent Dot or Circle on a True Spot Scope

I have also discovered that, for me and my aiming style, I cannot seem to focus through the "grind" on the lens of a standard True Spot scope lens. (A True Spot lens has a higher magnification region in the center and lower magnification surrounding that.) I still have to use a home-made circle to outline the grind. I tried using cellophane tape so that the only part of the lens that was "clear" was the hole, and I ended up with problems making sure I was aiming at the correct target/spot. Indoors, however, I really like the de-magnification of the other spots on a Vegas 3-spot or NFAA 5-spot target face. This allows me to be certain of which spot I'm shooting at and still have that positive view in the background, making what I'm looking at stand out.

In addition, a ¼″ grind is too small for me, even in a 4X or a 6X lens, and a ⅜″ grind is too large! The ⅜″ ring leaves me too much of a halo around the bull and thus allows me to float too far around the bull's-eye. By customizing the hole size and centering the hole on the lens, I can now also get exactly the right-sized halo I need for my aiming. I don't play with sight extension and thereby change the alignment of my scope housing through my peep sight. Of course, you can use a dot and circle in tandem, but I've found that you need to use a much smaller dot if you do this. The hole is what I concentrate on, but you still need to see the dot as well. This is another nice thing about making your own that allows finely detailed customizing of what and how you see to aim.

Recently, True Spot Scopes has come out with what they call the "Double lens" system, where you have, for example a 6X plain lens in clear color and then you have a negative 6X colored (or clear, your choice) lens on the outside that has whatever hole size you prefer. If you use my "experimental" option above to determine which hole size works the best, then it is easy to order that negative diopter lens with your correct hole size drilled into it. This ProActive approach to scope and secondary lens selection definitely saves you money.

Use of a Clarifier or Verifier Lens in your Peep Sight

Most people are aware of the fact that when you use a clarifier or verifier lens in your peep sight, that the dot in your scope must be substantially enlarged in order for you to see it. The same goes with the size of hole in the circle and the outer diameter as well. I have experimented with clarifier lenses, and frankly don't like them, but when I use one, I simply use the 1/2″ outside diameter cut-out with a slightly larger hole to look through. If using a dot, I increase the dot size to accommodate aiming the easiest and still not have to look around or over the dot to find the bulls-eye. I've learned, by shooting with a circle, I can look past the "dot" when I go back to that method and clearly see the center of the bullseye (X-ring) as if the dot in the scope isn't there at all. It is a fuzzy blur and the X-ring is nearly crystal clear, because that is where my focus is. Using the correct size of circle forces me to use proper back tension and relaxation in order to aim steadily. If I lose tension or a form element, then the "hole" dances around and I lose focus on the X-ring or center of the target. Since our eyes naturally seek concentrics, the lack of concentricity throws your psyche off and you start to work back and forth among round objects and you become confused as to what is going on. You know it isn't right optically, so try to use muscle power to straighten it out, when what is needed is proper alignment, back tension, and relaxation. This really is a let-down and start over situation, but most of us simply try to trudge our way through it instead of re-setting and starting all over from scratch.

How to Make Your Own Dots

Making custom-sized dots is very simple and easy. All you need to do is purchase a cheap set of drill bits ranging in size from 1/16″ to 1/4″, and then buy some cheap bits of 17/64″, 9/32″, 19/64″, 5/16″, and 21/64″ for making your "holes" in the circles. You can also purchase some brass compression bushings in 1/2″ and 3/8″ diameters and then go through your pile of "cut-offs" from aluminum arrows and get a few pieces of 2613 and 2712 and 2512 shafts to use as "cut-out makers" as well (*see photo*).

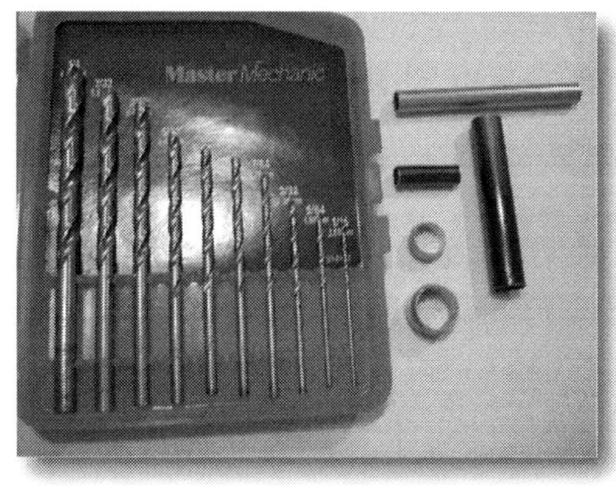

When you get your drill bits, it is a simple task of grinding the butt-end (the part that goes into the drill) off to a flat surface and lightly sanding off any burrs. You now have a complete set of "dot cutters."

The next step is to find a piece of soft wood, like pine, to use as a backing to your tape. *Hint* Don't use oak or any other hardwood; otherwise you will get a rough edge on the dot or circle.

Buy a roll of fluorescent red bumper reflective tape. This can be found in any hardware store, Wal-Mart, or any auto store. It comes in 2″ widths and it isn't very expensive. A roll goes a long ways; you can make a lot of dots and circles with it. You can also use red Department of Transportation tape if you can find it. I have found, however, that soft vinyl tape or electrical tape doesn't work well with this system. The bits aren't sharp enough to cleanly cut through this type of tape. Also, this tape doesn't have a protective backing, so you can't make spares without losing the adhesion qualities.

I like to keep larger dots and smaller dots on separate piece of tape, and then I also have 3/8″ and 1/2″ outer circles as well, with hole sizes going down from 5/16″ to 17/64″ on another piece.

Cut off a piece of tape about 2 or 3 inches long and place it tape side up on the wood board.

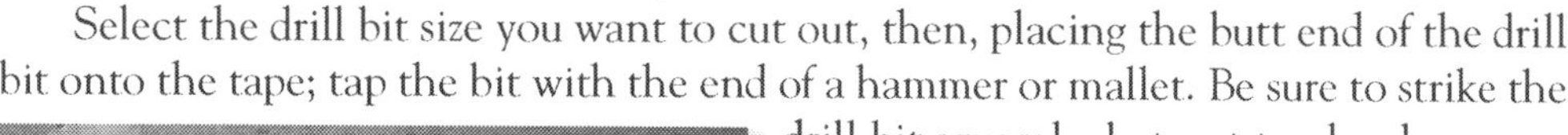

Select the drill bit size you want to cut out, then, placing the butt end of the drill bit onto the tape; tap the bit with the end of a hammer or mallet. Be sure to strike the drill bit squarely, but not too hard.

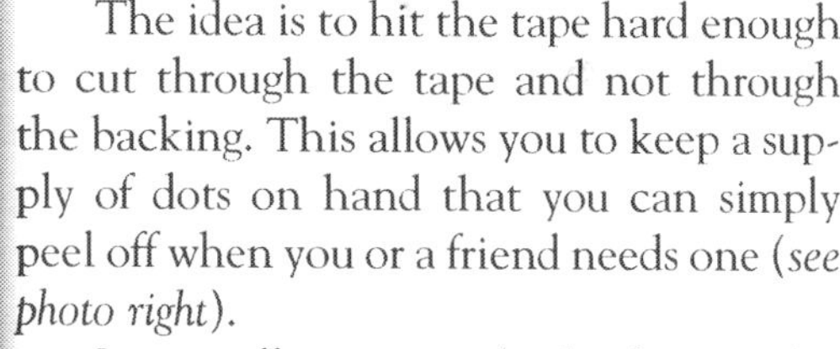

The idea is to hit the tape hard enough to cut through the tape and not through the backing. This allows you to keep a supply of dots on hand that you can simply peel off when you or a friend needs one (*see photo right*).

I normally start with the largest dot size I might use. For me, normally it is 11/64″. Make several dots of that particular size in a row of the tape.

Then select the next smaller size, move over on the same piece of tape, and tap out several of that size, leaving a little space between columns or rows (*see photo left*).

How to Make Circles

Making circles is a bit more difficult with the most difficult part being getting the inside hole centered in the outside circle. However with a little practice or using some ingenuity you can easily get them very close to center. As I mentioned earlier, I tend to look over the top, so if a hole is off center on the tape, the wide side goes to the

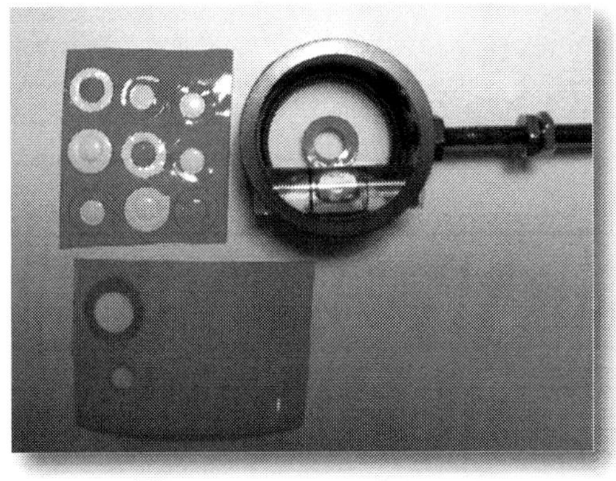

top. As long as the hole is centered in the lens or on the "grind" (True Spot scope), I've not had any problems with it. I think this is due mostly to the wide border not allowing me to focus in two places at once.

Place a piece of tape fluorescent side up on the softwood backing plate. Place the bushing or the piece of 2712 shaft on the tape. Using a hammer, strike the bushing or piece of shaft just hard enough to cut through the tape and not cut through the backing.

Using the drill bit or shaft size for the "hole" you want to cut, try to get it as close to center on the cut-out from #3 above, and then strike the drill bit or piece of arrow shafting to cut out the hole.

Make several each with ⅜″ and ½″ outside diameters with interior hole sizes that you have selected. I have found that smaller than 13/64″ is unfeasible. I'm having most of my best success with 6X and 8X lenses at 17/64″ or 9/32″. These sizes will differ from person to person and also with your selected sight extension distance and whether you are using a clarifier. The amount of sight extension and the use of a clarifier lens in the peep do affect how big of a circle you need to look through and how large of an outer margin you require in order to be comfortable with this system.

Placement of the Dot or Circle onto the Lens You can use a standard template provided by the manufacturer of the circles & dots that you purchase. You can also use a computer drawing program to make concentric circles of the size you need to use as a template to place your dots and/or circles onto the lens. You need to get the dot and/or circle centered onto the lens as close as you can. The more closely it is centered, the better, especially if you are trying to cover the "grind" on a True-Spot or similar lens. On an X-view lens, centering isn't too difficult due to the design of those lenses. If the lens has a hole drilled in it for the addition of a fiber-optic strand, centering is also not a problem.

Remove your lens from the scope and place it on your template, being careful to make sure the lens is indeed centered. Note: Some lenses can be sensitive to being moved around in the scope body. You should "index" that lens before removing it from the scope. Simply make a mark on the lens and scope body with a permanent magic marker (a small dot near the edge and below the top of the bubble will suffice). This insures that you get the lens back into the same spot as it was before you removed it.

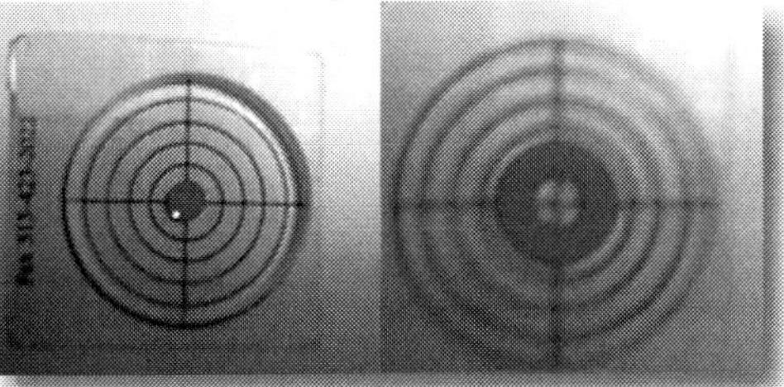

Remove a dot or circle by peeling it from the fluorescent tape. I like to use the end of a pin or needle, but you can use a sharpened pencil or something as soft. Remember, you can scratch the lens with a pin, so if using metal, be careful!

Lightly place the dot or circle onto the lens. You can still move it around a little, if need be. Once certain you have it where you want it, then press it down with the rubber eraser on the end of a pencil, or use something else that is blunt and soft (*see photos*).

Put the lens back into the scope, and try to get the index mark to the same spot as before.

Removal of the dot or circle is easy . . . simply use your fingernail to work it loose from any edge. If that doesn't work, take a toothpick and slice it off at an angle making a soft wooden chisel to lift up the dot or circle. Do not use a pin or something made of metal to do this. If you do, you run the risk of a major scratch on the lens.

Summary

While all this sounds complicated, once you have your punches made and have acquired the reflective tape, you will find that making your own dots and circles for your scope goes quite quickly. With some practice, you can make up a large batch of circles and/or dots in only a few minutes' time.

The last thing remaining is to go to the range and experiment to find which custom-sized dot or circle works best for you. Viola! You are no longer chained to what the manufacturers want to give you. After you have done this, you will have gained very valuable insight as to how a measly 1/32″ or in some cases, 1/64″ in hole or dot size can make a huge difference in how targets appear to you . . . as well as how well you can apparently hold on or float within, the center, without chasing the dot or pressing too hard to try to hold the circle centered and yet still see to "stare a hole" into the X-ring. Who would ever believe that a simple piece of fluorescent tape could be so useful for helping you to solve the big issue of aiming woes?

By customizing your dot or circle size to what works for you, you will find it much easier to learn to "Let it float and shoot the shot."

Section 9

Benchmarks, Goals, & Performance

In this book, Chapters 38 & 39 were devoted to the criteria by which a student selects a coach and a coach selects a student. In this section there is a focus on the information described in those two chapters. Had I placed this chapter right after Chapter 38, though, I thought it likely you would have glossed over it or that you might have thought I didn't think this to be important. It is here, the ultimate section and chapter, because part of becoming ProActive requires the application of what you are learning to the present as well as to plan for the future.

I do not coach elite archers. However, like any reasonably good professional educator, I had to first learn how to teach in order that I could teach how to learn! I realized early on that there is a real difference between a teacher with 30 years experience and a teacher with one year's experience repeasted 30 times.

Some archers are very difficult to coach; usually those who have been shooting for awhile. Also many beginners aren't willing to put in any time or dedication to developing a shot sequence or tracking their performance. I find this out during my initial interview of the archer and may make my decision at that point as to whether to take them on as a student of not simply based on those perceptions. I've had occasions where I've gone against my gut feelings only to have them proven correct and those coaching situations didn't last long; maybe one or two sessions.

What follows is a direct application of my Master's Thesis, "Improving Motivation Through Goal Setting." While writing this book, I quickly came to realize that the methods applied to students in school can be used to motivate toxophiles! It is the same situation: most shooters get bored with working on their game sooner or later. Most shooters sooner or later get tired of practicing. Most shooters eventually get caught up in trying to buy improvements instead of earning them by working on their form and execution. Some will switch from shooting on one side of the bow to the other in an effort to improve, while others, like me, are forced to make such change or to quit archery entirely. Many shooters don't know how to prepare for inevitable mishaps (this is especially prevalent among new archers) and most mid-level shooters do not have a real understanding of how to properly get really reliable sight settings, to measure, mark, and document equipment settings, and go about practicing for results instead of for score. Some of them are clueless as to their bow's mechanics or what their bows' settings are; they've always had a shop take care of it for them!! It is also self-evident that most archers today have little to no patience and aren't willing to really make a commitment to improve, but they are willing to read about it! I constantly have friends come up to me and say, "You'll never guess what I read about today," or they'll say "I was reading this article about YYY and it said that ZZZ will work, but it didn't say how to go about it." Thus, ProActive Archery went from a singular concept to help me, to a complete book to try to help as many archers as were willing to purchase the book and try out this concept.

And this chapter provides the keystone for becoming ProActive and really knowing yourself and your shot.

Tom Dorigatti

48

Tracking and Enhancing Performance with Benchmarks

Few archers have any concept of how to establish benchmarks, and set realistic goals and then keep tabs on their progress. They choose rather to just "fly by the seat of their pants" and just use their intuition as to whether or not they are progressing. Most of the time, this intuition is completely off-base.

For example, how many times have you been shooting fairly well for a month or two with a particular setup, then you have a bad round, and immediately say, "Well this isn't working, look at the crappy round I just shot!" So, you make a change or three, fail to mark down your starting point, and end up moving things around and becoming lost in all the changes. It may take weeks or months before you are back shooting the way you were before you mistakenly thought things were "all messed up."

What is worse, your "intuition" was based on the fact that you hadn't a clue as to what your past scores were, with the exception of the "bad one." You hadn't kept track of anything, you hadn't taken notes, you simply remember one (or maybe two) bad sessions, and so concluded that was a trend and it was time for a big change. You made the change, shot worse, or maybe slightly better, but once again, you didn't keep tabs on the real long-term results and are really only using your memory as the basis of comparison of past to present. I would, of course, hope that after getting this far into this book, you have made progress in becoming ProActive about your shooting and have taken steps to work on most of the above bad habits. Even so, even if you have given up working willy-nilly, I'll bet you have friends who operate just like that.

What you are about to be shown in this chapter works! I can tell you from real data from a verified long-term research project that "Motivation Through Goal Setting" worked for over 75% of the students who were in my classes while I was teaching in the public schools. In some of my classes this actually worked for over 95% of the students!

I have missed the boat with some of my archery students by not realizing until recently that I had "progress tracking devices" just sitting there for the taking. All that had to be done was to modify them to say the topic was "archery" and to reflect archery benchmarks, goals, and labels for tracking achievement! What I recommend is easy to use, only takes a few seconds of your time after a practice session or tournament, and will give you a visual and positive "image" of your real progress or, if a change isn't working, you will clearly see that and you can compare present to past performance in a matter of seconds. This is going to take most of the guesswork out of what your performance really is. You will have proof rather than intuition (which is just a fancy word for "guess" or "hunch"). You can, based upon your real performance, set goals that are reflections of your real performance. You can set goals that are more realistic and track them.

This is what ProActive archery culminates in, my friends. It culminates in you becoming ProActive by tracking your performance and having data so that you avoid the tendencies to go out and do something off the cuff without any thought.

I'm not going to repeat what was in Chapters 38 and 39, but I am going to share with you the results of the discussions in those two chapters and even more. Yes, some of what follows might be perceived as for "For Coaches Only" or "For Students of Coaches" only, however, if you are trying to improve your shooting are you not a student of the game? Haven't we really been talking about "self coaching?" (Gotcha!)

A Story to Start On

I keep track of my scores, X-counts, inside-out 5's, and all sorts of other data. Obviously, as the author of this book, I'd better practice what I preach. (Yes, my students will tell you that I also tell them that maybe I should practice more of what I preach, too, since I'm the king of tinkerers!) My personal journals and information are for my eyes only, because I'm quite loquacious when it comes to the comments therein, so it is better if others don't see my journal entries since there dates, times, places and, yes, even names in them. There are "lost journals" too, but while the pages may be lost, my memory isn't all that shabby just yet.

When this idea of using my Master's Thesis systems struck me recently, I thought I would go back and simply plot my past data on those tracking documents and get visual examples of what they could do, rather than a reading and remembering picture of what is really going on. The data, when placed onto the forms is striking, and quickly points out those things were nowhere near as bad as I had been thinking they were! The amount of real progress made over the months was startling, and way better than I had thought it was. Motivation was right there for the taking, but I hadn't conceived of having such striking pieces of evidence like this. So, I won't share my numbers with you, but will present you with a simulation of things and data that can come about if you partake of the opportunities presented. If doing this motivates me into realizing that things aren't as bad as I thought, I'm sure it will motivate many of you into becoming ProActive about your documentation and tracking of data. Maybe this should have been in the "Making Archery Fun" section, but this deserves its own special chapter. As is said, "a picture is worth a thousand words" and graphs are indeed pictures of what is going on relative to the data presented.

Finding Positives to Build Upon

One thing to remember is that no matter how bad things are going for you, you absolutely must find as many positives (things you are doing correctly) as you find things you are not quite doing up to snuff. If you dwell only upon your negatives, you will quickly lose your motivation and focus and it will be very tough to get them back. So the best thing to do is to mix few negatives with at least slightly more positives. It is possible to delude yourself by giving yourself too many positive strokes, but most people are far too negative. Here we need some dispassionate focus. Do I find myself in a funk from time to time? Absolutely, so I know full well what you are thinking about now.

Realize that no matter how bad your archery appears, find something positive to think about, start, and also end with. You had to have done at least one thing correct during that practice session or scoring round; find it and document it. While preparing for a practice session or while preparing your practice plan always ask yourself "What do I feel I am doing best?" Starting from something positive gives you a feeling that you are building on something good and that will go a long ways in making your practice session productive. The word "wrong" has a worse effect on you than the word "incorrectly," however phrases like "You need some work on . . ." or "Let's see if I can perhaps make a correction to this . . ." go a lot further and more quickly than either "wrong" or "incorrectly." It is really easy to "turn yourself off" for a practice, and end up completely wasting that session by being negative. As a coach, I hate the words "I can't..." or "I'm not..." If you can once, you can 60 times for an indoor round? If you can shoot a perfect 100 game, then you can shoot three of them in a row. It isn't really about 60 shots; it is about one shot 60 times in a row. We all can shoot one good shot; it isn't all that tough, is it?

Of course, for you students reading this, once again this is a two-way street, "I can't . . .", or "I don't like this . . .", "This isn't going to work." or worst: "Whatever!" are all complete turn offs for a practice session. If you have a negative thought on even one arrow, you have to religiously stop the shot, let it down, and re-set from the beginning. One piece of negativity leads to two, and it multiplies until you are so frustrated all you want to do is to get it over with and to go home. So you either quit in the middle, or you practice the bad thing over and over for that practice session and instead of gaining ground you lose it.

Archery Student Self-Evaluation

Many archers get their hackles up when self-examinations are recommended, thinking, "I already know what I'm doing. Why would I ever even dream of bothering with this self-examination thing?" Bear with me on this, and you will see why I highly recommend that you do. It will help you to isolate some things you may well never have thought about. You may well end up sharing it with some fellow shooters and they may pass it on to their friends, too.

I know for a fact that many of you won't be consulting an archery coach. Some don't have the money for it, while others don't really desire to enhance their skill level to quite that degree. Since you have purchased this book and are reading it you obviously want to improve, so take a leap of faith and continue reading. The worse you are out is a little time.

Archery Student Self-Evaluation Checklist

Student's Name ______________________ Date ______________

Instructions Circle your answers in the boxes next to the following questions. Feel free to ask questions as the purpose of this is to help you and your coach to develop a plan for your archery development. There arn't any right or wrong amswers. Please answer honestly.

Q1	What is your primary objective when you shoot a shot? X=X-ring, H=Hit target, G=make Good shot, A=Aim at X, S=Same execution as last good shot	X H G A S
Q2	Do you think the draw weight of your bow is too heavy for you?	Y N
Q3	Do you think you are drawing back the string correctly?	Y N
Q5	Do you know what "sky drawing is?	Y N
Q6	Do you have many people telling you what you are doing wrong?	Y N
Q7	Do you think your stance (essentialy foot positions) is correct?	Y N DK
Q8	Which of the following stances do you think you are using right now? O=Open stance, C=Closed stance, S=Square (even) stance?	O C S
Q9	Do you think about how you nock your arrows?	Y N
Q10	Do you think about bow hand position before you draw back?	Y N
Q11	Do you think about your release hand position before you draw back?	Y N
Q12	Do you think about your posture and balance before you draw back?	Y N
Q13	Do you raise the bow and pre-aim before you draw back?	Y N
Q14	Do you push the bow out and draw it back at the same time?	Y N
Q15	When you draw is your drawing elbow high or low?	HI LO DK
Q16	Is your bow shoulder high or low at full draw?	HI LO DK
Q17	At draw's end do you move your head to the string or string to your head?	ME HD
Q18	Is your release hand tense at full draw?	Y N
Q19	Is your draw elbow in line with your arrow? (IL=in line, OS=out short, OL=out long, DK=don't know	IL OS OL DK
Q20	Do you concentrate on the X-ring (X) or middle of the bull's-eye (M)?	X M
Q21	Does your sight sit fairly still (S), or go out the top (T) or bottom (B)?	S B T
Q22	Do you have tense arms, shoulders, and hands when aiming?	Y N
Q23	Do you know when the shot is going to go off?	Y N
Q24	Is it a surprise when the shot goes off?	Y N
Q25	Do you grab the bow when the shot goes off?	Y N
Q26	Does your release hand fly back when the shot goes off?	Y N
Q27	Do you ever see the arrow hit the target through your sight/aperture?	Y N

On the back of this sheet, please write the shot sequence you use, that is, the steps in order that you do from the time you go to the line until the first shot is in the target. Please number your steps.

So, given the fact that most shooters do not consult archery coaches, it doesn't mean that you cannot make use of a coach's tool. The form below is pretty much self-explanatory. It offers you a quick analysis of much of your shot sequence and helps you to see some things you might not otherwise notice. As I tell my students "You don't know where to start if you don't have a beginning. You cannot establish realistic plans or goals without a 'Benchmark.'"

Explanation of the Form This is the same form (left) I use to interview new students. The explanations below follow the question numbers, in order:

1. The first question is very important: Simply circle the response that applies to your mindset as you begin your shot sequence.
2. Answer honestly. My take? If you cannot draw the bow while sitting in a chair with your feet placed out off the ground in front of you, you are over-bowed and should crank your bow down.
3. Sky-Drawing? This is another good indicator that you are over-bowed and unsafe on range. In addition, this is costing you time and making you inconsistent with regard to how you set up for each shot. There are some venues where this is prohibited and you would be asked to leave the range if you continued to do it.
4. Is speed more important to you than accuracy? Be honest with yourself.
5. We all have a person who we would like to place ahead of on a leader board. This is to become a small part of goal-setting. Remember, however that the only person you really need to score higher than is yourself . . . as in shooting better than you did the last time (shooting a personal best).
6. Self-explanatory. How many do you listen to? How many things do they tell you to change all at once? Do you heed their advice and make all those changes?
7. Do you think your stance is correct?
8. Pick one that you think you might be using (refer to Chapter 17).
9. Do you think about how you nock your arrow?
10. Do you think about bow hand position before you draw back?
11. Do you think about the position of your release hand before drawing the bow?
12. Do you think about your body posture and balance before drawing the bow? Think carefully here. Do you shift your weight, hips, shoulders, or head at full draw?
13. Do you raise the bow and pre-aim it before drawing the bow back? . . . or do you "sky draw"?
14. Do you push the bow out and pull the bow back at the same time? Do you then "bend your elbow substantially" once you hit "full draw"?
15. Do you draw your bow with a high drawing elbow or a low drawing elbow? Realize that if you are drawing your bow with your elbow down against your torso or below shoulder height, you are likely well over-bowed. In this case, you are using your arms and not your back to draw back the bow.
16. Do you know if our bow shoulder is high or if it is low when you are at full draw?
17. Do you bring the bow to you, or do you move your head to get to the string or to get the string to the tip of your nose or to anchor?

18. Is your release hand tense or relaxed when you are at full draw?
19. Is your drawing elbow in line with the arrow when at full draw? IL = In-line; OS = Outside short; OL = Out long; DK = Don't know. If you haven't thought much about this, this alignment is a major key to consistent accuracy.
20. Do you concentrate on the X-ring (X) or the "middle of the bullseye" (M)?
21. Does your sight sit fairly still (S) go does it tend to go drop out the bottom (B), or rise out the top (T)?
22. Do you have tense hands, shoulders, and arms when aiming?
23. Do you know when the shot is going to go off? If you do, then you are likely punching your trigger or release and "command shooting." Not necessarily bad, but can lead to cases of target panic and inconsistencies.
24. Is there a surprise when the shot goes off? This is what you should work for. Be honest, you are only cheating the release, your scores, and yourself if you aren't honest in your assessment.
25. Do you grab at the bow when the shot goes off?
26. Does our release hand fly back when the shot goes off? Does it drop down and to the left or right? Does it say put and not move at all? Does it come forward and out slightly?
27. Do you ever see the arrow strike the target while you are still looking through your scope or sight aperture?

Okay, now that you have finished your evaluation, write down your shot sequence. That is, write the steps you follow, in order, from the time you go to the line until the shot is complete. Please number your steps. You now have a basis to analyze your shot sequence and to figure out a plan to build a more solid and consistent shot sequence; in an order that is recommended by most all of the top archery coaches and used by many of the top echelon and world class shooters. Yes, of course, the shot sequences vary, and so do the items on each shooter's list. The number of steps varies too, as we discussed in Chapters 25 & 26. Of course, as you work on this you must remember you can only do one thing at a time, only work on one thing at a time.

Not everyone has to have all those steps written down, but if you don't have a written benchmark of what you actually do, how can you begin to identify those which are automatic (not needing to be thought about while shooting), from those that you need work on and aren't consistent (do need to be thought about when shooting)? This is again, ProActive archery, but if you don't know where to start to work, how can you ever begin the process?

Your Ideal Archery Attitude and Mind Set

An ideal archer has a certain set of attitudes and behaviors. No one archer necessarily has all of these but each is worth exploring or emulating. (These are in no particular order or priority.)

1. Seldom, if ever use the words "I can't," "I won't," "This isn't going to work," or "Whatever!" Those are sure-fire ways to lose your focus and increase your level of frustration. Realize that any change is going to feel uncomfortable at first and your

muscles as well as your psyche are going to be fighting the change. Avoid the, "I was doing better before I made this change" mentality. I'll be giving you a means for getting proof of whether any change you attempt is a good one or not.

2. When someone observes something and relates to you what they saw, you should avoid saying, "No, I didn't do that." Accept that that is what they think they saw. What things look like from the outside and what they feel like from the inside are often at odds. If you really want to explore what you look like from the outside a camera can take still photos or even videos for you to check yourself. Caution You also shouldn't take everything people say as gospel. There are some who use trash talk or psyche jobs on you to throw you off. One really common one to try to throw someone off their game is the old "Do you know your arrows have a hop in them on the way to the target?" Whether they do or don't shouldn't derail you from what you are doing. Just make a mental note and ask someone you trust later to check your arrow flight. If someone was trying "mind games" on you, well, now you know (but they don't know that you know which is to your benefit).
3. Always "Fess up when you mess up." This means to be honest, especially to yourself. People make mistakes, and you are not going to shoot 100% of your shots perfectly; it isn't possible to do this. Remember the "good shot, bad result" possibility. A "good shot, bad result" can still be recorded as a "click" (good shot). That is to say, when there is a mistake made or a failure to communicate properly, own up to it and get on with the business at hand. Failing to acknowledge a mistake simply primes you to repeat it. You know what error you've made, so work on not letting it happen twice in a row.
4. Remember the "21 days of practice" rule of thumb on learning something new. You can track this in a fashion that gives you near positive proof of whether a change or something new is really working or not. This will take the opinion and guesswork out of the equation for you. Don't get caught up in the rush game and try to do two or three changes at once. This will be counterproductive and cost you dearly. I constantly battle with students and acquaintances over this issue. Their argument? "Well, it will be faster this way". My response may vary, but comes down to, "Oh, really? And which change will you write down as the one that worked and straightened it out and which ones are masking something else entirely?"

It is hoped that you realize that "being coached" and "self-coaching" are not simple processes. Most times these are not short term projects, but they are rather works in progress. These WIP's are likely not going to follow a predictable flow or process. There will be ups and downs and even diversions. Plans are written and plans are changed in order to accomplish goals and objectives. Here's how.

Establishing a Benchmark

Believe it or not, you already have at least one benchmark established if you've been keeping a record of your scores in a journal or database. If you don't keep a journal, you still have a benchmark established if you can look up the results of your last indoor our outdoor league scores! How much more simple can this be? If you don't have any of the above, then you need to shoot 5-10 practice scores and record your results based upon what you want to track. I'm going to provide you the tools you need to track your progress based on such.

A Final Story I had been shooting very, very well outdoors, but was still shooting in the 530's for Field Rounds, which while not so bad, only allowed me win on occasion, normally placing in the top five. I simply started working, not on my X count, but rather working on eliminating my wide 4's, those misses that were way outside the highest scoring ring on the Field Round. I set a goal to reduce and eventually eliminate the outer 4's knowing full well that by doing that, I'd be picking up more 5's and thus my final score would rise all by itself, without placing undue pressure upon myself to "shoot more 5's" or "shoot more X's." It worked! It wasn't long and almost all my shots that missed became inner 4's and controllable. The misses were much closer to being 5's, and of course the numbers of 5's and X's also increased. Once I got into the lower 540's then I worked on shooting "more 5's that didn't touch the white on the closer targets. In other words, I set goals of the "one bite at a time variety," in this case a goal of not touching the white on the Field face or the black on the Hunter face with any arrows from the Bunny/Birdie target through the 25 yard target. Of course, I had to be positive about this, so I recorded the inside outs and logged those, since those were the "positives" and I wanted to avoid counting how many touched the white or black (the "negatives"). So, that one-step at a time approach got me into the 540's, and then I worked on the next size of target face, and so on. Not only was this fun, but I could track my progress and was only working on one thing at a time. Dang it sure was fun having to make the decision as to which arrow to pull first and which to pull last when I had myself those 4-X 20's. Decisions, decisions, and those were feel good decisions, too. The good feelings bred more good feelings and you know where it goes from there.

Here's how I applied this to my indoor shooting. I had been shooting a lot of 300 scores, but the X-counts were running between 45 and 58. Not terrible, but that is too wide a range to be predictable and offer up winning scores indoors. So, what did I do about this (besides the "timing" program I told you about in Chapter 27)? This was a simple process. I added a new feature to my score tracking, that being how many times I had arrows touching the blue (as in not inside-out in the "5-ring"). To be positive, however I wanted to count how many "inside outs" I shot, so those were recorded! It wasn't long before my inside out 5's went up, and as a result of not thinking about X's all the time, but rather "letting it float and shooting the shot," my X-counts took care of themselves because I wasn't trying too hard and forcing my aim. In fact, the finish of this story is this: my very first 60X 300 was shot while I was simply focusing on shooting all of my arrows inside-out in the main bull's-eye. I wanted only an inside-out 300 with no arrows touching the blue! I ended up shooting a 60x 300. The 59th shot was by far the toughest of the league session, however. The 60th shot when off like a knife through butter. I wasn't focused on tightening up my aiming at all; I was focused on keeping them solidly in the white.

A Framework for Success

The series of graphs that follow are for you to use as examples of what you want to accomplish first. For beginners and mid-level shooters, I recommend starting with your total score and "inside-out 5's," for higher mid-level shooters (consistent 300 shooters with 50+ X-counts), I recommend Total Score and X-Counts for target and "Score and 12-rings" for 3-D shooters. For upper echelon shooters (consistent 300's and 55+ X-counts), I recommend two graphs, "300 Scores and X-counts," and the "X-counts and Clickers" graph, since your goals are higher X-counts and trying to improve upon those shots that qualify as "clickers" (see Chapters 41 and 42 for an explanation of "clickers"). You will find that by using these, you can create visual pictures of your performance. You can make new goals based upon your real past performance, your goals will be realistic, they will be achievable, and obviously, they will be measurable.

The first two graphs were created in Microsoft *Excel* as examples of how this program can be used for this purpose. You can, of course, draw the graphs with pencil and paper, but this way you can automate the process and you don't have to plot a thing. Of course, the data plots below also serve to show you what information you can track when you make equipment or form changes. Whether you score and plot the data manually or via computer the procedure is the same for all the graphs, only the names of which data you are tracking changes. It is really quite simple and only takes you a

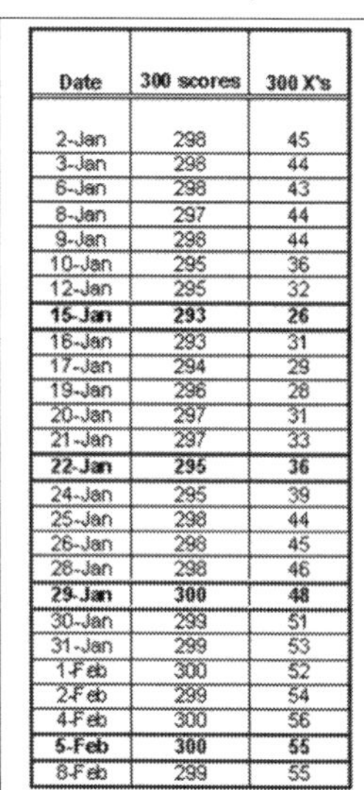

Date	300 scores	300 X's
2-Jan	298	45
3-Jan	298	44
6-Jan	298	43
8-Jan	297	44
9-Jan	298	44
10-Jan	295	36
12-Jan	295	32
15-Jan	**293**	**26**
16-Jan	293	31
17-Jan	294	29
19-Jan	296	28
20-Jan	297	31
21-Jan	297	33
22-Jan	**295**	**36**
24-Jan	295	39
25-Jan	298	44
26-Jan	298	45
28-Jan	298	46
29-Jan	**300**	**48**
30-Jan	299	51
31-Jan	299	53
1-Feb	300	52
2-Feb	299	54
4-Feb	300	56
5-Feb	**300**	**55**
8-Feb	299	55

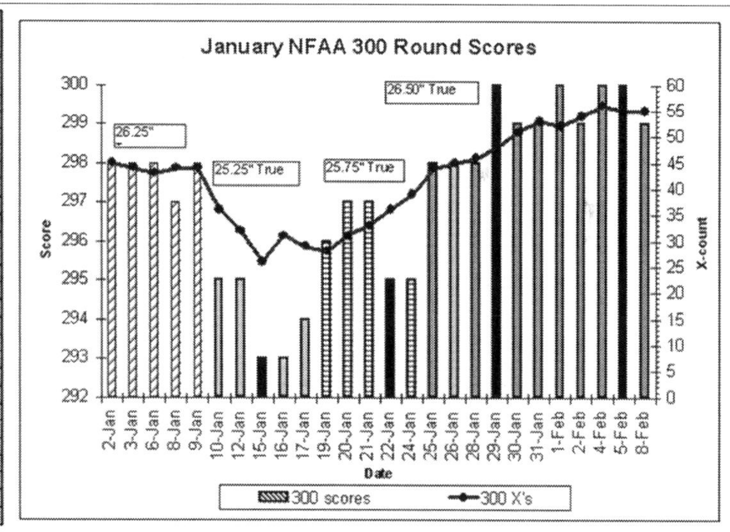

Notes: Jan 2 - Jan 8 Baseline. Draw length 26.25 True Draw.
Jan 10, Shortened Draw length 1 inch, To 25.25" True Draw. Tournament Sunday. X-counts are not solid, wide misses.
Jan 15: *Tournament*. Bow very jumpy and lots of tension. Seems either solid hits or real wid misses. Bow jumping around target picture jittery. X-count down,
Jan 19 - Lengthened DL 1/2" to 25.75" True Draw. Bow movement slower, X-count a bit better, but still below baseline.
Jan 22 - *Tournament*: Score up, but X-count down from baseline. Still too jumpy; struggling to get off the shot.
Jan 25 - Lengthened DL to 1/4" beyond baseline to 26.50" True Draw. Site picture much better.
Jan 28 - Sight settling down, misses are smaller. Will hold adjustments for a few more rounds.
Jan 29 - *Tournament*. First 300, 48X. Sight steady, not jittery. Will continue through Feb 5 tyournament at this setting.
Feb 1 - 4 300's in a row, X-count up in low 50's. Need work on exectuion, but sight picture steady.
Feb 5 - *Tournament*: 300 55-X. Will continue to track this setting.
Feb 8 - Sloppy round. Good X-count, but I got careless in 7th end and missed one.

few seconds to plot your data at the conclusion of your practice scoring rounds or tournament scores. I recommend you plot your tournament scores with a separate color so you can keep tabs on those. I don't recommend you put tournament scores on separate graphs from your practice scores. The primary reason is that one of your goals should be to eventually have little to no difference between your practice and your tournament scores. Remember, if you haven't been shooting 55+X counts in practice, it is highly unlikely you'll magically shoot a 60X score in a tournament. You need to track both on the same graph (*see graph previous page*).

I included the "data table" of the plotted scores on the left side. This is where the MS *Excel* program is getting its numbers from to plot the data. This is what is called, as I mentioned earlier, a "combination" graph; that being the primary Y (vertical) axis tracks one set of data (in this case Score), and the secondary Y (vertical) axis plots X-counts. Notice that the score is a bar and the X-count is a line with a dot for each data point. This works well for the data you will be tracking and is easy to work with. The horizontal axis is the date. You don't have to have a separate graph each month, especially if you don't shoot every day.

Notice that there is an area at the bottom for "notes" and what has been recorded there. The important things are that a change was made after a benchmark; in these cases draw length was adjusted and scores tracked with each adjustment. You can clearly see from the bars and lines that the 1″ shorter draw length resulted in an immediate drop in scores and X-counts. Here is one of those "pictures" of progress I was telling you about. In this example I only gave it one tournament and five practice rounds to determine that the change wasn't a gain, but a liability. The information is recorded so that you know what you tried and its result. Note that on 19 January, I "split" the difference on the shorter draw length, and scores started coming back up, but the X counts while rising, weren't at the benchmark level. Once again several scores were shot (I'd recommend 10, but only used 5 to save space on the graph).

On January 28, we made the change to a draw length ¼″ longer than the baseline and even had a tournament score in there and the results clearly indicate that this change was in the right direction. You have picture proof that a shorter draw length was not the thing to do, and that apparently the draw length of ¼″ beyond the benchmark (starting point) was indeed a good decision. What would you do next? You might continue tracking for several more rounds, and then maybe tweak the draw length by increasing it another ⅛″ and tracking again. You now have not only the benchmark of "where you started," but you also have a range of draw lengths that you know you cannot go below, and eventually, you will narrow this down to that range that works best for you at the time.

Next you would simply continue on, but with a new wrinkle to it. You now know exactly where you are at any given time. It is time to set a goal with regard to your score and your "counts." That is accomplished simply by putting in a red line a couple of points above where you have been shooting for total score, and another line for the secondary axis for a goal on your X counts. Remember, you eat the elephant one bite at a time. You could separate score from X-count, but most tournament archers will want to be tracking both. For beginners, I don't think that X count is what you should track; so I provide is a sample graph for tracking score and "inside-out" 5's, along with 3-D scores graph examples.

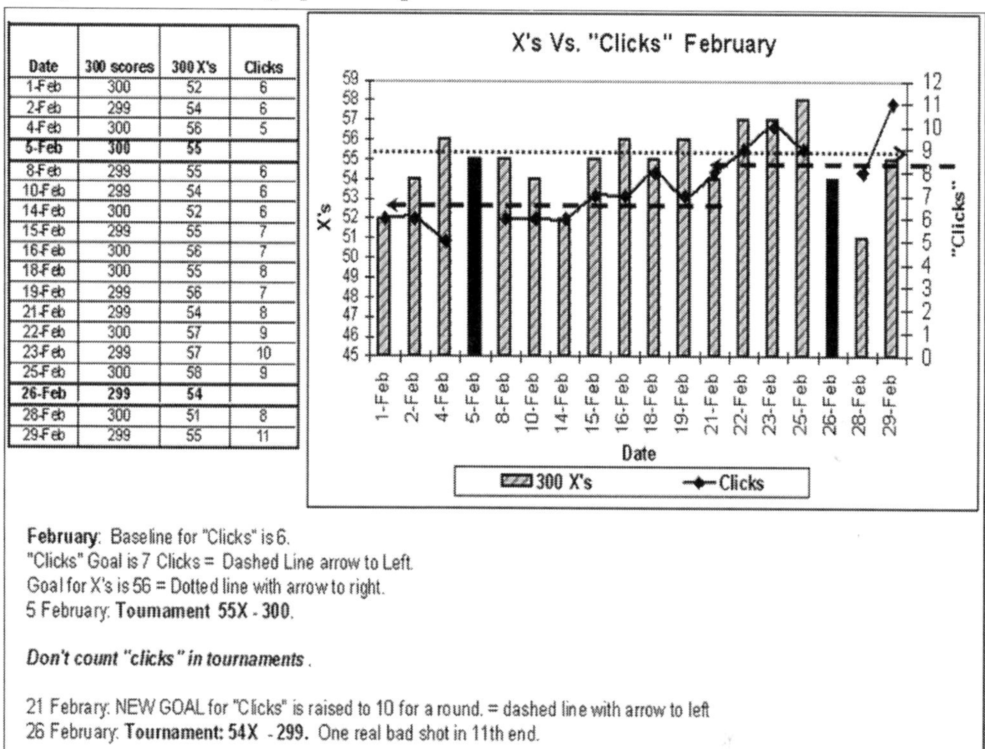

Date	300 scores	300 X's	Clicks
1-Feb	300	52	6
2-Feb	299	54	6
4-Feb	300	56	5
5-Feb	**300**	**55**	
8-Feb	299	55	6
10-Feb	299	54	6
14-Feb	300	52	6
15-Feb	299	55	7
16-Feb	300	56	7
18-Feb	300	55	8
19-Feb	299	56	7
21-Feb	299	54	8
22-Feb	300	57	9
23-Feb	299	57	10
25-Feb	300	58	9
26-Feb	**299**	**54**	
28-Feb	300	51	8
29-Feb	299	55	11

February: Baseline for "Clicks" is 6.
"Clicks" Goal is 7 Clicks = Dashed Line arrow to Left.
Goal for X's is 56 = Dotted line with arrow to right.
5 February: **Tournament 55X - 300.**

Don't count "clicks" in tournaments.

21 Febrary: NEW GOAL for "Clicks" is raised to 10 for a round. = dashed line with arrow to left
26 February: **Tournament: 54X - 299.** One real bad shot in 11th end.

This graph is intended for upper echelon or even professional archers who are at or nearly at the 58-60 X range on the NFAA indoor face, or the 300 – 30X range on the Vegas Face. This graph is adaptable to either round, or to field or hunter rounds, or even to given distances on FITA rounds or 900 rounds outdoors. I mentioned above the concept of placing goals as lines onto the graphs in a different color so that you know what those lines represent as I have done in this graph. You can see that this is a continuation graph from the above graph for January. Based upon the tracking record, I established an X count goal of 55X's (*see the dotted horizontal line*) and a "Clicks count" goal of 8 clicks (*see the dashed horizontal line*). The notes at the bottom explain the goal setting process. Always remember to have goals that are realistic, achievable, and measurable; otherwise it isn't a goal but rather a dream or, worse, a fantasy. You could make a short term goal for 60X, but if you are only shooting at a 52X level, how can you? The odds are you will never make it and will get discouraged rather quickly and abandon it. So, why not make it something you can get to, one step at a time?

The "Clicks" Tool

Let's talk about the "Clicks" thingy. You will recall that I mentioned earlier that there are only four outcomes for any one shot. I'll list those again:

1. *Good Shot = Good Result* (You need to repeat this one again and again and again).
2. *Good Shot = Bad Result* (Maybe you might check your sight or move it slightly if this happens a few times in a row). However if it only happens occasionally, then there may be other issues. I've known for years that an absolutely perfect shot could sometimes strike high and just out of the X or even just out of the 5-ring. But I knew it was a great shot, and a result of things being perfect, since I'm sighted in slightly high due to the fact I don't shoot all that many "absolutely perfect" shots; and neither to any of us!
3. *Bad Shot = Good Result*
4. *Bad Shot = Bad Result*

I also discussed what a "Click" amounts to and how to use "Clicks" to make your practice sessions more fun. A "Click" requires you to have a Hand Tally Counter. This tool is invaluable for a ProActive archer, or any archer wanting to improve their prowess. Unfortunately, many use them use them for tracking a "negative thing" as in they click it once for each time they drop a point or drop an X. Of course, their mindset is to try to not click it at all, which I guess is okay in and of itself. Make it more positive. We are conditioned to accept high numbers, since high score wins, correct? So, why not turn the clicks around and make them something to strive for more of? The more you "click" the better. Of course, you can still "click" during a tournament if you want, and it can be to keep count of how many you are "down" as a means of cross-checking the score keepers (they've been known to lose track and make mistakes).

The Rule of the "Click" Here is my hard and fast rule for being allowed a "Click": A click is a perfect shot, regardless of impact point. That means that in the above list, "Good Shot = Good Result" and "Good Shot = Poor Result" are eligible for you to "Click." The last two, do not qualify as a "click" no matter what. Some people quibble and want a "click" when they know they shot a bad shot and got an X out of it. They say, "Any X is a good thing, so I should click on that one." The key is a click is a "good or a great shot," and never are you allowed to "click" on a bad one in spite of that lucky "X" you just got (notice I said "got" and not "shot"). What is it you are trying to reinforce: good/great shots or being lucky? I don't think luck is something you can train, but shot making, yes! So, I hope this motivates you to become a ProActive "Clicker." Tracking your perfect shots can become addictive; it is just something you want to try for more of, and now you have a means to set a benchmark, make goals, and to keep track of them.

Other Graphs

The next graph and the others below are Sample Graphs of what you can make. Once again, I think that a beginner or low-to-intermediate shooter shouldn't track X's until they are shooting consistent scores of about 290-295. You would be asking way too much of yourself. Of course, you can if you want to, but the next graph, in my opinion, is better for you to start out with.

Notice on the blank graphs that the numbers are 1-31 along that horizontal axis. Those do not have to be the days of the month. They can be used for practice round numbers or the sequence of your practice sessions. The two blank rows of boxes at the bottom of the graph are for you to record your "X's (or inside out 5's) and your total score into. This gives you a "hard copy" of your data and shows what you have plotted into the graph. You can refer to the sample graphs to see how you to plot your numbers. Your total score is a Bar and filled in up to the score level you attained. Each line represents two points on the left and the right axes of the graph. You can make notes on the back of the graph and write changes similar to how it was demonstrated in the first graphic above (*above*).

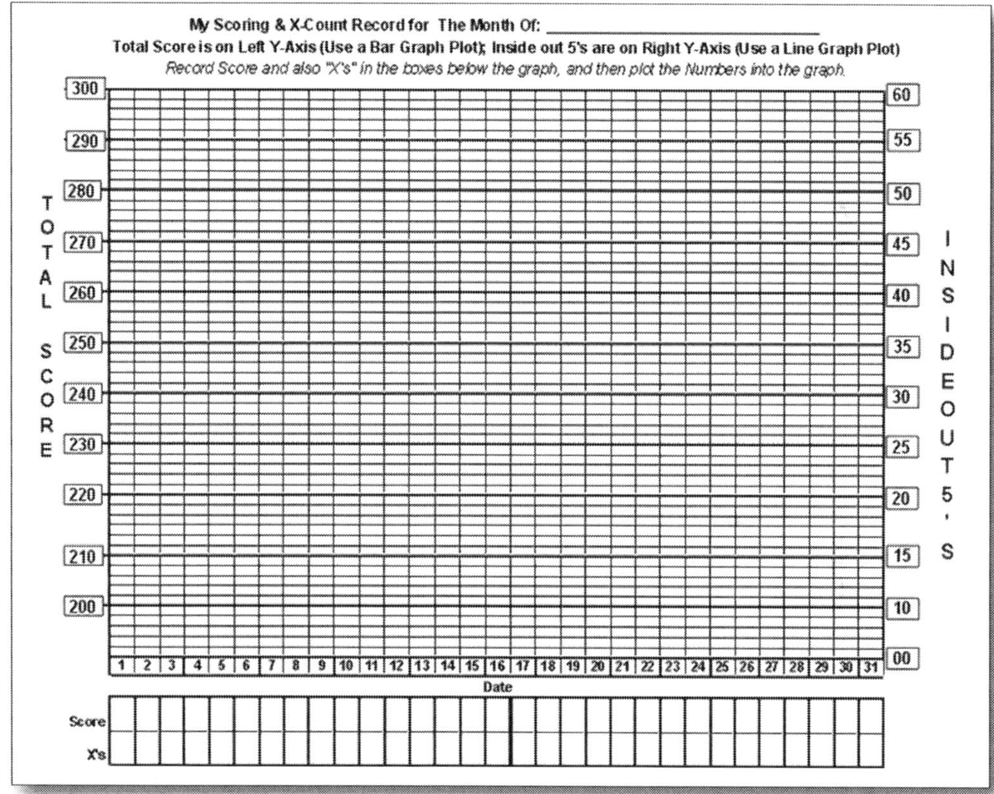

Since I believe strongly in walking before you can run, unless you are a consistent "300" shooter or consistently shooting above 260 on a field or hunter round, I'd recommend starting with this "Graph". It is really a Combination Graph that uses a bar graph for the total score on the primary Y-Axis, and a line graph on the secondary Y-Axis for your "inside out 5's" (or for field rounds, you can use "inner ring 4's") The reason we start with your total score and "inside out 5's" (for indoor NFAA rounds), is because I think that placing emphasis on X's for a beginner or mid-level shooter places too much pressure on you. Remember that I mentioned in my story that I was only shooting for the entire round to be free from any arrows touching the blue the night I shot my first-ever 60X indoor round? This allows you to concentrate on that, and not tighten up so much by concentrating on something that is, at present, probably beyond your capabilities. Remember the "One Bite of the Elephant at a Time". You need to learn to walk before you can run.

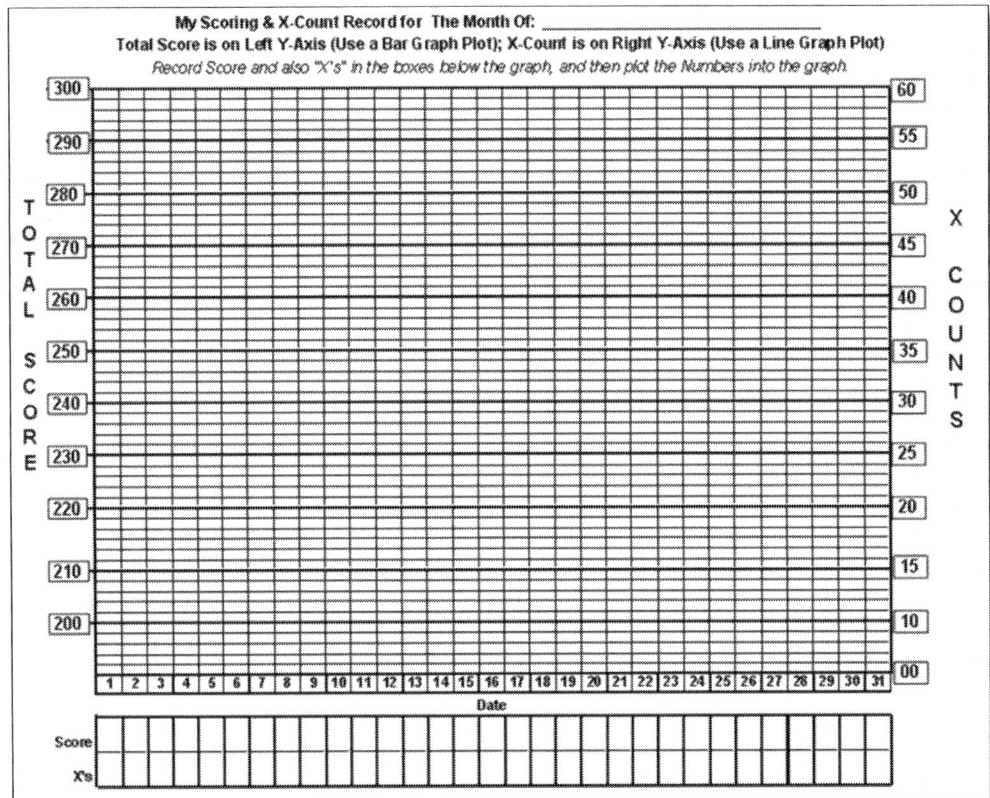

This particular tracking record isn't recommended for use by beginners. It is intended for mid-to-upper level shooters who consistently shoot scores of 290 or above. It can accommodate any round you choose as long as the total possible score is below 300 points, and of course fewer than 60 arrows are being shot. It works for 14-target units on the field course as well; since the total possible is 280 and you only shoot 56 arrows. If you are making your own graphs, just adjust your y-axis scales to accommodate what you are tracking and keep the scales consistent.

The next graph is a blank graph prepared for "X's Versus "Clicks." It shares the same format for plotting as all the other graphs. Only the names of the two Vertical (Y) axes are changed. Make your "goal lines" in different colors and styles for each side.

This graph demonstrates how you can adapt these "archery graphs" to track your 3-D scores and results. You can set benchmarks, establish goals, and then track achievement for your 3-D shooting, too. Of course, since 3-D is a different game, you should have separate graphs for this activity. One important variant for a beginner might be, rather than tracking score and 12-counts, to track score and 5's, set bench-

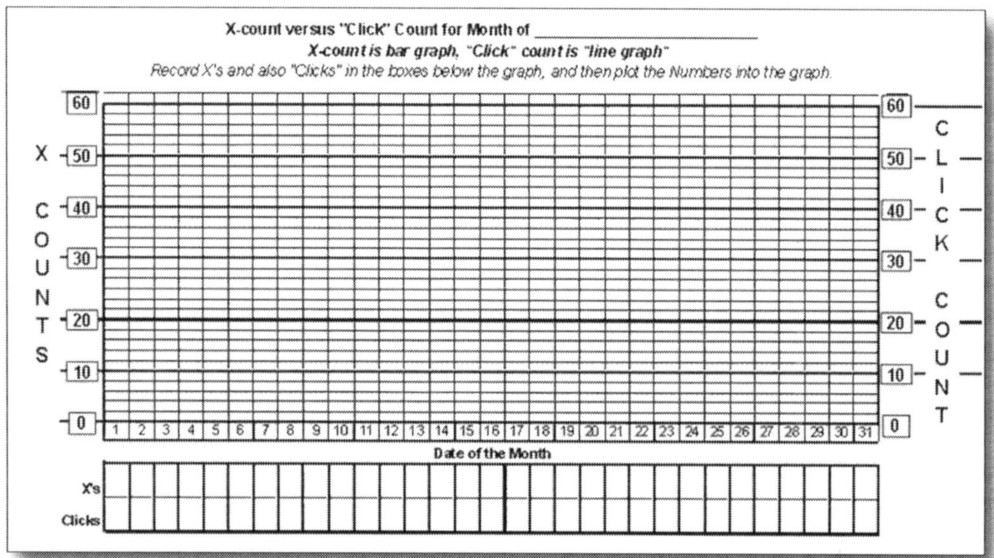

marks, and then work on elimination of the 5's and then once those are under better control, try to work on the 8's, and the move into the realm of tracking 12's. Since in the beginning you don't have the prowess to shoot a lot of 12's it is better to work from the outside in and track your improvement that way. Elimination of low arrow scores isn't going to come from trying to shoot more 12's; it will come in leaps and bounds by shooting fewer 5's and more 8's and 10's. All you need to do is change the axis from "12-Count" to "Number of 5's" and later on change it to "Number of 8's" as you progress on minimizing the larger misses.

Summary

So, there you have it. If my editor allows me to abuse the English language, I'll say, "That's all I got."

We have explored the world (or maybe my world) of ProActive Archery and how to go about our sport from a approach of describing building blocks and then taking a planned and organized approach.

I said at the very beginning that I've never won a world class event. I'm not a former Olympian. I'm not a former national or even a sectional champion (although I've been close to sectional champion several times over the years). I have, however, over the past 50 years of my archery career learned most everything about archery the hard way, by experimenting and solving my own problems by trial and test, and from listening, personal experience, and observation. In addition, you might be shocked at the amount of learning that took place while writing this book for you. In trying to clearly state what works, I have had to refine my thinking a great deal and, in doing so, have learned a lot.

Becoming ProActive was a way for me to replace hard work and preparation for pure or raw talent I did not possess and it became nearly an obsession. I had to figure

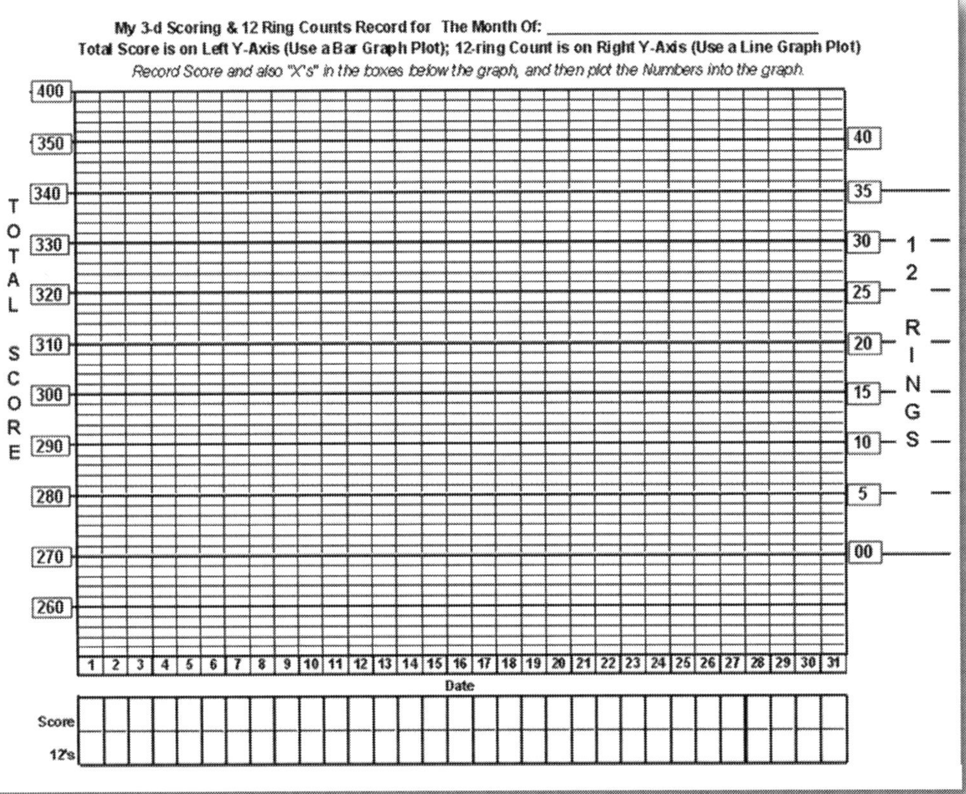

out how to prevent little things from wrecking my already weaker scores if I wanted to compete against those "better" and more talented than I was. Being prepared and diligent and observant eventually put me a cut above the competition a lot of the time, especially when conditions were less than perfect. This worked, not for National titles, or whatever, but it allowed me to move up leader boards to well above where I would have ever been without becoming ProActive.

I have been at the top of the game as I have mentioned before. I have also been to the bottom, too, because of medical setbacks and I had to figure out how to get back at least to the thermocline pretty much on my own. With the great help of great people such as Terry Wunderle and Larry Wise, I came to terms with many obstacles that were hindering real progress from the doldrums after medical issues almost took me completely out of competitive archery all together. I've had to go to extremes beyond what common sense would dictate to re-teach my muscles and body what my real body positions need to be. Getting there meant putting me well beyond what I felt was "normal" just so I could get my body to respond and then feel "normal." This is still a work in progress as all of my and your shooting development is. You simply need to understand the work in progress portion and how this all gets put together.

The goal for this book will be met if it helps even one archer become what they want to be, to become a better archer and a better person. Maybe they won't become a world or national champion. Maybe they won't even become a sectional or state champion. However, I feel with reasonable certainty that if even one of you becomes a more ProActive archer, you will have come a long ways and will have dramatically improved your enjoyment of the sport.

About the Author

Tom Dorigatti has been an avid archer and bowhunter for over 50 years. He has been hunting with a bow and arrow since he was 10 years old and started with rudimentary equipment, moved up to Recurve hunting bows, and finally on to target archery equipment in the late 1960's. Although bowhunting was his primary objective, target archery quickly took a front seat for the times when hunting season wasn't open.

Tom has been a member of the National Field Archery Association for 44 years and has actively participated in tournaments or on ranges in no fewer than 37 of the contiguous United States, Alaska, Hawaii, Guam, and the Azores. He has also been involved in managing archery leagues and tournaments, up to and including NFAA Sectional events since 1968. Tom has taken numerous small and big game animals with bow and arrow, the largest being a bull elk which he took with a 45 pound Recurve bow in 1971. He also has several Mule deer, Pronghorn antelope, and Whitetail deer to his credit. Tom has an Associate of Arts degree in Secondary Education, a Bachelor of Arts Degree, with majors in Secondary Education and biology and minors in Physical Science and French, and a Master's Degree in Teaching and Leadership. He also served in the United States Air Force as an Instructor Navigator and Standardization/Evaluation Navigator in KC-135A jet refueling tankers for Strategic Air Command. He has 22 years experience in private industry as an instructor, manager, and quality assurance manager. In addition, Tom has 10 years junior high and high school teaching experience in subjects ranging from biology, physical science, applied science, human anatomy and physiology, earth science and French.

He has written numerous articles for *Archery Focus* magazine and also written numerous archery and bicycling related puzzles for *Archery Focus* magazine and others. He is also author of a complete book of archery related puzzles soon to be released and hopes to write more books of puzzles.

Tom is also heavily involved in exercising with his greatest involvement being in competitive racquetball, and long distance road bicycling. Tom has logged over 7,300 and 6,600 miles in just the past two years respectively. He has taken week long bicycling tours in Colorado, Georgia, Florida, Wyoming, and Wisconsin. He will be out and about on the road again in 2012, taking at least one tour back in the Door County area of Wisconsin for a week. During the riding season, Tom can be found either at the archery range during bad weather, or out on the road bicycle.

Everything You Need to Know to Become a Better Archer!

Over 15,000 sold!

Written by your favorite **Archery Focus** authors—Rick McKinney, Don Rabska, Larry Wise, Ty Pelfrey, Dr. Lisa Franseen, Annette Musta, and others—**Precision Archery** covers every aspect of target archery. You'll find instruction on how to compete, how to perfect your form, and up-to-the minute advice on

- bow purchase, initial setup, and tuning
- fitness training to get and keep a competitive edge
- mental preparation and learning how to win
- how to adjust for wind, rain, and other adverse conditions
- the fine art of barebow
- how to work with a coach
- putting your shot together and taking it apart
- how to check out new equipment and work it into your shot

Nothing is left out, even the spirit of archery is addressed! If you are looking to take your game to the next level, this is the book for you!

216 pages • ISBN 0-7360-4634-8 • US $19.95

Available at Better Pro Shops and Archery Retailers!

27050124R10298

Made in the USA
Lexington, KY
25 October 2013